P9-CQI-464

ALSO BY W. TIMOTHY GALLWEY

The Inner Game of Tennis

Inner Tennis: Playing the Game

Inner Skiing (with Robert Kriegel)

The Inner Game of Music (with Barry Green)

The Inner Game of Work

THE INNER GAME
OF GOLF

THE
INNER
GAME
OF
GOLF

W. TIMOTHY GALLWEY

RANDOM HOUSE TRADE PAPERBACKS / NEW YORK

2009 Random House Trade Paperback Edition

Copyright © 1979, 1981, 1998 by W. Timothy Gallwey

All rights reserved.

Published in the United States by Random House Trade Paperbacks,
an imprint of The Random House Publishing Group,
a division of Random House, Inc., New York.

RANDOM HOUSE TRADE PAPERBACKS and colophon are trademarks
of Random House, Inc.

Originally published in hardcover in the United States by
Random House, an imprint of The Random House Publishing Group,
a division of Random House, Inc., in 1981. A revised edition of this
work was published by Random House, an imprint of
The Random House Publishing Group,
a division of Random House, Inc., in 1998.

A portion of this work was previously published in *Golf Magazine*.

Grateful acknowledgment is made to the following
for permission to reprint previously published material:
A.S. Barnes & Company, Inc.: Excerpts from *Power Golf*
by Ben Hogan, published by A.S. Barnes & Company, Inc.
Copyright 1948, 1976 by Ben Hogan. Reprinted by
permission of the publisher. All rights reserved.

Library of Congress Cataloging-in-Publication Data

Gallwey, W. Timothy
The inner game of golf / W. Timothy Gallwey.
p. cm.
ISBN 978-0-8129-7970-1
1. Golf—Psychological aspects. I. Title
GV979.P75G34   1998
796.352'01—dc21   97-41272

Printed in the United States of America

www.atrandom.com

1 3 5 7 9 8 6 4 2

Book design by Susan Turner

To Maharaji,
with gratitude for teaching me
the one thing
I most needed to learn

To be a student takes a lot of trust,
but not in the teacher.
To be a student takes a lot of trust
in you.

MAHARAJI

FOREWORD
LOOKING BACK

THROUGHOUT THE AGES THERE HAVE ALWAYS BEEN TWO STREAMS OF advice for people who wanted to improve a skill. I call one the river of "formulas" and the other the river of "feel." One current flows toward mastery in the outer world, the other toward mastery in the inner.

The river of formulas produces a formidable flow of technical instructions arising from the detailed analysis of any skill. This approach has dominated Western thought since the broad acceptance of Sir Isaac Newton's mechanistic view of the universe. In establishing the laws that govern the movement of physical objects, the Newtonian mind attempted to subject all physical movements, large and small, to the understanding of cause and effect. The resulting picture of the universe was like a huge mechanical clock whose little gears drive larger gears, which in turn drive the movements of the hands. This understanding gave its practitioners a new ability to predict and even control a particular class of physical phenomena that in turn led to the development of countless technologies in countless fields.

The game of golf, and specifically the mechanics of the golf swing, has been a favorite subject of inquiry for the Newtonian mind. The result has been not only the most intensive analysis of the components and sequences involved in this motion but, from this, a steady generation of technical instructions swelling into the thousands. In spite of the inevitable frustration of trying to understand, assimilate, and apply so many instructions, there has been an unending appetite for and belief in this kind of knowledge. This appetite stems from the same quest that fueled the technological Newtonian revolution: the desire to know and control.

It has always been somewhat disturbing to the Newtonians that human behavior, emotions, and aspirations could not be so easily known or controlled as the physical universe. Some have claimed that human behavior is, in fact, totally subject to cause and effect but that the variables are just too complicated to understand and manipulate fully. Human behavior presents two big problems for Newtonian scientists, whose methods of verification depend on shared observation and exacting rules of description. The first problem with studying human beings is that the "gears and levers" that turn the human clock are opaque, as they are confined within the body. You can't exactly cut open the living body to observe its workings. The best you can do is observe external behavior and try to make educated inferences as to the workings of the internal gears. The second problem with understanding human behavior in terms of cause and effect is that mysterious human potential called "free choice." The ideas of freedom and cause and effect seem to be mutually exclusive when applied to the same subject. So the inner human reality has been characterized as "subjective" and the outer reality "objective." In short, the methods of objective science simply did not lend themselves easily to the exploration of subjective realities.

But well before Newton—since the days of Socrates, in fact—men of wisdom have advised the human being to "know thyself." They claimed with authority and sincerity that this was, in fact, possible and spoke of a direct way of knowing inner reality. They were not scientific in the modern sense of the word but relied on faculties of knowing called by such names as "intuition," "insight," and "self-awareness." The purpose was not so much to know the outer world as to understand the dynamics of the one living in the world—to know the subject as distinct from the surrounding objective environment.

The second river of advice has been about mastering the human dimension of existence—the domain of thinking and feeling. Some call it the "mental side" of the game. I prefer simply to call it the "inner game." In this inner domain, much of what is important to understand, such as thought and feeling, cannot be directly observed by more than one person at a time. Though the results of thought, expressed in language, can be observed and analyzed, thought itself occurs too fast to be clearly observed. Few scientists or philosophers have claimed to understand the thinking process itself. As for feeling, it can be observed subjectively by each individual but can only be vaguely expressed in the outer world through word and gesture. In short, the individual can feel and feel richly, but can express, share, and compare what is felt in the inner world only partially—at best. Those who say that the human side of any activity, including golf, is important are often confined to speaking in metaphors and analogies. These are not exact and can only hint at the secrets of the game that is played from the inside out. This voice for playing the inner game has been strong and insistent for centuries, but hardly ever has it been the voice of the majority.

So these two streams, formulas and feelings, have moved through history as two great rivers, one seeming to swell as the other ebbs, sometimes crossing each other but rarely joining. It is sometimes difficult to tell if these rivers are moving toward the same ocean. It is not difficult to determine that human beings, to be effective, need something of what each stream has to offer.

Both these streams have influenced the way golf skills have been learned and performed. A few of the great teachers and players have been able to weave the wisdom of each into an integrated whole. I hope that as a result of reading, thinking about, and applying what you learn from this revised edition, you will be better equipped to forge such an integration.

When I first wrote *The Inner Game of Golf,* I knew almost nothing about the mechanics of the golf swing. I had been challenged to see how much golf I could learn just by adapting the "inner skills" that I had developed while playing and coaching tennis. The master skill was that of "relaxed concentration," which required an ability to pay close attention to the movements of ball and body and to make accurate observations of the results. It also involved the skill of trust in the body's capacity to learn and execute complex behaviors without following a complex set of instructions.

It is highly unlikely that any beginner who gets interested in the game of golf will escape being thrown into the stream of technical formulas. He or she could drown in the waters that flow from golf magazines, books, teaching professionals, and "knowledgeable" friends. The high probability of hitting some good shots, followed by some relatively poor shots, renders us vulnerable to this torrent of explanations and remedies.

But when I saw the wide disparity between my best shots and my worst, the claims from experts that there are right and wrong ways to swing the club became too compelling to ignore. So I flirted with technical instruction and admit to being seduced by a few of the leading technical formulations. I put the greatest hope in the notion that if I gripped the club correctly, assumed the correct posture, and held a single "swing thought" in mind, I would attain the "swing control" I obviously lacked. The simple assumption behind the promise of golfing technique was that by following the correct mental formulas I could control my behavior and get the desired results.

I understood that the game of golf was about control, and I was definitely subject to the pervasive human urge to increase control, an urge that, when unmonitored, becomes compulsive and then obsessive. Yet most golfers, myself included, would love a shortcut to mastery—hitting each ball to its desired destination with the grace, ease, and precision of perfection itself. And what then? Then, all who witnessed this mastery would stand back in awe and admiration. Yes!

So much for my dream. The reality was one of high hopes followed by mini-despairs. It ended in resignation and the belief that golf could be mastered only by those of great athletic ability who had the time to practice daily. The reality was that of imposing one set of instructions after another on a noncompliant body, then judging it when it failed to perform as instructed. The reality was the tightening of shoulders, legs, hips, and both sets of cheeks. The reality was that one tip led to another to another, which in turn led to unlearning the first three. Fortunately, my experience with the Inner Game of tennis made it possible for me to step out of the technology stream before I drowned in it. Though I would continue to dangle my toes in it from time to time, I never jumped in with both feet.

Instead, I wanted to see how far I could go without the benefit of technical expertise, and my editors set me the goal of breaking 80 while playing only once a week during the writing of this book. So the original edition became a narrative of my explorations of overcoming the inner obstacles of doubt, fear, and lack of focus that prevented natural learning. It also presented the basic inner skills that facilitate learning and peak performance.

The response of the golfing world to this inner approach to the game is noteworthy. As might have been expected, there was considerable resistance among some elements of the golf instruction establishment, whose authority stemmed largely from knowledge of the "swing mechanics." Then there were many pros who knew that the essence of what I was saying was true but didn't feel comfortable talking about it. Of course, players were skeptical about anything that did not seem in line with cause-and-effect mechanics as taught by their teaching pros or as endorsed by leading playing professionals.

But the book became a best-seller in the Newton-dominated

world of golf, so there were obviously enough golfers who knew that playing and enjoying golf is more than a matter of mechanics. They welcomed the book, passed it on to friends, and wrote thousands of acknowledgments to me about how it had reduced their handicaps and increased their enjoyment of the game. Sooner or later, many of the most skeptical golfers and their pros read the book and gave the Inner Game approach a try—if for no other reason than that golfers are a rare breed who will ultimately try anything that promises hope.

At the same time golfers were opening up to the mental side of golf, there was a general rise in the interest in sports psychology by athletes and their coaches. When *The Inner Game of Tennis* was published in 1974, it was considered revolutionary because it dealt directly and almost exclusively with the mental and emotional side of the game. Before then, people were nervous about expressing a need for help with the Inner Game and players who knew of its importance were reluctant to talk publicly about what they knew. The whole topic seemed to make most athletes feel just a little too vulnerable. Since then, we have witnessed the birth of a new field of study that now boasts thousands of practitioners, hundreds of facilities, and countless volumes of information about how to attain peak mental and physical states.

It was interesting for me to observe the evolution of golf instruction from the sidelines. I remember how surprised I was to see Bob Toski rise to popularity by teaching that the most important thing about the golf swing was to learn to feel it. Then there was the whole school of "imaging" led by cybervision, which taught people to learn to swing by watching slow-motion pictures of the best swing masters in the game. Without analyzing the specific movements of the swing or giving any instruction save "Watch, relax, and imagine yourself doing the same thing," it was as though the advice came straight from a single section of *The Inner Game of Tennis.*

In a recent *New York Times Book Review* article entitled "He's Tiger Woods and You're Not," author Lee Eisenberg states that there are several kinds of golf books. First, there's the instruction manual, of the cause-and-effect checklist type, usually written by leading players or their teachers. This genre of books has exploded in both volume and intricacy since the advent of the video camera, which reduces the swings of the best golfers to slow motion and provides as many freeze frames per swing as desired. This technology allows an even more minute analysis of a swing in motion and has further swelled the stream of technical instruction. At the same time, slow-motion videotapes revealed that the best golfers do a great deal that is individual or unique and that there are relatively few constants in the swings of the pros. In a book called *The Golf Swing*, David Leadbetter, one of the leading theoreticians and teachers of golf swing technique, said that the most definite conclusion he could draw from his years of study was "that there is no *definitive* method." Yet in golf, as in tennis, most teachers tend to ignore what is idiosyncratic and carve in stone whatever is not. The basic idea is to find a "model swing" that can be justified and then taught uniformly to everyone.

The *New York Times* article goes on to state that besides the books dealing with mechanical instructions there is another genre that deals with the mental side of the game, the leading examples of which are *The Inner Game of Golf* and books by Dr. Bob Rotella including *Golf Is Not a Game of Perfect*. Precursors of these books are Dr. Peter Cranford's *The Winning Touch in Golf*, Michael Murphy's *Golf in the Kingdom*, and Dr. Gary Wiren's *The New Golf Mind*. A more recent book in this genre is Fred Shoemaker's *Extraordinary Golf*. The point is that there is now a growing acceptance of the need for insight into the general domain of the Inner Game, and more information is becoming available to the average golfer. Furthermore, playing professionals as well as TV commentators are much more apt to express their thinking on the subject.

In spite of what might be called these "great advances" in golf instruction as well as advances in golf club and ball-making technology and a myriad of new training aids on the market, a very disconcerting fact has recently come to light. Generally speaking, the scores of golfers are not improving! At a recent conference of the PGA of America on Teaching and Coaching, *Golf Tips* magazine pointed out that "a question that arose repeatedly was this: Why is it that, despite the proliferation of golf schools, talented instructors, training aids, reputable instruction books and magazines, as well as high-tech, game-improving equipment, the handicap of the average American golfer is at best stagnant and—more likely—on the rise, according to United States Golf Association studies." For me the undeniable conclusion is that there is a big gap between what we know about the golf swing and our ability to help people learn.

I believe the answer to this problem will not be found in the further development of either technical or feel-based instruction alone. Nor does it help to study either field as if it were an independent area of mastery. No, in life they are integrated, and so, too, must they be in golf. The integration must be one that preserves the identity of each, a true marriage, in which each kind of knowledge works together and plays its appropriate yet distinct role. There can be no true marriage when each holds dogmatically to its own perspective and vies for dominance over the other.

I have kept two main purposes in mind while revising this book. In the last four chapters, I have attempted to articulate the next stage of development of the Inner Game, a step that goes beyond the basic need to have more kinesthetic or movement awareness in learning and performing golf. It introduces in greater depth the fundamental importance of knowing *why* you play the game as inseparable from *how* you play the game. Second, in the middle chapters, I have attempted to build a better bridge between traditional mechanistic golf instructions and the newer, feel-based kind of instructions. My hope is to create a better relationship between the "inner approach" and the "outer," two approaches that have been separate for far too long.

Consistent through both editions of this book is the idea that as golfers we are often our own worst enemies. No real progress in golf can be made without an honest acknowledgment of the inner obstacles that human beings put in the way of themselves and the expression of their potentialities. Whereas there is a more widespread belief in human potential than there used to be, it seems as hard as ever for most of us to own up to our tendency to get in our own way. And when we do acknowledge it, we tend to be so hard on ourselves that we become helpless to do much about it. Only if we find the courage and honesty to admit to our own self-interference and become more alert to it as it arises will we be able to make effective use of the plentiful technical information available. Without a better understanding of the human learning process and some compassion for the vulnerabilities as well as the aspirations of learners, all the technical information and all the positive thinking in the world won't help.

Building this bridge between inner and outer can bear much fruit in every game we play. It can also bring a greater respect for the ancient and wonderful game of golf by lifting it to a level of true recreation. It will also provide newcomers greater access to the game, lessening the frustration of the initial learning process while increasing the respect of those instructors who help people learn golf.

ACKNOWLEDGMENTS

THIS BOOK WAS COMPLETED WITH THE HELP OF MORE PEOPLE THAN I can name. I acknowledge and thank the following, who generously contributed time and energy: Jane Blalock, Marilyn Bowden, Tom Capelety, Tony Coleman, Ed Gallwey, Sally Gallwey, Al Geiberger, Molly Groger, Arch McGill, Michael Murphy, Tom Nordland, Gary Peterson, D.P.S. Rawat, Linda Rhodes, and Prentiss Uchida.

In addition, I acknowledge the valued assistance in design and production of this revised edition from Arnie Billingsley, Sean Brawley, Leslye Deitch, Tom Fitzpatrick, Larry Joseph, William A. Kasoff, John Kirk, and Sylvia Trujillo.

CONTENTS

FOREWORD Looking Back xi

ACKNOWLEDGMENTS xxi

ONE Golf: The Inner and Outer Challenge 3

TWO Breaking 90 with Back-Hit-Stop 17

THREE Overtightness: The Most Common Cause of Error 36

FOUR Overcoming Self-Doubt 47

FIVE The Awareness Instruction 69

SIX Discovering Technique 93

SEVEN The Short Game: Inner Putting and Inner Chipping 107

EIGHT Inner Swinging 131

NINE Of Slumps, Streaks, and False Expectations: Breaking 80 163

TEN Relaxed Concentration: The Master Skill 193

ELEVEN Playing Your Own Game 214

TWELVE Beyond Formula to Feeling 232

THE INNER GAME
OF GOLF

ONE

Golf: The Inner and Outer Challenge

As I laid down my tennis racket and cleaned off golf clubs scarcely used in twenty-five years, I felt two emotions. On the one hand, I had a keen sense of expectancy about exploring the application of Inner Game methods and principles developed on the tennis courts and ski slopes to the "royal and ancient" game of golf. On the other, I felt distinct uneasiness about grappling with the notorious mental obstacles evoked by the game. Somehow I sensed that, for me, golf could prove to be a dangerous game.

My uneasiness did not stem from a lack of confidence in the Inner Game. I knew that it had a real contribution to make, that its principles were grounded in basic truth, and that the methods and techniques had produced dramatic results not only in tennis and skiing but also in such varied worlds as music, business, education, health, and family life. Furthermore, I had received letters

from many golfers who had read *The Inner Game of Tennis* and reported that they had not only significantly lowered their handicaps but considerably increased their enjoyment. I sincerely felt
that the Inner Game would help golf and golfers in general and
from time to time even indulged in wishful daydreams about instant mastery of the game.

But golf is different from tennis, a sport that I had excelled in,
having played it all my life. My intention was to take up the game
and in a short period of time see how much I could improve my
present hacker level. I knew that helping others overcome doubts,
fears, and frustrations always seemed easy to me. But in learning
golf *I* would be the student. Sometimes I felt the pressure of possible failure, but I comforted myself with the knowledge that if I
really played the Inner Game I would inevitably learn more than
golf. Thus I could not really lose. Results would inevitably follow
learning.

"THE ONLY GAME I PLAY THAT I CAN'T LICK"

One of the first rounds of golf I played on my return to the game
was at the Hillcrest Club in Los Angeles in a foursome that included Dr. F., one of the best-known surgeons in California.
Somehow Dr. F., whom I had met at a celebrity tennis tournament, found time to play three times a week. On the first tee I felt
nervous in this unfamiliar atmosphere and admired Dr. F.'s seeming self-assurance. On the second tee, however, after a par on the
first hole, he pushed two successive drives out of bounds. Exasperated with himself, he slammed his driver to the ground and exclaimed disgustedly, "This is the most frustrating damned game
ever concocted by the mind of man!"

Sensing that his outburst did not come out of short acquaintance with the game, I naively asked, "Then why do you play so
often?"

Dr. F. paused, then finally answered, "Because I can't lick it."
He seemed surprised by his remark, and thought about it for a

moment before repeating firmly, "Yes, it's the only game I play that I can't beat!"

It soon became apparent that Dr. F. was frustrated not only by drives. Seeing him stand tensely over four-foot putts, I reflected that if he held his scalpel with as much apprehension and self-doubt as his putter, I'd never want to be on his operating table. Obviously, performing delicate surgery demands far more dexterity than is required to sink a four-foot putt, quite apart from the added dimension that the patient's life is at stake. Yet, clearly, golf unnerved Dr. F. more. Somehow I just couldn't imagine him angrily throwing his scalpel on the operating-room floor and calling himself a clumsy oaf, but this is exactly what happened on more than one three-putt green. As I watched all this, my respect for the challenge of the game was not diminished.

Dr. F. was not alone in frustration. Though I'd learned better in tennis, after almost every mis-hit golf shot I found myself subjecting my swing to critical analysis. I knew very little about the mechanics of the swing, but I tried to figure out what had gone wrong. Had I been off balance? Swung too hard? Maybe I'd been either too early or too late with my wrists. On the next shot I would try to correct whatever I thought had caused the mistake. But it seemed that every time I managed to fix one flaw, two more would emerge. The harder I tried to control my swing, the more mechanical and less rhythmic it became. The resulting shots were erratic, provoking my desire to try even harder for self-correction. Before long this cycle proved to be more like self-destruction than self-correction.

AWAY FROM THE GOLF COURSE, I took a fresh look at the game and asked myself what it was all about. The single word that came to mind was *control*. Basically, it seemed to be a matter of getting your body to do what you want it to do so that you can make the golf ball do what you want *it* to do. I saw the game as a stark challenge to a person's ability to control his or her own body. Since I had learned something from my experience in tennis about the problem of control, I decided to find a way of translating this understanding to golf.

WHAT I LEARNED ON THE TENNIS COURT

In short, what I learned on the tennis court was that the way most of us are taught to control our bodies simply doesn't work. Telling our bodies how to do something is not the most effective way to improve performance. Our muscles don't understand English, and our thinking minds don't really understand hand-eye coordination. Trying to make their bodies conform to the instructions of their last lesson, most tennis players inhibit free movement of their bodies and interfere with coordination rather than assist it. "Get your racket back early. . . . Meet the ball in front of you. . . . Don't roll the racket over on the follow-through," they say furiously to themselves during a match. Even when these drill-instructor commands are obeyed, they are usually performed with the stiffness and self-consciousness of a rebellious recruit and in a way that prohibits true excellence.

The quality of my teaching and of my students' performance took a major step forward the day I realized the extent of the disrupting effects of overinstruction. When my pupils' minds were free from both external and internal instructions, they could follow the ball better and had significantly better feel of their rackets. As a natural consequence, better results followed. In those early days of exploration of the Inner Game I was surprised at the improvement that would result after giving students the sole instruction "Forget everything you think you know about how to hit a tennis ball." Unable to forget anything they *really* knew, they could forget only what they *thought* they knew, and a natural ease would enter their game. But the Inner Game is not won with a single instruction, the inner opponent being far too crafty and well entrenched in our psyche to be dethroned so easily.

After several years the premise of the Inner Game of tennis

emerged clearly. The prime causes of error in tennis are within the mind of the player—in doubt, tension, and lapses of concentration more than in ignorance of mechanics. For this reason, as coach I found it far more effective to work from the inside out, trying to resolve the mental causes of error rather than to correct all the external symptoms. Over and over I observed that the removal of a single self-doubt could result immediately in numerous technical improvements in a tennis player's swing and overall game. The changes were spontaneous and unforced; they required neither technical instruction nor the constant demand for self-analysis that had characterized my early teaching.

On the tennis courts, methods for combating most mental problems facing tennis players had been found and proven effective. Now the challenge was to find practical ways to do the same under the physical requirements and mental pressures of the game of golf.

GOLF IS AN INNER GAME

As I began to play golf more regularly I realized that it would be a unique challenge to Inner Game effectiveness. What other game invites such tension and mental anguish? Like one's own children, golf has an uncanny way of endearing itself to us while at the same time evoking every weakness of mind and character, no matter how well hidden. The common purpose served is that we either learn to overcome the weaknesses or we are overwhelmed by them. Few games provide such an ideal arena for confronting the very obstacles that impair one's ability to learn, perform, and enjoy life, whether on or off the golf course. But to take advantage of this opportunity, the golfer must accept the challenge to play the Inner Game as well as the Outer Game. He or she must recognize not only sand traps and OB markers but the existence of mental hazards as well.

Perhaps the first task for the player of the Inner Game is to become aware of the mental factors evoked by golf. I found them to be many and multifaceted, but essentially they seemed to fall into five categories: the lure of the game to the ego, the precision it requires, the competitive pressures on the golfer, the unique pace of the game, and the obsession with the mechanics of the swing.

THE LURE OF GOLF

There is, I soon discovered, a seductive quality to golf found in few other sports. In moments of frustration many players vow to quit, but few are able to. For some reason, the two or three "triumphs" during a round are remembered long after the exasperating failures and dull mediocrity are forgotten.

I could see that some of the attraction of the game lay in the results that could sometimes be achieved by sheer luck. Golf is one of the few sports in which a novice can, on occasion, perform like a champion. A nonathlete playing golf for the first time can sink a fifty-foot putt on the first green and conclude that it is an easy game. Overconfidence can run rampant. Likewise, a reasonably well coordinated twenty-year-old may hit his first drive 250 yards straight down the middle of the fairway, and by the time he's walked up to his ball his ego is telling him that it will probably be only a short time before he's ready for the PGA tour. On a given day, my seventy-five-year-old father could score better than Jack Nicklaus on his worst. And on a given hole, even I, as a beginner, could occasionally hit a good drive down the middle, make an approach to the green, and sink the putt for a birdie—an outcome even the best pros would welcome. The problem, of course, was that this didn't happen very often for me—and in my naiveté my good holes would seduce me into thinking it was possible to be playing with the best. And the bad holes that inevitably followed would tend to plunge my vain hopes into despair. The same is not true of most sports. I am a better tennis player than golfer, but if I played Pete Sampras on my best day and he was having his worst, I would not win many points, much less games or sets. Realistic expectations about my abilities in golf were not so easy to come by in the early days.

After only a few hours on the driving range I realized that the compelling attraction of the game for me was also its major frustration. Even though I had played relatively little golf since I was thirteen, on occasion I would drive 230 yards, right on target. The sight of the ball soaring high and true was exhilarating; it filled me with a sense of mastery and power. The frustration lay in the fact that I couldn't repeat the experience at will. Fed by seemingly undying hope, I repressed my annoyance at failure and would reach for ball after ball. I wanted that feeling back to prove to myself that I could repeat what my body had shown me it was capable of doing. I was getting hooked by the game.

As I looked around the practice range I could see that others were caught in the same snare; there we were, spending hours and dollars trying for that elusive but tantalizing perfect swing that would give predictable results. Yet time and time again we were all faced with the dismal truth that we simply didn't have the self-control we wanted and somehow felt we should have. It wouldn't have hurt so much if we hadn't hit some excellent shots, giving us that cruel knowledge that the ability was there within us somewhere.

I began to understand and share Dr. F.'s fascination with the game. Golf seemed to raise my hopes only to dash them, to puff up my ego only to squash it. What kind of fun was this supposed to be? Could the game be beaten? What would that mean? Could I at least learn to enjoy the game and to play without frustration? I felt that to do only this would be a significant victory.

THE DEMANDS OF PRECISION

The most agonizing aspect of my own game was clearly its inconsistency. I was perfectly capable of hooking a ball forty yards left of center on one shot and then, with what seemed to be the same swing, slicing an equal distance on the next. Even more disconcerting was hitting a long drive down the middle on one hole, followed by a topped ball that barely dribbled off the tee on the next. I was used to inconsistency in tennis, but nothing on that order of magnitude! Although I might serve an ace and follow it with a serve four feet out, I wouldn't hit the bottom of the net with one shot and the fence on the fly with the next. Yet that's what golf felt like on some days.

It seemed to me that the precision required to play good golf demanded much greater mental discipline than was necessary for good tennis. The reason for the low margin of error was not hard to discover: the speed of the club head that is necessary to hit the ball a long distance. The speed of the golfer's arms on the downswing is not much greater than the speed of the tennis player's arm on the serve, but because of the greater length and flexibility of the golf club, the club-head speed is much greater than that of a racket. If a club head traveling over 100 mph contacts the ball with a face open a mere degree or two, the ball can be sent off target many tens of yards. With those odds, it's amazing that the ball ever does go exactly where we want it to.

In tennis, the serve is the only shot in which the player *initiates* the action, whereas in golf he does so on every shot. It is interesting to note that if you miss your first serve in tennis, you get another try. Golf is not so forgiving! Further, in tennis a much larger surface hits a much larger ball a much shorter distance. Moving from tennis to golf was definitely going to require some fine-tuning of my concentration.

The greater precision required in golf is also reflected in the manner in which the player addresses the ball. A tennis player can be pretty casual, or even a little flamboyant, as he sets up the service line, bounces the ball a few times, and serves. Most professional golfers display much more self-discipline. They seem to approach the ball in the same controlled, almost ritualistic way every time. Even their dress seems more meticulous. (I've often felt I could pick out the golfers from the tennis players at a cocktail party.)

Meticulousness has never been my strong suit. There isn't a family picture of me as a boy in which at least one shoe wasn't untied. I could usually solve all the problems given me on a math test but would seldom make a perfect score because of careless mistakes in computation. I wondered if I'd ever be able to achieve the degree of discipline that the game of golf seemed to call for. At the outset my only hope was to look at the game as a challenge to my ability to enhance this particular quality of mind. I can't say that I looked forward to the task.

The precision required in golf doesn't allow for release of the pent-up anger and frustration that one can find in more aggressive sports. Golf produces frustration, but it requires that you learn to deal with it in some way other than in your next shot. This presents a fascinating Inner Game challenge.

PRESSURE

If I have a mediocre day on the tennis court and lose a match 6–3, 6–3, I can always lessen the humiliation to my ego by telling myself that my opponent was playing particularly well that day. But the golfer stands alone. Blame or credit for the score rests on him or her, and usually there are three other people around to pass judgment. The ego thrives and dies in such a setup.

Every shot I take in golf counts. In tennis I can lose three straight points and still win the game; many lost points will never show up in the final score. Tennis forgives a few mistakes; golf forgives none. Thus, pressure can seem constant.

Because the game of golf is inherently a game of the golfer against himself, the Inner Game is intensified. The ego is both more challenged and more threatened. The player's spirits tend to rise or sink in direct proportion to his score, the sole product of his own efforts. Although I have seen many golfers avoid this pressure by blaming various weather and course conditions, golf clubs, balls, other players, family, or business affairs, I feel that few can fool themselves for long before facing the fact that golf is a game played only against the course and oneself and that one's score is a pretty true indication of skill.

Although I have seen many "fry" under this kind of pressure, I have also noticed that often it is this very same pressure that attracts golfers to the game. As a rule, most golfers prefer the tougher courses to easy ones and like to add to the existing pressure by betting money on the result "just to make the game more interesting."

Learning to perform at one's best under pressure is a clear goal of the Inner Game. The challenge of sinking a five-foot putt on the eighteenth hole to save par and the match is clearly a lot more mental than it is physical. And the player who can learn to perform with precision and power under such seeming pressure will learn an inner skill that can help him to cope with other situations in his life.

PACE

The pace of golf is unique and in obvious contrast to that of most sports. In tennis, for example, if my mind begins to entertain a flow of self-critical or negative thoughts, it is cut short abruptly by the need to respond to the oncoming ball.

But in golf we have too much time to think. Between shots a negative train of thought can become entrenched: What went wrong on that last shot? How do I correct my slice? What will happen to my score if I hit the next shot out of bounds? There is endless time to overanalyze and become confused, discouraged, or angry.

The tennis player is constantly caught up in the action—moving toward or hitting the ball. In four hours on the court I may play about sixty-four games or about four hundred points in perhaps twelve hundred to fifteen hundred separate shots. During the same length of time in golf I will hit—I hope—less than one hundred shots. If each golf shot takes me two seconds, then I am engaged in swinging the golf club for a total of only three minutes out of four hours of play.

Therefore, concentration in golf requires a unique kind of effort. In the first place, the ball just sits there and the pace of the game demands that the golfer be at an intense peak of concentration at the exact moment of the swing, supremely challenging his ability to keep from being distracted during the long intervals between shots. In tennis my concentration tends to build as the point progresses, reaching its peak as I become "lost in the action." But in the long stretches between golf shots it is easier to become lost in the thoughts on the surface of our minds.

I concluded that the walk between shots is one of the most critical parts of the game. Though this period of time is recognized by some pros as a potential mental hazard as well as a benefit, I feel its importance in most golfers' minds is generally undervalued. It is most often in the interval between shots that both the Inner and the Outer games are won or lost. It is during this time that the golfer's mental equilibrium can be destroyed by the momentum of negative thoughts or employed to shake off the tension of the last shot and to prepare for the next. The inner golfer learns to use the time between shots to relax the mind and to prepare it for the total concentration needed during the two seconds of the next swing. (This subject will be dealt with further in Chapter 8.)

OBSESSION WITH TIPS AND TECHNIQUE

I had long thought that the mechanics of the tennis swing had been exhaustively analyzed until I took a look at existing golf manuals. I wouldn't be surprised if more has been written about the mechanics of the golf swing than just about any other human movement. It has been dissected into amazingly minute segments and the information passed along to the already overloaded minds of students of the game. Hearing that I was taking up the game, a friend presented me with three volumes: *295 Golf Lessons by Bill Casper, 395 Golf Lessons by Gary Player, 495 Golf Lessons by Arnold Palmer.*

It is not difficult to see how superstition thrives on the modern golf course. So many players are in constant search of "the secret," and endless magic formulas are propagated by true believers. Ready to try anything to relieve frustration, the golfer finds his hopes rising as he hits a few good shots after trying a given tip. It works! he thinks to himself. "I've got the game licked," he exclaims, as my father has so many times confessed to feeling. But how long does any single magic formula help a given player? "The secret" is dropped after a few poor shots occur and hope wanes. Soon the golfer is open for the next tip. Of course, some modest tips can be truly helpful, but the all-encompassing ones only raise one's hopes for conquering a game that can *never* be mastered by a single tip. I am convinced that the happiest and best golfers are those who have realized that there is no single gimmick that works and that good golf is attained only by patience and humility and by continually practicing both Outer and Inner Game skills.

So HERE IS THE MENTAL SITUATION, as I see it, facing the brave soul who plunges innocently into the awesome game of golf. His ego will be attracted to the rich psychic rewards offered by success in the sport, and it will fear the imagined devastation that failure to perform up to a reasonable norm may bring. After he has played a few rounds, he will have hit enough good shots to provoke unquieting thoughts of heroism—if only he can learn to repeat consistently what he has shown that he can do on occasion. But unknown to the novice player, the mechanics of the game dictate that the probabilities of hitting those shots consistently are almost nil. Furthermore, he will be surrounded by prophets with both mental and technical golfing keys promising to deliver him from his evils and to unlock the gates leading into the heaven of good golf. Confused by the long lists of dos and don'ts, ranging from sound fundamentals to superstitious mental magic, he will tend to analyze each shot and to try to compensate for each mistake. Then he will compensate for the compensation. Between failures he will have all the time in the world to think and, while doing so, to increase his tension and doubt, while after success he won't be able to resist the temptation to analyze how to repeat it. Put this all together in the head of one man or woman who is already suffering the tensions of modern life and what you have is an intriguing but dangerous game.

THE INNER GAME OF GOLF

It is the thesis of this book that the secret to increasing control over our bodies lies in gaining some measure of control over our minds. A basic understanding of mechanics can help, and, surely, a certain amount of physical coordination is required to play good golf. But differences in talent do not account for the fact that most of us hit much better on the practice range than we do in the thick of battle on the course or for the wide variations in our individual scores. The aim of the Inner Game is to close the unnecessarily wide gap between our potential and our actual performance and to open the way to higher and more constant levels of enjoyment of the game.

THUS, THE CHALLENGE of golf lies as much in the relatively unexplained aspects of the Inner Game as it does in the Outer Game. There is a growing interest in the mental side of golf that is reflected in current books and magazine articles on the subject. Asking me to speak at a PGA meeting, a regional PGA educational director said that there was a general consensus that teaching pros were reaching a point of diminishing returns on analysis of the mechanics of golf and were turning their attention to the mental side of the sport. "We know a lot about the swing," one college golf coach said to me, "but not much about how to help golfers learn it."

This is not merely a matter of words. The issues of how to overcome self-doubt, lapses in concentration, self-anger, and low self-esteem are very real. Facing these handicaps for some is like noticing an unwelcome bedfellow; we'd rather roll over and forget that he or she is there.

But to play the Inner Game is not really a matter of choice. It is always going on, and we are playing it constantly in our various outer games. The only question is whether we are playing it consciously and whether we are winning it or losing it. Anyone who feels his performance is always equal to its actual potential, and fully enjoys and learns from his golf experience, has my hearty congratulations for winning the Inner Game. As for all others, including myself, though we may play very different outer games in different circumstances, there is still an enemy within and, thus, an Inner Game to be played.

The fundamental challenge to the golfer is to recognize the existence of interference and that winning the Inner Game may be more to the point than simply defeating the golf course.

This book describes practical ways to bring Inner Game principles and techniques to your golf game. These exercises are neither gimmicks nor tips; rather, they are ways to increase three primary inner skills: awareness, choice, and trust. Because many of the exercises were developed as I attempted to learn golf, some of this book consists of brief accounts of my own inner and outer struggles and the evolution of my game.

The next chapter begins with my efforts to gain enough consistency in my swing so I could take ten or more strokes off my 100-plus average score. I accomplished this with the help of a focusing technique I adapted from *The Inner Game of Tennis* called "back-hit-stop."

TWO

Breaking 90 with
Back-Hit-Stop

IN THE *INNER GAME OF TENNIS*, I WROTE, "RELAXED CONCENTRATION is the key to excellence in all things." I realized that golf was going to offer an even more difficult challenge to maintaining this concentration than tennis. When I first began to explore the Inner Game of golf, I was not aware that this subject was not entirely new. Since almost all golf instruction at the time seemed focused on mechanics, I was surprised when I ran across an article called "The Mental Hazards of Golf" in a 1929 issue of *Vanity Fair* by none other than the legendary Bobby Jones. The article was subtitled "Stray Thoughts on Worry, Nerves, Temperament and Lack of Concentration in the Game." Here are some excerpts:

> Golf is assuredly a mystifying game. Even the best golfers cannot step onto the first tee with any assurance as to what

they are going to do. . . . It would seem that if a person has hit a golf ball correctly a thousand times he should be able to duplicate the performance almost at will. But such is certainly not the case.

The golf swing is a most complicated combination of muscular actions, too complex to be controlled by objective conscious mental effort. Consequently, we must rely a good deal upon the instinctive reactions acquired by long practice. It has been my experience that the more completely we can depend upon this instinct—the more thoroughly we can divest the subjective mind of conscious control—the more perfectly can we execute our shots. . . . That intense concentration upon results, to the absolute exclusion of all thoughts as to method, is the secret of a good shot. Few great shots are played when the mind is fixed on the position of the feet, the behavior of the left arm, etc.

In playing a golf shot it always helps if the player can shut out from his mind all worry over the result of the effort, at least while he is in the act of playing the shot. . . . After taking the stance, it is too late to worry. The only thing to do then is to hit the ball.

It is not easy, even with the assistance of a first-class teacher, for a man to develop a sound golfing style. But it is possible and practicable for a person to cultivate a mental attitude toward the game which will enable him to get everything possible out of his own capability.

These statements rang true according to my experience teaching concentration in tennis. I realized that what I may have thought I discovered had, in fact, been around for a long time and had probably been discovered by many others, perhaps by everyone who had truly achieved excellence in his or her field. Yes, the problem is ultimately a simple one of control, but most things requiring excellence are too complex to be controlled, as Bobby Jones observed, "by objective conscious mental effort."

SELF 1 AND SELF 2

A major breakthrough in my understanding of the problem of control of mind and body came when, as a tennis instructor, I became aware of a constant commentary going on inside my head as I played. I realized that my students were subjected to a similar flow of self-instructional thoughts while taking lessons: Come on, get your racket back earlier. . . . You hit that one too late again. . . . Bend your knee on those volleys. . . . Uh-oh, here comes another high backhand like the one you missed last time. . . . Make sure you don't miss it again. . . . Damn it! you missed it again. . . . When are you ever going to hit those things? . . . Watch the ball, watch the ball. . . . What am I going to say to my doubles partner if I lose this match?

As I began to take a closer look at the thoughts going through my mind during a tennis match, I found myself asking, "Whom am I talking to, and who is doing the talking?" I was surprised to discover that there seemed to be at least two identities within me. One was playing tennis; the other was telling him how. I observed that the one doing the talking, whom I named Self 1, thought he knew all about how to play and was supervising Self 2, the one who had to hit the ball. In fact, Self 1 not only gave Self 2 instructions but criticized him for past errors, warned him of probable future ones, and harangued him whenever he made a mistake. It was easy to see that the primary feeling in the relationship between these two selves was mistrust. Self 1 didn't trust Self 2 to hit the ball, and, precisely to the extent that he lacked trust, he would try to force Self 2 to conform to his verbal instructions. I noticed that when I had more confidence in my ability to hit a shot, there was a corresponding decrease in instructions from Self 1 and that Self 2 would perform amazingly well without him. When I was on a streak, there was no talk in my head at all.

Once I became aware of Self 1, it grew increasingly obvious that this judgmental little voice barking away like a drill sergeant inside my head was not the best thing for my tennis game. Self 1 was more of a hindrance than the great help he wanted me to think he was. Thereafter I began looking for ways to decrease the interference of Self 1, and to see what happened if I trusted the potential of Self 2. I found that when I could quiet Self 1 and let Self 2 learn and play without interference, my performance and learning rate improved significantly. My Self 2 was a great deal more competent than Self 1 gave him credit for. Likewise, I found that when, as a teacher, I didn't feed the instruction-hungry Self 1 of a student with a lot of technical information but, instead, trusted in the capacity of *his* Self 2 to learn, the progress of my students was three or four times faster than average, and they learned with much less frustration.

In short, I found that Self 1—the verbalizing, thought-producing self—is a lousy boss when it comes to control of the body's muscle system. When Self 2—the body itself—is allowed control, the quality of performance, the level of enjoyment, and the rate of learning are all improved.

Although after a time I realized that Self 1 was really a composite of different ego-personalities that would surface at different times, it was still helpful to group all these elements under the identifying label of Self 1 as the source of our interference with our natural selves. I found that in order to *de*crease interference and *in*crease performance, it wasn't necessary to analyze *why* doubt, fear, judgment, and lapses in concentration occurred; it was sufficient to recognize their intrusion and then concentrate the mind on something real in the immediate environment. From this realization, a number of Inner Game concentration exercises were developed for tennis players.

Some readers of *The Inner Game of Tennis* have associated Self 1 and Self 2 with the popular two-hemisphere-brain theory, equating Self 1 with the rational, analytical left hemisphere and Self 2 with the intuitive right hemisphere. I don't make the same association because both right and left hemispheres are part of the human body. I look at Self 2 as the total human organism, the natural entity. Self 1, on the other hand, does not actually have a physical existence; it is a phenomenon of mental self-interference that can and does interfere with both right- and left-hemisphere functions. Self-doubt, for example, can be as crippling in a mathematics test as in a tennis match, on a golf course or in singing a song. But when the mind is concentrated and absorbed in what it is doing, interference is minimized and the brain is able to function closer to its potential.

When Self 1 and Self 2 are clearly defined in this way, the basic premise of the Inner Game can be expressed in a simple equation: $P = p - i$. The quality of our performance (P) is equal to our potential (p) minus the interference (i) with the expression of that potential. Or: Performance = Self 2 (potential) minus Self 1 (interference).

Thus, the aim of the Inner Game is not so much to try harder to persuade Self 2 to do what it is capable of doing but to decrease the Self 1 interferences that prevent Self 2 from expressing itself fully.

Still, I found that like most tyrants, Self 1 didn't like losing control and resisted efforts to minimize his influence. The process of decreasing his control in favor of Self 2 proved to be a challenging one, which required the development of concentration techniques designed to keep Self 1 occupied in noninterfering activity and consciously to allow Self 2 to hit the ball. Once Self 1 was focused in a concentration exercise, his interference with Self 2 decreased significantly and performance instantly improved.

THE MAGIC OF BOUNCE-HIT

What had become clear to me on the tennis court was that it was not so easy to follow Bobby Jones's admonition to "divest the sub-

jective mind of conscious control." Neither was it so easy to focus
to the extent of "absolute exclusion of all thoughts."

In tennis the most obvious focus for the attention is the moving tennis ball. But simply to encourage students to watch the ball
doesn't create the level of focus I was looking for. I found that
when I asked students to watch the ball's spinning seams, there
was a higher degree of focus and usually smoother shots. I found
even more success in a quite simple focusing technique I called
"bounce-hit," which proved effective for players at all levels.

Before giving the students instructions, I would usually introduce the exercise by saying that its purpose was not to improve results but to improve *focus*, an important Inner Game skill useful in
all endeavors. The exercise was to say out loud the word "bounce"
the instant the ball hit the court and the word "hit" at the moment
of impact with the racket. Once the player got locked in to
"bounce-hit," an almost immediate improvement could be seen in
the way he swung his racket and moved his feet and body, and
there was usually an observable increase in relaxation and fluidity
of movement. Players hit even more difficult shots with relative
effortlessness while their conscious mind was absorbed in the cadence of the bounce-hit focus.

I realized there were two basic criteria for the success of any
effective focusing exercise. First, it had to be interesting enough
to engage the attention of the conscious mind, distracting it from
its normal patterns of overcontrol and interference. Second, it
had to give useful feedback about ball and body to enable more
coordinated movement.

What I was looking for in golf was some simple focus of attention that in the same way would keep my conscious, thinking
mind out of the way of my natural swing and natural learning
process. And golfers I met who were familiar with *The Inner Game
of Tennis* were asking me the very question I was asking myself:
"What is the bounce-hit of golf?"

LOOKING FOR THE BOUNCE-HIT OF GOLF

Although I experimented with a number of exercises for focusing attention on the golf ball—such as watching a dimple, the label, or a speck of dust—none of these seemed to keep my mind quiet for long. The problem was that the darn ball just sat there. I would easily grow bored looking at it, and, if I forced the exercise, my mind became strained and my swing stiff. The bounce-hit magic seemed to have something to do with the mind's fascination with the movement and rhythm of the tennis ball, and this simply didn't apply to the golf ball. Also, in order to hit the golf ball, Self 2 didn't need moment-to-moment *visual* feedback; the ball wasn't going to go anywhere until I hit it. The very lack of motion of the golf ball, which gave one so much time to think and grow tense, was exactly what was impeding concentration.

Finally, I did find one focus that helped more than the others and is worth mentioning. Instead of looking only at the ball, I began looking at the back of the ball *in relation to* one of the blades of grass just below it. By keeping both in focus, I could tell if during the swing there was undue head movement. If the relative position of the ball and the background of grass changed a great deal, it was because I had moved my head a lot. This helped, but it still was not the answer I was looking for.

Eventually I came to the conclusion that the primary focus of attention in golf should be *not* the ball but the club head, the critical moving object. The movement was *there*, the feedback needed was *there*, the rhythm that fascinates the mind was *there*—not in the ball. But I couldn't follow the club head with my eyes; if I wished to focus attention on it, I would have to use my sense of *feel*, and I didn't know how difficult this would be. How much could I actually *feel* the club head moving during my swing? I decided to go out to the driving range to experiment with club-head awareness.

At first, I had relatively little sense of where my club was. I found that if I didn't worry about whether I hit the ball or not, I could feel it better. I tried shutting my eyes and swinging and found that my awareness of feel increased even more. The movement of the club head was becoming interesting enough to hold my attention throughout the arc of the swing. Whenever I would try simply to *feel* the club head and *not* to *control* it, the club seemed to swing itself, and I got excellent results—the same kind I had in tennis when my mind became concentrated. But when I split my attention—half to the feel of the club head and the other half to trying to control the swing—the results weren't so good.

BACK-HIT-STOP

To keep my mind focused on the club and away from the process of controlling it, I came up with the following exercise. Keeping my attention on the feel of the club head, I would say the word "back" the instant I felt the club reach its furthest extension at the completion of the backswing. I would simply sense its position without worrying at all whether it was in the "correct place." Then I would say the word "hit" the instant the club face met the ball. Finally, I would say the word "stop" the moment the club came to rest at the completion of the follow-through.

This exercise kept me in touch with the club head throughout the entire arc of the swing and was exacting enough to keep my attention away from the intrusion of Self 1 commands. Staying with the club until "stop" proved to be particularly effective in keeping Self 1 from prematurely jerking my head up to see where the ball had gone. The drill actually required more concentration than the visual bounce-hit in tennis. Precisely because it was more demanding, it was even more effective.

After only a few minutes' work with this exercise, there were often dramatic improvements in swing technique and results. The only real difficulty was in the tendency to want to control the swing instead of simply doing the exercise. It is natural not to want to give up all conscious control at once. But even with 50 percent of my focus occupied in "back-hit-stop," there was significantly less interference with the swing. Then, as my confidence grew, it was easier to risk focusing more on the exercise and to leave the hitting to instinct.

It was surprising to many golfers to whom I showed this exercise how unaware they actually had been of their club head. Although most had interesting theories about where it *should* be at the back of the swing, they were often six to eighteen inches off in their estimate of where it *actually* was. One thing I had learned in tennis was that it is more important to know where your racket *is* than to know where it *should be*. The tennis ball is hardly ever where it should be but always where it is. I told my students, "*Should* and *is* usually miss each other." The same is true in golf. What the body needs to control the path of the club head is not a lot of instructions but accurate, moment-by-moment feedback about its position. Back-hit-stop was effective in increasing this input, as well as in quieting Self 1. It took practice and trust, but it paid off in results.

One problem that emerged for some players practicing this exercise was a tendency to turn "back" and "hit" from nouns into verbs. This had the effect of putting them back into the mode of obeying commands. It was as if they were telling themselves, "Now get your club back, now hit the ball." I could usually tell when this was happening, as the normal overtightness and controlling effort would appear while the accuracy of the "back-hit-stop" suffered greatly. "The word 'back' is supposed to be used as a noun," I would remind them. "It is just used to denote the moment you feel your club reach the top of its swing, and 'hit' is another noun to denote the moment of impact." The same goes for "stop"; it is not a command to stop the swing but a word to mark its completion.

DA-DA-DA-DA

To help some people avoid the temptation to command I substituted the syllable "da" for each of the words. "Da" at the back and "da" at the hit and then "da" at completion. This made the rhythm of the swing even more obvious, especially when it was turned into a four-count cadence. "Da" at the moment of take-away; "da" at the top of the backswing, "da" at the moment of im-pact, and, finally, "da" at the end.

This four-count cadence had several added advantages. It gave an increased sense of rhythm and tempo as well as feedback about the position of the club head at four critical moments. It turned out to be a far more interesting focus for the mind because of the added sense rhythm. Consequently, there was less room for conscious control, better feedback for the swing, and a greater freedom in swinging the club.

This exercise can be practiced on the range to improve club-head awareness and to help discover one's natural rhythm and tempo. It can also be used during play on the course to keep the mind focused and clear.

I realized, as I had with tennis, that there is a very big differ-ence between *observing* your swing and *trying to control* it. Most important, I found out that it's hard to do both at the same time. When I kept to the discipline of this exercise, paying full atten-tion, I had much less tendency to overcontrol my swing, and, as a result, it seemed over time to gain control naturally.

Sometimes I felt that the Inner Game worked even better for others than for myself. Just when I was starting my search for the bounce-hit of golf, I got a phone call from a Mr. Dean Nims, from Des Moines, Iowa. He identified himself as the president of a paper company and an avid but frustrated golfer with an eighteen or nineteen handicap. He said he had read both of my Inner Game tennis books in the hope that they would help with his golf.

DEAN NIMS'S STORY

"I tried to come up with an exercise that paralleled your bounce-hit in tennis and finally settled on 'hit-bounce,' " Mr. Nims told me. "I would say 'hit' when the club hit the ball and 'bounce' when the ball landed, wherever it landed. The results were instantaneous and dramatic for me. Playing the McCormick Ranch Golf Course near Scottsdale, Arizona, I shot a 76 for the first time using this drill. It was unbelievable! I could see the ball much better, had much less tension, and didn't turn away from my shots after hitting them as I had done before. I'd never broken 85 before. Of course, I couldn't help thinking I had the game licked after that and would only use the drill when I thought I was in trouble. Then I'd get better again."

Later Dean came out to California to take some Inner Game golf lessons and to discuss with me the translation of Inner Game principles to business practices. A few months later I called Dean and he told me he was using Inner Game principles in most areas of his life. "I can't say I've won the game," he said, "but my golf has steadily improved—not only in my scoring but in my general attitude." His handicap had gone down to eight, playing little more than once a week, and he said he was enjoying showing the methods to others.

Dean told me about an eight-year-old girl who was on the range with her father one hot, humid summer day. The father was trying to instruct her, but she was unable to hit the ball in spite of all his help. They were both hot and frustrated when Dean introduced himself to them and showed the girl the da-da-da-da exercise. The girl seemed interested, took a swing singing out "daddy-da," and hit the first solid ball of her life. She continued to do so the rest of the practice session. Her father told Dean that his daughter had been in a junior golf program and, given the task of playing one hole, had been unable to get off the tee. The next day he called Dean to say that the girl was ecstatic. She had not only gotten off the tee, she had beaten her two competitors, both two years older.

But Dean also told me that a lot of adults he'd showed the exercise to had more difficulty.

"What's the problem?" I asked.

"They seem reluctant to really try something new and different, even though they saw what it did to my game. Some say they know they're lousy golfers and didn't expect to get any better, and some don't want to entertain the hope. Others who agreed to do the exercise had a hard time accepting that they were not saying 'hit' until way after the moment of contact. But when they realized that it was their thinking that kept them from saying 'hit' on time, and then could let go of Self 1 control, they'd experience a significant breakthrough."

As an aside, Dean told me about one of his salesmen who hadn't been performing up to his potential. "Although he wasn't a tennis player or golfer, he agreed to read the Inner Game books and discuss with me their application to sales. The next year his sales doubled."

The principle behind back-hit-stop and da-da-da-da is the same. Individual preferences, however, will emerge if you choose to experiment. The only important thing is to make a commitment to doing purely the concentration exercise. Don't try to add it to another tip or to other swing thoughts.

In both tennis and golf, I found that a person's level of focus does not stay constant. Often at the beginning it would start quite purely. There would be no expectations, and the person would let go of control to do the focusing exercise as an experiment. Then if he noticed the results of his shots—either whether they improved or got worse—control would often come back. As coach, I could see the increase of tension and hear that the words spoken were no longer in sync. Then, if I asked the student if he was on time, early, or late with the words or syllables, "I don't know" was often the reply.

When either you or another person notices that your voice is out of sync with your swing, it's a sign that you are losing focus. At that point, it is often interesting to notice quickly what pulled you off focus, for example, thinking about results, mechanics, memories of past shots, and so forth. Then determine to renew your focus on back-hit-stop or da-da-da-da. When these exercises are done with discipline, the result is almost always a freer swing made possible by less Self 1 control. Obviously, no exercise can promise a flawless swing every time, nor should it be a replacement for learning the important technical aspects of the golf swing, a subject that will be addressed in more detail starting with Chapter 5.

PRACTICING FOCUS

My recommendation is that you practice the exercises for at least a short time on the driving range and putting green before attempting them on the course. It is difficult enough to let go of conscious control over your swing in practice; it is almost too much to ask under playing conditions. Once you have found the exercise that works best for quieting your mind, you should stick with it and give it a chance to work. Eventually it will be difficult not to want to use it in the pressure situations. One can expect, however, that the greater the pressure, the harder it will be to quiet Self 1 and attain the same level of concentration as in practice. But then, that's just when you need it, so persevere.

When first learning how to use these exercises, it is a good idea to say the words out loud, and even to have an observer check your accuracy. When your voice is markedly out of sync with your club position, it will be because your mind has wandered—probably to the task of trying to hit the ball. Most players need some practice with this exercise before developing a concrete feel of the club head.

After a brief period of practicing back-hit-stop or da-da-da-da, your concentration will probably improve, and so your swing will be freer and you will get better results. At the first sign of success, be careful! Don't start thinking that these are magic words and that whenever you say them the ball will go where you wish. Remember that if it works, it's not the words that make it work but improved concentration.

Don't try to reduce the exercise to a magic formula, another superstition. If you do, the exercise will soon stop being effective, just like all other gimmicks. Then Self 1 will tell you, "Well, that sure doesn't work—throw it out. This whole thing is nonsense." Don't listen. Just remember that the words were just an aid to concentration and that it was the concentration that helped. Every time you succeed in blocking out Self 1 and allow Self 2 to hit the ball, you will get better results. But you have to make the effort *every* time; momentary relaxed concentration is easy, but it has to become constant and continuous. Techniques to help gain that concentration are only as effective as your steady use of them.

BREAKING 90

The positive effects of back-hit-stop and da-da-da-da were soon very apparent on my own golf game. As a result, primarily from doing this exercise, my average score dropped from about 95 to about 88.

When Joe Fox, my original editor at Random House, asked me to write about applying Inner Game methods to my own game of golf, I was hesitant at first. At that time I played golf fewer than four or five times a year and usually shot between 95 and 105. "Let's see if you can break 80 by the time you turn in the book and by playing no more than one round of golf per week," Fox challenged. He argued that many readers could not play more than that. At the time, I had slightly over a year to complete the book and break 80. Needless to say, I felt sufficiently challenged.

My game at the time was not hard to characterize. I hit a fairly long drive, but without consistency. Out of ten drives, no more than three would be likely to land in the fairway, four would have a moderate to severe slice, and three would be dubbed or hooked. Such a variety was not encouraging to me, even though distance itself seemed somehow to be a compensation. My mid and short irons were a little more reliable—but only a little. Even though I hit some greens and sunk some long putts, they were too few and far between. My game was not a cautious one. If I had a chance to cut off distance on a dogleg or hit through a flock of trees for the green, I would almost always go for it. I hated to play it safe and all too often was willing to give up prudence.

Still, hope was kept alive by the two or three spectacular shots I would hit every eighteen holes. Deep down there was a dream that I could repeat my best swings and that perhaps what I had learned in tennis about the Inner Game would bring me instant success in golf.

The day I accepted my editor's challenge, I set myself a regimen of no more than eighteen holes of golf per week and only one hour of practice on the range and putting green. In spite of a certain feeling of pressure about having to break 80, I started this golfing experience with high expectations. Somewhere in the more naive part of my mind I entertained the thought that perhaps I could discover such an effective concentration exercise for golf that I would be shooting par in a couple of weeks.

Such was not to be. Finishing my first round at Rancho Park in Los Angeles with a 98, I realized that despite my confidence as an Inner Game tennis professional, my abilities did not automatically transfer to golf. It wasn't until after a few weeks, once my dreams of glory had died down and my tension had subsided, that I began to apply focusing techniques in a disciplined way. By that time I had played three rounds and given myself three hours of practice. My scores averaged about 95.

When I made the decision to make the practice of focus a priority over my results, my first real breakthrough occurred. I decided that the discipline of whispering to myself the syllables "da-da-da-da" in cadence with my swing was worth committing to for at least my next ten rounds of golf. Near the end of the second month I had broken 90 once, and by the end of the third my score was averaging 88.

During this time, I focused almost exclusively on the rhythm and cadence of my swing, and I had the sense that my club head was doing the swinging rather than my trying to control it. I could feel my consistency increasing and with it my self-confidence. Soon I began to feel a little more like a golfer than like a tennis player trying to play golf. I also knew that I hadn't yet attained the limit of my capacity. I still had a lot to explore about both the Outer and Inner games of golf.

Not too much later I began to wonder what would happen if I were to play one of the great golf courses. Was I ready for it?

90 AT ST. ANDREWS GOLF CLUB, SCOTLAND

I flew to London on business but with the firm intention of heading up to Scotland to play the historic St. Andrews course. When my editor heard about my plans, he bet me ten dollars that I couldn't break 100 on the Old Course, whose generally adverse conditions of heather and weather make it one of the world's toughest.

The day I finally got a chance to play I flew to Edinburgh from the Inner Game Center in London and rented a car at the airport to drive to St. Andrews. I barely made my 1:00 tee time. I played in a threesome with Peter and Daphne, an English couple who live on the first tee at the Canterbury Golf Course in Kent. I felt nervous as I stepped up to the first tee, where crowds of onlookers line up to watch. The souvenir scorecard described the hazards on each hole, complete with pictures. They were formidable. The first hole presents only one hazard, called Swilican Burn, a wide ditch full of water right along the edge of the green. I made an effort to concentrate, targeted, and landed left of center on the fairway. From there I hit a seven iron twenty feet from the pin, but only ten feet from Swilican Burn. I wished I'd brought my own golf clubs; the putter of the set I'd rented at the caddie house was much lighter than my own. I kicked the thought out of my mind, focused on the heel of the putter head, and barely missed the putt. Par.

I'd come to St. Andrews on a day of rare good weather: 80 degrees, with a warm wind at our backs. Though I'd heard a lot about the beauty and majesty of this old course, I was nonetheless spellbound by its incredible meandering greens, like broad expanses of meadowland, and its treacherous and unusual traps. Some were eight to twelve feet deep; others had vertical sides that dropped six feet to fine white sand—more like small cliffs than lips. All bore provocative names: The Coffins, The Cat's Trap, The Principal's Nose. The sense of ancient tradition permeates the atmosphere; the town itself is built around the course, physically and culturally. I gave in to the magic of the place and the ambience of the day. I had anticipated pressure from my desire to make my one chance to play this course a good performance, not so much because of my bet with my editor as because I wanted to write about it in the book. (Self 1 was eager for renown.)

On the second hole I hit a hesitant chip shot for a bogey; I parred the third and bogeyed the fourth. Then I noticed that I wasn't nervous anymore and, mistakenly, I took this as a propitious sign. On the fifth hole I was a little discouraged to take three putts and a double bogey; I was getting casual, at St. Andrews of all places! I went to the sixth tee without really shaking off my three-putt green.

Thus far I hadn't been reading the descriptions of the hazards on the scorecards, and my caddie, a Scot with wild reddish-brown hair tucked up under a plaid ski cap despite the heat, hadn't told me about them either. He would simply point his crooked finger to tell me where to aim. Trusting his experience and my own Self 2 to hit where he pointed, I had managed to stay out of real trouble for five holes. On the sixth, aptly named Heathery, Peter read me the description of the hidden bunkers. For the first time my caddie, Fred, offered some advice, telling me to keep right because I'd been hooking. I aimed right for a draw, forgetting to do the da-da-da-da with my swing, and the ball landed deep in the heather, nestling neither on the surface of the thick heather nor on the ground, but suspended midway between the two. I knew I would need a heavy club to budge it, so I asked Fred if he thought I'd be crazy to use a driver. He shrugged and said it might work. I swung hard, but succeeded only in driving the ball down to the ground no further ahead of where it had been. I switched to a sand wedge and this time managed to scoot it along ten feet, still in the heather. "Making progress," Peter commented dryly. Using the sand wedge again for the next shot, this time I moved it twenty-five yards, but at least I was out of the heather. My three iron drove it 170 yards to the left edge of the green—but this green was no ordinary one. I was still thirty-three yards from the hole and would need to sink the putt for a double bogey. I hit fifteen feet past it, then missed the return putt, ending the fiasco with a quadruple bogey! Heathery had gotten to me!

It's this sort of experience that makes the hazards of St. Andrews so notorious. Daphne ran into similar trouble on the next hole, High. The green is guarded by a bunker about eight feet deep, and Daphne hit into it. Peter told her to keep her head down and swing through. She strained, but stayed in. After three swings she said, "Hopeless!" and picked up. She then had to ask Peter to haul *her* out of the bunker!

I ended the first nine with a 46, ten over par. I was feeling generally settled, not nervous, and strangely unbothered by the pressures I'd anticipated. Peter was playing better than I and was ribbing me a little; I found his chiding helped me increase my concentration. On the next six holes, I got two pars and four bogeys. On the sixteenth hole I pushed a drive OB and ended with a triple bogey.

Approaching the eighteenth hole after a bogey on seventeen, I was thinking that this would be my last opportunity to enjoy St. Andrews. I wanted to let out all the stops. Crowds were watching the golfers, mostly American tourists in plaid pants. I let go with my longest drive of the day and then hit a six iron twelve feet from the pin. I wanted to birdie the finishing hole but left it short.

Par on the first hole, par on the last. Almost poetic. I felt pretty good about both my Inner and Outer games. I'd scored a 90 and was able to find the often elusive balance between tensing too much and overrelaxing to the point of sloppiness.

Some barrier broke for me as I played those eighteen holes. I knew St. Andrews was one of the toughest courses I could play, for both Inner and Outer games, and I had survived it. It was as if I no longer felt that I had to prove anything. Being in Europe had jarred me out of my usual routine and given me new perspectives, and although my desire to do well at St. Andrews could have been an opportunity for a lot of interference from Self 1, it hadn't turned out that way. The obstacles of the course created a natural pressure that I welcomed. I felt a healthy desire to pit myself against them and take golf beyond the limits of mere score. In the place where the game began I got a better sense of what golf could be. Some underlying self-doubt I hadn't been aware of disappeared, and I felt the effects of this even in my business dealings before returning to the States.

Coming home, I felt again a humility and appreciation for what the Inner Game could teach me, with golf as a medium for discovering both my own potential and my existing limitations.

THREE

Overtightness: The Most Common Cause of Error

THE PRIMARY PHYSICAL CAUSE OF ERROR

THE SINGLE MOST COMMON PHYSICAL CAUSE OF ERROR IN GOLF, AND perhaps in all sports, is overtightness. It is generally understood by golfers with even a little experience that the overtightening of muscles in an effort to produce power is responsible for many poor drives. "Don't try to hit the ball so hard, dummy," is a familiar criticism from Self 1 on the course.

But it is equally true, though less recognized, that tightened muscles cause most slices, hooks, topped balls, and fat shots. Overtightening of the shoulders prevents a full backswing and follow-through, and overtightening of the hands turns the putter blade closed or keeps it open at contact, sending the ball off course. Involuntary tightening lies behind the dread yips in both chipping and putting.

Commonly, the observation of a beginning golfer watching the pros is, "Wow, they make it look so easy. They don't seem to be swinging hard at all." On almost any driving range the muscled jerkiness of the average golfer's swing is in obvious contrast to the pro's powerful fluidity.

Yet overtightness need not plague even the most inexperienced golfer. The purpose of this chapter is to explore the dynamics of this phenomenon and to give the reader some tools with which he can significantly reduce overtightness in his swing, whether he is a beginner or an intermediate or advanced player.

Actually, "overtightness" is an inaccurate word when applied to muscles, since no individual muscle unit can be over- or under-contracted. It is either relaxed or flexed. When the muscle fiber is relaxed, it is soft and pliable. When it is contracted, it folds in upon itself and becomes rigid enough to support many times its own weight. Strength is measured in the amount of weight that can be supported by contracted muscles. This is not the same as power. Power is the ability to *use* strength, and it requires a very sophisticated cooperative effort between contracting and relaxing muscles. Some muscles pull, while opposing muscles remain relaxed and pliant so as to allow the movement to take place.

What we experience as overtightness in golf is often the contracting of too many muscles—more than are necessary to accomplish the task at hand. For example, if all the muscles in the wrist are tightened before impact with the ball, there may be a lot of strength in the wrists, but little or no power will be generated because the tightness of some muscles will restrict the free movement of others.

Another kind of overtightness occurs when rigid muscles fail to release. For instance, the shoulder muscles involved in moving the club back on the backswing have to release fully to allow for other muscles to produce the forward swing. If they remain contracted because of tension, the muscles that initiate the forward swing have to fight against them in accomplishing their task. This creates a classic case of interference with the expression of power and control.

A third kind of overtightening stems from the mistimed contractions of muscles. If your arms are moving toward the ball and the wrist movement occurs at the optimum timing before contact, the momentum generated by this is added to the momentum of the arm movement and produces power. But if the wrist muscles contract at the top of your swing instead of just before contact, the momentum is lost and the club will not be moving much faster than your arms when you hit the ball.

Different kinds of errors in the swing are caused by overtightening in different parts of the body at different times. A restricted backswing is caused by overtightening in the left shoulder, restricted hip rotation by tightness in the hips, casting and scooping by tightness in the wrist and arms. Most of the subtler errors in the swing can likewise be traced to overtightness in certain parts of the body.

But to attempt to remedy the problem by analyzing each instance of overtightness would be exasperating and self-defeating. Literally thousands of muscle units are involved in the golf swing; their timing and coordination are exquisitely precise and are simply not accessible to intellectual understanding. The body coordinates these muscles in response to our general command to produce accuracy and power, but only when the execution of those goals is entrusted to it. The best conscious effort we can make is to be clear about our goal and to keep from interfering with its execution.

Though some experience of overtightness may be unavoidable in the process of learning the golf swing, by far the greatest amount of it comes from the ways in which we interfere with the workings of our bodies when we attempt to control the swing. This interference can be greatly reduced if we are willing to admit that it is present and notice it when it happens.

Just as instructing your muscles to contract is obviously futile, telling yourself to relax is not a solution. The command from someone else or from yourself to relax, often spoken as if to an idiot, only causes more tension and tightness. On the other hand, overrelaxing is liable to give you the swing of a wet noodle.

The first step in decreasing overtightness in one's swing is to determine if it is present. This may sound obvious, but trying to cure a flaw without really accepting and experiencing it almost always leads to greater problems. So the first step is to swing while focusing attention on your body as it does so. Don't try to do anything; just swing and see if you notice any overtightness, any lack of fluidity, or any forcing. In many cases, simply by paying attention to any restrictions in the flow of movement, you will begin to experience a reduction of overtightness without any conscious effort to loosen up. Ten or fifteen swings may be enough to produce a significant change if you are attentive and don't try to relax.

However, if you have played a good deal of golf, patterns of overtightness may have become so ingrained in your swing that it is hard to notice them. One can grow so accustomed to an over tight swing that it's difficult to feel it and therefore difficult to change it. The following exercises will help you detect tightness in your swing as it occurs; once it is brought to your awareness, it can be controlled.

HUMMING YOUR SWING

One day, quite by accident, I discovered an exercise that is remarkably effective in reducing overtightness. I was out late one afternoon hitting seven irons on the driving range while waiting for Tom Nordland, with whom I was going to do an Inner Game practice session. I was not concentrating on anything in particular, simply hitting balls and humming to myself. Suddenly, something struck me. I could hear differences in my humming, depending on how I was swinging the club. The experience was such a surprise that I wish everybody could become aware of it as spontaneously as I did. The next time you're on the practice tee, take a few swings and try humming to yourself while swinging. *Listen to the humming*.

I hadn't considered my swing particularly tight, but my humming told me differently. I could actually hear the tightness of my swing in the sound. While I was going back the sound would be nice and smooth, but during the change of direction my voice would become strained, and at contact my throat would constrict and the humming would increase in volume, in pitch, and, most noticeably, in tightness. Sometimes, when I really went after the ball, the hum would stop after contact and I would notice that I had also cut off my follow-through. Using a tape recorder, I later recorded the sound of my practice swing and compared it with a recording of a swing at a ball. The increase in tension was painfully obvious.

This phenomenon turned out to be very practical. I realized that I was amplifying feedback from my body by the use of sound. Overtightness that I previously was not very aware of now became glaringly apparent. The audible alterations in sound while swinging told me a lot about what was happening to my body. What to do? The answer was easy: Simply keep swinging and humming. Use this humming as a biofeedback machine to increase control.

For those who are not familiar with biofeedback methodology, it is a way of hooking up subtle physiological functions—such as blood pressure or even brain waves—to an electronic device that gives you feedback, either in sound frequencies or in visual patterns on a screen, enabling you to perceive slight changes. By simply attending to this feedback it is possible to gain control over bodily functions previously thought to be beyond volitional control. For example, we can learn to control our own blood pressure or temperature, though we won't know *how* we are doing it.

The sound method works in the same way. The sound amplifies the feedback you are receiving from the overtightening of muscles. By listening to changes in the sound, you can soon gain more control over subtle muscular tightness than you might have thought possible by simply trying to relax or to hit smoothly—efforts that often impel you to swing too loosely and with low club-head speed. The best way to use this exercise is to make no effort to swing more smoothly and simply keep listening while you hit balls on the range. Automatically, and in specific ways you won't understand—and don't need to understand—your swing will start changing. You will begin to hear less tightness in your humming, notice that you are making better contact with the ball, and get more distance while making no conscious effort to get those results. Just accept them and don't ask too many questions about how they happen. Otherwise, you will start thinking you know how to relax and giving yourself instructions about how to do it—which is one of the ways the overtightness was created in the first place. A name for this exercise might be "singing your swing"—or, if you don't mind bad puns, "hum, hum on the range."

It should be noted that although it is useful to hum loudly enough to make variations in sound easily audible for the sake of giving maximum feedback when first experimenting with the use of "singing your swing," later on I found it sufficient to hum in a voice audible only to myself. Even if the hum is very quiet, overtightness in the swing will usually change the sound. Muscles in the throat constrict with bodily overtightness, and the sound is choked off, giving you the necessary feedback. The principle behind this exercise has nothing to do with sound per se. It is *awareness* that is the curative and controlling factor, a subject discussed more thoroughly in Chapter 5. The sound simply serves as a device to increase awareness of what is happening, just as a biofeedback machine does.

MAXIMUM TIGHTNESS

I went to the practice range with two friends, Tom and Linda, both excellent golfers who were interested in learning to teach as well as to play the Inner Game of golf.

We started doing the humming exercise to try to locate any blockage to the fluidity of our swings. Watching my swing and listening to my hums, Linda observed, "The sound is mellow during your backswing, but then it has a sudden surge of tension on the way down toward the ball." She asked me if I could locate the tightness in my body that was responsible for the strain in my voice. I told her that I thought it was coming from my stomach, and she asked me to try to discover when the tightness occurred. I was able to notice the exact moment my stomach began to tighten and could give her numbers for the amount of tightness I felt on each swing. But when she asked me to lower the tightness, I couldn't.

Then she suggested that I deliberately *tighten* my stomach as much as I could. I found that after I released the contracted muscles, they seemed to relax more completely and I could start swinging without any contraction in my stomach at all. I realized that I had first learned this technique in a beginners' class in hatha yoga and that it had been used for thousands of years as a means of bringing about deep body relaxation.

To gain maximum relaxation in the body, first tighten it to the maximum extent, and then let go. For total body relaxation this exercise can be done on each part of the body from foot to head, holding the muscles in each part as tight as possible for five or ten seconds before releasing them. In a golfing situation you may not have the time to do all this, but it might help to tighten the stomach muscles and then let go and perhaps do the same with the arms and shoulders. The tightening will make it easier to relax many muscle units that might otherwise not let go, thereby giving the swing more flexibility and fluidity. An added benefit of this exercise is that it increases circulation of the blood and makes it easier to feel movement. There is one final benefit. When you tighten *before* the swing, you reduce some of your tendency to do so *during* it. A lot of our tightening comes from anger and frustration that build up at an unconscious level. By providing an escape hatch for these emotions, you reduce the chances of letting tension destroy your swing.

As EFFECTIVE AS physical techniques may be, they can't be expected to solve the entire problem of overtightness. If they could, golf would be a very easy game and not nearly so interesting. But because golf is a game of such precision, it takes the overtightening of only a few muscles at the wrong time to produce a slice or hook. Therefore, the more basic causes of tightness must be addressed and reduced.

"WHEN IN DOUBT, WE TIGHTEN"

In most cases, dealing with causes is more effective than dealing with symptoms. Most players admit readily that golf is largely mental, but when it comes to confronting the mental *cause* of physical error, we become shy. We'd rather stick to the physical symptoms, analyzing one error after another, satisfied if after each bad shot we can point to the technical mistake we made. But since it is so difficult to correct the myriad technical mistakes that can result from a single mental lapse, in the long run this is fatiguing and frustrating.

One becomes a player of the Inner Game only when one is willing to see the existence of mental self-interference. If there were no self-interference with the expression of our potential, there would be no Inner Game. It is only because doubt, fear, poor self-image, lapses in concentration, and anger are present in all of us that the Inner Game exists and is played by those who want to excel and to enjoy themselves doing so. Dealing effectively with these mental obstacles need not involve deep introspection or self-analysis. Golfers don't need to lie on the couch or repent their sins; they need only to be open enough to admit to the presence of internal interference and be willing to employ

pragmatic methods to reduce that interference. Once the understanding is there, relatively simple techniques can reduce tension
and cure many physical faults simultaneously without your even
being aware that this is happening. Such an approach is powerful
because it deals with causes rather than symptoms.

OVER THE YEARS I have done a lot of thinking and exploring on the
subject of the mental causes of errors in sports. In tennis it seemed
that the primary mental problem was fear of failure; in skiing it
was clearly fear of falling. In golf the anxiety and tension seemed
related most obviously to fear of failure and to its brother, fear
of success. But the simplicity of golf—just one action at a time—
encouraged me to delve further, and I now believe there is a more
basic mental cause of error.

One of the steps that led to the recognition of what I now believe to be the prime mental cause of error in all sports occurred
during an informal exchange on the golf range with Archie
McGill, a business executive and student of the Inner Game of
tennis, who, in his golfing days, played to a scratch handicap. The
brief lesson was a fortuitous one.

I had just hit a few drives when Archie stopped me and asked
me to put down my club and hold his finger as if it were my golf
club. I did so. He then asked me to hold his wrist as if it were my
tennis racket, and I did so. "Why do you grip the golf club so
much tighter than you do the tennis racket?" he asked. Not realizing that I was, I replied, "I don't know. I guess it's because I'm
more sure of myself in tennis."

"Right," Archie said. "When confronted with the unknown,
we tighten." This turned out to be an important moment for me.
The words registered and began ringing all the proverbial bells. I
looked at Archie, who himself had never made that connection
before and was realizing that he had said something of more than
superficial wisdom. "That's close to being a universal principle,"
I said.

This phrase captures a tendency that applies to many different aspects of human experience. When faced with the unknown or the uncertain—a common condition—human beings tend to enter a state of doubt and to tighten instinctively to protect themselves. Metaphorically, when we doubt our mental capabilities, we tend to constrict our minds or become closed-minded; when we doubt ourselves on the emotional level, we constrict our feelings. And on the physical level, when we doubt that we will achieve the results we want or think we may "do it wrong," we tend to overtighten our muscles.

I immediately recalled tennis players who tighten their shoulders, forearms, and wrists when confronted by a ball that they're not sure they can return. As I thought more about this response, it did seem a common tendency. When we have faith, we stay open. A child is constantly confronted with the unknown but is a sponge for all kinds of experiences until at some age he begins to learn to doubt himself. It is the questioning of whether we can meet a given challenge that seems to trigger the tightening action.

Doubt is the fundamental cause of error in sports. It is self doubt that causes the skier to tighten to the point of rigidity at the top of the run and the tennis player to tighten on deep backhands. And it is doubt that causes the stiffness in the putter's arms and body as he tenses over a three-foot putt. It was the problem, I realized, that had caused a lot of my own suffering and worry for a great deal of my life whenever I was in a challenging situation. In many ways I could see that much of the work I had been doing with the Inner Game up to now had been an attempt to solve the single problem of self-doubt. If self-doubt was the underlying cause of overtightness and overcontrol, I wanted to understand it better and learn what could be done to overcome it. I felt that if I could make some meaningful headway with this affliction, I would have made a meaningful contribution to golfers, to say nothing of the contribution to myself.

I tried out this idea on Archie. "Would you think it fair to say that self-doubt is the prime cause of error in golf?" Archie paused and reflected. "Absolutely," he answered. "And I do not know of a single golfer who can say that he has overcome it." Just about every playing or teaching professional I asked about this agreed that self-doubt is his biggest enemy and that it inflicts itself without warning not only on the weekend player but even on the seasoned tour player.

The next chapter explores the anatomy of self-doubt and the techniques for reducing its negative influence on one's golf swing.

FOUR

Overcoming Self-Doubt

I ONCE ASKED A LEADING PROFESSOR OF PSYCHOLOGY AT THE UNI-
versity of California at Berkeley where I could read something
substantial about the phenomenon of self-doubt. He hesitated,
then said that he remembered reading only two articles on the
subject. "Why do you think so much has been written about fear,
anxiety, and stress and so little about doubt?" I asked. His answer
was, "The only thing I can think of is because it is such an uncomfortable feeling."

In my experience it is a very uncomfortable feeling and one I
wish I were not familiar with. It is not within my interest or capability to take a scholarly approach to this subject, but I just want
to shine the light of some common sense on the subject, to understand it in a practical sort of way that might help those who
have tangled with this culprit on or off the golf course.

One of the reasons why doubt has not been more closely studied is that it is easy to confuse with fear. Doubt and fear are definitely friends, perhaps even relatives, but they are not identical twins. We often experience fear in the presence of a real or imagined threat—that is, when we are vulnerable to harm or imagine that we are.

But self-doubt relates neither to our vulnerability nor to danger, though it does question our competence to avoid danger or, even worse, our very sense of worth. No matter how much pressure we may feel is riding on a given putt, we do not feel anxiety if we do not first doubt our ability to sink it. Fear increases as our sense of our competence decreases. Therefore, if we can lessen our self-doubt, our fear automatically wanes.

In my dictionary, doubt is defined as "uncertainty of mind" or mistrust in the reliability of something. These are not complicated definitions. They are everyday occurrences. Whether doubt is useful to a person or not is determined by where it is directed. I can benefit myself by doubting the validity of many advertisements. Certainly this book has been saying: Don't buy into all that is said about the golf swing. But isn't it a different matter when that doubt is directed toward yourself?

I asked a teenager recently if he had experienced self-doubt, and he said, "Sure. Everyone does, don't they?"

"How would you describe it?" I asked.

"Well, it's a voice in my head that says I'm stupid and that I can't do something."

"And what helps when you hear that voice?"

"If I recognize it, then it's okay."

"What do you do when you recognize it?"

"I call it stupid!"

I THOUGHT THIS WAS a wonderful answer. Recognizing the voice meant to him that it wasn't exactly his voice but one he had a little separation from. And because of that separation, he could call it stupid. He did what many of us could benefit by doing. He doubted his doubt.

I first became aware of this voice that undermined self-confidence when I played tennis. Even as a child I would walk out onto the court for the first time that day and there would be uncertainty. "How am I going to play today?" would be the big question in my mind. I didn't realize at the time how important it was for me to play well, or why. That came later. Then, after I hit two or three balls, the voice would make some kind of assessment: "Oh, my backhand is off today," or "I'm having a bad day today." What is now interesting is how short a time it took me to make this assessment about how I was going to play all that day. Many golfers experience the same kind of uncertainty on the first tee. It's the first shot of the game, and they are uncertain what is going to happen. Then, based on the first few shots, either some confidence or some doubt appears.

OF COURSE, the voice of doubt does not stop there. After a few more missed backhands or golf shots, it makes another assessment, like "I'm a lousy tennis player (or terrible golfer)." Things get worse, and the voice concludes, "I'm not very good at sports," a not so judicial statement about one's abilities in all sports before the first set—or first nine holes—is finished. Finally, there's an awful feeling in your chest and you find yourself believing "There's something wrong with *me*." "I'm not a good enough person" is heard and sometimes believed.

It's not hard to see that when you believe in the power of these kinds of statements, they have a tendency to become self-fulfilling prophecies. When doubt is directed toward one's potential to learn and perform or toward one's very self, it can be quite detrimental. A needless questioning of one's value and potential as a human being, for whatever reason, may be the primary cause of the gap that exists between what a person is *capable* of doing and experiencing and what he or she actually *does* do and experience.

Self-doubt is like a shadow that creates an uncomfortable feeling of separation within ourselves and, if believed in, can affect every action that comes from that feeling. This feeling can be covered over by a false sense of self-confidence or lost in a frantic pursuit of proving to the world the opposite of self-doubt. People don't try to prove certainties, only uncertainties.

So let's see if we can shed some light on this shadowy subject. Can we understand something about what will undermine self-doubt instead of letting it undermine us? The first step is to acknowledge that we are not born in self-doubt. It's hard to find a very young child who doesn't believe in himself. Children may trip and fall when learning to walk, or the castle that they are building may topple with a misplaced block, but such occurrences are not yet occasions for questioning oneself. In fact, observations of children before school age show they have an unquestioning faith in their abilities. It is wonderful to behold and, I might add, terrible to undermine. So doubt is not our original state of mind but something learned or accepted somewhere along the way.

A second step is to acknowledge that doubt hasn't totally destroyed this original faith. All human action is based on an innate faith in the body's ability. A person cannot take a step without the conviction that he can take the next. To walk down a flight of stairs, the body flings itself out into space, taking fully for granted that one leg and then the other will move forward and support it. This faith does not function at a conscious level in the sense that we choose to have it or not have it; rather, it is an essential part of continuous movement.

If you begin to doubt that your legs will move correctly to carry you downstairs, hesitancy may ruin the natural continuity of the action. Then you might start *thinking* about how you *should* walk downstairs. To correct this, you might start giving yourself a set of instructions to correct your way of moving. If you allow doubt to build, it will eat away at your inherent faith, and the natural fluidity of your movements will deteriorate. Soon your movement downstairs will look as mechanical and self-conscious as many of the golf swings you see on the practice range.

A third step is to make an important distinction: the distinction between the voice of doubt and you. When doubt knocks at your door, no one says you have to open it, much less invite it in for tea. However, if, like me, you were raised in an environment of doubt and always having to prove yourself, it's possible to become so emmeshed in it that you can't tell the difference between yourself and the doubt. If you do invite it in, you may listen, but you don't have to believe everything it says.

Most golfers are aware that there is a conversation going on in their heads on and off the golf course. When speaking to audiences of businesspeople, I ask how many are golfers. "What would you do," I ask them, "if players in your foursome started talking to you the way you talk to yourself on the golf course?" There is instant recognition, some nervous laughter, and an array of proposals from "Hit them over the head with my driver" to "I'd never play with them again."

The value I find in recognizing this internal dialogue is that it allows me to separate myself from the undermining voice of self-doubt. What I call Self 1 is the one criticizing my swing on the court or the course; he is also the one making me try shots beyond my capability and then calling me stupid when I fail; more than anything he is the one trying to make sure I hit the ball "right" according to his most recent set of concepts about what is right. Self 2 is the one who has to hit the golf ball, the one being addressed by this criticizing, doubting, overcontrolling voice of Self 1.

There are many ways to characterize Self 1, but we all have to do that for ourselves. For me, Self 1 expects the worst of Self 2 and then, in compensation for the doubt, tries to overcontrol.

Most of us would not put up with someone else sowing seeds of doubt in our minds. If that person persisted, we would know he was trying gamesmanship on us and we would ignore him. But, for some reason, when the voice of doubt is coming from inside our own heads, we find it harder to ignore. Yet ignore it we must.

In my father's golfing days, there used to be a tournament called the "Boo Tournament" held at Pasatiempo Golf Club, near Santa Cruz, California. The rules of this tournament were the same as for other tournaments except for the suspension of one of golf's long-standing rules of courtesy: silence while your opponent is striking the golf ball. In this tournament you could say or shout anything to rattle your opponents, and they could do the same to you. What is notable about this tournament is that the average scores were no higher than in any other tournament at the club. Knowing they could expect any trick in the book and some that weren't, and being in no doubt about the intention behind the cajoling, many golfers quickly learned to tune out everything that came their way and focused more completely on each shot.

THE DYNAMICS OF SELF-DOUBT

The effects of self-doubt can be minimized if we attempt to see what it is. One of its characteristics is that it tends to strengthen as the challenge increases or as it represents increasing risk. For the golfer, progressing from low to higher challenges in the following imaginary sequence increases doubt:

1. Chipping in your backyard.
2. Driving at the driving range.
3. Hitting a drive to a wide fairway on the first tee of your club in a five-dollar Nassau with your archrivals.
4. Narrow fairway, trees on left, OB on right; eighteenth hole; par needed to win club championship; your competitor's drive has landed in the middle of the fairway 250 yards out.
5. You have a five-foot breaking putt to be the dark-horse winner of the U.S. Open; national television cameras are focused; thousands are watching in hushed silence; you've

never won a tour championship; you've been putting well all day, but choked on the seventeenth green, leaving a ten-foot putt short by three feet.

The first physical symptom of doubt is weakness. When a golfer stands over a crucial putt, he experiences weakness in his knees and wrists, light-headedness, and a general loss of feel and of muscle memory. In short, he loses command of his own resources. There are two common ways of reacting to this sensation: One is to give in to it; the other is to resist it. Giving in to the challenge, or avoiding it, decreases effort, motivation, and concentration and produces what I call "the unconscious mode," a state of mind characterized by inattentiveness, lack of motivation, lassitude, and sloppy performance. When this response to doubt becomes habitual both on and off the course, one's life becomes one of underachievement.

In our culture the more common reaction to self-doubt is to "try harder." Since our culture values achievement and censures laziness, most of us are encouraged by parents, teachers, or employers to overcome our shortcomings. "When in doubt, try harder," we are exhorted. In other words, we learn to compensate for doubt by exerting increased Self 1 control over ourselves. Although the "trying mode" could be considered a better solution than the "unconscious mode" (since trying tends to produce greater alertness of mind and stronger will to overcome obstacles), it nonetheless produces significant interference with the expression of our potential. Since you never try to prove what is certain, trying to prove oneself is, in effect, a mode based on doubt. It always creates mental tension and conflict, which are reflected on the physical level as overtightness; in turn, this restricts fluid coordination of muscles and thus limits the quality of our performance.

In many ways golf is a perfect vehicle for the trying mode. The challenge is so clear and the demarcation between success and failure so distinct that it is hard not to overcontrol. In tennis a double fault by a professional is not as big a failure as a topped ball or shank by a professional golfer. At every level of the game the difference between one's worst and one's best is embarrassingly large. When I am standing over a chip shot and entertain doubt about hitting a decent shot, I try harder for control, tighten in doing so, and to that extent make it harder for Self 2 to execute the shot. But when I don't doubt myself on a putt, I don't *try;* I simply putt in a spontaneous and natural way. The natural Self 2 effort expresses itself without overtightness, as when you walk down a flight of stairs or put food in your mouth—actions that don't generally call forth doubt but still require considerable coordination.

In short, "trying" is essentially compensation for mistrust in ourselves and generally leads to poor performance. Fritz Perls, the father of Gestalt therapy, observed that human beings are the only living species with the capacity to interfere significantly with their own growth. How? Mostly, Perls said, by *trying* to be something we're not. Perls was fond of remarking succinctly, "Trying fails."

FIVE COMMON TYPES OF TRYING TOO HARD IN GOLF

Basically there are five kinds of trying too hard in golf. All of them are compensations for a present or long-standing doubt and involve an overtightening of muscles that interferes with your swing. Once doubt is identified, practical steps can be taken to eliminate its influence.

Trying to Hit the Ball

As a beginning golfer I experienced the same doubt as almost every novice: doubt that I would hit the ball at all. Most golfers remember their initial experience of failure. We stood far above a small white ball that we were supposed to strike with a long, unfamiliar club in such a way that the ball would travel a long distance.

Both the ball and the club face seemed very small, and the chances of the two making contact seemed remote. Taking the club back farther and farther from the ball, we aimed, swung hard, and missed the ball entirely—an embarrassing and frustrating experience. This first association of failure remains with many throughout their golfing careers. Somewhere deep inside is that memory of missing the ball and thinking that it's really hard to hit. From this doubt comes some of our overtightening on the downswing and our tendency to *try* to hit the ball, instead of letting Self 2 swing the club.

I still find it remarkable to observe the difference in the swing of most golfers when the ball is not actually in front of them. An amateur who was having a tough time playing in a foursome including Sam Snead during a pro-am tournament at Rancho Canada Golf Course finally asked him for help. Snead replied, "The only thing wrong with your swing is what's wrong with most amateurs'; you don't hit the ball with your practice swing." Something about the presence of the ball invites doubt.

Trying to Hit the Ball Up into the Air

After the beginner has managed to make contact with enough balls, his focus often shifts to trying to hit them up into the air. It appears doubtful to him that swinging *down* on the ball will make it go *up*. Trying to lift the ball up by scooping under it is one of the most common causes of error cited by professionals.

On a round with a teaching pro, I bladed an approach shot over the green. What's happening? I asked myself. As if I'd spoken aloud, the pro said, "You're trying to lift the ball up into the air. You actually elevate your body as you hit the ball. *Don't try to lift the ball; let the club do it.*"

Trying to Hit the Ball Far

There has never been a golfer who has not once succumbed to the temptation of trying too hard to hit the ball far. During my first month on the driving range my favorite club was the driver! I had an almost compulsive urge to see if I could knock each ball past the last marker. Of course I couldn't, so I tried harder and fell into a familiar pattern: trying to muscle the ball to get maximum distance.

Equating power with physical strength and physical strength with the tightening of muscles, I would whale away, using, in particular, the muscles of my right arm, which had been developed through thirty years of playing tennis. Every once in a while I would connect and send the ball what seemed to be a mile. This would whet my appetite, and my overefforts would continue. But you can't be around the game for very long before you hear the platitude "Swing easy." I had to admit that the pros on TV didn't seem to be using as much effort as I did. The interferences caused by trying to hit with more power actually inhibit power. If you try to be strong, you only get in your own way.

The way to achieve power *without trying* is discussed further in Chapter 8.

Trying to Hit the Ball Straight

The closer we get to the pin, the greater our doubts about hitting the ball straight. This results in the kind of trying often called "steering." This is the kind of overcontrol that doesn't work any better in golf than it does in tennis, football, basketball, or baseball. When I try to steer a putt into the hole, I seem to flub it in the very act of trying to make sure it gets there. Sometimes after the putt I can feel the tightness that comes from the steering, and I realize that it corresponds exactly to the degree of doubt I had in my mind before putting. In the same "Mental Hazards" article quoted in Chapter 2, Bobby Jones described how he once hit one of his worst golf shots at a golf course called Brae Burn:

> The seventeenth hole is 255 yards and requires a very accurate brassie shot. The more serious difficulty there lies to the right, and this was the side I determined to avoid. But, as I addressed the ball, I was thinking more about keeping away

from the danger on the right than about driving to the green, and, as I hit the ball, I did something—Heaven knows what—that sent the ball an inconceivable distance into the very woods I was trying to avoid. I was very lucky to get out of that scrape with a four. This desire to *guide* the shot is the most difficult fault in golf to overcome.

Trying to Hit the Ball "Right"

Although the first four kinds of trying cause overtightness and introduce error into the swing, they are self-induced and relatively simple compared with the fifth kind of doubt. When trying hard to hit the ball far and straight fails, as it inevitably will, the golfer turns to trying to hit the ball "right" and in so doing involves himself in a web of such complexity that it is almost impossible to extricate himself from it. Once a player starts "taking apart" his swing and analyzing its mechanical elements, he not only lets himself in for endless self-criticism, doubt, and trying too hard, but handicaps himself in putting it together again. Every "shouldn't" invites mistakes, and every "should" challenges both our memory and our ability to make our bodies conform. Chapter 5 explains in greater detail this major pitfall of traditional golf instruction.

Most golf pros are aware of the difficulties imposed on students by too many "shoulds" and "shouldn'ts" of the golf swing. One professional I know wrote the following satirical piece about how easy it is to play golf:

IT'S AN EASY GAME: Everyone can learn to play golf. Once a player has mastered the grip and stance, all he has to bear in mind, in the brief two-second interval it takes to swing, is to keep his left elbow pointed in toward the left hip and his right arm loose and closer to the body than the left . . . and take the club head past his right knee . . . and then break the wrists at just the right instant while the left arm is still traveling straight back from the ball and the right arm stays glued to the body . . . and the hips come around in a perfect circle; and meanwhile, the weight must be 40 percent on the left foot and 60 percent on the right foot at the start . . . and at just the right point in the turn the left heel bends in towards the right in a dragging motion until the left heel comes off the ground . . . but not too far . . . and be sure the hands are over the right foot, but not on the toe more than the heel . . . and be sure the hands at the top of the swing are high and the shaft points along a line parallel with the ground . . . and pause at the top of the swing and count one, then pull the left arm straight down, and don't uncock the wrist too soon. Pull the left hip around in a circle . . . but don't let the shoulders turn with the hips. Now transfer the weight 60 percent to the left foot and 40 percent to the right . . . and tilt the left foot so the right side of it is straight . . . watch out for the left hand, it's supposed to be extended . . . but not too still or the shot won't go anywhere . . . and don't let it get loose or you'll smother the shot . . . and don't break too soon but keep your head down . . . then hit the ball. That's all there is to it!

Technical instructions are easy to give, but not so easy to execute. Because Self 1 is not designed to translate complex instructions into actions, doubt is incurred when it receives them and is expected to be able to make Self 2 perform them.

"WHATEVER YOU'RE TRYING TO DO, DON'T."

Once during an Inner Golf clinic I walked down the golfing range asking the participants what they were trying to do on their swing. There were varied answers: "I'm trying to keep from slicing"; "I'm trying to make sure I follow through"; "I'm trying to swing from inside out"; "I'm trying to keep my left arm straight"; "I'm trying to swing easy." And, of course, there was a beginner who said, "I just want to lift the ball off the tee!"

To each person I gave the same simple instruction: "Whatever you're trying to do, *don't*. Don't try to do it and don't try *not* to do it. Simply don't try at all and see what happens."

What happened was that each person improved—without trying to. The slicer sliced less, the left arm stayed straight all by itself, and the beginner was so exuberant over hitting every ball up in the air that she kept jumping up and down, saying, "This is easy, this is easy."

The less the golfer *tries*, the more fluid his swing will be and the easier it is for Self 2 to achieve the optimum coordination and timing that produce the true golf swing.

The very nature of Self 1 is to doubt Self 2. Self 2's attributes of spontaneity, sincerity, natural intelligence, and a desire to learn are beyond Self 1's ability to conceptualize. Instead, he says that they don't really exist and programs his computer with beliefs and concepts about the way you are in order to take Self 2's place. The self-image Self 1 creates is a cheap imitation of the living, limitless real you, the you whose capabilities and attributes surpass anything that Self 1 can conceive with his thinking mind.

THE LIMITATIONS OF THE TRYING MODE

Many people are perplexed at the suggestion that trying hard is a questionable virtue. Over and over in our culture we've been told, "If at first you don't succeed, try, try again." Hence, for many of us the word "try" means to succeed, and not to try has come to mean accepting failure. But the point of this chapter is that success comes easier when we make an *effort* but don't *try*.

Part of the difficulty of this concept is semantic. I use the word "try" to refer to the kind of Self 1 effort that is a response to self-doubt. "Effort" is the necessary energy expended by Self 2 in order to complete an act successfully and is based on faith, or self-trust. Faith is the natural underpinning of all successful acts, and it doesn't have to be learned. Babies don't *try* to learn to walk or talk, but they do make an effort. They don't overtighten when grasping your finger firmly; they use only the necessary muscles. (By the way, this would be a good image to keep in mind when gripping your golf club: hold it with the kind of firmness with which a baby grips your finger.)

When we realize that Self 1, having introduced doubt, attempts to take control over our acts himself, we are near the heart of the matter. Having weakened faith in Self 2, he makes his bid to take over as much as we will allow him to. His first ploy is to set himself up as your internal judge, to judge your actions as good or bad, and then to judge *you*. After bad shots, he tells you what you did wrong and what you should do next time to avoid the error again. After a good shot (which probably happened when you weren't thinking about any instructions) he wants to tell you how you did it so that you can do it again—but next time it almost never works.

Self 1's control is essentially coercive. He praises you and punishes you. He is a sergeant who wants to run the show and thinks that the private (Self 2) is stupid. He uses concern over results to entice you to depend on him. The natural outcome is that Self 2, who knew how to succeed all the time (or could easily learn), is so overridden that failure follows. No matter how familiar we may be with it, and no matter how far we've progressed in spite of Self 1, the fact is that control through self-judgment—that is, *trying*, with ego reward and punishment—is neither effective nor very satisfying.

Golf is traditionally a game played in silence. Few players will tolerate another person saying a word to them once they have addressed the ball. Then why are we so tolerant of Self 1's distracting voice chattering within our own head? If another person in the foursome were to remark, "You'd better watch out for that sand trap in front of the green," we'd probably accuse him of trying to psych us and try to ignore him. But if Self 1 whispers the same sentence in our heads, we listen as if he were a trusted friend and may even reply, "Thanks for reminding me: I'll try hard to avoid it." Of course disaster in one form or another usually follows. My own best golf is played when everything is quiet inside as well as out.

There is a state of mind more conducive to excellence than either the *trying mode* or the *unconscious mode*. The true professional in every field performs from a base of solid faith in his potential to act successfully and to learn to do what he hasn't yet achieved. He keeps his goals high, without letting himself become so emotionally attached to them that he fears failure. His sense of his own value is independent of external results. He doesn't listen to self-doubt, nor does he perform by rote. He dances to the tune of his Self 2 intuitions. In this state of mind his attentiveness to detail is sharp and selective. He sees each situation as it is, not as he would like it to be, and nonjudgmentally he perceives in each situation opportunities to propel himself toward his goal. Though he gets more done than most, his acts seem relatively effortless. What appears difficult to accomplish in the trying mode seems easy to him. This state of mind—what I call the *awareness mode*— is conducive to optimum performance and is a subject that will be discussed at greater length in the next two chapters.

THE DOCTRINE OF THE EASY

Obviously, golfers experience self-doubt and start trying hard when they look at the game as difficult. Part of this sense of difficulty is, of course, inherent in the exacting requirements for precision and power in the game. On the other hand, it is within almost everyone's experience that when we hit our best shots they seem easy, in comparison with the difficulty so often experienced during our worst shots. Some experts say that the golf swing is a natural movement. Others assert the opposite—that golf is difficult because the swing is so unnatural and contrary to instinct. This issue is worth some examination because it is the sense of the difficulty of the game that is responsible for much of our mental tension and our despair about significantly improving.

In his introduction to *Power Golf*, Ben Hogan took the position that golf was a tough game to learn:

> In order to develop a golf swing your thoughts must run in the right direction. Otherwise it will be impossible. Perhaps you will understand me better when I say that when you grip a golf club to take your first swing at a golf ball every natural instinct you have to accomplish that objective is wrong, absolutely wrong.
>
> Reverse every natural instinct you have and do just the opposite of what you are inclined to do and you will probably come very close to having a perfect golf swing. However, every golfer, even the so-called "natural player," learns the hard way. Some are just a little more fortunate than others in being able to learn a little quicker, that's all. . . .
>
> My approach to golf in this book will be positive rather than negative. In other words, you will not read anything in this book which will make you self-conscious and frighten you by emphasizing all of the faults you can acquire in trying to develop a golf swing.

At the other extreme is Ernest Jones, called on his book's jacket "America's foremost golf teacher," in a book called *Swing the Clubhead*. In the first chapter, entitled "Good Golf Is Easy," there appears a sequence of pictures of Diane Wilson swinging a wood with near perfect form at the age of five. The caption reads: "At her age Diane can swing so beautifully because she does not let her imagination interfere with the feel of the clubhead. She has shot a 71 for nine holes, and her father, a well-known professional, is now entering her in junior tournaments. Diane makes golf look easy because it is easy." Mr. Jones writes:

> If a five-year-old child can learn to swing, there is no reason on earth why you cannot. All you need to do is to repeat the action of that child. She was not distracted in her swing. Her

mind was not cluttered by the countless don'ts which fill the air whenever people talk golf. She merely took the club as it should be taken, in her two hands, and did with it what comes naturally. She swung.

So who's right? Is golf easy or hard, natural or unnatural? Tennis professional Vic Braden, my friend and occasional critic, has stated that one flaw in the Inner Game approach to teaching tennis is that it assumes that tennis is as natural as walking or talking and that in fact it isn't. Since tennis calls for movements that are not instinctual or "natural," he contends that tennis strokes must be learned through close analysis of patterns based on the laws of physics.

My own belief is that Hogan, Jones, and Braden are all correct. Golf and tennis are both difficult *and* easy. On the one hand, it is probably true that our genes do not carry instinctual information about the most effective way to hit a golf ball. It is also true that the most effective way to hit the ball is the opposite of what you might at first think. As we've discussed, students learn that hitting down on the ball makes it go up and that tightening muscles doesn't necessarily produce power. But whether the golf swing is natural or not, it is exacting enough to call for our full attentiveness in learning it. The true issue is not whether golf is natural; the point is that *learning is natural*. Even what might be called unnatural can be learned naturally. Natural learning is easy, but being taught something *un*naturally can make it very hard. Speaking, for example, would be virtually impossible if you tried to learn how to pronounce words by studying the necessary tongue positions. So however difficult golf actually is, we can make it harder or easier by the way we learn or are taught the game.

There is one other way in which we make the game harder for ourselves. What does "harder" mean? In this context it means close to the limit of our capabilities to learn. Hence, the lower the image we hold of our innate capabilities to learn or perform, the

more difficult a particular task seems. When we assume too readily that poor performance is based on a lack of innate capability—
that is, when we blame Self 2 for our failures—we automatically
make the game seem harder. The main point of this chapter has
been to establish that the more probable cause of error is Self 1 interference rather than Self 2 deficiency. Self 1 usually prefers to
blame the difficulty of the game, Self 2, or various external causes,
and it is this very perception of Self 1 that something is harder
than it is that sets the self-doubt cycle in motion. The doubt produces "trying," which produces tightness, which produces error,
which produces more self-doubt.

The "doctrine of the easy" states that acts done well are done
easily and that that which seems hard is usually not being done
well. Since it is always hard to perform with the interference of
doubt, the difficulty of golf lies not so much in the precision required by the Outer Game, but in the task of circumventing the
tension that results from thinking how tough it is.

Of course we think golf is hard because most of us make frequent errors. Since we have failed more often than we've succeeded in our attempts to hit almost every kind of shot, we are
likely to entertain doubt about how we will do on the shot confronting us. Some degree of mental tension is apt to be present
even if we do not remember our past failures consciously.

Below is a description of a technique that, with practice, can
reduce or entirely circumvent this kind of tension. I call the technique "easy link." It works to relax the mind in the same way as
associating with past failures works to produce tension. The technique is simply to remember or associate with a seemingly difficult task (in this case the golf shot) some action that is simple,
preferably one that has never failed. For example, when addressing a ten-foot putt, you might remember the action of simply
picking up a ball out of the hole. By vividly associating with this
easy act, there is no room left in the mind to associate the upcom-
ing putt with failure. Therefore there will be less tension and less
trying.

The first time this technique occurred to me I hit ten golf balls out of ten into a target across the carpet in my office ten feet away. What amazed me was that after doing so it didn't seem remarkable. It was easy to pick up ten balls.

Before trying the technique again I asked Molly, an Inner Game assistant, to experiment with it. First I asked her to make ten putts toward another golf ball about fifteen feet away. Measuring, I determined that her average putt landed about nine inches from the target. Then I said, "This time, Molly, I want you to think to yourself that all you are doing is reaching out and picking up that golf ball. Mentally I want you to associate these next putts with that simple action, not with the harder task of putting."

Molly got the idea and hit ten putts very close to the target ball—an average of only four inches away. Afterward she said, "The target ball somehow seemed more in my immediate world, not something out there. I had no doubt that I could reach out and touch it." Her stroke looked different, too; it was not consciously controlled, yet it was authoritative and followed through in a much less tentative manner. This technique uses a trick of Self 1 against itself. If doubt is engendered by association of a present action with past failure, why can't confidence be engendered by associating with an act you never fail at? I reasoned that it wasn't necessary, as it is sometimes suggested, to remember past successful golf shots; it would be more productive to associate with actions that you have *never* doubted you can do. Each time I succeeded in totally immersing myself in this concept, there was not a trace of doubt in my mind about sinking the putt, and Self 1 seemed to be entirely fooled. He didn't even become excited over shots better than my expectations; anyone can reach out and touch an object, and there's no need to congratulate oneself for that. And because the putt seemed easier, my stroke was easier, with no tendency to overcontrol.

This technique is easily adaptable to any part of your game. When I next had a chance to go out to the driving range, I asked Molly to come along.

I looked out at the yardage marker 150 yards away, a six iron in my hand. It just didn't feel right to associate hitting a shot that far with reaching out and touching it. Realizing that I was searching for something, Molly asked, "Well, what could you do in relation to that sign?" I thought for a moment. "Well, I know I could throw a tennis ball pretty close to it."

"Okay, you're just throwing a tennis ball to your student, who is right at the one-hundred-fifty-yard marker."

This association had the same magical effect for me. I held in my mind the memory of tossing a tennis ball and felt so comfortable inside that I didn't steer. Ball after ball went straight toward the marker. Only when I got sloppy with my technique or started thinking about my swing would accuracy desert me.

Then I asked Molly to try the same association. At first there was no noticeable improvement. I realized that she hadn't thrown a tennis ball much, so we tossed balls back and forth for a few minutes so that she could experience how easy it was. Her next shots were not only significantly straighter, but were more cleanly hit and had better distance. "It may be hard to play golf, but it's easy to toss balls," she said, grinning.

When I started experimenting with drives, fairway woods, and the longer irons, I found it natural to associate with throwing a baseball. Projecting a fairway to exist between two trees about thirty yards apart on the range, I would have thought that my chances of driving a ball into that opening were about fifty-fifty. There definitely would have been some doubt that I could do it consistently. But I had no doubt that I could throw a ball into a thirty-yard-wide opening, and neither would anyone else who has ever spent much time throwing. This association seemed to make it easy for me to let power out in the swing without fearing that I was losing control; I knew I could throw the ball hard and still keep it within the opening. The effect this had on the consistency of my drives was even more surprising than in the irons. There were no severe slices or hooks, simply straight balls, gentle fades, and a few slight draws—all in the fairway.

What excited me about all this was that I wasn't getting excited. This may not seem to make sense, but it was important to me. I had played enough to know that whenever I became aware that I was playing particularly well, the wave I was riding on would soon crash.

When I experimented with this technique on the putting green, I found I had the best results by associating mentally with reaching in the hole and picking up the ball. Another association I liked was that of threading a needle. Remembering that action not only relaxed my mind but concentrated it and automatically put in me a state of mind conducive to precise action. For chipping, I liked thinking about the simple action of taking the stick out of the hole.

Although there are other ways of circumventing self-doubt, this one is simplest to learn, for both the beginner and the advanced golfer. There are just three guidelines I found useful for successful association. First, the associated action should in some way include the target; that is, putting your hand in the hole is a better association than picking a daisy in a field. Second, the associated action should be not only a simple one but also one that you have actually done frequently. Details such as distance are not important; it didn't matter to me that my tennis students had never been 150 yards away, or that I had never thrown a baseball 240 yards. Third, it seems to help if the action is generically similar to the one you are doing, but not so close that you might try to physically substitute one for the other. The technique is *not* to swing a golf club the way you toss a ball. The association signals the mind to relax, but does not tell the body how to swing. It is effective in inducing a state of mind that is optimal for performing a physical action.

This technique is effective and simple, but it is not a panacea; don't expect it to make your ball go where you want it to every time. But when done with concentration and not as a gimmick, it can reduce the elements of self-doubt and tension that interfere with performance. Especially when you are prone to associate a particular golf shot with past failure, I recommend using this technique as a kind of shield to block out doubt. After a while you won't have the negative association any longer, and you can put away the shield.

IT IS LIKELY that if you succeed in convincing Self 1 that golf isn't difficult, it may start thinking that the game is easier than it really is. You'll know this is happening when, instead of getting overly tense, you grow too casual and sloppy. This is not a bad sign. Be thankful for being rid of your tension and make one adjustment: *Do the easy with full attentiveness.* For example, it is easy to pick up a golf ball out of a hole, but it requires effort and concentration to do it with maximum attentiveness. In this case, you might think of picking up the ball as if it were a valuable diamond you wanted to examine, or performing the act with maximum grace, care, and coordination. Since it is easy, you have no fear of failure, but since you want to do it well, it requires concentration. A commitment to attentiveness will result in the best from both worlds: you step closer to that state of mind in which performance is optimized, while avoiding the tension associated with past failure.

FIVE

The Awareness Instruction

THE PREVIOUS CHAPTER MADE THE CASE THAT SELF-DOUBT, FEAR OF failure, and self-judgment can significantly interfere with your ability to learn and perform. And one of the practices that invites all three of these inner obstacles is imposing on oneself a complicated series of technical instructions. When I first wrote this book, this was a rarely acknowledged fact. Golf instructors taught technique, and golfers tried to apply that technique to their swings. That's the way it was. Though it felt mostly awkward at first and frustrating much of the time, it was still generally accepted as the only way to learn. Now there is a greater understanding among players and professionals that the mind should be relatively free from instruction while you are swinging the golf club—at least during the round itself. Most golfers agree that carrying more than one instruction in your head at a time is counterproductive to good golf. Yet there is still a great deal to learn about how to learn golf.

Psychologists confirm that most of us learn more in our first five years than in all the rest of our lives. Yet small children don't go through this torturous process of self-evaluation, analysis, and trying to do it *right*. They don't have to *try* to learn; they simply do so. Until adults teach them otherwise, learning is so natural for children that they don't even know it's happening, and, in contrast with the experience of most adults, they have fun doing it. The talent to learn is one that we adults still possess, and if we can let go just a little of our attachment to conceptualization, it can be used and developed to great advantage.

This chapter explores a different and more natural approach to learning. It introduces the awareness instruction, which focuses attention on what you *are* doing instead of telling you what you *should* be doing. It shows that if you use awareness instructions, you can learn most golf technique directly from experience without being taught. This is a more empowering way for the student to learn and much more user-friendly.

HAS SOMETHING GONE WRONG WITH THE WAY WE LEARN?

Most of my life, I have been involved directly in the process of education. For seventeen years I was a student in the culture's educational system, which culminated in four years at Harvard University and a year on a government fellowship studying "Change in the Four-Year College" at Claremont Graduate School in California. After graduating from college, I taught high school English at Exeter Academy in New Hampshire and then became a training and education officer in the U.S. Navy. Still interested in the learning process, I went on to become one of the founders of a new liberal arts college in northern Michigan whose mission was to create an educational environment for students who wanted to accept leadership responsibilities in their lives. Five years later I took a leave of absence from formal education to reconsider my direction.

It was during this leave that I discovered a new and very different way to learn and to teach. I offer this brief history because I would like to address the problem of learning and teaching golf within the broader context of education in our culture at large. With a little understanding about the imbalance that permeates the way we learn and the way we are taught in formal settings, it becomes easier to apply whatever you learn about learning golf to learning in general.

If asked to state the imbalance concisely, I would say that institutional education has overemphasized conceptual learning to such a degree that the value of, and trust in, the natural process of learning directly from experience has been seriously undermined.

Based on the assumption that the mind is an empty receptacle that develops as it is filled with facts, conceptual learning is concerned primarily with the accumulation and ordering of concepts and theoretical information. Experimental learning has more to do with the development of innate potentialities and skills. The word "education" comes from the Latin *educare*, meaning "to lead out," and indicates that the potential intelligence sought already exists within us and needs to be drawn out. This drawing out by a teacher, a system, or an environment is the primary function of true education. Thus, talking, for example, is not a skill imposed on the child from without; rather, it develops from an innate capacity encouraged and supported by parents and the youngster's experience of his environment.

Balanced education requires a proper relationship between cognitive and experiential knowledge, but in the teaching of physical skills, learning through direct experience should take priority over learning through formal instruction in concepts.

As a result of formalized education, we tend to think that learning virtually ends when we graduate from school. We enter the workplace thinking that learning will happen only when we get sent to a training course. But our lives—at work, in relationships, and in any other activity that needs competence and understanding—require that we become better learners from our on-going day-to-day experience.

LEARNING FROM EXPERIENCE

I sometimes wonder what man's fate would have been if in the development process he taught himself to understand language before he learned how to walk. No doubt parents would have coached us when to shift our weight from left foot to right, and we would have spent a lot of time on the floor analyzing the causes for falling down again. Undoubtedly, many of us would have developed negative self-images about our motor skills and would still be tripping over our own feet.

Instead we learned from experience as a natural process, just as kids teach themselves how to balance on bicycles and skateboards. It is a demanding process that engages one's complete attention and is enjoyable, although the desired results are not always reached overnight. The foundation of the Inner Game approach to learning is that experience itself is the primary teacher and each individual must learn to learn directly from his or her own personal experience. Another person's experience, through teaching and instruction, can be helpful only if it does not compromise a student's all-important relationship with his or her own direct experience.

Learning is about change, making an inner change. The change can take place in a person's understanding, perceptions, and/or capabilities. It is provoked by new meaning given to experience. It is what enables us to grow and to cope more successfully with external changes.

Awareness is the primary faculty we have for *knowing* and learning from our experience. To some the word "awareness" sounds vague and impractical, but it is, in fact, one of those words that refer to something so basic that it is difficult to find a satisfactory definition. My *Webster's New Twentieth Century Unabridged*

Dictionary does not even contain the word as a noun. It briefly defines "aware" as an adjective meaning "knowing, cognizant, informed." As a synonym it suggests the word "conscious." It is by this primary faculty of being aware or of being conscious that human beings can know or learn anything. The entire evolution of life, from the single cell to the complex arrangement of cells called the human body, is based on the power of the living organism to be aware of external stimuli and to respond selectively to them. Yet throughout my education, I heard almost nothing about the power and fundamental role of awareness.

THE LAW OF AWARENESS

The Inner Game approach to learning is based on a fundamental and powerful principle of change. I call it the "law of awareness." In simplest form, this law states that *if you want to change something, first increase your awareness of the way it is.* In a more concise form: *Awareness itself is curative.* Whatever helps to increase awareness of *what is* will promote learning; whatever hides or distorts awareness of *what is* will block or distort learning.

Attention is the faculty of focusing awareness and the principal means of increasing awareness. Stated in simplest possible terms, where you focus your attention determines what you learn. An "awareness instruction," then, is an instruction to the attention to focus on a particular area for the purpose of becoming more aware of what is there. Unnecessary judgment, fear, or doubt about what is there will distort awareness and thus distort the opportunity for learning. It is the use of the awareness instruction in learning golf that I want to bring to your attention in this chapter. Before doing so, I want to take a critical look at what we are more accustomed to in learning golf, "the do-instruction."

THE DO-INSTRUCTION

The do-instruction is basically a command to *do* something or *not do* something. It is most commonly given in the form of "you *should* do this" or "you *should not* do that." As such, it carries with it an aura of rightness and authority that sets up the actions by the student to be judged by the giver of the command. When such instructions are not easily understood or easy to accomplish, they tend to evoke a fear of being judged that threatens the natural learning environment. It is only when the instructions are needed yet easy to understand and to follow that interference is not apt to be evoked. For example, to be told by a trusted instructor to stand with your feet about as wide apart as your shoulders is not apt to evoke fear or resistance. But could you say the same if you were given Ben Hogan's instructions about your downswing?

> All tension should be released from the right leg and hip. The right knee should break in toward the left knee. The wrists uncock, the right arm straightens and then turns over going forward over the left shoulder. This all takes place in that sequence and you will find that it will bring you to the complete finish.

Such instructions cannot help but create a sense of doubt in the student about his ability to put all this together. And with the doubt comes the fear of being judged for doing it wrong and often an understandable resistance, conscious or unconscious, to the instructor. When these instructions become internalized, as when Self 1 gives them to Self 2, the doubts and fears come with them and become part of our internal learning environment.

How do do-instructions incur doubt? How do you write your name? How do you tie your shoe? How do you walk down a flight of stairs? Think about one of these actions and see if you can come up with a set of instructions about how to perform it. Then try to do the action by following your own instructions. It's not easy if you described the action in any detail, but why?

The primary difficulty lies in our inability to translate any but the simplest verbal command into a bodily action. When asked to do more, we invite self-doubt because the brain cannot consciously control the body with words; the part of the brain that analyzes, conceptualizes, and instructs us verbally is incapable of moving a muscle and has only a limited capacity to communicate to the part of the brain that does control our physical behavior.

Besides the general tendency of the ego to resist being told what to do, there are five basic ways in which do-instructions engender doubt.

The first is the communication gap between teacher and student. The student doubts that he even intellectually understands what the instructor means. Teachers are notorious for developing their own jargon and assuming that everyone speaks the same language. For example, I'm still not sure exactly what the famous golf instruction "Pronate the wrists" means. Not knowing the meaning of the instruction obviously invites doubt that I can follow it.

The second is the internal communication problem with the student. Intellectually the student may understand, but his body doesn't. This is the most prevalent gap and a universal invitation to doubt. Because the mind understands, the student assumes that he should be able to make his body conform. He also knows that his teacher expects conformity. But unless the body can associate that instruction with an already familiar action, it can't conform. Without *muscle knowledge* of the instruction, the student finds himself unable to meet his own or his teacher's expectations and doubt increases.

Third, the student may understand intellectually and his body may understand, but the action called for is outside his present capability. For example, it was some time before my body was ready to deal with the subtleties of leg motion at the outset of the downswing. It's easier for instructors to see what's wrong in a person's movement than to know which particular correction should be focused on in a given development process. Doubt increases as the student is asked to do something out of line with his natural learning progression; this reinforces his "I can't do it" self-image.

Fourth, in many cases do-instructions given by teachers to students and by students to themselves are just plain incorrect.

Trying to follow commands that do not conform to the mechanics of golf or to the physiology of the body obviously causes doubt.

Fifth, there *are* do-instructions that are understood intellectually and in body language, are correct, are within the natural progression of learning, and are easy to accomplish. Such do-instructions need not cause doubt and can aid learning in some cases. But doubt arises when one tries to conform to too many of these at a time. Almost every time we receive a "should" instruction, there is a spoken or implied "shouldn't," which leads to another and then another, until the mind is clogged with more instructions than it can handle.

Much of modern physical-skill teaching relies heavily on do-instructions in spite of their inherent limitations and general misuse. In fact, most golf students feel cheated if the instructor doesn't tell them what they're doing wrong and what they should be doing. But it is this process that we have become so accustomed to that actually cheats us of recognizing our potential as learners. It persuades us subliminally to mistrust ourselves, and the resulting gap between our performance and our potential is large. Unfortunately, we learn from our teachers how to teach ourselves, and soon we all develop a Self 1 who continues to sow seeds of self-mistrust whenever we listen to it, whether or not we are taking lessons from a pro. To redress this problem is, in my opinion, one of the most important challenges before education in general, and it would be interesting if sports teaching could lead the way.

BEFORE ADDRESSING the alternative to the do-instruction in the teaching of golf, I should point out that there are excellent instructors of every sport who understand the limitations of do-instructions and who have developed the art of speaking a language the body can understand. The best teachers have always used image-rich language that invokes not an abstract description of a movement but a concrete picture or "feelmage" associated with acts already familiar to the body. Bob Toski's book *The Touch System for Better Golf* attempts to establish the primacy of feel and muscle memory in the swing. For example, he suggests that your swing should feel like a canoe building up momentum and then going over the falls and that "the left wrist should feel as firm through impact as it would if you were backhanding a rug-beater." Gary Wiren in *The New Golf Mind* points out that Sam Snead used to think of the word "oily" as he swung, thus engaging his right-brain hemisphere and avoiding the pitfalls of conceptual left-brain thinking. Unfortunately, as Ben Hogan pointed out, the golf swing is not easily associated with other common movements, so most of us do not have many useful analogies in our muscle memories.

THE AWARENESS INSTRUCTION

Fundamental to the Inner Game approach to teaching is a workable alternative to the do-instruction, one that engages the student in learning from experience and increases his self-trust. I call it the "awareness instruction." Simply defined, it is a command to the *attention* of the student rather than to his body. Instead of saying, "See if you can do this or that," it says, "See if you can *see, feel,* or *hear* what is happening right now and right here." The back-hit-stop exercise introduced in Chapter 2 involves an awareness instruction that requests that the student focus on the club, with special emphasis on its position at the back of the swing and at its completion. None of these three instructions calls for a change in *behavior*—they all simply call for heightened awareness of what is happening.

"See if you can *feel* whether the blade of your club is open, closed, or square at impact" is also an awareness instruction, circumventing the doubt about *doing it right* by involving the pupil's mind in the process of just noticing what is happening. The instructor might ask the student to shut his eyes, then arrange the club in different positions—open, square, and closed—until he can feel the difference in his hands while the club is motionless. The next step is the challenge to the student to see if he can feel the angle of the face at the moment of impact when the club is moving at normal speed. If the student thinks that this is a gimmick to help him to hit the ball square, he is apt to *try* to do it right and to be caught in the same trying mode as if he were simply told to make sure that his club was square at impact. But if he takes the awareness instruction for what it is—simply a request that he attempt to feel what is happening with the face, no matter what it is—then there is no question of right and wrong, the mind focuses on the experience, and soon experiential learning will take place as he learns to differentiate the sensations of the different angles of the club face.

Awareness instructions are radically different from do-instructions and tend to put the student in another frame of mind entirely. They engender a mode of learning that is free of doubt, frustration, and discouragement. They induce a natural state of learning, which, once rediscovered, progresses organically and rapidly. Most important, they strengthen the student's faith in his own capacity to learn from experience; the instructor's role is only to help him in focusing on the most relevant parts of his experience.

Let me add that when a student has been helped by an Inner Game teacher to regain trust in his ability to learn from experience, certain do-instructions *can* be given at appropriate moments in such a way that they neither cause doubt about their achievement nor undermine the student's basic trust in his own learning capacity. But so conducive are awareness instructions to learning that I use them 95 percent of the time and employ do-instructions only for simple tasks or when a high degree of trust in Self 2 and the teacher has been established.

Most do-instructions can be better framed as awareness instructions, and their translation becomes easy after a little practice. When I first heard the tip "On the downswing swing from the inside out," I was confused. Even after I understood the instruction intellectually, I had little confidence that I could do it, so of course I *tried*. I didn't get it right, so I tried again and, of course, only became tighter. A couple of times my friend Tom Nordland said, "That time you got it," but I couldn't feel the difference between those "right" swings and all the others.

The translation of this doubt-producing do-instruction into an awareness instruction might sound like this: "Just swing the club without trying to do anything, but feel whether, on the downswing, it's moving from outside the ball—that is, further away from your body—to inside—closer to your body—or the other way around." Before beginning, the instructor might move the student's arms from outside to inside and then from inside to outside to give him a *feel* of the difference. As soon as he can distinguish between these two broad categories of movement while actually swinging, the student can be asked to distinguish more subtle changes. He might be asked, for example, to see if he can tell after each swing whether it was more or less inside out than the last. In this case, in order to pinpoint his focus more subtly on the swing, awareness can be heightened by the use of a rating scale. If a downswing that is square to the target line is 0, a swing that is slightly inside out could be called a +1; more inside out, +2 or +3. Likewise, outside in downswings would be rated −1, −2, and −3. (With advanced golfers, the scale can be refined indefinitely to focus on smaller and smaller fractions of differentiation.) This fine-tuning of the student's attention creates more refined differentiation in feel and allows learning to take place. By experimenting, Self 2 discovers which stroke feels and works best for his body at his level of development.

Sometimes a golfer's swing becomes stuck in a groove, and, despite focusing on the downswing, it remains stuck. If the student feels that his normal swing is a −2, the instructor might say, "Why don't you see what a minus 3 feels like? . . . Now try a plus 3, a plus 2, a plus 1." After he has broken out of his rut by experiencing different swings, he can go back to swinging without trying, and if he sincerely doesn't *try* to swing "right" but sticks to awareness exercises, his body will automatically select the swing that feels and works best. Through such a natural learning process the student can groove his new swing without *thinking* about it but by concretely *feeling* it.

Here are some examples of translating do-instructions into awareness instructions. As you read them, try to imagine the difference in the way you might react to each instruction.

1. Keep your head still throughout the swing. It's imperative to keep it still. Keep working at it until you get it.

1. See if you sense any movement in your head during the swing. Notice whether there is more or less movement on each succeeding swing.

2. Early in the downswing, the right elbow should return to the right side. (Sam Snead)

2. During the next few swings, pay attention to your right elbow. Don't try to change it in any way; just see if you can tell what it does, especially after you begin the downswing. Notice any changes in its position.

3. Keep your left arm straight.

3. Notice whether your left arm is straight or whether it bends on each swing, and scale the amount on a scale from 1 to 5.

4. The most common fault of the inexperienced player during the downswing is hurrying into the downswing before the backswing is completed, rushing the right shoulder around before the club head reaches the hitting

4. On the next twenty shots, pay attention to your body and see if you can detect any rushing during the swing. If so, tell me how you rushed—that is, which muscles you used to rush and when. Don't try to avoid rushing; just

area, and turning the upper body into the shot too quickly. (Ben Hogan)

notice what you are doing, and any changes in degree.

5. Try to be certain the back of your left hand faces down the target line as you strike the ball. (Arnold Palmer)

5. Take a few swings paying attention to the back of your left hand. Notice if it is square, open, or closed in relation to the target line.

6. It is the consensus of *Golf Digest*'s professional teaching panel and advisory staff that the ideal position of the club shaft at the top is parallel to the intended line of flight. (*Golf Digest*)

6. Without looking, sense whether the shaft of your club is parallel to the target line, inside the line, or outside it. It might help if you shut your eyes during the swing to increase your sense of feel.

In each of these examples one difference between the two kinds of instructions is consistent. The do-instruction asks the golfer to achieve a certain result that he may or may not feel he can produce. Because there is a potential for success or failure, he is likely to be overconcerned with getting results and thus be open to doubt and to straining. Even if he succeeds, he will think that he has to remember that tip every time he wants the same results—along with all the other instructions already in his head. The awareness instruction, on the other hand, asks only one thing of the conscious mind: Pay attention to what is happening. There is no doubt because there is no right way or wrong way, and there is no fear of failure because there is no externally implied standard for success. Yet the body learns because it is now free to focus on what feels good and to see for itself what works.

One of the primary characteristics of the awareness instruction is that it is nonjudgmental. Awareness simply sees and accepts what is; it doesn't place a positive or negative value on the result. Some instructors who have tried to make awareness instructions work for them fall into the use of quasi-awareness instructions, such as "Are you aware that you're taking your swing back incorrectly?" or "Be aware that you're not turning." But it's impossible to be aware of *not* doing something because awareness can focus only on what *is* happening. What's not happening is a concept based on a judgment about what you think *should* be happening.

The most difficult thing about awareness instructions is to realize that they work, when all your life you've believed only in do-instructions. It's not hard to see that they circumvent self-doubt and frustration, but perhaps it's not so easy to believe that they get results. If it's any comfort, I have the same problem; even though they improve learning and performance whenever used, each time I am surprised. It blows my mind that a change for the better can take place so effortlessly. It is not always the change I anticipated, but that only makes it more interesting. Nothing but my repeated experience that awareness instructions do work has given me the confidence to rely so heavily on them. It is results, not theory, that warrants their use. Therefore, I don't suggest that you make a heroic effort to forget about results or to convince yourself that your score is really not important. What I do suggest is that you experiment with awareness instructions long enough and sincerely enough to discover their effects for yourself.

INTRODUCING AL GEIBERGER
TO THE INNER GAME

Ever since I heard of Al Geiberger's score of 59 at the Colonial Country Club in Memphis, I had wanted to meet him and talk with him about what he had done in the Inner Game to achieve such Outer Game success. When I called him, we made a date to meet at a private club in Santa Barbara.

I arrived at the club first and went to the pro shop to meet the club pro, with whom Geiberger had arranged to use the putting green and range. When I introduced myself, he expressed some curiosity about what I intended to do with Mr. Geiberger on the range. "You're not going to do anything that looks like teaching, are you?" he asked somewhat threateningly. I asked him what he felt would look like teaching.

"Well, I just don't want you showing him how to swing a golf club or him standing over you showing you how to address the ball or anything like that." I couldn't help being amused at the prospect of teaching Geiberger *anything* about how to swing a golf club, and, though I knew that he was certainly competent to teach me, I didn't want to learn that way. "No, I can assure you that what we do won't resemble that kind of teaching," I answered.

When Al arrived his bearing and manner reminded me immediately of Jimmy Stewart. He told me that he'd been interested in the mental side of golf for some time and that he was particularly open at this point; he had just had a disastrous time trying to learn the hows and how-not-tos of the parallel turn from a skiing instructor who'd made him dizzy with instructions. "Finally, I said, 'To hell with all this,' just skied down the hill and began to get the hang of it."

I asked Al about his Inner Game experiences in golf. He recalled that several times when he was practicing putting before a tournament and someone came up to talk to him, he would continue putting and be surprised that it would improve while he was engaged in casual conversation. When the interruption ended, he would say to himself, Now I'll get back to some serious putting— only to find that his performance would drop off significantly. "From this and other experiences," Al said, "I've come to realize that I perform best when I'm letting my subconscious mind hit the ball and my conscious mind is otherwise occupied. Is that what you're talking about in the Inner Game?"

"That's a part of it," I replied, "but it's possible to use the conscious mind in a productive way while still allowing what you call the subconscious mind, part of what I call Self 2, to control the hitting of the ball. You don't have to distract the conscious mind away from golf; you can involve it in a task that helps Self 2 in his task."

I offered to give Al an example of one way this might work in putting and began by telling him that I had found that one of the greatest single obstacles to performance among tennis players was trying too hard for results. "The same seems to be true in putting, where the goal desired is within immediate reach. The overconcern with results produces tension, tightening, and consequent loss of touch, which makes achieving the goal more difficult. So the key to increasing one's putting feel is to switch games—to change from the game called 'trying to get the ball in the hole' to an awareness game called 'see if you can *feel* where your ball goes in relation to the hole.' " The hole would still be the target, but the primary object of the game wasn't to drop the putt, but to be able to tell, without looking, where the ball stopped in relation to the hole. Only by focusing on the feel of the swing can you make an accurate guess.

At first Al had a hard time really letting go of trying to sink the ball. He would putt and guess, then look up to see where the ball had actually gone. If he had missed by what seemed to him too wide a margin, he would shake his head in mild disappointment. Finally, I insisted, "Al, don't try to get the ball into the hole. That isn't the game right now. Pretend that we're betting a hundred dollars a putt that you can come within six inches of telling me exactly where your ball comes to a stop."

"You don't *want* me to try to sink it? Should I try to miss it?"

"No, don't try to sink it and don't try to miss it. Just putt toward the hole and see if you can tell by feel alone where it goes."

This time Al prepared to putt with much less tension in his face. Instead of looking at the hole two or three times, he looked once, shut his eyes, and stroked the ball right into the cup. I caught it before it could make a sound and asked him where it had landed. "It was pretty good," Al said. His eyes were still closed, but there was more certainty in his voice. "Maybe it went three inches past the hole on the right edge."

"Nope, you're off a little. It went directly into the hole, though it probably would have rolled a few inches past if you'd missed. See if you can do better next time," I challenged. Al was beginning to see what this drill was about, but the surprise to him was that he was putting considerably better when he was sincerely playing the awareness game than when he was trying for results.

Thereafter Al became absorbed in the awareness game, and I could tell from the diminished tension on his face, both during his setup and after the putt, that he had let go of some of his concern about results. Most of his focus was now concentrated on increasing his feel in order to be more accurate in his guesses, and within a few minutes he significantly improved his ability to tell where the ball stopped. Simultaneously, his putting stroke became smoother and slightly less deliberate. Instead of looking at the ball, then back at the hole three or four times, he would sight once, close his eyes, putt, and then, even before the ball stopped, guess.

"How can you tell whether the ball went right or left of the hole?" I asked.

"I don't know for sure, but I can feel it."

"Putt a few more and see if you can discover what gives you the most accurate feedback about the direction of the ball," I suggested.

After three more putts Al decided that he could feel the direction by paying attention to the points on the thumb and forefinger of his right hand where they touched the leather of the putter handle. When I asked him to focus his attention on those points, he was able to tell me with amazing precision just how far to the right or left his putts went. As the accuracy of this feedback process increased, so did the accuracy of his putts, and soon they were considerably more consistent in their direction. Then I asked the same kind of question about how he could best determine the length of his putts. Although there were several factors here, by focusing on what seemed the most reliable feel he was able to increase the accuracy of his guesses, and automatically the accuracy of the length of the putts themselves increased.

As happens with almost everyone I have taught, after Al noticed the improved results he was getting during this awareness exercise, he would sometimes lapse into trying to repeat the "good results" by a conscious effort to control the putter. Inevitably, the results would be worse. "Can you feel the difference when you try?" I would ask. "Yes, I tried to sink that last one," he'd say. Then he would return to awareness-putting for a while until he couldn't seem to help trying again to sink the putt. There wasn't much for me to do, since his own experience was teaching him that trying for results instead of simply focusing on the feel of the stroke was giving him worse results. The fact that he could physically detect the difference, depending on which "game" he was playing, fascinated him. He seemed about to discover something important, but was a little afraid to accept the full implications of what he was learning.

"This might be really hard to do during a tournament," Al finally remarked after sinking three twenty-foot putts in a row.

"It's always hard to let go of long-standing patterns," I replied, "but the fact that it works makes it easier. I suggest you don't try it in a tournament until you have spent more time with the exercise on the practice green. Even if you don't radically change your approach to putting in tournaments, doing this exercise ten or fifteen minutes every time you practice putting can't help improving your feel for length and direction."

"That's the crux of putting—just feel of length and direction," Al agreed. I could see that he was wrestling with himself about his experience. Somehow he couldn't quite bring himself to trust not trying to control the putter and sink the ball, in spite of his clear experience that he putted best when his Self 2 was engaged. On the other hand, he had experienced such surprising results that he couldn't dismiss the difference.

"Let's go to the driving range," Al suggested. There we started with an exercise similar to awareness-putting. I asked him to swing without looking where the ball went and then see if he could describe its trajectory. At first Al was surprised that this exercise was so difficult. He said that he was in the habit of looking at the ball in flight to determine what, if anything, he had done wrong on his swing. I knew that this was a traditional method but suggested to Al that perhaps there was a better one. "What if you could actually *feel* the first tendency of the swing to leave its groove? Then wouldn't it be possible for correction to take place even before the ball was hit? I don't know much about the mechanics of the golf swing, but I feel confident that if I could feel the difference between a hook and a slice or even between a draw and a fade, I could then control which kind of shot I produce. On the other hand, I'm not sure that even if I correctly analyze a given error, I will succeed in trying to correct it on the next swing."

Al agreed that during a tournament round most pros don't attempt to make mechanical corrections, though perhaps they might modify their address to the ball if something seemed wrong there. "We save mechanical corrections for the practice range," he said.

So with renewed motivation we began the awareness game, beginning with an eight iron and then moving on toward the longer clubs. As with putting, after he had developed by feel a general awareness of where the ball went, I asked Al to try to be more specific. "What part of your body is most reliable in telling you whether you're getting a fade or a draw? And how can you tell the height of the trajectory?" These questions piqued Al's curiosity. He had never really tried to locate what cues from his body gave him this feedback, since he had relied primarily on his eyes and his analytical mind to figure out what his swing was doing. As time passed, he became more accurate and confident in his descriptions of his trajectories, and it was easy to tell that he was more aware of his swing. Increased control was inevitable. "I think you're on to something here, Tim," he said, "but what about the fundamentals? Surely you have to teach the fundamentals."

I answered that of course I felt the fundamentals were important for advanced players as well as for beginners, but that before we discussed how to deal with them, I wanted him to give *me* an Inner Game lesson. Al agreed, and I told him of a simple awareness process that I had used in both tennis and skiing. It seemed to me that in golf, too, it would be useful in correcting errors and reinforcing strength.

"First you ask the student to forget about results and simply focus on the kinesthetic sensations of his body while swinging the club. When you see that the student is not trying to hit the ball but is simply focusing on the feel of his body, ask him if he is more aware of any particular part of it. My experience is that if there is an important flaw in the swing, the part of the body that is critically related to that error will draw itself to the student's attention. On the other hand, if there isn't an error, generally the part of the body that is critical in controlling the optimum swing will receive the student's focus and be reinforced. When the student locates the part of his body that is in the foreground of his attention, he can then be asked exactly *what* he is feeling there. For example, if he is most aware of his right shoulder, he may answer that he feels a little tightness or jerkiness there during the swing. At that point the coach may ask him to take a few more swings while focusing his attention on his shoulder to see if he can locate the exact moment in the swing in which the tightness occurs. It's important that the coach not give the student the impression that the tightness is "bad" and should be eliminated, only that it is there and that we want to find out more about it. Perhaps after a few swings the student determines that the tightening occurs just at the beginning of his downswing. At this point his feel has progressed from general body awareness to a specific "where," then to a specific "what," and finally to an exact *"when."* The final step in the process is to discriminate the *degree* to which the action is occurring. To help the student do this, the coach might say, 'I want you to take a few more swings paying attention to whatever is happening in your right shoulder at the moment your downswing begins, and specify the degree of tightness you feel. If you feel the same tightness as on the last few swings, call it a five; if there's more, give it a number from six to ten, depending on how much; if there is less, number the degree of tightness from four to zero.' By helping the student differentiate between degrees of tightness, his body unthinkingly starts to select the kinesthetic sensation that feels and works the best."

"So you never try to help him actually make the correction even if you can see what's wrong?" Al asked.

"No, because the whole point of the exercise is to help the student recognize that his body has the inherent capability of correcting itself. It's not that a novice golfer can't benefit from outside instruction; of course he can. But most of us have become so reliant on external authority to correct ourselves that we've lost confidence in the extremely sophisticated mechanism we have within us for self-correction. This process is designed to strengthen that confidence, and it also allows the student to gain more from external instruction at those times when it is useful."

After this explanation, Al watched me take a few swings with a seven iron and then began to give me an Inner Game lesson.

After five swings Al asked me if I was particularly aware of one part of my body, and I answered that I seemed to focus on my right hand. I also remarked that my shots seemed to lack consistency and that I really couldn't tell if they were going to go straight, draw, or fade. "Don't worry about that," Al said. "Just tell me what you are noticing about your right hand." I said that its grip seemed a little loose, and he asked me exactly which part of the hand. After a few more swings I said that I could actually feel my fourth and fifth fingers leave the club handle. "When does that happen?" Al asked. "At the back of the swing, before coming down," I answered. Of course I realized that this was probably a flaw in my swing, but, sticking to the process I'd outlined, Al said, "Don't try to hold the club any tighter; just keep swinging and give me a number that indicates how loose your hand is on the club at the back of the swing. Zero will mean that your fingers didn't leave the club at all, and a plus figure means the degree of firmness of your grip."

I took about ten shots, calling out numbers after each one: "Three, two, three, zero, one, zero, minus one, minus one, minus one, minus one." "The last four shots were the best I've seen you hit," Al said. "They felt more secure somehow," I replied, "but it also felt as if I was getting less power." "It may have felt that way," said Al, "but in fact they were a good five to eight yards past the others."

Al was not surprised that keeping my hand on the club produced better results; in fact, he said, the standard instruction to combat this common error is "Keep the last two fingers of your right hand firm on the grip." But he admitted that while watching my swing he hadn't picked up the fact that my fingers were coming free and that the Inner Game method had been an effective way of detecting the error.

"What if you had seen the error and given me the traditional instruction and I had asked you *how* firm I should hold my fingers?"

"Yes, I see what you mean; the numbers do make it more precise."

"Not only that, but the big difference is that now I don't have to try to remember to do something right and therefore won't tighten up or become frustrated about my fingers. All I have to do is to feel what's happening and get feedback from the results. This state of mind is very different, even though the technical correction may be the same, and it will help me maintain poise and self-control."

Al remembered a lesson he had recently given his son and how frustrating it had been when the boy couldn't seem to master a particular mechanical detail. "I threw his whole swing off by trying to get him to do one simple thing right. Finally, I told him to forget about it and just swing the club, and his rhythm began to return. Maybe the Inner Game approach wouldn't tie him up in knots the way I did."

A LESSON IN LESSON TAKING

After a round at Los Robles Greens in Los Angeles, I went out to the range to hit some balls and was joined by Pete, one of the golfers in the foursome I'd just played in. Pete was a long-iron hitter with a ten handicap who seemed to rear back and attack the ball. On the sixth hole he'd hit a nine iron 150 yards downwind and sunk it for an eagle. He said he'd been having trouble with his drives; he was slicing all of them. I asked him if he wanted to try an Inner Game exercise that wouldn't tamper with his swing but would help his concentration. He agreed, and I explained the back-hit-stop exercise to him. At first he couldn't do it at all, but when he started paying attention to the club head instead of trying to correct the slice, there was an immediate, dramatic change in the trajectory of the ball. "Wow," he said, "it works! That's the first draw I've hit all day."

"Okay, but don't try to do it again. Just let the club head go where it wants."

Again Pete hit a draw. "This is incredible. I thought the stiff shafts of my new clubs were making me slice and that I had to learn to really come through with them."

"The problem seems to be more that you *thought* there was a problem. Most of our problems come from trying to correct problems, and when we stop trying to correct them and just pay attention to the club head, the body makes its own corrections."

I could see that this was an entirely new idea to Pete and that he wasn't buying it easily. Still, he went on practicing the back-hit-stop, and I returned to practicing with my five irons. Jack, another of our foursome, came over to offer Pete some help, and they began a very technical discussion. Pete started slicing again. Soon I heard him say to Jack, "Hey, watch this. I don't know why it works, but you ought to try this back-hit-stop stuff."

After a while Pete came over and offered to give *me* a lesson. He wanted to teach me how to hit down into the ball on my irons, to take a divot from inside out and make the ball jump off the club.

He gave me about four do-instructions and I felt pretty awkward, but I was eager to learn. I knew that my irons weren't going as far as I could hit them. Actually, the lesson turned out well. He'd give a command like "Hit a goddamn divot this time!" and I'd translate this mentally into "Let's see how much earth my club takes." Then there'd be a divot and Pete would say, "Good, do you see what that does? The ball jumped off the club, and look how far it went." Then he said, "Okay, this time stand farther away from the ball, and make the divot go in this direction." He placed a cigarette 30 degrees outside my target line. It didn't look possible to me; I'd never come close to swinging in that direction. All right, Self 2, I said to myself, somehow swing so that the divot goes toward the cigarette. I haven't the slightest idea how to do it.

After a few swings Self 2 got it. Pete was jumping up and down saying, "That's it! You're hitting it inside out!"

I knew that Pete's technical information was helpful, but I also realized that if I'd tried to follow his instructions literally, I'd probably have ruined my swing. I had to smuggle his tips safely past Self 1 somehow and hope that Self 2 got the picture. This wasn't easy, particularly because I didn't want Pete to think I wasn't trying to do what he was asking, and I had no idea whether Self 2 would do it. But Pete must have thought I was trying hard to do exactly what he said, because the results got better and the swing easier, and in the process I picked up a good ten yards per club on my irons. Pete left feeling that back-hit-stop had cured his slice and that his technical advice had helped put distance on my irons.

I finished the practice realizing that what another person has learned from experience can help Self 2 to learn and that it is possible to circumvent the doubt and overcontrol that usually attend do-instructions.

SIX

Discovering Technique

CHAPTER 5 ATTEMPTED TO SHOW THAT THERE IS A FUNDAMENTAL difference between the awareness instructions and the traditional technical instruction, or what I called the "do-instruction." I hope it's now clear that increasing proficiency at any skill is a function of awareness, choice, and trust. Whatever interferes with any of these functions will inhibit the process of learning. If one's self-confidence is undermined in the process of receiving instructions, the possibility for learning will be impaired. If on top of this there is pressure from the instructor to do it "by the book" at the risk of displeasing him, Self 1 has the opening to inject fear, doubt, and distraction into the learning environment. It is ironic how often instructions designed to help the student will do precisely the opposite.

By using awareness instructions alone, you can make a great

deal of progress in evolving a golf swing that is truly yours. But a large question may remain in your mind: Am I supposed to throw out all the technical knowledge I have accumulated over the years? Am I supposed to ignore all that I am being taught or might read? In short, what is the role of technical knowledge in learning golf according to the Inner Game philosophy of learning?

This chapter attempts to answer that question by suggesting that there is a way to integrate the best of the Outer and the Inner, technical knowledge and learning from experience. What I hope to provide here is a way to use both awareness techniques and technical information to help you *discover technique for yourself*. The purpose of all good instruction is to help the individual learn better and better ways of doing something. I first introduced this concept of the "marriage" of awareness and technique in the revised edition of *The Inner Game of Tennis*, and it is equally applicable to any sport. In the next two chapters, I will try to illustrate the integration between awareness and technique in my discussion of the specific skills of putting, chipping, and swinging. First, I have some general comments on technical instructions as they relate to learning from experience.

To me it makes sense to build any system of instruction on the best possible understanding of the natural learning process you were born with. The less the instruction process interferes with the process of learning built into your very DNA, the more effective your progress is going to be. Said another way, the less fear and doubt are imbedded in the instructional process, the easier it will be to take all the steps in the natural learning process.

WHICH CAME FIRST, THE EXPERIENCE OR THE TECHNIQUE?

In the effort to understand how to use technical knowledge or theory I believe that it is most important to recognize that, fundamentally, *experience* precedes technical knowledge. We may read books or articles that present technical instructions before we have ever swung a club, but where did these instructions come from? At some point did they not originate in *someone's* experience? Either by accident or by intention someone hit a ball in a certain way and it felt good and it worked. Through experimentation, refinements were made and the golf swing finally became a repeatable one.

Then, perhaps, in an attempt to repeat that way of hitting the ball or to pass it on to someone else, the golfer attempts to describe that swing in language. But words can only represent actions, ideas, and experiences. Language is not action, and, at best, it can only hint at the subtleties contained in any complex behavior. Although the instruction can now be stored in the part of the mind that remembers language, it must be acknowledged that remembering the instruction is not the same as remembering the swing itself.

It is, of course, very convenient to think that by giving ourselves a correct instruction like "Swing from the inside out," we will hit wonderful draws over and over. We have been taught to trust Self 1's conceptual process of learning technique more than Self 2's natural process. Self 1 wants the credit for the good shot and wants to ignore the role of Self 2. This sets us up for disappointment when we give the same instruction again and the same good shot does not occur. Since we think the instruction was correct, the conclusion we come to is that we failed to obey it properly and that led to the error. Then we may get angry at ourselves for this "failure," make disparaging remarks about our abilities and call ourselves stupid, or blame ourselves in a variety of other ways.

But maybe the error was in not trusting Self 2 more. It is as if we think of ourselves as an obedient computer rather than as a human being. Consequently, we are apt to lose the direct access to the muscle memory that carries the most complete knowledge of the desired action. In a society that has become so oriented toward language as a way of representing truth, it is very possible for us to lose touch with our ability to feel and with it our ability to "remember" the way the shots felt. This remembering is a fundamental act of trust in Self 2 without which excellence in any skill cannot be sustained.

When the verbal instruction is passed on to another person who does not have in his bank of experience the action being described, it lives in the mind totally disconnected from experience. Then, as the student continues to learn in this way, there will be an ever-widening split between the memory of theory and the memory of action. And if we use an instruction to pass judgment on our shots instead of attending to the lessons of experience, the gap between experience and the instruction is further widened. The instruction, used as a conceptual "should" or "should not," puts a shadow of fear between Self 2's intuitive knowledge and the action. Many times I have observed golfers hitting perfectly decent shots but complaining about them because they thought they did something "wrong." By the time they have brought their swing into conformity with their concept of the "right" way to do it, the shot has lost both power and consistency as well as naturalness.

In short, if we rely too heavily on instructions, we lose touch with the ability to feel our actions and undermine our natural learning processes and our potential to perform. Instead, if we swing the golf club while relying on the instincts of Self 2, we reinforce the simplest neural pathway to the optimal shot.

By using awareness instructions, you can learn a great deal of technique naturally by paying close attention to your body, the club, and the ball. The more awareness you can bring to bear on any action, the more feedback you get from experience and the more naturally you learn the technique that feels best and works best for you or any given player at any given state of development. We may need to learn how to feel again and learn how to learn again. The saying of an old master is pertinent here: "No teacher is greater than one's own experience."

HOW TO MAKE THE BEST USE OF TECHNICAL INSTRUCTIONS

So the question remains: How can one person's greater level of experience help another person? The short answer is that a valid instruction derived from experience can help me if it guides me to my own experiential discovery.

For the student, the question is how to listen to technical instructions and use them without falling into the Self 1 traps of judgment, doubt, and fear. For the teacher or coach, the question is how to give instructions in such a way as to help the natural learning process of the student and not interfere with it. If the teacher succeeds in this effort, then he will have taught more than golf, and the student will walk away with skills that can be used for the learning of any skill.

HOW DO YOU LEARN TO GRIP THE CLUB CORRECTLY?

Let's say you've read a set of instructions about how best to grip the golf club. There is not much doubt involved in learning the grip. It may feel a little awkward, and you may not have much understanding of why the club should be held in the prescribed manner, but those problems diminish with time. You look for the grip that suits your hands. The instructions are there to "get you into the ballpark" so you can go on to discover what will work best for you.

But how firmly should you grip the club? You will probably not find a technical description that is more specific than "Grip the club firmly but not in a death grip." Or perhaps "Grip the club with the same firmness of a handshake." You can tell that there is no way you are going to learn the best amount of pressure to apply to your wrist by reading about it in a book. The book can give you a hint, but after that you are going to have to learn directly from your experience. And that is probably how the person writing the book had to learn, too.

Just as the originator of the instruction discovered from experience what was too firm and what was too wobbly, so the individual golfer has to find out the same way—by experimentation. This can be done only by paying close attention to the feel of your hands, wrists, and arms during your swing. You don't need to put your findings into words; *it is the feel itself, not the description of the feel, that you will remember.*

A "discovery" frame of mind is very different from a "dogmatic" frame of mind. If I try to define "firm grip" and obey it as an instruction, in the effort to grip the club "correctly" and "firmly," I will usually overtighten the wrists. This prevents them from moving as freely as they need to through the ball and thereby robs me of both power and accuracy. Then, in an effort to get more control and more power, the dogmatic Self 1 is apt to let the tightness move up the arms to my shoulders and neck until the swing is generally constricted.

Soon someone will tell me that I should relax and not try to hit so hard. But how much should I relax? Do I know how to relax? If I can't "feel" the overtightness, I am not going to be able to find the proper amount of relaxation. It just can't be spelled out in words.

So I believe the best use of most technical knowledge is to communicate a *hint* of a desired destination. The hint can be delivered verbally, demonstrated in action, or observed in a picture or video, but it is best seen as an *approximation* of a desirable goal waiting to be discovered firsthand by the individual golfer through paying close attention to his own experience.

If you asked a group of golf instructors to write down all the important elements of a golf swing, most would find it easy to distinguish at least fifty instructions. Imagine the difficulty for the golfer who must deal with this complexity. No wonder self-doubt is so easy to come by! On the other hand, understanding the swing and remembering its feel is like remembering a single picture. The mind is capable of that, and it can recognize when one element in one picture is slightly different from another. The other advantage of using awareness to "discover the technique" is that it doesn't tend to evoke the overcontrolling and judgmental tendencies of Self 1.

HOW TO WATCH THE PROS

When I was a child, I used to play touch football, and I noticed that I played a lot better when I'd just come home after my dad had taken me to see the San Francisco 49ers play. I hadn't studied Frankie Albert's passing technique, but I had picked up something, and it made a difference when I played. I think most people have had experiences very similar to this.

Although it is obvious that we can learn a great deal by watching better players play golf, we have to learn how to watch. The best method is simply to watch without assuming that the way the pro swings is the way you should swing. In many cases, asking a beginner to try to swing like a pro is like asking a baby to walk before it has crawled. Formulating technique while watching the pro or by trying to imitate him or her too closely can be detrimental to your natural learning process.

Instead, allow yourself to focus on whatever most interests you about the pro's movements. Self 2 will automatically pick up elements of the swing that are useful to it and discard whatever is not useful at the time. Observe how each new swing feels and how it works. Allow the natural learning process to lead you toward your best swing. Do not force yourself to make the change. Just allow Self 2 to "play around" while it searches for new swing possibilities. In doing so, it will use what it is ready for from the "hints" picked up in its observation of the pro.

Self 2 has very good instincts about when it is time to work on any particular element of your swing. In learning how to learn by watching pros play, you may want to alternate between external observation and experimentation on the range until you have the confidence that you can access the particular swing technique you are working on.

Throughout this approach to learning, the ultimate choice stays with you as you alternately shift attention between observation of the pro's swing and focus on your own. There is no judgment necessary in the process. You see differences between what you are doing and the external model, but simply notice them, and continue to observe, feel your own movements, and check the results. This "learning mind-set" lends a freedom to search for the feel that works for you.

In summary, I do believe that someone who has discovered his or her best swing can help you discover *your* best swing. Knowledge of technique learned by one person can give another an advantage in discovering what technique works best. But it is dangerous to make that person's swing or any swing description into your standard for right and wrong. Self 1 easily gets enamored of formulas that tell the body what position it should be in and when. It likes the sense of control it gets from doing it by the book.

But Self 2 likes the feeling of flow—sensing the whole swing as one thing. The Inner Game encourages you to keep in touch with the Self 2 learning process you were born with while avoiding getting too caught up in trying too hard to make your movements conform to an outside model. Use outside models in your learning, but don't let them use you. Natural learning is and always will be from the inside out, not vice versa.

With this approach I do not have the feeling that I am fitting myself or my students into an external model. After an Inner Game tennis lesson, a golf professional told me what he liked about this approach: "What I consider to be the right technique for my swing is ever-changing day by day. My model is always being destroyed and rebuilt as I learn more and more. My technique is always evolving."

Self 2's nature is to evolve every chance it gets. As your technique evolves, you will become better at learning technique and you will be able to make big changes in a short period of time. As you discover Self 2's learning capabilities, not only will your golf swings improve but you will have increased your capacity to learn anything.

THE LADDER OF EFFECTIVE WAYS TO LEARN GOLF (FROM LEAST EFFECTIVE TO MOST EFFECTIVE)

Strategy Number 1: Trying to Figure It Out on Your Own

You think you're a good athlete and things come naturally to you, so you'll just rely on your knowledge of other sports and figure things out as you go along. What happens to such a player? He starts with the enthusiasm that's natural for a person who is going to be independent and learn on his own. But he doesn't know how to learn. He makes good shots, and he makes bad shots. Every time he makes a good shot, he thinks, What did I do right? Every time he hits a bad shot, he tries to figure out what went wrong. He is caught in this culture's good-bad mode of learning, but he is basing his own rules of "good" and "bad" on relatively little experience. What he doesn't know he fills in with unfounded assumptions. His thinking is both judgmental and groundless. His criteria for right and wrong are founded on an all-too-narrow base of experience. He becomes superstitious: "Before that last good shot, I wiggled this way or waggled that way, or thought this particular thought before starting my swing . . . and it worked. Now I've got the secret to the game!"

Confident in his new discovery, he addresses the next ball with high hopes and expectations. In this state of mind, it is not unusual for him to hit another good shot—not because of the wiggle, waggle, or special thought but because of his momentary self-confidence. Maybe two or three good shots, then the inevitable flub. "What went wrong with that one?" he wonders. "Maybe I didn't wiggle or waggle enough. Maybe I didn't think my thought strongly enough." So he redoubles his efforts, but now doubt has crept in. Another shot misses the mark. "Maybe it's something else I'm doing wrong." The latest "secret to successful golfing" is discarded after three holes, and the same thinking that dreamed it up in the first place is now looking for the next secret. Uncertainty sets in. Just enough good shots are being hit to make him think that his latest explanation of cause and effect is grounded in reality. At the same time, inexplicably poor shots are fueling the uncertainty. Frustration deepens. Amazingly enough, some players hold on to this approach throughout a lifetime of golf. To compensate for the continuous disappointment of broken beliefs, they brag to their friends that they are self-taught and don't really need the help of a teacher.

Strategy Number 2: Taking Lessons from a Golf Professional Who Understands Only the Mechanics of the Game

This strategy starts with the commonsense assumption that if you don't know how to do something, someone who does know can teach you. If you don't know the law, you go to a lawyer. If you don't know mathematics, you go to a math teacher. This is a sensible approach, and, if you have enough humility, it can work much better than Strategy Number 1. The instructor, like any trained expert, understands the game and will be willing to pass his knowledge on to you for a reasonable fee. This is the same kind of knowledge you can find in a golf magazine or book. It is cause-and-effect knowledge, based on a mechanical understanding of the golf swing (even though the theories of mechanics vary greatly among experts and they disagree vehemently on certain elements of the proper swing).

The underlying fallacy of this approach is the assumption that someone who knows the mechanics of a golf swing therefore knows how to help someone else learn how to play golf. Although, typically, both professionals and students share this assumption, it is not necessarily true that if a person can describe, demonstrate, and correctly analyze the golf swing, he can teach it to another person. The conceptual knowledge of a golf swing can indeed be passed via book, article, or qualified golf professional, but, as explained earlier on, there is quite a gap between knowing something conceptually and being able to do it. Fortunately for golfers, the PGA and many golf instructors have been making strides to understand the learning process better and to improve ways of helping students learn.

The biggest downfall of learning from the professional in the traditional way is that the student becomes overly dependent on both the professional's knowledge and the learning process. When things go wrong, he will return to the pro or refer to one of his many instructions. The student undoubtedly will be caught up in the process of analyzing each bad shot just as he did in Strategy Number 1. The natural learning process is still missing. Most of golf simply cannot be learned by imposing external instructions on the swing elements. Fortunately, the body is such an amazing learning mechanism that, over time, it will begin to learn in spite of the interferences that are an inevitable part of learning by instruction and analysis.

Strategy Number 3: Natural Learning Without the Help of a Professional

Almost anyone who does not interfere with natural learning is capable of developing a good game of golf without taking lessons. The fundamental skill is nonjudgmental awareness—a way of looking that does not judge good or bad, a way of focusing attention without consciously trying to correct. Learning by this method requires trust, not in a formula but in your body's ability to learn directly from experience, without judgmental analysis. Though golf may be more complicated than riding a bike, for example, it can be learned in much the same way. When you can relax in face of the challenge of golf and are not overwhelmed by the shoulds and shouldn'ts of external models, you are much better able to feel what is happening in your swing. Your attention naturally gravitates toward what needs to be noticed. By trusting that attention, and giving freely of it, learning takes place. The process is continuous as your attention shifts spontaneously to the next focal point. You are learning to stay out of the way of the natural learning process, secure in the knowledge that you'll be hitting shots that work and shots that don't. Improvement will be gradual, but natural, and you will skip the frustration that drives so many away from the game. Moreover, you will be able to employ these skills of focus and trust in the development of other skills. Strategy Number 3 is the primary method described in this edition of the book and the one I used to learn the game while writing the original version.

Strategy Number 4: Natural Learning
Plus the Help of an Inner Game Coach

Even though I am capable of focusing my own attention, I have been consistently surprised at the relative effectiveness of using a focus suggested by another person. As individuals operating within our own mind-set, we inevitably develop blind spots, areas of our behavior that we simply overlook or ignore. We become accustomed to what we repeat, and this familiarity breeds unconsciousness. So, as effective as natural learning is, there is no substitute for the help of another pair of eyes, especially if they belong to someone who understands the natural learning process.

The value of Inner Game coaching, even when done by individuals without any special knowledge of the mechanics of a particular sport, has been driven home to me by how much I have learned from my students. Though few of them know much about the mechanics of golf, most have begun to absorb the principles of natural learning. First, I would coach them, then I would ask them to coach me. I would ask them to watch my swing, not for the purpose of correcting anything but just to observe. I knew that their attention would spontaneously focus on some aspect of the swing. It might be my posture at setup, an aspect of the backswing, or the follow-through. It might be balance, tempo, or some little detail that didn't seem significant enough to mention. Whatever it was, I would ask them to tell me. Recently, a student said she saw that the first thing I did on my takeaway was to make a slight movement with my right hand that opened the club face. I had no idea what I was doing and no idea if it was working or not. My response was twofold. First, I had to be careful not to jump to any conclusion about whether this movement was helpful. Second, I had to focus my attention on that movement and notice if it increased, decreased, or stayed the same, trusting that any necessary learning would take place.

The big difference between this kind of coaching and that of the traditional professional is that the first holds up a mirror. The Inner Game coach says focus here or focus there, without any hint of trying to induce a preconceived change. It is this noncorrective attitude that helps the student make nonjudgmental observations of his own swing, increase the sense of feel, and trigger the natural learning process.

Strategy Number 5: Natural Learning with the Help of a Golf Professional Who Understands How to Coach Natural Learning

The coach who understands the natural learning process, but not the mechanics of the golf swing, can still help the student get the most out of his or her own learning abilities. But the professional who grasps both the mechanics and the Inner Game can be even more helpful, since the student will be able to keep faith with his own learning capabilities while benefiting from the teacher's experience.

Whereas the Inner Game coach might just give the focusing instruction "Notice the extent of turn made by your left shoulder," the knowledgeable professional can give a hint about the direction of change he expects to take place. He might believe, for example, that to gain maximum power it is important to take a complete backswing and that, in most cases, the shoulders should turn until the back of the left shoulder is just behind the ball. But how would he "coach" the learning of this movement? Not with an emphasis on "doing it right." The emphasis should be on exploration. He might say, "Notice the degree of turn of your shoulders during your backswing. Let me know if the back of your left shoulder [pointing to the exact spot] stops turning before or after the ball." He might ask the student to scale −3, −2, −1 for positions in front of the ball and +1, +2, +3 for after the ball. After the coach is confident that the student is able to feel accurately what her shoulders are doing, he might add the suggestion "As you keep exploring this turn, you will probably find the position you are looking for in the vicinity just behind the ball." If this instruction is given in such a way that it does not cause the student to stop exploring and to start "obeying," the learning can take place naturally and with firsthand knowledge of what works. It will be more confident, quicker, and more lasting. Under such instruction, a student gets the best of both worlds. He retains his trust in his own natural learning abilities yet benefits from the pro's knowledge. The dignity and joy of Self 2 learning are kept intact at the same time that experience and knowledge of golf are brought to bear unobtrusively.

SEVEN

The Short Game:
Inner Putting and
Inner Chipping

MUCH HAS BEEN WRITTEN ABOUT THE IMPORTANCE OF THE SHORT game in golf. It accounts for nearly half the strokes taken in any given round, yet it often gets only a small fraction of the attention and practice. Even more important, the simple back-and-forth movements of putting and chipping are the easiest places to build the foundations of both your Inner and Outer game technique and to understand the relationship between the two.

The short game is clearly the place where mental focus comes most into play. Awareness and feel are critical. It is also where a little yip in your chip can cost you a quick stroke while sending a piercing dart into the heart of your self-confidence. A putt that misses by a hair's width is still a missed putt, and sending it that last millimeter will count as a full stroke the same as your 200+ yard drive. The ultimate goal of every shot is to hit the golf ball in the hole, but the only time you actually succeed is on your last shot on each hole.

Finally, the short game is the great equalizer in golf. Every golfer has the *physical* ability to sink a chip or a putt and on occasion will hit shots that the pro would gladly accept. Age and lack of skill can put a three-hundred-yard drive out of reach, but not the hope of holing a thirty-foot putt. If you don't happen to live near a practice range, or perhaps don't feel like spending another five to seven dollars for a big bucket of balls, there's always the backyard lawn, a grassy park, or a living-room carpet. Each will provide you with a learning environment for practicing this crucial part of the game of golf.

This chapter is about developing your awareness and trust skills in putting and chipping. It also explores how to integrate technical knowledge in a way that does not undermine what is most important—your feel and your self-confidence.

INCREASING AWARENESS
OF THE PUTTING SURFACE

Almost all golfers could make a significant improvement in their putting by *seeing* the putting surface more clearly. The most common mistake is to *look too hard* and *think too long* about the line of the putt. Near the hole, the final target, tension tends to increase; we know that a small error can add a stroke to our score, so we tend to strain as we look back and forth between the hole and the ball trying to fix the line in our minds.

But this isn't how to see something well. The eyes work best when they are relaxed. As with other tryings, "*trying* to see" fails. Even a slight tension in the mind can cause a tightening of the muscles that regulate the shape of the lens. In effect, this means that staring or tensing the eyes will actually make the hole appear either farther away or closer than it actually is. Tension can also make the hole look smaller and distort the slope of the green. The eyes don't need help to see; you don't have to squint or stare.

What we see *comes* to our eyes, not the other way around. When looking at the hole, don't take a "hard" look, as in straining to see detail. It is better to use "soft" eyes that are receptive and allow the important details to come to you. This will also allow a more tension-free stroke. In this state it is natural for our eyes to move around; trying to hold them still prevents them from absorbing information. Only when you are relaxed and receptive does the light reflected from external objects fall on the most sensitive part of the eye, and only then are details seen in full clarity.

Thinking too much can also hinder the seeing process. Most golfers feel they should mentally calculate the break when they line up a putt: "Let's see, it's a downhill lie, so I should hit it soft, maybe with a longer, smoother swing. . . . There's a break to the right, so I guess I should aim about six inches above the hole. . . . But I left the last putt like this short, so I don't want to hit it too soft. . . . I wonder what the effect of the grain will be . . ." This kind of thinking can interfere with seeing.

It's not your intellect that needs to analyze the putt because, as I hope you now believe, it is not your intellect that can direct your putter to hit the ball effectively. You can see the slope of the green and the distance to the hole without saying to yourself, "It's eight feet downhill, with a break to the right." To translate the situation into words invites intellectual analysis and Self 1 interference with your stroke.

The other possibility is to observe the putting surface, including any changes in its contour, and let Self 2 pick the line. Often I stand in front of a breaking putt and think I know how much break to allow for. But then I let Self 2 make the decision and often watch the ball take a completely different line to the hole.

Self 2 doesn't learn how to read greens by looking at the green alone. It learns most by observing the balls roll over the surface of greens with different contours and different kinds of grass. A good way to educate Self 2 is to roll golf balls across a given contour and study the shape of the trajectory of the ball's path relative to what you imagined it would do. When the ball does something you didn't expect, take a closer look at the green to determine the cause.

GOING TO SCHOOL ON OTHER GOLFERS' PUTTS

It is commonly felt that you can learn a lot about the contour of a particular putt if one of your opponents has a line similar to yours and is putting first. But it is to your advantage to go to school on *every* putt both before and after your own. If you do this exercise, it will not only sharpen your awareness of the speed of this particular green but give Self 2 further information that will help you in the future. Estimate the length and slope of each player's putt; then, before the putt is halfway to the hole, decide whether the ball is going to stop short or beyond the hole and by how much. This gives Self 2 valuable practice in reading greens, as well as precise information about the relationship between the speed of the ball and how far it travels. I find it's also more fun than just standing around pretending to be interested when I'm not and keeps me from analyzing my last putt or worrying about what will happen when it's my turn.

INCREASING AWARENESS OF DISTANCE

I have found that it's not necessary to try to calculate the number of feet to the hole of any given putt. But it is important to allow yourself to increase your awareness of distance. Standing behind the ball, I sometimes divide the line between the ball and the hole in half and then divide those segments in half one or two more times. If the green is contoured, my eye doesn't follow a straight line to the hole but whatever line Self 2 is picking out to allow for the break. Having visually focused my attention on the distance in this way, I will take a practice swing or two, without any effort to control the force of the swing. I don't rehearse the swing in the normal way of trying to repeat the "right" amount of force. I really don't know how hard I should hit the ball, so I ask Self 2 to show me. This active admittance of not knowing is important. "Show me how hard to hit this one," I say as Self 2 takes a few swings. I can tell when it is comfortable that it has found what it was looking for. Even then I don't try to reproduce that swing but let Self 2 make any adjustments it wants to in the final swing. It takes some trust, but when I don't interfere, I usually find out that my trust was well placed. I don't believe there is anything magical about this, and Self 2 definitely improves with experience on different kinds of greens.

Another way to sense distance is to walk to the hole with your eyes shut and attempt to put your putter handle in the hole. This brings "distance" to the body in a way that is more than just visual and adds to the information Self 2 can use in doing its calculations. As you get good at this exercise from short distances, you can test your distance awareness from longer and longer distances from the hole.

A SIMPLE SOLUTION TO A COMPLEX PROBLEM

Self 2 has to calculate both the direction and the force with which to hit the ball, and these variables are related to each other in a way that is almost impossible for the conscious mind to grasp. When a problem is clearly too hard for me, I sometimes find it easier to trust Self 2, and then the putt comes out much better than I expected. The best putter on the 1996 Tour was Brad Faxon. When asked for advice about what to think about while putting, he was quoted in *Golf Magazine* as saying, "Believe it or not, I'm not really thinking about anything when I putt. . . . It's hard to teach. I let my instincts take over. I like to see which way the break is going and use it. When I'm putting well, I feel as if I can make everything." A better statement of trusting Self 2 in putting will be hard to find. Yet other pros still like to rely on the technical aspects of putting.

JUST HOW TECHNICAL IS PUTTING?

At one L.A. Open, I ran into a touring pro who had the negative experience of falling from a consistent top five place on the tour to a position well down in the pack. We were introduced in the locker room, where he made the following comment about *The Inner Game of Golf*.

"I read your book," he said, "and I think what you have to say applies pretty well to the golf swing, but not to putting. Putting is just much too technical for the Inner Game to work." If anything, I expected quite the opposite, so I asked him, "Tell me, how old were you when you putted the best?" The pro thought for some time and then, with an almost nostalgic look, said, "I guess I've never really putted better than on certain days when I was fifteen or sixteen years old. I used to go out with three adults and one-putt sixteen out of eighteen greens. When they saw that I was in that kind of a zone, they would let me putt their balls as well. And I would generally sink them from wherever they were on the green."

I then asked what I thought was a question with an obvious answer: "Well, just how much technical knowledge could you have had at fifteen years old?" His answer truly shocked me. "Oh, of course I had very little technical knowledge. It's true that I putted best at the time, but that really doesn't count because at that age I didn't know how technical putting really was."

This conversation has stuck with me over the years as an example of just how deep belief in technique can go. It was particularly poignant because with all his accumulated technical wisdom about putting, it was his deteriorated putting game that was largely responsible for his declining standing on the Tour. When belief in technique becomes stronger than belief in our fundamental abilities, there will inevitably be loss in both confidence and performance.

Of course, not all touring pros who have technical know-how

put their primary belief in it. Jack Nicklaus, in *Golf My Way*, writes, "Such is putting! 2% technique, 98% inspiration or confidence or touch . . . the only thing great putters have in common is touch, and that's the critical ingredient . . . none of them found it through mechanizing a stroke, nor do I believe they could maintain it in that way." That says it very clearly, and I believe the principle behind what Nicklaus is saying applies to more than putting.

But the question remains: How do you develop this "critical ingredient" called "touch"?

BODY AND CLUB AWARENESS

After you have begun to learn about reading the green, the greatest challenge is to increase awareness of body and club while putting. Developing feel in putting can be broken down into two simple components: feel of distance and feel of direction. Feel in putting, as with any golf swing, is transmitted primarily through the hands, wrists, arms, and shoulders. What is different about putting is that these are the only necessary transmitters of feel. Because most putts do not require great force, the legs and the hips are not required to be in motion. They simply provide a solid and stationary base for the delicate movement of hands, arms, and shoulders. It is because putting requires such precision that simplicity is the most important characteristic of the putting stroke. The less unnecessary movement there is in the rest of your body, the easier it is for Self 2 to focus attention on the critical arm and hand movements. You want to eliminate all unnecessary variables in the stroke so that the remaining essentials can be felt and translated into precision in both distance and direction.

The grip of the club is your feeling contact with the putter. Therefore, you want a grip that (1) allows your two hands to act as one and (2) allows for maximum feel of the putter's movement. I like to get as much skin as possible in contact with the handle to allow for maximum feel. I also like to have the back of my left hand and the palm of my right hand parallel to give me a better feel for direction. Within those guidelines each individual can explore and discover the grip that gives the best touch.

The way you stand over the putt is also important to maximizing feel. If you were to stand in a different way on each putt, you would make it harder for Self 2 to learn consistency. You want to stand in a way that is comfortable, again so that you are not robbing yourself of an ounce of awareness of the movement of the stroke itself. For the same reason, you will probably want to have the ball in the same position in your stance. Most professionals advise that it be placed just far enough toward your front foot so that the putter is at the bottom of its arc or just barely on its way up at the moment of contact with the ball.

Don't be afraid to experiment with different grips and postures. Often a change will increase your sensitivity to the feel of your body. Similarly, changing putters can often increase your awareness of different putting sensations. This is one reason why golfers often putt better for a short time after switching putters.

If you continue to follow the principle of simplicity in putting, the stroke itself will begin to resemble a pendulumlike motion. The shoulders, arms, and wrists can form a relatively firm and consistent triangle as they rock back and forth in a rhythmic and steady motion. Again, the fewer unnecessary movements there are in the motion, the more feel you will gain of the stroke.

THE TOUCH GAME

I devised the "touch game" to increase my own sense of feel in putting. It is a simple awareness game, yet it is the most effective practice I have found for this purpose. The minds of most golfers, even when just practicing putting, have one dominant thought: Try to get the ball in the hole. The difference between success and failure in putting is so definite and the goal so precise that putting tends to make us very goal-oriented. But too much goal-orientedness will rob you of feel—the feel you need to reach your goal. So the touch game changes the goal of putting. Here's how it works:

You putt the ball without looking where it goes, and then you form a mental image of where you *guess* the putt has come to rest. Success is not defined as getting the ball in the hole but as *knowing* where the ball went. In other words, if the putt goes right of the hole six inches and stops eight inches beyond the hole and you guessed it right, by feel alone and without looking, then you win! If the ball went in the hole and you thought it went two inches left, then you lose!

There is only one way to win this game, and that is to feel as accurately as you can what effect a particular putting stroke has had on the ball. You do not try to sink the putt, nor do you try not to. You trust Self 2 to make the putt, and you're totally absorbed in trying to feel what happens. Where the ball ends up compared to where you thought it did is the measure of just how aware you were of the feel of your body and putter.

This is a very challenging and beneficial learning game. It takes the tension out of the putt by changing the game's external goal. At the same time it gives you an ever-increasing awareness of the two all-important variables in golf—distance and direction. After a little practice, most golfers find that they are quite accurate in knowing where their putts end up without looking. At the outset of this practice, I suggest you divide the touch game into its two components. First, just play for accurate sensing of distance. Then, switch to direction. Go back and forth between the two games until you feel you want to combine them.

PUTTING WITH YOUR EYES SHUT

To get the most benefit out of the touch game, I recommend putting with your eyes shut. Even though it is more difficult to make precise contact with the ball at first, this disadvantage can soon be overcome and you will find that closing your eyes gives you a much greater sense of feel and surprisingly good results. It proves how much putting is a matter of touch and shows that after the putt is lined up, there is little need for the eyes.

The Next Step: Knowing How You Know

After you have gained an ability to feel where your putts go, you can take another step to heighten both feel and control. After making your initial guess about where your ball ended up, ask yourself, "How did I know?" With this question you are searching for the "feel clues" that contributed to your guess. For example, you may have guessed that your putt went six inches left of the hole. When you ask yourself what made you guess that, you might realize that you sensed the putter blade was slightly closed at impact. Then, on the succeeding putts, you put extra attention on the club face at impact, trying to "read" even more accurately its effect on the ball. Because the goal is not trying to get the ball in the hole, you do not try to control the putter face, you simply observe it. You attempt to feel if it is more closed, less closed, or the same as it was during the preceding putt. This requires a lot of attention, which almost always increases feel and control. Without conscious effort, the law of awareness will tend to bring the putter into proper alignment.

But let's say the putter face doesn't change its angle of impact and you continue with the awareness process. You then ask yourself, "If the putter is square at address to the ball, at what moment in the putting stroke does it change?" In this way you search for the source of this critical variable. When awareness is at the source, it will tend to change naturally in a way consistent with the desired results.

It is also possible that the club face is not the only variable contributing to your leftward putts. As you continue the touch game, you discover another indication—a sensing of a right-to-left direction (a push or pull) in your putter stroke. Then you apply the same awareness process to the direction of your swing as you did to your club face. You simply notice the direction of your next putts and again guess at the results. Learning to sense this direction is a very different process from "trying to keep it straight," which ends up in a tendency toward Self 1 control and overtightening of muscles that decrease feel. The awareness *without effort to correct* increases feel and as a result increases true control.

The process of attempting to increase your awareness of particular sensations—no matter what they are—is the same. In all cases, you are trying to trace the *feeling* that contributed to the result back to its source. Then you focus attention there and allow the change to take place where it is most needed.

The Touch Game

The beginner can go a long way toward achieving the foundation of feel by playing a simplified form of the touch game. I recommend the following exercise for the more advanced golfer who is getting ready to play a round: Line up three or four balls a few inches apart. Putt the first, and look where it stops rolling. Then putt the second without looking. Guess if it went farther, the same, or not as far as the first putt. Then check. Do the same with the remaining balls, comparing the feel of "distance" to that of the first putt. The same exercise can be done with regard to direction by guessing whether the second and following putts are right or left of the first ball. Again, the idea is not to hit the "target" ball but to use it as a reference for feeling distance and/or direction. The advantage of using the first ball as a reference as opposed to the hole is that it takes away all implied pressure of "succeeding" and "not succeeding."

SOME CRITICAL VARIABLES
IN PUTTING AND CHIPPING

This process of discovering and then attending to the variables that are affecting your stroke applies equally to putting and to chipping. By using the touch game, any golfer will find subtle changes taking place in the short game, making it more consistent and reliable. Listed below are a number of critical variables that can be attended to that apply to both putting and chipping. Focusing attention on one of these variables at a time without trying to make any changes can provoke spontaneous swing improvement.

- Awareness of the alignment of feet, hips, and hands
- Awareness of the club-head speed
- Awareness of the direction of the path of the club head
- Awareness of the length of the backswing and the length of the follow-through
- Awareness of the angle of the club face before, at, and after contact
- Awareness of the spin imparted to the ball
- Awareness of the position of the ball between your feet

DISCOVERING YOUR PUTTING/CHIPPING TECHNIQUE

The natural way to learn putting and chipping technique involves using awareness and trust together to move toward one desired learning goal—control over distance and direction in the short game. Awareness is used to focus on the critical variable, and trust allows you to let go of technical controls and trust Self 2's sense of feel and the natural learning process. After you gain firsthand familiarity with this process, it is possible to incorporate knowledge of technique into the equation. As stated in the last chapter, technical knowledge will not be used as a direct instruction (except in the case of easy-to-follow instructions regarding grip and ball positioning). Instead, technical knowledge will be used as a "hint" to the student about the learning that is likely to take place as the student increases awareness of his or her current putting or chipping stroke.

The chart on the following pages is divided into three

columns. The one on the left describes a commonly desired outcome of a putting or chipping stroke. This column represents what might be your end goals in achieving control over distance and direction. The second column lists a few of the critical variables that contribute to achieving the goals in the column on the left. These variables are to be taken not as instructions but as places to focus your attention in order to discover the technique for achieving your desired outcomes. For example, it is very important that you not read the phrase "any unnecessary movements" as an instruction to limit your movement. Instead, read it as an instruction to *look for* or *sense actively* any unnecessary movements. Follow the law of awareness—if something needs to change it will as you increase your awareness of it. Also, this is not meant to be a complete list of critical variables, but it should be enough to give you some practical examples. You can compile your own list based on your understanding of your own short game as it continues to evolve.

Finally, the column on the right represents some hints based on the technical knowledge about the short game commonly held to be valid by golf professionals. This list is also not complete and of course can vary depending on the professional who is asked. This column is meant to give you a hint about the direction of desired change. I believe this is the most effective use of technical knowledge in a verbal format for the person who wants to discover putting and chipping technique. It is there to prompt and/or validate the spontaneous change that occurs while you are paying attention to the corresponding critical variable. To the extent that you treat it as a hint and not an instruction to obey, Self 2 will be able to guide you to the technique that works best for you and produces your desired outcomes.

Inner Putting and Chipping Chart
for Self-Discovering Technique

DESIRED OUTCOME	CRITICAL VARIABLES FOR FOCUS	LEARNING GOAL (TECHNICAL HINT)
Consistent, simple motion	Unnecessary movements, especially in wrists, legs, and head	Approximately like the motion of a pendulum made by rocking your shoulders—left shoulder down, right shoulder up on the backswing, and vice versa on the forward stroke
	Unnecessary variations in movement of arms or hands	
	Consistency of grip	Backs of hands square to putter face
	Consistency of stance	Weight favors front foot
	Consistency of preputting routine	Have the same routine
	Position of ball in stance	Left eye over the ball at address
	Change in distance between elbows	Keep distance consistent
	Speed of backswing compared to forward swing	Keep them even
Stability	Movement of head during swing	No head movement until ball is well on its way
	Stability of lower body	Knees and hips slightly bent, no movement from waist down
	Distance between feet	Approximately shoulder width

Stability *(cont'd)*	CRITICAL VARIABLES FOR FOCUS	LEARNING GOAL (TECHNICAL HINT)
	Stability of triangle made by shoulders, arms, and wrists	Keep the triangle intact throughout putt
	Center of gravity	Keep it low and even—belt-buckle level
Control of distance	Length of backswing	Backswing and follow-through approximately same length
	Length of follow-through	
	Applied force (acceleration)	Smooth as possible acceleration
	Sound of ball on putter face	Solid
	Quality of contact with ball	Strike ball on putter's sweet spot
Control of direction	Contour of path to hole	Putt toward apex in a breaking putt
	Position of ball in stance	Under your left eye; beneath your sternum. Contact at bottom of arc
	Direction of shoulders, hips, knees, and feet	Parallel to target line
	Angle of putter face through impact	Keep putter face square to target line through impact by working back shoulder under forward shoulder

Control of direction (cont'd)	CRITICAL VARIABLES FOR FOCUS	LEARNING GOAL (TECHNICAL HINT)
	Position of hands relative to ball at setup and at impact	Slightly forward of ball
	Angle of lead wrist	Constant angle
	Direction of putter movement in relation to path to hole	Straight line, except on long putts when it works from inside the target line at the back of swing to inside at completion

MORE AWARENESS EXERCISES FOR INNER PUTTING

Looking at the Hole

After you have practiced the touch game with your eyes shut and have gained confidence that Self 2 can make solid contact with the ball without looking at it, a new possibility opens up for your putting. The technique is simple. Look at the *hole* while putting instead of the ball. The effectiveness of this technique depends on how developed your sense of feel is in your putting movement. It is best to control movement through feel rather than through vision. And since you know where the ball is, the best place for your eyes is on the target and/or on the intended line of the putt. After all, where does an archer look?

I tried this technique first on the putting green and then on the course with very good results. Once I learned to "see" the ball with my hands, I could keep my eyes on the hole and see both at once. With the target in my immediate vision, I felt more confident that Self 2 could find the *feel* that would put the ball where my eyes were focused.

A second advantage of this technique is that it avoids the tendency to lift your head up to see where the ball is going. And because the putting stroke is so short, looking at the hole does not restrict necessary body movement.

A third and not unimportant advantage is that I found the technique helped my confidence. When I am looking at the hole, I can imagine that it is an easy matter to place the ball into it. I imagine that I am just reaching out to touch the hole or to take something out of it. This reduces the tension that arises from assuming that I am attempting something "hard." With reduced fear of failure, there is also less chance of steering the ball or having a breakdown in my wrist or a dreaded yip. I also find that the more I use "soft eyes" to focus on some interesting aspect of the hole, the more I keep myself in the present and allow for a tension-free swing. You can always find something about the hole to engage your specific interest. Perhaps it is the richness of the dirt at the back of the cup, the light reflecting off several blades of grass at the point of desired entry, or the hole's oval shape. The particular focus doesn't matter. What is helpful is finding something that engages your visual attention and allows Self 2 to make the putt without any interference from Self 1.

One-Handed Putting

One way to notice the effect of doubt on performance is to putt one-handed. First take a few strokes and ask a friend to notice if your hand wobbles. Then putt a ball toward the hole. If there is no wobble, it's not a bad way to putt. Try it in competition on the course. Any wobble? Doubt has a greater effect on our small muscles, and with no left hand to steady them, their movements become more obvious.

Now that you have a clear feedback system, you can work to decrease the effect of doubt. Keep putting and simply observe the wobble with detached interest, noticing everything about it without trying to suppress the doubt or curb its effects. If you can do this, the wobble will diminish by itself. The doubt will have no fuel; you will realize that doubt doesn't have to be fought and that it will go away if you don't resist it but stay focused on what *is*.

Listening

Hearing can be more of an asset than it is generally given credit for in golf. It can give you input that you don't get from other senses, especially about the contact you are making with the club. By listening to the sound of the ball as it is struck, you can learn to discriminate whether it is being hit inside, outside, or directly on the sweet spot. As this awareness increases, so does the percentage of solid putts.

This exercise reminds me of the blind golfer who was playing in a foursome and was being ribbed by the other players. After one of his opponents left a sixteen-foot putt five feet short, he remarked, "That has to be the worst putt I've ever heard!"

Threading the Needle

Precision in putting is as much a state of mind as it is a technical accomplishment. One of the ways I find the state of mind that produces precision is to imagine that I am threading a needle. I think of the delicacy required, the accuracy of hand and of eye required to put a thread through the narrow teardrop at the end of the needle. Immediately, my mind is focused and geared for precise movement. I notice if my left and right hand move the club at exactly the same moment, if the club is resting just above the grass so it touches it but without the slightest friction. These are simple things to notice, but they require a fine-tuning of the attention that prepares for the surgical accuracy required in putting. In this way, I feel less that I am accomplishing precision by "doing things right" and more that I am simply uncovering the precision that is already there and expressing it. The first attitude makes me tense as I think of what I have to do to be precise. The second attitude is knowing that Self 2 is capable of great precision and that I can relax and appreciate the expression of this quality.

INNER CHIPPING

Chipping is like putting in that it requires only a short swing, with at least part of the shot rolling along the putting surface. But it also shares many components with the full swing, and I've been able to learn a great deal about golf just by chipping on the lawn. I like to take a bunch of balls out to the front yard and chip them toward a target, trying to find a rhythm and feel that works for me. Most of the important elements of the game are there, and I can hit several hundred balls in less time than it would take me to play nine holes. In a relatively short time I can explore my awareness of alignment and posture, rhythm, tempo, and most of the aspects of body and club awareness. The touch game works as well with chipping as it does with putting. And there is an almost endless list of critical variables I can focus on. Here are just a few:

- Awareness of weight distribution on my feet
- Awareness of the position of the ball in my stance
- Awareness of the position of my wrists and hands in relation to the ball
- Awareness of the distance of backswing relative to follow-through
- Awareness of where the club makes contact with the ball
- Awareness of the smoothness of transition from back to forward motion
- Awareness of the acceleration of the club's forward movement
- Awareness of the direction of motion relative to the target line
- Awareness of the angle of the club face
- Awareness of the angle of both front and back wrists
- Awareness of back-hit-stop
- Awareness of the tightness of the grip
- Awareness of the sound at impact
- Awareness of any jerkiness in the swing

- Awareness of the angle of takeaway and the angle of descent

CHIPS AND TIPS

Tips are Self 1's favorite weapon against the awareness progression, and there is no harder task than ridding ourselves of the hunger for tips. Self 1 constantly offers hope that there is some one thing it can do that will work.

Perhaps I hit a putt while thinking about something specific, and the ball goes into the hole. "That's it!" says Self 1. "You thought that thought and the ball went in! It works!" If you think the same thought on the next hole and sink the putt again, you're really in for trouble. You'll be sure you have The Answer and will probably start telling other people about it, too.

Of course there isn't any such tip; there is no thought, no technique, no theory, in either the Inner or the Outer Game, that is going to make the ball go in the hole. Taken as such, a tip is really nothing more than a superstition, and it carries the implication of a superstition that if you *don't* do it, something terrible will happen.

On the other hand, it is perfectly consistent with the principles of natural learning to find a focus of attention that works for you one day and move to another on the next. Focusing on a critical variable is very different from following a tip. Focus does work, and the particular variable you focus on can and will change.

Chipping on the lawn today, my attention goes naturally to the back of my left hand. As long as I let it rest there, the feedback I receive seems to give me maximum feel about where my leading edge is and lets me feel confident. This doesn't mean it's my secret for chipping; it's merely what my body finds useful today. I have to be willing to let go of it and may have to find another focus tomorrow.

A lot of golfers try to figure out how long the chip shot will be in the air and how far it will roll along the ground: "Where should my shot land on the green?" I suggest that it is good practice to try to guess at the shot's trajectory but to avoid thinking, "This is what I am going to try to do." Many combinations are possible between the variables of height and force applied. I suggest that you line up your shot, then guess what its height will be and where a shot of that height should land to make it to the hole. But don't try to get that result. Just let Self 2 do it, then watch the loft, where the ball lands and how it rolls. With each effort, Self 2 will get more experience and thus more skill.

The human body and the energy that moves it make the ball go in the hole, and we have no choice but to rely on them. All we have to learn is to concentrate the mind and keep ourselves out of the way of the body so it can either do its job or *learn* to do it better than it now can.

WHAT TO DO WHEN YOU LOSE THE FEEL

Nowhere is feel more crucial than in putting and chipping. Everyone experiences days when the club feels like an extension of the body and control seems simple, and everyone has times when the feel just isn't there—especially when playing under pressure.

The greatest cause of loss of feel is self-doubt, usually brought on by missed putts. Using the doctrine of the easy can help by taking your mind off negative associations with past putts and bringing positive associations into your swing.

But the basic strategy for increasing feel is consciously to switch games from a game of results to one of awareness. Usually, it is overconcern with results that leads to overcontrol and decreased feel, so change your goal to increasing awareness. Pick any awareness technique and increase your focus on whatever feel is there. Don't judge it as good or bad; merely observe it. Feel will pick up immediately, and improved results will follow as a matter of course.

Another reason for losing feel is boredom. When a player becomes bored, awareness declines, and although his swing may be so grooved that it achieves satisfactory results for a while, he will soon stop learning, and shortly thereafter performance will drop off. Boredom is best combated by taking conscious risks and concentrating on enjoyment. Experiment with a radically different putting stroke, or even change putters. It doesn't have to be a *better* stroke or putter, just a different one; it is the change that will increase awareness and decrease the boredom.

Equally effective is putting for pure fun. Playing the results game without ever giving yourself a break is dull and, ironically, leads to a decline in results. Take a break. Do whatever is necessary to introduce pleasure and excitement into your putting. Use your imagination; risk a few failures. An increase in feel is the inevitable result of an increase in the quality of your experience. Results will inevitably follow.

CHIPS AND YIPS

For some reason the chip shot seems to invite a tendency to mis-strike the ball. The ball is hit thin and sculled along the ground, or it is hit fat with an embarrassing thud that reveals that the "big ball" (planet Earth) was hit before the little one. And when doubt raises its ugly head, the dreaded yip can enter, seemingly grab the club, and make such an awkward stab at the ball that both score and pride have a hard time recovering.

The best preventative first aid against the yips is back-hit-stop or da-da-da-da. These focusing exercises are simple yet usually engaging enough to distract the mind from doubts. But I am among those golfers who did not find the occasional yip so easy an obstacle to overcome. It was not unusual for me to stand over a chip shot and feel quite uncertain. I would take five or six practice strokes mainly for the reassurance, only to stand over the real ball—and yip. I really hated the sensation and hated the result. I hated it much more than hitting a drive out of bounds or failing to get out of a bunker. I even hated it more than missing a short putt. It was especially embarrassing when I was playing with people who knew I had written a book on "the mental side of golf." I think the yip gods took a special pleasure in inflicting their tortures on "the Inner Game guy."

Welcoming the Yips

I tried many remedies for the yips, both technical and nontechnical. Some of them worked for short periods, but none cured the disease. Finally, the only way out that I could find was not to fight them. Like all manifestations of Self 1, the yips don't do well in the light of awareness. I would say to myself, "Okay, if you are going to yip, I am going to feel exactly how you do it. If you show yourself on this shot, I will study you with full awareness and without judgment." With this statement I declared that I would not be pushed around by a yip—even if it happened, which it usually did, at the most inopportune moments. When I caught the yip in action, I could feel a kind of weakness occur in my right wrist a split second before impact. That weakness wasn't real, but it seemed real, and the result would be that my club face would not move squarely through the ball but either stub the ground behind it or open at the last instant, sending the ball way off to the right.

I believe it was my intense dislike for yipping that made this error so enduring. And it wasn't until I could accept a yip or two without feeling terrible about it that the yips seem to decide to leave me more or less alone. Again, as with other habits, awareness itself is curative. But the awareness has to be accompanied by a true acceptance, without judgment, for the magic to work. I remember Mike Murphy's comments on yips when we played Pebble Beach together. "The most excruciating moments in all golf," he called them. "The short putts or easy chip shots that are impossible to miss unless you do something grossly wrong will make something inside you say, 'You'll do the impossible. You *will* miss.' And blink! You hit the ball sideways. It's the simplest movement fouled up, the most insidious opening to your demons. Those are the real character testers."

So the short game is a great place to learn the fundamentals of Inner and Outer golf. Here you can develop feel and consistency that will stand you in good stead whenever you are close to the green. And here you can also learn to overcome whatever demons of doubt might have crept into your game. It's not only a place to test character but a place to build a little.

EIGHT

Inner Swinging

THE PHYSICAL REQUIREMENTS OF A CONSISTENT GOLF SWING ARE both precise and complex. The demands of power and accuracy accentuate the central problem facing the golfer on each swing, exacting control of the body. The development of a swing to meet this demand can be either daunting and frustrating or a relatively easy and natural process. We have a choice. As earlier chapters pointed out, if you give the control to Self 1 by trying to impose all the shoulds and shouldn'ts, dos and don'ts, you will travel the path of complexity. If, on the other hand, you can find your way to the natural learning process that you in fact already have, then the continuous improvement of your swing can be quite simple and enjoyable. The rest of this chapter is an invitation to explore Self 2's natural learning process—learning from experience—as it applies to your golf swing.

As with Inner putting and chipping, the golf swing can be best learned by developing feel and learning from your own swings. This is done by *paying attention* to certain critical swing variables without trying to make any changes. Change takes place as a spontaneous result of increased awareness—at whatever level of proficiency your swing may be. Technical knowledge can be used to identify which critical variables to observe and to give a hint about the direction of change that might occur.

This chapter looks at the golf swing in terms of several important learning outcomes: increased balance and stability; improved rhythm, tempo, and fluidity; increased power; and increased accuracy. Not all the variables for each of these outcomes will be discussed, but each will be discussed enough to allow the golfer to begin to make desired swing improvements. The principal aim is to apply a *method of learning* that uses focused awareness and trust as the primary tools. Once you feel comfortable with this method, you may use any source of sound technical knowledge, whether it is from your professional, or a golf instruction book, magazine, or video, to help you improve any aspect of your golf swing now and in the future.

INCREASING THE FEEL OF YOUR SWING

The first step to making any improvement in your swing lies in *increasing* the feel in your swing *as it is*. This is not a complicated process. Anyone can do it. Some people say, "I can't feel what I'm doing wrong," or "I can't get back the feel I used to have." Some even say, "I can't feel anything." Let's start with the last statement. If you think you can't feel your swing at all, shut your eyes and take a swing. Did you take the swing? How do you know? You didn't see it, smell it, or taste it, and probably you didn't hear much of it. So if you know you took a swing, you must have felt something. That's where you start. You feel whatever you feel. Maybe you feel something tight or loose, a little jerky or quite fluid; you may feel balanced or off balance, awkward or coordinated, fast or slow. The important thing is to feel without judgment of right or wrong. Why? Very simply because if you start judging what you feel as wrong, you are apt not to want to feel it. There's an old saying, "If you can't feel it, you can't heal it." It's a corollary to the law of awareness: Awareness itself is curative.

You might say, "Well, I'm very aware of my slice, and it doesn't change." I suggest that you are aware that you slice because you observe the ball taking wild turns to the right. But that is far different from *feeling* your slice. Feeling your slice is different from analyzing the cause of the slice. Really feeling it during the swing would mean you could tell without looking whether one particular ball sliced more or less than the one before it. And it would mean you could tell another person how you knew that you sliced more or less. Analyzing is intellectual speculation. Feeling is knowing. Knowing adds real control. This approach aims to shine more light on your swing through developing your feel.

One more distinction: Feeling your swing does not mean trying to feel the way it felt on that round in which you shot ten strokes below your handicap. You can feel your current swing only the way it is—not the way it was or the way you think it should feel someday. It's a funny thing about *should* and *was;* you just can't *feel* them. Why? Because they don't exist. Only the swing you swing right now exists—and it won't for long—so pay attention while it's happening.

First Step to Greater Feel: Shifting from Broad to Narrow Attention, Then Back to Broad

Where do you start in this process of learning to increase the feel of your swing? Just take a few swings. Allow your attention to focus on the general feel of your swing. Don't try to focus on anything in particular at first. Just sense your body during these initial swings. In reality, there are thousands of things happening in your swing whether you are a total beginner or a pro. But you won't be able to notice all of them at the same time. One or two particular things will stand out. Without your planning it, some part of Self 2 will select a few sensations to serve up to your conscious awareness. Start with the feeling that was the most obvious, and focus attention there. If it was a feeling of tightness, then on the next few swings you can focus attention on exactly where in your body that tightness occurs and when.

Once you locate them in time and space, you can notice any changes in the degree of tightness. Don't be surprised if, within a few shots, you can't find the tightness anymore. It probably diminished on its own as you paid attention to it. Why? Because it felt better when you didn't tighten. Relaxing is a natural response to feeling overtightness. That's how simple natural learning is.

Let's take another example. Maybe you felt your right elbow doing something at the top of your swing. Okay. So you pay attention to your right elbow. Now you have to be careful here. You may think you know what your right elbow should or shouldn't do at the top of your backswing, but you can't let that get in the way of your attending to what it *is* doing. If you try to make your elbow "do it right," it will be hard to ever really know what it is doing. When you can catch it in the act of doing whatever it is doing, only then does it have a chance to self-correct.

But you will have to discipline your attention to make as accurate an observation as possible, without any "good-bad" judgment. Observe and allow any change that's going to take place to do so. Maybe on one swing the elbow goes higher and on the next it stays lower. How it feels, how it affects each shot, and whatever understanding you may have of the golf swing will all come into play in the process of natural change. You don't have to force it. Soon the change will stop, your elbow will find the location that feels best and works best for you at this time in your swing development, and then you move on.

You can use this same method to go through every single part of your body from head to feet and every part of your swing from setup to finish. The process is effective as long as you stay interested. When you lose interest, forget about focusing on anything at all and just hit the ball without any particular focus. That's a good way to take a break. Then, when you feel like focusing again, do it. (For beginners, I don't recommend narrow focus right away. It's best to keep your attention on the overall feel of the club for a while. Only when broad focus gets boring and something in particular presents itself would I recommend shifting to narrow attention.)

As the next step in swing development, you may want to make an improvement in one of the basic elements of a sound swing. We start with balance and stability.

IMPROVING BALANCE AND STABILITY

Balance is a good place to learn about natural learning precisely because it is so natural. You can't learn to balance a bike by reading a book or being taught how to balance. You have to feel the difference between balance and imbalance. At first you can feel only the big differences—and by that time it is usually too late because you've already fallen. But with attentiveness, you learn to feel smaller or more subtle differences in balance and learn to make automatically subtle adjustments that enable you to ride without falling. In golf, learning to maintain balance is a prerequisite of obtaining consistent power and accuracy in your swing. And you learn this balance in the same way: by feeling it at ever-increasing degrees of refinement.

Finding Your Balance by Finding Your Imbalance

If you notice that you were off balance only at the end of your swing when your right leg has had to spin around to keep you from falling, then, as it is with riding a bike, it is too late. You have to find where the imbalance *begins* to occur in your swing. The process is simple. Look for any instance of being off balance in your setup and/or your swing. When you find one, don't do anything about it. Simply bring attention to the moment and place in your swing where the imbalance occurred. Chances are it will not repeat itself. If it does, keep your attention focused on the same place until Self 2 finds out how to self-correct.

Focusing on balance is not only a good place to begin to develop trust in natural learning, it is also an easy exercise to use with practice swings. Just take a few initial swings without any intention other than to notice balance and imbalance. Could you detect anything other than perfect balance in the swing? If so, where? Perhaps you noticed a slight sense of imbalance on your left foot at the follow-through, or maybe you noticed your arms pulling you slightly ahead of yourself on the downswing. What you are able to feel will depend on how experienced a golfer you are and just how aware you are of the swing. But the process itself is the same. Once you detect an imbalance, just focus attention on the exact time and place you noticed it and allow the self-correction to take place.

In the process of looking for moments of imbalance, you may fix more than your balance. You may notice, for example, that imbalance during your backswing has something to do with the speed with which you take the club back. Then you can shift your focus to the speed of your takeaway. You may find that after a few swings both tempo and balance self-correct.

Learning Stability

Stability and balance are very closely related. Almost every golf teacher and playing professional will say that the importance of having a stable setup posture and a stable lower body during the swing cannot be overemphasized. The details of the setup posture are not within my area of expertise, but they are readily available in every golf instruction book or magazine. (You can find a few of them in the Inner Swinging Chart on pages 150–152.) But the fundamental importance of stability in the swing is the same as it is with putting and chipping. It is only by having a dynamic stability in the lower body that the shoulders, arms, and hands are allowed to generate club-head speed and direction.

You learn stability the same way you learn balance: by noticing instances of instability and placing attention there until changes occur that contribute to increased stability. There are many elements of your initial setup to which you should pay attention. Critical variables include the distance between your feet in relation to your shoulders, the degree of bend in your knees and hips, ball position, weight distribution, and relative position of shoulders, hips, knees, and feet. Technical instructions can give you a clue, but you must discover for yourself the feel of the posture that will result in balance and stability. If you are trying to remember what a book said when you stand before the golf ball, you may or may not be in the best physical posture, but you can be almost sure you will *not* be in the best mental posture. But if you take the attentiveness to feel your way into *your* best posture, what feels stable and natural for you, then it is more likely you will stay focused in the feeling mode and produce *your* best swing.

Stacking

One of the most important elements of swing stability is the relative position of shoulders, hips, knees, and feet. To describe the proper positions and then attempt to get your body to conform to them during the swing would be nearly impossible. But I can imagine my feet, knees, hips, and shoulders being stacked like a pile of dominoes or poker chips. Then as I swing, I can notice if the stack stays straight or if one part or another gets out of vertical alignment. Being a tennis player, I found I had a tendency to sway a bit from left to right during my swing, and my center of gravity would sometimes swing outside my feet. I was able to achieve greater stability by observing the moment and degree of weight shift to the right until it didn't happen anymore. Learning stability by means of simple awareness may have saved me a lot of pain and suffering.

DISCOVERING YOUR RHYTHM

Rhythm is easier to experience than to define. When your golf swing is rhythmic, you know it, and when it's not, you can tell immediately if you are at all aware. Because we can feel rhythm, we can increase control over it.

Do not start by trying to swing "rhymically." Just swing the way you swing and notice the rhythm. Getting caught up in mechanics or even focusing too narrowly can take the music out of any swing. Rhythm is one aspect of the swing that you definitely don't want to try to match to someone else's or try to mold to some concept of what is "correct." You already have a rhythm. You walk with a rhythm, breath with a rhythm, and dance with a rhythm. It is a matter of experimenting with different rhythms, and, when you find yours, it will feel comfortable and more confident. But one caution: Don't just choose a rhythm that happened to produce a good result on one or two golf shots. You are looking for something that beats in time with your own inner pulse, so look inside for what feels best to you.

Harriet, a young woman who came to me for an Inner Golf lesson, felt that although she tried hard to swing correctly, something was keeping her from getting good results. Watching her take a few swings, I found my attention drawn to the full stop she took at the back of her swing. Deliberately obeying all the "rules," she took the club back, stopped as if to shift gears, and then swung forcefully down toward the ball.

I asked Harriet if she liked to dance, and she nodded. "Then do a dance called the 'golf swing.' Forget about results for a while, and all the rights and wrongs; just create a movement that has a pleasing rhythm to you." This was easy for her; inside of five minutes, her swing was completely different. She lost none of her effective elements of technique but picked up so much rhythm and timing that her stroke really became a swing. Not only did her power and consistency increase, but her obvious enjoyment in the movement itself was striking. "For the first time swinging this

club isn't a chore that I'm worried about doing right, but something I like doing," Harriet said. "But I'm surprised that the results are there, too. It's like hearing that you can do what you've
always really wanted to and it will work out okay." This seemed to
me an apt definition of how the golf swing can be.

The golf stroke, like the tennis stroke, is basically a two-beat
rhythm: back and forth. These two beats are fundamental to most
movement—the rhythm of breathing, for example. We don't have
to force it; it is there. Two common errors in swinging—failure to
complete the backswing and forcing or rushing the downswing—
are fundamentally errors of interference with that natural rhythm.
Either we want the swing to descend before the backswing has
been completed or we doubt that the transition will happen without help and so we force it.

The club will come down and accelerate itself as the tension
produced by the full backswing builds to its limit and begins to
uncoil. The key is to let the swing's rhythm control itself.

Not only is paying attention to rhythm tension-reducing, it is
also a good way of freeing the body from the awkwardness and
stiffness that result when you try to perform according to do-
instructions. Like balance, it can also distract Self 1, in playing
conditions, from anxiety over results. Self 1 doesn't really have
many ideas about how to achieve balance and rhythm, and consequently it offers less interference in the guise of advice.

HEARING YOUR RHYTHM

An adaptation of the da-da-da-da exercise in Chapter 2 is useful
for "hearing your rhythm." After a few swings, insert "da's" at the
key places in your swing, such as the moment the club is all the
way back, the moment of impact, and the moment of swing completion. You can add as many da's as you like, but remember to
keep your awareness on the club head so that you can say each one
at the exact place in your swing that it represents. By listening to
the da's, you can sharpen your sense of rhythm. Do this exercise

for about five minutes at a time as part of your range practice. Your own rhythm does not remain static from day to day, so it's not a bad idea to locate it again each time you play. Let the body find its own sense of rhythm for a particular day, or even for a particular shot. Your job is simply to let it happen and to stay attuned to it. If you do so, your swing will gradually find a basic rhythm that is suitable to your body size and type, temperament, and skill level.

DISCOVERING YOUR TEMPO

Tempo means rate of motion. In the golf swing it is determined by the relative speed of the arms on the backswing and downswing. You can feel your tempo by sensing the rate of your backswing, downswing, and follow-through.

Little is needed to improve tempo other than to become more aware of it and to be alert to Self 1's slightest tendency to interfere. Self 1 can't really describe tempo; however, Self 1 can destroy it by speeding it up beyond the natural pace of your Self 2 swing or by slowing it down too much through overdeliberateness. But simply being aware of the tempo of your swing can keep Self 1 from interfering.

As I experimented with my own tempo, I found that if I took the club back too slowly, I increased my tendency to swing down harder with my right arm. Although in point of fact the speed of the backswing shouldn't affect the speed of the downswing, my Self 1 *thinks* it does, so it makes up for a slow backswing by giving it the gun on the way down. I noticed that as I let the tempo of my backswing increase just a little, a slight momentum would build at the top of the swing that would heighten my sense of coil and increase my confidence that the club would descend at a reasonable speed. When my club came to rest at the top, I felt more inclined to force the club down to the ball. Bringing the club down willfully is nowhere near as effective as letting it descend as a response to the coiling of the backswing.

When practicing on the range, it is useful to explore different tempos, but when actually playing I would not recommend experimenting; merely be aware of your tempo as a focus for your attention. Consciously trying to influence tempo is likely to throw off your timing or some other aspect of your swing. If you think you would like a faster or slower tempo on a particular swing, translate that desire into a muscle thought by moving your arms in the desired tempo before the swing and then trust Self 2 to do it.

EXPERIMENTING WITH DIFFERENT TEMPOS on the practice range will give Self 2 a chance to explore the feel of various speeds and choose what is best for you.

Take a few swings with your attention on tempo but without trying to change anything. Using a scale of 1 (slow) to 10 (fast) as a measure, rate your present backswing and downswing. How can you best differentiate between variations in speed? For me the left arm gives the best information about tempo. Without a club in your hand, feel the rate of your arm moving back and then the rate coming down. Which is faster? By how much? Paying attention to the speed of the left arm gives a valuable clue, especially since—at least in my case—it is the overeager right arm that destroys the tempo.

After you have determined what your present swing's tempo is, experiment with several different ones (back 7, down 3; back 3, down 7; back 5, down 5; back 8, down 8; and so forth). By consciously swinging in these different ways, you are broadening the scope of your experience. Often this is a valuable method for going beyond our present limits, both physical and mental. Then let go of conscious control and let Self 2 swing, calling out the numbers corresponding to the speeds you feel. At first you will probably notice some variations. Self 2 will be experimenting for a while to discover what feels and works best. Gradually, it will stabilize at a consistent tempo as the learning process is completed. Then you should keep swinging for a while to groove your new tempo.

THESE THREE GENERAL ASPECTS of the swing—balance, rhythm, and tempo—are similar in that they relate to the whole swing and are too complex for Self 1. To focus awareness on them, you don't have to break down the swing or analyze its parts. Therefore, they are excellent focal points for attention during play, when focus on a specific part of the body or aspect of the swing could throw your stroke off balance. Trying to conform to specific mechanical details during a swing under pressure is asking for trouble, yet too often this is what we try to do in moments of self-doubt.

It is also worth mentioning that experiencing balance, rhythm, and tempo provides much of the enjoyment of golf.

SETUP POSITION

Accuracy in golf begins with the way you set up to the ball. Your initial alignment of feet, knees, hips, and shoulders relative to the target line makes Self 2's most difficult job—controlling direction—much easier.

My main suggestion on this subject is that you allow yourself to experiment and don't become locked into an absolute doctrine. Use awareness exercises to experiment with alternatives in ball placement relative to your feet (both in and out and forward and back), with open, closed, or square stance; shoulder or hip alignment; head position; and amount of knee bend. The goal in each of these experiments is to find a position that (1) is comfortable for *your* body, (2) allows you to swing freely from a stable, centered platform, and (3) gives Self 2 a vivid sense of the target line.

When setting up while on the course, it is especially important to let your body sense its position in relation to the target. Before hitting each ball, your body needs to know where the target is not only visually but through feedback from the position of your feet, hips, and shoulders. Let it *feel* the target line, not just *see* it. One way to facilitate this is to move your feet in place several times before settling into your final position. This simple action, plus attending for a few seconds to the alignment of hips and shoulders, will tell your body where you want it to hit the ball and thus help Self 2 determine what kind of swing will accomplish the result.

When a beginner first hears all the so-called rules of a correct stance, he can grow so concerned that he's doing something wrong on the setup that he's tense before he even hits the ball. After some experimenting I found that even if I didn't obey those rules, my Self 2 could hit the ball straight. This was a great relief to me. I even played around with radically open and closed stances, with the ball much too far in front or back. In the most extreme positions I couldn't hit the ball straight, but in all the moderate positions Self 2 seemed to be able to make the adjustments necessary to hit the ball toward the target. This built up my trust in Self 2 and made me feel a lot less intimidated by instructional dogmas. It also made it far easier to relax over the ball.

Still, there's no need to make it harder for Self 2 than necessary, especially if you are looking for consistency, so let him show you what's easiest for you. Use professional instruction if it helps, but make your Self 2 the final authority. After all, Self 2 is the one—not your teacher—who has to hit your shots.

INCREASING ACCURACY

Control over the direction of the ball is a major focus of golf instruction. But there are only two factors that influence direction: the angle of the club face at impact and the path of the club head. From an Inner Game perspective, it stands to reason that the key to increasing your control over direction lies in increasing your feedback from these two critical variables.

A golf ball can be hit out of bounds with a perfect grip, a perfect stance, a straight left arm, and a still head—in short, with everything right, except that the club face is too open or closed in relation to the target. Conversely, a ball can be hit accurately with an awkward grip, terrible stance, bent arm, and wobbling head—as long as the club face is square at impact. In fact, one of the few universally agreed-upon principles for accuracy in every golfing situation requires the club face to be square to the target at impact. For this reason, awareness of the angle of the club face is crucial in learning to increase accuracy. If the club face is either open or closed at impact, it will impart a sideways force to the ball, as well as sidespin, and produce either a slicing trajectory (open face) or a hooking trajectory (closed face).

Learning to sense the angle of your club face at impact on drives requires a greater degree of concentration than on putts because of the higher speed of the club face. Realizing that your club face was open after you see your ball slice into the woods won't help you change it. The art of control comes from being able to acquire information from your body early enough during the swing so that the body can correct any misalignment *before* impact. This correction cannot be made consciously, but Self 2 can perform subtle last-minute adjustments below the threshold of conscious awareness if he is trusted to do so.

The path of the club head in relation to the target—not the angle of the club face—should determine the ball's initial direction. But sensing that direction is one of the most difficult kinds of awareness to achieve in golf.

Hit a few balls and guess their direction without looking. Ask a friend to check your accuracy. If you can't feel where the ball is going, it's hard to control it.

It took me a long time to truly sense my club-head direction by feel alone; I always had to look at my divot mark. Obviously, it was too late when I did so, but at least it told me that I was off line and that I should pay more attention in practice to this aspect of the swing.

One of the best ways to focus on your club-head direction is to practice making vastly out-of-line swings—far outside-in or far inside-out. Only by feeling the enormous difference between these two extremes did it become easier for me to sense the smaller differences.

There is much speculation about the cause of outside-in swings. To me, one reason seems predominant: It's more natural. Since the body is standing inside the target line, it is natural to swing across your body or in the direction of the body. If you try hitting from an extreme inside position to the outside, your body is in the way. You can experience the same unnaturalness by trying to throw a ball outward to the right of your body (assuming you're a right-hander). It's much easier to throw a ball across your body, to the left.

An extreme outside-to-inside swing, which is therefore the more common error of the two, is destined to start the ball off the club head to the left. To compensate for this, the club face is usually open at contact, producing the beginner's banana ball, which goes left off the club face before curving widely to the right. In an attempt to correct for the slice, the golfer often opens his stance toward the left; then the swing becomes even more outside-to-inside and the slice correspondingly greater. Various compensations for this problem produce many of the swing patterns that test Self 2's ingenuity in hitting even a few decent shots.

Control of this flaw can best be gained by learning to sense the difference between outside-in and inside-out swings and by learning to sense the difference between an open and closed face, both at setup and during the stroke itself.

CLUB PATHWAY AWARENESS EXERCISE

Exercises to develop control of accuracy and speed require subtle degrees of concentration and should be used only on the practice range when learning is more important than performance.

Learning to discriminate the feel of the path of the club in relation to the target can be developed by aiming for different targets on the ball itself. Imagine the face of a clock on the top of the ball, with the point closest to the target representing the noon position. For an inside-to-outside, or draw, swing, aim at the 6:00 to 7:00 position on the ball and follow through in the 12:00 to 1:00 position. For an outside-to-inside, or fade, swing, aim at 5:00 to 6:00 and follow through at 11:00 to 12:00: It may help to imagine that you yourself are the ball. Which point of contact would give you the best trajectory to the target?

For true accuracy, awareness of the angle of the club face and of the path of the club head must be integrated. The effects of the spin imparted to the ball by an open or closed club face will cause it to veer to the right (open) or left (closed). Even with a square club face you will fade if the club comes through a little outside-in; if a little inside-out, you will draw. But these awarenesses have to be developed separately on the practice range. In play, it's best to surrender control and trust Self 2 to integrate what he has learned about both aspects.

INCREASING POWER

The first error most beginning golfers make is to try for power. By attempting to force power into the stroke, Self 1 tightens too many muscles and, in so doing, restricts other muscles necessary to swing the club head through its arc. Overtightening freezes portions of the swing, and, even if it doesn't lock the wrists completely, it definitely throws off timing and rhythm.

Compensation for this error causes the second major impediment to power and the one most common among more experienced players. After many painful lessons learned from trying to hit the ball too hard, and with the encouragement of one of the most popular golf tips, the player tries to "swing easy." Fear of relinquishing control causes him to swing with too slow a tempo or, worse, to decelerate as he approaches the ball. Learning to swing the club at different tempos is invaluable to the serious golfer, but slowing down the swing because of overcaution robs it of both power and accuracy.

Releasing optimum power on the swing comes from learning how to express your potential for it on the one hand and discovering how not to interfere with it on the other. The actual bodily process of producing power is extremely complicated, as it involves the contracting and relaxing of pairs of opposing muscle groups with a rapidity and timing that stagger the imagination. Self 2 can regulate this process perfectly if not interfered with.

As a way to quiet Self 1, I find it useful to think of the generation of power as a flowing river. Strength lends additional power to the muscles if used properly, but it's more important to generate a river of energy that can flow through your body. Overtightening restricts this flow and decreases power. I find that reminding myself before I swing to use energy, not strength, often results in a more powerful drive.

Whereas strength is a function of the development and reflexive abilities of our muscles, power is generated by muscles contracting and releasing, and so it has more to do with coordination than with force. Therefore, though it is the speed of the club head that imparts power to the swing, this velocity is the result of a complex and well-timed sequence of muscle contractions that build up tempo from one muscle group to the next. It starts in the legs. The velocity of our leg movement is not great, but built on it is the forward momentum of the hips, which in turn pulls down the arms. The arms are also pulled down by their own muscles, and their velocity is the sum of the momentum building throughout the body and their own power. Then the wrists pick up that force, adding to it the momentum of their own uncocking.

Obviously, the intricacies of momentum are far beyond the abilities of Self 1 to master, especially in the two seconds it takes to swing a golf club. The entire sequence has to be coordinated by unconscious parts of the nervous system. All that can be grasped consciously is that the power swing is really a series of momentums, each building on another. No single one of them is very fast in itself, but the total velocity imparted to the ball is enormous when the timing is right. Imagine a man standing on the flatbed of an open railway car moving at 60 mph who shoots a gun in the same direction at 800 mph. The speed of the bullet when it hits its target is 860 mph.

The timing of the muscle-releasing process is more important to power than the strength of any single muscle group. This is the reason why trying for power by flexing different muscles to the maximum can, in fact, impede the velocity of the club head.

EXERCISES FOR INCREASING POWER

To explore your own potential for power, swing your club with the intent of increasing the flow of energy through your body. Pay attention to anything that seems to be restricting this flow. Wherever you find the flow in your body restricted, pay attention to whatever is happening there. As you focus on it, it will free itself of its own accord. Don't tell yourself to relax, as this will probably produce more tension. Do this exercise until you experience your body as a channel through which energy is flowing unrestrictedly. It doesn't help to push the flow; the best you can do is let the water build up behind the dam and then let it release. For me the exhilaration I experience with this release is one of the greatest enjoyments in the game.

Increasing the stability of the swing will also enhance power. Beginners seem to believe that power comes mostly from the hands and arms. The experienced player knows, consciously or unconsciously, that the momentum that ends with the high speed at which the club head strikes the ball begins in the feet. Imagine what would happen to your power if you were suspended in a harness two inches above the ground. How much club-head speed could you generate? No matter how strong you are, the results would not be impressive.

To get a feel for the amount of stability you do have and how to increase it, here is an exercise you can do with the help of a friend. Take your normal setup position as if you were about to hit

a drive off the tee. Ask your friend to test your stability by pushing you in the upper body, front, back, and sides to see how easy
it is to topple you off balance. Teachers of the martial arts are famous for using this technique to demonstrate to their students the
value of a stable center.

Now make a conscious effort to ground yourself. Settle into
your center as you did in the balancing exercise and let your belly
hang as if it's resting on the ground, but without changing your
physical posture. Relax any tension in your upper body. Ask your
friend to try again to topple you, using the same amount of force.
Unless your posture is already very stable, within a few minutes
you'll experience a measurable increase in your stability. The
greater the stability of the setup position, the more power and accuracy are introduced into the swing.

In golf the drive is one of the few opportunities we have to
release our total power in action, and to me it's worth even a
lost ball now and then to experience that sensation fifteen or so
times a round. Driving is my favorite part of the game for this
reason—not because I let myself swing fully but because I allow
myself to enjoy it fully. I've found that almost everything I let myself enjoy fully I soon am doing well because enjoyment and
learning go hand in hand. When they don't, usually it's because
not much learning is taking place, and performance inevitably
suffers.

There are many focal points on which to concentrate the attention that will aid in the production of more power, and any of
them are helpful during practice on the range. Stick with one area
for at least five minutes, but let Self 2 help you to find the focal
point that it wants to stress.

TARGETING

In *Golf My Way*, Jack Nicklaus writes of the importance he places
on visualizing the target and the shot before hitting it:

Inner Swinging Chart for Self-Discovering Technique

DESIRED OUTCOME	CRITICAL VARIABLE	LEARNING GOAL (TECHNICAL HINT)
Increased balance and stability	Balance/imbalance	Remain in balance with little or no movement of head.
	Degree of head movement	
	Distance between feet	Approximately as wide as shoulders
	Weight distribution	Even distribution on balls of each foot at setup
	Firmness of legs	Firm legs, knees in
	Degree of knee bend	Knees slightly bent at setup
	Degree of bend of waist	Slight bend at waist
	Location of center of gravity	Keep it low, at belt-buckle. Should never go outside the feet
	Stacking (vertical alignment) of feet, knees, hips, and shoulders	Turn upper body over stable lower body. Keep vertical alignment as if swinging in a barrel.
Increased fluidity of swing	Tightness of grip	As you might hold a bird or a tube of toothpaste
	Smoothness/jerkiness, at takeaway	Smooth, one-piece takeaway
	Speed of transition between backswing and downswing	Complete your backswing before starting your downswing.
	Degree of tightness of right biceps at transition	

DESIRED OUTCOME	CRITICAL VARIABLE	LEARNING GOAL (TECHNICAL HINT)
Better tempo and rhythm	Speed of backswing	Arms, shoulder, and hips complete the backswing at the same time
	Aliveness of arms	Arms swing through to opposite side of body
	Cadence	Slight bow out of elbows at address to relax arms
Distance: Increased power	Speed of club head at impact	Head slightly behind ball at impact
	Weight transfer during swing	Stance a little wider than shoulders
	Plane of swing, vertical to horizontal	Almost full weight on back leg at the top of the swing and almost full weight on front foot at finish
	Radius of clubhead pathway	As extended as possible
	Extent of turn of shoulders and upper body	Shoulders turn twice as far as hips; back faces target
Direction: Increased accuracy	Alignment of feet, knees, hips, and shoulders to target line	Parallel to target line at address
	Club face relative to target line	Bottom leading edge is perpendicular at set up and impact. Club face looks at target through impact.

Direction: Increased accuracy (cont'd)	Direction of swing path relative to target line. Inside out, outside in.	On or near target line
	Angle of back of left wrist at impact	Similar to position at address
	Degree of bend in left elbow	Little if any bend until just after impact
	Direction of shoulders at impact	Square to slightly open at impact

I never hit a shot, even in practice, without having a very sharp, in-focus picture of it in my head. It's like a color movie. First I "see" the ball where I want it to finish, nice and white and sitting up high on the bright green grass. Then the scene quckly changes and I "see" the ball going there: its path, trajectory, and shape, even its behavior on landing. Then there's a sort of fade-out, and the next scene shows me making the kind of swing that will run the previous images into reality. Only at the end of this short, private, Hollywood spectacular do I select a club and set up the ball.

Much has been written on the subject of visualization and mental rehearsal. These techniques can have a powerful effect on performance, but many people, including myself, don't "see" pictures distinctly when they visualize. The primary advantage to targeting in this way is that it can give Self 2 a clear goal in a language that it understands: imagery. Before putting, telling yourself in words that you want the ball to go into the hole is much less effective than actually picturing the ball doing so. You will get the best results if you think of it as a way of communicating a request to Self 2. If you make it an order in the form of a picture from Self 1 to Self 2, you will induce doubt, and you will *try* to accomplish what you visualized; probably you won't get the results you visualized, and you will soon abandon the technique.

To me this is the most important issue in visualization: using it to make a demand on Self 2, or as a gimmick, undermines trust in Self 2 and your proper relationship to it. *Asking* Self 2 by offering an image of the results you want is very different from *demanding* them, and affects the success of the technique as well as your general state.

When visualizing the target, it is best to hold the image in your mind throughout the swing. If you were shooting an arrow, throwing a baseball, or bowling, your eye would constantly be focused on the target. Since this is impossible with the golf swing, the best one can do is to "remember" the target constantly. "Remembering" does not mean trying to steer the swing; it simply means holding the position of the target as vividly as possible in your mind so that Self 2 can direct the swing.

SELF 2 TARGETING

I have so much respect for Self 2 that sometimes I think that picturing where I want my drive to go is presumptuous of me. I figure he knows better than Self 1 where to hit the ball. When I feel this way, I stand behind the ball and look down the fairway, letting Self 2 do the looking. I also let him decide whether to hit a fade or a draw to the left or right side of the fairway. It's exciting and requires more trust than willpower. When I address the ball, I don't really have any idea where it's going, and I don't find out until it rolls to a stop. This is a good antidote to overcontrolling, especially to steering. How can I steer if I don't know where I'm going? Letting Self 2 pick the goal is quite different from simply stepping up to the ball and hitting it anywhere; you make a conscious choice to let Self 2 make the decision and then trust it to execute the shot. Self 2 understands whether or not I'm sincere in surrendering the target as well as the shot-making. When I have faith, he almost always surprises me pleasantly—often with a much better shot than I could imagine.

I remember one particular shot that seemed impossible to me on a day when I was playing Pebble Beach with Michael Murphy. I had admired Mike's book *Golf and the Kingdom* and had looked forward for a long time to playing with him. The fact that Pebble Beach put on its best weather for us was a much-appreciated bonus. I had been playing pretty well up to the twelfth hole, a tricky, well-trapped par three of 184 yards, where I hit a three iron that faded into a trap ten yards in front and to the right of the green. The ball came to rest directly under the trap's six-inch border. There was no way I could hit it toward the green without ricocheting off the border. "What on earth can I do in a situation like this?" I asked Mike, a much more experienced golfer. "Well, there's not much you can do but blast it out of the trap and hope you can chip it close enough on your next shot to sink the putt and settle for a four." This made perfect sense, but somehow I just couldn't do the reasonable thing. Okay, I said to Self 2, I sure as hell don't know how to hit this shot. I don't even know where to aim. You hit it. When I addressed the ball, I found myself facing a good seventy degrees left of the pin. I swung down, without the slightest preconception, through a point about two inches behind the ball with three-quarters force. Almost immediately after contact with the sand my club banged into the trap border, but the ball itself bounced off the border in a direction thirty degrees to the *right* of the pin, and, by virtue of spin and the break of the green, started a long curving roll toward the hole. I stood in awe as I saw it finally stop two inches from the cup. "I guess you should have hit it just a tad harder!" quipped Mike.

I leave it to my readers to do their own experimenting with Self 2 targeting. The key to success is a relaxed mind, faith, and the effort to surrender to Self 2. Of course, not all your shots are going to turn out the way you would like, and when this happens, how you deal with the situation is important. If you blame your lack of coordination or intelligence, or berate yourself in any such way, you can expect repeat performances. If you don't sense the immediate cause of the error, don't dwell on it or try to analyze it; it is almost certainly due to some kind of self-interference. All you can do next time is trust Self 2 more and put more effort into relaxed concentration. When you do, the past error doesn't affect the next shot.

BODY-AWARENESS SCAN

To take full advantage of the curative faculties of awareness, a good practice is to tune up your body about once a month with a body-awareness scan exercise.

Begin by focusing your attention on your feet. Does anything draw your attention? Now focus on your calves, knees, thighs, lower body, upper body, right arm, left arm, wrists, and head. This tuneup will give you information about which areas require specific attention and will keep you from neglecting problems that may be affecting your swing.

GUIDELINES FOR AN INNER GAME PRACTICE SESSION

Ideally, every practice session will be an enjoyable learning experience. The guidelines below are not meant to be followed rigidly but rather will give you an idea of the different components of a productive practice session.

Five Minutes of Pure Play

This period is for the purpose of warming up and preparing the mind and body for learning. Play is a good first step in most learning situations. Don't set any performance goals or try to practice anything. Don't try to focus on anything in particular or try to hit "good" shots. Make no judgment on any of your results—you are not going for results. This is the time to take all the pressure off yourself. I sometimes even like to hit half swings, one-handed swings, hooks, and slices. The idea is to loosen up both mentally and physically. And have fun!

Twenty Minutes of Focused Swinging

This is the time to practice focusing on critical variables. You might want to start with self-generated variables you begin to notice (see p. 204). Next, think about a desired outcome for the practice session and start to focus on a variable recommended by your pro or one of the variables mentioned in the Inner Swinging Chart. Don't worry about results at this time. Trust that Self 2 will learn equally well from the good and from the bad. Your challenge with *all* awareness exercises is twofold: nonjudgmental focus of attention and letting go of conscious control. Simultaneously.

Generally speaking, I don't like to spend more than about five to seven minutes on any one variable at a time. But the best rule of thumb is to stay with it as long as it seems interesting to you and learning is taking place. I like to use three or fewer variables in the twenty-minute learning session. With each exercise, attempt to increase the awareness of feel for whatever aspect of the swing you are focusing on. Give any changes a chance to take place. Next, let the learning groove itself for a few shots, and then move on to the next focus. It's also a good idea to alternate between broad and narrow focus. You don't have to make sure that any swing change that takes place happens every time. You are primarily training your nervous system by giving it a range of focused experience.

Five Minutes of Play

Break from your period of focusing with a return to play. But here the play might be a little more results-oriented. You might want to swing with unrestrained power or hit with the same club to different targets.

Remaining Time: Performance

Use whatever time you have left to simulate playing conditions and to emphasize performance. Imagine actual golf holes; visualize the shot and select a club for each situation. Allow a longer period of time between shots, aligning yourself toward a different target for each one. Introduce psychological pressure by imagining more pressure than you would normally feel on the course. (This technique has the advantage of making real pressure less hard to handle.) Or set a goal for yourself and determine not to end the session until you achieve it.

DO YOU WANT A PERFECT SWING OR THE ABILITY TO SCORE WELL?

Vijay Amritraj, undoubtedly the greatest tennis player who ever played for India, introduced me to Gene Malin, a highly ranked seniors tennis player, on the first tee at Spanish Hills Golf Club in Camarillo. The fourth player was Vijay's accountant, George, who was the last to hit. Before he did, Vijay whispered in my ear, "Don't be fooled by his swing."

I didn't know whether to expect a great swing and a not-so-good result or the other way around. The swing was astonishing! George stood over the ball, bent at the waist at almost a ninety-degree angle, with brand-new titanium clubs, waited for what seemed ten seconds without making the slightest motion, then, in an instant, reared up to an erect position, pulled his club back at lightning speed to about a half-swing position, and, without the slightest pause at the top, slashed into the ball, literally jumping forward as he did so, at one point with both feet off the ground. To call this the most idiosyncratic swing I had ever seen would be a major euphemism. His first drive went sky-high and about 150 yards out. He reached down and picked up his tee as if he'd gotten the kind of results he usually expected. The relatively smooth drives of the three tennis players were in the fairway between 225 and 250 yards out.

Then George hit a three wood, with the same swing, about 200 yards, and a wedge within ten feet of the pin. Standing over his ball, he bent down so far that he could grasp the club a foot from the blade with his right hand. He sunk his putt for a par as if he had conducted business as usual. The tennis players, who had far better swings, came in with bogeys and a supreme wonderment about how they had been beaten by George.

A teaching pro would not know where to start correcting George's swing, and, as you might expect, he had never gone to one. Yet hole after hole he hit the fairways, chipped and one-putted more often than not, and came in with the lowest score.

I don't think George knew how "bad" his swing was. I don't think he cared. He knew what he wanted, and he felt confident he would get it. When he didn't get the results he wanted, he vented his feelings, but he did little analysis of what was wrong. He knew his swing was an aberration that would be better next time. At most he would say, "I wanted to draw that one, but I faded it." After watching him swing many times, we three tennis players would laugh in amazement that such a swing could produce the results he got.

George was very clear about his priorities. How his swing looked was not high on his list. Scoring was. A reporter once asked Ben Hogan who had the best golf swing he had ever seen. Hogan supposedly scratched his head, searched his mind for a long time, and finally said, "Oh, some guy I never heard of at some driving range in North Miami Beach." In golf as well as in life, it's very easy to get so caught up in the subgoals that you forget the goal itself.

YOU CAN'T CORRECT A BAD SHOT, SO WHY TRY?

Last summer I spent a few days with the PGA pros playing on the European circuit. A teaching pro named Jos, whom I had introduced to Inner Game methods, had been with the Tour for nearly the entire season. He had worked individually with over thirty of the touring pros, after which many of them made dramatic improvement in their scores. One Scottish pro who had never placed in the top twenty came in second in the next tournament after working with the Inner Game methods for less than a week. The next day, a full-page article about the "magic" of the Inner Game of Golf appeared in one of the London newspapers.

Interestingly, Jos, who gained a reputation for working Inner Game magic, never corrected anyone's swing. In fact, he knew very little about the mechanics of the game. His initial promise to his clients was that he would not do anything to change their swings—only their scores!

One evening, mid-tournament, I was asked to make a brief presentation to the pros. They listened attentively, looking for answers to questions about staying focused and keeping the pressures of tournament play from having a negative influence on their game—yet in private conversations, most of the pros asked about what really seemed to be on their minds: "How do I make a correction in my swing?" Their questions were usually preceded by descriptions of "technical failures" that I couldn't have commented on if I wanted to. But behind the complex descriptions of what had gone wrong, all the questions were the same: "There I was on the xth hole; I was striking the ball pretty well, when all of a sudden I [totally nonunderstandable technical jargon describing the swing mistakes they had made. And, of course, the ensuing bad results] tried to correct it by [more incomprehensible descriptions of technical manipulations to correct their swing], but I could never get myself back to my normal swing. So how can I correct a mistake like that?"

Finally, the answer dawned on me. You can't. Why? Because the swing that you want to correct has already occurred. Nothing you can do will change it. Thinking that any particular fault in a given swing needs to be corrected seems very natural, but it's based in doubt. What is the doubt? That the incorrect swing will happen again unless I actively do something about it. But you don't know that to be true! Yet the expectation that it will happen, no matter what you may do to try to prevent it, becomes a self-fulfilling prophecy. And in the process of "correcting," you can easily overcompensate and bring on the opposite problem. Attempting to correct prematurely for a golfing error is one of the greatest mental errors both professionals and weekend players make. We not only try to correct bad swings, but we try to repeat good ones. Both attempts are doubt-based. Neither one allows for true learning. Playing golf this way is playing in a *reactive* mind-set. Instead of hitting each shot as a perfectly new shot, which it is, I am swinging in reaction to past shots—good and bad. I assume that my swing will go off again unless I intervene and I assume that I can analyze what is wrong and correct it.

The only time it might be advisable to try to correct your swing is after the competition is over, and then only if you or another person has noticed enough repetitions of the stroke error that correction is called for. There are two kinds of stroke error— those you are aware of when they happen and those you aren't aware of until you see the unwanted result. If you are even aware of the approximate location of the swing error, Self 2 can correct it, without any manipulation from Self 1. The correction takes place spontaneously and really isn't a correction. A new swing is made, and the felt "error" is dropped. Trust in Self 2 means that you expect it to swing correctly, even more so after a faulty swing. Why? Because it's the nature of Self 2 to learn from experience, and it will if you don't let doubt and Self 1 control get in its way.

When I was playing tournament tennis and made an unforced error, I understood that the actual cause of my error was a momentary lapse in focus. I let the error be a wake-up call to come back to the present moment. I would make a conscious effort to let go of the past shot and focus my attention in the present moment. At the same time, I would ignore Self 1's inevitable comments on what I did wrong and how to correct my stroke and simply determine to trust Self 2 more. I admit this was counterintuitive. Just when my swing seemed to let me down, I would trust more. Every time I did this, I felt a kind of inner exaltation, not just *when* I hit a good shot but in knowing that I was not allowing myself to get pulled into the endless Self 1 cycle of error and correction.

CREATING YOUR SWING

It is very tempting to think you will excel at golf by training your-self to swing the same way every time. By repeating the same swing every time, you think you'll get the same result. This widely held belief is based on the observation that consistency seems to result from a foundation of similar elements—a steady balance, a steady rhythm, a steady movement through the striking zone. Good shots from the same player tend to look very much alike, from drives to putts. But to think of them as merely repetitions is an error. This is not so easy to explain. There is a distinct differ-ence between *creating* a shot and *trying to repeat* a shot. Creation is free. It is not bound by the past, although it learns from the past. Only machines repeat themselves. Repetition soon gets boring, and with the boredom comes lack of attentiveness.

Creating your swing takes your full commitment to each shot. Even though you may get the exact results you are looking for, there is an element of the unknown. You don't know exactly how you will do it because you have never taken that swing before. The moment is a new moment, and you, in that new moment, are a slightly different person, hoping you have learned from past moments and therefore looking through slightly different eyes. Making new swing after new swing is the way of the creative golfer. A creative swing is not necessarily different from the last swing; it is just not an exact repetition. In this mode you are more awake and more exhilarated by each swing. The swing evolves or-ganically, probably without your even knowing it. This is the way of nature and the way of natural learning.

Pursuing a swing that is repeatable could be a self-defeating effort. When something is the same every time, we have a hard time attending to it. For example, a constant noise in the room soon becomes unnoticed. The same is true of a golf swing. Swings that are merely repetitions are harder to feel. And when you lose feel, you lose control. I believe this is why people so often putt better temporarily when they make a change in their putter. The difference of the feel increases awareness. Increased awareness gives increased feel. Increased feel gives increased control. I believe this is also why players who practice the same shot too long often lose feel and are discouraged by the fact that they hit the first fifty balls better than the last fifty balls.

I suppose it is possible to make yourself into a kind of machine that can simply stamp out the same kind of shot at will. I know tennis players like that, and some are quite successful. I don't know what kind of a temperament it takes, but whatever it is, it's not for me. To get out of the numbing routines of machine golf, I recommend hitting the ball in a number of different ways on the driving range. Without making any effort to get good results, explore different ways of swinging the club. Don't even look for a better way to swing. In fact, it's fun to try swinging "wrong" by exaggerating whatever errors you have a tendency to make. This exercise accomplishes two things. First, it helps you be non-judgmental. You find that when you swing at the ball in the most horrendous way, lightning does not strike you down, you do not die of a heart attack, and, in fact, nothing at all happens except that the ball goes wherever it goes. Sometimes it will surprise you and be a better shot than you make when you are trying to swing correctly. The second and equally valuable result of this exercise is that it increases swing awareness. After five or ten minutes of unorthodox swinging, when you return to trusting Self 2 to hit the ball, you will feel the swing much more vividly. And again, the increased feel will increase Self 2 control and ultimately improve results.

NINE

Of Slumps, Streaks, and False Expectations: Breaking 80

As I learned to become more and more aware of my golf swing, my shot-making ability clearly improved. On the range and course I was hitting with greater distance and consistency than ever before. After six months, my score was holding consistently between 86 and 90 on courses of average difficulty. More experienced golfers said that scoring in this range was quite remarkable given that I'd been playing seriously for less than six months and only once a week. I began to think I was ready for a more challenging course, as I had thought before playing St. Andrews.

PLAYING PEBBLE BEACH WITH MICHAEL MURPHY

I had admired Michael Murphy's book *Golf in the Kingdom* and had been a friend of his since the early seventies. I knew he was an accomplished golfer, so it was with mixed feelings of friendship, respect, and some trepidation that I called him to make good on his casual offer to play Pebble Beach with him someday.

As we confirmed a date to play, both Mike and I admitted to being a little nervous, knowing that it is always easier to share a philosophy about Inner Golf than to succeed in demonstrating it on the golf course. The day before leaving Los Angeles for this course, I opened the paper to a cartoon that seemed expressly designed for the two of us. It pictured two yogis, scantily clad, sitting on their respective beds of nails. One was saying to the other with a contemplative expression on his face: "You know, there is only one true test of humility, and that is to play Pebble Beach from the back tees, with the wind blowing in your face . . ." When I showed it to Mike, we both laughed and felt more relaxed because we both knew that humility was the worst that could happen to us. Nonetheless, we decided not to play from the back tees!

Except for an occasional round, Mike hadn't played in several years, but I was amazed at the ease of his swing and at the degree of concentration he mustered when he was near the pin. He didn't hit so many greens in regulation, but he got a lot of pars and ended the round with a birdie on the treacherous par-three number seventeen and a par on the long par-five eighteenth, giving him a respectable 82.

As for myself, I had decided that I didn't want Pebble Beach to intimidate me, nor did I want to fall into the trap of trying to impress Mike Murphy. Both of these had the potential to get to me if I let them. We had invited my father, who lives in Carmel and loves the Pebble Beach course dearly, to play with us. Just as we reached the club, I said to him, "I'm going to go for the enjoyment of the play today, no matter what games Self 1 wants to play.

Pebble Beach is too beautiful and the companionship of Mike too rare to ruin the day worrying about how I'm playing."

By and large my resolve carried the day. It was threatened only at the times I began scoring better than I'd expected and started thinking about the possibility of breaking 80 at Pebble Beach. The thought "Wow, this would be great in the book" almost did me in a couple of times.

I had some jitters to overcome on the first hole, where I hit a long drive that was treacherously close to the woods on the right of the fairway. My only possible shot to the green was to stroke a four iron low and to the left, hoping to fade it into the green, which was invisible from where I stood. The only problem was that I didn't know how to hit a four iron low and fade it on purpose. It was my first chance to take a risk, and I did: "Self 2, I hope you know how to make this shot because I don't, and I'm going for it." The shot ended up fourteen feet from the pin. Dad was on in three and sank a fifteen-foot putt for a par. Mike was on the fringe in two and two-putted. I was in the garden spot, with a chance for a birdie. Self 1 was a little intoxicated by my unlikely approach, and I failed to notice how fast the greens were, so I hit my first putt past the hole by six feet. Coming back, I was thinking about making a par to at least tie the others, which proved to be an unnecessary and damaging thought, and I had to settle for a bogey. This showed me how little detached I really was. I had a sinking feeling in my stomach as I missed that putt and let my disappointment show. Mike responded to this: "That's good, Tim; it shows you care. One thing about this game; no one has too difficult a time really caring."

Mike and I both parred the second hole, but I hit an eight-iron approach on number three over the green and across the road, a misjudgment that cost me two strokes. Self 1 said, "That's not fair. You hit a good shot. It never occurred to you it could go OB. That's going to ruin your chances." I thanked Self 1 for his comment and remembered my initial intention to enjoy the day and do my best. The two-stroke penalty might teach me not to assume that you are ever out of the reach of trouble on the course, especially on one like Pebble Beach.

Mike finished the first nine with a double bogey on the ninth hole, which made his score a four-over-par 40. I was three over par after the third hole, and finished the round with par, bogey, par, par, bogey, bogey, for a 42. I was pleased with my score but more pleased that I was truly enjoying myself quite independently of the number of strokes I'd taken.

On the second nine I started with three pars in a row, while Mike went three over par. On the twelfth hole, I made that impossible sand shot described in Chapter 8 that ricocheted off the lip of the trap to within two inches of the cup. When I hit my longest drive of the day on the 555-yard fourteenth hole, Self 1 whispered innocently, "You know, Tim, in spite of your forty-two on the first nine, if you keep going like this you could break eighty. You can get a par on this hole easily. Then you could afford a bogey on one of the next four holes and still come in with a forty-two–thirty-seven for a seventy-nine." I was attracted to this thought, and on my next shot I was overconfident. I hit a clean three wood 220 yards, but it faded and dropped three feet outside the OB markers, on the front lawn of one of those beautiful fairway homes. My next shot came close to repeating the error, but landed three feet inside. Self 1 had managed to sabotage his dreams with a single shot.

Dad could see the disappointment on my face and consoled me with a story about Arnold Palmer, whom he had seen hit three shots on the same hole into an overhanging limb, each going OB near where I had. "The next day of the tournament that limb was missing from the tree," he said, "and it didn't look as if it had been sawed off!" I three-putted the green and carded an 8, but Dad's story made me feel better.

I was able to forget quickly and reengage my interest in enjoying each swing. I shot pars on the next two holes and bogeys on the last two, giving me a 42–42, 84. Mike shot a 42 on the second nine, which gave him an 82 for the day.

Throughout the day, I noticed that Mike took a lot of care with each shot. Even on two-foot putts he would study the lie carefully and prepare himself mentally as fastidiously as on more difficult shots. I realized that, for him, caring was a discipline that made the game of golf what it was. After a shot had gone astray, he would usually say something like "I lost consciousness in mid-swing" or "There was a big gap in my awareness on that shot; I wasn't very present."

Still, it seemed to me that caring too much can be as much a problem as not caring enough. Sometimes I care so much that I overtighten and mis-hit; other times I care too little and lose concentration and accuracy. For centuries Zen masters have wrestled with the problem of balance between these two extremes, and they eventually generated the ideal of "effortless effort"—caring without caring. To the Western mind this paradox is enigmatic. It defies intellectual logic but appeals to an intuitive sense that it is the true synthesis between the two extremes of caring too much and caring too little.

The answer here also seems to lie in the *nature* of the care—that is, what is doing the caring, and what does it care about? If what I am caring about is what Mike thinks of me as an Inner golfer, or what my score will be, Self 1 is doing the caring and is more interested in my image than in my experience. But if my caring takes the form of a natural desire to do my best for the fulfillment inherent in the action, then Self 2 is caring about expressing himself to the fullest, which is appropriate to the situation at hand. Effortless effort: the absence of Self 1 trying and the natural expression of Self 2 effort. It's a state of mind that can be achieved only by constantly choosing Self 2 over Self 1 whenever the choice is clear. Golf is an arena in which both selves vie constantly, and, more than in almost any other game, the feel of the action and its results gives a strong indication of whether it was Self 1 or Self 2 who was in control.

AFTER THIS IMPORTANT ROUND at Pebble Beach, I began to see that there might be more to mastering golf than course management and shot-making ability. I continued to score in the high eighties for a long time but seldom dipped below 85. I was about halfway through my experiment when I began wondering if breaking 80, the goal I'd promised my editor, was realistic. I asked myself a difficult question: Why wasn't my score improving in proportion to the obvious improvements in my shot-making ability? I was ready to explore an important area for anyone who wants to learn the most important lessons that the game of golf has to teach. It was time to delve into the underlying motivations and mind-sets that golfers bring to the game. Some of these are unconscious and not easy to uncover.

HOW DO YOU GET OUT OF A SLUMP?

Shortly after I began this inquiry, a friend of mine named Al asked me a simple question that began to focus my thinking. We had been walking together while watching an LPGA tournament at Rancho Park Golf Course in Los Angeles. Pointing out one of the pros who had been playing well early in the Tour and then had seemed to fall apart, he asked, "How do we get out of slumps?"

My first response was more immediate and intuitive than analytical. "By not getting into them," I answered. Al paused. I knew what his next question would be, and I didn't know how to answer it.

"But what if you're already in one?" he asked on cue.

I'd thought a lot about the causes and cures of slumps but had no pat answer.

"Slumps don't exist," I found myself saying. "We create them in our minds. Some people say they're in a slump after two poor shots in a row; others don't feel they're in a slump until they've played poorly for two months. Therefore you're in a slump when you think you are. The deeper you think it is—the more deeply you believe in it—the harder it will be to get out of it. A slump is a belief that poor past performance is going to continue, and the best thing to do is not to believe it. Stay in the present, and let each shot, good or bad, stay in the past. The past doesn't have power over the present unless you surrender that power to it. If you find that you *have* been believing that you're in a slump, stop believing this the instant you recognize it. You created the belief, and you can un-create it."

I was a little surprised at the length of my answer, but it rang true. Al looked satisfied. "Just forget the bad shots and make each shot a new one," he concluded. "Yes, all the past is good for is that maybe it taught you something."

We each went our separate ways to watch the women professionals. But three hours later at the sixteenth hole, Al approached me again. "Tim, I have one other problem I'd like to ask you about. I'm a twelve-handicap; I play about twice a week. The other day I was playing in my usual foursome here, and I started off the day with par, birdie, par, par, birdie, par. By the time I reached the seventh hole, all I was thinking was, When is this going to end; it can't keep up much longer—and of course it ended on that hole. My question is, When you've got a streak going, how do you keep yourself from thinking it's going to end?"

I was struck by the parallel between Al's two questions, though he didn't seem to make any connection between them, and realized something I'd never seen so clearly before.

"That damned Self 1 gets us going both ways!" I exclaimed. "When you're playing badly, it tells you you're in a slump and will never get out, but when you're playing better than usual, it tells you that you're in a streak that can't last. It isn't even logical. On the one hand, it tries to get you to believe that negative experiences in the immediate past are bound to continue, but when the immediate past is positive, it tells you that your performance is bound to change for the worse!"

How do you get out of a slump, and how do you continue a streak? These two questions put side by side reveal something I find curious. The clear assumption behind the first is that once

I'm "in a slump," unless I do something about it, I'm likely to stay in it. Therefore I ask, What should I do to get out of it? The second question assumes that if I am in a hot streak I need to do something to stay in it. Very interesting. When I'm playing below my expectations, I assume that the poor performance of the immediate past will continue unless I (Self 1) intervene. But when I am playing well, I do not assume that the good performance will continue unless I intervene. Self 1 is telling me that I have to do something to make the streak continue.

Even though each question seems logical on the surface, they all arise from opposite assumptions about how the past affects the future. It is as if Self 1 uses a faulty logic to convince us to expect the worst from ourselves in either situation! At the same time, I could see that Self 1 was establishing the importance of its own intervention. How many times have I seen players look for remedies to get out of slumps, and those remedies just dig the hole deeper? It's the spinning-your-wheels syndrome—the more you accelerate to get your car out of a rut, the deeper you dig the rut.

The key to understanding streaks and slumps seems to lie in the phenomenon of expectations. If I hit two bad shots in a row, what do I expect will happen on the next if I don't do anything to correct consciously? Do I expect to hit another bad shot, or do I expect that I will be more likely to hit a better one? In short, do I expect to learn from the past mistakes or to repeat them? This seemed to be a question worthy of further exploration. The golfer's assumptions about how the past affects the present lead to a set of expectations that clearly has great impact on his ability to perform in the future.

One day I played in a foursome, one of whose members commented as we walked down the first fairway, "Last week I ruined my stroke, and now my swing is totally out of sync. I'm really going to have to work it out during this round." How did he know this?

Similarly, if I start out with three poor shots, a voice inside may tell me, "You're way off your game today. Your swing is all screwed up." If I believe this, I do have a bad day all day—or at least a struggling one. All that really happened was that I hit three poor shots, and this doesn't say anything about my swing or about the future. But unconsciously I have set up negative expectations for myself, and, as often as not, I strengthen them by telling my partner, "I haven't played in two weeks, and last time I couldn't hit my hat, so don't expect much from me today."

What is particularly interesting about expectations is that they are a belief about the past that can affect the future. Expecting the best from yourself or another often contributes to that desired outcome. Expecting the worst can be equally self-fulfilling. The effects of "negative expectations" have been well documented, and an entire school of "positive thinking" has found broad appeal to those interested in succeeding at any enterprise.

THE EXPECTATIONS GAME

A step toward understanding the impact of expectations on performance emerged from a conversation with my father about his enjoyment of golf. When I asked him when he enjoyed the game, his answer was straightforward: "I enjoy golf when I play equal to or better than my expectations." I realized that for him this was very true, so true that my mother could come very close to "reading" his golf score by observing the expression on his face when he came home. She didn't have to ask how he had done and would sometimes tell me accurately, within a stroke or so, what he had scored that day. But, of course, she asked anyway.

I also noticed that Dad would often score very well on the first nine only to "even things out" by scoring poorly on the second nine. Surprisingly, this happened just as frequently the other way around. A terrible start would very often be balanced by a better-than-usual ending. Expectations alone seemed able to cause a swing of four or five strokes one way or the other. Interesting. I began to wonder if my expectations were keeping my score in the mid-eighties. I began to think more about the dynamics of expectations and their impact on my own performance.

I reflected on a somewhat painful round of golf I had recently played. Determined to break 80 and meet or exceed the expectations of my editor, as well as my own personal goal, I decided to play nine holes, and, if I broke 40, I would finish the round. I started well: par, par, par, birdie, par, bogey, par. I was even par going into the eighth hole. If I shot par in the next two holes, I would card my first 36 for nine holes. My tee shot on the five-par eighth hole was long, but it rolled into a fairway sand trap. Having a good lie, and with high expectations, I took out my four wood, hoping to reach the green. I then proceeded to hit three consecutive shots out of bounds and ended the nine holes with my accustomed six over par!

This got me thinking. If I am involved in a game that aims to meet or exceed my expectations, how can I "win" this game? At one level, the answer was obvious—I shouldn't set my expectations too high! If I feel confident I can shoot in the nineties, and that is all I expect, then most of the time I can meet my expectations and win the game. But if I shoot par on the first nine? Now my expectations are apt to shift. I might start thinking I can shoot in the high seventies or low eighties for the round. But what if I let myself succeed in shooting in the low forties on the second nine? What is going to happen? I'm going to feel great because I really busted my expectations! I'm going to celebrate my success, and probably I'm going to brag a little to my friends. And then— when I play next weekend—my expectations have changed. They have become higher! Now I must shoot in the low eighties to equal or exceed my expectations and those my friends have for me. That's going to be hard, and the probability of disappointment is greater. So what does Self 1 do? While telling me all along that I might break 80 if I try hard, it makes sure I shoot high enough on the second nine to bring my score back toward my handicap!

So what underlying purpose is served by projecting expectations? The only one I can think of is to preserve some sense of certainty about the future. Golf is clearly a game filled with uncertainties. And if I care about my results, I want to have some range of certainty about them. The part of Self 1 that feels uncomfortable with uncertainty and likes to project doubt creates an expectation. But because its purpose is to create certainty, it wants to be right. To be right, it does what it can to make its prediction come true. Expectations can create an identity, and remaining true to that identity can be a very strong motivating force. The reason you form an identity is to gain a sense of continuity or certainty. Surpassing the expectations of a formed identity can therefore feel threatening to one's stability. And sometimes this sense of stability is more important to a person than performance. There's a definite conflict of interest here that can have a significant impact on Self 2's performance.

Just as I was pondering the role of expectations in my own game, a poignant example of their impact on golf learning and performance came to my attention from a golfer named Harry Graham.

THE MAN WHO DIDN'T KNOW
WHAT "PAR" MEANT

Harry Graham approached me after an Inner Game learning demonstration, during which a forty-year-old man who had never held a tennis racket before learned to serve and keep the ball in play, using proper footwork and changing grips, in about twenty minutes.

"Seeing how easily you helped him learn tennis," Harry said eagerly, "I was thinking that you might be able to help me with my golf."

"What seems to be the problem?"

He proceeded to tell a story that I might not have believed if I hadn't been convinced of his sincerity.

"About five years ago," Harry said, "I took up golf for fun and relaxation. I used to get off work at three and be able to play a round before dark. I worked on the weekends when my friends played, so I always played alone. About a year went by before I had the chance to play with some other people. I was surprised that they all shot in the high eighties or low nineties, and they were astounded that I'd shot seventy-four. 'How do you do that, after playing for only a year?' they asked in astonishment. 'If you're that good already, you could probably easily learn to break par and earn your living on the Tour. You should start taking lessons and go for it.'

"I didn't know how I'd done it; I didn't think it was any big deal to shoot par. I'd done it lots of times. In fact, that's what I thought 'par' meant—the score you were expected to make."

I looked at Harry incredulously.

"I thought par meant a kind of average score and felt quite happy about being average after only one year. Of course, I was playing every day, mainly because I thought the game was so much fun and it really was a nice break from work."

"Well," I said, "that sounds wonderful. What's the problem?"

"Well, I got to thinking about what my friends had said and decided maybe they were right. It *would* be a nice way to make a living, doing what I enjoyed the most, so I began taking lessons and working on the mechanics of my swing. To make a long story short, my problem over the last four years is that I haven't broken eighty-five once and don't enjoy the game anymore. I've tried everything, and nothing has worked. I'm very frustrated."

"Well, I can't make you forget what par means," I replied. "Once you know, you know. But you can make a choice to return to your original attitude toward the game, when you were playing for your own reasons and weren't trying to measure yourself against the expectations of others."

Harry and I talked for some time about natural learning and after a while he felt he could enjoy the game again. After I left him, I realized his story was a rare testimony both to the inherent power of Self 2 learning and to the power of expectations to impede it.

"THE THREE-BALL PLAYER"

While teaching tennis I ran into the same kind of identification with a certain level of performance, the same phenomenon, though perhaps not quite so rigid as it is in golf. When giving a demonstration of Inner Game methods, I would often ask for a volunteer from the audience who was a "three-ball player." When someone asked what that meant, I explained that a three-ball player was someone who, after he has hit the ball over the net three consecutive times, says, "Wow, that was a long rally!" People laughed, recognizing similar thoughts in their own experience. "What happens then?" I asked. "You miss!" was the unanimous reply. In fact, you don't always miss, but you do tend to get nervous. And if you hit another ball or two over the net, you're apt to get really nervous and say, "This isn't like me . . . it's got to end soon." What's interesting about this internal conversation is that the limit does not lie in the ability to hit more balls over the net; it lies in the phrase "This is not like me."

In the tennis demonstration, I found that changing the "expectations game" and replacing it with another game could dramatically alter the probabilities of going beyond one's expected limits. I would rally for a few minutes, with the volunteer who generally lived up to his or her expectation of hitting only three or four balls over the net before missing. Then we would have a short "coaching conversation" that went something like this: "How many balls would you like to be able to hit consecutively over the net?" Answer: "Ten would be great." "How about a thousand or, even better, never missing?" I would ask. "But that's an impossible goal." "We're not setting a goal but a direction," I would reply. "Wouldn't you like to move toward the direction of never missing?" "Okay. Sure. Sounds good to me." Then I would tell the volunteer to forget all about goals and instead concentrate on doing a simple exercise to increase her focus of attention, a skill she could use either on or off the court. At that point I would introduce the bounce-hit exercise. While focusing on saying "bounce" each time the ball hit the court and "hit" each time it hit either racquet, the three-ball player would start hitting ten or more balls without missing and without showing any signs of anxiety at passing a limit. Each time an error would occur, I would return the focus to the ball, not the miss, by asking whether she had said "bounce" or "hit" on time. After doing this exercise for a short time, the player could often return fifty or more shots before finally missing out of sheer exhaustion.

Focusing techniques such as bounce-hit also work in golf, as described in earlier chapters, though usually not so dramatically. This is partially due to the fact that in golf there is more time to think about your expectations and to lose your focus. It is also harder because of the handicap system, which creates such a strong tendency to form limiting self-identifications with specific levels of performance.

DON'T LET YOUR HANDICAP
BE YOUR HANDICAP

Golf can be a setup for creating limiting expectations. More than almost any other sport, it lends itself to precise measurement. It's one of the few sports where every shot is scored. This is not true in tennis, in which only winning or losing shots are counted, and these are erased by the game, and the game is erased by the set. The match is won by the person who won the most sets, which is not necessarily the person who won the most points or even the most games. In medal play, not only does every golf shot contribute to your score but the common practice of keeping a handicap means that every shot you take contributes to your handicap, a calculation based on all your past scores for a certain period of time.

When I play to a handicap, I have "evidence" upon which to

base my expectations. Not only do I have evidence to form my own expectations about my performance, but those expectations are also held by the golfing community, which uses them to equalize my chances in handicap tournaments. When both you and "the world" believe in what can be expected of you, that can be quite a difficult barrier to break. For some reason, however, it seems to be more difficult to break this barrier on the side of lower scores than higher.

We tend to identify ourselves with our handicaps, thus making expectations about our performance even stronger. This fact comes home to me every time I play with strangers. After we exchange names and the social amenities are over, the first question asked is "What's your handicap?" This is a thinly veiled way of asking "How good are you?" Most people's response to this question will be "I'm a fourteen handicap," "I'm a four handicap," and so on. This is just like saying "My name is Bob, and you can expect me to shoot an 86 on this round . . . I'm an 86 kind of person!"

During the time that I had a twelve handicap, I played a round that brought this home to me sharply. The stranger with whom I was playing asked what my handicap was, and we made a small bet. I was playing exceptionally well that day for a twelve handicapper, a fact that did not escape the attention of my companion. He made several sarcastic comments during our round, and I myself felt self-conscious about the discrepancy between my handicap and my performance.

At the end of the day the man owed me a dollar. When I thanked him, he asked caustically, "What're you thanking me for?" I told him I'd enjoyed the opportunity to play.

"Well," he replied in a disgusted tone, "I didn't. I never enjoy playing with sandbaggers." With that observation, he walked away.

Driving home after the game, I felt angry at the man's insinuation that I had lied about my handicap. Having told him truthfully that my handicap was twelve, should I have played only as well as a twelve handicapper and fulfilled both our expectations?

Self 1's interest is in creating a self-image, and he loves to define himself. But his definitions are only limited imitations of your true Self 2 potential.

ARE EXPECTATIONS NECESSARY IN GOLF?

If playing the expectations game can limit my performance and enjoyment of the game, the question then arises: "Do I have to play the expectations game?" When I asked myself this question, I remembered a saying that had been passed along to me by a much-respected friend. "Blessed are they who have no expectations, for they shall not be disappointed." I wondered if it were possible to have neither low nor high expectations, nor anything in the middle, but to have *no* expectations. "Why do I need to have expectations in the first place?" I asked, realizing that the question itself was pushing my expected boundaries of thought. Maybe having expectations wasn't as much a necessity as I had thought but could be more of a choice.

I decided to look up the dictionary definition of "expectations." Its primary definition in my *Webster's Unabridged Dictionary* is "a looking forward to an event as about to happen." It is different from "hope" in two ways. "Hope" originates in desire and requires no reason to believe that what is hoped for will actually occur, while "expectation" is founded on some reasons that are thought to make the event probable. Also, as the dictionary points out, "Hope looks forward to some good; expectation looks forward to good or evil."

Now, in some situations in life, I actually need a bit of certainty in order to take intelligent action toward my goals. But this is not so much the case in golf. I don't really need to know that I am going to have a good day or a bad day. And do I really need to predict whether my next shot is going to be one of my best or my worst? Not really. If I want to know, all I have to do is wait a few moments. But if I want to know, I am apt to predict the worst, or at least not the best, and then my negative prophecy is apt to come about. What I have done, perhaps without knowing it, is to place my intolerance for uncertainty ahead of my desire to perform. To the extent that I don't need to be certain, I can be free of the limiting impact of expectations.

In short, the expectations game puts you in a double bind. To win it, you have to be "right" about your predictions about the future. And it's easier to be "right" and to "win" the expectations game if you keep your expectations low. But in order to keep your expectations low, you have to keep your scores high, so you thus have a game that is structured in such a way that it tends to keep players within a certain band of mediocrity. It is by its very design a limiting factor in the quest of excellence. One might then ask, "If negative expectations have a negative impact on performance, then how do you free yourself from them?" This can be a tricky matter. There is a common tendency for people to think they should simply replace negative expectations with positive ones. But it may not be as easy as that. If a person expects to slice by simply programming himself into saying to himself, "I expect to hit this straight . . . I expect to hit this straight," and so on, it probably won't work. Why? Because it is a positive thought that is meant to counter a negative one. Obviously, you believe the negative one to be true or you would not be trying to manipulate it away. So, in fact, you are reinforcing your negative belief in the very act of trying to counter it. There must be a better way.

WHAT IF . . .

While teaching tennis, I learned that it was difficult to combat negative programming head-on. If a person was convinced that he was a defensive volleyer, for example, it was hard to get him to attack the ball at the net just by telling him to do so. Even attempts at reprogramming were difficult if the negative self-concept was a long-standing one. Although *I* might have the faith that the student's Self 2 was capable of hitting aggressive volleys, his mind would prevent its expression.

One day I found a way to circumvent this, and the student's potential immediately began to develop. Since the same technique has proven effective in golf, I will explain it by means of an Inner Game lesson I gave to a golfer who told me that he'd always had a jerky and unrhythmic swing.

Since many people exaggerate when they tell a teacher what's wrong, I expected that when I saw Jeff's swing it wouldn't be as unathletic as he had described. I was wrong. Although he had played for over ten years and had an eighteen handicap, it seemed miraculous that he could break 100. "I have to agree with you, Jeff; those swings are not the epitome of smooth, coordinated movement. You weren't exaggerating." He looked a bit relieved that at least I could appreciate his concern. "But, of course, what I don't yet know is how you'd like to be able to hit the ball."

"Well, I'd like to be able to hit more smoothly and rhythmically—the way the pros do."

"Different pros swing in different ways. How would *you* like to be able to swing?"

"I'd like to be more—"

"No, don't *tell* me, *show* me. How would you swing?"

Jeff started hitting shots. Immediately, there was a marked increase in fluidity and rhythm, a different swing altogether. I gave no sign of surprise but, in a deadpan tone, remarked now and then, "Uh-huh, you'd like to swing a little more like that. . . . Yeah, I see, more like that . . ."

By the time Jeff had hit fifteen balls, his swing had transformed itself from that of a hacker to that of a swinger. I couldn't restrain my enthusiasm any longer. "Well, too bad you can't swing like that, Jeff. Maybe someday!" Jeff looked shocked as he realized what had happened. In his mind he hadn't been hitting smoothly; he was simply showing me how he would like to *if he could*.

Jeff's next swing was a disaster, a replay of his earlier tight and awkward swing. "Right, that's how you do swing," I said. "Now show me again how you'd like to be able to."

Again the smooth swing appeared. Jeff looked confused. The swings were completely different, yet he hadn't been taught anything new. "Which one is the real me?" he asked.

"It's your choice," I replied. "Both swings are there. The tight one is the one you thought was yours for over ten years, but the other one's been there all the time waiting to be let out."

That's how powerful negative programming can be. Self 1 is quite literal in his instructions. He will tell you a thousand times that you can't putt, and it will seem that you can't. Since everything you do to improve is based on the premise that you can't putt, nothing works for long; the identification with bad putting is too strong. Yet years of "I can't putt" can be circumvented by a single "But *if* I could . . ."

Likewise, a skier who hesitates going down a slope well within his capacity can be asked, "How would you ski if you weren't afraid of falling?" His style changes dramatically. A businessman who has been struggling with a decision to the point of desperation is asked, "If you knew the right decision, what would it be?" In both cases the "what if" often releases the potential that was being blocked by negative thinking.

Obviously, this trick can't be used to develop something that is not already within you. All it does is avoid the expectation that something is not there which in fact *is*. It works only when there is some trust between instructor and student, for it is embarrassing for the student to see that what he had been striving for was available all the time.

There are a couple of ways to use this trick on the practice range. One is to hit the way you'd really like to, regardless of the outcome, as suggested in the putting chapter. A good way to make this exercise more enjoyable and more acceptable to Self 1 is to practice what I call the "movie-star drill." Pretend that you are starring in a movie about a golfer whose form you admire. You don't have to get the same results as that golfer; you merely have to pretend that your swing resembles his and the director will splice in the shot later. Don't try to analyze how Jack Nicklaus swings and copy it; Self 1 will say, "I can't." Simply act the part of Jack Nicklaus.

We all tend to set expectations for ourselves that are commensurate with our past performance, even if they are optimistic ones. But when you play "what if" as Jack Nicklaus or Nancy Lopez, you'd be surprised what can sometimes be released when you really get into the role. You may not duplicate their swings, but parts of you that couldn't project beyond the self-image barrier of being only a weekend or average player emerge as soon as the barrier is circumvented in this way. Hidden parts of yourself are encouraged to simulate the attitudes and mannerisms of the pro.

EXPRESSING QUALITIES

Self 1 tends to notice a quality that seems to be missing from our golf swings or our characters and tries to replace it with some concept of the way we *should be.* All my life I've battled with my image of my own carelessness, and particularly in golf I've often wished I were more precise. Naturally, I've tried to improve in this regard, but until recently nothing seemed to work to make me more precise.

While working on this chapter it occurred to me that attempting to be precise puts me in the trying mode. Thereafter I stopped trying to put precision into my putting and chipping, which suffered most from this failing, and focused my attention on whatever precision was already there. My goal was to allow any precision I did possess its full expression. Through simple awareness my putting and chipping improved radically because I was giving all my attention to it.

On a piece of paper, list five or more qualities that describe your golf swing—not its results, but the swing itself. Here are a few sample self-portraits: Tony—tight, overcontrolled, correct, careful, muscled; Margo—powerless, cautious, unsure, precise, smooth; Jim—loose, off balance, wild, floppy, flowing.

Next, list some attributes you would like to see in your swing but which you feel it lacks. They don't have to be the opposites of your existing qualities, merely different. Tony's list might include "fluid, uninhibited, graceful, effortless, and unthinking." Write down each of these desired qualities four times, encouraging Self 2 to express their essence as you write. The experience of expressing the word as you write it is much richer than simply writing the word. Like golf, writing is a physical action and can therefore serve as a channel for the expression of Self 2 potential.

Another game that can be played with pencil and paper is one I call "paper golf." On a blank sheet of paper, mark points on the left-hand side to represent tees and draw circles on the right side to represent holes. Placing the pencil on the tee, close your eyes and draw a line to the center of the circle. After you've done this a few times, pick one desired quality from your list and draw the line from "tee" to "hole" expressing that quality. Do this a few times for each attribute you feel you lack. How do these lines compare with the first set of lines? How do they compare with each other? Take a look at the shape of the lines, as well as their accuracy. Which qualities were the most fun to express? Next time you're on the driving range, take your list with you. Consider each quality separately and reflect on it. Search your memory for an image that expresses it. (For example, Tony might picture a river as he thinks of fluidity or of a sapling bending in the wind as he thinks of gracefulness.) Then hold the image rather than the word in your mind as you swing. Don't *try* to express that quality; simply allow for the possibility that it already exists within you and let out whatever wants to express itself. Even if you think that little of the desired quality is coming through, notice whatever is there. Realize that you didn't force it to be there; it was already inside you. Continue with one quality until you have realized it to your satisfaction, then go on to another.

You will find that some of these desired qualities may improve your performance significantly, while others may make it worse. That's fine. You're not after performance right now; you're attempting to release certain generally desirable qualities. Then, when you are actually playing, the qualities you may need in a particular situation can emerge without conscious summoning.

Examples of qualities that you might want to consider include daring, trust, precision, finesse, mastery, gracefulness, coordination, rhythm, balance, power, straightness, and cleanness. The beauty of this exercise is that you discover parts of yourself that you had assumed didn't exist. This widens the scope of your possibilities; you don't have to develop a set style but can adapt it to fit the circumstances.

One day, after working at expressing various qualities that I hadn't associated with myself, I conceived the idea of expressing "Tim Gallwey." It was quite a different experience; instead of *being* Tim Gallwey, I tried to express my picture of "him" as detachedly as I had the other qualities I'd chosen. This experiment may sound odd, but it gave me a feeling of freedom, a sense that I wasn't limited by any qualities or even by the self-image conglomeration that is known as "Tim Gallwey." What I am is something more than my self-image and the qualities I can discern about myself. I can choose to present and express any of them.

39-39 AT PERFECT LIBERTY

One day I went out to play Perfect Liberty, a new golf course that had, so far, only nine completed holes. I didn't really have time to play eighteen holes, but I promised myself that if I broke 40 the first time through, I'd play them a second time. I was becoming increasingly aware that my last chance to break 80 before submitting the manuscript to my publishers was approaching. I had maybe another four weeks, and knowing this didn't exactly reduce the pressure.

I was playing with Tom Nordland and two other golfers, all of whom were going to complete the round. To walk away after nine holes would be embarrassing, but before we started I told them the conditions I'd imposed on my game.

I started with a bogey on the difficult uphill first hole, hitting a four iron to the fringe of the green but failing to get down in two. Still, I felt relaxed going to the second hole and absorbed in the awareness technique I had chosen.

I parred the next five holes and could feel the tension mounting as I approached the eighth tee. I was aware of the score and that breaking 40 was within reach, although the last two holes at this course had often been my downfall. A three wood well hit on the dogleg eighth hole would put the ball into a dry water hazard in the middle of the fairway. Although I'm not particularly fond of my two iron, Self 2 selected it as the best club for the situation. "The ball is already there, ten yards short of the water hazard . . . I can see it there. . . . Now, how would you like to swing this two iron?" I asked myself.

I heard the answer in my own head: "As if I knew how." And that's exactly how I swung. I hit it as if it were my favorite club. I felt wonderful as I swung; the swing was effortless, the crack off the club was clear, and I felt almost no vibration from the impact in my hands. The shot was clean, and the ball landed uncannily near the exact spot of grass where I had pictured it. I could do nothing but marvel at seeing what Self 2 can do without interference from Self 1. That shot gave me added confidence in the technique, and I parred the hole after missing a twenty-foot putt by half an inch.

To say I was truly confident on the ninth tee would not be accurate. The thought did pass through my mind: Wow, you could hit the drive OB and *still* break 40.

"That's right," I answered, overlooking the fact that this thought could have come only from Self 1. "I've got it made." Of course, my drive faded just enough to hit on the top of the hill a few feet on the wrong side of the OB marker. I waited to see if by luck it would roll down, but it stayed put, as if defying me.

Two shots later I was on the fringe of the green, needing to chip close enough to one-putt to break 40. I remembered how only a few months earlier this situation would have scared me to death; at the very least I would have been thinking of some technique to keep me from yipping. But I hit the shot without a thought. Confidence in myself and in this latest technique was growing, and I felt very little pressure. The chip almost went in; I had only a two-inch tap for my 39, and a chance to play another nine, and a hope to break 80.

From time to time during the second nine I thought, I should be feeling more pressure than I am . . . I wonder when it's going to hit. But it never did. I didn't play spectacularly, but I made only a few mistakes. I missed a few birdie putts, failed to get out of a sand trap once, and hit another drive OB, putting me three over par, with a 78 for the round.

However, my enthusiasm for breaking the "80 barrier" was dampened by the fact that I did so playing the same nine holes twice. The second nine would not be completed until October, and for this reason I didn't feel I'd legitimately broken 80. But it felt good just the same.

THE CHOICE TO ACCEPT THE UNCERTAINTIES OF GOLF

Expectations can be a setup for disappointment. They can make it harder for me to break through to new levels of performance. And what do they provide in return? The promise of a temporary and, quite often, illusory sense of certainty.

It's true that sometimes I need to be somewhat certain about some things. If I deposit $1,000 in the bank, I expect that I can withdraw it on demand. If I stop at a red light, I expect that it will soon turn green. In these two cases my expectations about the future are firmly grounded in experience and reason. But when I'm standing on the first tee and I haven't hit a golf ball in a week, how grounded can any expectation be? Can I say to myself that if I just think, Swing easy and smooth, I can expect to hit it long and down the middle of the fairway? Or if I remember, Take a full turn until your left shoulder is just past the ball, is that a solid basis to expect a good first drive? Or even, "I will faithfully focus on da-da-da-da, to the exclusion of all other thoughts." Will that produce a result to meet my best expectation? Maybe if I envision the result and the perfect swing and then just let it happen? No! None of the above. Why not admit it? Nothing will bring true certainty into that shot. So why can't we give up on certainty? Self 1 is the kind of guy who doesn't like surprises. Then don't take him to the golf course!

Here is the alternative: Accept the uncertainty. Learn to tolerate it. Things change. Shit happens. Beauty happens. What's wrong with a little uncertainty? Doesn't it go with the territory of life? Doesn't it definitely go with the territory called golf? Besides, what's wrong with a few surprises? I've learned to like surprises. I'm surprised when that first drive goes down the middle, and I'm surprised when it doesn't. Actually, I can be relatively certain that in golf exactly what I expect will *not* happen. If I want to break through to a new level of understanding or a new level of performance, then I throw out the expectations game as a useless and limiting mind-set. This is easier said than done, but very much worth the effort.

Once I learn that I can be free from my own expectations, I can begin letting go of my unneeded expectations of others. Just as I want myself to be predictable, I want others to be predictable, too. When they are not, then I become disappointed, even upset. But why should I need them to be the way I expect? Sometimes I need them to keep their promises—that's a different matter. But they don't have to be the way I think they are going to be just so my little view of the world can have more stability in it. I'm coming to terms with the fact that there is very little in life that is stable, so I'm going to enjoy the part that is and let the rest be as unstable as it wants. This way I can see the possibility of freedom from the expectations game on or off the course.

MY FRIEND TOM NORDLAND was an excellent golfer who wanted to learn how to become an Inner Game instructor. We played many times during the period that my editor gave me to break 80. When I finally did, Tom asked if he could write an account of his observations of the evolution of my golf game. I offer his narrative below.

TIM BREAKS 80!

It has been two years since Tim and I first played golf together. When I moved to Los Angeles from Minnesota, I thought I had done so in order to become involved with Inner Tennis, so it was a pleasant surprise when I learned that Tim was going to write a golf book.

When we started playing together, Tim had a long way to go. His swing was upright and uptight, and he had a unique way of lifting his arm and cocking his wrists as he swung the club. Although his typical shot was a slice, sometimes he would overpower the ball with his stronger right arm and pull the ball far to the left. He could hit the ball a long way when he connected just right, but his swing allowed for little consistency. His short game was equally erratic and showed that he hadn't played much. He would take mulligans and "gimmes" and fix his lie if it wasn't to his liking. I gradually let him know that serious golfers don't touch the ball between tee and green and that they count every stroke.

At the start, Tim's scores were consistently in the mid- to high nineties. Gradually, as he played more and practiced Inner Game exercises, his scores started dropping, breaking 90 and then moving toward 85. His improvement came from the fact that though he was playing only once a week, he was able to use concentration techniques he had transferred from tennis to golf effectively. But I had wondered if he would lower his score much more unless he played more and took some lessons. Although he had originally planned to take a lesson once a month, his first experiences with professional instruction weren't satisfactory. "My head gets clogged up with instructions, and I just don't have the time to devote to taking my swing apart and putting it back together," he said. So much for lessons.

Then Tim's business commitments began interfering with the regularity of his golf. When I reminded him of the need to play the game frequently if he hoped to improve, he replied, "There are a lot of golfers who can't play regularly. I'd rather prove that the average golfer can continue to improve with Inner Game techniques as well as the guy who can play all the time. Anyone knows that with enough practice he can improve. Besides, I can practice concentration anytime I remember to."

Tim started playing less and scoring better. I think it was after he came back from playing St. Andrews that I first noticed a change in his swing. Suddenly, he *looked* like a golfer rather than like a tennis player trying to play golf. He was hitting the ball straighter and more solidly than he ever had, and with less effort. He had developed some consistency. I don't know how it happened; there was simply a breakthrough. Tim said that he'd known it had to happen.

For a few months, Tim was playing in the low eighties consistently, and I thought that it wouldn't be long before he broke 80, having played a scant forty rounds from the time he was shooting in the high nineties. Then he was laid up with an illness that drained his energy and kept him off the course for three months. When he resumed, his scores shot up to the high eighties and he had to regain the consistency he'd attained earlier gradually. He took the setback as an Inner Game challenge and seemed more interested than discouraged. By the following summer he was again shooting fairly consistently in the low eighties.

We played Camarillo Springs Golf Course, northwest of Los Angeles, with Jon Wright and Al Forbes. The course is a relatively short par-71 but fairly challenging, especially with the strong wind that was blowing that day. We all knew that this was a "must" situation for Tim; time had run out on his book deadline. It was a real pressure situation, but Tim looked calm and composed as we teed off.

On the first hole, number ten, Tim reached the green nicely with a drive and a midiron and two-putted easily. He had hit both shots with authority, and I sensed he was up for the challenge. On the next hole, number eleven, he was explaining his "doctrine of the easy" drill to Jon, tried to cut across a dogleg, and hit his drive out of bounds by a few feet. He reached the par-four hole in two with his second ball, but three-putted for a triple bogey! I hoped he wouldn't be too discouraged, and his five-iron tee shot on the next hole, a par-three, showed that he wasn't. He hit it about eight to nine feet away and sank it for a beautiful birdie. He also birdied the next hole and almost birdied the fourteenth, leaving him one over par after five holes. He was playing beautifully.

After hitting the next three holes in regulation and getting easy pars, he came, still one over, to the par-three eighteenth, which was about 180 yards into a strong and sometimes gusting wind. Tim hit a three wood and skied it about halfway, his first really bad shot of the day. His fifty-yard pitch shot was held up by the wind and landed short in a trap; he blasted out fourteen feet from the pin and missed the putt for a double bogey and a 38, three over par.

On the first six holes of the front side Tim made only one bogey, the rest being pars. Some of them were tough because of the strong wind, but Tim was playing without error. His concentration was relaxed and steady. If he didn't reach a green in regulation, he was usually close enough to chip and putt for par. I was amazed by his accurate chipping all day long. During this interlude I wanted to ask him how he was feeling, but I didn't want to increase the pressure on him. Usually in such situations we made it a point to tease each other, but today was different. I sensed that Jon and Al felt the same way. We talked about Inner Game drills and concentration and avoided talk of his score.

The third-to-last hole was the crucial one. It was a medium-long par-three (155 yards), but again the wind made it difficult. Tim hit a six iron, didn't catch it fully, and landed in a water hazard. After taking a drop on the line of flight into the hazard, he was still forty to fifty yards from the green and lying two! I had been in similar situations before and knew that if he got nervous here and missed his recovery shot, he could easily get a double or triple bogey and blow the round. I watched with interest.

Tim didn't take much time and hit a beautiful, fluid approach shot, pin-high about six to seven feet from the hole, as nice an approach shot as I've seen under those circumstances. At that moment I knew that he was going to break 80. Though the putt lipped and he got a double bogey, it didn't matter; he had proved he could handle the pressure. He was now only six over with two holes to play. Neither tensing nor playing safe, he made pars on the last two holes, hitting the greens in regulation and two-putting. After he hit his second shot 150 yards to the green on the last hole and thus assured himself of his goal, we watched in amusement as he spent several minutes quacking at a flock of ducks in an adjacent pond. I wished I'd had a camera. The picture of the serene golf course at dusk, the lovely pond with its mallards, the mountains in the background, and the happy golfer with his bag on his shoulder seemed to symbolize something about the game, the recreation it offers and the reasons we play it.

"UTMOST SINCERITY"

When I began experimenting with expressing qualities, I naturally asked myself what was the most important quality to enhance golf. Many people would say self-confidence, and until recently I would have agreed, if self-confidence is defined as reliance on Self 2. But there is an even more necessary quality on which the other attributes are based.

On the afternoon that I spoiled my chances for my best nine holes with four out-of-bounds on the eighth hole at Perfect Liberty Country Club in the Malibu Hills, one of the Japanese priests who tend the grounds approached me and asked how my book was going. "You believe in using your brain more than your arm?" he asked.

"I believe in both arm and brain," I said, "but I want to play with less ego interference."

"That's the most important thing," he said diffidently. "We like to say, 'Always use *utmost sincerity.*' If I could do everything with utmost sincerity, it would be very beautiful."

The phrase struck a deep chord in me. Utmost sincerity is what's left when you stop trying to *be* anything, when there are no more expectations or pictures to live up to. For me it sums up something I've valued highly ever since I began my excursion into the Inner Game. For the first thirty years of my life I dedicated myself to making something of myself—to being something more than my current self-image. The day I really became a player of the Inner Game I turned 180 degrees from this pursuit to that of discovering more and more of what I already am. By and large this has been a process of "un-becoming" my images of myself. It's like peeling off layers to get closer and closer to a simple core.

And what's at that core? Sincerity—something I can't describe. No matter what pictures I paint of this core, they are inaccurate. It can't really be pictured because it's so profoundly basic, but the closer I get to it, the more I can sense that it is natural, strong, and universal.

When that sincerity is the part of me that's predominant, I don't need to know if I'm going to play good or bad golf. I don't have to limit myself with expectations. I don't require any special results. Paradoxically, at times when I don't feel I need good results, I can't seem to avoid them. The minute I grow greedy for them and try to hold on to them or make them happen, I tighten a little, try to force them, and find that they tend to slip away. But the more I experience utmost sincerity, the more I realize that it is this quality—not the results—that feels good, and when I am in that mode I'm content to be what I am and to enjoy it as it leads me beyond my Self 1 limitations.

TEN

Relaxed Concentration: The Master Skill

OVER THE YEARS I HAVE BEEN ASKED TO COACH INDIVIDUALS AND teams in a wide range of activities about which I had relatively little knowledge. Once when coaching the British Davis Cup tennis team, the Olympic pentathlon coach asked me to help train his team in riding, swimming, running, shooting, and especially fencing, none of which I had ever done competitively. After working with PGA golf professionals in Texas, I was asked by the Houston Philharmonic to give a coaching demonstration, and knowing full well that I had never played any orchestral instrument, they picked their tuba player for me to work with. I accepted these invitations and many others, sometimes wondering what gave me or my clients confidence that I could help. Gradually, I realized that there was a common denominator in the achievement of excellence in all things. There is one *master skill* underlying the myriad of specialized skills required to excel at anything. I call it "relaxed concentration," and I call it the master skill because with it one can learn to improve any skill, and without it, it is difficult to learn anything. It is not easily defined or taught, but it can be learned and even successfully coached.

Everyone has experienced the state of relaxed concentration at one time or another during moments of peak performance or experience. In those spontaneous but all too elusive moments of heightened alertness and perception, actions seem artlessly excellent and life seems simple and whole. Even in complicated, demanding situations, the effort needed is clear and actions flow out of us that are uncannily appropriate. Golf shots are made as if they were the easiest ones imaginable, and we wonder what we ever thought was difficult about the game.

What is going on in your mind during your best performance, during a peak learning experience, or during a moment of total enjoyment? How does this state compare with your normal frame of mind during average or less-than-average performances? I made my initial observations about this on the tennis court and found that, when playing badly, my students' minds were filled with (1) a lot of self-instruction, (2) self-judgment, (3) various thoughts and feelings stemming from doubt and fear of failure. Yet when they were playing at their best, they reported that their minds were relaxed, absorbed, and quiet, free of these tensions. Often they would say that they weren't thinking at all and that their bodies seemed to know without conscious thought how to hit the ball.

WHAT IS RELAXED CONCENTRATION?

It is simply the capacity to focus totally. It occurs when commitment, abilities, and attention can be channeled in a single direction. It is being truly conscious and free of fear, doubt, and confusion. It is what enabled Ted Williams to say that sometimes he could see the baseball so well "that it almost stands still for me." Martial artists from East and West have long known that when totally focused, the mind is not interrupted by what we call "conscious thinking," and it is then that the most precise action occurs. Or as the master in Eugen Herrigel's *Zen and the Art of Archery* says, "A single conscious thought through the mind diverts the arrow from its course toward the target."

A more academic but insightful description of this state in both play and work has been written about extensively by Professor Mihaly Csikszentmihalyi of the University of Chicago. Calling it the "flow state," he writes,

> In the flow state, action follows upon action according to an internal logic that seems to need no conscious intervention by the actor. He experiences it as a unified flowing from one moment to the next, in which he is in control of his actions, and in which there is little distinction between self and environment, between stimulus and response, or between past, present, and future.

He goes on to say that the experience of this flow state is so *inherently* enjoyable that it is often sought for itself rather than for any extrinsic rewards that may result from it. He points out that this state has been experienced on the battlefield and in concentration camps, proving that it is attainable even during almost unendurable activities. Presumably, then, it might also be possible on the golf course!

And, of course, there are many descriptions from artists and athletes of all kinds, including golfers, who refer to playing "in the zone." Chess players, mountain climbers, race-car drivers, creative problem solvers, dancers, public speakers, even people in love have given similar descriptions of this elusive state. They praise it; they recommend it; they proclaim both its intrinsic value and the amazing results it often produces. Yet my experience of such people is that they are often surprised and humbled by the achievements they attain in this state, giving less credit to themselves than to something that is at least a step beyond their control. They usually shy away from trying to teach the attainment of this state, knowing intuitively that no words or formulas can promise to take student or teacher through the door to this valued experience.

Just as the state of relaxed concentration is often credited for contributing to one's best performances, the lack of it is frequently blamed for one's poorest performances. This holds true from the highest levels of athletic competence to the lowest. Likewise, when relaxed concentration is in the workplace, both individuals and teams work smoothly and effectively. But in its absence there is fragmentation of thought and action, leading to miscommunication and the inevitability of breakdowns in teamwork and performance. In both the individual and the team, divergence and conflict arise that prevent coherent, coordinated action.

There is no magic formula or method that automatically puts a person into the optimal state of mind. It may be that the state we look for is already there but that by mentally trying to figure out how not to think, we are, of course, thinking and thus endlessly chasing our tail. It's interesting that Self 1 will even propose ways to get rid of Self 1. It is even more interesting that we would believe it might succeed.

THE PARADOX OF "LOSING ONESELF IN ACTION"

For a long time I was curious about descriptions of the state of relaxed concentration, like "I was totally lost in the action," "It just seemed to all come together at the right time," "I seemed to disappear and something else took over," or "I was playing out of my mind." These descriptions sound as if a person is being taken over by some alien force. But as I started to experience relaxed concentration a little more, I began to reach the conclusion that this "something else" that was taking over was not alien at all but was *me*. If anything was alien, it was the sensation that Self 1 was temporarily lost during total concentration. It sounded strange to hear myself say things like "I wasn't there and I never felt more at home."

So who is "lost" when we "lose ourselves in action" and who is found? For those who have followed the notion of Self 1 and Self 2 throughout this book, there is an easy explanation: Self 1 is lost—at least for a time—and Self 2 is found. Relaxed concentration is the natural state of mind of Self 2. Consequently, Self 2 is often more visible in the very young, who have not yet developed their Self 1 patterns of interference. For most adults, although it might seem easy when it is happening, a true state of relaxed concentration is usually not achieved without some degree of effort to focus attention and to prevent oneself from being swept away by Self 1 habits.

CONCENTRATION OF THOUGHT

Although conscious thought is often blamed for pulling us out of a state of relaxed concentration, one could reasonably ask, "Is there not such a thing as concentration of conscious thought?" Cannot thought itself be either focused or scattered, coherent and purposeful or disoriented and chaotic? How many times have you been in a conversation or at a meeting and suffered as the train of thought that starts out in one direction gets diverted into another direction, only to be switched to another, then another topic, seemingly without the choice or consent of those involved? Such fragmentation of thought is so commonplace that it often goes unnoticed. There's just that uncomfortable feeling at the end of the conversation that much was said but little accomplished. Of course, the same holds true *within* an individual. Concentration of thought cannot occur unless the thinker has learned to direct the flow of thought, slow it down, and, possibly, bring it to a stop. In this respect, thought is like the engine of a car; it needs brakes as well as an accelerator. And it helps if the driver has both hands on the steering wheel.

THE PRACTICE OF RELAXED CONCENTRATION

It is impossible to learn much about concentration without practicing it, and it is not until you start practicing it that you become aware of what it is, what its benefits are, and, perhaps, how unconcentrated you have been. Control over one's attention is a fundamental freedom. I was shocked at first to find how little control I consciously exercised.

When it comes to making the effort to practice, it is important to remember that the goal is *relaxed* concentration. Many people know that it is important to concentrate on what they are doing. Tennis players are repeatedly told to "watch the ball, watch the ball, watch the ball." We have all been told countless times to "pay attention to what we are doing" by parents, teachers, managers, and coaches. So we try to concentrate. But if we try too hard because we *doubt* that we will be able to achieve the desired concentration, then we will be subject to the law of doubt. When in doubt, tighten. The focus becomes forced and anything but relaxed. When you try too hard to concentrate, you will soon get tired because you are not actually receiving the benefits of the concentration. It's only a matter of time before distraction comes and you are happy to be distracted from your painful effort, and the time is usually pretty short. But relaxed concentration doesn't have to be forced. It is natural. It takes a *small but constant* effort to keep conscious and present enough to your immediate experience so that you don't get pulled away. It requires a nonjudgmental recognition when you do get distracted, followed by a gentle return to focus.

Can relaxed concentration be taught? I don't think so. Can it be learned through practice? Yes. In fact, I can think of no waking moment when a person cannot practice relaxed concentration— driving a car, standing in line, having a conversation with a friend, cooking dinner, solving a problem, hitting a ball, or walking the course between golf shots.

Human beings have the capacity to be conscious, but they can also lapse into unconsciousness. This choice is always present, and therefore so is the possibility of practicing staying conscious. The moments that we miss when unconscious do not come back so we can experience them again consciously. If we miss them, we miss them.

You can't make relaxed concentration happen any more than you can make sleep happen. It occurs when you allow—not force—yourself to become interested in each moment of your life. Undertaking to learn this master skill is a supreme challenge, but one with inestimable personal benefit.

STEPS IN CONCENTRATION

Discipline

The first step is to make a disciplined effort to focus your attention. Doing the simple back-hit-stop exercise requires such discipline. Your attention may want to fly away into thoughts about how to hit the ball or what will happen if you miss. One purpose of the exercise—indeed, of all the exercises in this book—is to provide a focus for your attention on something specific *here and now*, away from the interferences of past, future, should, shouldn't, and what might have been. Here and now the mind can begin to quiet itself, and the quieter it grows, the more feedback it gives Self 2 about what's happening.

Imagine that the mind is like a lake. When its surface is calm, reflections of trees, clouds, and birds can be seen clearly and in rich detail, as can whatever is in its depths. But when the surface is ruffled by the wind, it does not reflect clearly. Objects look darker, less distinct, even distorted. Likewise, the mind that is restless or agitated cannot make clear contact with reality, and then we have a difficult time dealing with our surroundings. Hence, quieting the mind is the first step in concentration.

Interest

Concentration reaches a deeper level when the mind becomes interested in its focus. It is difficult to keep your attention on something in which there is little interest. When there is discipline but no interest, it takes so much effort just to keep the mind still that concentration is generally superficial and of short duration.

Each individual needs to find his own focus of interest. Interest increases as you get into the subtleties; details are always more interesting than vague impressions. The path to this state of interest is to become ever more receptive to experience and to sustain your effort to make contact with what you are focusing on. If you try to force interest, it will evade you.

Absorption

A third level of concentration could be called absorption. It is a deepening of interest to the point where you begin to lose yourself in what you are attending to. A person becomes so absorbed that he is hard to distract. A golf professional absorbed in addressing an important shot won't hear people near him talking or be aware of cameras or his competitors because they are not relevant to his immediate task. This level of concentration is pleasurable as well as conducive to excellence, for you literally leave worries, doubts, and troubles behind. Most great athletic performances are accomplished in this state, where even the most strenuous action somehow seems effortless. There is no room for anxiety because your mind is so focused that you don't even hear doubt knocking at your door.

In an interview, Jane Blalock, an LPGA player, described the experience of absorption vividly: "It doesn't happen all the time, but when I'm playing well sometimes it's as if my eyes change. I can feel it. I just feel like Dr. Jekyll and Mr. Hyde—a transformation happens, I'm a totally different human being. I don't hear anybody, I don't see anybody, nothing bothers me, nothing is going to interfere with what I'm about to do."

In this state we experience an intensified contact with reality. Relevant details are seen more clearly: Golf balls and holes seem more distinct than usual, and actions flow with an uncommon ease even in the midst of extreme exertion. You just seem to know the best thing to do with each change in the situation.

Once absorbed in experience, one sometimes slips into a state that is difficult to describe because the "observer" who would describe it is no longer there. It's like falling asleep; you don't really know you did until you've awakened. But in this case it is falling awake, and you may not know it happened until you're looking back on it. As strange as it may sound, this state of absorption feels like the most natural thing when it happens. It is simple, effortless, and uncalculated.

THE ACT Δ

From my own experience and the descriptions of others who have performed in an optimal state of mind, there seem to be three essential characteristics of relaxed concentration: (1) heightened awareness or perception, (2) strong and undivided desire or choice, and (3) heightened trust in potential and an absence of self-doubt. Awareness, choice, and trust are not merely ingredients but skills that can each be developed by practice. They become doors to relaxed concentration. As such, I see them as primary Inner Game skills that automatically increase performance, learning, and enjoyment in any activity.

Awareness skills increase our ability to focus our minds non-judgmentally in the present moment, on details relevant to our purpose. *Choice skills* develop our ability to clarify goals, both short-term and long-range, and to find the energy and determination to overcome the inner and outer obstacles in order to achieve what we really want. They involve learning what your true goal is and making the effort to trust and be aware. *Trust skills* decrease doubt and give us confidence in our true potential. They involve learning to count on what is reliable for a particular end and to let go of dependence on what is not reliable. In Inner Game terminology, this means that the golfer learns to trust Self 2 to hit the ball rather than Self 1.

From this description it is easy to see that the three skills are interrelated. None can exist without the others, and a heightening of any one will automatically heighten the other two. However, the concentration produced by their combination is only as strong as the weakest link in the triad.

AWARENESS SKILLS

The essence of awareness skills is learning to see things as they are—that is, nonjudgmentally. When a golfer sees his swing in terms of "good" or "bad" he will not have a clear picture of it as it *is*. Awareness never judges; only Self 1 does. True awareness is like a flawless mirror; this principle is basic to Inner Game understanding. Awareness is curative only when there is no judgment, and when it is combined with purpose, effective action and learning can take place.

If the game of golf has to do with the controlling of a ball and a club with a body, and we understand that better control is accomplished by increasing awareness, then the priorities for one's attention are narrowed to the ball, the club, the body, the course, and the target. Since the course, target, and ball (before contact) are immobile, they do not require the greatest concentration of the player's mind. Nevertheless, they should be observed, but not in a judgmental way. Your lie is not "bad," nor are the lake or the OB posts; nor are the trees you went into on your last round. Neither are they "good." They are best observed without attributing positive or negative values to them. Your lie is the way it is: in a divot, in the rough, buried in the sand, or sitting up smartly in the fairway. It's important to see the situation in clear detail. Negative judgments tend to obscure your vision of what you wish wasn't there and to cause doubt and tightening. Positive judgments tend to make you feel it's unnecessary to see details, and you become too casual.

Clearly, the most important focus for attention in golf is the body and the club. Golf is a game in which the sense of feeling is far more important than the sense of sight.

I can't resist telling a story about a blind golfer whose lifelong dream was to play a round with Arnold Palmer, his idol. Finally, after a tournament, he had the courage to introduce himself and ask Palmer. Understandably, Arnie was noncommittal. "Well, sure, sometime that would be fun," he answered, and then began talking to someone else. But the blind man would not be dissuaded so easily. Again he asked, and again he was put off politely. Finally, he made one more try, and, with a number of people standing around, he challenged Arnie: "Mr. Palmer, I know you're not the type to turn down a fair challenge. I have ten thousand dollars I'd like to wager on a single eighteen-hole medal-play match with you. Will you accept my challenge?"

"Sir, with all due respect," Palmer answered, "I don't want to take that money from you. Thanks anyway."

"Mr. Palmer, I'm not kidding. If you don't accept my wager, I'll feel justified in letting it be known that you weren't sure you could beat me."

Arnold Palmer has never been criticized for being uncompetitive. People were looking on and he was slightly annoyed by the persistence of the stranger, so finally he agreed: "Okay, if that's the way you want it, I'll play. Ten thousand dollars. You name the course and the time, and I'll be there."

"Very well," said the blind man. "I'll meet you on the first tee of Pebble Beach tomorrow at *midnight*."

According to the story, which may or may not be true, Arnie blushed, smiled, and capitulated. The blind man withdrew his wager, and they played a friendly daytime match.

FOCUS ON CRITICAL VARIABLES

Obviously, the blind man felt confident that he could play with feel alone. And, in fact, with just a little assistance, many blind people have learned to play excellent golf. This should tell us something about the relative importance of vision and feeling in golf. So where do you focus your attention? Not on thinking, not on seeing or even visualizing, but on feeling. It's okay to envision where you want the ball to go, but I question whether you want to en*vision* how to hit it. If anything, you may want to "en*feel*" how you are going to hit it. During the swing, it is feel, and not thought, that will control your movements.

How do you learn feel? By feeling whatever you can. In any activity you increase awareness by focusing attention on critical variables. A variable is anything that changes. A critical variable is a variable that is critically important to desired results. A few of these variables were itemized in Chapters 7 and 8. In golf, most of these variables must be attended to through the kinesthetic sense of feel or touch. People in our culture are more accustomed to being asked to look or to listen than to feel. When asked to feel something closely, whether it's an emotion or a physical sensation, they are often uncomfortable. The person being asked to feel the path of the club head may respond by asking, "What do you want me to do differently?" or "What do you want me to think about?" But there is a difference between doing, thinking, and feeling. This is a little cultural barrier that must be crossed to achieve relaxed concentration in golf. Though I was born and raised in California, I do not consider myself a stereotypical "touchy-feely" type. But I have to admit that golf is a game where you want to be very touchy-feely, not in relation to the people you play with but in relation to your own body and swing. To a great extent, excellence in golf is a function of how aware you are of the sensations of your body during the setup and swing. When you practice relaxed concentration in golf, give full and total attention to the feel of your swing during the few seconds of each and every shot. The much-discussed benefits of muscle memory are not derived so much from "good memories" as from vivid *feeling* experiences. In short, control in golf is inseparable from relaxed concentration on how the swing feels shot by shot, in practice, and on the course.

There are two ways to find a focus of attention on your swing. The first is to use a focus recommended by your teaching pro or perhaps one or more of the critical variables recommended in Chapter 8. The other, and by no means less valuable, way is to use a focus that is self-generated. You simply start attending to whatever catches your attention spontaneously. If you just pay general attention to how your swing feels on a given day, something in particular will stand out. Maybe you notice a jerkiness in the rhythm or a good feeling of release of your wrists just before impact with the ball, an imbalance at the completion of swing, a feeling of awkwardness, and so on. Whatever stands out, pick that as your variable to attend to. Without judgment and without trying to make any kind of change, allow yourself to become more attentive to that particular variable. You can do this by feeling exactly *when* and *where* the variable occurs in the swing and then *to what degree*. If you can do this without any conscious control, the law of awareness dictates that beneficial change will result from your heightened awareness alone. When change has taken place, that particular variable will vary less and become less interesting. Something else in your swing will probably stand out. Attend to that. The focus can be as specific as the angle of the club head at impact or as broad as your rhythm throughout the swing. Generally speaking, I find a very narrow focus of attention more useful to practice on the range and practice green and a broader focus more conducive to play on the course. But I leave this to each player's experimentation.

CHOICE SKILLS

Choice is inseparable from concentration. You can't force concentration, and you can't be forced to concentrate. We attend only to what we have a desire to attend to. If our desires are scattered in several directions, our attention will be, too. Desire is like a force that has both strength and direction. About any particular desire a person can ask what its source is, where it is directed, and what its strength is. It is your desire to hit the golf ball that will direct your attention to the relevant components of the intended action—the ball, body, club, and target. The strength or singularity of your desire will contribute to the quality of concentration. If the desire is weak or confused, then focus will be more easily distracted; if it is strong and sincere, it will overcome both external and internal obstacles to reach its goal.

Without desire, there is no goal and no action. You can be very much aware of the ball sitting on the tee, but unless you have some urge to hit it, you won't. People generally have many different desires at the same time, somewhat like a boat that has many different forces acting on it. Maybe there is a twelve-mile-an-hour current from the west, a three-mile-an-hour tide from the southeast, and a twenty-mile-an-hour wind from the north. Perhaps the boat has a five-horsepower engine and the captain at the tiller is steering due west. The boat moves with a speed and direction that is the result of all these forces. Similarly, if a golfer has a small desire to shoot his best score ever, another to play it safe and not make a fool of himself, another to do only what he has to do to beat Joe, and a final desire not to break his normal expectations (see Chapter 9), the actual force and direction of desire brought to bear on a given shot will somehow be the result of these divergent desires. Confused desires diminish focus and are counterproductive.

Choice or commitment is like the engine in the boat. It allows some degree of maneuverability within a set of forces that it does not yet control. Here the analogy breaks down a bit because the winds, tide, and current represent unconscious desires that the captain of the boat has no control over. But human beings, by becoming aware of unconscious desires, can bring them under the control of conscious choice. Ultimately, when all the desires are moving in a similar or harmonious direction, full concentration can be achieved.

Choice, like awareness and trust, is a given. We can't *not* choose. We can pretend we don't, but to pretend you don't choose is a choice! Why would a person do that? In my experience, the answer is simple and somewhat embarrassing. I realize that choice has consequences. I don't like some of the consequences of my choices, so I choose to forget that I made the choice in the first place. Now I can pretend that the consequences are not my fault. I can even blame them on others, on destiny, or whatever else is convenient. Ouch. Painfully true. Of course there are consequences for not accepting the consequences of your choices. Your boat stops going in the direction you steer it and instead seems to be at the mercy of winds and currents outside your control.

This point is illustrated by a conversation I had some time ago with a student who persisted in asking for advice on a certain matter. Guessing that he wanted to avoid responsibility for his own choice, I declined. When he continued to persist, I asked him, "If you were the only person in a car, would you rather be in the driver's seat with your hands on the wheel or in the backseat where you couldn't reach the wheel?" Without hesitating, he said, "Oh, I'd much rather be in the backseat." "Why?" I asked, incredulously. "Because one way or the other, I would probably get into an accident. But if I were in the front seat, with my hands on the wheel, then it would be my fault."

OVERCONCERN ABOUT RESULTS

We come now to a very critical point in understanding the game of golf. What is the importance of results? In golf every single stroke you take is counted, tallied into your score for the round, and then averaged into your ongoing handicap. And the goal of each hole is precise: a little white ball going into a little dark hole. Very specific. Very measurable. By design, golf brings out our goal-orientedness. And the game is played mostly within cultures

that themselves are very goal oriented, though most of our
day-to-day goals cannot be measured with the precision of golf. If
you look at most advertisements for golf equipment, training aids,
or golf schools, most of them will entice you with the promise or
suggestion of lower scores.

The question I would like to pose in the context of how to
practice relaxed concentration is: Is it possible to be too goal oriented in golf? Does being goal-oriented produce the best scores?
Do you think concentration comes easily to those who put everything into attaining good scores? Does it produce the deepest
concentration? I don't think the answer to this question is easy,
but for every serious golfer, it is worth asking.

THE PEL Δ

Granted, the rules of golf say that the goal of the game is to get
around the course in as few strokes as possible. Performance is
obviously important in all goal-oriented activity. But is it the only
goal? It may be the only goal that is measured and scored. But is
it the only result that counts? It is difficult for some golfers to see
it any other way. But if you think about it, if all you really wanted
was a low score, then the easiest courses would be the most popular. But it is usually the case that the most difficult courses are the
most expensive and the most sought after. This is not consistent
with a single-minded desire for low scores. "Well, challenging
courses are more fun," the golfer replies. Yes, I agree, and often
more beautiful. Does that mean there is another goal—fun or enjoyment perhaps? Is that a real result of golf? Or do you consider
enjoyment just an incidental by-product of a good score? If you
had to choose between having a low score and having a good time,
which would you choose? Regardless of your answer, it is a fact
that for the four to five hours you are playing eighteen holes of
golf you are somewhere between misery and ecstasy. And human
beings have a built-in preference toward the enjoyment side of the

range of experience. So, almost by definition, enjoyment is a goal that comes with us while we're playing golf.

These questions are quite relevant to the subject of relaxed concentration. Generally speaking, those who value the inherent enjoyment in a given activity have an easier time finding a consistent focus.

Thus far, we have established at least two universal goals in golf: a performance goal (to score well) and an enjoyment goal (to have the best possible experience). Is there another? What about learning? Can you learn something valuable while playing a round of golf? Is what you can learn confined to golf, or can you learn things that will be useful outside of golf— like relaxed concentration, or confidence, or self-discipline, or honesty? And is it the person with the lowest score who necessarily learns the most? Obviously not. In any particular round of golf, learning and score are clearly distinct achievements.

So now we have three goals—performance, enjoyment, and learning—that are all present in golf. In fact, if you think about it, they are present in all activities in play or in work. Now comes an important question. Are these three goals related? Do they belong in a triangle indicating mutual interdependence? The obvious answer is yes. If a person is performing at a certain level but fails at learning and at enjoying the activity, what will soon happen to the performance level? Likewise, if a person does not enjoy the activity, it may be possible to keep up high levels of performance over the short haul but not the long one. On the other hand, if learning is happening, it is only a matter of time before it is bound to have impact on performance. Most great athletes and great performers in every field genuinely love what they do because of the experience that it brings them—not just because of the extrinsic results.

You can take performance, enjoyment, and learning as three mutually supporting aspects of sports or work, a relationship I will refer to as the PEL triangle. Many work teams who get caught up in the performance momentum alone don't get the necessary support from the other two sides of the triangle. This can have serious consequences if you are working in an environment of change. Learning is exactly that capability which enables us to adapt to change. It saves much more time than it takes. Thinking you don't have time to learn from mistakes is very time-consuming. Furthermore, learning from experience doesn't really take time because it happens while you are working. It's more a matter of attitude and personal and cultural priority, not time, that gets in the way. I have introduced the concept of balancing the PEL triangle in many work teams, and in almost every case a surprising improvement in *performance* has resulted along with the intrinsic benefits of increased learning and enjoyment at work.

The fact is that these three goals are the inherent goals of Self 2, so the simplest way to balance the triangle in any activity is simply to learn to *choose* Self 2. Given the chance and just a little encouragement, Self 2 always goes for enjoyment and learning. Its best performance is the natural result. This is inherent, but it is definitely a choice. Every such choice strengthens your connection with Self 2 and increases the probabilities of spending more time in a state of relaxed concentration.

TRUST SKILLS

Trust is the third component of relaxed concentration. Trust is the glue that holds awareness and choice together. It is the leap of faith that allows us to have greater and greater access to the potential that lies unactualized within us. Doubt is the great disrupter of that access. Self 1 is fundamentally a doubt-maker. When I listen to the conversation in my own head, I can reach no other conclusion than Self 1 simply does not like to trust Self 2. Obviously, this doubt undermines the flow of relaxed concentration. "Can I really do this?" it asks, even midswing, midsentence, or midthought.

Do you ever wonder why Self 1 doubts you? Perhaps it is in

doubting that Self 1 creates a role for itself. "You aren't really capable of living this life on your own, making your own choices correctly, and certainly not capable of hitting a golf ball correctly, so let me help you," it suggests. And how often do we doubt this doubt-maker? If someone else said the things about us that we say to ourselves in our own heads, would we tolerate it? Probably not. We would object or at least try to avoid that person. But when the little voice of self-doubt knocks at our door, we invite it in for tea and extended conversation. "You are probably going to miss this three-foot putt," it whispers. Your knees and wrists weaken. "Remember that last one you missed and how bad it felt?" "Yeah, I remember," we say. "What should I do to make sure it doesn't happen again?" "Well, whatever you do, don't leave it short again," self-doubt advises. You hit the ball four feet past the hole. "I told you that you'd miss," it says mockingly. "Next time concentrate more! And make sure you stay relaxed!" it might say. Is this a voice that is really out to help you? It's worth a thought. Do you really want to engage in conversations with it? Has it really ever helped you? Why not doubt the doubt-maker? Why not trust ourselves?

In his famous essay "On Self-Reliance," Ralph Waldo Emerson wrote, "Trust thyself, every heart vibrates to that iron string." I loved that quote from the first time I read it. But what does it mean to trust oneself? Not an easy question. Self-trust is such a basic act that it is sometimes easier to know it by its opposite. It is also easier to see in young children before it has been undermined. In a child, trust shows up as a simple and endearing quality. No one calls it egotistical or overconfident, as will happen all too soon. Trust is there when the child makes mistakes and when the child doesn't. Doubt does not seem to enter the picture at all, and, as a consequence, focus, learning, enjoyment, love, laughter, and all the human treasures are available to the child and are readily seen by others.

Trust is what enables us to relax enough to be ourselves. It is what makes it possible for you to go to sleep at night, or to laugh in the face of your worst nightmares, or to know that you are still all right even after three triple bogeys in a row. Trust does not make every shot we hit go long and true, but it allows us to think straight regardless of where the balls may go. In the face of the most challenging situations, trust allows us to pay attention to priorities and to access the capabilities we need. Trust is what allows us to learn and to acknowledge that we need to. Trust is the one and only channel we have to be who we really are, and, as such, it is the only true ticket to enduring enjoyment. For each individual, trust in oneself is an available choice at every moment. It is a choice because, after childhood, it doesn't just happen automatically.

Before going ahead, I must make it clear that I am not claiming that blind trust in itself is a virtue. The virtue is to learn to trust what is trustworthy. Obviously, it is not a virtue to trust a three-year-old to cross a street in traffic. And was it a virtue to trust the leader of your country if you lived in Germany in the thirties? Misplaced trust is the cause of much hurt, suffering, and loss of independence. But the greatest misplacement of trust of all occurs when we trust someone who tells us, directly or indirectly, that we are not worthy of our own trust. We can learn to trust others only to the extent that we can first trust ourselves. After all, if I can't trust myself, how can I choose who or what I *can* trust? I'll make a mistake, won't I? I'll pick the wrong book, the wrong leader, the wrong religion, the wrong things to believe. No. Life demands trust in life; existence demands that we trust our existence. It's the only way it works. And it does work.

TRUST AND CONTROL

I said in the foreword and in the first chapter that golf is a game about control. Trust takes place in the practice of letting go to Self 2 control. When I give total focus to the movement of my club head, to the feel of my swing, I have to trust that the ball will be hit, even though I can no longer hear the voice of Self 1 telling me how to do it. If I don't let go of the control of the swing, I can't really be fully aware of it. Why? Because I can't *feel* my swing at the same time I am *thinking* about how to swing. So trust and awareness go hand in hand. It is by letting go of Self 1 control that I gain control of my swing. Sometimes it is easier to trust when I am not aware. When I am unconscious, it's easier to swing freely, even wildly, without inhibition. But I cannot learn to swing well without bringing awareness into my swing. So I have to learn to be aware and let go at the same time. This is the heart of the Inner Game experiment and practice. Such is the practice of self-trust in golf. It does not guarantee that every ball will go long and true. Nothing will. But it does guarantee that you will not be at war with yourself and that you will learn to sustain greater and greater levels of relaxed concentration. This is the challenge of the Inner Game of Golf.

ELEVEN

Playing Your Own Game

YOU COULDN'T EXPLAIN THE
PRESSURES OF GOLF TO A MARTIAN

IF YOU ASK MOST GOLFERS IF GOLF IS A PRESSURE-FILLED GAME, MOST will agree that it is. But have we given much thought to where the pressure actually comes from? I contend that in golf itself there is *no* pressure. If we want to discover where the pressure comes from, we have to look somewhere else than the game of golf itself. Allow me to present my case.

Imagine, if you will, that a Martian has just landed his space-craft somewhere near the eighteenth green at Pebble Beach during a Pro-Celebrity golf tournament. The president of the United States is standing over a five-foot, downhill, breaking putt. That he is feeling pressure is quite obvious from the fact that his hands, wrists, and knees are trembling noticeably. Perspiration is on his forehead as he tries to summon his concentration for what he hopes will be his last stroke of the tournament. The Martian is watching with great interest as the crowd stands in hushed silence. Unable to contain his curiosity, he turns to you and asks, "Tell me, sir, why is it that the leader of this, the most powerful country in the world, seems to be overcome by fear?"

Without hesitation, you give the obvious answer: "Well, sir, that's a downhill, breaking putt! It's not as easy as it looks."

The Martian acknowledges the point respectfully. "Yes, I can appreciate the difficulty of the task," he replies. "I'm quite sure I would not be able to succeed myself. But if I may ask, what dreadful thing must happen if he is to miss? It must be quite frightening. Perhaps this is a kind of symbolic war and your country's enemy becomes the victor if he fails in this task? Or maybe his youngest daughter must be sacrificed to the gods if this shot is missed. . . . There must be something causing such dread in such a great and fearless leader."

"Well, you see, there is a lot of pressure on this last putt. If he misses, he will have to add another stroke to his score. It might affect his standing in the tournament, and it might even raise his handicap," you explain. "Yes," replies the Martian. "I am familiar with all the rules of golf and understand scores, handicaps, rankings, and the like. But nowhere have I read about the consequences of a high score or a high handicap. If there is no money involved in this match, what is actually at stake? What is won or lost?"

Now, answering the Martian becomes a little more difficult. You could try telling him that if the president misses the shot, people might consider him a "choker." Or you could say that it would be a blow to his self-confidence or self-esteem. You can imagine the Martian's response: "I didn't see anything about losing self-esteem—whatever that is—in the rules of golf." And he would be perfectly right. You can't really explain the pressures we feel playing golf because they have nothing to do with the game. The rules of golf just say you hit a ball with a stick, follow the rules, and count the number of strokes it takes you to go around eighteen holes. So where's the pressure?

As hard as it might be to explain to the Martian, the fact remains that plenty of pressure is felt on the golf course, and not just by professionals whose careers are on the line. Whatever is at stake, it is not a part of the game of golf but of the meaning that the players bring to the game. Put another way, the pressure is to be found in the games we play while we are playing golf, games made up in the culture and passed along quite efficiently from generation to generation. The reason the Martian can't understand is that he is not a part of the culture.

The importance of this distinction between the game of golf and the games we play while playing it is that while we cannot easily alter golf's rules, we are free to change the rules of our Inner Games. They are all individual or cultural inventions, and we can uninvent them or make up totally new games. If we don't like feeling the pressures that some of these games bring with them, and if we don't like the way they can limit our performance, this just might be worth a try.

"GOLF IS A MICROCOSM OF LIFE"

After a lecture on the Inner Game of Golf as part of a UCLA Extension Continuing Education program, a middle-aged businessman approached me and asked urgently, "Can you give me a particularly strong concentration exercise that can keep me from becoming nervous on the last two holes?"

"Are you sure it's a concentration focus that you need?" I asked, guessing that he might be looking more for a gimmick than for a real solution to his problem.

"Yes," he said. "There's really nothing wrong with my game until I get to the end of the round. I've been playing all my life, and I love the game. I have a four handicap, and I believe in everything you say about the Inner Game, but I never par the seventeenth or eighteenth holes. Sometimes I'll even double- or triple-bogey them."

Over a cup of coffee, Joe began to speak about his game in general. "You know," he said, "I don't really have problems dealing with pressures in my business or home life; I seem to be able to handle anything that comes my way pretty easily. In a funny way, golf is the only part of my life that *really* matters to me. Every time I play, it's like a microcosm of my life. When I tee off on the first hole, I'm born. On the first few holes I'm growing up; on the middle holes I'm in my prime. And then . . ."

"Then at the last holes you approach death. No wonder you have trouble concentrating!"

Joe laughed. "I suppose you're right," he said. "Seriously, though, can you give me something to help maintain an old man's concentration through the eighteenth hole?"

"Well," I ventured, "don't you think that maybe if you reconsidered the meaning you attribute to the game—"

"No!" Joe cut me off abruptly. "Don't take away my game! That's what gives meaning to golf for me. Even if letting go of it were the only way I could score better, I wouldn't do it. I want to win the game *I'm* playing," he said with intensity.

"GOLF HAS MADE ME SOMEONE"

Several years ago, I received a call from a highly ranked player on the LPGA Tour. She had been the winner of many major tournaments in her career and told me she needed only a few more victories to be included in the Hall of Fame. She asked if I would have time to help her with the mental aspects of putting. I agreed to meet her on the putting green at the Riviera Golf Club in Brentwood, California. After we introduced ourselves and chatted informally, she explained that the only time she had difficulty with putting was on the final holes of major championships in which she was in contention: "Then, sometimes my hands tremble a little and I lose the feel of my stroke."

Not seeing how I was going to reproduce these circumstances so we could work on the problem as it occurred, I began asking her a few questions. "What is the goal of golf?" I asked. "To get around in as few strokes as possible," she replied succinctly.

"And why do you play?" I asked.

"That's a good question," she said, and then proceeded to give one of the most elegant answers I had ever heard. "First, I love the environment that the game is played in. Second, I love expressing a God-given talent. And third, I love competition." Her answer was so straightforward and so sincerely uttered that I have never forgotten it. I also didn't see that these motivations were potential sources of pressure.

"So far your hands aren't shaking," I said. "You will probably always be able to enjoy being on a golf course, expressing your talent and enjoying competition. These are not things you are apt to lose. Tell me, are there any other reasons you play?"

She thought for quite a while this time. "Well, yes," she said. "I owe something to golf. Golf has made me who I am today. Somebody. And I have many fans, and they count on me to do well. I don't want to let them down."

"Now how are your putting hands?" I asked.

"Trembling a bit," she admitted. "There is a lot at stake here. And getting into the Hall of Fame means a lot to me."

I was particularly interested in the sentence "Golf has made me who I am today." "If it is golf that made you someone, then golf can make you no one again," I remarked, pointing out the obvious. "Now I can understand why your hands might be shaking when you are in contention for a title. Someday your ability to compete will wane, and then what happens to who you are?"

The most poignant part of the conversation for her was not just how much meaning she had attributed to the Hall of Fame but how much she felt she owed to her fans, who somehow would also lose something if she didn't win. What became clear was that golf was one thing and "what's at stake" was something else. And this something else was not real but made up. When I hear TV golf announcers commenting that "the leader is six under par walking down the sixteenth fairway, and the pressure is really mounting," or something to that effect, I wonder how they know this. They say it as if it were as factual as a statement about the weather. But it's not. It's a matter of belief—a belief that is widely reinforced by everyone who believes in it—but, still, only a belief.

In fact, if you placed an elderly lady who had never played golf on the eighteenth green at Pebble Beach, gave her a putter, and asked her to try to putt the ball into the hole, she would probably experience no jitters at all. She might make the putt or miss the ball entirely. She would not "know" what was at stake. No, the pressure is not in golf. It is in the beliefs and meaning we bring to the game.

KATHY INVENTS HER OWN GAME

When I first met him, Joe worked as a human resources manager for the Coca-Cola Company. He had asked me to design a seminar on coaching skills for the managers in his division. The seminar I designed included a demonstration of the Inner Game as it applied to tennis, and Joe, upon seeing the results, wanted to know if they applied to golf as well. Joe, who was a low-handicap golfer, was also a Ph.D. in psychology and very interested in the learning process and what interferes with it. My work with Coke lasted for a period of six years, and Joe and I became close friends as well as collaborators on the Inner Game as it is applied to corporate management. During this time Leslye, my partner and adviser, also developed a close relationship with Joe, his wife, Kathy, and their two children. It was therefore particularly disturbing when we heard that Kathy had been diagnosed with a cancer that she had a low probability of surviving. There was little Leslye or I could do to bring comfort to this situation. Mostly we watched with the greatest respect and admiration as both of them lived with this fact. Neither giving up hope nor denying the seriousness of the disease, Joe and Kathy lived more fully, with greater intimacy and joy, than ever before. Their attitudes were the same—whatever happens, let's make the most out of our time together.

One of the things Kathy chose to do with her time was play an occasional round of golf with Joe, who was a near scratch golfer. One memorable afternoon Joe asked Leslye and me to join them for a round in Atlanta. Kathy was an advanced beginner, and, weakened and sobered by her condition, she didn't feel obliged to obey all the rules. She played for the pleasure of being in nature, for the camaraderie with her husband, for health and exercise, and for the joy she could find in the game. She swung at the ball with the abandon of a free spirit. If she hit a great shot, it brought a smile to her face. If she hit a terrible shot, it brought a smile to her face. If she got a little tired, she would just pick up her ball and carry it until she felt like hitting again. If she felt like hitting a couple of balls from the same place, then that's what she would do. She certainly was not worried about her score, her handicap, or impressing the people she played with. She seemed to take as much delight in the fortunes and misfortunes of the others in her foursome as she did in her own game.

What struck me is how independent her enjoyment was from her performance. And how easy it was for her to break all the rules of the game, written and unwritten. It was no big deal. She had given herself permission to follow her heart, to do it her way. Deep down we all knew that we were capable of doing the same thing. We could give ourselves the same permission to enjoy the game. It was a privilege to play with her and an inspiration to all who witnessed her.

ALMOST PERFECT LIBERTY

One of the most exhilarating moments in all my golfing experiences occurred one evening on the ninth tee at Perfect Liberty Golf Course. Starting at 4 P.M. after a day of writing, I had been unusually concentrated in my practice of "da-da-da-da" and wasn't aware of my score at all. As I approached the ninth tee, I checked my card and found that I had taken only thirty-two strokes—even par. I had a good chance to score my best nine holes ever. Of course I started thinking how good such a success story would look in the book. Looking down the narrow fairway, a longish downhill hole with OB on either side, I remembered that I had ruined many a good score on this hole before.

Then something clicked inside me; I realized it *really* didn't matter one iota whether I hit the ball OB or not. This may not sound like an event of epic importance, but it was to me. For a moment my heart knew what I grasped so well intellectually: The results in golf were not real. There was something else that was much more real, and how I scored on the course wasn't it. I can't say what made this perception so clear, but I remember an incredible sense of freedom as I stepped up to the ball and, concentrated but without concern, took a full swing. The ball left the club with a crack that seemed louder than any I'd heard before and soared off to the right, heading right toward the OB markers on the side of the hill. I remember thinking that it looked as if it would go OB and at the same time knowing more certainly than my eyes could see that it wouldn't. Part of this was knowing that it really didn't matter if the ball *did* go OB, and part of it was the feel when I'd hit it. But before the ball even began to draw, hit the side of the hill, and roll down onto the fairway, I let out a loud whoop. I felt a sense of victory that didn't come only from seeing a shot land well. Externally, I've hit better shots; internally, it was my best ever. In that moment there was a triumph that went far beyond managing to swing a stick correctly to make a ball go where I wanted it to. I had broken through an illusion. I felt as if I'd been freed from a tyrant. I could see that I had been trying to please the tyrant demanding external results because he rewarded me with praise and pride when I did what he wanted and punished me with feelings of self-contempt and helplessness when I didn't. But with that drive I had told him I didn't want to play his game anymore. He had taken the fun out of games and the art out of work, and he was an obstacle to getting the very results he demanded. His rewards weren't real and offered nothing but the illusion of happiness. I saw all this clearly as I walked to my ball. I felt no stronger, not even more confident, merely a lot less vulnerable.

The sun was setting behind the hills as I sank a four-foot putt for a par. I had scored my first par-36 for nine holes, and I felt no excitement. Yet I felt wonderful. I'm not ashamed to say that my eyes teared in gratitude.

For me, and obviously for many others, the illusion of the game had become so powerful that it had seemed real. Many people don't even like to speak of golf as a game. "You're going to have a hard time convincing the average golfer that his score isn't the most important thing," cautioned my father. "It's the score that makes them feel good." But it's believing that the results are so important that also creates most of the misery I see on the golf course. There *is* more to golf than the score. I've felt it, and I know there must be others who recognize that games are far more than results.

BREAKING THE GOLF ILLUSION

The illusion that the score is the most important thing about playing golf is so strongly engrained in most of our minds that it would be fatuous to think that it might be dispelled simply by some words written in a book. Intellectual assent to this proposition would not be hard to come by, but the real challenge is to break the hold that the score has on us at the visceral level—in our gut. Before we start down this path, let me say that I am not one of those people who thinks you should play golf without keeping score or that children should not be given grades in school. I have no quarrel with the rules of golf, just with the absurd meanings we have attributed to some of them.

First, forgive me for saying the obvious, but *golf is a game*. We all know this to be true when we are in our right senses. But sometimes we seem to forget the meaning of "game." "Game" means a "pretend" reality. "Game" means that we are going to make believe that it is important to hit a little white ball into a little black hole. I suppose if we really did believe it was important to have black holes filled with white balls for some reason, we wouldn't take them out once we had accomplished the task.

Monopoly is also a game. And if I land on Boardwalk with a hotel on it and have to pay $2,000 in Monopoly money, I may express exasperation, complain that I am going bankrupt, and make all kinds of gestures to represent my feelings about my misfortune. But I never for a moment think that my "real-life" bank account has been diminished. I never really think that anything meaningful has been lost when I lose the game. And I can't imagine losing sleep over the fact that my technique in the game needed work. But golf is a different story. We're not playing with Monopoly money anymore. We let our score and our performance be the measure of our self-esteem. We put our self-respect up for grabs—and something in golf is always ready to do the grabbing.

For those of you who know that golf is a game but still find yourselves pushed around by its pressures, as if the game were playing you, I have a strong remedy for you to try. I first concocted this remedy for Tom, a friend of mine who played to a four handicap and called me one day for "an Inner Game tip" just before he was going to play an "important match" with three of his friendly competitors. He should have known better than to ask me for a tip, and he didn't. But I could hear an intensity in his voice that gave away his intent to get a low score and impress his friends. So I advised him to forget about the competition for one round and "hit each ball for maximum enjoyment." He listened. A long pause followed as he thought about my proposition. Then he answered with undiminished intensity, "Okay. I'll try." His voice gave his thoughts away. What he was really saying was "Wow, maybe that will work." And "work," of course, meant "score better."

That brought out the devil in me. I adjusted my prescription slightly. "Yes, hit every ball for maximum enjoyment. But there are two more instructions you must follow. The first is that you may not under any circumstances score less than 86!" This time there was a short silence while he made sure he had heard me correctly, then an audible gulp on the other end of the line as the implications that he would have to shoot ten strokes higher than normal sunk in. "What's the third instruction?" he asked hesitantly. "The third instruction," I answered without the slightest expression of sympathy, "is that you may not tell anyone you are playing with about these instructions."

It was only because Tom was a good friend and a sincere student of the game in all its dimensions that he graciously accepted the challenge. "Okay. I'll do it," he said in a voice that was noticeably more sober.

That evening he called and I was eager to hear his report. "So did you follow the instructions?" I asked, not knowing what to expect. "Yes, I did," he replied succinctly. "And it wasn't exactly easy. Do you want to hear what happened?"

"I'm all ears."

Tom told his story with a mixture of pain and triumph. It was quite a story. The gist of it was that he started off the first nine feeling very relaxed with nothing to lose. By the time he got to the eighth hole, he was one under par and three strokes ahead of his nearest competitor. He then began thinking about his promise to come in with an 86. "I started looking for opportunities," he said. "Like when I was on the green, forty-five feet away from the pin, I said to myself, 'Now here's a good chance to three-putt without anyone expecting anything.' Then I would get up to the ball, barely taking aim, and nail it right into the hole. This must have happened three or four times," he said almost apologetically, "and when I arrived at the sixteenth tee, I was four under par. I couldn't miss a shot even when I tried."

"What did you do?" I asked, almost hoping that he had decided to forget the exercise and finish with his best score in a long time.

"I did what you said," he replied without emotion. "I teed the ball up on number sixteen and decided to see how far out of bounds I could hit it without it being obvious to the others what I was doing. In the last three holes, I was able to drop six shots per hole to par."

"Wow" was all I could manage to say.

"I tell you what," said Tom. "I wouldn't trade the experience for any score I could have made." I wondered what he could possibly mean. "Just to watch the reactions on the part of my friends! It was amazing." He went on to explain that when the second ball went out of bounds, they were joking with him and took some delight in the return of his mortality. Then, after a few more wasted strokes, there began to be some concern expressed. Finally, there was utter dismay. "They were truly suffering. I kept up the act and looked appropriately distraught, but they, they were beside themselves. They stopped kidding me and offered help; then they were simply silent. They ended up totally depressed. And all the while I was just watching how seriously everyone was taking it.

I didn't let on until we were sitting over beers in the clubhouse. I don't know how long it will last, but I don't think any of us will take the game so seriously again for a long time. I don't know what we learned, but I don't think we'll ever get quite so caught up in the delusion of golf again."

RE-CREATING THE GOLF ILLUSION

Games are simulations of reality devised by man to create a "safe" environment in which to hone skills and develop qualities useful in real life. Because the consequences of a game are not real, it is safer to experiment and take risks that, if taken in the "real world," might be too costly.

So on the one hand it is too bad when we take a game and make it more real than life. On the other hand, it is equally in violation of the spirit of any good game not to play it *as if* the consequences were real. What does this mean? It means that to get the most out of the learning experience and enjoyment that games and sports have to offer, you have to pretend the consequences are real. If you don't, there is no reason to exert yourself, to dig deep for an effort of utmost sincerity. There is no reason to go beyond yourself. And that is the point of the game, to provide an environment in which you can safely go beyond previous boundaries. That's what makes it a learning experience. It's also what makes it fun. So the key is to pretend that the game is real while knowing that it is not. You re-create the illusion, but you don't get caught up in it. We knew how to do this as children playing cops and robbers and hide and seek. We had the right idea. Play it as if your life depended on it; then, in an instant, be able to leave it and laugh, no matter the outcome. Could it not be the same with golf? I wondered. Play *as if* each shot of the round were of the greatest consequence, and walk off the course, treating the best or the worst of scores with knowing disregard.

BALANCING THE PEL Δ

In the last chapter, I stated that to attain a true state of relaxed concentration there must be a balance between the three aspects of any human endeavor: performance, experience, and learning. When Self 2 emerges over the ego-centered interferences of Self 1, three things always occur: The person performs at or near his or her best, a natural enjoyment arises from whatever he or she is doing, and the person learns.

Golf is just one of the activities in which we have gotten so caught up in the importance of results that we sacrifice the enjoyment and learning legs of the PEL triangle. Instead of a mutually supporting balance, our triangles are lopsided, with one really long leg in the direction of performance and two stunted ones representing our commitments to the quality of our experience and of our learning. The irony is that in the process of sacrificing all for the sake of performance, we sacrifice performance as well. Why? Because, over the long run, high-level performance requires continuous learning and is sustained by enjoyment. It's nearly impossible to perform consistently if you're on a roller coaster between elation and deflation.

So if you want to escape the "golf illusion," I recommend that you balance your PEL triangle. This means that you can play more than the "performance game" while playing golf. You can play the "learning game" and the "enjoyment game" as well. After all, it takes four to five hours to play a round of golf. Why not go for maximum enjoyment and maximum learning as well? Yes, I know that no one keeps score in these games. But they count nonetheless. You take something home with you when you win these games—something perhaps more valuable than a score. If you are able to set and achieve learning and enjoyment goals in golf, it is very possible that you will find it easier to bring the same balance into your work life and other activities. This is natural— the way it was meant to be. And it works. I truly believe that if we aren't enjoying and aren't learning, something is wrong and we should step back, whether we are on the golf course or in the workplace, and ask ourselves, "What is really important to me?" During twenty years as a business consultant, I have introduced this concept of balance to work teams at many different levels in a number of different kinds of organizations. Never once have I found a team whose members did not think they were overbalanced in their emphasis on performance results compared to learning and enjoyment. Time and again, efforts to rebalance the triangle have resulted spontaneously in improved performance.

A PRO LEARNS AGAIN TO ENJOY THE GAME

Recently, I played with a former golf pro who had virtually given up the game since he had failed to qualify for the pro tour the year before.

Barry was raised on golfing technicalities and knows a hundred dos and don'ts for every swing in every possible situation. Predictably, his swing was mechanical, tight, and now, returning to the game, anything but consistent. He just couldn't seem to keep from hitting thin. He was obviously uptight and becoming more tense as the day wore on and his former game refused to return. He was using the back-hit-stop exercise but admitted, "I really have no idea where the club is at the back of my swing. Nothing works for me, anyway."

"Then when do you say 'back'?" I asked.

"I say it when I think the club should be there, but I don't feel it."

I asked if he wanted to try another exercise.

"I'd try anything at this point," he said.

"All right, why don't you try hitting the next drive as if it really doesn't matter at all how well you hit it or where it goes. Just hit it any way you want to."

Barry proceeded to drive fifty yards farther than anything he'd hit all day, but he didn't look self-satisfied as he watched the shot—only surprised.

"What are you going to do next time?" I asked.

"I'm going to try to do the same thing again and hope for the same results."

"Maybe you'll get them, but the odds are you won't. You weren't going for results when you hit that shot, and if you start thinking to yourself, Hey, this method really works!, it probably won't. You can't use 'not caring about results' to get specific results, can you?"

Barry looked puzzled. "Then what do you suggest?"

"Well, you could change games for a while. Up till now you've been playing the achievement game—hitting the ball 'right' to get the best results."

"Until recently that's the only game I'd ever played—especially on the golf course."

"There is another game, and it's not the only one to play, but it's a good one to try when you're frustrated. It's called 'fun-o,' and there are only two rules. One is that you hit each shot in whatever way is the most fun for you in that particular situation. The second rule is that you relinquish entirely any concern for results. You still play golf—that is, you go for the hole with the least number of swings—but your goal is the enjoyment you get out of each stroke, regardless of the outcome."

We all played "fun-o" for the rest of the round, and soon Barry was acting like a kid out of school. When I asked him what he was doing differently, he said, "I'm just doing the opposite of everything I've been told throughout my golfing career. It feels terrific. I'm using my right hand instead of my left and slapping at the ball as if it were a hockey puck."

Barry enjoyed his rebellion for a couple of holes, whacking wildly at the ball. Then he grew tired of this and started hitting it the way he'd always wanted to. By the end of the round he was a different person.

After the game Barry told me, "I really dreaded playing again; I was sure it would take me a long time to reach my former standard. Frankly, even as a kid I got into this game as a way to achieve success. I was always afraid of failure, so I practiced all the current techniques for hours every day. In twenty years of golf, I don't think I ever really played for fun before."

PLAYING YOUR OWN GAME

In the final analysis of the game of golf, we can be sure of only a few things: the hitting of a ball with a club over a course and into the hole. The goal of the game is crystal-clear: Get the ball in the hole. Looking at the simplicity of the physical game of golf, I realize I succeed only eighteen times a round. In that, I am equal to everyone who plays the full course. We vary only in how many times we *fail* to get the ball in the hole.

The second thing we can be sure of is that the meaning golfers attribute to this physical game is a matter of the golfer's choice. There is no inherent meaning in the game. The rules of the game give it no meaning. People give it meaning. When each of us first learned the game, we could not help but pick up on the meaning attributed to it by the person who taught us. And where did that person find meaning? You can choose to ignore the question of meaning, but it won't go away, and it will affect every shot you take and most of what you think and feel while playing the game. This is where the mental side of golf exists—in the agreed-upon meaning of the game.

But did you ever consciously agree with anyone? Did you ever say to yourself, "Yes, golf is a game where I have to prove something about myself . . . to my dad, my mom, my friends, or myself," or "Now I'm going to spend four hours to see if I can live up to my own expectations of myself," or "Golf is my chance to show that I am better than someone else"? Did you say, "If I can't learn to break eighty before I die, then my life is not worth living"? And did you ever wonder why you care so much about whether you're hitting the ball right, according to the current definition of "right"? Fragments of most of these games are in all of us, and they continue in varying degrees whether we like it or not. I'm not saying that these additional meanings are good or bad. But have you ever actually made a conscious choice about the meanings you are accepting?

There can be great benefit in making the choice consciously. There is something to be gained in stepping back each time you play and asking yourself, "Why am I playing?" There is an old saying, "If you don't stand for something, you will fall for anything." In the culture of golf, there are many things to "fall for." Many of them have the capability to drive people crazy or, if not crazy, at least closer to misery than enjoyment.

THE FUNDAMENTAL OF GOLF: WHY DO YOU PLAY?

The foundation of mastering the mental side of golf is to take a stand on why you are playing. Once you decide that you are going to play for the fun of it, or for the friendship, or whatever, the other Inner games will come knocking at your door, the games you and the rest of us have been playing unconsciously. You will at least have a choice. In the choice to play your own game while playing golf you accomplish something more important than your score. You accomplish a measure of human dignity. If you feel pressure, you know that it is the pressure you created. If you feel joy, you know why. And if you can play your own game on the golf course, and allow others to play theirs, then it becomes more possible to do the same in the rest of your life.

TWELVE

Beyond Formula to Feeling

RECENTLY, THE PUBLISHER OF THE 1946 GOLF CLASSIC *LIVE HANDS* BY E. M. Prain asked me to write the foreword for the book's republication. Noting that the original foreword was written by Bernard Darwin, a renowned golf writer and former captain of the Royal and Ancient Golf Club of St. Andrews, I wondered, "Why me?" and barely took the invitation seriously. It was only because of Leslye's advice that I even opened Prain's book to read a few pages. There were five short chapters. The first one, entitled "Searching for Formula," showed me that the golfer's compulsion to look for a simple "secret" of the game was not a new one at all and that I was not the first writer to express the irony of being caught up in the complexity of mechanics while looking for the single cure-all technique.

In his elegant English style, Prain describes the endless search for a formula that will unlock our dreams of being the golfer we think we could be:

> The trouble with the rest of us (all but the best players) is that we are always groping. We cannot grow as we should like because we have not roots. We are the earth's most changeable disciples, ever ready to try some new tag in the hope it will prove our salvation, equally ready to desert it for another if it does not give us what we want.

A scratch golfer himself, Prain describes the futility of his own search: "I do not know how many times I felt I had found Excalibur. One day my salvation lay in the movement of my hip, the next in the way my shoulder turned, and again I felt I had found it when I opened my somewhat closed stance."

Prain's search for formula takes on religious overtones: "I know the hopeless feeling which assails the changeable disciple. How fleeting are the moments of success and how often the new half-built castle tumbles about him in ruins." Many of Prain's golfing friends, caught up in the search for formula, would set out to enjoy the game, but soon after they teed off found themselves playing "as if under a cloud." As he explains, "In the course of one swing they were trying to do six or seven different things. But all that they achieved was an exaggeration of certain actions of that swing which deprived the whole of rhythm."

Had I not known when these words were published, I'd have thought they were written by someone who had read *The Inner Game of Golf*. It seems as if our appetite for formulas in golf and in life is as unending as the cycle of hope and disappointment that these illusory mental constructs engender. We want encapsulated wisdom. We want to read the formula in a book and apply it to our lives. We don't particularly want to think about the formula; it's enough to know that someone who calls himself an expert has thought about it. Our job is simply to follow it. A formula is a mental construct that tells you what to do in a given situation. In the face of uncertainty, the formula gives direction and certainty. If golf really worked that way, we would all be scratch golfers by now. And if life worked that way, we would all have happy lives.

My passion to transcend formulas does not come from a life free of them. Precisely the opposite—I was brought up with formulas for everything. Being Irish, I also had a bit of the rebel in me, so I turned against traditional formulas only to come up with untraditional (but equally problematic) formulas. Finally, I've arrived at the point where I'm ready to give up on formulas once and for all, except as they apply to routine matters like filing a tax return or installing a piece of software. As noted in Chapter 6, "Discovering Technique," I still believe that it is important to understand the technology of anything that you want to do excellently. But understanding and following formulas are two different things. I don't hit the ball with my understanding. My understanding contributes, in the background, to my execution. But in the execution itself, I am either following formula or following feeling. I am either coming from the mind or from the gut.

I have chosen feeling over formula. I want to play from feeling, write from feeling, live from feeling. Why? Because it feels *good*, and it works. At least that's my experience. By feelings I obviously do not mean the fears and doubts that Self 1 generates. These are what create the uncertainty that has me looking for formulas in the first place. So I am not talking about Self 1 emotions, positive or negative, as the source of play. Rather, I am talking about the feelings generated naturally by Self 2. You can see them in young children all the time—not learned feelings but self-generated impulses, desires, instincts, and responses that are the most human part of human beings. For me, the whole point of quieting Self 1 thinking is not to hit the golf ball better but to access more easily the natural feelings of Self 2. All of us have these feelings, and all of us enjoy them. But most of us have been conditioned out of our belief in their value and, especially, in their practicality.

I want to enjoy and follow the feelings that come from the

natural wellspring of my life. When it comes to golfing, this means my priority is to find the feeling and swing from it. As I stand before the ball, I am not thinking about how I should swing, nor am I trying to remember how the swing should feel. No. The first and most important thing I have to do is reach for the urge to hit the ball. This may sound strange. "I know I want to hit the ball, and I know where I want to hit the ball, and sometimes I even know how I want to hit the ball," I can imagine the reader saying. Yes, so do I. But I don't always *feel* it. There's a big difference between having an idea about where or how to hit the ball and responding naturally to the desire to do it.

It's like the difference between thinking that it's time for dinner and feeling hungry. Either will get you to the dinner table and through the act of eating a meal. But is there not a significant distinction between the meal eaten in conscious response to hunger, the water drunk in conscious response to thirst, and following the formula "It's time to eat and time to drink"? For some it doesn't matter. For much of my life, it didn't matter to me. With the attitude that I wanted to accomplish everything quickly, I often tried to read a newspaper, watch TV, and get something else done all at the same time. It was even okay to eat in the car while driving to an appointment. But when I eat from the feeling of hunger, the meal itself becomes important because there is a unique enjoyment in feeling and fulfilling the hunger.

In the same way, there is a unique enjoyment in hitting the ball exactly the way you want to. Not the way you think you want to but the way you feel you want to in the very moment you're hitting the ball. I don't have to name this feeling—in fact, it's better if I don't. Naming the feeling might turn it into a formula. I just have to go with the feeling, whatever it's called, and let it express itself in my shot. With each shot I execute this way, I become more myself. I become more human. There is a sweet satisfaction to each shot, from drive to hole. Only when I am willing to take this seeming risk of putting feeling first do I know that I am playing golf and not being played by golf. I become more important than the game. And that is the way it should be. I do not want to be a pawn in my own game. I want to be the player. When finding the feeling and expressing it take priority over everything else, the results are usually a happy surprise. On those occasions when the ball goes off course, I usually realize in a flash that I was also off course. I left the purity of the feeling and added in a little strength that wasn't felt, a little formulation to compensate for some doubt or fear generated by Self 1. Good. I thank the shot for showing me, for holding up the mirror. And I draw from the shot renewed motivation to reach for the purest urge the next time I swing.

Does Self 1 go away? No. Though it may offer less in the way of mechanical formulas, Self 1's next ploy is something like "Now, that was the right feeling on the last shot. You should try to feel that way the next time, too." Of course, I fall for that a few times because the Self 2 shot did feel great, so it's easy to believe that I should feel like that all the time. But my "feeling part" doesn't work that way, does it? If I like a certain feeling, Self 1 wants to reduce it to a formula—a repeatable sameness. I liked it, so I want to capture it, make it be there on demand. Press the button and say, "Now feel just like you did when . . ." In doing this, I am actually leaving the domain of feeling and reentering the domain of thought, the part that tries to reproduce mentally what it has experienced nonmentally.

The moment I try to reproduce a feeling, I take a step away from where natural feelings originate. I need to learn a little old-fashioned humility. I need to be willing to feel whatever is there at the moment, not just what I expected to find. The feeling I experience on the first tee may be quite different from the one I feel on the eighteenth, so why try to hit the eighteenth-tee shot with the first-tee feeling? Standing over the putt on the thirteenth green, I might not be able to retrieve the same sensation that sank the forty-foot putt on the twelfth green. I can't really control the spontaneous nor should I want to. But I can learn to reach for that place where the spontaneous occurs. I can sit at its door and listen to the music that plays there, to the drum that beats, and I can acknowledge the originality and sweetness of the song. And I can express that song in my swing as well as in my walk from one shot to the next.

This for me becomes true play. This is the way I can enjoy golf. And this is the only thing I have found to be more compelling than formulas. Thoughts about the golf swing still enter my mind, and that's okay. They have something to teach me, but nothing important. The minute I begin to think they have something important to tell me, the minute the result of the shot becomes more important than my connection with what I have called my Self 2, I have set myself up to be trapped once again, to be played by the game instead of being the player of the game. Initially, I was surprised to discover that even though I was putting feeling first, I still wanted to compete. I like competition and the challenge it provides. Competition serves a valid purpose and heightens my enjoyment. But there's true competition and false competition. False competition is the striving of Self 1 based on the (supposed) need to prove something to someone. As false competition pressures fall away, I find within myself the true competition—the striving for excellence. I was interested recently to learn that the word "competition" is from the Greek word meaning "to seek together." Two opponents seek excellence together while competing.

Maybe some readers would like me to name more specifically the feelings I am referring to. I leave them unnamed so that Self 1 can't so easily judge or manipulate them. I seek to protect their integrity by keeping them out of the domain of language. Then I am freer to hit each ball with the genuine enthusiasm of the moment and not from a particular feeling Self 1 tells me I *should* have. I call the feeling I hit the ball from "felt desire."

It is satisfying in itself when that urge is expressed accurately, and the satisfaction is independent of where the ball goes. It is this enthusiasm itself that I value the most. It is of life, and it is living. Here words begin to fail. My choice to play this way is part of my choice to live my life with utmost sincerity and with the enthusiasm that I recognize was a natural part of my early life—and the life of every child. While pitching and chipping one day, I was thinking about Prain's title, *Live Hands*. My hands did feel more alive, and I was much more aware of their subtle and very complex movements. But I had no desire to interfere or manipulate. The more connected I am with this living feeling, the more alive I feel—my hands, my legs, and every other part of my body. I noticed my body learning technique without needing to analyze what it was learning. Things work that way only when feeling is given top priority.

I feel an enthusiasm in writing about this, but not that of a salesperson or an evangelist. It is something I have to offer, something that I have discovered that seems of utmost importance to me. It is not important to me that it be important to you, but I wouldn't want to keep it a secret either. Take from it what you will. If what I am saying is valid for any reader, it is because the reader already knew it to be true before reading these words and the words are just a reminder. That is what they are to me. I need this reminder because so much of what I run into every day is the result of formulaic thinking and behavior. We are trained to believe that formulas will take us where we want to go, in golf, in work, in relationships, in life. So attached do we become to our particular formulas that we will fight bloody, cruel fights to defend them and to promote their global acceptance.

A DIFFERENT KIND OF ENJOYMENT

I spent many long hours rewriting Chapter 9, trying to bring together my understanding about the impact of expectations on the golfer and his golf—not an easy subject, as you might have gathered. By five in the afternoon my brain was tired and my body restless for movement. Too much writing, not enough doing, I said to myself. Off to the nearest golf course I went in the hope of getting in at least nine holes before dark.

I had just been given a set of irons by the Southern Cal representative of Spalding, and I was eager to try them out. The West-lake golf course was a relatively short but challenging 18-hole course with only two par-five holes. Par was 67. I decided to play with only a five iron, a seven, a pitching wedge, and a putter. This would give me a good chance to try my new irons and allow me to move quickly. It would also ease any indecision about club selection! I started on the tenth hole and hit two five irons to the green and left my twenty-foot putt an inch short. The next hole was 420 yards, and two five irons left me ninety yards short of the green. But my first shot with my new pitching wedge landed a foot from the pin for an easy tap-in for par. "My clubs haven't learned how to miss yet," I said to myself. By the time I met up with other players on the fifteenth hole, I had barely missed three birdie putts and was even par. The two foursomes in front of me looked slow, and I didn't feel like waiting. So I doubled back and played holes twelve, thirteen, and fourteen again. Three more pars. By now I could hear Self 1's voice quite distinctly calculating having my best round and trying to remember what I had just written about how to keep a streak going. I could also hear it rehearsing how it would brag to certain people about my "accomplishment." But there was also another voice present: "What do you really want to accomplish?" it asked. Fifteen was a 520-yard par five, and I hit my first off-line five iron of the day. It wasn't really bad, but it came to rest in the root system of a tree on the left edge of the fairway. I hit another ball, this time as well as any I'd hit all day. I played both balls in. I had to take a stroke penalty for an unplayable lie on my first. I ended up with a bogey on my first and a par on my second. One over. "What do I want to accomplish?" I asked again. My answer surprised me. "Really nothing at all. I just want to enjoy the experience."

What was the experience? I want to tell you about it because it taught me something important. The experience I was having while playing this round was not exalted. I was not on a high. I might even have said I wasn't experiencing much at all. I would just stand up to the ball and hit it. I didn't think about it or spend time lining up my shots or envisioning where I wanted the ball to go. I wasn't doing any Outer Game technique or any Inner Game technique either. I was just hitting the ball and watching it fly straight. There was not even the hint of wanting to say "YES" with the affirmative gesture of having conquered something. The whole thing was no big deal at all. The closest word to describe the feeling was "contentment."

I remembered having a similar feeling years ago when I was playing in the zone in tennis. But at that time in my life I remember feeling something was missing. I was missing the feeling of "I did it." I missed the feeling of accomplishment that comes from trying something and having it work. But on the course at Westlake, I didn't miss the feeling of conquering, the feeling of triumph. I liked the simpler, less dramatic feeling that was almost unnoticeable but nonetheless there. It felt constant and true, not something that would crumble easily. So my only choice was just to keep on appreciating that simple state as long as it lasted—not because it was producing par golf but because it felt comfortable. Self 1 made its effort, and I made my effort. I ended with pars on the last two holes, and the simple feeling just continued.

After another day of hard work at the computer, the urge to play overtook me again around 5:30. It had rained most of the day, so the Westlake course was almost empty. This time I wanted to try out my three iron. So I took it, my seven, my wedge, and my putter, and, playing quickly, I was able to complete a full eighteen holes. I played the last two in the dark, chipping in on the eighteenth for a birdie. My game was not quite as consistent as the day before. I bogeyed seven of the eighteen holes but birdied three, giving me a 71 for the first time ever. What was nice was that there were only momentary interruptions of the simplicity, each one reminding me that I had to keep alert to Self 1's effort to enter and make things more complicated. At the end of the day, I felt I had learned how to play golf. Definitely not the final word on how to swing the club or on shot-making, but a very satisfying reason to play the game for the rest of my life.

THE FUTURE OF THE GAME

Though the rules of golf are relatively static, the use and meaning of the game vary with each individual and are affected by changes in the culture. I believe that in the next few years there will continue to be significant changes in the way golf is taught and played.

Already golf instructors I have spoken with admit that there is relatively little more to be learned about the mechanics of the golf swing; what teaching professionals need most is to learn how to help their students put into practice what is already understood about the swing. The focus is shifting slowly to the art of learning as opposed to debating the content of what should be taught. There is a growing admission on the part of even the master technicians of golf that breaking down the elements of the golf swing and putting them back together again is a difficult and generally ineffectual way to master the game. There is also a growing recognition of the role of tension and other mental obstacles in golf. In short, we are seeing a shift of attention from the physics of the game to its psychology.

This shift from the outer to the inner in golf reflects a general rebalancing occurring in the culture at large. There is a growing realization that physical control over our external environment is limited. Without an ability to solve problems on the mental level, technology cannot get to the root of the causes of war, crime, famine, or our general dissatisfactions. It seems clear that the breakthroughs of the next age must come in the form of advances in our individual and collective abilities to tap existing human capabilities and to overcome the negative internal forces that interfere with their expression.

As our culture undergoes a necessary rebalancing of its outer and inner games, sports in general can find a new raison d'être. Potentially, sports have a greater value to a culture than as a mere outlet for releasing tensions or providing heroes. They can become the laboratory in which research and experimentation about human motivation, performance, and self-interference take place. Ancient cultures used sports to benefit and strengthen themselves. The Inner Game is hardly a new one, but we are pretty rusty at playing it. Sports can be a safe arena in which we relearn its importance and increase our skill at it. Sports can be both the showcase and the laboratory in which the culture can learn increasing self-control.

Golf has a particular role to play in this scenario. Admittedly, its players are not known for their openness to change; indeed, it is said that it is a conservative game played by conservatives. But it is, in fact, a game popular with a broad cross section of the population and one that demands self-control. A businessman who learns how to cope with stress on the golf course can save his management a lot of suffering and his business a lot of money. Likewise, a student can grasp the elements of learning and self-confidence on the golf course in such a way that it has a permanent effect on his life. Everyone should learn to respect that thin line existing between what is real and what is a game. As a culture, we would then come to understand the true value of competition. In short, the Inner Game aspects of the game of golf described in this book are exactly those issues that the culture at large needs to grapple with. If golf allows itself to become a medium for such experimentation, it would more than justify its existence.

This shift of attention will have a great significance for golf instructors. It will no longer be sufficient for a teacher of the game to be a good player and to know the mechanics of the swing. Forward-looking teachers will attempt to develop an understanding of the learning process. If they do, they will be more valued than in their old roles as swing mechanics, for they will be teaching such valuable inner skills as concentration, self-trust, will, and awareness. Such teachers will be recognized as making valuable contributions to the quality of a student's entire life.

But how many better ways are there to engage in the universal and ageless contest against oneself? If the game is played as Bobby Jones claimed to play it—as a conquest of oneself—it becomes truly recreational. It is a break from the routine and patterns of daily life that can truly enrich our existence. What players learn about themselves on the course can be transferred to every aspect of their lives and thus benefit the culture of which golf is only a small part.

Such a perspective would give the game a significance that would make it worth all the time and effort we enjoy putting into it. Although I don't expect a new way of looking at the game to take place overnight, it could happen quickly in this current era. But whether it comes gradually or as a revolution, it *will* take place, and golf will become more fun, more natural, and more in tune with the way games are meant to be played—in dynamic balance between the inner and the outer.

Penguin Books
The Levant Trilogy

Olivia Manning was born in Portsmouth, Hampshire, spent much of her youth in Ireland and, as she put it, had 'the usual Anglo-Irish sense of belonging nowhere'. She married just before the war and went abroad with her husband, R. D. Smith, a British Council lecturer in Bucharest. Her experiences there formed the basis of the work which makes up *The Balkan Trilogy*. As the Germans approached Athens, she and her husband evacuated to Egypt and ended up in Jerusalem, where her husband was put in charge of the Palestine Broadcasting Station. They returned to London in 1946 and lived there until her death in 1980.

Olivia Manning's publications include the novels *Artist Among the Missing* (1949); *School for Love* (1951); *A Different Face* (1953); *The Doves of Venus* (1955); *The Balkan Trilogy* (1960–65), which consists of *The Great Fortune* (1960), *The Spoilt City* (1962) and *Friends and Heroes* (1965); *The Play Room* (1969); *The Rain Forest* (1974); and *The Levant Trilogy* (1977–80), which consists of *The Danger Tree* (1977, *Yorkshire Post* Book of the Year award), *The Battle Lost and Won* (1978) and *The Sum of Things* (1980). She also wrote two volumes of short stories, *Growing Up* (1948) and *A Romantic Hero* (1967). She spent a year on the film script of *The Play Room* and contributed to many periodicals, including the *Spectator*, *Punch*, *Vogue* and the *Sunday Times*. Olivia Manning was awarded the CBE in 1976.

The Balkan Trilogy and *The Levant Trilogy* form a single narrative entitled *Fortunes of War* which Anthony Burgess described in the Sunday Times as 'the finest fictional record of the war produced by a British writer. Her gallery of personages is huge, her scene painting superb, her pathos controlled, her humour quiet and civilized. Guy Pringle certainly is one of the major characters in modern fiction.'

Olivia Manning

The Levant Trilogy

Volume One: The Danger Tree
Volume Two: The Battle Lost and Won
Volume Three: The Sum of Things

Penguin Books

Penguin Books Ltd, Harmondsworth, Middlesex, England
Penguin Books, 40 West 23rd Street, New York, New York 10010, U.S.A.
Penguin Books Australia Ltd, Ringwood, Victoria, Australia
Penguin Books Canada Ltd, 2801 John Street, Markham, Ontario, Canada L3R 1B4
Penguin Books (N.Z.) Ltd, 182–190 Wairau Road, Auckland 10, New Zealand

The Danger Tree first published in Great Britain by Weidenfeld & Nicolson 1977
First published in the United States of America by Atheneum Publishers 1977
Published in Penguin Books 1979
Copyright © the Estate of Olivia Manning, 1977

The Battle Lost and Won first published in Great Britain by Weidenfeld & Nicolson 1978
First published in the United States of America by Atheneum Publishers 1979
Published in Penguin Books 1980
Copyright © the Estate of Olivia Manning, 1978

The Sum of Things first published in Great Britain by Weidenfeld & Nicolson 1980
First published in the United States of America by Atheneum Publishers 1981
Published in Penguin Books 1982
Copyright © the Estate of Olivia Manning, 1982

This collection published as *The Levant Trilogy* 1982
Reprinted 1983 (twice)
Copyright © the Estate of Olivia Manning, 1982
All rights reserved

Printed and bound in Great Britain by
Richard Clay (The Chaucer Press) Ltd,
Bungay, Suffolk

Except in the United States of America, this book is sold subject
to the condition that it shall not, by way of trade or otherwise, be lent,
re-sold, hired out, or otherwise circulated without the
publisher's prior consent in any form of binding or cover other than
that in which it is published and without a similar condition
including this condition being imposed on the subsequent purchaser

Contents

1. The Danger Tree
2. The Battle Lost and Won
3. The Sum of Things

VOLUME ONE

The Danger Tree

To Reggie, with love

One

Simon Boulderstone, aged twenty, came to Egypt with the draft. For nearly two months, as the convoy slid down one side of Africa and up the other, he had been crowded about by other men. When he reached Cairo, he was alone.

He had two friends on board, Trench and Codley, who had been his family, his intimates, the people nearest to him in the world. The sense of belonging together had been deeper than love – then, at Suez, a terrible thing happened. He lost them.

As the three were disembarking, Simon had been ordered out of the lighter and put in charge of a detachment of men whose officer had gone down with jaundice. He shouted to Trench and Codley 'See you on shore' before joining the men who had been holed up in the corridor all morning. They were weary of waiting, and they had to wait longer. It was mid-afternoon before Simon reached the quay and discovered that his friends had gone. No one could tell him where. There was an emergency on and each truck, as it arrived, filled up with waiting men and went. Simon was not only alone, he had missed his transport. It seemed, too, that he had reached the most desolate and arid place on earth.

The sergeant to whom he spoke said Trench and Codley might have gone to Infantry Base Depot, or they might have gone to one of several transit camps that were in and around Cairo.

'Wherever they are,' said the sergeant, 'they won't be there long. Things are in a bloody mess. Just heard Tobruk's fallen. What bloody next, I'd like to know?' He gave Simon a travel warrant and directed him to take the afternoon train to Cairo and report to Abbasia barracks.

'Anyone in particular?': Simon hoped for the reassurance of a name.

'See Major Perry in Movement Control. I'll phone through to him. Good bloke, he'll fit you up.'

Simon, waiting at the station, was numb with solitude. Everything about him – the small houses packed between dry, enclosing hills, the sparking glare of the oil tanks, the white dockside buildings that reflected the sky's heat, the dusty earth on which he stood – increased his anguish of loss. He had never before seen such a wilderness or known such loneliness.

The train came in, a string of old carriages foetid with heat and human smells, and set out slowly through the Suez slums and came into desert. Simon saw a lake, astonishingly blue, with sand all around it, then there was only sand. The sand glowed when the sun set. The glow died, the darkness came down – not that it mattered for there was nothing to see. Simon tried to open the window but the two Egyptians in the carriage said 'No.' One, holding up his finger in an admonitory way, explained that sand would be blown into the carriage. As the journey dragged on, the heat grew and Simon felt that he was melting inside his clothes. He longed to leave the train, imagining the night air would be cool but when he reached Cairo, the outer air was as hot and heavy as the air of the carriage.

Waiting for a taxi, he breathed in the spicy, flaccid atmosphere of the city and felt the strangeness of things about him. The street lamps were painted blue. Figures in white robes, like night-shirts, flickered through the blue gloom, slippers flapping from heels. The women, bundled in black, were scarcely visible. The district looked seedy and was probably dirty but the barracks, he thought, would be familiar territory. He hoped Major Perry would be there to welcome him. When he was dropped at the main gate, he found he was just another young officer, another problem, adding to the overcrowded confusion of the place. He pronounced the name of Perry, to which he had clung as to a lifeline, and found there was no magic in it. He was told by the clerk in the Transit Office that the reporting point for his unit was Helwan. The barracks had been turned into a transit camp. And where was Major Perry? The clerk did not know. The major could be at Helwan or he could be at Heliopolis.

'All sixes and sevens these days,' the clerk pushed his hand-kerchief impatiently across his sweaty brow and Simon appealed to him:

'But can you put me up?'

'I'll try,' the man gave Simon a second glance and as an afterthought added 'Sir.'

Simon expected no better treatment. He had been picked for an early commission on the strength of his OTC training but to the clerk, a corporal in his late thirties, he must have looked like a schoolboy.

He waited in the half-lit hall while men walked about him, knowing their way around. Fifteen minutes passed before a squaddie came to carry his kit to a room on an upper floor. The stark gloom of the passages reminded him of school and soon, he thought, he, too, would know his way around.

He was led to a room, furnished with a hanging-cupboard and three camp-beds, at the top of the barracks where the ceilings were low. A single lightbulb, grimy and yellow, hung over naked floorboards.

The squaddie said, 'If you're lucky, sir, you'll get it to yourself.'

'Not bad,' said Simon, still with school in his mind, 'but it smells strange.' The smell was like some essential oil, almost a scent, but too strong to be pleasant, carrying in it a harsh-ness that suggested evil and death.

As Simon sniffed inquiringly, the squaddie said, 'They've been fumigating.'

'Really? Why?'

'Look, sir,' the man went over to a wall that may have been white in the days of Cromer and Wolseley but was now cracked and grimy grey: 'Take a shufti.'

Simon bent towards one of the cracks and saw, packed inside, objects the size of lentils, blood dark and motionless.

'What on earth are they?'

'Bugs. Live for centuries, they say. Can't get rid of them. You ought to see the new chaps when they come here – they swell up, red, like jellies. And itch, cor! But you'll be all right. This stuff keeps them down for a couple of months.'

Feeling the fumigant rough in his throat, Simon went to the

open window and looked out on a parade ground surrounded by the flat-fronted barracks building. A long wooden balcony, an outlet of the lower floor, ran immediately under the window and he could see blankets folded at intervals, indicating an overflow from the dormitories.

'There seems to be a lot of chaps on leave here.'

'Not exactly leave, sir. Ex-leave you might call it. They're stuck, waiting for transport 'cos trains've stopped running into the blue.'

'Why's that?'

'It's the emergency. The trains have wog drivers a'corse, and they're scared. The war's come too close and they think they'll run into the fighting and get shot at. If you're wanting a bite, I'd get down if I were you, sir. The mess shuts about nine.'

Simon was lucky – he had the room to himself, but when he woke in the middle of the night, he would have been glad of company. The murderous smell of the place reminded him why he had been brought here. He had fought mock battles on Salisbury Plain but now the battles would be real. The shot would be real and the bullets could kill a man. The desert itself was not so strange to him because his brother had been out here for nearly eighteen months. Hugo had sent home letters about brew-ups, desert chicken, bully splodge and flies. He was very funny about it all. He said as soon as you got your food you slapped a tin lid over it but even so you found that inside there were more flies than food.

Hugo had survived well enough and Simon did not expect to die. Yet men were dying out there; young men like Simon and Hugo.

Rising at daybreak, Simon was fortunate enough to find an army truck going to Helwan. While the civilian world was still asleep, he was driven out of Cairo into the desert again. In this country it seemed the desert was everywhere. The sun lifted itself above the houses and lit the streets with a pale, dry light. The truck driver, dropping him at the camp outside Helwan, told him if he did not get a lift back, he could take the train. He made his way among huts, over trampled, dirty sand, till he came on a large brown building like a misshapen mud pie.

Here, in a small room, in front of a small table, he found Major Perry.

The major, with fat bronzed face and white moustache, was over-alert in manner and looked as though he belonged to an earlier war. Half rising, thrusting out his hand, he said at the top of his voice, 'Got notice of your posting – got it here somewhere. The corporal'll dig it out,' and then began apologizing for being old and overweight. 'Wish I had your chance. I'd like to be out there givin' the hun a bloody nose. You'll have to do it for me. Poor show – this latest! You heard? Tobruk's fallen.'

'Yes, sir. I suppose things are pretty bad, sir?'

'You're damn right, they're pretty bad. We've lost the whole garrison and we'll be lucky if we don't lose the whole Middle East. Still, we're not beaten yet. It's up to you, Boulderstone. Fresh blood and fresh equipment: that's what we need. Give us both and we'll manage somehow. They've got Hitler's intuition and we've got Churchill's interference: 'bout evens things up, wouldn't you say?'

Simon said nothing. He was baffled by this equating Hitler and Churchill and he could only suppose the major was slightly mad. To divert him, Simon said he was out of touch. He had spent the last two months on the *Queen Mary*, dependent for news on the radio bulletins. The last one he remembered spoke of 'strategic withdrawals'.

'Strategic, my arse!' Perry snuffled so forcefully that he gave out a strong smell of drink, so Simon realized he was not mad but drunk. He had probably gone to bed drunk and got out of bed still drunk, and the drinking was carrying him through a state of near panic. 'This isn't the old Sollum Handicap, y'know – it's a bloody rout. Bloody jerries coming at us in our own bloody tanks. The stuff those bastards have picked up would have driven Rommel back to Benghazi.'

'I heard there was a shortage of transport, sir.'

'Shortage of transport! There's a shortage of every bloody thing the army's ever heard of. You name it: we haven't got it. Except men. Plenty of men but no equipment for them. No rifles, no tanks, no field guns. And the men are exhausted. Damn well had it.' Perry paused, blew out his lips so Simon

13

saw the nicotine brown under-edge of his moustache, and deciding he had said too much, his tone dropped. 'New blood, that's what we want. Too many chaps have been out there too long, fart-arsing this way and that, till they don't know if they're back or tits forward. Now you, Boulderstone – in ordinary times, you'd have a month in camp, but these aren't ordinary times. We need you out there. We've been refitting a lot of old trucks and there'll be a convoy starting soon. I think we can get you out there at the double.'

'That's what I'd like, sir.'

'Keen, eh? Good man. Might get you away by Tuesday.'

'Till then, sir – am I on leave?'

'On leave? Why not. Forty-eight hours. Give me a tinkle mid-way and I'll let you know what's doing. You can draw your pay and have a couple of nights on the town. How's that, eh? Know anyone in Cairo?'

'My brother has a friend, a girl. I could look her up.' Simon had not thought of looking up Hugo's girl but now, thinking of her, he blushed and grinned in spite of himself.

'Ah-ha!' Perry's wet, blue eyes that had been sliding about in wet sockets, now fixed themselves on Simon's young, pink face. 'Good show. And if you get a bit of ... I mean, if anyone offers you a shake-down, that's all right so long as you ring Transit and release your billet. I know you chaps think Cairo's the flesh-pots, but two things are in short supply here. One of 'em's *lebensraum*.'

'What's the other, sir?'

'Ah-ha, ah-ha, ah-ha!' Perry snuffled wildly then held his hand out again. 'You don't have to worry. Not with your looks, you don't. So good luck. Enjoy yourself while you've still got the chance.'

Hugo's girl lived in Garden City. Simon, leaving the shabby purlieus of the Cairo station for the shabby splendours of the city's centre, thought he could find it for himself. He would probably see it written up somewhere.

The main streets impressed and unnerved him. The pavements were crowded and cars hooted for any reason, or no reason at all. Here the Egyptians wore European dress, the women as well as the men, but among them there were those other Egyptians whom he had seen flapping their slippers round the station. The men came here to sell, the women to beg. And everywhere there were British troops, the marooned men who had nothing to do but wander the streets, shuffling and grumbling, with no money and nowhere to go.

It was Sunday. Some of the shops were open but there was a lethargic, holiday atmosphere about the streets. Simon had once gone on a school trip to Paris and here, it seemed to him, was another Paris, not quite real, put up too quickly and left to moulder and gather dust. There was nothing that looked like a garden or a Garden City. He would have to ask his way but was nervous of approaching people who might not know his language, and he was shy of the soldiers who never knew more than they needed to know. He looked out for an officer to whom he could speak with ease. He saw officers of every allied country – Poles, Free French, Indians, New Zealanders – but the sort he wanted, English, young, of low rank like himself, did not come along.

Something about Simon, his air of newness, perhaps, or his uncertainty, attracted the beggars and street vendors. The women plucked at him, holding up babies whose eyes were ringed in black that he mistook for make-up, but, looking closer, he saw were flies. Swagger sticks, fly-whisks, fountain pens were thrust at him as if he had a duty to buy. 'Stolen,' whispered the fountain-pen man, *Stolen!* The sherbet seller clashed his brass discs in Simon's face. Boys with nothing to sell shouted at him, 'Hey, George, you want, I get. I get all.'

At first he was amused by these attentions then, as the sun rose in the sky, he grew weary of them. A hot and gritty wind blew through the streets and sweat ran down his face. A man pushed a basket of apricots under his nose and he dodged away, shaking his head. Abandoning Simon, the man swept the basket round and pressed it upon a squaddie who spat on it. It was a pretty gilt basket full of amber fruit and the seller was proud of it. He persisted, 'Abbicots, George, mush quies. Today very cheap', and the squaddie, putting his hand under the basket, knocked it into the air. The apricots rolled under the feet of the passers-by and the seller scrambled after them, lamenting, almost sobbing as he gathered them up from the filthy pavement. The squaddie gave Simon an oblique stare, aggressive yet guilty, and hurried into the crowd. Simon wondered if he should go after him, remonstrate, take his name and number, but how to recognize one British private among so many? They looked alike, as though they had all come from the same English village; not tall, skin red and moist, hair, shorts and shirts bleached to a yellow-buff, slouching despondently, 'browned off'.

Simon's self-reliance weakening as the heat grew, he stopped a taxi and asked to be driven to Garden City.

The girl was called Edwina Little and Hugo, writing to Simon, described her as 'the most gorgeous popsie in Cairo'. The phrase had stirred Simon even though he was about to marry his own girl, Anne. Hugo had instructed him to draw five pounds from his bank account and buy a bottle of scent from a shop in the West End. The scent, monstrously expensive it seemed to him, was called *Gardenia* and it was to travel to Egypt in the diplomatic bag. Simon scarcely knew how to explain his intrusion into the Foreign Office but the man in charge of the bag took his request lightly.

'Another votive offering for Miss Little?'

'You don't mind, do you? I mean – is it really all right?'

'Perfectly. Perfectly. We'll slip it in somewhere.'

Because of this romantic mission, Edwina had remained in his mind as a sublime creature, luxurious and desirable, but more suited to an older brother than to a minor like himself. Letters between England and Egypt were so slow on the way that Hugo knew nothing of Simon's posting and had had no chance to offer him an introduction to Edwina. In going unintroduced, Simon felt a sense of daring that added to his excitement.

The road sloped down to the river and on the embankment the driver shouted: 'Where you go now?'

'Garden City.'

'This *am* Garden City.' The driver, a big, black fellow, had a Sudanese belligerence: 'What number he wanting?'

The taxi slowed and they spent a long time driving round

curving roads, looking for one house among a great many others, all giving the sense of a rich past and present disrepair. The driver stopped from boredom and Simon protested, 'This isn't the right number.'

The Sudanese swung round, his face working with rage, 'This *am* right number. You pay or me clock you.'

Simon laughed, 'Oh, all right.' Walking noiselessly down the sandy road in the comatose air of mid-day, beneath the heavy foliage of palms and trees, he was startled by a banging of car doors and a forceful English voice giving orders. Making towards this uproar, he turned a corner and saw a tall man in khaki shorts and shirt, with a wide-brimmed khaki hat, directing passengers into two cars. His commanding shouts of, 'Move up. Now you get in there. That'll do for that one,' led Simon to suppose he was approaching a military operation. Instead, he found the first car held two women and an old man with a toy dog on his knee. The tall man was now intent on filling the second car. Both cars, Simon saw, stood in front of the house he was seeking. Hoping to avoid the man's eye, Simon edged in through the garden gate but was detected.

'You looking for someone?'

'Miss Edwina Little.'

The man frowned and though not more than thirty years of age, spoke like an angry father. 'Friend of yours?'

Simon would have resented the tone had he not heard in it a plea for reassurance. He answered mildly, 'Friend of my brother.'

From the balcony above him, someone whispered, 'Hello.' Jerking his head up, he saw a girl who had placed her arm along the balcony rail and her cheek on her arm. Looking down, smiling, she begged of him, '*Do* tell me who you are.'

Her hair, brown in its depths, golden where it had caught the sun, hid most of her face and her bath robe, of white towelling that enhanced the warm shade of her skin, hid her body except for the arm and the rising curve of her breast, yet the impression she gave was one of extraordinary beauty. He could scarcely find breath to say, 'My name's Simon Boulderstone. I'm Hugo's brother.'

'Are you?' She spoke with wonder, bending closer to him,

while he, lifting himself on his toes, could smell, or thought he could smell, the rich gardenia scent which had come to her in the diplomatic bag. He started to tell her that he had arrived only the day before but the tall man, his voice now pained and querulous, broke in on him.

'Really, Edwina, you said you were ill.'

'Oh, I *am* ill,' she pushed her hair back to smile at Simon. 'You see, I have a headache and can't go on Clifford's trip but I'll be better when I've had a rest. So *do* come back later. Promise me you'll come back later.'

'Of course, I will.'

Gathering her wrap close to her neck, Edwina stood upright, calling to Clifford, 'Take him with you, darling.'

'We're pretty crowded...'

'And bring him back safely.' Edwina waved to everyone in sight, gave a special smile to Simon, and went into the darkened room behind the balcony.

Clifford grumbled, 'If she wants you to come, I suppose we'll have to manage it somehow.' Returning to the command, he ordered the man with the dog to get in beside the women. Seeing the old fellow meekly giving up the front seat, Simon said, 'Oh, no...' but Clifford, placing himself behind the wheel, ordered him sharply, 'Get in. Get in. We're late in starting as it is.'

Feeling at fault, Simon was silent as the cars set out but he looked covertly at Clifford, wondering who and what he was. With his wide khaki hat, he appeared, at first glance, to be an officer in one of the colonial forces but Simon now noticed that he had no insignia. He was a civilian. His looks, too, deteriorated on examination. His thin, regular features sank towards a mouth that was small, hard and narrow as the edge of a coin.

Feeling Simon's regard, Clifford said, 'Always happy to have you chaps along. No point in coming out here and not seeing the sights.'

Simon, with no idea where he was being taken, agreed, though the main object of the trip for him was the return to Garden City.

'Interested in Egyptology?'

18

Simon, thinking of his local cinema with its Tutankhamün décor, said, 'I think so.'

'That's right. Learn what you can, while you can. This is the Nile.'

Simon looked out on the wide, grey-silver river moving with the slow lurch and swell of a snake between banks of grey and yellow mud.

Pointing with his thumb at some small boats that were going by as indolently as driftwood, Clifford said, 'Feluccas.' Simon watched the white triangular sails of the feluccas tilting in the wind. The same wind blew through the car like the breath off a molten ingot.

'Over there, at sunset, you can see The Pyramids.'

Simon looked but saw only the bleary haze of the heat. They had crossed the river into suburbs where life was coming to a standstill. It was an area of large modern houses and avenues where trees held out, like inviting hands, patellas of flame-red flowers. A few cars were still making their way home-wards but the homeless – vagrants, beggars and dogs – had thrown themselves down under the trees to sleep the afternoon away.

Clifford gave Simon a sharp, accusing glance. 'What's happening out there?'

'Where?'

'The desert, of course. Where else? What the hell are you chaps up to? Not long ago we were at Benghazi – now, where are we? There's a rumour we've even lost Mersa. That right?'

Simon said he knew nothing, he had just arrived with the draft, a fact that seemed to cheer Clifford who relaxed in his seat and laughed, 'Thought you looked a young 'un.'

The passengers in the back seat had not spoken during the drive out of Cairo. Looking round at them, Simon noticed that one of the women – a pale, dark-haired girl – was not much older than he was. Too thin, he thought, but he was attracted by the glowing darkness of her eyes and smiled at her.

'I'm Simon Boulderstone.'

'Hugo's brother?'

'You know Hugo?'

Simon turned in his seat, expecting to hear more from someone who knew Hugo, but the point of contact seemed merely
to disconcert her and she spoke as though avoiding it, 'I'm
Harriet Pringle. This is Mr Clifford's secretary, Miss Brownall.'

Miss Brownall, a wan-faced, elderly virgin, bent forward as
her name was mentioned and watched his eagerly, waiting for
him to speak, but he could think of nothing to say, and giving
her a smile, he turned away again.

Clifford waved at the windscreen and said, 'There you are!'
and Simon, seeing the blunt, battered face of the Sphinx,
gasped in amazement. Then came The Pyramids. He had been
told he would see them at sunset but not that he would see
them that very afternoon. And there they were, taking shape
like shadows out of the haze – or, rather, one was taking
shape, then another, smaller, pyramid sifted out from behind
its neighbour and there were two, growing substantial and
standing four-square on the sandy rock. To see them better,
Simon put his head out of the window then, blinded by the
dazzle of the outside air, drew it in again.

The sun was overhead now and, with every inch it rose,
the heat increased. The car, Simon felt, was a baking-tin,
baked by the furnace outside. The roof pressed like a weight
on its occupants and Simon envied Edwina who could sleep
off her headache in bed. If he had stayed in Cairo he, too,
might have been sleeping – but where could he sleep? Not in
that barracks room with its smell of death. His head nodded
and hit the side of the car. He sat up and heard Clifford speaking to the other three.

'They say Wavell's made plans for the evacuation of Cairo
but, plans or no plans, it'll be plain, ruddy murder. It's already
started. Every foreigner in Cairo's piling into the trains, going
while the going's good. I don't mean the British, of course. The
real foreigners. The crowd that came here from Europe.'

Harriet Pringle said, 'We came here from Europe.'

'I mean the foreign foreigners. Dagos. The gyppo porters are
having a high old time at the station. I was there yesterday, saw
them chucking the luggage about, roaring with laughter, bawl-

ing, "Hitler come". It's all fun now but wait till the hun really gets here.'

The old man with the dog said, 'I don't know. Not a bad fellow, your gyppo. He may laugh at us but there's no taking advantage. No insults, no rude words. I don't think they will harm us.'

Clifford let this pass but said after some minutes, 'You're not taking yourself off then, Liversage? Some of us, with jobs and homes here, will have to stay put, but you're free to go any time.'

Liversage cheerfully agreed, 'Yes, I'm free to go, but I won't unless they make me. I was pushed out of Sofia and pushed out of Greece, but now I'll stay where I am. I don't think they'll bother about an old codger like me,' and dismissing the matter, he leant into his corner of the car and closed his eyes.

Simon, surprised by this talk of flight, said, 'I heard there was an emergency but I didn't know things were so bad. I mean, if it's like that, it's a bit odd, isn't it, going on a sightseeing trip?'

'Not really. No point in moping about in town. The trouble is, they're keeping us in ignorance of the true situation. Bad policy, that, in my opinion. Ignorance breeds fear. I'd say, "Tell people the truth. Trust them to keep their heads." By people, of course, I mean us. Not the wog. I wouldn't tell the wog the time o'day.'

Liversage mumbled through his sleep, 'Merry fellow, your wog. Can't help liking him.'

Ignoring this, Clifford said, 'First, we'll take a look at the Saccara pyramids. That over there's the step pyramid. Dangerous. No one's allowed inside. But there's another one ...'

Miss Brownall squeaked her alarm, 'Not the one with the bats?'

Clifford, with his air of authority, in his uniform that was not a uniform, asked sternly, 'And why not the one with the bats?'

'Oh dear!'

The car turned left on to a track in the sand and shapes could be seen through the limitless fog of the distance. Approached, they were revealed as heaps of unbaked bricks that had once

21

been pyramids. Now they stood like patient, waiting animals as Clifford made a dashing swerve in front of them and braked to a stop. The following car, trying to imitate the swerve, skidded and nearly rammed Clifford's car. His expression fierce, he threw open his door but finding all well, he contented himself with the voice of leadership, 'All out. All out.' His followers, struggling from beneath the heat of each other's elbows, emerged to a more spacious area of heat.

Fly-whisk in one hand, torch in the other, Clifford pointed both objects at the largest and best preserved of the pyramids, 'We're going in this one,' then realized that Mr Liversage was still in the car. Going smartly to it, he looked at the old man, saw he was asleep and let him remain. The rest he led to a hole in the pyramid's flank.

Harriet Pringle, loitering, last in the queue, seemed reluctant to enter. Simon paused so she could precede him into the dark, ragged opening in the bricks, but she shook her head, 'I don't like the look of it.' The pyramid's outer casing of stone had been looted away and the inner structure had sunk on itself like a ruined plum-pudding. 'I don't think it's safe and I'm afraid of bats.'

Simon laughed, 'I'll go ahead and scare them.'

For a few yards they were able to walk upright, then the roof sagged and they had to bend to get under it. Ahead of them Miss Brownall was giggling and from the scuffling, scraping and grunting, it was clear that the others had been forced down on to hands and knees. Harriet stopped, then something caught in her hair and she turned and ran back to the daylight.

Simon went on until he could feel space about him and heard people breathing. The air was cold. Clifford had switched off his torch to heighten the drama of arrival in the central chamber and the party stood in darkness until the stragglers arrived. As Simon joined them, Clifford relit the torch and shone it upon him: 'All here?' Then he saw that Harriet was not there and said with displeasure, 'Where's *she* gone?'

'Mrs Pringle turned back.'

'Oh, did she!'

Wisely, too, Simon thought as he looked about him. The

chamber was empty except for a stone sarcophagus of immense size. Everything else had been looted, even the sarcophagus lid. Not only was there nothing to see but Simon realized that to enter the place was foolhardy. The apex of the pyramid was breaking through the roof plaster and poised over their heads were several tons of bricks that could be brought down by the slightest earth tremor. Clifford, moving imperturbably beneath this peril, flashed his torch on to the decayed walls, saying, 'Wonderfully fresh, these colours. Book of the Dead, y'know!'

The others stood as though not daring to move and their murmurs sounded to Simon more apprehensive than admiring. Miss Brownall was slapping her bare arms and one of the men from the second car, feeling the chill, had wrapped a scarf under his chin and up over his trilby hat.

'Well, Miss Brownall,' Clifford humorously asked, 'who do you think was buried here?'

Miss Brownall said she could not say but the man with the scarf answered for her, 'I would presume, yes ... yes, I would presume it was Ozymandias, King of Kings.' His precise enunciation did not suggest a joke but Clifford looked suspiciously at him.

'Didn't know there was an Ozymandias.' To prevent further discussion Clifford made a quick move to an entrance in the further wall. 'Now, this is interesting. Another passage. Let's see where this leads.'

As the others filed after him, Simon made his escape and came thankfully out to where Harriet was sitting on the ground, her back to the pyramid, sifting sand through her fingers. She had collected a small pile of blue beads and scraps of mummy cloth. 'Look what I've found.'

Simon sat down beside her and took the opportunity to ask, 'Who is Mr Clifford? Is he very important?'

'In a way, I suppose he is. He's an agent for an oil company, but he's not as grand as he'd like to be. He doesn't belong to the set that plays polo and gives gambling parties so, to show his superiority, he's taken to Ancient Egypt in a big way.'

'I suppose he *is* English? Which part does he come from?'

23

'You mean his accent? It's a Clifford accent. He's English but doesn't come from England. The Cliffords have lived here for generations. The men go home to find English wives so the family maintains its Englishness. Their traditions are English, but their money is not. I wonder, if the gyppos turned on us, which side he'd be on?'

'Turned on us? You don't really think they'd turn on us after all we've done for them?'

Harriet laughed at him, 'What have we done for them?'

'We've brought them justice and prosperity, haven't we? We've shown them how people ought to live.'

With his face close to her, seeing his clear skin, the clear whites of his eyes, the defined dark blue of the iris, she thought, 'How young he is!' Until now she had taken it for granted that her generation was the youngest of the adults but she realized that in the two years of her marriage, a yet younger generation had come into the war. They arrived in Egypt, fresh and innocent, imbued with the creed in which they had been brought up. They believed that the British Empire was the greatest force for good the world had ever known. They expected gratitude from the Egyptians and were pained to find themselves barely tolerated.

'What have we done here, except make money? I suppose a few rich Egyptians have got richer by supporting us, but the real people of the country, the peasants and the backstreet poor, are just as diseased, underfed and wretched as they ever were.'

Aware of his own ignorance, Simon did not argue but changed course. 'Surely they're glad to have us here to protect them?'

'They don't think we're protecting them. They think we're making a use of them. And so we are. We're protecting the Suez Canal and the route to India and Clifford's oil company.' Disturbed by Simon's troubled eyes, Harriet stood up asking, 'And where is Clifford? What are they doing in there?'

'Exploring another passage. I must say, he's pretty brave. The roof's so shaky, it could come down any minute.'

'He's showing off. He's challenged by you.'

'Me? Why me?'

'Because you're a fighting man and he ought to be, but isn't.'

'Oh, he needn't worry about me. If he wants to keep out of it, all I can say is good luck to him.'

They could hear Clifford's voice as the party returned. Harriet opened her hand, full of tiny blue beads, and scattered the beads over the sand: 'They've been here for two thousand years. Now they can stay for another two thousand.'

Clifford, coming out frowning and blinking in the brilliant light, looked sardonically at her. 'So, young lady, you were afraid to come with us?'

'Yes.'

Nonplussed by this admission, Clifford turned on the others. 'Right. Back to the cars. I'll show you a very remarkable tomb.'

'The funny one?' asked Miss Brownall.

'Yes, the funny one.'

Clifford spoke sternly and he looked stern as he swung the car away from the dark mounds that had once been pyramids and headed them into the dazzling, swimming nothingness of the desert horizon. Silver mirage now hid the sand and, from it, oddly elongated rocks and stones stood up like wading birds. Everyone except Clifford was silent, stupefied by the atmosphere inside the car. Simon imagined them cooking, their flesh softening and melting into fat, while Clifford talked away. Apparently unaffected by the heat, he described the tomb he said he had discovered. It was – and here Miss Brownall gave eager agreement – unlike any other tomb anyone had discovered before. Absorbed by his own discovery, he ran the car off the track and Harriet, clutching at a metal handhold, cried out that her fingers were burnt.

'Is it always as hot as this?' Simon asked.

'This is only the beginning. Next month will be worse. They used to think Englishwomen and children could not endure such heat but now we have to stay here, we find we endure it quite well.'

An outcrop of rock was appearing in the distance and Clifford said 'This is it. *Now* you'll see something.'

The cars stopped and the passengers struggled out again. They were immediately assailed by flies that settled with sticky feet on to sticky hands and faces. Clifford, flapping his whisk about, said, 'Don't know what God was thinking about when he created flies.'

Miss Brownall, modest in her knowledge, asked, 'Weren't they created to plague the Egyptians?'

Harriet agreed. 'The plagues came and never went away again.'

Simon began to describe the millions of flies he had seen, a black blanket of flies, all heaving together on the banks of the Red Sea, but Clifford, having no interest in this talk, ordered the party to follow him into the rock tomb.

Simon remained a moment to observe a fly motionless on the back of his hand, its mottled grey and black body covered by transparent wings that gave it a greasy look. It seemed too large, like a fly seen through a magnifying glass. He tried to shake it off but it remained, heat-struck, and having no heart to kill it, he brushed it away.

'Don't lag behind, chaps,' Clifford shouted. 'Come on. Stick together –'

They passed through an opening into the semi-darkness of a large cave. The masons had squared it up and plastered the walls, then the artists had marked in the areas to be decorated but they had done no more. Some of the spaces had been roughly brushed in with red or white. Clifford, pointing to them, said, 'Have you ever seen anything like this? Isn't it extraordinary?'

There was a questioning silence then Harriet said, 'Not really. It's merely unfinished. They started to decorate it then, for some reason, the work came to a stop.'

Miss Brownall drew in her breath as though she feared for Harriet's safety and Clifford did indeed look angry. 'Why should they stop?'

'The usual reasons. Demand falling off. New religions taking over. New ideas. Or prices going up and the tomb-makers going out of business. It's interesting to see that in ancient Egypt things ended just as they have always done.'

'Perhaps. Perhaps not.' Clifford was discouraging but one of the men from the second car said, 'I think Mrs Pringle is right. It's just an unfinished tomb.'

Clifford grunted, 'That's merely supposition. Anyway, there's more to see.' He led the way down some rough steps into a small, lower cave where shelves had been cut in the rock. Here the walls were unplastered and there were no painted guidelines or panels. Looking about the empty tomb where no soul had sought instruction and no instructions were given, Harriet felt sorry for the builders who had been forced to abandon their work. While Clifford flashed his torch about, trying to whip up interest in a place that had ceased to be interesting, Harriet looked up and saw they were all crowded together beneath a gigantic stone that was poised, ready to be lowered on to the hole when all the shelves had been filled. She murmured in horror and sped up the steps and into the safety of the open air.

Simon, hurrying after her, asked, 'What's the matter? Are you all right?'

'Yes. It was that stone. If it had suddenly slipped, we would have been buried alive down there.' At the thought of their death in the darkness and heat of that underground hole, she was convulsed with fear. 'No one would ever have known what had happened to us.'

Clifford, his followers behind him, approached Harriet with a satisfied smile. 'You're very jittery, aren't you? That stone's been propped up there for over a thousand years. Did you think it was waiting to come down on you?'

She knew she was jittery. She had come jittery out of Rumania and then out of Greece, and now she lived in expectation of being driven out of Egypt. She said, 'I'm sorry. I was silly. I'm inclined to be claustrophobic.'

Appeased by her admission of weakness, Clifford smiled benignly and said they would go to the Fayoum and have their picnic under the trees. The promise of picnic and trees pleased everyone and the oasis, when they came to it, gave them an illusion of relief. There was shade from the massed foliage of palms, sycamores, banyans and mangoes, but it was heavy rather than cool. The sunlight, falling in shafts through the branches, lit dust motes in the air. Dust veiled everything, the dust of the road silenced their feet. Women, walking bare footed with pots on their heads, moved with a dream-like quiet, their black draperies grey with dust. Small houses stood by the road, simple cubes of whitewashed clay, with unglazed windows from which came the smoke of burning cow-cake. The warm, dry smell of the cow-cake smoke hung everywhere on the air.

Where the road opened into a Midan there was a sphinx, its nose rubbed off by time, and here the cars stopped under the trees. Car rugs were spread out on the sand, packets of cakes and sandwiches were taken from the boot of Clifford's car and everyone sat down, waiting for Miss Brownall to make tea on a spirit-stove. Sitting in the steamy shades, they watched camels plash by, grunting morosely, heads held high in contempt of the creatures they were forced to serve.

No one was hungry except Simon who had had nothing since his canteen breakfast, but he was reluctant to eat food to which he had not contributed.

'Tuck in. Tuck in,' Clifford shouted at him, and everyone who had brought food urged it upon him. Simon tucked in.

The heat now had a leaden weight so even the flies were stilled. The sun had passed its meridian and the light was taking on an ochre tinge that gave to the trees and the sandy air an antique richness. They all sat bowed, drowsy, and Harriet felt they had lost the present and were in some era of the remote past. Then Miss Brownall came round with cups of tea. They roused themselves and began to talk. The man who had spoken of Ozymandias, unwound his scarf from his hat and, sipping his tea, watched Harriet from the corners of his eyes. After some moments, he began fidgeting across the rug towards her, making an introductory mumbling and creaking in his throat that at last became words.

'This ... yes, this is the young person who knows things. She can tell us what's going on. She's in the American information office.'

The man to whom he spoke was the one who had backed Harriet's opinion of the cave. He was thin and elderly and his raw, pink hands, tightly clenched, were nervously pressed into the ground at his sides. He smiled on Harriet, saying, 'Oh, I know. I know she's in information.'

The two of them gazed expectantly at her and she introduced them to Simon. The man with the scarf was Professor Lord Pinkrose; the other was called Major Cookson. The major was so absurdly unlike a professional soldier that Harriet laughed slightly as she spoke his name. As for information, she had no more than anyone else.

Pinkrose's face went glum. A pear-shaped, elderly man, he was wearing an old-fashioned tussore suit that buttoned up to his chin. His nose, that rested on top of his scarf, was blunt and grey like the snout of a lizard. His eyes, too, were grey – grey as rainwater, Simon thought – and looked coldly on Harriet when he realized she had nothing to tell. He was about to turn from her when he remembered he had another question to ask. 'Have you any news of Gracey? ... any news? Every time I ring the office, I get a girl saying, "Mr Gracey is not available," and that's all she says. It's exasperating. Over and over. "Mr Gracey is not available." It's like a machine.'

Gracey was the head of the organization which employed Harriet's husband, Guy Pringle. She said, 'It is a machine; an answering machine. There's no one in the office. The place is locked up. I've tried to contact them, too. Guy's in Alexandria in an out-of-the-way place and if the advance goes on, he could be cut off there.' Harriet, her anxiety renewing itself, spoke with feeling. 'It's Gracey's job to order him to leave but Gracey's not here. He's taken himself to a safe place as he always does when things look bad. I went to the office and found the porter. He told me Gracey's gone to Palestine.'

'Gone to Palestine! Gone to Palestine!' Pinkrose seemed baffled by the news and then became agitated. 'You hear that, Cookson? You hear that? Gracey's gone to Palestine.'

'So have a lot of other people.'

'But he said nothing to me. *Nothing*. Not a word. This is disgraceful, Cookson. To go off without a word to me. Did you know he had gone?'

Cookson shook his head. 'I never see Gracey these days. Now I'm on my uppers, most of my old friends have faded away.'

Pinkrose, caring nothing for Cookson's lost friends, interrupted him. 'I'd no idea the situation was so serious. No idea. No idea. No idea at all.'

Harriet watched Pinkrose with a smile, quizzical and mildly scornful, while Pinkrose's small, stony eyes quivered with self-concern. She had known him first in Bucharest where, sent out to give a lecture, he had arrived as the Germans were infiltrating the country and had been abandoned then just as he was abandoned now. He was, she thought, like some heavy object, a suitcase or parcel, an impediment that his friends put down when they wanted to cut and run. Looking beyond him to Cookson, she mischievously asked, 'And what are your getaway plans this time, Major Cookson?'

Cookson gave a wry, sheepish smile, not resenting the question. In Greece, where he had had money invested in property, his house had been a centre of hospitality. When the Germans came down on Athens, he had chartered two freighters, intending to take his friends to safety. Pinkrose had been among those invited. They had kept their plans secret but had been discovered and Cookson was ordered by the military to include anyone who chose to leave.

Now, having spent the money he had in Egypt, he existed on a dole from the British Embassy. He had been brought by Clifford merely as a driver of the second car. His clothes were becoming shabby, he looked underfed and Pinkrose, who had been his guest in the past, treated him as an inferior. For a time those who knew Cookson's story had no wish to speak to him but now, seeing him so reduced in the world, Harriet looked on him with pitying amusement. He answered humbly, 'I have no plans, and if I had any, I've no money to carry them out. Those freighters cost me a fortune and I didn't get a penny of compensation from the army.'

'Still you got away with all your possessions while we were allowed only a small suitcase. You even had your car on board.'

'My poor old car,' Cookson sighed and smiled. 'The Egyptian customs've still got hold of it. They refuse to release it – not that it matters. I couldn't afford to run it.'

Harriet, having decided the past was past, smiled with him, realizing that now they were almost old friends, while Pinkrose went on with his fretful mumblings, the more angry because he had been left in the lurch for a second time.

A crowd of children had gathered to watch the strangers. Mr Liversage, enlivened by his tea, went over to them and trailed his dog backwards and forwards in front of them, his manner gleeful, expectant of applause. The children stared, confounded by the laughing old man and the old, bald toy dog which was a money-box in which he collected for charity. At first they were silent then one of them opened his mouth to jeer and the others took up his contempt with derisive yells and shouts of 'Majnoon'. Stones were thrown at man and dog and Clifford rushed in, wielding his fly-whisk like a flail, and scattered the miscreants. That done he ordered his party to rise. 'Wakey, wakey. We've a long drive back.'

As they moved and dusted themselves down, a passenger from the second car, a university professor called Bowen, said, 'Isn't this where that chap Hooper lives? He took over a Turkish fortress and spent a mint of money on it.'

'Hooper?' The name brought Clifford to a stop. 'Sir Desmond Hooper? Now he's the one who could tell us what's happening out there. He's always wining and dining the army big shots.'

Bowen, a small, gentle fellow, nodded. 'Well, yes. He might know more than most people.'

'Then why don't we look him up? Call in for an early sundowner?'

'Oh, no,' Bowen, aghast at the idea, had the support of Cookson and Mr Liversage, when he realized what was being argued, said firmly, 'Can't do that, my dear fellow. Too many of us. Can't march an army into a chap's house, don't you know! Simply not done.' Pinkrose, however, eager for news and concerned for his own safety, felt differently. 'Why not call in? Why not? These aren't ordinary times, no need to stand on ceremony these days. It's disgraceful the way we're kept in ignorance. If Sir Desmond Hooper knows what's going on, it's his duty to tell us. Yes, yes, his duty ... it's his duty, I say.' Pinkrose spoke indignantly, carrying his anger with Gracey over on to the innocent Hooper.

The others – Simon, Harriet, Miss Brownall and a girl from the second car who was also one of Clifford's employees – took no part in the discussion but waited for Clifford's decision. Harriet, entertained by it, was not unwilling to see the Hooper fortress in the anonymity of so much company.

31

Pinkrose's agreement settled the matter for Clifford. 'We'll go,' he said. Bowen begged, 'At least ring him up first.'

'Ring him up? Where from? We'll get more out of him if we take him unawares.'

Clifford spoke to one of the camel drivers and was directed towards the river. The fortress was soon evident. Larger and more complex than most desert fortresses, it stood up above the trees, a white-painted, crenellated square of stone behind a crenellated white wall. The wall enclosed a row of palms from which hung massive bunches of red dates. A boab, looking out through the wrought-iron gates, seemed doubtful of the party but Clifford's masterful manner impressed him and he let them in. They drove between extensive, sandy lawns to an iron-studded main door where three safragis lolled half-asleep. One of them, rousing himself with an air of long-suffering, came to the first car and inquired, 'What do you want?'

'Lady Hooper.'

'Not here. Layey Hooper.' The safragi made to walk away but Clifford shouted, 'Sir Desmond, then.' The safragi had to admit that Sir Desmond was at home.

Mr Liversage refused to leave the car but the others – even Bowen's curiosity was stronger than his discretion – followed the servant into a vast hall where the parquet was as deep and dark as the waters of a well. The house was air-conditioned. Enlivened by the drop in temperature, they seemed all to realize suddenly the enormity of their intrusion into the Hooper household. Harriet had an impulse to run back to the car but the safragi had opened the door of a living-room and, feeling it was too late to retreat, she went in with the rest. The room was as large as a ballroom and made larger by its prevailing whiteness. Walls, carpets, curtains and furniture were white. The white leather and the white-painted surfaces had been toned down with some sort of 'antiquing' mixture which Harriet noted with interest. The only colour in the room came from half a dozen paintings so startling in quality that she took it for granted that they were reproductions. Moving to them she saw they were originals.

She said to Clifford in wonder, 'They're real.'

'I don't like that modern stuff.'

'They were painted before you were born.'

'I don't like them any the better for that.'

Clifford, disconcerted by his surroundings, was in a bad temper.

Sir Desmond entered and looked at his uninvited guests with bewildered diffidence. Deciding they were friends of his wife, he said, 'I'm afraid Angela's not here. She's out on a painting expedition.' Then he noticed Bowen, 'Ah, Bowen, I did not know you were here.'

Bowen, identified, blushed and tried to excuse himself, 'I'm sorry. So wrong of us to interrupt your Sunday peace. It's just ... we ...' Struggling to find an excuse, he twisted about in anguish.

'Not at all. Sit down, do. Won't the ladies sit here!'

Harriet, Miss Brownall and the other girl were put into the seat of honour, a vast ottoman so deep they almost sank out of sight. The men found themselves chairs and Sir Desmond, placing himself among them, asked if they would take tea.

Clifford said they had had tea and his manner left the occasion open for a more stimulating offer, but Sir Desmond merely said, 'Ah!' He was a tall, narrow man with a regular, narrow face, dressed in a suit of silver-grey silk. His hair was the same silver as the silk and his appearance, elegant, desiccated yet authoritative, was that of an upper-class Englishman prepared to deal with any situation. He looked over the visitors who, dusty, sweaty, depleted by their travels, were all uneasy, except Clifford. Clifford's assurance was such that Sir Desmond dropped Bowen and addressed the younger man : 'Well, major, what brings you into the Fayoum?'

Clifford blinked at the title but did not repudiate it. 'We're just exploring a bit. Voyage of discovery, you might call it.'

'Is there anything left to discover in this much-pillaged country?' As he spoke Sir Desmond noticed that Clifford had on his shoulder not a crown but a plain gold button and his voice sharpened as he inquired, 'What are you? Press? Radio? Something like that?'

'Certainly not. I'm in oil. The name's Clifford. The fact is, Sir Desmond, rumours are going round Cairo and we don't like the look of things. And we don't like being kept in ignorance.

The station's in an uproar with foreigners trying to get away and I heard even GHQ's packing up. What we want to know is: what the hell's happening in the desert?'

'I don't think I can answer that question, Mr Clifford.'

Rancour came into Clifford's voice. 'If you can't, who can?'

The telephone rang at Sir Desmond's elbow. He answered it, said urgently, 'Yes, yes, hold on,' and, excusing himself, went to take the call in another room. A scratch of voices came from the receiver on the table. Clifford tiptoed to it, bent to listen but before he could hear anything, a safragi entered to replace it on its stand.

Bowen was indignant. 'Really, Clifford, what a thing to do! And I think we've stayed long enough. Let's slip away.'

'No, no.' Pinkrose was impressively impatient, 'This may be the very news we're waiting for.'

'It may indeed,' said Clifford.

The light was deepening towards sunset. The safragi who had attended to the telephone, opened the windows and the long chiffon curtains blew like ghosts into the room.

Bowen complained, 'It's getting late . . .' but Clifford silenced him with a lift of the hand. Before anyone else could speak, a car, driven at reckless speed, came up the drive and braked with a shriek outside the house. They heard the heavy front door crash open and from the hall came the sound of a stumbling entry that conveyed a sense of catastrophe. A woman entered the room shouting, 'Desmond. Desmond,' and seeing the company, stopped and shook her head.

The men got to their feet. Bowen said, 'Lady Hooper, is anything the matter?' She shook her head again, standing in the middle of the room, her distracted appearance made more wild by her disarranged black hair and the torn, paint-covered overall that protected her dress. Lady Hooper was younger than her husband. She was some age between thirty and forty, a delicately built woman with a delicate, regular face. She looked at each of the strangers in turn and when she came to Simon, she smiled and said, 'I think he'll be all right.'

Two safragis carried in the inert body of a boy. The three women hastily struggled out of the ottoman and the boy was put down. He lay prone and motionless, a thin, small boy of

34

eight or nine with the same delicate features as his mother: only something had happened to them. One eye was missing. There was a hole in the left cheek that extended into the torn wound which had been his mouth. Blood had poured down his chin and was caked on the collar of his open-necked shirt. The other eye, which was open, was lacklustre and blind like the eye of a dead rabbit.

Sir Desmond entered and anxiously asked, 'My dear, what has happened?'

'We were in the desert. I was sketching and didn't see ... He picked up something. It exploded – but he'll be all right.'

Harriet could scarcely bear to look at Sir Desmond but he answered calmly enough, 'My dear, of course. I expect he's suffering from shock.'

'Do you think we should rouse him? Perhaps if we gave him something to eat ...'

'Yes, a little nourishment, light and easy to swallow.'

'Gruel, or an egg beaten up. What do you think?'

Sir Desmond spoke to the safragis who glanced at each other with the expression of those who have long accepted the fact that all foreigners are mad.

There was an interval in which Sir Desmond telephoned a doctor in Cairo and Lady Hooper, sitting on the sofa edge, held the boy's hand. Sir Desmond, finishing his call, spoke reassuringly to her, 'He's coming out straight away. He says Richard must have an anti-tetanus injection.'

'There was Dettol in the car. I bathed his face.'

One of the safragis returned, bringing a bowl of gruel and the visitors watched with awe and amazement as Sir Desmond, bending tenderly over the boy, attempted to feed him. The mouth was too clogged with congealed blood to permit entry so the father poured a spoonful of gruel into the hole in the cheek. The gruel poured out again. This happened three times before Sir Desmond gave up and, gathering the child into his arms, said, 'He wants to sleep. I'll take him to his room.' Lady Hooper followed her husband and Clifford, knowing he was defeated, was willing to depart.

Outside, beneath the palms and the roseate sky, he gave a long whistle. 'Now I've seen everything.'

'They couldn't face the truth,' Bowen sighed in pity. 'They couldn't accept it.'

'They'll be forced to accept it pretty soon. And we never heard what that phone call was all about.'

Mr Liversage lay asleep in the car. Bowen elected to move him over and sat beside him while Miss Brownall joined her friend in the second car. Remembering the boy, no one spoke as they drove through the Fayoum. The trees merged, dark in the misty evening. Lights were flickering inside the box-shaped houses. It would soon be night. As the oasis was left behind, the boy's death lost its immediacy and Harriet thought of all the other boys who were dying in the desert before they had had a chance to live. And yet, though there was so much death at hand, she felt the boy's death was a death apart.

Bowen murmured, 'A tragedy. An only child.'

'And the last shot in the old locker,' said Clifford. 'They're not likely to have another.'

The sun had almost set when they approached Mena and the last, long rays enriched the sand. It glowed saffron and orange then, in a moment, the colour was gone and a violet twilight came down. The passengers were sunk together with weariness but Clifford had still not had enough. A few hundred yards before the road turned towards Mena, he drew up and said, 'There's an ancient village about here. Let's take a shufti.'

'Is it really worth the effort?' Bowen asked.

'Oh, come on!' Clifford rallied the party, insisting that if there was anything to see, it must be seen. They wandered about on the stony mardam and found the village which was sunk like an intaglio in the sand. Jumping down, they walked through narrow streets between small, roofless houses. The dig must have been a students' exercise for the dwellings were too poor to yield more than a few broken pots and it was hard to understand why anyone had chosen to live in this waterless spot. In the deepening twilight, it was so forlorn that even Clifford was glad to move on to the Mena House bar.

While Bowen and Simon were buying the drinks, Clifford moved eagerly round the officers in the bar until he found a group known to him. Putting his head among them, he said, 'Just come from the Hooper house. Their kid's been killed by a hand grenade he picked up. You won't believe this, but old Hooper tried to spoonfeed the boy through a hole in his face.' Tomorrow the story would be all over Cairo.

When their drinks were finished, Harriet said to Simon, 'Shall we climb the great pyramid?'

'Is it possible? Goodness, I'd love to, but can you manage it?'

'I've done it twice before. The last time, I was wearing a black velvet evening dress which hasn't been the same since.'

They went out to the road that was lit only by the lights of the hotel. The pyramids were no more than a greater darkness in an area of darkness. Harriet led Simon to the noted corner from which the ascent was easiest and as they climbed on to the first ledge, the local Bedu sighted them and came running and shouting, 'Not allowed. No one go up without guide. Law says you have guide.'

Simon paused but Harriet waved him on. As they scrambled upwards the Bedu shook their fists and wailed, 'Come back. Come back,' and Harriet laughed and waved down at them. Standing on one ledge, she jumped her backside on to the one above then swung her legs up after her. She was very light and moved at such speed, she passed Simon and was first at the top. There she waved again to the guides who were still making half-hearted complaints before they drifted away.

The apex of the pyramid was missing, purloined to provide stone for other buildings, and now there was a plateau some twelve yards square. Harriet, seeing it as a dancing-ground, held out her arms to Simon as he reached it and they circled together for a few minutes, singing 'Run rabbit' until they were overcome by laughter. They went to the edge of the square and sat, looking into the darkness of the desert. The sky was fogged and there was nothing visible but the blue quilt of lights that was Cairo. Speaking as a soldier, Simon said sternly, 'There ought to be a proper black-out.'

'You could never enforce it. It would take the whole British army to get the Cairenes to black their windows. Besides, it would be no use. A pilot told me that the Nile is always visible. They'd just have to follow it. The lights frightened me when we first came here but nothing happened and I got used to them.'

'You mentioned my brother. You didn't say much about him. Didn't you like him?'

'Hugo? Of course I liked him. I liked him very much. We met him in Alex. He was in the Cecil bar and he looked so young and alone that we went over and spoke to him. He talked about the desert. He said he was sick of it but he had to go back next day. He asked us to have dinner with him because it was his twenty-first birthday.'

'Really!' Simon was entranced by this information. 'You were with him on his twenty-first?'

'Yes, we went to Pastroudi's and had a great time.'

'How splendid!' Simon waited, expecting to hear more about this momentous dinner-party, but Harriet had said all she meant to say. The numinous sequel to that dinner was not for Simon. It had been the night of full moon. Passing through the black-out curtains at the dor, they had entered the startling brilliance of the night and stood together to say good-bye. Hugo, his handsome, smiling, gentle face white in the moonlight, thanked them for giving him their company on his birthday. Guy wrote down a telephone number saying, 'When you come back on leave, let's meet again,' and a voice inside Harriet's head said, 'But he won't come back. He is going to die.' She felt neither surprise nor shock at this foreknowledge, only the certainty that it was true.

Simon broke into her memory, saying, 'I must try to find him but I'm not sure if I can. I don't know what it's like out there.'

'I don't know either. It's strange, living here on the edge of a battlefield. It's like living beside Pluto's underworld.'

Simon, knowing nothing about Pluto's underworld, moved to a more desirable subject. 'You know Edwina's Hugo's girl. She's really something, isn't she. She's very beautiful.'

Harriet laughed, saying only, 'I hardly know her. She's an archivist at the Embassy.'

'I say, is she?' Simon could not have said what an archivist did but the word impressed him. He wanted to hear more about Edwina but felt the need to curb his interest. 'Actually, I'm married. My wife's called Anne. We were only together for a week and then I had to go to Liverpool and join the draft.

She came to the station to see me off and she couldn't speak. She just stood there, crying and crying. I said, "Cheer up, the war can't go on for ever," but she only cried. Poor little thing!'

Simon's voice faltered so Harriet feared that he, too, would cry. She wanted to agree that the war could not go on for ever but she had no certainty. She stood up and said, 'The others will wonder where we are. Having come up at top speed, there's nothing to do but go down again.'

The cars no longer stood outside Mena House. Harriet sent Simon to the hotel desk, expecting a message had been left, but there was no message. Clifford's party had gone and she and Simon were left behind.

Abashed, Simon said, 'But Edwina told Clifford to take me back to her. She made me promise to return.'

'I see.' Harriet could imagine Clifford seizing the chance to decant a rival, even such a young and temporary rival as Simon. If Edwina asked where Simon was Clifford could say, 'He went off with a girl,' and that would be the end of Simon.

'It was my fault. I shouldn't have taken you away like that.'

'It was an experience. I've been hearing about the pyramids since I was a kid but I never expected to go up one.' Simon smiled to show he did not blame her but it was a dejected smile. Harriet, thinking how few experiences might be left for him in this world, felt enraged that Clifford, so much concerned for his own safety, could abandon Simon who would soon be risking his life. She said, 'Don't worry. We'll find a taxi and I'll drop you off in Garden City.'

'But can I just barge in like that?'

'Of course. If Edwina invited you ...'

'Yes, she did invite me.'

They waited outside the hotel until a taxi, coming from Cairo, was willing to take them back. Harriet was relieved to see a light in the living-room of the flat where Edwina lodged. Simon, too, looked up, delighted, never doubting that Edwina was there.

He said, 'I say, I'm terribly grateful. We'll meet again, won't we?'

'I expect we will.'

The safragi who opened the door of the flat seemed to confirm Simon's expectations. Inviting him in, the man grinned in an intimate, insolent manner as though conniving at some act of indecency. He said, 'Mis' Likkle here,' but Simon found the person in the living-room was not Edwina. It was a man in late middle age who rose and gazed on him in courteous inquiry.

'Miss Little invited me here.'

'Did she? I'm sorry, but she has gone out to dinner. She's usually out at this time.'

Apologizing, Simon began to back from the room but the man said, 'Do stay. I'm Paul Beaker, one of the inmates. If Edwina's expecting you, I'm sure she'll be back quite early. Why not have supper with me!'

Supper with Paul Beaker offered a bleak alternative to Edwina and Simon hesitated, considering refusal, reflecting on the possibility of her return. There was a snuffle behind him and he realized the safragi had waited to observe his reception. He said, 'Your man thinks I'm some sort of joke.'

Beaker, looking over Simon's shoulder, ordered the safragi away and explained to Simon, 'This is an Embassy flat and we live here in a sort of family freedom that is incomprehensible to the Moslem mind. Hassan can no more understand the innocence of our proximity than you can understand his grins and giggles.'

Beaker, a fat man with a broad red face, raised the glass he was holding and said, 'Have a drink. *Do* have one. It will give me an excuse to have another.'

Simon was handed a tumbler of whisky. Pouring in a little water, Beaker asked, 'That all right?'

Simon, who had never before drunk anything stronger than beer, supposed it was all right as Beaker was drinking the same thing. Beaker, before he had even reseated himself, started to drink with avid satisfaction.

The room was sparsely furnished with sofa, two armchairs, a table and not much else. 'Rather a makeshift place,' Beaker said as Simon placed himself on the edge of an armchair, intending to leave when his drink was finished. 'The chap who holds the lease, one Dobbie Dobson, does not want to lash out on furniture. It's expensive and hard to get and who knows how long we'll all be here! I, myself, am leaving in a few weeks. I've been appointed to the university of Baghdad. I'm not a diplomat. I'm a professor of romance languages.' Doing his best to keep Simon entertained, the professor ruminated about the flat. 'Not a bad flat, really. It's designed for a Moslem family. This would be the audience room, then there's another room behind here, the hall's there and you see that baize door? It leads to the gynaeceum, the women's quarters. It's all arranged so the women of the house could pass from one end of the flat to the other without being seen by the visitors in here.'

Simon, uncertain whether Beaker was speaking of past or present, thought of the women moving secretly in the hidden rooms, then thought of Edwina and his cheeks grew pink. 'Do you mean Edwina is kept behind the baize door?'

Beaker laughed. 'Oh no, no indeed. Would one dare? No, I mean that it was in accordance with Moslem custom. Edwina *does* have her sleeping-quarters behind the baize door but no restrictions are placed upon her. She comes and goes as she likes.'

At the mention of Edwina's sleeping-quarters, Simon's blush deepened. He lowered his head to hide it while Beaker refilled the glasses and asked, 'You been out of England before?'

'Oh, yes. I once had a week in Paris.'

'Paris, eh?' Beaker laughed as though the name had some peculiar connotation for him. 'And now you're going into the desert, is that it?'

Simon, who was listening for Edwina's return, realized he must explain himself. He told of his journey round the Cape then asked if the professor had ever met his brother, Hugo.

'Yes, I seem to remember a young fellow called Hugo, one of Edwina's swains. So he's your brother! And you're joining him at the front. Bit worrying for your people to have two sons out there, isn't it? Are you their only children?'

'Yes, just the two of us,' Simon was suffused by the memory of his home and said, 'We live in Putney – not really Putney, more Roehampton.' He saw the street of small Edwardian terrace houses, all alike except that the Boulderstone home had a conservatory leading from the living-room. Mr Boulderstone had built it himself and said it added to the value of the house. Warmed and activated by the whisky, he told Professor Beaker about the conservatory that was filled with his mother's geraniums and a very old sofa. In the summer she would sit among her plants, mending clothes and knitting and listening to talks on the radio. The clouded glass, the scents, the summer warmth of the conservatory came back to him so vividly that he described them to Beaker as though they were important in the scheme of things. There was one remarkable thing in the conservatory. When the local mansion was being demolished to make way for a housing estate, Mr Boulderstone had acquired an old vine which he planted against the wall outside, bringing the main stem in to spread under the glass roof. He told his family that the vine was a Black Hamburg, like the vine at Hampton Court that produced great bunches of purple grapes, but, whatever Mr Boulderstone did, his vine had nothing but small green grapes like bunches of peas. He bought the vine buckets of blood from the abattoir. He puffed sulphur over the bunches but they never got bigger. Sometimes a sour flush of mauve would come over the grapes but they tasted as bitter as aloes.

Beaker, gazing intently at Simon's glowing face, seemed deeply interested in all this, encouraging Simon to talk so by the third whisky he was as far back in memory as his infants' school. When Beaker made to refill his glass Simon said, 'Oh no, I'd better not. I've got to find my way back to Abbasia barracks somehow.'

'Why not stay here,' said Beaker. 'We often put you chaps up. There's a small spare room.'

Thinking of Edwina, thinking of the abominable, death-smelling room at the barracks, Simon said, 'Oh, I say, thanks. But I've got to ring Transit.' When he rang Transit, he found a message had come for him from Major Perry. He was to be at Kasr el Nil barracks at six the next morning.

He said to Beaker, 'I'm afraid, sir, I've got to make an early start.'

'Don't worry. I'll give you the alarm clock. We're used to chaps making early starts.'

Simon settled thankfully back into the armchair and let Beaker give him another drink. But that, he knew, was enough. Hassan came in to set the table and Simon now was happy to accept Beaker's invitation to supper. Four places were laid but only Beaker and Simon sat down. Beaker asked him about the long voyage out to Egypt and Simon tried to describe the wonderful communion that had existed between him and his two friends, but already the deathless friendship, the understanding, the intense sympathy, the very smell of the ship itself, were fading from his mind like illusions that could not survive on dry land.

While he was talking, the front door opened and shut and Simon's voice dried in his throat. Paused in expectation, he realized that Beaker, too, was listening for Edwina's return. Then a male voice shouted, 'Hassan', and Beaker twitched nervously. 'Dear me, that's Percy Gibbon. I didn't know he would be in. He *will* be cross that we started without him.'

Percy Gibbon could be heard talking in Arabic to the safragi while Beaker, awaiting him, made an effort to appear sober. When Gibbon entered, Beaker began in a confused and fussy manner, 'So sorry, I really thought ... I really did ...' Gibbon held up an imperious hand and Beaker's apology limped to a halt.

Gibbon said, 'There are more important things to worry about.'

'Oh, really, are there? You've heard something?'

'Nothing that I'm free to impart.'

A very subdued Hassan put down Gibbon's soup and Gibbon bent to it, his nose just above the plate. It was a very large nose, the cheeks falling back so sharply that, from the front, Gibbon's face looked all nose. His mouth was small and his weak, pinkish eyes seemed colourless behind brass-rimmed glasses. Having downed his soup, he blinked at Simon. 'One of Edwina's, I suppose?'

Simon said, 'Not really. I only arrived yesterday. I came out on the *Queen Mary* with the draft.'

Gibbon frowned down in disapproval. 'That's something you should keep to yourself.'

Beaker, having incited information from Simon, now sided with Gibbon. 'Dear me, yes. Quite right. People are on edge. Rumours and so on. Unwise, I agree, to tell anyone anything.'

Gibbon said nothing. A dish of sliced lamb with carrots and

sweet potatoes had been put on the table and he shovelled nearly half of the lamb on to his plate. He ate briskly, repeatedly sniffing as though he had a cold in the head. He took no more notice of Simon and as soon as the meal was over, he jumped up and took himself out through the baize door.

Simon asked in a low voice, 'What does he do?'

Beaker, too, spoke quietly as though fearing a reprimand. 'Don't know. Whatever it is, it's very hush-hush. I've been told he breaks codes.'

'He must be very clever.'

Beaker laughed and let his voice rise. 'He certainly thinks he is. My theory is that he's modelled himself on one of those Byron heroes. You know: "Vital scorn of all", "Chilling mystery of mien", "Haughty and reserved manner" – that sort of thing.'

Simon nodded, too sleepy to speak, and Beaker suggested that having to make such an early start, Simon might be wise to go to bed. He was put in a room behind the baize door. It was as bare as the barracks' room but for Simon, it was another thing. It was a room in a household and what was more, it was near Edwina's room. The whole corridor behind the baize door had been redolent of flowers.

He was roused some time after midnight by the noise in the living-room. Several people were talking and laughing, then came the plink-plink of a guitar and a voice rose high, pure and dulcet, singing in a language Simon did not know. From the long, melancholy notes, he guessed it was a sad song of love and he murmured to himself, 'Poor little thing.' Then the voice warmed into impetuous emotion and he knew the singer was Edwina. The song tantalized him with the memories of young women he had known in England and the women he had met that day. He saw in his mind not only Edwina, but the dark girl called Harriet and the woman with the dead boy in the Fayoum House. Even Miss Brownall entered his thoughts with a certain seductive pathos because she was a woman and tomorrow he must go where there were no women.

While he lay listening, in a state of ardent anguish, a door was flung open in the corridor and Gibbon bawled out, 'Shut up. I do an important job, not like you bastards.'

The guitar stopped. The song devolved into giggles and Simon returned to sleep. Professor Beaker's alarm clock wakened him to darkness and silence. He had no idea how he was to find his way through the unknown, sleeping city but down by the river a taxi was parked with the driver curled up on the back seat. He reached Kasr el Nil barracks as the first red of dawn broke across the sky, and saw the convoy strung out along the embankment.

There was no sign of movement. He had had to go first to Abbasia for his kit and was relieved to find himself in time. He wondered if he looked a fool, turning up in a taxi but, reaching the lorries, he realized no one knew or cared how he had got there.

The lorries were a mixed lot, made up from one unit or another, but on most of them the jerboa, the desert rat, could be discerned through the grime. They had arrived sand-choked from the desert and were returning sand-choked, but here and there a glint of new metal showed where a make-do-and-mend job had been done. Among the men packed on board them, he recognized faces he had seen on the *Queen Mary* and he felt less dejected. Finding the sergeant in charge, he said, to show he was not a complete novice, 'I suppose a lot of your chaps were on leave when the trains stopped?'

'That's right ...' there was the usual pause before the 'sir' was added.

It was up to Simon to take over now. He counted the lorries and said, 'Thirty. That's the lot then, sergeant?'

'That's the koulou ... sir.'

The sergeant strolled off with the blank remoteness of a man to whom war was an everyday affair. Simon, with no idea of what lay ahead, looked about him as though seeing everything for the last time. There was an island in mid-river, one end of it directly opposite the barracks. In the uncertain light it looked like a great schooner decked out with greenery. The light was growing. The island, touched by the pink of the sky, was taking shape, its buildings quivering as though forming themselves out of liquid pearl. Palms and tall, tenuous trees grew from the shadows at the water's edge. Nothing moved. The island hung on the air like a mirage or an uninhabited place.

45

A wind, cool enough to be pleasurable, blew into Simon's face and he said to himself, 'Why, it's beautiful!' The whole city was beautiful and for a few minutes the beauty remained, then the pearl hardened and lost its lustre. The sun had topped the horizon. The air was already warm. The terrible crescendo of the day had begun.

Major Hardy, arriving at the barracks square, chose to place his staff car half-way down the column. Simon, given no order to join him, climbed in beside the driver of the leading lorry. Trying to sound knowledgeable, he asked, 'How are we going out, corporal?'

The corporal, whose round, sunburnt face was even younger than his own, replied, 'Oh, the usual way, sir,' and Simon waited to see what way that was. It proved to be familiar. They went, as Clifford's party had done, past Mena House and the pyramids. The corporal did not give the pyramids a look and Simon, seeing for the second time the small one sliding out from behind the greater, felt less wonder and said nothing. When they passed the excavated village, only Simon noticed it. They were travelling slowly so the lorries would keep together. At first the pace – it seldom exceeded ten miles an hour – was tolerable but when they faced the open desert, with the sun rising and shining into the cab window, tedium came down on them. Until then, Simon had still been attached to the known world but now it was disappearing behind him. He felt apprehensive, disconnected and rootless, and asked himself what on earth he was doing, going off like this into the unknown? Then, it came to him that, though he was vulnerable, he was not alone. He was a man among other men who, if they had to act, would act together. Yet the apprehension, fixed in his stomach, could not be moved. To reassure himself, he asked the driver, 'What's it like out there?'

'Oh,' the driver, called Arnold, dccked his head in a deprecating way, 'not bad, sir. You get browned off, a'course, but it's got its moments.'

Arnold had been one of those stranded in Cairo and had to find his battalion. He had no certainty he would do so. 'Never know what's happened when you're away. Don't want to start with a fresh mob, not when you're used to your own lot.'

This statement conveyed a sense of confusion ahead and Simon asked, 'How do you find your way around in the desert?'

The corporal laughed. 'You get a feel for it, sir.'

The sun rose above the cab roof and mirage hid the sand. The sky, if anyone could bear to look at it, had the molten whiteness of mid-day. They touched on the edge of a town. It was like a holiday scene with small, white villas, date palms and walls hung with purple bougainvillaea, then came the white dazzle of sand and a sea, in bands of green, blue and violet, that seemed more light than water. They passed abandoned camping sites where regimental flags hung over emptiness, then drove between two shallow lakes, one of them green, the other raspberry pink, both dotted with floating chunks of soda. Simon could not hide his astonishment.

'What a weird place!'

'It's only Alex, sir.' Outside the town, Arnold tentatively asked, 'Time to brew up, sir?'

'Good heavens, yes. I should have thought of it, shouldn't I?'

'That's all right, sir.'

The red flag was hoisted and the convoy drew into the side of the road. Numbers of army trucks and cars were going east. It seemed that that day only the convoy was going west. Looking down its length, Simon saw Major Hardy getting out of his car. The major was merely a passenger to the front but Simon, with no great confidence in his own power to command, felt it would be politic to treat him as if he were in charge. As Simon strolled down to the car, the major, spreading a large-scale map out over the bonnet, lifted a dark, lined face with a bar of black hair on the upper lip and gave him a stare of acute irritation. Simon started to introduce himself but Hardy interrupted him. 'Your section's brewing up. Better get back to see fair play.'

The sergeant, whose glum, folded face was kippered by the sun, was demonstrating, with an air of long-suffering, how to make a fire and boil water for the brew. The new men looked on as two large stones were set up to form a hob for the brew can, which was a cut-down petrol can. The water came from the convoy's reserves but the sergeant said sternly, 'You don't use it, see, if you can get it from anywhere else.' He packed scrubwood between the stones and set it alight. Down the convoy, other fires were being started for other sections. At intervals, at the roadside, groups of men stood and watched for water to boil.

'Now,' said the sergeant, 'y'puts in yer tea, see.' He broke open a case of tea and threw two large handfuls on to the boiling water. 'Right. Now y'lifts it off, see.' He lifted the can as though his dry, brown hands were insulated against heat. 'Right. And now – where's yer mugs?'

The mugs stood together on the sand, a concourse of mugs, one for each man in the section and a couple over. Vincent trailed condensed milk from mug to mug, giving an inch or more of milk, and then the sergeant splashed the brew can over them. The men, picking up their tea mugs, moved into groups as though each had sorted out the companions natural to his kind. Already, Simon thought, they had ceased to be a collection of strangers and soon they would be wedded into twos and threes of which each member belonged to the others as he had belonged to Trench and Codley. Feeling himself solitary and apart, he looked for Arnold but Arnold had his own friends, men who had been with him, stranded, in Cairo. The sergeant brought over one of the spare mugs and two bully beef sandwiches. 'Spot of char, sir?', then remained beside Simon who, deeply gratified, asked him where he had been before he went on leave.

'Mersa. The jerries were just outside.'

'Where do you think they are now?'

The sergeant snorted. 'A few yards up the road, I reckon.'

Simon saw that he was not, as he had thought, sullen or remote. He was dejected by defeat. 'We had Gazala. We had Tobruk. It was hunkey-dorey. Looked like in no time we'd be back in Benghazi, then this happened.'

'What *did* happen?'

'Came down on us like a bat out'a hell.'

Arnold called, 'Blue flag, sir?'

'Oh, yes. Yes. Blue flag.'

Looking towards the horizon where the heat was thickening

48

into a pall, Simon could imagine the German tanks appearing like monstrous bats, advancing with such speed and fury, the convoy could be wiped out before it had time to turn round. But the horizon was empty and even the eastbound traffic had stopped.

'Quiet, isn't it!'

Arnold said, 'Jerry's too busy to bother us,' and as he spoke, a Heinkel, returning from a reconnaissance flight, dived over the convoy. He braked sharply. The Heinkel, returning, sprayed the sand like a gesture of contempt. The bullets winged harmlessly into the sand. The plane flew off.

As the sun began to sink, Simon was concerned about the routine for the night. At some place and point in time he should give the order to make camp but before the need became an anxiety Arnold said, 'Think we should leaguer here, sir?'

There was a glimmer of white on the coast. The glimmer grew into a village of pleasant holiday homes with a bay, like a long white bone, that curved into the desert's cinderous buffs and browns.

'Who lives out here?' Simon asked.

'No one, now. They all moved away long ago.'

The lorries were positioned into a close-rank formation that served as camp and defence. Arnold, smiling as though he had begun to feel a protective affection for Simon, asked him, 'Permission to bathe, sir.'

Simon followed as the men, running between the dunes, shouting at each other, pulling off their shirts and shorts, went naked into a sea as warm and clinging as milk. Lying on the sea, in the haze of evening, he looked back at the village and was surprise to find it was still there. Had he been asked as they covered mile after mile of sand, 'Where would you choose to be?' he might well have chosen this oasis beside the white shore, with its villas under a shelter of palm trees. He raised his head to look westwards into the foggy distance of the desert coast and seeing nothing, he had an illusion of safety. The enemy must be further away than the sergeant imagined. Content filled him and he smiled at the man nearest to him. 'We didn't expect this, did we?'

The man laughed and twisted his head in a movement of appreciation. 'Dead cushy,' he said.

That night, startled out of sleep by the rising moon, Simon felt the earth vibrating beneath him. He sat up, uncertain where he was, and saw the brilliant whiteness of the houses patterned over by the palm fronds. There was a booming in the air, distant but heavy, and he knew it must be artillery. Pulling himself down into his sleeping-bag, he put his hands over his ears and sank back into sleep.

For most of the next day the convoy seemed alone in the desert. Occasionally a dispatch rider passed on a motorcycle and once a staff car came up behind them and went by with the speed of a police car. Then, in mid-morning, a pinkish smudge appeared on the horizon. Simon asked Arnold what he thought it was.

'Could be a sandstorm.'

The smudge, pale and indefinite at first, deepened in colour and expanded, swelling towards the convoy until, less than a mile away, it revealed itself as a sand cloud, rising so thickly into the heat fuzz of the upper air that the sun was almost occluded. Inside the cloud, the dark shapes of vehicles were visible. The first of them was a supply truck, lurching, top-heavy with mess equipment. The procession that followed stretched away to the horizon. Like the convoy, it moved slowly, creaking and clanking amid the stench of its own exhausts and petrol fumes. As they reached and passed it, Simon felt the heat from the vehicles that followed one after the other on the other side of the road.

Transports carried tanks that had lost their treads. Trucks towed broken-down aircraft or other trucks. Troop carriers were piled with men who slept, one on top of the other, a sleep of exhaustion. Guns, RAF wagons, recovery vehicles, armoured cars, loads of Naafi stores and equipment, went past, mile after mile of them, their yellow paint coated with sand, all unsteady, all, it seemed, on the point of collapse. As they moved nose to tail, they gave an impression of scrapyard confusion yet somehow maintained a semblance of order.

A staff car, that had pulled on to the wrong side of the road, brought the convoy to a halt. Major Hardy, striding towards it, shouted, 'What's going on? Is the whole damned army in retreat?'

Another major looked out of the disabled car, his face creased with weariness, and shouted back, 'No, it damn well isn't. The line's holding a few miles up the road. The Aussie 9th Division is rumoured to be on its way – and it better be. They're a mixed bunch back there: 8th Army, Kiwis, South Africans, a few Indians. How long they can hold out is anybody's guess.'

'But where's this lot going?'

'Ordered to prepare defences further east.'

'Where? The back gardens of Abou Kir?'

'Likely enough,' the major wiped the sweat from his face and gave a grin. 'We'll fight on the beaches.'

'This convoy's to report to 7th Motor Brigade. Any idea where that is?'

'Search me. Could be anywhere. It's hell and plain bloody murder where we came from.'

The obstructing car was pushed off the road to await a mechanic and the convoy went on, moving westward when it seemed that everything else in the world was going east. The breakdowns become more frequent. Every few hundred yards there was a halt and men were sent to push some vehicle away while Major Hardy questioned anyone he could find to question. He became more flustered, finding no one who knew or cared where the convoy might find its divisional headquarters. He shouted at Simon, 'Don't dog my heels, Boulderstone. Get a move on or we'll have another night on the road.'

They made what progress they could. Structures appeared beside the road, temporary and flimsy but suggesting that at last, among the muddle of wire and piled up stones, the tired newcomers might find their destination. Some sappers were at work on a crack in the tarmac and Simon, seeing them before Hardy had a chance to get to them, ran to make the usual inquiries. From their manner, he was uncertain whether they were telling him the truth or not. One sapper said, 'The Auk's down the road. Been standing there all day without his hat, just watching this ruddy circus go by. He'll tell you where to go.'

Simon doubted that but asked, 'What does he look like?'

'The Auk? Great man, ruddy hero. Big. Big chap. You can't miss 'im.'

The sappers, still laughing, stood back to let the convoy bump its way across the broken surface and drive on towards a red blur where the sun was beginning to set. The booming that had disturbed Simon the night before, now started again; a much more ponderous sound. Stars of red and green were rising into the sunset and Simon asked Arnold: 'Is that the front line?'

'No, the front's a good ten miles on.' They drove another mile. 'Think we'd better get down, sir?'

It was time to leaguer. The men sprang from the trucks, shaking the cramp from their legs, cheerfully congratulating each other as though they had reached home. The westbound traffic had been stopped by its own congestion and the dust had begun to settle. The air cleared but there was not much to see; only a vast plain, crimsoned by sunset, from which two columns of smoke, black as soot, rose into the blood-red brilliance of the sky.

Two

At eight a.m., the hour when the Egyptian sun exploded in at the edges of shutters and curtains, Harriet Pringle heard an uproar outside her bedroom door. The noise was only one woman's voice – the voice of Madame Wilk, the proprietor of the pension – but so heightened was it by panic and outrage that Harriet jumped out of bed, certain that calamity was upon them.

Madame Wilk was shouting into the telephone, 'They were seen. How do I know who saw them? It is known everywhere. I am telling you – thousands of them, all broken and useless, the men dead to the world. I have friends in Heliopolis and they rang me. They said, "They're still coming. A terrible sight, a whole army in retreat." ' Madame Wilk, her indignation growing, began to thump the door beside her, Harriet's door. 'Get up. Get up. You're finished, you British. The Germans are here already. Oh, oh, oh, what shall I do?' The voice rose into a funereal wail of such agony that Harriet opened the door.

Outside, Madame Wilk stood with the receiver in her hand, a shrunken little monkey of a woman with large brown eyes, faded and swimming with tears. She was a Copt, married during the first war to a British officer who had gone home leaving her with nothing but a British passport. Now she realized that if the British were finished, she, too, was finished, and the tears overflowed from her wrinkled eyelids and trickled down her withered cheeks. 'All my shares is gone. What have I? What is to happen to me?'

'What will happen to any of us?' Harriet asked.

'You? – you will run away, but me! What can I live on? Here I have worked, I have saved for my old age. I bought my pension, I bought shares because of my good sense, and now what are they worth? Nothing. They're worth nothing.'

Major Perry, putting his head out of the room opposite, said 'They'll recover. The exchange goes up and down like a bally yo-yo.'

'What good my shares recover and me not here where my shares are?'

Major Perry's laughter distracted Madame Wilk so Harriet was able to close her door. She hurried to take her shower and dress so she could find the truth of this latest, frightful, rumour of retreat, then went out to the long hallway that was the heart and centre of the Pension Wilk. The hall served as dining-room and sitting-room (not that anyone would sit there for long), and the tables and chairs, lined along one wall, almost blocked the passage. Guest-rooms opened off on either side. They were small but each had a shower-room attached and this enabled Madame Wilk to claim for the pension 'luxury' status.

Windows were shuttered during the daylight hours and meals had to be taken by artificial light. Harriet found this oppressive but had to accept that in Egypt the sun was an enemy. If it were not excluded, the indoor heat would be intolerable. Still, she felt a sense almost of triumph when she found that a door in the hall had been left open and daylight shone on the breakfast tables. The door, propped open at dawn for the sake of ventilation, had to be closed, locked and bolted before the guests were up. Harriet had often heard Madame Wilk's voice raised when a safragi had forgotten to shut it, but this morning, with other things to scream about, Madame herself had forgotten the door. Walking through it for the first time, Harriet could see why she was so concerned to keep it shut. It led on to a flat roof. The Pension Wilk was at the top of a tall block of flats and Harriet, going to the edge of the roof, found that only a single rail ran between her and the drop down to the street. Conscious of daring, she stood by the rail and looked towards Giza, half expecting to see the defeated army wandering in past Mena House. But there was no army. She saw nothing but the pyramids, that were visible only in early morning and at sunset, looking as small as the little metal pyramids that were used as pencil sharpeners.

The morning was so still, it did not relate to war. The traffic had not started up and she could hear, from a hundred yards below her, the bell of a camel and the slap of the camel-driver's bare feet.

She moved round the roof, astonished by the extent and clarity of the view in this early sunlight. Soon the town would be hidden under heat but now she could see the small houses washing, like a sea of curdled foam, up to the cliff-face of the Mokattam Hills. Above them Mohammad Ali's alabaster mosque, uniquely white in this sand-coloured city, sat with minarets pricked, like a fat, white, watchful cat.

Once, before history began, a real sea had filled the basin and beaten up against the cliff. It drained away and then the ancient Egyptians had come to give to the human spirit beauty and dignity. As she reflected on those first Egyptians, cries came from the minaret nearest to her and at once all the air was filled with the long, wailing notes of the muezzins calling the faithful to prayer. The kites, roused from sleep, floated up from the buildings in unhurried flight and began to glide with gentle, dilatory grace just above the roof tops. Harriet looking down on them, saw they were not as they seemed from below, a muddy brown but, catching the sun on their feathers, they gleamed like birds cast from bronze.

She was startled by another voice that joined with the muezzins, the voice of Madame Wilk. 'Come in, Mrs Pringle, it is forbidden to be on the roof.'

'I'm quite safe, Madame Wilk.'

'It is not for you to be safe, Madame Pringle. If you fall and are killed, the police will make trouble for me. So, at once, come in.'

Harriet went in and Madame Wilk banged the bolts into place, saying, 'Ah, I have too many worries.'

Harriet sat down to partake of a breakfast that was always the same. It began with six large, soft, oversweet dates served in a little green glass dish. The next course would be a small egg that might be boiled, fried or poached but always had the same taste of damp and decay.

Harriet was, like most of the pension guests, on the lookout for somewhere to live, yet as she thought of having to leave Egypt, of having to move once again to an unknown country, even the Pension Wilk seemed a desirable resting place.

On her way out, Harriet stopped beside Major Perry's table to ask, 'How did Madame Wilk get the idea we are in retreat?'

Perry, whose face had been drooping, reacted to the question like a bad actor. Puffing out a stench of stale alcohol, he laughed, 'Ha, ha, ha. You know what Cairo's like! Some surplus equipment was returned to the depot at Heliopolis and the locals got the wind up. Just the usual scare and rushing to the telephone.'

'I didn't know we had any surplus equipment.'

'Stuff to be broken up for spares. The desert's littered with it.'

'So there's nothing to worry about?'

'Nothing, girlie, nothing. When we get reinforcements, it'll be as right as rain.'

Harriet laughed. 'That's fine, only it doesn't rain here, does it?'

Guy and Harriet had arrived in Egypt during another 'Emergency', almost exactly a year before the present one. Then, as now, the Germans had reached Sollum and were likely to come further, but the fact did not mean much to the refugees who had suffered a much more acute loss. They reached Alexandria still mourning for Greece and their memories of Greece, and Egypt evoked in them disgust and a fear of its strangeness.

Their train had drawn into the Cairo station at midnight and those who had money in Egypt found themselves taxis and went to hotels. The rest, having nothing but useless drachma, waited about, bemused, not knowing where to go or what to do. Eventually an army sergeant took charge of them. Telling them that quarters had been requisitioned for them, he had led them a long way through back streets to a building as discouraging as a poor law institution. Here they were shown one dormitory for the women, another for the men and a single cold shower to be used by both. The dormitories with their iron bedsteads, army blankets, dismal lighting and smell of carbolic, had a prison atmosphere but no one complained. The refugees felt they had to put a good face on things and look grateful, imagining, until the manager brought round the bills, that they were the guests of the military. They learned later that the place had been a brothel until closed down by the army medical corps and the brothel-keeper, put out of business, was free to recoup his losses at the expense of the refugees. They would have paid no more at a first-class hotel and Guy, trying to make light of things, said, 'Now we know what it means to be "gypped".'

No food was served in the building and the new arrivals, gathered next morning in the hall, expected the sergeant to return and lead them to an army canteen. He did not come. No one offered them help of any kind. It came to them gradually that now they must look after themselves.

The Pringles, standing in the hall with the others, were surprised to see Professor Lord Pinkrose near the door. He was reputed to be a rich man but, ever ready to conserve his wealth, he had joined the penniless crew that looked to the army for succour. And here he was, breakfastless like the rest, but having an air of knowing what he was about. With him were two men whom Guy had employed as teachers at the institute in Bucharest.

They were called Toby Lush and Dubedat. Toby, in his usual get-up of old tweed jacket and baggy 'bags', was clicking his teeth impatiently on his pipe stem. He could not stay still.

Seeing the manager, he held to him, saying. 'We ordered a taxi for ten o'clock. Not here yet. Keep an eye out for it, there's a good chap.' The other man, Dubedat, elevated his thin hooked nose, his expression stern, disassociating himself from Toby's restless shuffling and gasping while Pinkrose, gripping his trilby hat, looked down at his feet. The hat, that was usually on his head, had left an indentation upon his strange, dog-brown hair.

The manager detached himself from Toby who said, 'I think he'll fix things for us.'

Pinkrose, lifting his grey lizard face out of the folds of his scarf, sniffed. 'I sincerely hope so. I made an appointment for ten-thirty and would not wish to be late. It is impendent upon us ... yes, yes, impendent upon us to show respect for the man who holds the reins.'

Harriet whispered to Guy, 'What do you think they're up to?'

Guy, adjusting his glasses to look at them, said, 'Why should they be up to anything?'

'Oh, they're up to something, all right.'

Seeing Guy beaming on them with such good will, she said, 'Have you forgotten that Pinkrose reported you as unfit for Organization work?'

'Did he? Oh, yes, I believe he did.'

'You know he did. As for the other two clowns – they went out of their way to discredit you in Athens.'

'They behaved badly,' Guy agreed but his expression remained benign.

The brothel had not been air-conditioned and the refugees were drowning in the indoor heat. Guy's face glistened and his glasses kept sliding down his nose. A big, untidy man with books in every pocket, he could not but be amiable. Cast up here together in this wretched billet, he saw Pinkrose, Dubedat and Lush as companions in misfortune and bore them no grudge.

Making a sudden bolt out into the street, Toby Lush came back in a state of blustering excitement. 'It's here. It's outside the next door house. It's been there all the time.'

When the three were gone, the Pringles began to realize that they could not stand for ever, lost and purposeless, in the dismal hall. Others were beginning to venture out into the dazzle and unnerving unfamiliarity of the Cairo street. They needed money. They had eaten in the army canteen at Alexandria and that had been their only meal in four days. They needed food but, even more, they needed reassurance.

Guy said, 'I ought to report to the Organization office, wherever that is.' Harriet thought it would be easier to find the British Embassy. They set out. Reaching a crowded main road, they felt hostility in the heat and tumult and became reckless. They stopped a taxi and were grateful to the driver for taking them in. He drove them to the Embassy where Harriet had to remain outside as hostage while Guy went in and borrowed the fare. They had stopped beside an ornamental wrought-iron gate but Guy was not allowed that way. A porter directed him to a small side building which was the chancellery.

Harriet, gazing through the gate at the dry lawns and flower-beds, wondered how plant life survived at all under this blaze of sun. In Athens, when they left, gardens and parks had been massed with flowers. In the olive groves, under the trees, the flowers stood as high as one's waist. Would she ever see the like again?

Guy, who had gone nervously into the chancellery, came out waving an Egyptian pound note. 'We have a friend here.'

'Who?'

'Old Dobbie Dobson.'

They went joyfully in to see Dobbie Dobson who greeted them just as joyfully. They had not known him well but now it seemed wonderful that they had known him at all. Taking both of Harriet's hands, he put her into a chair and smiled at her. The greetings over, the Pringles seemed to come to a stop. They wanted nothing more than to sit for a while in Dobson's air-conditioned office, among the furnishings of Spanish mahogany, the polished brasswork, the sense of order and richness, and regain themselves, but Dobson had to hear what had happened to them.

Pulling themselves together, they described their escape, making humour out of the hungry voyage, the vermin, the lice in the cabins, the passages boarded up because the freighters

58

had been prisoner transports, the useless lifeboats, with rusted-in davits. Dobson laughed with them.

'Well, well, you're safe,' he said. 'That's the main thing.'

Looking out at the lawn running down to the river, Harriet glimpsed the possibility of a settled life in Cairo. But it was only a glimpse. Such a life had not been offered them here and she was too tired and on edge to pursue the thought of it.

They had not seen Dobson for seven months and it seemed to them he had aged beyond that time. He was putting on weight while Harriet and Guy had grown sadly thin. He had lost his tufts of baby-soft hair and the skin was beginning to darken beneath his eyes. Only his diplomat's charm had remained untouched by this injurious climate. He said, 'Well, now, you'll be wanting money.'

Guy agreed he needed money but more than that he wanted to know how the Organization stood in Egypt. Who was in charge?

'You probably know the director. His name's Colin Gracey. He was in Athens at one time.'

Guy stared at Dobson and Harriet stared at Guy. Dobson could not have spoken a more disastrous name but, knowing nothing of affairs in Athens, he was merely puzzled by their dismay. Guy was too discomposed to speak and Harriet explained that Toby Lush and Dubedat had bolted to Athens, fearing an invasion of Bucharest, and had made themselves so useful to Gracey, he had actually put Dubedat in charge of the institute.

'Oh, no!' To Dobson this seemed beyond belief.

'Yes. Gracey was supposed to be an invalid – he had some sort of back trouble – and he managed to get a flight to Syria, leaving Dubedat and Lush in charge. I will say that Guy won in the end, but that won't help him now.'

'So there was a struggle for power in Athens!' Dobson looked at Guy. 'I can't think Gracey will hold it against you. You'll have to see him, of course.' Dobson, with no wish to involve himself in Guy's situation, was now extending tact rather than friendship.

Before Guy need speak, an Embassy servant came in with

cups of Turkish coffee. The concentrated caffeine in the small cups was as stimulating as alcohol to someone who seldom drank coffee. Guy, as he emptied his cup, sat up sharply, his expression decided. 'I won't see Gracey and I will not work for him.'

Harriet, worn out by strain and their three hungry days, could scarcely keep back her tears. 'What are we to do? Where can we go?' Her voice broke on these questions and Guy hung his head. Yet he remained obdurate. He knew his own worth and had expected to find here a responsible director who would appreciate his qualities. Instead he was again subordinate to a man he despised. Having once overcome Gracey's hangers-on, he would not now come to terms with his cabal. He said, 'I'm as highly qualified as Gracey, which is something he doesn't like. The only qualification he looks for is willingness to flatter him and do his work for him. I won't flatter him.'

Harriet said, 'But others will. Now we know where those three were going this morning. "The man who holds the reins" – Gracey! How on earth did Pinkrose know that he was here?'

'I told him,' Dobson admitted. 'Pinkrose rang the Embassy this morning, about ten o'clock, and he was put on to me.'

'And wasted no time going to see Gracey,' Harriet put a hand on Guy's arm. 'Darling, you'll put yourself in the wrong if you don't go too.'

Guy, seeing her eyes were wet, conceded a little ground. 'If he wants to speak to me, he can send for me. But I won't work for him.'

Harriet appealed to Dobson. 'Guy's in a reserved occupation. What happens if he refuses work offered him? Will he be placed under arrest?'

Dobson laughed. 'Nothing as dreadful as that, but he'll have no salary.'

Seeing them displaced, homeless, moneyless and futureless, Harriet put her face down into her hands and Dobson, touched by her desolation, turned his persuasive charm on to Guy. 'I really think, my dear fellow, you should just go and see Gracey. After all, he *is* your senior official. It would be the courteous thing to do.'

Guy, shaken by this mention of courtesy, raised troubled eyes and at that moment the servant returned and handed Dobson an envelope. Passing it to Guy, Dobson said, 'This is for you; an advance on salary, sanctioned by Gracey.'

'He knows I am here?'

'Yes. While you were paying off the taxi, I spoke to the finance officer and he got on to the Organization office. I knew you would want some cash.'

Guy held the envelope for a few moments then put it into his pocket, saying, 'It's due to me. It does not change things, but I will go to the office. As you say, it would be courteous to do so. Where can I find Gracey?'

'The offices are on Gezira. They're rather splendid.'

This fact did not impress Guy. 'We'll have something to eat and see him after that.'

'Don't go too early. Offices here shut for the siesta and don't open before five.'

Coming out to the chancellery with them, Dobson squeezed Harriet's shoulder. 'Cheer up. You're safe and well. As they say in the RAF: "Any prang you walk away from is a good prang". And Egypt's not too bad. You probably think it's weird but it has a certain macabre charm.'

He recommended them to a restaurant at Bulacq, noted for its river fish, and waved them away. The restaurant was underground with bare wooden tables and the fish tasted chiefly of mud, but food was food, and the Pringles were restored. Harriet, over coffee, commended Guy to his face for his warmth, good humour and generosity, telling him he had only to be himself with Gracey and Gracey would be won by him. He could get anything he wanted. And he should stop and think how fortunate he was. His sight unfitted him for the army, that was true, but he could be directed into a much worse job. While other young men were fighting a war, he was only asked to teach and lecture. The times being what they were, personal pride was out of place. Guy was forced to agree. He said, 'Well, if he offers me something, I'll take it,' and seeing him relent Harriet began to imagine the meeting with Gracey would put everything right. And so it may have done had Gracey been in his office at five o'clock.

There were two girls, Armenians, in the outer office and they apologized for Gracey's absence. They admitted he was due in at five, but could not say when he would arrive. One girl said, 'Sometimes he does not come at all.'

Questioning her, Guy discovered that Gracey had gone out that morning with three English visitors, one of them a lord. He had not been back since. The Pringles, if they wished, could wait in the hope that he would come in for his letters.

It was evident from their manner of speaking that the girls had very often to apologize for Gracey. Waiting for nearly two hours, the Pringles realized that here, as in Athens, Gracey treated the Organization as a mere extension of his social life.

'But it is a splendid office,' Harriet said, trying to soften Guy's resentment of Gracey's behaviour. 'A flat like this would be wonderful, wouldn't it?'

The office was at the top of a block of flats that jutted into the river at the northern end of the island. The river, reflecting light into the rooms, grew red with sunset and in the distance the pyramids came into view. It seemed to Harriet they could do worse than remain in Egypt and live in a place like this, but Guy said, 'Don't be silly. We could never afford to live here.'

The sun set, darkness came down, the lights were switched on and the girls prepared to leave the office. But the Pringles could stay.

'Sometimes Mr Gracey is very late.'

Guy decided they would stay another fifteen minutes. At the end of that time, when he was about to give up, Gracey strolled in and stopped at the sight of him. With no one to warn him that there were visitors in the office, he looked startled and seemed about to take to his heels. Guy stood up. Gracey, unable to escape, gave him a cold nod and said, 'Please sit down,' then went into his office where he could be heard slitting envelopes and shifting papers about before calling to the Pringles to enter.

He had adopted an air of languid dignity, unsmiling and weary. At first glance his appearance was not much changed. His fair, classical head looked youthful and his long, delicate body moved with grace but gradually the youthful impression crumbled. His hair was more grey than gold and his face had dried and was contracting into lines. Egypt had aged him, as it had aged Dobson, but more than that : it had depleted what Dobson had retained. In Athens, a spoilt invalid made much of by Cookson and Cookson's friend, Gracey had been all smiles and charm. Now he did not smile.

'Well, Pringle, what are we to do with you?'

Guy was silent, leaving Gracey to answer his own question. Gracey, apparently having no answer, frowned as though it were inconsiderate of Guy to survive the Greek campaign.

During the afternoon, which they had spent at the Metro cinema, Guy had reflected on all Harriet had said at luncheon. He knew he was privileged to be reserved in a congenial occupation. Unlike most men, his chances of surviving the war were high. The least he could do was submit and accept what came to him. Having decided this, he had one moment of weakness as they set out for Gezira : 'If only it wasn't Gracey!'

Harriet said, 'You despise Gracey, so the greater the glory in swallowing your pride and obeying him. Your political beliefs should tell you that.'

'Nonsense. You're thinking of religion, not politics.'

'What's the difference?'

'Darling, you're being silly.'

Gracey said, 'I suppose you want to stay in Egypt?'

'Is there any choice?'

'No, not really. Men have been turning up from all over Europe. I've had to make jobs for them or get some other director to take them. They've gone to Cyprus, Turkey, Palestine, the Sudan – anywhere they could be fitted in. I've had my work cut out, I can tell you.' Gracey looked aggrieved at the thought of the effort expended on the men from Europe and his glance at Guy seemed to say, 'And, now, here's another one.'

'There's not much scope for the Organization in Egypt,' he said. 'Here they have the Public Instruction system – the PI, as it is called – that's been employing English teachers for years. There's no point in duplicating their work. We have the institute, but that merely offers straightforward teaching. I can see no opening for a lecturer like yourself.'

'I'm prepared to teach.'

'The fact is, we're overstaffed. We've a number of excellent Egyptian teachers of English.'

Harriet said, 'I believe Lush and Dubedat came here this morning. May I ask if you've taken them on?'

Gracey, challenged, lifted his chin and looked remote. 'I owe a lot to them. They did yeoman service for me in Athens.'

'So you're employing them here! What about Lord Pinkrose?'

'Lord Pinkrose is not seeking employment at the moment. He feels he should take a holiday and as this is a sterling area, he has the means to do so. He has, I believe, a considerable private fortune on which to draw.'

'If you cannot employ me,' Guy said, 'I must be repatriated. That is in my contract.'

'Contracts, I'm afraid, don't count for much these days. I cannot repatriate you. There's no transport for civilians. The evacuation ships, and they are few and far between, take only women and children.'

'Then I suppose I can be released from my contract and find other work.'

'There's no question of your being released. The Organization holds on to its men. You'll just have to wait till I can think of something for you.'

'Very well.'

The strain between the two men was evident and Harriet made an attempt to improve the situation by asking about Gracey's health. Was his back any better?

'I'm glad to say it is. Much better.' Unable to resist the chance to talk about himself, Gracey relaxed slightly as he described his treatment by a French orthopaedic surgeon in Beirut. 'Most successful, I must say – but not at first. The spine was in a bad way. It did not respond to rest so he put me into a plaster jacket and that did the trick. I wore it for three months. Not very pleasant and not flattering to the figure, but I had to bear with it. I still get a twinge or two if I exert myself. I have to take care but so long as I *do* take care, and rest, and don't overdo it, I can jog along. So ...' Gracey rose and extended a hand to Guy. 'Come back in a week. By then I hope I shall have something to offer you.'

Away from the office, Harriet said, 'I think he was glad to get rid of us. Perhaps he really doesn't know what to do with you.'

'It's his job to know what to do with me.'

'Oh darling, don't quarrel with him. He's probably not as bad as we think.'

Guy shrugged, bemused by the fact that Harriet, more critical of the human race than he was, was also, in her way, more tolerant. If he lost faith, he lost it completely. Harriet had not much faith to lose.

Returning to their dismal quarters, Harriet knew the thing they most needed was a place of their own. She spent the week going round small hotels and pensions, finding them filled by army personnel. She was near despair when she was offered a room in the Pension Wilk. Madame Wilk, however, required a months' rent in advance and the Pringles, handing over most of their money, faced a period of anxious penury. The pension provided meals, of a sort, but between meals, if you had no money to spend, there was little enough to do. A general evacuation still threatened and Harriet, fearing they might leave Egypt with all its sights unseen, persuaded Guy to take the tram-car out to Mena House. Guy would scarcely give the pyramids a glance. He found them neither beautiful nor useful and said he did not like them.

Harriet, becoming cross in the heat and glare, asked: 'What *do* you like?'

They had wandered into a 'dig' left idle by war and Guy, tripping on the uneven ground, gave a disgusted glance about him and pointed to some small trucks used for transporting rubble. 'I like those. They remind me of the tips on the road to Dudley.'

The pyramids observed, not much remained. The museum was shut for the duration. Someone told them about the City of the Dead, a favourite gharry trip by moonlight, but Guy rejected it as 'a morbid show'.

When he returned to the Organization office, he was told

that Gracey had left Cairo. He had, in fact, left Egypt. Only one of the girls remained in the outer office and she looked embarrassed as Guy faced her, dumbfounded by Gracey's defection. He had gone to the office in hope of employment to fill his empty days, and now what was he to do? Where had Gracey gone? Gracey had gone to Palestine. As Palestine did not come under the authority of the Cairo office, Guy asked, 'Has he gone on holiday?'

'He say "on a tour of inspection".'

'What does that mean?' The girl shook her head. 'How long will he be away?'

'I do not know how long. Perhaps a long time. It depends.'

'On what?'

'On what is happening. The war, you know. If the Germans come too close, people go to Palestine.'

'I see. And who is doing his work while he is away?'

The girl shook her head again. Guy, at a loss, asked for a piece of paper and wrote the address and telephone number of the Pension Wilk. He asked her to let him know when she had news of Gracey's return. She looked sadly at the paper and said in her small, mournful voice, 'I am so sorry but after tomorrow I shall not be here. The office is closed when Mr Gracey is away.'

Until then the Pringles had scarcely given a thought to the emergency. The English residents in Cairo were flustered but to the refugees, still caught up in the tensions of the Greek defeat, the desert war seemed a trivial matter. Calamity for them was the German occupation of Athens and many of them wept as they heard the final broadcast from the Greek radio station: 'Closing down for the last time, hoping for happier days. God be with you and for you.'

The silence that followed was, for them, the silence of the civilized world.

Most of the refugees had no wish to stay in Egypt. Most of them went to Palestine and from there managed to make their way to India, Persia or South Africa. Some, it was rumoured, even managed to get back to England. Those who could not afford to travel on their own, began to talk about a possible official evacuation, seeing it as a solution of a vacuous life spent mostly in small underground bars, the only places they could afford where they were out of the appalling sun.

The bars, that had adopted names like the *Britannia* or the *George* to entice in the troops, sold Stella beer for which Guy acquired a taste. His closest friend in those dire days was Ben Phipps who had been a freelance journalist in Athens. Now, having reached a major war zone, he decided to offer himself to the London papers as a correspondent. He sent out eight cables to Fleet Street, claiming to be an expert on Middle East affairs, but replies were slow in coming.

Resentful of his own displacement, Ben Phipps was scornful of the English who lived richly in Egypt. 'A bloody good thing if the whole lot are given the boot. Let them know what it's like to live out of a suitcase.'

'What good will that do us?' Harriet asked.

Ben's small, black eyes jumped angrily behind pebble glasses. 'We'd all be in the same boat. That's what.'

Harriet had to agree that calamity had its uses. If they ended up together in Iraq or the Sudan, Gracey would have no more power over Guy.

Two days later a London evening paper cabled, appointing Ben Phipps its Middle East correspondent. A dramatic change came over him. He no longer despised the English who had done well in Egypt. He no longer hoped for a general evacuation. Though the Middle East situation had had for all of them as much structure and relevance as a cage full of flies, Ben now talked knowingly of desert strategy and the need to hold the Levant as bulwark against the loss of the Persian Gulf oil.

He left Cairo kitted out in khaki shorts and shirt and carrying the old portable typewriter he had brought from Greece. Guy and Harriet went with him to the train. 'Off into the blue, eh?' he said with relish, looking pityingly at the Pringles who would be left behind.

Guy, unable to believe his friend had gone, said he was sure he would be back in no time. But not only Ben Phipps had gone. One by one the remaining refugees found means to go elsewhere. Soon no one known to the Pringles was left in the bars. There was no one with whom to talk through the slow, dispiriting hours between meals. No one with whom to discuss the tricks by which the penurious supported life in Cairo. No one to ask for news.

This idle and purposeless life disturbed Guy and Harriet in different ways. Harriet longed for a home more spacious than the small, cluttered room at the pension but Guy, who had often in his youth had no home at all, only wanted employment and friends. Perhaps he wanted employment most. He was ashamed to be idle while other men were at war. He tried to outwit his workless state by planning lectures, concerts for troops, productions of Shaw or Shakespeare, but could do none of these things. He was without status, acquaintances and the means to carry out his plans.

Soon after Ben's departure, Guy picked up with Bill Castlebar who lectured at the Cairo university. Castlebar occasionally went to the bars but preferred the Anglo-Egyptian Union which he recommended to the Pringles. Because they had once or twice mentioned Dobson, he was uncertain where they belonged in the social hierarchy and gave his advice with a hint of irony. 'You may think you're a cut above the Union, but there are worse places. The Sporting Club has more to offer, of course – polo, racing, gambling, swimming. You'd meet the local nobs there but it costs a lot of money to play with them. Perhaps you can afford it?' Reassured on this point, he said, 'The Union's not smart but the conversation's a great deal livelier.'

'Can one get beer there?' Guy asked.

'Get beer! You can not only get it, you can get it on tick. *They let you sign for it.*'

Introduced into the Union, the Pringles sat under the trees and knew they had found their asylum. The Union, that shared the vast lawns of Gezira, existed to promote friendship between the Egyptians and their British rulers, but few Egyptians appeared there. The British scholastics, from the university lecturers who were fairly well off to the PI teachers who lived just above the poverty line, kept the place going. There was a club house and library and a belt of ancient trees of immense height that shaded the outdoor tables and chairs. As Castlebar pointed out, you could sit there all day and no one questioned your right. In a country where the ruling caste was expected to maintain aristocratic standards, the Union succoured the English poor.

Here Guy found company, the company usually being Castlebar and Castlebar's friend Jackman. He was immediately at home with them and Harriet accepted them, realizing that they were exactly the sort of dissidents Guy would pick up wherever he went. He was entertained by Castlebar who wrote limericks, but had a much greater respect for Jackman. This puzzled Harriet until she learnt that Jackman had told Guy, in the greatest possible confidence, that he had fought in Spain in the International Brigade. Harriet felt an instinctive doubt of this claim and said, 'Why don't you ask Castlebar if it's true?'

'Castlebar knows nothing about it. Of course it's true, but he has to keep it dark. It wouldn't do him any good in a place like this if it got around.'

Six weeks passed without news of Gracey and Guy, existing in a state of desperate suspension, began to hate his director and so see Cairo as a centre of waste and imprisonment. He discussed Gracey with Castlebar and Jackman and they encouraged him in a revolt of ribaldry.

If they did not know Gracey, they knew about him. In Cairo, he lived as the permanent house guest of a rich Turk, Mustapha Quant (called by Jackman 'Mustapha Kunt') who maintained him in decadent splendour in a houseboat on the Nile. Their stories about Quant, Gracey and the parties given for male friends only were a delight to Guy who felt justified in ridiculing his director to all comers.

Harriet, made uneasy, said, 'Let's stop talking about Gracey,' but Guy had reached the point of anxiety in which talk was the only release. It was terrible to Harriet to see Guy's good sense overthrown. And if Gracey did not return, he might be held here in a despairing limbo until the war ended.

He exploded out of this condition one morning, coming from the shower, flapping his bath-towel about in his excitement, shouting, 'Listen to this.'

> There's Wavell of the desert,
> There's Tedder of the planes,
> But I'm Gracey of Gezira,
> I'm the man that holds the reins.

I live in style with Mustaph,
Our houseboat it is fine,
But if Rommel looks like coming here,
I move to Palestine.

'Don't you think it's funny?'

'Not very. And for God's sake don't put it around.'

'Of course I won't,' Guy assured her but when he composed another verse, he had to recite it to Jackman.

They say Christ walked on water
On the Sea of Galilee,
But I'm Gracey of Gezira,
No water walks for me.

The song, for Guy was now singing it to a music-hall tune of no originality, amused not only Castlebar and Jackman but anyone sitting near them at the Union. Harriet, torn between pride in Guy and fear of reprisals, begged those who heard the song not to repeat it. 'If it got back to Gracey, Guy could be in real trouble.'

'Who would tell Gracey anything?' said Jackman, pulling his long nose and shifting his thin backside about as he sniggered, acting amusement without any amusement in his eyes.

People who barely knew Guy congratulated him on his temerity in composing the song. The word 'temerity' alerted Guy to his own rashness yet he remained defiant. Life was precarious and he might not have any future to worry about.

Then the atmosphere changed. The British had retaken Sollum and were chasing Rommel out of Egypt. Though Cairo seemed to them as empty and crowded as a railway junction, they would have to settle down there. Harriet started looking for a job.

Guy learnt of Gracey's return from Toby Lush. Toby, coming along the crowded pavement with his trotting walk, saw Guy and was about to rush across the road when Guy caught his arm. 'Where have you been?'

Toby sprang back, pretending to ward off a blow. 'Hey, old cock, don't eat me.' His face slopping about like bilge water in his attempt to appease Guy and also impress him, Toby said that he, Dubedat and Pinkrose had gone on a sightseeing tour of upper Egypt. 'Pinkers hired a car and I did the driving.

Amazing what we saw. Gracey joined us two weeks ago and we all came back together.'

'Perhaps now Gracey'll let me know what he has in mind for me.'

'He will, old cock, but you've got to realize he's a lot on his plate. Trouble is, you said you didn't want to work in Cairo.'

'I said nothing of the sort.'

'Been a bit of misunderstanding, then, but don't worry. I'll put in a word for you. And I say,' Toby became alert and encouraging, 'what's that song you wrote: "Gracey of Gezira"? The old soul roared when he heard it. He said it'd be the institute's theme song.' The 'old soul' was Dubedat.

Aware, at last, of his own unwisdom, Guy said, 'Don't tell Gracey about it.'

Toby spluttered on his pipe with joy, 'Don't worry. You know Gracey. He's got a great sense of humour. He'll love it.'

When Guy went to Alexandria, Harriet, who had started work at the American Embassy, remained in Cairo. With two incomes, the Pringles could keep their double room at the Pension Wilk and be together at weekends. They regarded the mid-week separation as temporary. Either Guy would be permitted to return or Harriet would go to him.

At the Embassy, Harriet was known as the Assistant Press Officer. The title sounded important but she was merely a stop-gap employee and, sooner or later, the press office would be taken over by a team flown out from the States. The team was slow in coming. Harriet had been in her position for nearly a year when the latest, and most fearful, emergency arose in the desert. By then she had become as knowledgeable about the war as Ben Phipps. She was generally held to have inside information and people would stop her in the street to ask for news. But she was still temporary, and not only temporary but a member of an inferior race.

Having grown up in the belief that Britain was supreme in the world and the British the most fortunate of people, she had been shocked to find that to the Americans she was an alien who rated less than a quarter of the salary paid to an American-born typist. She protested to her superior, a Mr

Buschman, saying, 'I'm not an alien – I'm British.' Mr Buschman liked this so much that he managed to get her a rise in salary. The rise was not great but it reconciled her to her alien degree and the working hours that had been imposed on the staff after Pearl Harbor. Entering the war with the enthusiasm of late-comers, the Americans decided on an 'all-out' war effort. The other Cairo establishments closed from noon till five o'clock, but the Americans decided to work through the afternoon. Given an hour for luncheon, the employees returned to the Embassy when the whole city lay motionless in a stupor of heat.

Mr Buschman, a young married man, neatly built, not tall, with a flat, pale, pleasant face, was both fatherly and flirtatious with Harriet. He once tried to span her waist with his hands and nearly succeeded. Then he measured it with a tape and said, 'Twenty-two inches. I like that.' He asked her what she weighed. When she said 'Seven stone', he worked it out and said, 'Exactly one hundred pounds. I like that, too.'

And Harriet liked Mr Buschman. She particularly liked the way he called her 'Mem' as though she were Queen Victoria, and she felt an affectionate trust in him until the day when the German radio put out a threat to Cairo. At half-hourly intervals, a voice said, 'Tonight we will bomb Cairo off the face of the earth.' The threat was in English and Arabic and Harriet's translator, Iqal, bringing her this item, said, 'You see, Mrs Pringle, how they are seeking to frighten us!' Short and stout, with the heavy shoulders of a water-buffalo, Iqal shrugged so that his shoulders rose in a hump behind his head. 'We are not much frightened, I think.'

The American staff did not seem frightened, either. Mr Buschman made no comment when he went through the news sheets that contained the repeated threat to destroy Cairo but when she left the office that evening, Harriet saw the Embassy cars gathered outside, prepared for flight. Next morning, the cars were not there. The Embassy seemed empty except for Harriet, Iqal and the Levantine girl typists. When Iqal came in with the first news sheets, Harriet asked him, 'Where is everybody?'

'You do not know, Mrs Pringle?' Iqal was eager to tell her

72

what she did not know. 'Our American friends went for a night picnic in the desert, but now the danger is over, doubtless they will return.'

Iqal's grin held only a trace of irony. To him the actions of his employers were above criticism but Harriet was struck through by a sense of betrayal.

'Mr Buschman said nothing to me about the danger.'

'Nor to me, Mrs Pringle.'

Harriet had to realize that so far as Mr Buschman was concerned, she and Iqal were equally alien and equally dispensable. Now, with the Afrika Korps outside Alexandria, the Embassy cars were again assembled, packed and ready for a getaway, but this time she was less hurt by the sight of them. Mr Buschman remained, as he always was, cordial and kind, but she knew now that his cordiality had its practical side. He was concerned for the safety of the American staff but need not worry about aliens. The American staff had diplomatic protection and could leave, if they had to leave, in their own time. Their preparations were against the possibility of bombing, street-fighting or an Egyptian rising, all the risks of a base town caught up in active warfare.

The Americans, protected and prepared, remained calm. Only Iqal showed disquiet. On the morning of Madame Wilk's outburst, he said to Harriet, 'What do you British do with my country, Mrs Pringle? You come here to rule yet when the enemy is at the gate, you run away.'

'I haven't run away, Iqal.'

'No, but many have. And what of your officers who disport themselves at the Gezira swimming-bath! Where are they now?'

Harriet made a wry face, knowing that one of the sights at Cairo at that time was the queue of officers, half a mile long, waiting to draw their money from Barclay's Bank. Having confounded her, Iqal was at once contrite and good-humoured and showed her a news item he had been holding back. 'See here, Mrs Pringle,' he began to giggle wildly, 'here they say the Afrika Korps reach Alexandria tonight. They send a message to the ladies of Alexandria and this is what they say: "Get out your party dresses and prepare to defend your honour."

Oh-ho, Mrs Pringle, oh-ho!' Iqal's thick dark finger quivered with excitement as he pointed to the item. 'These Germans are not deceived. Alexandria is a place of brott-ells.'

'How do you feel about a German occupation, Iqal?'

Faced with this direct question, Iqal at once became grave and declamatory. 'You ask me, Mrs Pringle, how do I feel? That is an interesting consideration. What do these Germans promise us? – they promise freedom and national sovereignty. What are those things? And what are these Germans? They are invaders like all the invaders that have come here for one thousand four hundred year. They come, they go, the English no worse than others. But to govern ourselves! – that we have forgotten, so how do we do it? And why should we believe these Germans, eh? For myself, I am brushing up my German to be on the safe side, but all the time I am asking myself, "Better the devil we know". In their hearts, Mrs Pringle, the Egyptian people wish you no harm.'

'You mean, too many people are doing too well out of us?'

'Ah, Mrs Pringle, I see you know a thing or two.'

'Well, one thing I do know, the Germans won't get to Alexandria. The British always fight best with their backs to the wall, and we can't afford to lose the Middle East.'

'Can't afford? Deary me, Mrs Pringle, how many people can't afford? The French, the Poles, the Dutch – could they afford?'

'Don't forget, Iqal, we have the Americans with us now.'

At this mention of his employers, Iqal sobered and nodding in reverential appreciation of this truth, he whispered, 'Ah, it is so!'

Harriet worked in a basement area too large to be called a room. Mr Buschman sat at a desk between the French windows at the back. Harriet, who had an alcove to herself, was in charge of a map of the eastern hemisphere that covered the whole of one wall. Her daily job was to mark the position of the combatants with pins. There were blue-headed pins for the allied forces, red for the Russians and Chinese, and black for the Axis. Recently, having had to order them, Harriet had obtained yellow pins for the Japanese.

On the morning when news came of Pearl Harbor, Harriet had gone to work in high spirits, seeing the war as more or less over. She found Mr Buschman in quite a different state. White-faced and trembling, he said over and over again, 'The bastards! The God-damn bastards!'

Harriet said, 'Well, it's something definite. You'll have to come in now.'

Mr Buschman struck his desk in rage. 'Definite? God-damn, it's definite all right. We'll make the bastards pay. We'll blow them right out of the water.'

But the Japanese were advancing and Harriet, sticking yellow pins into Wenchow and Gona, began to feel that the only change brought about by the American intervention in the war was the change in her working hours.

That day, leaving the office at one o'clock, she met Jackman who asked her the usual question: 'Any news?'

Harriet shook her head.

'Where's Guy! Not still in Alex? I'd get him out of there if I were you.'

Jackman drooping, with concave chest and shoulders hunched, kept his hands in his pockets as he talked. He had a thin, almost aesthetic, face, not unhandsome, but spoilt by a surly expression and the long nose that he was always stroking and pulling as though to make it longer. Looking at the ground in his hang-dog way, he said, 'I can tell you this, Rommel won't bother to take Alex. He'll cut it off by going round the back. When that happens, it'll fall of its own accord. No help for it. No supplies. Nothing. They'll be starved into surrender. You ring Guy and tell him to take the next train to Cairo. Here he'll have a chance. There – not a hope in hell. Tell him if he tries to stick it out, he'll only end in the bag. And a lot of good that'll do him, you or anyone else.'

Jackman began to make off while Harriet was asking, 'What are we to do?' He looked over his shoulder to shout at her, 'When they get here, grab a car and race for the canal...'

'*If* they get here.'

'Nothing can stop them now.'

Harriet was the only guest taking luncheon at the pension. At the other end of the hall, almost invisible in the weak electric light, Madame Wilk sat at her table. Two tables away from Harriet sat Miss Copeland who appeared at the pension once a week. Today was her day. She would lay out a little haberdashery shop on one of the tables then, sitting in the silence of the deaf, she waited to be given her luncheon, tea and supper. After that she packed up and went to some mysterious living place. She sold sanitary towels to the younger women at the pension, passing them over, wrapped in plain paper, with a secrecy that suggested a conspiracy. No one knew how long she had lived in Cairo. Harriet, who was curious about her, had learnt that years before, when Miss Copeland still had her tongue, she used to tell people that she was related to an English ducal family. Some people got together and wrote to the head of the family on Miss Copeland's behalf, but there was no reply. She was now very old and her skin, tautly stretched over frail old bones, had the milky blueness of chicken skin. Each week it seemed she could not survive to the next, yet here she was, silent and preoccupied, remote from the panic of the times. She went through her luncheon with the intensity of someone to whom a meal was a rare and wonderful treat.

Luncheon ended, as breakfast had begun, with six dates in a green glass dish. Harriet took her coffee over to Madame Wilk's table and whispered, although Miss Copeland was in no danger of hearing her, 'Does she know about the emergency?'

Madame Wilk gave her head a severe shake.

Miss Copeland's cottons, tapes, needles and pins were laid out this week, as every week, in orderly rows beside a red and white chequered Oxo tin for money, when there was any money.

'What's to be done about her?'

Madame Wilk spread her hands. 'God knows.' She and Harriet kept their heads together, fearing to disturb Miss Copeland's happy ignorance of events. She might have to be told, but not yet.

Harriet set out for work through streets coagulated with heat and empty of movement. Labourers and beggars lay in a sort of sun syncope, pressed against walls, arms over eyes, galabiahs tucked between legs to avoid any accidental exposure of the parts that religion required them to keep hidden.

Sweat trickled like an insect between her shoulder blades

and soaked the waistband of her dress. She could smell the scorched smell of her hair. And about her there were other smells, especially the not altogether unpleasant smell that came from waste lots saturated with human ordure and urine. Cairo was full of waste lots; dusty, brick-strewn, stone-strewn, hillocky sites where a building had collapsed from age and neglect. The smell that came from them was nothing like the salty, pissy smell of an European urinal. It was rancid and sweet like some sort of weed or first war gas. Harriet thought of phosgene, though she did not know what it was like. She had read somewhere of soldiers mistaking the smell of a may tree for poison-gas.

On her solitary walks to afternoon work, Harriet had had odd experiences, induced perhaps by the mesmeric dazzle of the light. Once or twice, she had lost the present altogether and found herself somewhere else. On one occasion she was in a landscape which she had seen years before, when riding her bicycle into the country. It was an ordinary English winter landscape; a large field ploughed into ridges that followed the contours of the land, bare hedges, distant elms behind which the sky's watery grey was broken by gold. She could smell the earth on the wind. There was a gust of rain, wet and cold on her face – then, in an instant, the scene was gone like a light switched off, and she could have wept for the loss of it.

Once an old man, white bearded, of noble appearance, had stopped her and held out his hand. He was wearing priestly robes and a green fez. They talked for a while about life and her reasons for being in Egypt, then he asked her to marry him, saying he had had many wives in a long life but never one who would go out in the heat of mid-day without a covering on her head. She asked how it was his fez was green while all others were red and he said he had had it specially made for him to indicate to the world that he was a descendant of the prophet. He was a jocular old man and they parted with a lot of laughter.

Now, reaching Suleiman Pasha where the shop blinds were pulled down but doors were ajar in case custom should come, unlikely though it was, Harriet saw ahead of her a single living creature. It was a man in khaki shirt and shorts, a lost

British soldier, hung over with baggage. When he reached the Midan he sank down on the steps of an office block and began pulling the straps off his shoulders. Beneath the straps, under his armpits, in every crevice of his clothing the cloth was black with sweat. He was wiping his face when Harriet approached him.

The large buildings of the Midan threw one side of the square into shadow so deep it gave an illusion of darkness. Although the sky was a pure cerulean blue, the eye, reacting against excess of light, covered it with a dark film. The banks and office blocks, ponderously imitating western buildings, seemed as flimsy as theatre flats. The whole Midan might have been made of cardboard, not painted but blotted over and bloated with grey, black or umber dye, uneven and dimmed by dust.

Seeing Harriet, the soldier called out, 'Excuse me, miss. You English? I thought so. Strange how you can tell.' He plashed his hand over his pink brow, drew it down his cheeks and shook the sweat from his fingers. 'I missed the transport, went to the barracks and they say I got to wait till seventeen hundred hours. Thought I'd look around but what a place! I was just saying to m'self, "Where do you go now, chum? What's to see and do around here?"'

Harriet, looking about her, wondered what there was to see and do in the wide, empty streets of Cairo at this hour. She told him: 'There's the Rivoli cinema not far from here. It's air-conditioned and so chilly, you might catch a cold. I've caught cold myself there.'

'Can't be too chilly for me.' The soldier rose and looking her over said with jaunty fervour, "Spose you wouldn't come with me?'

She smiled, knowing to these lost men an Englishwoman, any Englishwoman, was not an individual but a point of contact with desirable life. 'I'm sorry. I have to go back to work, but I'll walk part of the way.'

'Right-e-o.' He put the straps back and with all his belongings lurching around him, went with her towards Fuad al Awal. Eyeing her with some curiosity, he said, 'Funny meeting someone from England, just like that! What you doing here, then?'

'Egypt's full of English people. My husband has a job here.'

'Oh, yes?' At the mention of a husband the soldier retreated into respectful silence and Harriet, to start him talking again, asked how he had come to miss his transport.

'It was like this, see. Me and my mates went down into one of those bars and had a few beers and I passed out. Not in the bar, mind you. I went in – well, if you'll excuse me mentioning it – I went in the toilet. They didn't know I'd passed out, did they? I mean, I could've gone after a bint, couldn't I? Can't blame them, can you?'

'No, it could happen to anyone.'

'That's right.'

She could see how pained he had been at finding himself deserted and how much he needed company, but she was late already. Pointing to the cinema, she said regretfully, 'I have to go the other way.' Before she turned the next corner, she looked back and saw him standing like an eager dog, staring after her, hoping she would change her mind.

At the Embassy the only sign of life was the hopping of the hoopoes in and out of the garden sprays. Mr Buschman always played golf in the middle of the day and, coming rather late to the office, would put salt tablets into a large glass of water and drink it with a grimace. Lined up on his desk in different coloured boxes were pills and capsules which he called vitamins. Harriet had never heard of salt tablets or vitamins and Mr Buschman, amused by her innocence, said, 'They're sent out to us through the bag. They look after us, you see.' The vitamins were distributed among the American staff but not, of course, the aliens.

Looking over the news sheets, Mr Buschman laughed aloud. ' "Defend their honour" – that's rich!'

Harriet had tried to ring Guy from the pension and had been told that all the lines to Alexandria were engaged. She decided that if she could not reach him by telephone, she must go to him, and she said to Mr Buschman, 'I've been trying to get in touch with my husband but can't get hold of him. He ought to leave Alexandria...'

'Don't worry, mem. He'll leave when he's ordered to leave.'

'There's no one to order him. The director's gone to Palestine, the office is shut – but he doesn't know this. He's alone up there. He'll just wait expecting to receive orders that won't come, and he'll be trapped.'

Harriet gulped and Mr Buschman, putting a hand on her shoulder, said, 'Hey, hey, mem, don't cry. Give the girls his number and tell them to ring it every five minutes till they *do* get through.'

'But, Mr Buschman, if they can't get him, I'll have to take a day off and go up to Alex and tell him how things are.'

'You do just that, mem,' Mr Buschman gave her shoulder a squeeze and his kindness, his concern, his ready willingness to help her, rayed from his face like love. Much moved, Harriet asked him to come over and look at the wall map. She pointed to the two sets of pins, one in the desert, the other in the Ukraine, converging on the Middle East like two black claws. 'You see what it is, Mr Buschman: it's a giant pincer movement.'

Mr Buschman stared at the map and slowly shook his head. 'Looks like it. But don't forget, mem, that's only a map. There's a mighty big bit of territory between those pincers.'

'Yes, they've a long way to come but the Germans move quickly.' Harriet had seen the German news films in Bucharest. She had seen the golden-haired boys standing up in their tanks, singing, 'What does it matter if we destroy the world? When it is ours, we'll build it up again,' as they drove with all speed on to Paris. She thought how quickly they could eat up that almost unguarded territory between the pincers. 'If the Ukraine collapses, what's to stop them? We can't even keep them out of Egypt.'

Nonplussed, Mr Buschman stared, rubbing his hand across the back of his neck, then went back to his desk leaving Harriet unassured. She saw the Middle East cracking between the pincers like a broken walnut and asked herself: what would happen then? She tried to work out on the map the strategy of defeat. The British troops, she supposed, would retreat into Iraq and make a last stand in defence of the Persian Gulf. But suppose there were no troops? Supposing the whole 8th Army was caught between the converging pincers and not one man remained to retreat and defend what was left? What would they do then? There was almost relief at the thought of it.

Responsibility would cease. They would not have to run away again.

The exchange girls, unable to reach Guy, told Harriet: 'It's the business men. They ring all the time because they are nervous. And they're already talking to each other in German.'

Harriet decided to appeal to Dobson. When she left her work, other people were returning to theirs. It was the rush hour and the most oppressive time of the day. Heat, compacted between the buildings, stuck to the skin like cotton wool. The roads were noisy with traffic and the workers, unwillingly roused out of their siestas, were rough and irritable. Bunches of men hung like swarming bees at the tram-car doors, clinging to rails and to each other. When a car swerved round a corner, several were thrown off but falling lightly, they picked themselves up and waited to get a handhold on the next. The richer men, to avoid this rabble, fought for taxis and Harriet, knowing she could not compete, decided to walk down to the river.

The pavements were more crowded than usual. Some of the men were so new to commerce that they still wore the gala-biah but most of them had managed to fit themselves out with trousers and jackets. Some had even taken to wearing the fez. Many were pock-marked or had only one seeing eye, the other being white and sightless from trachoma; many were enervated by bilharzia, but they were all rising in the world, leaving behind the peasants and the back street balani from whom they derived.

Harriet stopped to look in the windows of a closed-down tourist agency. She saw, dusty and cracking with heat, the posters that used to draw the rich to Egypt: the face of the Sphinx, the lotus columns of Karnac, the beautiful and tranquil Nile with the feluccas dipping in the wind. She sadly thought, 'Good-bye, Egypt,' but at that moment a familiar sensation came into her middle and she knew she was in for another attack of 'Gyppy tummy'. The sensation, that was not altogether pain, appeared in her mind as a large pin – not an ordinary pin but, for some reason, an open safety pin – which turned slowly and jabbed her at intervals. She thought over what she had had for luncheon. In this country one ate sickness. She could not blame Madame Wilk who was always telling the cook to wash his hands. The cook would reply, 'Saida, we wash our hands all the time. It is our religion to wash our hands.' And so it was. Harriet had seen the men at the mosque putting a finger or two into the pool and giving a token splash inside their galabiahs. Madame Wilk said, 'What am I to do? I can't follow them when they go places.' Nor could she. So Egypt was not only the Sphinx, the lotus columns, the soft flow of the Nile, it was also the deadening discomfort and sickness that blurred these sights so, in the end, one cared for none of them.

Harriet reached the Embassy's wrought-iron gates as the sun was dropping behind Gezira and a mist like smoke hung over the river. Passing into the mist, she realized it really was smoke. The atmosphere was heavy with burning. Inside the Embassy gardens, she saw a bonfire and the Embassy men and women, Dobson and Edwina among them, bringing out trays and bags of papers. Servants were feeding the papers to the fire and the gardeners were poking them about with rakes to keep them alight. This activity was solemn, yet not quite solemn. Edwina was making some remark and everyone laughed. They had their immunity, after all. Whatever happened, they would get away alive.

Dobson looked towards her and she waved to him. He crossed to the gate with a smiling amiability as though the paper burning was a social ceremony and Harriet might be welcomed in. Instead, as she was about to speak, he came out to join her and suggested they stroll along the embankment. 'My eyes are watering from the smoke. Let's get out of it.'

Dobson's air was, as it always was, insouciant and she said, 'Just now I was thinking of the pre-war tourists who seemed to be immune to bacillary dysentery. And you, you're immune to the enemy.'

Dobson laughed. 'One of the perks of the profession.'

'Well, I want your help. Guy's not immune, as you know, and he's on the outskirts of Alexandria where he'll have little idea of what's going on. I can't get through to him on the phone. What are we supposed to do?'

Dobson came to a stop and stood with his back to the embankment wall. At this end of the river walk a group of banyans had grown from the path and, dropping their branches down, had rooted themselves on all sides. There was a whole complicated cage of banyans, their silvery, tuberous trunks looking immensely old. The intertwining of branches to roots and roots to branches had left a central cage and Dobson stepped into it, looking up at the knotted roof as though seeing the banyans for the first time. While he stood there, apparently reflecting on Guy's position, a rain of charred paper fragments came floating down and with half his attention on the paper, he said, 'I suppose Gracey's in touch with him?'

'No,' Harriet spoke sharply to regain Dobson's whole attention. 'Gracey's gone, probably to Palestine. Anyway, we've no means of contacting him. The office is shut.'

'Oh!'

Smoke darkened the sunset but the smoky air was rich with the rose colours of evening and through it, wavering like a child's kite, a half sheet of headed paper sank and settled, just out of reach, in the banyan branches. Peering up at it, Dobson said, 'Oh, dear!'

'Is it a fact that Rommel is only one day's drive from Alex?'

'So it seems, but there's no immediate cause for anxiety. If Alex is evacuated, the military will bring the English civilians out, I'm pretty sure.'

'But there may not be time to evacuate the civilians. And if the town is cut off, no one will get away.'

Dobson smiled. 'We've got a navy, you know.'

Harriet was not sure whether he was laughing at her or not. Probably in the face of the fall of Alexandria, Guy's fate seemed to him, as it would to most people, a minor matter. But it was not minor to her and Dobson, all in all, was a kindly man. After a moment's reflection, he said, 'I'll tell you what I'll do. If I can get the Embassy line cleared this evening, I'll give him a tinkle and advise him to be on the alert.'

'Thank you. But much better to tell him to come to Cairo.'

'I can't very well do that. Not my territory, you know, but I'll warn him that the situation's serious.'

And that, she realized, was as much as she could hope for from Dobson, who now had to get back to his bonfire. But the bonfire was dying in the twilight and the girls were going home. Dobson paused inside the gate to say, 'Though there's no cause for panic, I really think you'd do well to leave Cairo. Most of the women and children are being packed off. There's a special train taking anyone who wants to go. It leaves about nine tomorrow morning.'

'But if there's no cause for panic ...'

'No *immediate* cause. No one's being forced to go at the moment, but there could be a God-almighty flap if and when they are. If you leave in good time, you'll be spared the turmoil. We just want to clear the decks, in case ... Then, if the situation rights itself, you'll have had a free holiday in the Holy Land.'

Harriet said nothing.

'I'd get to the station early, if I were you. Bound to be a bit of a crush.' Dobson smiled, taking her silence for acquiescence. Good-natured though he was, he could be self-important in office and now, satisfied that he had disposed of her, he nodded her away. 'Good-bye. And perhaps we'll meet at Philippi.'

Three

It took a couple of days for the convoy to disperse. It had arrived during a lull in the fighting. When they leaguered, the gunfire had stopped but next day, at first light, the men were awakened by a thudding uproar that seemed to be less than a mile away. Simon, sitting up in alarm, was taut with protest: the noise was too close and he was not prepared for it. Surely he should have been given time to brace himself against an onslaught like this? He got out of his sleeping-bag to see what was to be seen and there was nothing but rising billows of smoke on the horizon. The guns must be three or four miles away.

Realizing this, his nerves subsided but he was dispirited by the arid desolation around him and suffered, like everyone else, from fear of what would happen next. Those who could locate their units were the lucky ones. They were packed into trucks to be delivered to friends, in places where they knew the routine of life. They went cheerfully and the other men said to each other, 'Lucky buggers!' Half the trucks went with them so the remaining men, with gaps in their leaguer, felt exposed to the unknown.

At mid-morning, having nothing much to do, they were distracted by signs of activity near by. Traffic today was mostly driving westward. Different sorts of transport trucks were bringing up supplies and waiting to deliver on to an area a hundred yards west of the convoy's camp. Simon, asking the sergeant what was going on, discovered that this area was to form a service depot for the battle a few miles up the road. Engineers took over the area and put down oil barrels that marked tracks for the lorries. The lorries then moved on to the mardam to deliver their goods. Service lorries came next. Gradually, as though the positioning of the black barrels gave meaning to the desert, the enclosed sand was occupied by vehicle workshops, tank repair units, dressing stations and supply dumps.

The men who were still in the camp stood and watched as the empty sand flats filled with men and materials. The service units seemed aware of an audience and moved about like stage hands, displaying their efficiency. Simon and the others, grouped together to hide the embarrassment at their enforced idleness, saw the supply base grow before them.

The Spitfires and Hurricanes went unheeded until a plane of a different kind dived over the camp and spattered the ground with bullets. The men threw themselves down, trying to dig themselves in, for the first time aware that here, idle and useless though they were, they could die as easily as the men at the front. Simon, being the only officer among them, ordered them to get spades from the lorries and dig slit trenches. They did this with enthusiasm. The sand digging was easy enough, the trenches were completed in an hour and their occupants, again with nothing to do, stood deep in them, resting their arms on the sand, bored by their own inactivity and envious of the activity of others.

The traffic changed direction again. Trucks that had gone up to the front were returning with wounded and taking on supplies. Smoke and dust hung in the growing heat. Seeing

85

the orderlies and stretcher-bearers moving, as grey as ghosts in the dusty distance, the men of the convoy grumbled resentfully. Couldn't they go and offer a hand? Simon consulted with the sergeant but the men were untrained in the work in progress and the trained men would have no use for them.

The gunfire was an unending reverberation against the senses. The distant smoke clouds rose so thickly that the sun was a white transparent circle behind haze, but the loss of light did not bring any diminution of heat. By mid-afternoon most of the men had lost interest in the service depot and, prodding down into the trenches, slept until sunset when the canteen truck came round. The sound of the guns was dying out. The trucks, leaving the depot, were going eastwards again and the men of the convoy relaxed into a new friendliness, feeling they had survived an ordeal.

The sergeant came over to Simon and said in a sociable way, 'In case you don't know, sir, my name's Ridley.' The fact they were among the remnants left in the camp had brought them together and Ridley, become confiding, said he had seen Major Hardy leaving the camp soon after daybreak. According to Ridley, the major had driven off to divisional headquarters on a ploy of his own.

'Been sick, see,' Ridley said. 'Jaundice. The brass-hats all get it, comes from all the whisky they put down. Well, he was in hospital a long time and when he came out, he found he's been replaced, which doesn't surprise anyone. What he wants, if you ask me, is to get on to staff but he's a toffee-nosed old bumbler and I bet they don't want him.'

'What do you think will happen to the rest of us?'

'Can't tell you that, sir, but let's hope we stick together.'

At dawn next day, the guns started up again and the service units were out sweeping and tidying their areas as though attempting to make a habitat of a bit of desert. The men of the convoy, expecting another day of tedium, watched disgruntled till the canteen truck came round. While they were eating their sandwiches, Major Hardy's staff car came into the leaguer. This was indeed a diversion. The sergeant, who knew everything, had said to Simon, 'We won't see his nibs again.' They all stood and watched Hardy's legs come out of the car as though his emergence were a special entertainment laid on for them. Standing beside the car, he called Simon to him. He was a changed man. Until then, keeping his distance, he had had the ruffled atmosphere of one who nursed a grievance.

'Boulderstone,' he said, addressing Simon with easy confidence. 'This area will be evacuated at six a.m. tomorrow. The trucks are to move to another camping site a few miles back. Any questions?'

'Yes, sir. Are you coming with us, sir?'

'I am. I am now your commanding officer.'

Before Simon could make any comment, Hardy dismissed him and returned to the car where he sat examining papers for most of the daylight hours.

Next morning, taking his place in the leading lorry, Simon found Arnold at the wheel. He was surprised that Arnold was still with the remnants left in camp. He said, 'I thought you went with the trucks.' Arnold had gone with the trucks but his unit had moved. No one could tell him where it was and so, after dark, when the men were asleep, Arnold had made an unobtrusive return to the camp.

'And you're staying with us?'

'Looks like it, sir.'

'Splendid.' Arnold was someone Simon knew. Arnold had given him help on the outward trip and could be relied on to help him now. Arnold, known and helpful, brought a sense of continuity to a disrupted world.

They sat together in comfortable silence, awaiting the order to move. It did not come. Time passed and the cool of daybreak took on the sting of morning. At last, Simon jumped down from the cabin, intending to approach Hardy but was stopped by the sight of the major, face drawn, hands shuffling through the paper that lay, disordered, on the car bonnet. He gave Simon a look of such rancour that Simon made off to where Ridley stood with a sardonic smile on his narrow, kippered face.

'What's the hold-up, sergeant?'

'If you ask me, sir, the old fucker's lost his notes of the route.'

Whatever Hardy had lost, he had now found and coming

over to Simon and Ridley, fussily important, he ordered Ridley's truck into the lead. Climbing back into his cabin, Simon found Arnold drooping under the heat from the roof. As they were about to start out, the canteen truck came round and the men, getting down for their tea and bully, could see Hardy haranguing the sergeant.

Everyone was eager to be off. The patch of desert where they had leaguered was like most of the desert elsewhere, yet it had become hateful to them. They seemed to imagine that, once on the move, their world would change. By the time they set out, the track was under mirage and the convoy went at a crawl. Heat fogged the distance so there was no horizon, nothing to separate the silver mirage fluid from the swimming, sparkling white heat of the sky. They might have been moving in space except that objects – petrol cans, scraps scattered from falling aircraft, abandoned metal parts – stood monstrous and distorted out of the mirage.

The wind, blowing hot into the cabin, roused Simon to painful awareness that here he was and here, for God knows how long, he would have to remain. Pushing the sweat streams back into his hair, he said, 'It's so bad, I suppose it can only get better.'

'Oh, surprising how you get to like it, sir.' Arnold, though he was no longer in the lead, peered from habit out of the windscreen for sight of the piles of stones, trig-point triangles or oil barrels with which the engineers marked the line of firm sand.

It was late afternoon before the mirage folded in on itself and dwindled away. Arnold gave a murmur of satisfaction, seeing them still on the track, and Simon said, 'Good show, eh?'

Arnold smiled and Simon, wanting to know more about him, asked, 'You came round the Cape? What was it like?'

'Not bad. We didn't see much till we stopped at Freetown. Then at Cape Town, they took us a trip up Table Mountain. It was smashing.'

'The scenery, you mean?'

'The scenery wasn't bad, either. But it was the flowers. Never saw anything like them.'

'We weren't allowed ashore. They'd had the British army by

the time we arrived and we just had to stay on board. It was a big ship – the *Queen Mary*. A liner.'

Arnold, too, had come out on a liner but could not remember what it was called. The lower deck had been packed like a slave ship, the hammocks slung so close it was impossible to move without rocking the man on either side, but he had discovered there were splendours higher up. Sent to the saloon deck with a message, he had looked in through an open door and seen a real bed, gilt chairs with tapestry seats and a carpet on the floor.

He commented without envy. 'The officers had it good.'

'Only the brass hats. There wasn't elbow room in our cabin. They'd put in extra bunks and your face nearly hit the one above. Did you have any special friends on the ship?'

Arnold nodded but paused before admitting their names. 'Ted and Fred. Chaps I dossed down with.'

That, it seemed, was the most Arnold would give away for the moment. They drove a few miles in silence then Simon questioned him again, wondering if he had felt about Ted and Fred as Simon had felt about Trench and Codley. Arnold said, 'Ted and Fred were all right,' and another mile passed before he explained how the three had been drawn together. They had occupied three hammocks, in a cubby beside the engine. 'You see, I had the middle place.' Only that fact, he believed in his humility, had admitted him to the team. They had taken possession of two square yards of deck space and each morning, first thing, one of them would go to the space while the other two queued in the canteen.

'Ted and Fred: they were special, weren't they?'

Arnold gave an embarrassed grunt and excused his emotions by saying, 'They were my mates.'

'What happened when you reached Suez?'

Arnold had had better luck than Simon. His relationship with Ted and Fred had survived for nearly a month in Egypt. There had been no emergency in those days, so the three went to a base depot for acclimatization before being sent to a camp at Mahdi where they shared a tent and waited for their movement orders. If no order arrived by mid-day, they were free to get passes out of camp and take the tram-car into Cairo. They usually went to a cinema but often enough they just walked about, grumbling to each other. They were browned off, not only because they were there, but because they felt no one cared whether they were there or not.

Ted and Fred were town-bred boys and did not find Cairo as strange as it seemed to Arnold. He had grown up in the Lake District and, wandering aimlessly through foetid, filthy, noisy, sun-baked streets, he longed for his own green countryside. Months passed before he was reconciled to the desert but now he said, 'The desert's all right when you get to know it.'

They had been nearly a month at Mahdi when Ted, who was the boldest of them, said to the sergeant, 'What are we here for, sarge, mucking about in camp?'

The sergeant seemed to like his cheek. 'You'll find out soon enough, my lad,' and a week later, when two men were needed to make up the complement of an out-going truck, he picked on Ted and Fred. Arnold, who had visited the zoo on his own, came back as the truck was moving off. He ran after it, shouting, 'Where are they taking you?'

Ted and Fred, looking at him over the back flap, could only shrug their ignorance. Ted grimaced, comically rueful, but Arnold knew they were gratified at being chosen while he was not. The truck turned out of the compound and that was the last he ever saw of Ted and Fred.

'I bet you missed them?'

Arnold stared ahead for a minute or two before he whispered, 'I didn't know how I was going to go on living.'

'Were you on leave in Cairo?'

'Not leave, exactly,' Arnold had developed amoebic dysentery in the desert and had been sent back to base hospital. While he was away, his company had been 'whacked up' giving covering fire during the evacuation of Gazala.

'Suppose I was lucky, really. A lot of my mates copped it.'

'What do you think happened to the rest?'

Arnold shook his head. 'Could have been sent to join other battalions. That happens when a company's badly whacked up. Anyway no one knew where they were.' And so Arnold was displaced and, like Simon, uncertain what lay ahead for them.

Whey they stopped to brew up, Simon drank his tea standing

beside Arnold, feeling not only that their uncertainty was a bond but that there was sympathy between them. But he feared their attachment could not last. They could be separated by circumstances: even if they had the luck to remain in the same unit, they would be divided by rank.

He asked, 'What about Ridley? – How did he lose his outfit?'

Simon learnt that Ridley had been wounded during the retreat from Mersa Matruh. Discharged from hospital, he found his company had been broken up so, like the other men left in the convoy, he belonged nowhere.

As they started again, the staff car pulled out from its position between trucks and Hardy, his head out of the window, shouted that he was taking the lead. He turned inland and they drove for an hour before being signalled to stop. When the convoy came to a standstill, Ridley jumped down from his truck and, coming to Simon, whispered fiercely, 'Christ, if we leaguer here, we're sitting ducks.'

Simon thought Ridley was right. The flat, bare mardam offered no protection and there was nothing in sight but a group of trucks some distance south. There was nothing to mark this stretch of desert, but Simon supposed it had some meaning for Hardy. Feeling that Ridley expected him to act, he went to the major and asked, 'Are we to camp here, sir?'

'No. Tell the men to stand to. I've something to tell you all.'

Papers in hand, the men drawn up in front of him, Hardy did his best to convey amiable authority. 'I've called a halt so I can put you in the picture. We're a mixed lot, as you know, and some of you are new to the desert. Others are not at their best, having returned from sick leave, but I think we can make ourselves useful. Orders are that we join with another detachment to form a mobile column. There's a number of such columns down south – Jock columns they are called, after Colonel Jock Campbell, VC, who thought them up. Clever man. As I said, we'll be at the southern end of the line – away from the big dogfight, I'm afraid, but with a job to do. We're to swan about and sting the jerries whenever and wherever we get the chance.'

'Sounds exciting, sir,' Simon said.

'Could be. Could be.' Not wanting to overdo the amiability,

Hardy jerked up his head and asked, 'Any questions?'

'I'll say there are,' Ridley whispered to Simon then, raising his voice, he adopted an obsequious whine quite different from his usual sardonic tone. 'Do we go south straight away, sir?'

'No, we'll stick around here for a few days and wait for supplies. We need extra officers and, of course, artillery.'

'This stinging the jerries, sir: how're we to set about it?'

'Ah!' Hardy examined his papers and seemed relieved when he found the answer. 'It'll be a matter of swift raids and counter-attacks.'

'I *see*, sir,' Ridley respectfully said though, in fact, the answer did not tell them much. There was an uneasy silence then everyone listened, awed, as Ridley managed to bring out another question. 'Sir, how'll the column be made up? Number of trucks, guns and the like, sir?'

'I think I can answer that,' Hardy, his manner stern and competent, consulted his papers again but this time the answer was not at hand. Giving up, frowning his annoyance, he made a blustering attempt to extemporize. 'There'll be gunners, naturally. Artillery officer, of course. Enough infantry for close protection. Four lorries, I'd say – could be six. And ... and so on.'

'What about hardware, sir?'

'Hardware? I suppose we'll have to take what we can get.'

'Plenty lying about, sir.' Ridley, with satisfaction in his own knowledge, began to advise on things they might find useful, but Hardy would have none of this. Cutting through Ridley, he said, 'Carry on, Boulderstone.'

'Sir. Where are we making for, sir?'

The major had marked his command by putting on an impressive pair of field glasses. He now raised them to look at the only trucks in sight and after long contemplation said, 'Yes, those are our chaps.'

He pointed into the south-west and as the men looked with him, their faces shone red with the setting sun.

Hardy seemed pleased with himself and shouted, 'Get a move on, Boulderstone. No time to waste.'

The trucks filled. Simon was in the lead again. They set out to find company and cover before the night came down on them.

Four

Dobson had been right. There was going to be a scramble for the special train. To make matters worse, the train was late and those packed together on the platform were in a state of agitated anxiety, expecting tumult.

Cairo had become the clearing house of Eastern Europe. Kings and princes, heads of state, their followers and hangers-on, free governments with all their officials, everyone who saw himself committed to the allied cause, had come to live here off the charity of the British government. Hotels, restaurants and cafés were loud with the squabbles, rivalries, scandals, exhibitions of importance and hurt feelings that occupied the refugees while they waited for the war to end and the old order to return.

Now they were all on the move again. Those free to go, or of such eminence their persons were regarded as sacrosanct, had taken themselves off days before. It was said that the officers of General Headquarters had left in staff cars but, whether that was true or not, there were still officers at Groppi's. Now it was the turn of the English women and children who had obstinately remained in spite of warnings. The warnings had become urgent, and most of them had decided to leave.

Harriet was not among them but she was not far from them. Where she stood, awaiting the Alexandria train, she could look across the rail at the vast concourse packed on the platform opposite. She saw people she knew. She saw Pinkrose, hanging on to his traps and pushing first this way, then that, trying to find a position that would give him an advantage over the others. In his determined search and frequent mind changes, he thrust women from him and tripped over children, and so enraged the volatile Greeks, Free French, Poles and German Jews that they shouted abuse at him and blamed him for their fears. Hearing none of this, aware of nothing but himself, he struggled back and forth, losing his hat, regaining it, clucking in his agitation.

The train was sighted and a groan went through the crowd. The train came at a snail's pace towards the platform. The groan died out and a tense silence came down on the passengers who, gripping bags and babies, prepared for the battle to come. As the first carriages drew abreast of the platform, hysteria set in. The men who had been castigating Pinkrose for loutish behaviour, now flung themselves forward, regardless of women and children, and began tugging at the carriage doors. The women, suffering the usual disadvantage of having to protect families as well as themselves, were shrill in protest, but the protest soon became general. The carriages were locked. The train, slow and inexorable as time, slid on till it touched the buffers at the end of the line.

The scene was now hidden from Harriet by the arrival of her own train. Hardly anyone was risking the move to Alexandria and choosing among the empty compartments, she heard the clamour as the special train was opened up. She also heard the gleeful yells of the porters throwing luggage aboard. 'You go. Germans come. You go. Germans come.'

Iqal might have his doubts about the German promises but the fellahin had heard there were great times ahead. The wonder was, Harriet thought, that they were all so tolerant of the losers. Even when poor, diseased and hungry, they maintained their gaiety, speeding the old conquerors off without malice. No doubt they would welcome the new in the same way.

Harriet's train moved gently out. The uproar died behind her and she passed into the almost silent lushness of the Delta. Here was a region of dilatory peace that lived its own life, unaware of war and invaders. All over the Delta that stretched north for a hundred miles, black earth put out crops so green the foliage was like green light. Now, in high summer, this vibrancy of green was exactly as it had been when the Pringles first arrived. Then it had been Easter. Greece was aflower with spring but in Egypt there was neither spring nor autumn, only the heat of summer and the winter's soft warmth.

Flat, oblong fields were divided from each other by water channels, and each produced crops without respite. Vegetables, flax, beans, barley, tobacco, cotton: all lifted their rich verdure repeatedly out of the same blackness for which Egypt had once been called the Black Land. Between the crops there were fruit trees: mangoes, pomegranates, banana palms, date palms, and sometimes a whitewashed tomb, like a miniature mosque, or a white house with woodwork fretted like a child's toy.

Men, women and children went on working without looking at the train. Their persistence was leisurely and the train, too, was leisurely. Harriet was able to watch a water buffalo trudge a full circle, turning a water wheel that had outworn generations of buffaloes.

When, a year ago, she first saw the Delta, it was evening. The refugee ship had arrived early in the morning but people were not allowed ashore. They had to be questioned and given clearance. They were hungry. They had been told to bring their own food but in Athens the shops were empty of food, and there was none to be found. Harriet had brought some oranges on the quay and these had kept the Pringles and their circle of friends going for three days. Oranges had been the main diet in Athens for some weeks before the end and that was how they had existed; on oranges, wine and the exaltation of the Greek spring.

Berthed by the quayside at Alexandria, the passengers saw nothing but cases of guns and ammunition. No food. Then two soldiers had come to stare up at them and the passengers shouted at them in all the languages of Europe. The soldiers came to the edge of the quay, asking what it was the refugees wanted. 'Food,' shouted Harriet.

Food? – was that all?

The men went into a shed and came back with a whole branch of bananas. They broke off the fruits and threw them up over the ship's rail and everybody scrambled for them. Harriet caught one and took it to share with Guy who sat where he had sat for most of the voyage, placidly reading the sonnets of Shakespeare.

'Half each,' she said and he smiled as she peeled off the green skin and broke the pink flesh, then watched as she bit into it.

'What does it taste like?'

'Honey,' she said and the sweetness brought tears into her eyes.

Allowed to land, they were taken to an army canteen for bacon and eggs and strong tea. 'Tea you could trot a mouse on,' said Guy. The sun was low when they boarded the train and they journeyed into a country stranger than any other, yet suffocatingly familiar. The heat, the airless quiet, the rich oily colours reminded Harriet of old biblical oleographs seen at Sunday school. It was the 'Land of the Pharaohs', a land she had known since childhood.

'Look, a camel,' someone shouted and they all crowded to the window to see their first camel of Egypt lifting its proud, world-weary head and planting its soft, splayed feet into the sandy road. The workers were leaving the fields. A string of them wandered along the road, slowly, as though it did not matter whether they went home or not.

The sun set and twilight merged and darkened the fields. Half-way between Cairo and Alexandria, the train stopped at Tanta. A Greek girl called out, 'My God, look at Tanta!' They looked and experienced the first shock of Egyptian poverty. Tanta station was in a culvert overhung by the balconies of gimcrack flats where washing was strung on lines and rubbish was heaped for the wind to blow away. Fat men in pyjamas lay in hammocks or stood up sweating and scratching and leering down on the women in the train. Many of the refugees were Athenians, used to a city of marble. In Alexandria, where it rained, the bricks had been baked but there was no rain in the Delta. Tanta was the dun colour of unbaked clay.

Beggar children whined up at the train, banging on it to demand attention. As the train pulled out, they ran beside it, their bare dirty feet slapping the ground until they were lost in the twilight. Then darkness came down and there was nothing to see but the palm fronds black against the afterglow of sunset.

Here was Harriet at Tanta again. The same fat men sprawled on the balconies, the same children whined at her, the same smell of spice, dung and death hung in the air, but none of it disturbed Harriet now. Tanta was a part of Egypt. It was the nature of things, and her only thought was to get the journey over. If asked, she would have said she did not dislike Tanta as much as she disliked Alexandria. Though she deplored her mid-week separation from Guy, she dreaded the time when her job would end and she would have to move from Cairo. Built on a narrow strip of land between a salt lake and the sea, Alexandria, she felt, was depressing and claustrophobic. Castlebar, who went each week to tutor the son of an Alexandrian Greek banker, had said to Guy, 'You'll enjoy it. The fashionables are quite amusing,' but Guy was not among 'the fashionables'. His college was not even in Alexandria. It was beyond the eastern end of the long Corniche that ran from the Pharos, all round the old port, and stretched in an endless concrete promenade, until it was lost in desert. Guy was in the desert. He taught English at a business college where the sons of tobacco and cotton barons wanted to learn a commercial language. When Guy organized a series of lectures on English literature, a deputation of students came to tell him that they did not need to know about literature. They did not want English, as Guy understood it. They wanted something called 'commercial English'.

Alexandria was famous for its sea-breeze but the breeze could often bring in a summer mist. When Harriet left the train, she found the sun hidden by a moisture film that increased the greyness of the streets. The townspeople were queuing up outside banks or hurrying from shop to shop, buying as though against a siege. There was unease in the air, the same unease that Harriet had felt in Athens when the Germans reached Thermopylae. In Cairo people were saying that the rich business community of Alexandria had appointed a reception committee to prepare a welcome for Rommel. That was probably true but the rich were stocking up before the invaders came to empty the shops. Cars, packed with supplies like the cars outside the American Embassy, stood ready for those who thought it wiser to flee. Some of them were lagged with mattresses as a protection against aerial bombardment.

Harriet took a bus along the Corniche. There was a drabness about the streets and she felt that some bright constituent was missing. She realized that the young naval men, who went about in white duck, as light-hearted as children, were missing from among the people on the pavements. She supposed that shore-leave had been stopped.

That day no one had time to lie on the beach. The long grey sea edge, usually full of bathers, was deserted except for a few small boys. The vacuous greyness of the town depressed her. She realized she had become acclimatized to Cairo's perpetual sunshine and rumbustious vitality. Here the long sea-facing cliff of hotels and blocks of flats had a winter bleakness as though all life had moved away.

In Cairo, the German occupation was still merely possible: here, apparently, it was a certainty. She decided she would stand none of Guy's heroics. She would take him back to Cairo that very night.

In normal times, Guy would have been on leave. The college had shut for the summer but, feeling he had no right to take leave, he had remained to conduct a summer course in English. Only a few students, eager to excel or to gain his favour, had enrolled but they were enough to give him a sense of purpose. He would argue that the school was part of the college curriculum and he could not abandon it. She would argue that it was not and he very well could.

Again calamity presented itself as a solution. I would deliver Guy from Alexandria and from his wretched lodgings. If she had to come here, they would live not in one of these expensive Corniche flats but in the same sleazy hinterland where he was living at the moment. Not much caring where he lived, he had taken a room in a Levantine pension of the poorest kind, a place so dark and neglected, everything seemed coated with grime. One day, watching him as he talked to the landlord, she had seen him rub his hand on the knob of a bannister then pass the same hand over his forehead. She had berated him, telling him he might pick up leprosy, smallpox, plague or any of the killer diseases of Egypt. Guy, who believed all disease was a sickness of the psyche, said, 'Don't be silly. You only catch what you fear to catch,' and, fearing nothing, he saw himself immune.

When she left the bus at the end of the Corniche, she had still to walk half a mile to where the college stood isolated in a scrubby area of near desert that was now being built up. The building had once been a quarantine station for seamen. Staring out to sea, grim faced, lacking any hint of ornament, it might have been a penitentiary. And for Guy it was, in a way, a penitentiary. He had been exiled here for his song, 'Gracey of Gezira' – or so Harriet believed. He had brought his exile upon himself.

No one, not even a boab, was in the hall. She walked unchecked down to the half-glazed door of the lecture hall and, looking in, saw Guy at a desk, bent over a book. The shutters had been closed against the sun and had not been opened when mist covered the sky. The amber colour of the electric light made his face sallow and he looked very drawn. He had lost weight and his cheeks, that had been smooth with youth when they married, only two years before, now showed a line from nostrils to chin. Time and the Egyptian climate had told on them both.

From the silence, she guessed they were alone in the building and she was reminded of another time of danger when Guy, who had been the beloved mentor, waited in vain for his students. During their last days in Bucharest, with the Iron Guard on the march, the students were wise to stay away.

As she opened the door, he turned his head and at once he was young again. He jumped to his feet, animated by surprise and pleasure. 'Well, this is the nicest thing that's happened to me for a long time.'

'I've come to take you back to Cairo.'

He laughed, treating her statement as a joke. She looked at the book on his desk. It was one she had given him for his last birthday and she said, 'Good heavens, you're not trying to lecture them on *Finnegans Wake*?'

'Not all of them, but I have two exceptionally brilliant chaps who are interested in English for its own sake. Pretty rare in this place. I promised them a seminar on Joyce. I'm certain that Joyce got a lot of his funnier pieces from students at the Berlitz School. I get the same sort of things here. Look,' he pulled some students' papers out of his desk and read, ' "D. H. Lawrence was theoretically wrong" – Joyce would have loved that. And here,

Thou wast not meant for death immoral bird...

'Darling, you've got to come to Cairo, at least for a few days.'

'You know that's impossible. I have my summer school and . . .'

'Which you're keeping open for only two students?'

'Well, I had ten to begin with. They thought if they humoured me by joining the class, I'd repay them by marking up their exam papers. When they found it didn't work, they faded away. But there are two left and they're exceptional.'

'Well, exceptional or not, the fact is you're keeping this place open for a couple of students? Here you are, at a time like this, waiting to discuss *Finnegans Wake*?'

'Why not? What do you expect me to do?'

'I expect you to have some sense. Don't you realize the Germans are less than fifty miles from Alex?'

'Oh, darling,' he took her hands and squeezed them. 'Little monkey's paws! You aren't frightened, are you? You weren't frightened in Greece when we had nothing in front of us but the sea. Here we have the whole of Africa.'

'I'm frightened for you. A lot of good having the whole of Africa if you're cut off here. If you're waiting for orders, you'll wait for ever. There's no one to give orders. Gracey's bolted, as usual. So, for that matter, have Toby Lush, Dubedat and several thousand others. I saw Pinkrose going off on the special train this morning. The least you can do is come to Cairo. If you hang on here, you'll end up in Dachau. In Cairo, we stand a fair chance of getting away.'

'Don't worry, darling. We've always got away before.'

'That's the trouble. You're overconfident. We've got away twice – but it could be third time unlucky. They move so fast, you could be caught before you knew they had reached Alex.'

'I can't argue now, darling.' Guy put an arm round her shoulder and led her to the door. 'The students are due any minute. You get back to Alex. Get yourself something to eat and I'll see you later. I'm going to the Cecil to meet some men.'

She asked suspiciously, 'What men? What time?'

'Six o'clock. You'll find Castlebar there. And I'm having supper with a chap you don't know. Called Aidan Pratt. If you get there before I do, introduce yourself. Be nice to the poor fellow. He's very shy.'

'All right. Six o'clock. And be prepared to come back with me.'

Guy laughed and shut the door on her.

The sun was breaking through the mist and the promenade was in sunlight when she reached the bus stop. Guy had said, 'I can't argue now,' implying, she hoped, that he would argue later, but later there would be Castlebar and this man she did not know and Guy, always high-spirited in company, would be too volatile to discuss unwelcome reality. He had an impulse to take risks, and then there were the two students, the ambitious swots who roused his old obstinate loyalty and could detain him there until it was too late.

'Bloody students!' She saw them as voracious creatures who would devour him if they could. And, in time, he would be devoured. She felt rage that he should be wasting his learning on this wretched place.

As there was no bus in sight, she decided to walk the length of the Corniche and so pass the dead centre of the day. Walking, that in Cairo meant bathing in sweat, was pleasant enough here where the sea wind tempered the heat, but the walk was monotonous. It was a dull shore with rocks that were rotting like cheese. At one point where the sea washed under the cheesey, crumbling rock shelf, holes had been cut so the waves, beating through them, made a booming sound. Or so it was said. Harriet had never heard it. The holes were very ancient and were no longer a diversion. Today the water splashed through them with a half-hearted plip-plop that she thought a fitting comment on the wartime world. The sun was dropping and the light deepening. This was the evening when the conquerors of the Afrika Korps were to force their pent-up ardour on the ladies of Alexandria.

The conquerors had not yet arrived but there was a British soldier leaning against the sea wall. He looked like a man with all the time in the world but his baggage showed he was waiting for transport.

She stopped to lean beside him, staring with him at the flat, almost motionless sea where no ships sailed, and said, 'You off to the desert?'

He muttered, 'Ya.' He was older than the soldier she had met

101

in Cairo and he did not marvel at meeting a young English-woman.

'I suppose you've no idea what's happening out there?'

'Nope. Heard nothing for days.'

'Do you think Rommel will get here?'

'He'll get here if he can, won't he? If not, not. There's no knowing, is there?' He spoke dully, sodden with boredom, so, knowing she would get no response from him she walked on. The barrage balloons were beginning to rise over the town. By the time she reached the harbour, there were a dozen or more kidney shapes hanging in mid-sky. She had an hour to get through before going to the hotel so walked on till she was opposite the Pharos, then she sat on the wall, her legs hanging above the sand, and watched the pleatings of ruby cloud that were forming round the horizon. The Pharos, newly painted, reflected the sky. The scene absorbed her so it was some minutes before she realized she was an object of prurient excitement among the boys on the shore below. They were dodging about in their ragged galabiahs, the eldest not more than ten or eleven, bending down, sniggering, as they tried to see up her skirt. She shouted 'Yallah' but they would not be driven off. She lifted her legs over the wall and sat the other way but the boys ran up the steps to stare at her from the road. At last, sick of their antics, she jumped down and went to the Cecil.

The atmosphere inside the hotel was forlorn. The cosmo-politan patrons had gone with the rest and even the bar, the venue of British naval officers, was empty except for three army captains who stood together, constrained and sober, and another who sat by himself. This last was near the door, watch-ing for someone, and she guessed from his vulnerable air, his expectation and his disappointment when she came in, that he was waiting for Guy. He must be the shy Aidan Pratt. From her experience of Guy's acquaintances, she guessed that this man had asked Guy to dinner not simply for the pleasure of his company. He had a need of his own. He wanted to confide in Guy, or ask his advice, or get something from him. Guy had probably promised him the evening and he, supposing he would have Guy's company to himself, had not bargained for

102

her, or for Castlebar. Guy was, as usual, double-booked, and not only from forgetfulness. His engagements crowded upon each other because he brought down on himself more dependence than any normal person could support.

Knowing the man would not welcome her company, she wandered back to the foyer and sat there as the lights came on inside and the twilight deepened outside. Guy did not appear and, feeling solitary and exposed, she returned to the bar and approached Aidan Pratt. When she spoke, his surprise was almost an affront.

'Guy Pringle suggested I join you here.'

He stared with animosity until she explained that she was Guy's wife, then he stumbled to his feet, attempting to recoup his discourtesy with a smile. He was a heavy, handsome young man with limp and oily black hair. He was still in his early twenties, but his eyes were contained in hollows of brownish skin that aged him. They were large eyes, very dark, and his smile did not dispel their desolation. His aura of depression repelled her. She, too, had hoped to have Guy to herself. He was, she realized, another victim of Guy's reassuring warmth. Each one imagined himself the sole recipient. Guy would remake the world for him, and for him alone. They clung to him and, in the end, he evaded them or asked her to protect him from them. 'You answer the telephone, darling ...' Deeply buried, there was in him an instinct for preservation and the instinct might save him in the end.

Aidan Pratt asked her what she would drink. From the bar, he looked intently back at her, perhaps wondering if he could confide in her, treat her as a surrogate for Guy, and she realized she had seen him before. When he brought back her drink, she asked if they had met somewhere. He shook his head but his smile took on vitality as though her question had pleased him.

When he sat opposite her, she felt his whole personality on edge. His face was moist, not from heat, because the bar was air-conditioned, but from nervousness. His uniform of fine gaberdine was expensively tailored but he fidgeted inside it as though troubled by its fit. She asked where he was stationed. He was on leave from Damascus.

'Damascus? Then how did you come to know Guy?'

'Doesn't everyone know Guy?' he gave a laugh. 'Last time I was here someone told me a story: two men were wrecked on a desert island. Neither knew the other but they both knew Guy Pringle.'

'Yes, I heard that story in Cairo.'

'I met him here, in this bar, on my last leave. Next day I went out to the college and we walked to Ramleh, talking all the way there and back. A memorable day. We arranged to meet here again the following evening. I waited three hours before I discovered he wasn't even in Alex. He'd gone to Cairo for the weekend.' As Harriet showed no surprise, he asked, 'Does that sort of thing often happen?'

'You remember the bread-and-butter fly that lived on weak tea and cream? If it couldn't find any, it died. Alice said, "But that must happen very often," and the gnat said, "It always happens." '

'Always? He makes a habit of letting people down?'

'He doesn't mean to let them down. He takes on too much. People persuade him to do what he hasn't time to do so, inevitably, *someone* is let down.'

Aidan's mouth tightened and he said with slight hauteur, 'As you are here, I suppose we can depend on him tonight?'

'Yes, he'll turn up sooner or later. I want to take him back to Cairo.' She thought it an odd time for anyone to come here on leave and said, 'Things are pretty bad, you know.'

'You mean, worse than usual? Isn't it the same old romp as last time? They reach Sollum and then they're driven back?'

'They're much nearer than that. They said they'd reach Alex tonight.'

'Obviously you didn't believe them or you wouldn't be in Alex yourself. Still, you're right. He oughtn't to stay out where he is. A lot could happen before he got wind of it.'

'I'm glad you agree with me. How long are you staying here?'

'Not long. I could only get forty-eight hours so I return tomorrow.'

'I envy you. I wish we were safely in Damascus.'

'Oh, Damascus isn't all that safe. We have our troubles. The Free French are in control but a good many Syrians don't want them. We often hear pistol shots. People get killed,' he paused and dropped his voice. 'Friends get killed. A friend of mine looked out to see what was happening and a bullet went through his head.'

He glanced at her to see how this information affected her, and quickly glanced away. The loss of a friend and, she would guess, no ordinary friend! So this was the tragedy he was nursing within himself! She said, 'I'm sorry,' but of course it was Guy he wanted. Only Guy would hear the whole story because only Guy could give the true, consoling word. She added, 'Very sorry,' and as she spoke, he made a gesture, so poignantly conveying his loneliness and heartbreak that she knew she had, indeed, seen him before.

She was puzzled by the familiarity of that gesture. He stared down at the floor. There was nothing more to be said but then, at the most opportune moment, Guy entered the bar.

His glasses pushed into his hair, his arms stretched over an insecure burden of books and papers, he hurried to them, saying delightedly, 'So you found each other all right!' He bent to kiss Harriet. 'I didn't tell you who he was. I knew you'd recognize him and I wanted to surprise you.'

Looking again at Aidan, Harriet did recognize him. 'Of course, I knew I'd seen you before. You're the actor, Aidan Sheridan.'

Aidan, revivified by the arrival of Guy, made a denigratory movement of the hand. 'I was Aidan Sheridan. Now I'm Captain Pratt of the Pay Corps.'

He could not suppress Harriet's admiring memory of him. 'I saw you play Konstantin in *The Sea Gull*. I went with a friend to the gallery and we sat on a narrow plank of wood and gazed down at you, spellbound. It was all new to me – I'd never seen Chekov before. I was very young and at the end I went out crying.'

Aidan flushed darkly and caught his breath. He was moved by her memory and several moments passed before he could say, 'I was young, too. It was my first big role. At that age it is bliss to have a dressing-room to oneself. On my first night, sitting in front of the mirror I said to myself, "Now it's all beginning!"'

Guy beamed on his wife and friend, letting them discuss

Chekov for a while, but eager to have a part in the felicitations, he soon took over to compliment Aidan on other parts he had played: Henry V, Romeo, Oswald ...

'Did you play Hamlet?'

Aidan shook his head. 'That was to come.'

Guy, knowing he had asked the wrong question, hurried on to another subject: his own production of *Troilus and Cressida*. Describing it, he longed to be in the theatre again and said, 'I must produce another Shakespeare play.'

'Gracey would never let you,' said Harriet.

'If it's for the troops, he couldn't very well refuse. Or why not a Chekov play? Why not *The Sea Gull*?'

'Really, darling, for troops?'

'Well, why not? The men get sick of those concert parties. One of them told me they'd welcome a real play. They're not fools. They want something to think about. *The Sea Gull* is about wasted youth. It would have meaning for them.'

Aidan sombrely agreed and Guy turned excitedly to him. 'You would play Konstantin, wouldn't you?'

Startled by the suggestion, Aidan gave an ironical sniff. 'My first youth is passed. Trigorin would be more up my street these days.'

'Then, would you play Trigorin?'

'You're not serious? I couldn't act with amateurs.'

The statement had a finality that shocked Guy into silence. Harriet laughed and Aidan again blushed darkly, this time with shame, realizing that his vanity had betrayed him.

'But you are an amateur,' Harriet spoke with friendly reasonableness, not wishing further to deflate his unhappy ego. 'You are an amateur soldier among professionals, aren't you?'

'I suppose I am.'

Guy, having made a rapid recovery, said, 'But you would help and advise, wouldn't you?'

'Willingly, if I'm around. But I can't get here as often as I would wish.'

Harriet, wanting to put a stop to this talk of productions said, 'And quite probably Guy won't be here, either.' She looked at Guy, insisting that he listen to her. 'Be sensible. Jackman says Alexandria will be cut off. Rommel will simply march round behind it and it will fall of itself. They could be here tomorrow. Come back to Cairo, just till we know what's going to happen here.'

'Darling, you know I can't abandon my students like that.'

'What students? Did those two turn up this afternoon?'

'No, but that doesn't mean ...'

'It means *they've* abandoned *you*. I bet they're taking German lessons.'

Guy laughed. 'If the worst happens, I'll jump on a jeep. The army will take me out.'

'The army won't get out. It'll be surrounded, too.'

'Then it'll be another Dunkirk. The navy will rescue us.'

Dobson had said the same thing and Harriet, for the moment let the matter drop. Guy asked Aidan if he had met Catroux who was, according to gossip, the illegitimate son of a royal personage. Did Aidan think this was the truth? Aidan discussed Catroux with avid interest, as though the general were his own achievement or an important part of his own life. Harriet could imagine that the name of Catroux dominated Syria as other names dominated Egypt. There had been Cunningham, Ritchie (the troops sang 'Ritchie, his arse is getting itchy'), Freyberg, Gott. Now there was Auchinleck. She saw them as larger than life, archetypal heroes, who had power over other men, and over civilians, too. When they decreed that Egypt should be evacuated, everyone must pack and go. The war had deprived people of free will. They must do what they were told.

Aidan, while talking, came to a sudden stop and gazed with unbelieving displeasure as yet another intruder arrived to claim Guy's attention. Castlebar had come to the table. Harriet could feel, almost like a physical force, Aidan's will to remove Castlebar but Castlebar was not to be moved. Confident of Guy's welcome and not unwelcomed by Harriet, he sniggered a greeting and sidled round the table to seat himself on a chair with his back to the wall. Guy, happy in the belief that Aidan and Castlebar would be drawn to each other, introduced the one as 'the famous actor' and the other as 'the famous poet'. Ducking his head, Castlebar gave Aidan a sidelong stare of dislike which Aidan, more directly, returned.

As Guy went to the bar to buy drinks, Castlebar put a packet of Camels on the table in his usual manner. The packet was placed central to his person, the open end facing him, a cigarette pulled out and propped up so it could be taken and lighted from the one in his mouth. Thus, there was no wasted interval between smokes. His thick, pale eyelids hid his eyes but all the time, he was observing Aidan as he might an enemy.

The two men were physically alike. They had the same heavy good looks but Castlebar was some ten years older. His sallow skin was falling into lines, his hair was greying and his full, loose mouth sagged as though pulled down by his perpetual cigarette. His lips were mauve and had the soft, swollen look of decay. Harriet, sensing their distaste of each other, supposed that Castlebar resented Aidan's youth while Aidan saw in Castlebar a debased analogue of himself.

Guy, certain that his friends were enjoying each other as much as he enjoyed them, began to plan a whole evening for them all: a few drinks here, then to Pastroudi's for a bite and on to Zonar's for coffee and drinks then, if they wanted to go on drinking and talking, they could come back to the Cecil where Aidan was a resident. Neither man interrupted this exuberant programme but at the end, Castlebar said, 'Sorry. Nothing I'd like better but I'm going back on the early train.'

'Take the later train.'

Castlebar shook his head, stared down for some moments then stammered, seeming to force his voice through impeding teeth, 'Don't want to hang about here. Not even for love of you, dear old boy. My Greeks were in a panic. They had packed and would leave at the first sound of the guns. They thought I was mad to come up here but they owed me a bit – a whole quarter's tuition in fact. Thought I'd better make sure of it.'

Harriet fervently said, 'Thank God someone's got some sense.' She gave an ironical laugh as she looked at Guy. 'Castlebar may drink too much and smoke too much, but he's not taking silly risks.' She turned to Castlebar, 'Can't you persuade Guy to come to Cairo. He thinks the navy will rescue him.'

'The navy?' Castlebar lifted his eyelids and gave Guy a startled stare. 'Don't you know the navy's gone?'

108

'Gone?' Harriet was alarmed. 'Gone where?'

'No one knows. The Red Sea, I'd imagine. My Greeks were in a state about that. They say the whole Fleet upped anchor this morning and deserted the town.'

'Good heavens, that shows you ...' Harriet turned on Guy but Guy, adept at dodging her anxieties, jumped to his feet and the others watched him as he went to make much of a big, stooping, paunchy fellow who had just entered the bar.

'Who's he found now?' Castlebar spoke with indulgent exasperation. 'Your husband's crazy. Here he is sitting with friends who hang on his every word, but he's not satisfied. As soon as he sees someone else, he rushes over to them.'

'It's Lister. I met him at Groppi's. His job's in Jerusalem but he comes here all the time to fill up with food.'

Aidan, his face contracted as though with pain as he saw Guy bringing Lister to the table, said to Harriet, 'He gathers people as he goes.'

Lister, limping on a stick, smiled as he joined the company, his round blue eyes giving an impression of innocent, almost infantile, amiability, but Harriet knew he was more complex than he seemed. In the midst of his fat, pink, glossy face there was a cherub's nose and a very small mouth covered by a fluffy moustache. He was wearing a pair of old brown corduroy trousers and a shirt that had faded to yellow, and only his cap and the crown on his shoulder indicated that he was not a civilian but an army officer. He sank into a chair as though the few steps from bar to table had exhausted him, and pushed his right leg under the table, out of the way of harm. Getting his breath back, he lifted Harriet's hand, brushed it wetly with his moustache and asked, 'How is my lovely girl?'

'Not too happy. We've just heard that the navy's left Alex.'

'Good God!' Lister's little mouth fell open. 'What next? You'd scarcely believe it, I didn't know till I got here that there's a flap on. No one tells us anything in Palestine. I'm in Intelligence but there hasn't been a signal from GHQ ME, for a week.'

Harriet said, 'The rumour is that GHQ ME has left Egypt. They've been too busy evacuating themselves to send you a signal.'

'That's probably it. Jerusalem's packed out with evacuees, but it's always like that when the Germans cross into Egypt. To tell you the truth, you're safer here. Palestine's a cul-de-sac and if we move on to Syria, we'll meet the German 6th army on its way down from Russia. Where do you go then? Better off here, I say. You can always go down the Nile.'

Castlebar sniggered. 'You mean, *up* the Nile.'

'Yes. This must be the only country in the world where south is up.' Lister's big, shapeless body quivered as though he had made an enormous joke.

Guy, putting out his hands to Lister and Castlebar, urged them to tell some limericks. Between them, he said, they had the best collection he knew. 'Come on, let's have a flyting.'

'Oh!' Lister, choked by his own laughter, flapped a hand in protest. 'I'm too far gone. Been at it all day. I can't remember anything.' His nose, that was still the nose of infancy, glowed with the drink he had taken. 'Took a taxi from the station to Groppi's, rang Harriet (I'd've given you a fine repast, m'girl), had lunch at the Hermitage, went back to Groppi's for a few cream cakes, then I thought why not pop up and see old Pringle? Knew I'd find you in the bar.'

Aidan, pushing his chair back from the table, looked at Lister in frowning distaste. Castlebar, as he noted this, gave Harriet a sly grin and said to Lister, 'Bet you intend a visit to Mary's House?'

'Oh, oh, oh!' Lister averted his eyes as though deeply offended but his laughter overtook him, his body collapsed in on itself and tears ran down his cheeks. When he had recovered enough, he said, 'Did you know: when they got a direct hit, all the chaps taken to hospital said, one after the other, "I got mine at Mary's House," and a little sweetie of a nurse said to the doctor, "Mary must've been giving a very big party."'

It was an old story but they all laughed except Aidan, whose frown grew darker. The drinks were renewed and Castlebar was persuaded to speak a few limericks. His poetry was a mild mixture of nostalgia and regrets but his limericks had a dexterity and obscene wit that convulsed Lister, who soon attempted to rival them. Lister's humour was scatological and Harriet, bored, said as soon as there was a pause, 'Darling, don't you think we should eat?'

'Yes,' Guy had a couple of inches in his glass, 'when I've finished this,' but he made no attempt to finish it. Washing it slowly round and round, he gained time by leaving it unfinished.

He invited Lister to Pastroudi's but Lister, shaking his head, tittered mysteriously and left them to guess where he was going. When it seemed the 'flyting' would end, Castlebar insisted that Guy must contribute to it. 'Do Yakimov,' he urged and Lister agreed. 'Oh, oh, must have Yakimov.'

Yakimov, dead and turned to dust in the dry Greek earth, led a post mortem life in Guy's repertoire of comic characters. Harriet, hungry but resigned, listened with fear that the performance might fail and pride that it did not. She was the only other one of the party who had known Yakimov in life and so the only one who, watching Guy's rounded, sunburnt features take on Yakimov's slavonic mask, marvelled at the impersonation. The change, for her, verged on the supernatural. For the others, there was a funny story. Guy imitated Yakimov's delicate, fluting voice, but the voice was not as exact as the face. 'Ee-a knew a lay-dee who played a most unfair game of ... cro-o-o-*quet*. She would put her skirt over her balls and move them about with her foot, *just* wherever she liked ...'

Here the laughter began. Harriet had heard the story so often, both from Guy and Yakimov himself, she could have reproduced every intonation. She ceased to listen but, instead, watched the two inches of beer going round and round as Guy spoke. If in a hurry, he could open a throttle in his throat and put down a pint without pausing for breath. If he wanted to linger, no one could make his beer last longer.

When he recovered from his mirth, Lister bent forward to say in a half-whisper, 'Heard a strange story at Groppi's this morning. You know Hooper, the one that married a rich girl who paints a bit? Well, she took that boy of theirs into the desert and she was so busy with her painting, she didn't notice the kid had picked up a live hand-grenade.'

Harriet sat up, realizing she was about to hear of the tragedy

111

she had witnessed – when? With all that had happened since, it seemed an age ago. She said, 'I was there. I saw her bring the boy in. We all realized he was dead, but the Hoopers couldn't believe it.'

Lister opened his eyes, amazed. 'So – is it true? – Did they really try and feed him ...' He circled a finger over his cheek '... through some hole in his face?'

'Yes.'

'A weird story!'

Castlebar sniggered. 'Egypt's a weird place. Feeding the dead's an ancient custom, but it still goes on.'

'Goes on, does it?' Lister asked with awe.

'Oh yes, they all go up to the City of the Dead, taking food to share with the corpse under the floor. They set up house there and stay till the dead relative's got used to the strangeness of the afterlife. I like it.'

'Yes.' Lister, too, liked it but he could not keep his laughter back. He and Castlebar laughed together while Aidan, who had been shocked by the feeding of the dead boy, regarded them with horror. Guy was putting down his beer. The party had to break up. Castlebar was catching his train. Lister, with his secret intention in mind, began determinedly to get himself to his feet. He could scarcely put his right foot to the ground. 'Gout,' he explained and bending unsteadily over Harriet, he kissed her hand again. 'Look me up when you come to Jerusalem. You don't need to stay in that ghastly refugee camp. I'll use m'influence and get you a room at the YMCA. We'll have some fun. I'm the life and soul of the YMCA smart set. I'm always in trouble because I keep a few bottles in the wardrobe.'

Castlebar and Lister left the bar together and Guy, reluctant to part from them, went with them as far as the foyer.

Aidan said in disgust to Harriet, 'What extraordinary people! Why does Guy waste his time with fellows like that? And repeating limericks to each other! An odd occupation!'

'The English do become odd here. Ordinary couples who'd remain happily together in Ealing or Pinner, here take on a different character. They think themselves Don Juans or tragedy queens, and throw fits of wild passion and make scenes in

112

public...' At Aidan's movement of inquiry, Harriet laughed. 'No, not Guy and me. We're only apart from circumstances. We're thought to be an exemplary pair.'

'But Guy? With those people, he was not himself. He was acting the fool, wasn't he?'

'Yes, in a way. But what's he to do? He's stuck at that commercial college, wasting his talents. He's not allowed to leave the Organization and Gracey can't, or won't, give him a job worthy of him. Other men are at war, so he must take what comes to him. He cannot protest, except that his behaviour is protest. He must either howl against his life or treat it as a joke.' As she spoke, protest rose in her, too. 'This is what they've done to him – Gracey, Pinkrose and the rest of them. He believes that right and virtue, if persisted in, must prevail, yet he knows he's been defeated by people for whom the whole of life is a dishonest game.'

Aidan looked at her with new interest. 'He's not happy, and I don't think you are, either.'

'Can one except to be happy in these times?'

'No. We have no right ... no right even to think of happiness,' Aidan sighed and looked to the door for Guy's return, and Harriet began to feel curious about him, wondering what she would make of him if she knew him better.

The three of them set out for Pastroudi's restaurant. Alexandria had been blacked out by the military and the darkness enhanced the disturbing emptiness of the streets. A shudder passed through the air and the ground seemed to move beneath their feet. Harriet, unable to account for this phenomenon, came to a stop and said, 'Is it an earthquake?' She had experienced one in Bucharest but this, she realized, was something different. The shudder and vibration were repeated and went on as though a distant steam-hammer was pounding the earth. The two men, walking indifferently through it, made no comment until Harriet asked, 'What is it?'

Aidan told her, 'It's a barrage. They're preparing an attack.'

'Who? Them or us?'

'It's very close. Probably us.'

Guy spoke as though the vibration was a commonplace. 'I'd guess twenty-five pounders, wouldn't you?' He looked to

113

Aidan who said, 'And the new six pounders. I'd say, 5.5 inch howitzers, too.'

Harriet, surprised that Guy should have heard of a twenty-five pounder, asked how far the barrage was from them.

Guy laughed. 'At least forty miles. I don't think Rommel will make it tonight.'

Aidan said seriously, 'If they break through, they could make it before daybreak.'

'But they won't break through. I must say, I'd like to take a troops' entertainment out to our chaps.'

Harriet said, 'Darling, really, you're mad!' She did not know whether Guy's courage came from his refusal to recognize reality, or a refusal to run from it, but the idea of taking an entertainment to men engaged in a desperate delaying action seemed to her typical of his mental processes.

The moon was pushing up between sea and sky, throwing a long channel of light across the water. The promenade was a spectral grey in the moon glimmer. Not a soul, it seemed, had come out to enjoy the cool of evening, but when they pushed through the heavy curtains into Pastroudi's, they found the restaurant crowded, noisy and brilliantly lit. The Alexandrians were eating while there was still something to eat. Uncertainty and fear raised the tempo of chatter into an uproar. Aidan had booked a table but they had stayed so long at the Cecil, the table was lost to them. They had to wait in a queue and while they waited, the air-raid warning rose. As the wailing persisted, people shouted to each other that it must be a false alarm. The Luftwaffe would never bomb a town that was about to fall into German hands. The warning added a sort of hilarity to the noise. No one took it seriously until the manager strode through the room shouting, 'What do you do? You know the regulations. Downstairs, everyone. M'sieurs, m'dams, into the kitchens, I beg you.'

His alarm infected the diners and they began pushing their way down into the hot and clotted, greasy atmosphere of the basement. The kitchen staff and waiters, fitting themselves in between stoves and sinks, left the central space clear for the customers. The lights were switched off. The wailing ceased and there was an interval of attentive silence before people began to complain that the precautions were unnecessary. They had left their food for nothing. It was, as they had said, a false alarm. A man called them all to go back to their dinners but before the fret and grumbles could lead to action, a bomb fell. It was a distant bomb, but a bomb, nevertheless. The silence was the silence of fear, then a moan passed over the kitchen.

Guy said, 'That was the harbour. They're bombing the French warships.'

Ah, that explained the raid. And who cared what happened to the French ships that had lain there immobilized since the fall of France? Then a second bomb fell, much nearer, so close, in fact, that the pots and pans rattled and cries went up. People began struggling towards the stairs as though hoping to find some other, safer place, and Guy put his arms round Harriet to protect her and she pressed to him, less afraid of the bombs than of the fear around her.

A third bomb fell, further off, a fourth, so distant it could just be heard, and at once the panic died. The raiders had passed over. People relaxed and took on the gaiety of relief, telling each other that they could now go back and eat in peace. But the manager was on the stair and would not let anyone pass. They had to wait for the All Clear before the lights were switched on and they could return to their spoilt food.

Harriet was due back in her office next morning and had to catch the last train. Leaving the restaurant, Guy was intercepted by a man who wished to gain favour for a stout youth who came lagging after him. The son had to take a book-keeping examination and the father pleaded for him. 'I feel, Mr Professor, sir, he should have an extra understanding of this subject.' The subject was not part of Guy's curriculum but he listened patiently and gave what advice he could. The conversation ended with an invitation to cakes and liqueurs. When could the professor come? Any day of that week or the next week or the week after would be suitable. The whole future was open to him so there was no excuse, no chance of escape. Harriet made off before the invitation could be extended to her.

In the hall she could hear the man shouting, 'So, then, you come Thursday week, professor, sir?'

'If Rommel doesn't get here first.'

'Very funny, professor, sir. You make a joke, eh? You make a joke?'

Passing out through the black curtains, they found the city adazzle with moonlight. Harriet was reminded of another night of full moon, the night of Hugo Boulderstone's twenty-first birthday. Just as tonight, they had left the blacked-out restaurant and entered this startling light that cut the buildings into shapes of silver and black. Harriet remembered Hugo's face white in the moonlight and the voice that told her they would never see him again.

Now Guy, his head full of productions and plays and all the theatre talk of the dinner-table, stopped to declaim, 'On such a night as this ...' and pausing, turned expectantly to Aidan Pratt who took the lines up, speaking them in a voice so charged with emotion and melodic resonance that his two listeners marvelled:

> In such a night
> Troilus methinks mounted the Trojan walls
> And sighed his soul out to the Grecian tents
> Where Cressid lay that night ...

At the end of Jessica's speech, he bowed to Guy, inviting him to continue.

Guy, in his rich, pleasant voice, said, 'In such a night stood Dido with a willow in her hand ...' and broke off to add, 'And on this very shore.'

'Somewhere further west,' Aidan gravely amended and Harriet turned to hide her laughter.

Walking towards the station, Guy persuaded Aidan to recite other speeches from other plays, adding others himself and so, quoting and counter-quoting, the thought of the invaders was lost in the poetic past. They left the sea behind and came into the gimcrack district near the station where a whole family might occupy a corner of a room. One of the last bombs had fallen here. Three houses had collapsed together on to the basement where people had been sheltering. Some of them had survived but were trapped inside. They were calling through cracks in the masonry, pleading to be released.

Neighbours, mostly of the balani poor, stood in the road before the ruin, grinning with embarrassment because the pleadings were in vain. No one had the means to move the vast mountain of rubble heaped on top of those who cried.

Guy, Harriet and Aidan, coming upon this scene, felt they should act or conduct action but realized they were as helpless as the rest. Seeing a policeman at the rear of the crowd, Guy asked what was being done for the prisoners. When would they be released? The man put on a show of official competence on hearing an English voice and said, 'Bokra.' Guy did not think this good enough. Something should be done there and then. The policeman said that the civil authorities had no rescue team and no machinery for lifting heavy material. They usually depended on the good will of British servicemen, but now the servicemen had gone away. The people in the basebent would have to wait and see if help came. In an earlier raid, survivors were similarly trapped and had been still crying out a week later.

'What happened in the end?' Harriet asked but no one had the answer to her question.

The survivors, overhearing what was being said, set up a more furious wailing and the policeman, going to the rubble, shouted in to them to be patient. Very soon, perhaps that very night, the whole German army would be here to dig them out. At this, the prisoners began to curse the British for bringing the house down on their heads.

Guy said to Aidan, 'If we organized these fellows into a gang, they could clear the site by passing the stuff from hand to hand.' When the policeman returned, Guy repeated this plan in Arabic and the bystanders, realizing what he had in mind, wandered off in all directions.

Soon there was no one left to form a gang and the policeman, twisting his face into a grimace of pity, apologized. 'Those very poor men, effendi. Those men not strong.' Guy had to agree. The fellah, weakened by hunger and bilharzia, could not do much. The policeman said, to reassure him, 'Bokra police come. Bokra all very nice.'

Harriet said, 'Bokra fil mish-mish,' and the policeman could not keep from laughing.

Guy appealed to Aidan, 'What's to be done?'

'Nothing, I'm afraid.'

That being so, they had to go on, with the cries of the abandoned prisoners dying away behind them.

Harriet's train was about to leave and she had no time to argue with Guy but, leaning out of the carriage window, she pressed him, 'Darling, when will you come to Cairo? Tomorrow?'

'No, not tomorrow. I'll come at the weekend.'

Aidan was smiling with satisfaction that, at last, he had Guy to himself. The train began to move. Before it was under way, Harriet heard him beginning to tell Guy about his friend in Damascus who had gone out to see what was happening and died with a bullet in his head.

Five

The Column did not form itself as rapidly as had been expected. The infantry was there but the guns and gunners had not arrived. Hardy was also expecting another lieutenant. Simon, who for the moment was in charge of both platoons, told Ridley that he had heard there was a serious shortage of artillery. Ridley mournfully agreed. 'We could be hanging about here till Christmas.'

Simon oversaw the digging of slit trenches and he envied the men because they had this occupation, but the digging was easy and the job quickly done. After that, boredom was general. They were occasionally strafed by a passing Messerschmidt but they were too far back to rate serious attention by the enemy. There were no diversions and nothing to do but camp chores. The day's events were the visits from the mobile canteen and the Naafi truck that sold cigarettes and beer.

Early in the morning, the men kicked a ball about – there was a belief that the enemy never attacked men at play – but as the heat increased, activity lost its pleasure and the players flagged. After the mid-day meal, the old soldiers would fit up a ground sheet or blanket to form a bivouac and the new-comers soon copied them. Everyone in camp slept through the afternoon. Simon, who had regarded sleep as a time-wasting necessity, now discovered it could be bliss. Whenever he had nothing better to do, he would get into his sleeping-bag, which protected as much against heat as against cold, and hiding his face from the light, would sink into sleep. Sleep devoured boredom. Sleep devoured time. Here, he thought, they were all like the Cairo beggars who at noon gave themselves thankfully to oblivion.

But there were enemies that could deprive one of sleep. The flies were the worst. The newcomers became, after a while, in-ured to the bite of mosquitos and sand-flies, but nothing could repel the tormenting flies that buzzed and hit one's face and dragged their feet over sweaty flesh. Simon told Ridley of the black blanket of breeding flies he had seen on the Red Sea shore and Ridley described the fly traps that the men con-structed from wire. 'At Mersa,' he said, 'we caught the buggers by the million.' When the traps were full, there would be a mass burning of flies but the flies lived off the dead and the stench of the pyre would linger about the camp for days. For this reason fly burnings were now forbidden.

After sleep came the evening and the men longed for even-ing as a parched man longs for water. When the sun touched the horizon, the pressure of heat lifted and the flies disappeared.

At the end of their first day at the new camping site, Hardy's driver put a folding table and chair outside the HQ truck and Hardy sat down with his radio to listen to the news. When Simon came within hearing distance, Hardy said, 'You can get yourself a chair from the truck, Boulderstone,' and so, each evening, Simon joined Hardy beside the radio set. After a while, attracted by the sound of the radio, the men began to collect at a distance, at first respectfully standing but, as the entertainment became a habit, seating themselves in groups, smoking and even occasionally making a comment which Hardy ignored. He sometimes grunted or gave, when a news item disturbed him, a bitter, coughing laugh. but he said nothing to Simon who, isolated at the table, would have pre-ferred to be with the men.

The Column was joined by a gunner officer called Martin and a third chair was put out at sunset. Martin was a sandy Scot with an inflamed skin and a bristling red moustache. As he was a captain, Hardy could not ignore him altogether but neither man had much to say. On his second evening, Martin brought a bottle of whisky to the table and sent the driver to find glasses. When he poured drinks for himself and Hardy, he made a grudging movement in Simon's direction but Simon said he only drank beer. That was Martin's first and only gesture towards Simon who was then ignored by both officers. With them, but apart from them, Simon wondered if there was any creature in the army more wretched than a subaltern who had no contact with his seniors and was not allowed to consort with his men.

Talking to Ridley about the non-arrival of the guns, he said, 'We might have been living it up in Cairo all this time. Why were they in such a hurry to get us out here.'

Ridley, solemn with the consciousness of his own wisdom, said, 'We've got to be here. That's the point, see.'

'Even if we're doing nothing?'

'Lots of chaps out here are doing nothing, but they've got to be here. What'd happen if they wasn't?'

Simon laughed. 'I see what you mean.'

'After all sir, it's experience.'

'Pretty dreary experience, sarge.' Simon's early apprehension had begun to fade. So little had happened that he began to think that nothing ever would happen and he wrote home to say what an odd business it was, living here in the desert, like nomads, with nothing to do. In his opinion, they were worse off than the nomad Arabs who sometimes passed the camp. The Arabs had tents, and tents were homes of a sort, but the army men slept under an open sky. For several nights Simon was worried not only by the lack of cover but the intrusive magnificence of the Egyptian night. The stars were too many and too bright. They were like eyes: waking in mid-sleep, finding them staring down on him, he was unnerved, imagining they questioned what he was doing there. And there was the vast emptiness of the desert itself. The leaguered trucks formed a protective pale but as there were only four trucks, they could not join up. Between them could be seen dark distances that stretched for ever – and what might not come out of the distance while they slept? Some men found the space about them so threatening, they would seek refuge under the lorries. This was a fool thing to do, Ridley told them. There were freak rain storms, even in summer, and lorries had been known to sink into the wet sand and smother the men while they slept.

But in spite of their fears, the dawn came too soon for them. The guards, whose watch had been spent in the last bitter hours of the night, had the job of rousing the camp. Their shouts of 'Wakey, wakey' sounded a note of heartless relish for the men dragged out of sleep. Getting themselves up in the steel-cold daybreak, they could see no reason in their lives.

The first warmth of sunlight lifted the spirits. For a while the sand was the colour of a lightly cooked biscuit, stones threw shadows as long as sword blades and the whole desert was as airy and exhilarating as an endless seashore. Simon thought, 'If only the sun would stand still ...' but the sun inched up and up till its heat was an affront to the human body. The water ration those days was a gallon per man and this had to serve for washing, shaving, washing of clothes, cooking and drinking. Simon was tempted at times to drink the lot and leave himself unwashed.

Hardy, speaking as though he had given the matter long thought, told Simon to find himself a batman. 'Got any preference, Boulderstone?'

'I'd like to have Arnold, sir.'

'Arnold?' The choice seemed to surprise Hardy. 'You think he could cope?'

'I've found him very capable, sir.'

'Indeed? I don't know much about him but Ridley thinks he's a bit of a wet.'

Simon said, 'He's all right, sir,' and Arnold was granted him. He understood Ridley's doubts about Arnold but he also understood Arnold. What he knew of him, he had discovered by direct questioning. Unquestioned, Arnold was not one to reveal himself. Simon had several times found him gazing at some desert creature – a spider or lizard or a beetle rolling a ball of dung before it – and realized that his interest went beyond curiosity. On the last occasion, Simon asked, 'What did you do in civvy street, Arnold?'

'Student, sir.'

Simon had to ask three more questions before he discovered that Arnold had studied Natural History at Durham. He had taken his degree a week before the outbreak of war. He not only observed the desert creatures, he was forced to observe the games the men played with them. The men would catch a couple of spiders – not tarantulas that were dangerous to handle, but the big white spiders, of fearful appearance but harmless – and goad the creatures into fighting each other. Or, a more popular and spectacular sport, they would pour petrol round a scorpion and light it so the creature was ringed with fire. They would then gleefully watch its attempt to break out until, in the end, unable to endure the heat, its sting would droop slowly and penetrate the scales on its back. While the other men whooped with joy, Arnold would watch as though he shared the creature's agony.

Simon thought it wretched sport but he recognized the men's need for some sort of diversion in this God-forsaken wilderness. Arnold, helplessly shifting his feet or twisting his hands together, felt only for the animal world. Usually he was silent but once he burst out, 'Why do you do it? Why do you do it?'

The men laughed at him and said, 'Look what he'd do to us if he got the chance!'

'And why not? We don't belong here. This is his habitat – his home, I mean. We've no right here. He has to defend himself against us. Why not leave the poor things alone?'

Arnold was a joke. The men said, 'Poor old Arn, he's sand-happy,' but the officers were less tolerant. The outburst had been talked about and Martin said to Simon, 'I don't know why you want that squit as a batman. You can't trust those quiet types and that one, he's nothing but an old woman.'

Ridley was held to be the most knowledgeable man in camp. He was in Signals and so had the means of picking up information. At work in the HQ truck, he gossiped with other transmitters, picking up and purveying all the rumours, scandals and jokes of the line. When not at work, he talked to the drivers of the supply trucks that visited the camp and if they had nothing to tell him, he usually had something to tell them.

Simon, for some reason, was a favourite with Ridley who would come to him first with any news worth passing on. Ridley was ready to help Simon because Simon accepted help and advice with gratitude and humility. Ridley could sort out the noises that came from the forward position and could tell Simon which was the sound of a field gun and which a medium or ack-ack. He warned Simon about minefields and uncharted areas where a jerry can or an old baked beans tin might be a booby trap, set to blow your head off.

Simon was troubled by this information and not understanding why, he brooded on it until suddenly, like a returning dream, he remembered the dead boy in the Fayoum house. All the incidents of that day had become remote for him and the people he had met seemed to him beings of an unreal world. He now knew the real world was the fighting world where his companions had a substance and significance that set them apart from the rest of mankind. Only Edwina had circumstance in his world because she was Hugo's girl and Hugo was constantly in his mind. One day, feeling he now knew Ridley well enough, he asked him, 'Could you discover the whereabouts of a Captain Hugo Boulderstone?'

'With respect, sir – a relation of yours?'

'My brother.'

'Ah!' Regard for this near relationship lengthened Ridley's long face. 'Shouldn't be difficult. Not what you'd call a *common* name.'

Soon after, Ridley discovered that there was a Captain Hugo Boulderstone attached to the 6th New Zealand Brigade at Bab el Qattara. Simon eagerly asked, 'What chance of getting a lift down there?'

'Couldn't say, sir. You'd have to bring it up with the major.'

Simon brought it up that evening, beginning, 'Do you think, sir, I could get a lift down to Bab el Qattara? I'd like...'

'Don't be a fool, Boulderstone,' Hardy interrupted him, 'you can't get a lift anywhere. You're not out here on a sightseeing trip.'

Next day Ridley had word that the Bab el Qattara box had been evacuated and German forces had moved in.

'That doesn't sound too good, does it?' said Simon.

'There's no knowing. Chaps think the Auk could be up to something.'

Two field guns and two anti-tank guns and their gunners joined the Column which was now complete except for the lieutenant due to take over the second platoon. He arrived next day when Simon was helping Arnold, whose job it was to collect rations from platoon headquarters. Simon and Arnold were both on-loading the section's water-cans and sacks for supplies when a staff car drew up a few yards from the truck. Simon had thrown off his sweat-soaked shirt: his shorts needed a wash and his desert boots were covered with sand. Arnold looked no better than he did and the lieutenant, fresh from the discipline of base camp, eyed the pair of them with acute distaste. Wearing his best gabardine, carrying gloves and cane, he had obviously got himself up to present himself to the officers of the Column. Extruding his superiority, he shouted, 'I say, you fellows, is Major Hardy about?'

Recognizing the voice rather than the man, Simon said, 'Good God, it's Trench,' and would have embraced him, had not the new arrival taken a disgusted step back.

'Who the devil are you?'

'Don't you recognize me? I'm Simon Boulderstone. Where've you been? We've been waiting for you.'

Trench's fair hair had bleached white under the Egyptian sun. With his fine, regular features and military moustache, he could have posed for a portrait of the ideal young officer, but at that moment he lacked the calm assurance for the part. Instead, disconcerted, he looked Simon over to make sure he had not lost officer rank then, smiling sheepishly, he gave a halting account of his movements since leaving the ship at Suez. He and Codley had been taken to Infantry Base Depot to await a posting. Giving Simon a reproving glance, he muttered, 'How is it you're doing what you're not supposed to do?'

'What do you mean?'

'You're loading a truck.'

Simon laughed. In that moment it was revealed to him that Trench was an ass. His friend, whom he had admired beyond all other men, was one of those asses who thought familiarity with the men was 'bad for discipline'. He was a 'spit and polish' officer, a sort of man Simon despised.

'You need to get some service in,' Simon said. 'When you've been out in the blue for a bit, you'll be glad to do anything to break the monotony.' He turned to Arnold and winked at him. 'OK, Arnold, carry on. Don't forget oranges and cheese. Try and bag some fresh meat this time. If they offer you pilchards again, tell them where they can stuff them.'

Arnold saluted with uncustomary smartness. 'Sir. We could do with some Cruft's Specials, sir.'

'They'll let you have plenty of those.'

'And it's our turn for jam, sir.'

'Good show.'

Arnold's manner was deferential and Simon, seeing him off, gave him every possible attention, apparently forgetting that Trench was waiting to be led to Major Hardy. The truck went off. Simon, turning away from it, saw Trench with surprise. 'You still there? Come along then, I'll take you to the HQ truck.'

They walked together in silence, both knowing that the old intimacy was lost to them. Some time passed before they thought about it again or understood how, or why, it had ever existed.

The Column, completed, was ordered to prepare for a move and Hardy made an inspection of weapons. As he walked with Martin between the ranks, Ridley asked in the obsequious whine he reserved for senior officers, 'Think we'll get a scrap, sir?'

'Could be. Could be.'

'Make a nice change, sir.'

Hardy was giving nothing away but Simon felt his apprehensions revive. Bored during the waiting days, he would have wished for action. Now action threatened, he thought longingly of boredom. Doing his best to appear calm, he asked Ridley, 'What's it like, being under fire?'

'You don't feel so much at the time. It's the thinking about it, is worst.'

'You mean, you get your blood up?'

'That's right. Couldn't've put it better m'self. Back here you think you don't hate jerry, but when you go in, it's different. P'raps you see a pal cop it – a decent bloke, p'raps, what's done you a favour. You think "Right you bastards, I'll get you for that" and so you go in fighting mad. You get to hate them like hell. You got to, y'see, you wouldn't be no use if you didn't.'

The thought of being injected with hate, as with a drug, did nothing to reassure Simon. Hate could make you reckless but recklessness did not make you safe. During the night before the dawn departure he woke several times. Hearing the other men stirring and muttering, he knew they were as tense as he was.

Next morning delay would have been welcome, but this time they started as the first cherry red strip of light appeared between the black earth and the black sky. Simon felt no inclination to talk. He was beside Arnold in the leading truck and the leading truck was the one that copped it if they struck an uncharted minefield. As the strip widened, the desert was flushed with red. Simon had been provided with a compass for this journey which took them over sand flats as featureless as mid-ocean. The sun rose and the hours passed. Soon enough they were in the dusty glare of noon, the most painful hour of day, with mirage stretching like water over the track. A hill appeared in the distance, not high but unique in this part of the desert.

Simon stirred himself to ask what it was. Arnold said, 'It's the Ridge, sir.'

The Ridge, as they drew near it, could be seen in detail, a long, narrow outcrop of rock, its flanks fluted as though innumerable rivulets had run down it for centuries. Simon had been told that they were going south of the Ridge so he imagined the journey would soon be over. As they came level with the rock, a wind sprang up and ran along the rock base lifting the sand like the edge of a carpet.

'We're in for a bit of a storm, sir,' Arnold said. 'Think we should call a halt?'

Simon was uncertain but as they rounded the eastern end of the Ridge, the sand had thickened like a fog in the air and Arnold advised him, 'If we brew up now, sir, it could be all over by the time we're finished.' He put up the flag and the Column was halted. Simon, running back to consult with Hardy, was thankful to find they had done the right thing.

They drank their tea, bunched together with backs to the wind, waiting for the storm to die down. Instead, it grew worse and Ridley said morosely, 'Could go on for days.'

Breathing sand, eating sand, blinded and deafened by sand, the men crouched by the trucks for shelter and picked sand from their noses and the interstices of their ears. Ridley became more gloomy. 'Known this go on for *weeks*,' but at sunset, when the air glowed as though the sand had become incandescent, the wind dropped and the world became visible again. In the slanting light the Ridge with its fluted sides looked like a monstrous millipede. Beneath it, there was a large encampment and Simon would have been glad to leaguer to its rear but Hardy decreed that they make another mile before darkness fell. As they moved off, guns opened up behind them and Simon, his stomach muscles contracting, felt he should have written home before leaving camp. He thought of his mother first, then remembered his wife. He should have sent letters to both of them, preparing them for whatever happened to him, but in terms that made light of it all. He tried to think of his wife but the few days of their honeymoon had disappeared into the past. He made an effort to recall her face and saw instead the long, fair, drooping hair of Edwina Little. Troubled by his infidelity, he took out his wallet and gazed at the photograph of Anne and all he could feel was that her face was not the right face. He wanted to see the laughing, sunburnt face that had leant towards him from the balcony in Garden City but the truth was, no face could distract him now. The whole of the pleasurable world had dwindled out of sight, leaving him with nothing but a sense of loss and an awareness of the danger he was in.

The Column leaguered in a service area where supply dumps and transports were camouflaged with nets. It looked safe enough, rather like a vast workshop, but the trucks had just drawn up when the guns started again and hammered their senses as they sat round Hardy's radio waiting for the news. The newsreader announced that later in the evening there would be a commentary on 'The Alamein Line'. Simon asked Hardy, 'What's that, sir?' and Hardy, who would not admit ignorance, said, 'If you pay attention and listen, Boulderstone, you'll find out.' This admonition was so familiar to Simon, it occurred to him that Hardy had been a schoolmaster in his civilian days. The commentator told them that the Alamein Line stretched from the coastal salt lakes to a mysterious hole in the desert called the Qattara Depression and his description suggested that there were bodies of well-armoured troops in close formation for forty miles. None of the officers questioned this but Simon, who had seen nothing of such a line, spoke to Ridley before going to his sleeping-bag. 'I say, sarge, you heard that about the Alamein Line. Where exactly is it?'

Ridley, as much at a loss as he was, gave the matter thought and said, 'This is it, I reckon. There's the South Africans up north and a couple of Indian divs down south, and the Kiwis are under the Ridge, and our chaps are in between. They're a bit thin on the ground but it's a line all right.'

Ridley seemed satisfied but Simon, who had pictured the front as a carnage of gun-fire, bursting shells and barbed wire hung with the dead and dying, felt disappointment as well as relief. 'It's not much of a line, sarge.'

'It's all we've got. Still, it's not what we've got but what they haven't got that'll make the difference. It said on the intercom today that the Auk's trying to make an army out of remnants. That's it – remnants. The Auk's a great bloke but I don't fancy his chances.'

'Do you fancy anyone's chances, sarge?'

'Ah, now, sir!' Ridley pulled himself up and spoke with confidence, 'We'll do for them, yet – you wait and see.'

Driving next morning into open desert, the guns booming behind, the Column was as exposed as a fly on a window-pane. Arnold, peering out for markers, also kept an eye on the sky but it was not till mid-morning, when they had stopped to brew up, that enemy aircraft observed them. Ridley was carrying tea mugs over to the officers when three Italian Macchis buzzed the trucks. Before any of the men could drop to the ground, bullets were spitting about them. The officers sprang back and Hardy, the eldest of them and the most alarmed, lost his balance and fell, his voice rising in a thin, protesting cry, 'Oh, my wife and kids!'

The Macchis, having strafed the Column from end to end, flew off. No one had been hit. Ridley helped Hardy to his feet and everyone behaved as though the fall had been an unfortunate trip-up and said, 'Bad luck, sir.' Simon, thinking he alone had heard Hardy's cry, decided it must never be mentioned, not even to Arnold.

Driving on, they came into a region where rocky outcrops, miniatures of the great Ridge, rose, one after the other, out of the flat mardam. These outcrops changed in colour, the usual Sahara yellow taking on a tinge of pink and the pink growing and deepening until the rocks and sand had the faded rose colour of old red sandstone. Hardy called a halt between the rock ridges and the Column leaguered in a wide, flat area, like a rose pink ballroom aglow with sunset. In the distance, when evening cleared the air, a dramatic range of high ridges could be seen on the horizon. Hardy, consulting his maps, told the officers that the range marked the terminal of the line. Beyond it was the Depression and the Depression, it seemed, could not be crossed. So the Column need go no further. 'Tomorrow,' he said, 'the men'll make slit trenches and dig in the vehicles.'

They had arrived.

Six

Rumour came to Cairo of a battle fought inside Egypt at a railway halt called El Alamein but, it seemed, nothing had been settled. The Germans were still a day's tank drive away and their broadcasts claimed they were merely awaiting fresh supplies. Any day now the advance would begin again. Egypt would be liberated and Rommel and his men would keep their assignation with the ladies of Alexandria.

Though the situation had not changed, the panic had died. Those who were, or believed themselves to be, at risk, had gone. Those who remained felt a sense of respite but were warned they might have to leave at short notice. They were advised to keep a bag packed.

When Harriet, returning for luncheon, found a note at the pension to say Dobson had rung her, she supposed the evacuation order had gone out. She took out the small suitcase, the only luggage she had brought out of Greece, and put together a few toilet articles. The suitcase was already packed. She could leave in minutes, but she did not intend to leave without Guy. She thought of a dozen arguments to bring down on Dobson when he telephoned again and his voice, when she heard it, startled her. His tone was jocular. Instead of ordering her to the station, he invited her to meet him for drinks at Groppi's: 'Come about five-thirty.'

'You sound as though you had good news?'

'Perhaps I have,' he spoke teasingly. 'I'll tell you when I see you.'

Back at the office, she looked through the news sheets, but they gave no cause for rejoicing. Whatever Dobson would tell her, it could have nothing to do with the war.

That morning she had heard that her job at the Embassy would not last much longer. The promised team from the States was about to fly to Egypt. Mr Buschman, not caring to tell her himself, had sent her a typed note. Dispirited, she went to the wall map where the black pins converged upon the Middle East.

She had taken it over during the great days of the Russian counter-offensive when everyone was saying that the Russian winter would defeat Hitler as it had defeated Napoleon. Marking the Russian advances, she rejoiced as though pushing the enemy back with her own hands. Guy had picked up a new song from one of his left-wing friends and repeatedly sang it to what was, more or less, the tune of *The Lincolnshire Poacher*:

To say that Hitler can't be beat
Is just a lot of cock,
For Marshal Timoshenko's men
Are pissing through von Bock.
The Führer makes the bloomers and his generals take the rap,
But Joe, he smokes his pipe and wears a taxi-driver's cap.

In the desert, too, the Germans had been in retreat. The British troops, who had been making a hero of Rommel, now turned their admiration on to Stalin and the Russian generals. But that had all passed. Harriet, bringing the black pins closer to the Kuban river, thought, 'A few more miles and they'll have the whole Caucasus.'

Inside Egypt, the black pins stretched from the coast to a hatched-in area of the desert named on the map 'Qattara Depression'. When Mr Buschman wandered over to see who was where, she asked him what this Depression was. He stood for some moments, rubbing his small, plump hand over the back of his neck, and then gave up: 'All I know is, it's the end of the line.'

'But why is it the end of the line? Why don't they come round that way? If they did, they could surround the whole British army.'

'Too right, mem. They surely could.'

Harriet asked Iqal about the Depression but he had never heard of it.

'How is your German these days?'

He smiled an arch smile, the runnels of his face quivering so he looked like coffee cream on the boil. 'I brush it up now and then, but I don't know! These Germans should make more haste.'

'I told you they wouldn't get here.'

'That is true, Mrs Pringle, and perhaps you spoke right. But on the other hand, perhaps not. It says in the broadcasts they regather their forces and then they come – zoom! So what is one to think? See here, Mrs Pringle, they exhort us, "Rise against your oppressors," they say, 'Kill them and be free.'' '

'You don't think the English are oppressors, do you?'

Iqal raised his great shoulders. 'Sometimes, yes. Sometimes, no. When they break through the palace gates and tell my king

131

what to do, what would you call them? Are they not oppressors?'

'We're fighting a war, Iqal. If the Egyptians really felt oppressed, they would turn on us, wouldn't they?'

'Ah, Mrs Pringle, we are not fools. My friends say, "Time enough when the Germans are at the gate – *then* we cut the English throats."'

'Oh, come now, Iqal, you wouldn't cut my throat?'

Iqal giggled. 'Believe me, Mrs Pringle, if I would cut your throat, I do it in a kind and considerate manner.'

'You wouldn't hurt me?'

'No, no, Mrs Pringle, indeed I would not.'

Harriet reached Groppi's when the sun was low in the sky. She passed through the bead curtain into the brown, chocolate-scented cake and sweet shop as the great round golden chocolate boxes were reflecting the golden sky. The garden café, surrounded by high walls, was already in shadow. It was a large café, sunk like a well among the houses, with a floor-covering of small stones and it disappointed people who saw it for the first time. A young officer had said to Harriet, 'The chaps in the desert think Groppi's is the Garden of Sensual Delights – but, good grief, it isn't even a garden!'

It was, she said, a desert garden, the best anyone could hope for so far from the river. It was a garden of indulgences where the Levantine ladies came to eye the staff officers who treated it as a home from home.

The ground was planted, not with trees, but with tables and chairs and coloured umbrellas. But under one wall, where there was a strip of imported earth, zinnias grew and an old, hardy creeping plant spread out and up and covered lattices and stretched as far as the enclosure that stood at one end of the café site. This creeper sometimes put out a few copper-coloured, trumpet-shaped flowers that enhanced the garden idea. But this display, and there was not much of it, would have died in an hour without the water that seeped continually through the holes in a canvas hose. In spite of the water, the mat of leaves hung dry and loose, shifting and rustling in the hot wind. Only the tough, thick-petalled zinnias thrived in this heat.

132

When Harriet entered, the safragis were taking down the umbrellas, leaving the tables open to the evening air. At this hour people were crowding in, searching for friends or somewhere to sit. Dobson must have arrived early for Harriet found him at a vantage point, in front of the zinnias. He had seen her before she saw him and was on his feet, beckoning to her, his smile so genial she wondered if he had news of a victory.

She asked, 'Has anything happened?' He did not answer but waved her to a chair. Whatever he had to tell, he was in no hurry to tell it.

A safragi, his white galabiah given distinction by a red sash and the fez that denotes the effendi's servant, wheeled over a gilded trolley laden with cream cakes. Harriet asked for a glass of white wine. Dobson urged her to choose a cake, saying, 'Do join me. I think I'll have a *mille feuille*. Good for you. You've lost weight since you came here.'

'I really hadn't much weight to lose.'

Dobson put his fork into his *mille feuille* and said as the cream and jam oozed out, 'Yum, yum,' and put a large piece into his mouth then asked, as he sometimes did, about her work at the American Embassy.

'Coming to an end, I fear.' Harriet gave a wry laugh. 'Perhaps we're all coming to an end. Iqal was joking about cutting our throats – perhaps not just joking. He seemed to resent that occasion when the ambassador drove a tank through the palace gates.'

Dobson, putting more pastry into his mouth, swayed his head knowingly, swallowed and said, 'We're always having trouble with Farouk. He's a fat, spoilt baby, but he's a clever baby. The other day H.E. waited over an hour for an audience. He thought the king was with his ministers but instead he had a girl with him. She put her head out of the door and seeing H.E. there in all his regalia, she went off into screams of laughter and slammed the door on him. When he eventually got in, he found Farouk sprawled on a sofa, languid and irritable – post coitum, no doubt. He thought, with the hun so close, he could tell us to clear out. H.E. explained why we must hold Egypt at all cost. Farouk scarcely bothered to listen and at the end, he

133

sighed and said, "Oh, very well. Stay if you must. But when your war's over, for God's sake, put down the white man's burden and *go*." '

Dobson, having told his story, looked over the garden as though expecting another guest. Harriet hoped she would now hear why he had invited her here, but before anything more could be said, two Egyptian women stopped to speak to him. He jumped up, became at once diplomatically effusive, and they talked together in French. The women, dressed in an embellished version of Parisian fashion, wore black dresses to which they had added brooches, necklaces and sprays of flowers. Their skirts ended an inch above the knee but their sleeves, as required by the prophet, came down to their wrists. They flirted with Dobson, their eyes enhanced by eye-veils, and moved their heads, giving small, rapid turns this way and that so their earrings danced. Harriet had heard that Dobson, the only bachelor among the senior diplomats, was regarded in Cairo as 'quite a catch'. One of the women invited him to a cocktail party and he accepted as though overwhelmed by the thought of it, but when the women moved away, he fell back in his chair with a long, exhausted sigh. 'My policy is to accept everything and go to nothing. Where's that husband of yours?'

'Are you expecting him?'

'Certainly I'm expecting him. I rang him first thing this morning and asked him to be here at five-thirty. It's now nearly six and I ought to be back in my office.'

'You want to see him about something? Is it important?'

'It is for him.' Dobson laughed, making light of Guy's non-appearance, but it was an aggravated laugh. Harriet looked anxiously towards the entrance, fearing that Dobson would go and the important matter be nullified, all because Guy could never turn up on time. She said to excuse him, 'People make too many claims on him so he ends up with more engagements than the day will hold. The result is, he's late for everything, and made later by all the telephone calls he makes to explain why he'll be late.'

Dobson thought this very funny. 'How does he get away with it?'

'If he didn't get away with it, he'd have to learn not to be late. People spoil him and make him worse than he need be.'

The afterglow of sunset was taking on the green of dusk. The evening star appeared as from nowhere, radiating long rays of white light, and the coloured electric bulbs were lit among the creepers. All about, in the high house walls, windows were thrown open and people looked down on the brilliant garden.

Harriet said, 'When we first came here from Greece, those lighted windows frightened me. I thought, "What a target we are!"'

But at that moment, the lights meant nothing but the passing of time, and her fear was the fear that Guy would not turn up at all.

Dobson said, 'Ho, there he is!' forgiving Guy on sight for being three-quarters of an hour late.

Guy, lost between the tables, was dishevelled as ever. He had broken his glasses and mended them roughly with adhesive tape. At least, Harriet consoled herself, he hasn't brought anyone with him.

When Dobson waved to him, he came over at a hurried trot, breathlessly explained how someone or something had detained him. Dobson, all irritation gone, said, 'Don't worry. Don't worry at all. What are you going to drink?' When at last the table was resettled, he said impressively, 'Now, then!' They were going to hear what this meeting was all about.

'I've received a telegram from Bevington.'

'Our chairman?'

'Lord Bevington himself.' Dobson started to laugh so that his body was shaken by a sort of nervous hiccups. 'I remember when Bevington came here on a visit. It was my night on duty at the Embassy and I'd just got my head down when the boab looked in – huge, coal-black fellow – and croaked at me, "De lord am come!" Dear me, I said to myself, it's the day of judgement ... Well, now! first things first. Colin Gracey has been given the push.'

'He's leaving the Organization?'

'You needn't be surprised. Pinkrose cabled the London office and accused him of neglect of duty, incompetence, cowardice in the face of the enemy and, most heinous crime of all, going

135

to Palestine without letting Pinkrose know. He also, as a make-weight, said he had evidence of immoral practices.'

'Really!' Harriet was interested. 'What immoral practices? The houseboat? Mustapha Quant?'

'Probably. A Turk was mentioned.'

Guy looked troubled. 'They can't simply take Pinkrose's word for it. There must be an official inquiry.'

'There has been an inquiry. In any case, Pinkrose's complaints were only the last of a series made by British residents. Pinkrose carried most weight because he is known to Bevington who cabled the Embassy for confirmation. I cabled back that Gracey had indeed fled and the office was shut. This clinched it. We were informed that if Gracey returned he should be handed a letter ordering him to Aden which is, I believe, the Organization's Devil's Island.'

Guy took off his glasses and, the tape giving way, the lenses fell apart. He asked, 'But who will replace him? Are they flying someone out?'

'No.' Smiling blandly, Dobson watched Guy fidgeting with the broken frame then said, 'Bevington has chosen a London-appointed man – the only one left in Egypt.'

'Guy?'

Dobson turned his smile on to Harriet who threw back her head and laughed with delight. Dobson looked to Guy for a similar reaction but Guy, though he had flushed with pleasure, looked disturbed. 'Is this really fair to Gracey?'

'You don't have to worry about Gracey. He's not likely to take himself to Aden. Even before he left here, he was inquiring about a possible passage to the Cape, saying that the exigencies of life in a war zone were telling on his health.'

Guy still did not seem satisfied and Harriet, taking the glasses out of his hand, said, 'Forget Gracey. What you have to think about is the Organization. If Bevington has chosen you for the job, it's up to you to do it. Don't waste concern on Gracey.'

As he reflected on this, Guy's expression lightened and he realized that he had before him a whole new area of activity on which to expand his energy. All he had to do now was settle matters at the Commercial College. As Harriet had suspected, when the need came, these matters could be settled easily enough.

Guy said, 'I've a couple of excellent Greek teachers who can take over the English department. I'll be back here as soon as they're installed and my first aim will be to get the Institute on its feet.'

'And,' said Harriet, 'you'll have to tidy yourself up. Here,' she returned his glasses, neatly mended with tape, and said, 'Order a new frame for them,' then she took his hand and said with affectionate pride, 'I don't know how you do it, but you always win in the end.'

Dobson had to leave them but, standing up, he said, 'I don't know how you feel about that pension of yours but I have a room free in Garden City. It was Beaker's room and he's left a few sticks in it. If you like to look at it ...'

'Goodness, yes. How wonderful!' Overwhelmed by the day's good fortune, Harriet could not speak above a whisper.

It was arranged that next evening, when she left work, she was to look at the room.

Dobson said, 'Bless you both,' and made off through the garden, walking with a backward tilt as though his heels were lower than his toes. Looking after the short, plump figure, Guy said, 'There, I always said Dobson was a really nice fellow.'

'Have I ever said anything else?'

The Organization men, feeling themselves inferior, had been inclined to jeer at the diplomats who, in times of danger, saw the Organization as another and unnecessary problem.

Now Guy said, 'I'm afraid we felt they were another order of being – but, really, they're not bad when you get to know them.' He was rapidly taking on confidence and vitality as he considered the responsibilities that lay ahead. The lines on his face had faded and he was alert with a new consciousness of authority. Harriet thought, 'He may one day be eminent.' Guy, catching her considering glance, said, 'We'll have more money now, so let's have a Pernod on the strength of it.'

Dobson told Harriet that the flat belonged to the Embassy. He explained why it was divided into two parts and led her through the baize door into what had been the harem quarters. He usually let these rooms to Embassy staff but if no Embassy person needed accommodation, he was free to let to friends.

'So I had Professor Beaker and now ...' he gave Harriet a humorous little bow, 'I hope to have Guy and Harriet Pringle. What could be nicer! But you'd better look the room over before deciding. It's not at all grand. The main part is protected because the servants' rooms are above it, but this wing is immediately under the roof. I'm afraid it gets rather hot.'

When he opened the door, the heat, as though too big for the room, rolled out and wrapped itself round them like an eiderdown. The servants had not bothered to pull down the blinds so heat came in, not only through the ceiling, but also the window. The woodwork, which had been sun-baked for a century, seemed to crackle with heat and the floor shook as they walked upon it.

The room was furnished with a divan bed, two chairs and a hanging cupboard. The professor had rented this furniture from a store in the Muski and the Pringles could add to it if they wished.

'I know it's not much, but it's rent free. You only have to pay your share of the housekeeping. So – what do you think?'

Harriet, trying to think of some adequate expression of gratitude, gave a little sigh and Dobson, mistaking her hesitation for uncertainty, said, 'I'll leave you to consider and look around.'

Harriet, left to herself, absorbed the atmosphere of the room that was square and not very large. The window looked out on the leaves of a tree that filled the whole window space. The heat muffled her but, entranced by the thought of living here with Guy among congenial people, she did not mind the heat. She sat on the edge of the bed and stared at the tree then, hearing a telephone ringing, she was struck with fear that someone else was wanting the room and she hurried back to Dobson to lay claim to it.

Dobson, his call finished, came into the living-room and she said at once, 'It's a wonderful room.'

'Oh, hardly that, but if you want it, it's yours. I'm sorry

Edwina's not here. She's out with one of her young men, but do sit down. Hassan has squeezed some limes for us. Will you have gin and lime, or just plain lime and water?'

'Lime juice! What luxury!'

Dobson, thinking she referred to the work of squeezing the limes, said, 'Oh, it's not so difficult. We have a little machine thing.'

Settling down with his gin and lime, he asked if she had heard any amusing gossip lately. Unable to think of any, she put her question about the Qattara Depression.

Dobson, being able to answer it, looked pleased. 'The Depression is just an immense salt pan but it's got the jerries foxed. They know if they tried to cross it, their tanks would sink into it. Tweedie, the military attaché, drove out to take a shufti and he said you can see the German engineers climbing down to it and poking sticks into the surface. Until they find a way across it, it acts as a strategic terminus.'

'But couldn't they go round it?'

'Too far. Five hundred miles or more. Tweedie thinks they're overstretched as it is.'

'You think that's why they've come to a stop? You don't think they're simply waiting for the Caucasus to collapse? If the German panzers came down through Persia, they'd meet up with Rommel and surround the British forces. 8th Army could be wiped out.'

'Dear me,' Dobson laughed. 'You certainly believe in facing up to the worst.'

'If Hitler got the Baku oil and the Middle East oil – what would happen then?'

Dobson cheerfully considered this possibility – Harriet realized that cheerfulness was a form of diplomatic courtesy – but she could see he was bored by her suppositions. 'I imagine our troops would have withdrawn to Upper Egypt long before that happened. We'd battle on.'

'For ever? Like the Hundred Years War?'

'It's possible:' Dobson spoke as though the war was a tedious subject, better not discussed. Harriet finished her lime juice and said she must go. Taking her to the door, Dobson said in the

139

tone of one making a confession, 'I may say that, in my cable to Bevington, I mentioned that Guy was the only Organization man in Rumania who stuck it out to the end.'

'Thank you, Dobbie. Guy needs a friend.'

'Needs a friend! But no one has more friends.'

'There are friends and friends. There are those who want something from you and those who will do something for you. Guy has plenty of the first. He's rather short of the second.'

'Do you mean that?'

'Yes. He collects depressives, neurotics and dotty people who think he's the answer to their own inadequacy.'

'And is he?'

'No, there is no answer.'

The next day, when Harriet brought some of her belongings to the flat, she found Edwina in the living-room. The two girls had met at parties but had talked only once, during a dance at Mena House when they happened to be in the cloak-room together. Edwina, putting on lipstick of a violent mulberry colour, caught Harriet's gaze in the looking-glass and winked at her as though they shared a joke. She said, 'This colour's a bit much, isn't it?' Harriet did not think so and Edwina said, 'Some people say I'm fast, but I'm not really. I only want a good time.'

And why not? Harriet asked herself. Drawn to Edwina's easy good nature, she would have talked longer but Edwina, besieged by all the excitements awaiting her, threw her lipstick into her bag, saying, 'Well, back to the fray. Let's have a chat some time,' and was gone. The time did not come. Though they were the same age, Harriet and Edwina did not meet on common ground. Edwina was unmarried and reputed to be the most eligible girl in Cairo. Even the plainest English girls were sought after and Edwina, a beauty even if not a classical beauty, had so many invitations to dinners and parties, she could not, with the best will in the world, find time for other girls.

Now she greeted Harriet like an old friend, saying, 'Oh, I'm so glad you've taken the room. What fun it will be, having you here!' Pushing the sun-bleached hair away from her eyes, she observed Harriet with such warm and welcoming admiration that Harriet felt the world would change for her. 'Yes,' she said, 'what fun!' and life, that had been dark with war and defeat, for a moment took on the brilliance of Edwina's good times.

Edwina said, 'How sad, I have to go and change but we'll see such lots of each other now we're sharing a flat, won't we?'

Of course. Of course. Harriet, going to her room, heard Edwina singing under the shower. Putting her things into the hanging-cupboard, she noticed a dry, herbal scent in the air, like the scent of *pot-pourri*. She thought it came from the dried-out wood, then saw that the window had been opened and noises, gentle and monotonous, told her that there was a garden outside. She heard the hiss of water and realized that the water was drawing the scent from dry grass. And there was a thin thread of pipe music repeating the same phrase over and over again.

She took a chair to the window and standing on it, tried to look through the tree's dark, glossy, ovoid leaves but they grew too thickly and there was nothing to be seen but the blur of sunlight beneath the lowest branches. The sun was sinking and its rays, piercing in between the leaves, filled the room with a dusty glow. Close to the tree, she saw that its head of leaves was dotted with green fruits that here and there were taking on a flush of orange or pink.

Looking into the tree, feeling protected by its presence, hearing the delicate pipe phrase endlessly repeated, she felt comforted as though by the prediction of happiness to come.

When she returned to the living-room, Dobson wandered from his room, naked except for a bath-towel worn round his waist like a sarong. 'We're very informal here,' he said.

She asked about the garden outside her window and was told it belonged to the owner of one of Cairo's big stores. 'A very rich man,' Dobson said with satisfaction.

'Someone's playing a pipe out there.'

'That's the snake charmer, a frequent visitor. He's a bit of a joke among the safragis who say he can always produce a sackful of snakes because he brings them with him. He charms the same snakes every time.'

Harriet was pleased to hear that the snakes were not killed

but led this enchanted life, perpetually charmed by pipe music.

At the end of the week, when she left the pension and brought the last of her things to the flat, Dobson asked, 'And when are we to be joined by the great man himself?' Edwina entering, as he spoke, wanted to know who the great man was, saying, 'Why have I not met him?'

Harriet said, 'You'll meet him soon. He is my husband.' She expected him to turn up for supper that evening and had told him he would see Edwina, but Edwina was dressed for some much more sumptuous occasion than supper at the flat. Waiting for her escort, she asked Harriet to join her on the balcony. The French windows had been opened and the first cool air of evening was drifting into the room. Outside there were some old wickerwork sofas and chairs. Sitting in the mild, jasmin-scented twilight, looking over the palms and sycamores and mango trees that grew in the riverside gardens, Harriet felt that she and Guy had at last found a home in Cairo.

Edwina had brought out the grocery lists which she made for the senior safragi, Hassan, and showing them to Harriet, said, 'You can take a turn at the housekeeping if you like, but you have to keep an eye on Hassan. He expects to make a bit here and there, but it mustn't be too much. Also, he's inclined to pay more than he need at the market to show what a great house he works for, so you have to keep a check on prices. They all take advantage any way they can and Hassan's no worse than most.'

'There are just the four of us: you, Dobbie, Guy and me?'

'No, there's one more: Percy Gibbon,' Edwina seemed to regret the addition of this fifth person but said no more about him. 'I do look forward to meeting Guy,' she sighed. 'I wish I had a nice husband like that. Dobbie says he's a pet.'

Harriet, flattered, wondered if, among the young, expugnable officers who took her out, Edwina could ever find one she would wish to marry. Lulled into a sense of well-being by Edwina's amiable chatter about food and market prices, Harriet forgot that her companion was going out and felt a sense of shocked deprivation when Hassan came out to announce, 'Captain come, sa'ida,' and Edwina jumped to her feet. Again she lamented that she must go, but she was eager for the evening's entertainment. Standing a moment against the light of the room, she gathered together her sequinned scarf and her little, glittering evening bag, then smiled and went away, leaving behind her scent of gardenias.

The snake charmer did not return for several days but Harriet, coming back from the office one afternoon, heard a more complex and powerful music filling the flat.

Dobson's room led off the living-room, the door stood ajar and as she paused near it, Dobson looked out and said, 'You haven't seen my gramophone, have you?' He invited her into a room that was larger than the other bedrooms but as sparsely furnished. The only thing remarkable in it was an old-fashioned box gramophone with a horn of immense size. The horn, made of papier maché, lifted itself towards the ceiling, opening in a mouth that was more than four foot wide.

'I've never seen anything like it.'

Dobson was delighted by her astonishment. 'Magnificent, isn't it? It must be the only one of its kind in the Middle East. I bought it from Beaker who got it before the war, when you could get anything sent out. He didn't want the bother of transporting it to Baghdad so I was happy to take it from him. It's hand made. The needle is amethyst so it will never wear out.'

The record had ended and lifting it, holding it delicately by the edges, Dobson turned it over, saying, 'I'll put it on again so you can hear the quality of the sound.'

The gramophone had to be cranked up by hand. Dobson, in his siesta garb of a towel round the middle – worn not from modesty but to ward off stomach chills – turned the handle so his fat little belly protruding above the towel edge, his narrow soft shoulders and his soft pale arms, all quivered with the effort. He looked, Harriet thought, as plump and bosomed as a woman but he was quite unabashed by the fact. Placing the needle to the moving record, he stood back and the music unrolled like velvet about the room.

Harriet, not knowledgeable about music, guessed it was Mozart.

'Yes. The Clarinet Quintet. Exquisite, isn't it?'

All through the late afternoons and evenings of mid-summer the questing notes of the clarinet filled the flat as Dobson played and replayed his new record.

Harriet's job might end any day now. It ended, as things were liable to do these days, without warning. Harriet was at the map, advancing the black pins across the Kuban river at Krasnodar when Iqal came up behind her and said in a hurried whisper, 'Important gentlemen have come from America. I warn you, one is about to enter.'

She turned and said, 'I think he's entered already.'

The man, as neat looking as Mr Buschman but younger, seemed oddly pale and composed among the hot, sunburnt people in the basement. He was dressed as Mr Buschman dressed in a dark poplin suit of elegant cut, a white silk shirt and a narrow black tie. Mr Buschman had not returned from golf and the new arrival came straight to Harriet with hand outstretched. 'As you see, we are here at last. We touched down half an hour ago.' Unmoved by the ancient world, unmoved by war, he smiled with sublime self-assurance, showing perfect teeth. Seeing the map, he asked, 'How's it going?'

'On and on and on.'

'It'll go better now.'

'You're going to blow them right out of the water?'

He was much amused. 'You've said it, mem.'

Harriet put the pins down. 'The Germans have crossed the Kuban river. You might like to mark it up.'

'Oh, give them to my secretary. She's in the john at the moment. She'll just love playing with those little pins.'

Harriet said good-bye to everyone and turned her back on the map as she would, if she could, have turned her back on the whole weary conflict.

Guy, when he entered the Institute as Director, found in the hall a notice that said Professor Dubedat and Professor Lush would, on alternate evenings, give lectures on Shakespeare, Milton, Wordsworth and other outstanding figures of English literature. Apart from this promise, little remained of the cultural activities that had once filled the six rooms and lecture hall of the building in the centre of Cairo. The place had a run-down appearance. Three Egyptian teachers remained to take dwindling classes and these, when they heard that a new Director had arrived, came to Guy with complaints and questions.

'Where, may I ask, sir,' one of them asked, 'are these professors called Dubedat and Lush? Of their lectures we have not heard one word.'

Guy did not know. He called a meeting of all the remaining staff – a Coptic secretary, the two Greek women who looked after the library and the three teachers – and gave them a talk, impressing on them the importance of the work he required them to do.

Harriet, sitting at the back of the hall, wondered again at Guy's ability to stimulate enthusiasm and make possible what before had seemed impossible. She had felt the same wonder when, producing *Troilus and Cressida* in Bucharest, he had overcome the apathy of the stage-hands and infused the cast with his own energy. And that had been simply for one evening's entertainment. Now he had a task much more worthy of his spirit. He told the staff that he was working on a new curriculum for the autumn term when there would be not only classes in English but lectures by such notables as Professor Lord Pinkrose, the famous poet William Castlebar, Professor Beaker from Baghdad and half a dozen of the English professors at Fuad al Awal University.

As Guy brought out these names, Harriet was astounded to realize he knew them all and had already approached them. Even Pinkrose had written from the King David Hotel, Jerusalem, to say that when it was safe for him to return to Egypt, he would be pleased to repeat the lecture that he had given at Phaleron before a brilliant audience on the day Germany declared war on Greece. Guy read this letter aloud with such emphasis that the audience, deeply impressed, broke into applause. Then, the library! Up till now the librarians had followed the out-of-date procedure of keeping the books guarded behind a counter and handing them out on request. All that would change. The library shelves would be thrown open to borrowers to pick and choose and browse at will. Guy was making a list of a thousand recently published books which he intended to order and which, sooner or later, would turn up. He laughed and said, 'Later rather than sooner, I imagine,' and the audience applauded again.

The English librarian, a Miss Pedler, was among those who had gone to Palestine, and the library had been kept open by the Greek women, both married to Egyptians, who now began calling out the names of books that the library needed.

'Write them down. I'll see we get them.'

Guy said he intended setting up a library of gramophone records which would be lent to musical groups in the forces as well as the Institute. He planned a weekly Institute evening when there would be music, poetry-readings and plays.

'And dancing?' one of the teachers excitedly asked.

'*And* dancing. One very important thing – we will need more teachers. Put it among your English-speaking friends. Tell them the work is regular and the pay good.'

The Egyptian teachers laughed, throwing themselves about in their chairs and shouting, 'Professor Pringle, sir, we have had no pay since Professor Gracey went away.'

Guy said that would be put right. No one mentioned the German advance or questioned his certainty that the Institute would remain and the British remain with it. Harriet, who might once have feared that Guy promised more than he could perform, was now confident that what he said he would do, he would do.

Walking back to Garden City, he asked her, 'Was I all right?'

'You were splendid.'

Guy had been so absorbed by his new authority that Harriet had had no chance to ask him what he thought of the move to Dobson's flat. When she spoke of it now, he said, 'The room's all right but that tree is a nuisance. It cuts off the light.'

'I love the tree. What do you think of Edwina?'

'She seems a nice girl. A bit of a glamour puss.' Guy laughed at the thought of Edwina and Harriet felt she could be thankful that glamour was an abstraction which did not much affect him.

'What do you think of Percy Gibbon?'

'That fellow who sits at the table and never speaks?'

'Yes. I feel he resents our being there.'

Guy laughed again, unable to believe that anyone could resent his being anywhere. 'I suppose he's shy, that's all.'

Guy was too busy to observe the life of the flat. There was scarcely time in the day for all the tasks he had set himself. He had a trestle-table sent from the Institute so he could work at home. The table was put up in the Pringle's bedroom where it was very much in the way. Guy, whose sight was poor, could not bear the room's penumbra and, looking round, found the room next to them was empty. He asked Dobson if he might put the table in there. The room was so small that Dobson had not thought it tenable for long, and said, 'Use it by all means, my dear fellow.'

Spreading out his papers in the spare room, Guy heard the door open and, looking round, found Percy Gibbon regarding him with malign disapproval. 'This is where I do my exercises,' Gibbon said.

Guy genially replied, 'Carry on. You won't disturb me.'

Percy did not carry on but slammed the door violently as he went.

During the time they had been in the flat, he had once spoken to Harriet. When she had said at the breakfast-table, 'I heard a rumour that we've lost the Canberra,' he lifted a face taut with reproof and said, 'If you heard that, you should keep it to yourself.'

Later, Harriet said to Dobson, 'I don't think Percy Gibbon likes us. He seems to feel we have no right to be here.'

'He's the one who has no right to be here. He asked me to let him stay for a few days while he found a place of his own. That was a year ago, and I can't get rid of him. He complains about his room, about the servants, about everybody and everything. I've suggested, very tactfully of course, that he'd be happier elsewhere, but he says he hasn't time to look for another place.'

'He's pathetic, really. He's in love with Edwina.'

'Surely you're joking?' Dobson laughed aloud at the thought of Percy in love but Harriet, who had seen him looking at Edwina with desperate longing, could only pity him.

Seven

Simon first felt the Column had taken on identity when he heard one of the men refer to it as Hardy's. Soon Ridley and Arnold and all the rest of them were calling themselves Hardy's Lot, speaking of Hardy as though he were another Popski and they his private army.

If Hardy himself had had any qualities on which to hang reverence, they would have made a hero of him, but everything about the major discouraged worship. He had little contact with the men and his remote manner suggested a self-sufficiency in which they had no faith. Simon had been right in suspecting that Hardy had been a schoolmaster before the war. According to Ridley, he had been the headmaster of a small prep school in Surrey. Simon, who had had a form-master not unlike the major, realized that Hardy was a timid man whose silence and withdrawn manner hid nothing but inefficiency. The form-master, Bishop, kept his distance with the boys and they did not know what to make of him. Some of them were ready to believe he was a superior person but when he left after only one term, the school porter told them, 'Poor chap, he wasn't up to it.'

Having known Bishop, whom he did not like, Simon felt he already knew Hardy and oddly enough, for that reason, did not dislike him. Instead, remembering the lost papers and the shuffling hands, Simon felt protective towards him. He could imagine Bishop in the same position and felt that Hardy, a middle-aged man, uprooted from a regular job, was worse off than any of them.

The day after they had leaguered among the pink rocks at the southern end of the line, Simon supervised the digging of slit trenches. One of the men called Brookman, a big, heavy fellow who had told Simon that before the war he had been in 'the fruit', was giving out his usual street-trader's patter. Throwing a rock to his butty, he shouted, "Ere y'are, gran, you can eat 'em with no teeth.' The butty pitched the rock back and

Brookman, leaping into the air, let out a thin, anguished howl:
'Oh, my wife and kids.'

This gave rise to so much laughter, Simon could see how
the story had gone around. Ridley, of course, was the culprit.
To Brookman, Simon spoke sharply. 'Cut it out, Brookman,
anyone can be caught off balance. You're a married man yourself, aren't you?'

Brookman, startled by Simon's unwonted severity, mumbled,
"Speck you're right, guv,' and there were no more jokes about
Hardy's wife and kids.

They were supposed to be in the front line but the only
thing out in no-man's-land, apart from the junk yard litter left
by earlier fighting, was a small hill in the middle distance. At
night, yellow flashes of fire and Very lights marked the German positions to the north, but there was no sight of the
enemy during the day.

Simon's nerves had subsided but, at the same time, he felt
a sense of let-down at the thought of returning to the sleepy
boredom of the earlier camp.

Seeing Hardy with his field glasses up, he asked him, 'Why
don't they come on, sir?'

Hardy continued to stare towards the German lines as though
he might find the answer out there, then he said, 'I suppose
they had to stop some time. Jerry's only flesh and blood, after
all.'

'But if they could get this far in less than a month, why not
finish the job?'

'My guess is, they made it too fast. If they've outrun supplies,
they could be stuck for some time to come.'

A few mornings later, while the dew still hung on the camel
thorn, half a dozen enemy trucks were sighted, travelling slowly
and cautiously round the base of the hill. They were first seen
by Ridley, who ran to Martin. Martin gave the order to open
fire and Ridley, coming over to Simon grinning his self-satisfaction, said, 'This is it, sir. Get your head down and cover
your ears.'

Simon followed Ridley into a slit trench and, bending his
head against the sand, protected his ears. The sound that came
to him through his hands was the most fearsome he had ever

heard. The gunners, who had had little to do till then, made up for their inactivity. As the firing persisted, Simon felt physically pummelled by the uproar but imagined he was taking it well until, the action over, he found to his consternation that his cheeks were wet. While he was scrubbing away his tears, someone put a hand on his shoulder. He swung round, angry and ashamed, but it was only Arnold.

'It's all right, sir. It takes you like that first time.'

'What happened?'

'We got one truck and the others made off double quick.'

Climbing up from the trench, Simon could see the solitary German truck smouldering at the foot of the hill. Three bodies were sprawled about it and he said to Arnold, 'What about those chaps? Shouldn't we do something to help them?'

'Nothing we can do, sir. The others hauled the wounded on board before they scarpered. Those chaps have had it.'

Simon, sent out to investigate, took Arnold and three men with him. This was his first venture on foot into open desert and though the area ahead was much like the area of the camp, he had a disturbing sense of offering himself as a target. He could imagine all the guns of the Afrika Korps trained on his party and he said to Arnold, 'Walking ducks, aren't we?'

'On a job like this, sir, they usually leave you alone.'

Whether this was true or not, the burial party went unmolested to the truck and examined the bodies. The Germans, though newly dead, were already stiffening in the heat. Simon looked at them with awe. They were not simply the first dead Germans he had seen, they were the first Germans: and, more than that, they were the first dead men he had seen in the whole of his life. One lay face down and when turned over, Simon saw he was a youth very like Arnold. Going through the uniform pockets, he found the usual things: identity papers, letters, snapshots of mum and dad, but no girl friend or wife. Too young for that, Simon thought and said to the men, 'All right, get on with it.'

The graves were not deep. No point in remaining longer than need be out here, yet, because it was customary, the men tied

150

some sticks together to form crosses and placed one at each head. And, Simon thought, what a fool business that was! You killed men and marked the spot with the symbol of eternal life. Walking back, he said something like that to Arnold who replied, 'They'd have killed us, given the chance.'

'That's what they said about the scorpion.'

'I know, sir, but you don't have to kill scorpions. The other's different – it's what we're here for.'

Following the attack on the enemy trucks, there was a long period when no enemy was seen. Ridley had discovered that the New Zealanders had been moved to an encampment near the Ridge and Captain Hugo Boulderstone was still with them. As the days passed vacuous with sun, heat and the drone of flies, Simon decided to make another application for leave to visit his brother. The major, his glasses trained, as usual, on nothing, turned fiercely at Simon's request.

'You mad, Boulderstone, or something?'

'I just thought, sir . . .'

'It's not your job to think. Your job is to stand by and await orders.'

Going back to his bivouac, he murmured to Ridley, 'The major does great work with those field glasses.'

Ridley, inflating his cheeks, let the air break through closed lips but that was his only comment. Now that Hardy was in command, Ridley did not openly criticize him and Simon felt the need to justify his remark.

'I asked for leave to visit my brother and he jumped down my throat.'

'Not surprising, sir, if you don't mind me saying so. They say on the intercom the Kiwis are up to something.'

'An attack?'

'Could be, but don't worry, sir. Might be no more than a twitch.'

A few days later, waking before dawn, Simon heard the rumble of distant artillery and the thud of aerial bombardment, and knew this was the attack. He imagined Hugo in the midst of it. He sat up on his elbow and saw Ridley, wearing nothing but his drawers, peering between the leaguered lorries in the direction of the hill. A waning moon, a big, lop-sided face, cast a dismal half-light over the camping area. Going to Ridley, Simon whispered, 'What's up?'

Ridley whispered back at him, 'Don't know, sir, but it's my belief jerry's up to something over there.' He nodded towards the hill where lights, faint, as from a dark lantern, were moving on the upper slopes.

'Think I should wake the major, sarge?'

'No point. Can't do much before sparrow-fart.'

But Simon, unable to contain his information, went to where Hardy lay and finding him awake, excitedly reported what had been seen.

'Who saw these lights?'

Simon had to admit that Ridley saw them first. 'But I confirmed it, sir. I thought you'd want to know at once, sir.'

'Quite right, Boulderstone. When it's light we'll let them know we're here.'

Rising before dawn, prepared for the noise of gunfire, Simon stood with the other officers beside the HQ truck, seeing the hill appear in the sudden, startling whiteness of first light. They could see black figures moving quickly as though to take cover before day would reveal them.

Martin shouted an order to the gunners: 'All right, give them half a dozen rounds.'

As the guns opened up, the figures fell out of sight. Hardy, surveying the hill through his glasses, said, 'No sign of life now. Probably only a patrol but I'll get through to air reconnaissance and advise a check.'

Soon after, a Leander, slow and sedate like an elderly mosquito, went over the Column and several times circled the hills. Half an hour later the report came that the hill was still occupied and there were signs that the enemy was turning it into a miniature fortress. The ground before it on the east, had been disturbed as though mines had been laid, and store puts for weapons had been dug on the western side.

The guns started again and continued their fire at intervals during the afternoon. After the four o'clock brew-up, Simon and Trench were ordered to report to Hardy. The HQ truck was dug into the shelter of a rock ridge and Hardy and Martin were lying on top of the ridge, both training field glasses on the hill.

Simon and Trench, standing a couple of yards apart, did not look at each other as they waited. Though circumstances forced them to associate, they did not do it willingly. Each felt in the other an awareness that something was wrong, though neither could have said what it was. Even now, sharing the anxiety of the summons, antagonism was alive between them.

Hardy, turning his head to look at them, gave a long sigh of dissatisfaction, saying, 'The enemy's still in position. I hoped our fire would rout them but there's more of them than we thought. The trouble is, we're short of ammunition.' He said something to Martin then slid down from the ridge and spoke to his two lieutenants. 'There's nothing for it, I'm afraid, but to send in the infantry. Make a direct attack, give them a blow, a real knock-out, that'll drive them off the hill.'

Both young men said, 'Yes, sir,' sounding as enthusiastic as they could. Simon, glancing obliquely at Trench, saw him staring at his feet, his fine, long mouth half open, obviously uncertain what was expected of him.

Hardy said, 'You'll lead your platoons into action tomorrow, starting out before dawn.'

Simon again glanced at Trench and seeing his lips quiver, thought, 'He's more scared than I am.' For a moment, he felt a gleeful sense of triumph, then his own fear came over him. When they met later for the evening meal, Simon, for the first time since Trench joined the Column, felt able to speak freely to him. 'Do you think we should leave letters or write out cables, or something?'

'You mean, for our people?'

'Yes. I've got a wife, too. What do you think?'

They had heard of men writing letters, letters that often enough proved to be letters of farewell, and they self-consciously considered whether or not to do the same thing. Trench decided, 'I don't think we should. It's a bit like asking for it.'

'You're probably right.'

Sharing the immediacy of the attack, their antagonism seemed to have gathered itself together and vanished like the mirage. They began reminding each other of incidents during their days on the *Queen Mary* and almost at once their old sense of intimate understanding came back. Remembering their laughter on board ship, they started to laugh again, recalling Codley's jokes. Their excitement was like a renewal of love but it was a febrile excitement. They could not put from their minds the fact that at daybreak they would be under fire. Yet the laughter, like alcohol, gave them a sort of courage and they were still together, scarcely able to bear the thought of being separated, when Hardy came round the camp. He stopped beside them. 'Boulderstone? Trench? Try and get some sleep before the balloon goes up.' He spoke kindly, as he might to his own children, and both men were emotional with gratitude and a willingness to obey him to the end.

Simon did not expect to sleep but he was sleeping when the guard's voice roused the camp. 'Wakey, wakey, you lazy bastards.' Sitting up in the darkness, he found Arnold standing beside him and asked, 'For God's sake, Arnold, what time is it?'

'Three ak emma, sir.'

The reason for waking at that hour was too shocking to contemplate. The men rose groaning and swearing at the intense cold. Simon, in a daze, could not contemplate the ordeal ahead but maintained a sort of half sleep, stumbling as he pulled on his sweater. Hardy was also up and when the two platoons assembled he came, fully dressed, to tell them that Martin and his artillery would accompany them and give them covering fire. The sappers would go in first to check whether or not mines had been laid at the base of the hill.

Waiting for the all clear, the men silent behind him, Simon had to swallow down the nausea that rose from the pit of his stomach. If it forced itself up, where, he wondered, could he go to vomit unseen? But it remained what it was, a phantom nausea, a sickness of the nerves, and as soon as they moved, he forgot about it.

The enemy seemed to be on the alert. Repeated gun flashes dotted the German positions and the men, who were in close order, instinctively kept closer than need be as they marched into no-man's-land. The moon had set and they moved by starlight. There was little to see and Simon thought it unlikely that anyone had seen them, yet, a few hundred yards from their objective, a flare went up from the hill-top, blanching the desert and revealing the two close-knit platoons. Immediately there was uproar. Red and yellow tracer bullets, like deadly fireworks, passed overhead and machine-guns kept up their mad, virulent rattle. Simon shouted, 'Run for it,' but the men had not waited for an order. They were running for their lives through the shrieking, whistling, rustling, thunder-filled air.

Pelting towards the hill, Simon told himself, 'We're running straight into it,' but the hill itself was cover. Simon's platoon had arrived without loss and he called to Trench, 'What about your chaps?' Trench's breathless voice came to him from the darkness, 'All right, I hope.'

There was no let up by the gunners on the hill but now Martin's artillery was sounding a reply and Simon, crouching with his men, waiting for the barrage to cease, began to hope that the guns would settle the matter. Then Martin came over and, speaking under the noise, instructed him to take his platoon to the left of the hill and advance upwards till battle was joined. Trench and his platoon would go to the right. In a low, grumbling tone that suggested the whole business was something of a bore, Martin told both the young men, 'The order is: accept no more casualties than the situation justifies.'

Simon's voice had become a croak as he asked, 'Casualties, sir?'

'Pull yourself together, Boulderstone. D'you imagine there won't be casualties? Now – go in and show fight.'

The firing had stopped but as Simon started to move off, Martin seemed to change his mind. He said, 'Wait.' No sound came from the hill and for an elated moment Simon imagined the enemy had been wiped out, then the machine-guns began again.

The sky broke and a livid light showed them to each other. Looking from one drawn face to another, Simon thought, 'We're mad to be here.' Ridley, head hanging morosely, was waiting to fix up a field telephone. Martin was also waiting, no one knew for what. Arnold gave Simon an affectionate, reassuring smile as though he had been through all this before and he knew it would be all right.

'Now,' Martin whispered, 'get on with it. Give the hun a bloody nose. Should be a piece of cake but if you hit a snag, send a runner back and we'll sort you out. *If we can.* Off you go, and good luck.'

Glancing back, Simon had a glimpse of Trench's face miserably contracted and he thought, 'Poor old Trench.' He, himself, was revivified now action had begun. Reaching the left flank of the hill, he drew his revolver and ordered his men to fan out. They made their way crabwise up the grey, cinderous lower slopes. Their feet, sinking into the ground, made little noise but the defenders were prepared for them. As the first of them came in sight of the machine-guns, hand grenades showered down on them. They bent double, drawing together for mutual protection while Simon shouted, 'Fan out ... fan out,' not expecting to be obeyed.

A palisade of flat stones and rocks had been built at the crown of the hill. Seeing a head rise above it, a hand lifted to pitch a grenade, Simon fired, and was amazed to see the man leap up and fall backwards. His shot, his first shot with intent to kill, had found its mark. He had wounded someone, or even killed him. Either way, he'd put one jerry bastard out of action. The satisfaction intoxicated him. In his excitement, he lost all sense of danger and did not hear Arnold shouting, 'Keep down, sir. For God's sake, keep down.' In an ecstasy of joy, he rushed into a fusillade of machine-gun bullets, thinking he had discovered the thing he had wanted all his life.

His euphoria faltered when a bullet whined past his ear. He realized the ground about him was bouncing with bullets and Arnold's cries suddenly made sense. He threw himself down behind a rock and saw that the other men had taken cover. The cover was not much. The upper slopes of the hill were littered with rocky outcrops but so low that the men were lying behind them with their heads down. The battle now settled into a give and take of rifle fire, then a howl of anguish went up. The Germans had hurled a mortar bomb. Arnold, dodging from rock to rock, reached Simon and lay down beside him. 'Three chaps hit, sir. Two badly. One of them a gonner.'

'Who is it?'

The dead man was Brookman and Simon asked himself

how many casualties the situation *did* justify? The machine-gun fire, having died down, opened up on the right-hand side of the hill. He realized that Trench was getting it and he was free to act. He said to Arnold, 'Run back. Tell Martin we've been under heavy fire but there's a lull. Say I propose to rush the enemy lines. Ask for further orders.'

Arnold went down the hill in leaps and Simon ordered the others to fix bayonets and wait. If they went in soon, they could draw the fire off Trench. Here was an opportunity to rush the palisade and perhaps behind it there was no more than a token force. He became impatient of the delay and looking down the hill, saw that Arnold had just started the ascent. Bent low, he was taking it cautiously. Simon shouted to him to hurry and, eager to comply, he straightened himself, ran forward, threw up his arms and fell.

Simon called to him, but he did not move. Screaming his name, Simon ran down to where he lay, white faced, eyes open. He had been hit in the chest. In spite of the fixed stare, Simon believed that something might still be done for him. Testing his weight, finding him light enough to carry, Simon lifted the thin, young body on to his shoulder and went at a half-run down to the foot of the hill.

Astounded by the sight of him, Martin shouted in fury, 'You damned fool, what do you think you're doing?'

'It's Arnold. He's my batman and driver. He's been shot in the chest.'

'Put him down at once and get back to your men.'

'You'll look after him, won't you?'

'Get back, I tell you. You could be court-martialled for this.'

By the time he reached the hill-top, the Germans had leapt the palisades and had met his platoon in hand-to-hand combat. Coming face to face with a blond, pink-skinned German youth, Simon fired in a fury, saying, 'Damn you. Damn the lot of you,' and the pink face opened and spilt out redness, like a pomegranate.

This was hatred, all right. Simon felt he could do battle with the lot of them but the defenders had already had enough. They turned, scrambled back over the palisade and stumbled down the western side of the hill. Their trucks awaited them and as the victors bawled after them in triumph, they piled in and drove towards the main German positions.

Returning to base, Ridley caught up with Simon to say, 'Not a bad show, sir.'

'Not too bad, sarge.'

'You heard, sir? Mr Trench copped it.'

'Dead?'

'Dead as mutton, poor bloke. They say, just before he was hit, he was putting up a tremendous fight.'

'Just what I'd expect,' Simon said, ashamed that he had expected nothing of the sort. He could not understand now his earlier contempt for Trench. Trench and Arnold had been his friends and he had lost them both. He wondered, as Arnold had wondered when Ted and Fred went from him, how he could live without them.

The engagement had cost the Column eight men, all told. The bodies were brought back and buried before supper. Hardy said to Simon, 'You acted unwisely, leaving your men, but I understand your desire to help Arnold. You did pretty well, so we'll forget what happened. Have you anything to say?'

Looking back over the events of the day, Simon could think of nothing. He shook his head. Bereaved and very tired, he only wanted sleep.

Eight

A new general came to displace Auchinleck. The displacement was discussed in Cairo but no one could say why one general had gone and the other had taken over the command. Harriet, walking in Suleiman Pasha, saw Auchinleck on the opposite pavement. It was, she learnt later, the very day on which he was leaving Egypt for good. She stopped to watch him. He was a very tall man with a grave, handsome face and a broad brow: the ideal of those leaders, those demi-gods, whom she had seen as ordering the lives of common men, yet he, too, owed obedience and had been sent away. Though she had not met him and would probably never see him again, she felt a profound sadness as she watched him disappear into the indifferent crowd.

Harriet, too, had lost her import, small though it was. No one now asked her for news because she knew no more than anyone else. If, among all the rumours that spread out from civilian ignorance, she learnt of some true event, she could not act upon it or pin it to a map. She wanted to replace her job at once and put it about that she was free and looking for work, but there was little work for English women civilians in Egypt.

She asked Guy if she could take up Miss Pedler's job in the library but before anything could be decided, Miss Pedler returned. Most of the evacuees, tired of life in the Jerusalem camp, were finding their way back to Cairo though nothing had happened to change the situation from which they had fled. The very fact that nothing had happened was satisfactory enough. An invader who was so long in coming might not come at all.

Even Pinkrose had returned. The Pringles, going into Groppi's to meet Aidan Pratt, saw Pinkrose sitting in front of a plate of cakes. It was mid-day, the sun burnt through the canvas of the umbrella, but Pinkrose was muffled like a Bedouin and perhaps for the same reason. He hoped his hat, scarf and woollen suit would protect him against the heat. His hat pulled down to his eyes, his scarf up to his nostrils, he was intent on four cakes, creamed, candied, decorated with fruit and sweets, the richest that Groppi could provide. His problem was which to eat first.

When Guy and Harriet stopped beside him, he did not lift his head but put out a hand as though warding them off. He slid his eyes up at the intruders and said, 'Ah, Pringle, it's you!' Having accepted the invitation to lecture, he had to accord Guy some slight civility.

Guy said, 'You know I've been appointed Director here?'

'Yes, yes, I gathered that. Um, um, I gathered that.'

'I feel I have you to thank for the appointment. It was, I believe, the result of your cable to Bevington.'

'Oh, was it!' It was clear from Pinkrose's tone that this was not the result he had intended. A gleam of satirical contempt

159

for Guy's simplicity came into his stone-grey eyes but he had nothing to lose by accepting gratitude, so nodded and said, 'Is that so?'

'There are some letters for Gracey in the office. I would forward them if I knew where he was. I was wondering if you could let me have his present address?'

'Present address? Present address?' Pinkrose, eager to be at the cakes, was losing patience with this conversation. 'I really can't say. I heard ... indeed, I was *told*, the Director in Jerusalem told me, that Gracey is trying to get himself shipped down to the Cape. How and when I cannot say. I fear I cannot help you, Pringle. No, no, I cannot help you.' He twitched all over in his desire to shake off the Pringles, then he remembered that Harriet had once been a source of information and he raised his head slightly to ask her, 'The desert situation has settled down, eh? The Germans have outrun their strength. No bite left in them, eh? No bite. No bite.'

Harriet, never unwilling to disquiet Pinkrose, did not resist this opportunity. 'I don't know about the desert. No one is giving it much thought these days. The chief worry now is the Ukraine. The High Command expects it to collapse before the end of the month. When that happens, the enemy will come down on us like the wolf on the fold.'

Pinkrose, his grey colour becoming more grey, looked stunned, then falteringly asked, 'Haven't we got troops in Iraq?'

'A handful. What could they do against twenty panzer divisions?'

'Twenty? Did you say twenty? No one told me they were likely to come that way.'

'People here are living in a fool's paradise. They think if the desert situation's all right, they're all right. They forget we're threatened on another front.'

Pinkrose was sunken in his seat, gazing at the cakes as though they had failed him, then a laugh jerked out of him. '*Now*, I understand. Yes, yes ... You wish to frighten me. Well, I will not be frightened. No, I will not be frightened. So you can take yourselves off. If you wish to spread alarm and despondency, you can spread it elsewhere.'

'Why should I wish to frighten you, Lord Pinkrose?'

'That is easily answered,' Pinkrose's voice was shrill with triumph. 'I was one of those whom the major invited on to his ship – *you were not.* You pushed your way on board. Yes, yes, you pushed on board. It would have been a pleasant trip – a very pleasant trip, indeed – but a crowd of you pushed on board and spoilt it all. Four people settled themselves in my cabin. *Four* of them. They made things very uncomfortable for me, and for the major's other guests. You young people think only of yourselves. So, take yourselves off ...' Pinkrose lifted his cake fork and waved them away.

As Harriet drew breath to protest, Guy gave her a little push and they both went to a vacant table. Out of Pinkrose's hearing, Guy said, 'Why try and frighten the poor old thing?'

'I said nothing that wasn't true. He may be a great deal more frightened before this war is over. If we're cut off here, what will happen to him or to us? Or anyone else? Who would repatriate us? Who would care if we lived or died? We'd be lost, the dregs of the wartime hierarchy, beggars, dependent on Moslem charity. And we can be thankful that the Moslems are charitable. We'll have no other friends.'

'Darling,' Guy lifted her right hand and put it to his lips. 'Little monkey's paw. The Russians won't give in so easily. The Ukraine will hold, you wait and see.'

'How do you know? What makes you so sure?'

'I am sure.' He did not explain his certainty but squeezed her fingers, conveying his confidence by the pressure and warmth of his flesh. He looked at her hand before putting it down and said, 'Thin little hand!'

'Too thin. I keep getting these stomach upsets.'

'That won't do,' he said and quickly changed to a subject that disturbed him less. 'Who do you think came into the office this morning? Toby Lush. He came, ostensibly, to congratulate me on my appointment but they want work, the pair of them. They had a pretty dreary time in camp while Gracey and Pinkrose were living it up at the King David Hotel. They said that Gracey never bothered to contact them and when they bumped into Pinkrose, he pretended not to know them.'

'You surely won't employ them, will you?'

161

'Why not? What are they but poor derelicts of war? I'll find a use for them.'

Aidan Pratt, on what he called 'a brief assignment', had tried to ring Guy in Alexandria and, not finding him there, had traced the Pringles to Dobson's flat. Getting Harriet on the telephone, he asked her to come with him to the Muski. He wanted to buy a gift for his mother. When she agreed, he said as an afterthought, 'I suppose Guy wouldn't come?'

Harriet had once persuaded Guy to go with her to the Muski but at the entrance to the narrow, half-lit Muski lanes, he had turned back saying that nothing would get him in there. He felt, she realized, as she had felt inside the ruined pyramid. Though she said, 'I'll ask him,' she knew Aidan would be disappointed.

Seeing him coming towards them as though half-fearing rebuff, she whispered to Guy, 'Do come with us ...'

Guy was quite decided against the Muski. 'I couldn't possibly,' and Aidan, sensing his refusal, said with humorous humility, 'Not coming? I suppose you have more important things to do?'

'I wouldn't say important. I've work to do.' Guy greeted Aidan with his usual amiability but he could not stay long. They talked for a few minutes but there was no lingering over the wine in his glass. Draining it in one long draught, he said, 'I'll see you later,' and went without arranging time or place.

'Is he always so *engagé*? I'm not likely to see him later – my train goes at six.'

Harriet said to excuse Guy, 'He's more than usually busy at the moment, getting the Institute back on its feet.'

Aidan gave a baffled laugh and agreed that they set out for the Muski straight away. They found a gharry waiting outside Groppi's and took it to Esbekiya Gardens. Aidan, Harriet realized, had recovered from the first pain of his friend's death and she found him easier company. Moving through the afternoon heat as through a tangible fume that smelt of sand and the old gharry horse, she tried to compensate for Guy's absence. She told him what she knew about the places they passed. The Esbekiya, she said, still had the sunken look of a lake bed and in the old days, when the Nile rose, it used to be filled with water. Now the square was a turn-around for the tramcars but a few of the old houses remained with trees dipping over the garden wall as though to reach the water that was no longer there. Napoleon had lodged in the mansion that had been turned into Shepherd's Hotel. She thought there was still a hint of the oriental, pre-Napoleonic richness about the square but it had become a centre for raffish life and raffish medicine. On the seedy terrace houses that had displaced most of the mansions, there were advertisements for doctors who cured 'all the diseases of love' and promised to the impotent 'horse-like vigour'. Gigantic wooden teeth, bloody at the roots, were hung out as a sign that cheap dentists were at work.

Aidan, his dark and sombre eyes turning from side to side, asked, 'Why has it become so run-down?'

Harriet pointed to the small, dry garden in the centre and told him that the assassin of General Kléber had been impaled there, taking three days to die. 'After that, who would want to live here?'

The Muski ran from the top of the square and Harriet said they should pay off the gharry because now it would be more fun to walk. Alerted by the word 'fun', Aidan jumped down to the road as though making an effort to enjoy himself.

Asked what he thought of buying, he was unsure: 'Jewellery, or a piece of silverware or perhaps a length of silk.'

The Muski offered such things in plenty and Harriet, who knew the shops, thought Aidan would quickly find what he wanted. There she was wrong.

The lanes were quiet under the heat. The shopkeepers lay indolently in the shade at the back of their open-fronted shops, sleeping or passing amber beads through their hands. Most of them ignored the visitors, knowing who came to buy and who came merely from curiosity, and Harriet saw they had little or no faith in Aidan's intentions. She began to feel they were right.

He fingered the bales of silk and rayons and put them contemptuously aside. They did not compare, he said, with the Damascus silks. Harriet took him into a small, glazed-in shop where scent was sold. The scent could be put into plain bottles or phials of Venetian glass decorated with gold. He agreed the phials were pretty but the scents – rose, musk, jasmin or sandalwood – were too sweet for Aidan's taste. Then Harriet thought she knew the very place to interest him: it was a large shop without windows, like a great tent. Here, in the half-light, the shelves and floors were packed with old silver and plate, engraved glass, Victorian ornaments, Indian toys, Burmese temple birds, Staffordshire dogs, horses, swans and human figures. Harriet particularly liked some iron trays painted with flowers and buildings and fanciful scenes that could be set on legs to serve as coffee tables, but Aidan shook his head. He turned over some rugs and said, 'Not the best of their kind.' In the middle of the shop there was a glass case filled with antique jewellery made of pink gold and rose diamonds. Harriet, who could not afford to buy them herself, handled the elaborate brooches, rings and pendants, and admired the large diamonds that looked more valuable than they were. 'I'm sure your mother would like these.'

'Much too showy for her.'

They set out again. Passing a window that displayed a broken Grecian head and some small Egyptian tomb finds, he stopped. 'There might be something in here.'

'Those things are terribly expensive.'

'I'll just have a look.'

Harriet stayed outside, feeling he was by nature secretive and more likely to make up his mind if left alone. When he was slow in returning, she wandered to the end of the lane where the bazaar opened out into an ordinary shopping street. Between lane and street there was an Arab café with three wooden tables and benches set out on the road. The proprietor, in a grimy galabiah, sat with one leg under him and his back to the house wall. Harriet asked if she might sit down while awaiting a friend. He did not ask her what she would drink but waved her to a bench, mumbling the conventional courtesy that everything in his house was hers.

Weary from her long walk in the heat, Harriet sat down gladly and watched the street beginning to fill with the early evening shoppers. Somewhere nearby there was a dry goods shop and the whole area was filled with a scent of pulse and spices, the scent of every back street in Egypt. A loudspeaker, fastened to the wall above her head, was telling one of the endless sagas of the Arab world. She heard the name Akbar and knew it was about the great hero whose father was a king and whose mother was Sudanese. Being blacker than his fellows, he felt he must do courageous deeds to prove himself, but being also lazy, he often lay in his tent and could be roused only by the gentle persuasions of his mistress who was the most perfect of womankind.

There was a mosque among the shops, its minaret intricately carved and rising ochre-coloured against the deep cerulean of the sky. She could not tell whether it was made of sandstone or merely encrusted with sand. When she first arrived, she had meant to visit all the main mosques of Cairo but soon found that here it was easier to make plans than to carry them out. If one waited till tomorrow, or the next day, or next week, it might be less hot and one's body might be more willing to exert itself.

As Aidan came towards her, smiling his success, she said, 'So you've found something!'

He did not show her what it was but, sitting down, suggested they take mint tea. He did not speak while they drank it but, putting his cup down, he hesitantly asked, 'Tell me about Guy. Can he possibly be as artless and warm-hearted as he seems. He must have his *terra incognita* – his complexes, hang-ups, impediments? What should one call them? Megrims?'

Realizing he wanted nothing more than to talk about Guy, she said, 'He's probably more simple than you think. I'll tell you something that happened in Bucharest just after we were married. I was about to step on a bus when Guy pulled me aside so that another woman – a woman of my own age – could step on in front of me. I was thunderstruck. And what annoyed me most was the simpering amusement of the woman when she saw Guy hold me back. I was furious and he was bewildered by me. He explained, as though to a child, that one had to be courteous to other people. I said, "What you did was damned discourteous to me," and he said, "But you're part of me – I don't have to be courteous to you."'

Aidan seemed at a loss as he imbibed this story but eventually said, 'Yet, because of Guy's intrinsic goodness, you were able to overlook what happened?'

165

'I didn't overlook it. I'm still angry when I think about it.'

'But he did not mean to offend you. Such intrinsic simplicity has its admirable side.'

'Yes, if you're not married to it.'

'I understand.' Aidan smiled as though the story had brought them into sympathy and putting his hand into his side pocket, he took out a small green box. He pushed it towards her and said, 'See what I bought.' She opened the box and found inside, packed in cotton wool, a cat, less than two inches high, made of iron, sitting upright on a block of cornelian. Harriet realized why Aidan had taken so long to find what he wanted. The gift he sought must be unique, and he found the one thing she would, if she had the money, have chosen herself. She replaced the lid and pushed the box back again. He held it and looked at her, then put the box before her. 'Keep it for me.'

'But isn't it for your mother?'

'Yes. I will tell her I have it but I can't risk the posts. You must look after it till I can take it home.'

'I'd rather not. It's much to valuable to have around.'

'Please. I can't hold on to things. If I keep it, I'll put it down somewhere and forget it. I've lost the sense that anything's worth keeping.'

'You've *lost* the sense? You weren't born without it – you lost it?'

'Yes, but at the time that was the least loss. I lost much more – everything I had, in fact, including the sense that anything left had value.'

'What happened?'

'Oh,' he stared down at the table and made the gesture he had made when he spoke of the death of his friend. 'It's not easy to talk about ... I may tell you another time.'

'Have you told Guy?'

'Not yet. When we went for our walk, he did most of the talking.'

'Had it anything to do with the war?'

'Yes, everything.' He paused then said in a bitter half-whisper, 'The war has destroyed my life.'

'It hasn't done any of us much good.'

'I'm not so sure of that. There's a chap in our unit – he used

166

to be a bus driver and now he's a major. He feels he's found his feet at last. He's enjoying every minute of the war. But for me, it was a disaster. My career had just started when war broke out. When it's over – if it ever is over – I'll be verging on middle-age. Just another not-so-young actor looking for work. In fact, a displaced person.'

'We're all displaced persons these days. Guy and I have accumulated more memories of loss and flight in two years than we could in a whole lifetime of peace. And, as you say, it's not over yet. But we're seeing the world. We might as well try and enjoy it.'

'Yes, but there are some memories that are beyond human bearing, except that we have to bear them.'

'You won't tell me?'

'Not now. Not now. I have to catch that train.'

They walked till they found a gharry. Harriet asked to be put down in the Esbekiya where she could find a tram-car to Kasr el Aini. The green box was still in her hand and unwilling to keep in temporary custody an object she so much coveted, she asked him to take it back.

'No. One day I'll ask you for it.'

'Very well.' He wished to imply that their friendship would continue and she said, 'I'll keep it safe for you.'

'Did you know that the line into Syria is open? If you and Guy could come to Beirut, I'd meet you with a car and we could drive to Damascus, visiting Baalbec on the way. There are some impressive sights up there. And the Damascus bazaars are more mysterious than the Cairo ones.'

Speaking, his face came alive with enticement intended, she felt, for Guy – and that was the trouble. Guy did not want to see impressive sights. He would rather pass his spare time, if he had any, talking and drinking in a basement bar.

'Guy may come ...'

'If he doesn't, you come without him.'

She smiled and said, 'One day, perhaps I will.'

Nine

There was no work for Harriet in Cairo, not even voluntary work. In Athens the English women had organized a canteen for troops but in Cairo the ladies of the Red Cross jealously kept a hold on paramilitary work and the provision of comforts for the men. Outsiders were expected to remain outside.

Finding nothing to do, she wondered if she could take over the housekeeping at the flat. She did not think that Edwina would willingly give it up but found her glad to be rid of it.

'Darling, how sweet of you. It would be divine – and save me *so* much effort. I often don't know how to get everything done.'

Harriet, when the accounts were handed to her, found that Edwina had merely muddled through them and the servants had bought where they pleased. Edwina said, 'If you have trouble with Hassan, I'm always here to help,' but Harriet thought she could manage Hassan. There would be a new regime and Edwina would be left free for her main occupation, her social life.

Edwina's promise of friendship was frequently repeated but it developed no further. She would have a few words with Harriet while awaiting a telephone call or the arrival of the evening's young man, but the talk was always brief and interrupted. Harriet who had been anticipating the pleasant, gossipy intimacy that can exist between women living in proximity, now knew that Edwina would never have time for it. Her afternoon break, between one o'clock and five, was spent at the Gezira swimming-pool. More often than not she was out for dinner and at breakfast time she came to the table exhausted by the effort of getting herself out of bed. Sitting opposite Harriet, hair over one eye, she would blink the other eye and grin in rueful acknowledgement of her frail condition. Sometimes the activities of the previous night prostrated her altogether. Dobson would say, 'Poor Edwina has another migraine,' but however badly she might feel in the morning, she would be up and dressed, her languors forgotten, by the time her evening escort arrived. They would go off with a great deal of laughter and Harriet could imagine that laughter served as conversation for most of the time. Edwina had once told her that she only wanted a good time, and the lost and deprived young men who came on leave – a leave that might be the last they would ever have – had nothing else to give her.

One day, when Edwina had pleaded a migraine for the third time in a fortnight, Harriet asked Dobson, 'How do the girls she works with feel? Don't they mind her being absent from the office?'

Dobson, who regarded everything Edwina did with amused tolerance, said, 'Not really. To tell you the truth, she can get away with anything. She's rather special, isn't she?'

Harriet agreed, being herself spellbound by Edwina's special quality. She was only regretful that that quality was squandered among so many futureless encounters. She said one evening while they were together on the balcony, 'Don't you get bored, going out so often?'

'Well, yes, but what else is there for me? You're lucky. You have that nice husband. You've something to stay in for.'

Harriet supposed she was lucky even though, staying in, she spent most of her evenings alone. She said, 'We're young at the wrong time.' The war, with all its demands, took precedence over their youth and when it was over they, like Aidan Pratt, would be young no longer.

Then, a week or two later, a change came over Edwina. She started taking supper at home. When the telephone rang and some eager young man begged for her company, she could be heard sweetly excusing herself, pleading her usual headache before returning with a sigh to the sitting-room. Harriet, realizing she had been expecting a different caller, concluded that someone of importance had entered Edwina's life.

Percy Gibbon eyed her as though her change of habit brought him both terror and hope, but Edwina was unaware of him. She was abstracted as though all her senses were intent on something remote from anything about her. After supper she would go to her room or sit, saying nothing, on the balcony. Now there was no wink or grin of complicity for Harriet but when they both took their coffee out into the scented air, she occasionally gave Harriet a wan smile and seemed about to confide in her. But there were no confidences. One evening, when Guy had gone to work in the spare room and Dobson had returned to the Embassy, and the two girls sat on the swaying, sinking wickerwork sofa, Harriet tried to distract Edwina with a story about Hassan.

'You know Hassan's been stealing the gin from Dobbie's decanter and filling it with water! I spoke to him about it and he swore that it was the afreets. Well, I thought I could catch him. I emptied the gin out and put in arak which becomes cloudy when you add water. Next day the decanter disappeared. When I spoke to Hassan, he said the afreets had broken it.'

'Oh, dear!' Edwina put her head back and laughed, but it was not a real laugh, rather a distracted and almost soundless effort to show appreciation while her mind was elsewhere.

Percy Gibbon, who had been moving restlessly about in the sitting-room, came out as though decided on a course of action, and spoke aggressively to Edwina, 'I suppose you're going out later?'

Edwina answered with gentle indifference, 'I may.'

Percy gave a disgruntled snort and rushing to the front door, left the flat. Harriet said, 'I believe he wanted to ask you out.'

'Poor Percy,' Edwina said, as though Percy were a little dog accidentally trodden upon. Harriet thought: Yes, poor Percy. Poor ugly creature. How changed he might be if he could only change his looks!

The telephone started ringing, Edwina listened till she could bear it no more and cried in anguish, 'Why doesn't Hassan answer it?' She leapt up, went to the hall and came back to say the call was for Guy. When she sat down again, she had a wet glint about her eyes.

'Who were you expecting?' Harriet asked.

'Oh, no one in particular.' Edwina, bemused, said, 'It's getting late,' then throwing back her head, she broke into an Irish song: 'My love came to me, he came from the south ...' Her voice was light but clear and melodious. When she reached the line: 'His breast to my bosom, his mouth to my mouth,' she caught her breath and came to a stop, fearful of breaking down.

Guy, returning from the telephone, had paused to listen and as the song died, he came on to the balcony, praising her singing as one who knew what singing should be. He had heard she could sing but did not know she had a voice of that quality. He said, 'It's a lovely voice. A moving, beautiful voice. If I get up a troops' entertainment, you will sing for them, won't you?'

Edwina, disturbed by her own song, could only nod her agreement.

Guy was about to enlarge on his plans for the concert but as he spoke, the telephone rang again and Edwina, whispering an excuse, ran to it. This time the call was for her.

Harriet said, 'Are you serious about this entertainment? Haven't you enough to do?'

Guy said, 'I never have enough to do,' and returned to his work-table.

Next day Harriet met Edwina's new friend and realized he was, indeed, a man apart from her everyday admirers. He was older than most of them, being in the late twenties, and his manner suggested a man of substance.

When he called for Edwina, she was still in her room. Instead of waiting in the background, nervous, expectant and barely noticed, he threw himself on to the living-room sofa and talked as though putting the company – this being Dobson and Harriet – at its ease. Dobson maintained his insouciance in the face of this affability but once or twice, losing his hold on himself, he sounded surprisingly deferential.

When introducing the new arrival to Harriet, he had said, 'You know Peter, don't you?' so it was evident that if she did not, she ought to know him. Peter, fixing his very dark eyes on Harriet, seemed satisfied by what he saw.

He was short, square built, ruddy and black haired, with a broad saddle nose and a firm mouth. He had the look of a farmer, and not a young farmer. In spite of his youth, he was as bulky as a man of fifty. Gripping Harriet's hand, he sank back in the sofa, pulling her down beside him. He had been talking when she came in and he went on talking, at the same time putting an arm round Harriet's waist and every now and then giving her a squeeze. All young attractive women, she realized, were his women, and he had no doubt at all of his right to them, or his attraction for them.

With her eyes on a level with his shoulder, Harriet could see that he was already a half-colonel, and he was complaining of this fact. 'I've been three months at GHQ and I've risen faster than I did in three years in the blue. Not from merit, mind you. Far from it. I'm a fighting man. I'm no good dealing with all that bumf. No, I'm pushed up so Sniffer Metcalf can be pushed up further. To promote himself, he has to widen the base of his pyramid. If he can fit in another major, we all go up a step. You may think that our most important aim and object is to shove Rommel back to Cyrenaica? Not a bit of it. The only thing that occupies our department is the one burning question: can Sniffers graft his way up to Major General before some busybody at the top sniffs out Sniffers.'

Peter's laughter was loud and long and he was squeezing Harriet with his head on her shoulder when Edwina entered, subdued and virginal in a long dress of white slipper satin. Her toilette indicated a very grand dinner ahead.

'Ah, there you are, then!' Peter, jovially paternal, still holding on to Harriet, looked Edwina up and down then, releasing Harriet and jerking himself forward, he pointed at Dobson. 'And I'll tell you something else ...'

This new subject, whatever it was, was stopped by Edwina who gave a scream and said, 'Oh Lord, m'heel!' and taking off one of her white shoes, she examined the high, narrow heel.

'Anything wrong?' Peter asked.

'Well, no ...' Trying to put the shoe on again, she dropped a pair of long, kid gloves. She let them lie until Peter, getting his heavy body out of the sofa, retrieved them. As though the shoe were beyond her, she handed it to him and balanced, one hand on his arm, while he fitted it on to her foot.

Harriet, used to seeing Edwina in control of her escorts, disliked seeing her as she now was; flustered, silly and on edge. Her skin, its golden colour enhanced by the white satin, had an underflush of pink and she looked away from Peter, afraid to meet the emphatic stare of his black eyes. His manners were casual yet, Harriet felt, whatever he did was right because he did it. Then, as Edwina fidgeted with her bag and scarf, he gave her a slap on the rump that was more heavy than playful. Her scream this time was a scream of pain and Peter said, 'Sorry, old thing,' and led her away.

'Who is that fellow?' Harriet asked, resenting Edwina's abasement.

'Don't you know? He's Peter Lisdoonvarna.'

'What an odd surname!'

Dobson laughed at her ignorance. 'My dear girl, he's Lord Lisdoonvarna but, as you must have heard, titles are *de trop* for the duration so he's just plain Peter Lisdoonvarna.'

'I see,' said Harriet, who did see. Edwina had found her desideratum and the chance of such a marriage had quite overthrown her. 'It's remarkable to be a lieutenant-colonel at his age. I suppose he was promoted because of his title?'

'Certainly not,' Dobson was shocked by the supposition. 'While he was a field officer, he never rose above lieutenant. He was moved to base – very much against his will, I may say – and you heard what he told us: rapid promotion followed. That sort of thing goes on at GHQ. He laughs at it but I gather he's pretty disgusted. Some relative must have pulled strings to get him away from the front line.'

'I didn't know that could be done.'

'It can't be in theory, but I imagine a bit of fixing does go on. It's not unreasonable in his case. He's an only son and there are no male relatives. If he were killed, the title would die out.'

Thinking of Edwina's song, Harriet said, 'I suppose he's Irish?'

'Anglo-Irish. The best sort of fighting man. The best in the world, I'd say. A terrible waste, putting him into an office. But, then, it would be a terrible waste if he didn't survive.'

'Edwina seems very attracted. Do you think she stands a chance with him?'

Dobson did not question what Harriet meant, but said, 'Who knows? There have been less likely marriages, and these are not ordinary times. She might land him, but I only hope she keeps her head.'

The rich owner of the next door garden sent Dobson a basket

of mangoes which he placed on the breakfast table.

Harriet, spooning the pulp out of the rosy mango shell, said, 'Gorgeous, gorgeous, and perhaps from our own tree.'

Reminded by this, Dobson told the Pringles they would have to give up the spare room because he had a friend coming to stay.

Guy said, 'Oh, not the spare room. Let's give up that damned tree. I hate the sight of it staring at me through the window.'

'You can say that,' said Harriet, 'when you're in the very act of eating mangoes?'

Dobson, smiling slyly, said, 'Still, Guy may be right. His could be an instinctive dislike. People here call the mango "The Danger Tree". You know that in England someone dies every year from eating duck eggs? — Well, in countries where a lot of mangoes are eaten, someone dies from mango poisoning every year.'

Edwina, who had been putting out her hand for another mango, withdrew it, saying, 'Dobbie, how could you! What a horrid joke!'

'It's not a joke. The stems are poisonous and sometimes the poison seeps into the fruit. It doesn't happen often but people *are* killed by it.'

Harriet joined with Edwina's indignation. 'You're an awful liar, Dobbie. If it were true, you would have told us straightaway.'

'Ha!' Dobson smiled. 'Had I told you straightaway, you would have said, "The greedy fellow wants to keep his mangoes for himself."'

Percy Gibbon gave his usual angry grunt and left the table. Guy, helping himself to another mango, said to Harriet, 'You see, I was right. The tree's a bad tree. We must give it up.'

Harriet knew she would have to give it up. Guy seldom asked anything for himself so when he did, he must have his way. She did not speak and he added persuasively, 'You don't really mind giving it up, do you?'

'No, I don't mind. Not really.' Harriet asked Dobson when they would have to move.

'Soon, I'm afraid. I don't know exactly when she's arriving but, of course, the place will have to be scrubbed out.'

The room had not been scrubbed out for Guy and Harriet who had taken it dust and all. Speaking of the friend who would soon arrive – a female friend, it seemed – Dobson had betrayed the same deference that had been induced in him by Peter Lisdoonvarna. Dobson's friends belonged to a higher social order than Dobson's lodgers and Harriet, who was not likely to know her, did not ask the newcomer's name.

Peter Lisdoonvarna returned three days later. This time Edwina, ready dressed, was waiting for him but Peter was in no hurry to take her away. Settling down in the sofa, he gave Dobson more military gossip and was enjoying himself so much that Edwina's gaze became strained in an effort to appear interested. When at last he shuffled out of the sofa, Edwina was up before him but they were not yet on their way. Peter stood in the middle of the room then, without warning or explanation, went to the dining-table and thumped his fist down on it. He shouted, 'Glory to the bleeding lamb,' then, marching round the table, repeatedly banging it, his voice growing louder and louder, he bawled, 'Glory to the bleeding lamb, I love the sound of Jesus' name. His spirit puts me all in a flame, glory to the bleeding lamb.'

As this went on and on, Harriet laughed to console Edwina but Edwina did not laugh: she looked hurt and amazed. At last, coming to a stop from sheer exhaustion, he said, 'I'll tell you about that,' and threw himself back on to the sofa. 'We've got this sect in the village at home. I forget what they call themselves – the holy somethings or other. Not Rollers, no, not Rollers. Well, that's what they do, the whole lot of them, men and women, children, too: they march in a circle round and round the room, all yelling out, "Glory to the bleeding lamb," etc. They go on till they're drunk with it,' and unable to control his exuberance, he rose and returned to the table, hitting it and starting the chant again. Edwina sank into a chair but this time a few rounds were enough and, pulling her to her feet, he took her off, leaving the air still tingling with his voice.

'How can Edwina stand it?'

Dobson shook his head. 'I agree, he's a boisterous fellow, but he's young. He'll grow out of it.'

Peter's appearances were irregular. He would call for Edwina three nights running then be out of sight for a week. Edwina stayed in, listening and yearning for the telephone to ring. Harriet, concerned for her, said after one of his absences, 'Don't worry. He'll ring tomorrow.'

'Who?' Edwina looked startled.

'Why, Peter, of course.'

Edwina, apparently unaware that anyone could read her obsession, gazed in wonder at Harriet's percipience, then, free at last to speak, her emotion overwhelmed her and she cried, 'Oh, Harriet, I do long for him.'

'I know. I can see you're attracted by him.'

'It's more than attraction. I . . . I adore him. I know he's not very good looking but he's fascinating.'

'Yes, with all that energy and confidence, he's compelling – but you must admit, Edwina, you're a bit dazzled by the title.'

Edwina made a wry face, laughing at herself, but said, 'Any girl would be dazzled, wouldn't she? I mean – surely you would be?'

'I don't know. I've never been offered such a thing. But Edwina, between ourselves, do you think he is likely to share his title with you?'

Edwina shrugged and sighed, her face abject. 'I can't say. He's never serious. When someone's joking all the time, how do you pin them down?'

'And you have tried to pin him down?'

Edwina had to agree and Harriet asked her, 'Does he tease you?'

'He does, rather.'

'I'm afraid it's a form of sadism. He's too sure of you and some men don't want to be sure. They're excited by uncertainty. If you could hide your feelings, pretend that all the jollity bores you, show an interest in someone else – it might sober him up.'

Edwina fervently agreed. 'You're right. Yes, I'm sure you're right.'

'Let him be the anxious one.'

Edwina said, 'Yes,' but she still drooped in her desire for one person, and one person only.

'Next time, when he rings, don't jump at his invitation. Say you have another engagement.'

'I'll do that.' Resolved, Edwina looked at Harriet with glowing admiration. 'Harriet, how clever you are!'

'Not clever, just growing old.'

Harriet felt a flattering sense of achievement but when next the telephone rang, Edwina ran to it and, lifting the receiver, said, 'Peter, oh, Peter!' Listening to her rapturous voice, Harriet knew that in future she might as well keep her advice to herself.

Dobson expected his guest to arrive on Sunday. On Saturday evening when Harriet was moving their things into the small, spare room, the low sun, richly golden, spiked in between the mango leaves. The ceiling, baked all day, exuded heat. Smothered and dizzy, Harriet could not imagine that Dobson's guest would tolerate for long the monastic simplicity of this room or the heat that was condensed here during the day, but if she did choose to stay, then the room would be her room, the tree her tree, and Harriet might never come in here again. She looked back at the tree that looked in at her and said, 'Good-bye, mango tree.' She dropped down to the bed, putting off the arduous business of moving clothes, and was half-asleep when she was startled by uproar outside the door.

Looking out, she found Percy Gibbon, naked, in an evident state of sexual excitement and beside himself with rage, beating his hands on Edwina's door and shouting, 'Open up, open up.'

'What on earth are you doing?'

'She's in there with that bally lord.'

'What if she is? It's none of your business.'

Percy, his face distorted with indignation, pointed to the baize door that was held ajar by Hassan and Aziz who clutched at each other in mirth. Percy's condition, which had been farce, became scandal as soon as Harriet appeared, and Hassan put up a long 'Uh, uh, uh!' of shocked enjoyment.

'What do you think they think of it?' Percy asked.

'What do you think they think of you? Look at yourself. Can't you see they're laughing at you?'

177

Percy observed himself and his anger crumbled at the sight. He began to whimper, 'It's her fault. It's all her fault.'

'Go back to your room.'

Harriet spoke imperiously and when he obeyed, she turned on the safragis, ordering them away with such scorn, they fled together. She decided to put a stop to their insolence. She knew that they saw the inmates of the flat as immoral and ridiculous, and they were contemptuous of a way of life they could not understand. Recently she had realized that the safragis supposed Dobson's tenants lived off Dobson's charity. A Moslem household was always full of dependants and hangers-on and Edwina, Percy and the Pringles were despised for their supposed penury. Dobson, she suspected, was aware of this and did nothing to discourage it. He ruled that no money should be paid to him in front of the servants but Guy, who could never remember such trivial proscriptions, had recently thrown a bundle of bank notes across the table while Hassan was in the room. 'Our share of the housekeeping,' said Guy and Dobson whipped the notes out of sight, but Hassan had seen them and his eyes rolled in astonishment.

Hassan now knew that the lodgers paid their way. He had seen money change hands and to him money was power. Harriet, wife of the man who had paid the money, had taken on stature and she decided that in future Hassan and Aziz would keep their contempt to themselves.

It was Wednesday when the guest eventually turned up. She came at teatime when Harriet was setting out for the midsummer reception at the Anglo-Egyptian Union. Guy had agreed to go with her but, as usual, some engagement detained him and he telephoned to say he would come later. The reception was a tea party merging into an early evening wine party. He said, 'It'll go on all night, I'll get there as soon as I can.'

Descending into the small front garden, where poinsettias grew like weeds, Harriet saw two gharries at the kerb. One, it seemed, had been hired to take an excess of luggage and Hassan, Aziz and the boab from the lower flat had been called out to unload it. The cases, mostly of pigskin or crocodile, were elegant and their owner, a tall woman in a suit of pink tussore, looked as elegant as the cases. She was paying off the drivers and her voice had a disturbing effect on Harriet who would have kept out of sight had there been any point in doing so. Knowing they had to meet sooner or later, she let the gate click and the woman turned.

'Hello. I'm Angela Hooper. Do you live here?'

'Yes. Can I help you with your things?'

Angela Hooper said, 'We've met before, haven't we?' Apparently recalling nothing more distressing than some past social occasion, she held out her hand. 'How nice to see you again. I knew if I came to Dobbie's, I'd find congenial company.'

Neither Dobson nor Edwina were at home so Harriet went back to the flat and showed Angela to her room. 'I'm afraid it's very hot about this time of day.'

'Oh, I'm conditioned to heat. I don't mind what the place is like. I just want to be among friends.'

Harriet showed her the bathroom then went to the sitting-room. Feeling it would be discourteous to leave a newcomer alone in the flat, she waited while the cases were brought up and stacked along the corridor.

Angela Hooper, when she joined Harriet, was in no way discomposed by her unfamiliar surroundings, but gazing at Harriet, her eyes brilliant with vivacious inquiry, she said, 'You were going out, weren't you? Anywhere exciting?'

'Not very. In fact, rather dull. There's a reception at the Anglo-Egyptian Union. They serve wine later but the chief entertainment is the tea party because the Egyptian guests, who come early and go early, are more likely to be there. I don't suppose you would care for it?'

'Why not? I'm ready for anything. Let's see if we can stop the gharries.' She ran to the balcony and shouted down to the gharry drivers who had lingered in hope of a fare back to the centre of town. Catching Harriet's arm, she said. 'Come on. I've had the most boring journey. Let's go out and see life.'

It was now too late for the tea party but, as Guy had said, the drinking would go on all night. On Bulaq Bridge the gharry steps were boarded by two small boys who had made necklaces by stringing jasmin florets on to cotton. Clinging to the gharry

179

with dirty hands and feet, their galabiahs blown by the river wind, they shouted, 'Buy, buy, buy,' and swung the necklaces like censers in front of the women. Their arms were hung with necklaces and the scent overpowered even the smell of the gharry. Angla bargained with the boys who were glad of any reward for their day's work. Taking the money, they sprang down, leaving a heap of jasmin in her lap. Twilight was gathering and Angela, looking up into the glowing turquoise of the sky, said, 'Oh, what fun to be back in Cairo!'

So she was back in Cairo! But where, Harriet wondered, had she come from? And why had she taken one of Dobson's small rooms when she had her own splendid house in the Fayoum?

She said, 'I've been out here a long time. I love Egypt. I don't really want to leave.'

'Are you leaving?'

'I don't know. I've been thinking about it. There's talk of sending some of the English women and children home by sea. That would mean round the Cape. It could be an interesting trip, or it could be the most excruciating bore. So ... to tell you the truth, I'm rather *bouleversé*. I don't know what to do.'

The Egyptian guests had left the Union and the English had settled down to an evening that would be like every other evening except that the committee had provided a carafe of wine for each table.

The lights had come on in the club house. Inside, men could be seen moving round the snooker table while outside people were sitting beneath the darkening foliage of the trees. The club house lights shone out on to the grass and the beds of bamboo and the plants that climbed up between the windows. Jasmin scented the air.

Harriet and Angela found a vacant table at the edge of the lawn and as soon as they sat down a safragi brought over a carafe and four glasses. Angela picked up the carafe, which held little more than a pint of red Latrun wine, and laughed at the man. 'This is expected to go far, isn't it?' Looking round to disseminate her laughter, she said, 'And that's all the party fare? Dear me! Let's have something more festive,' and ordered a bottle of whisky.

Those sitting near by were displeased by her ebullience until they realized who she was, then they gave her smiling attention. She was known to be a rich woman and the rich did not come often to the Union. And she was not only rich but had been the centre of the extraordinary story of the Hooper boy's death. Clifford, two tables away, rose to get a better view of her and Harriet feared he might come over to join them. He thought better of it but when he sat down again, he bent towards his companions and talked eagerly, probably describing, all over again, his visit to the Fayoum house.

The Union shared its lawn with the Egyptian Officers' Club but the lawn went far beyond both clubs, stretching eastwards into a belt of heavy, ancient trees. Behind the trees some players were performing an Arabic version of *Romeo and Juliet* and voices, though remote, reverberated on the night air. There was a frenzied shout of 'Julietta' and, in response, a flat, sonorous and solemn 'Nam'.

'Oh dear, deathless passion!' Angela was shaken with laughter and Harriet, observing her, reflected, as others were certainly reflecting, on the dead boy. Angela knew she had met Harriet somewhere but did she realize where and when? If so, what was the nature of her cheerfulness? Was it defensive, or hysterical, or had she already recovered from that tragic afternoon?

The moon was rising from behind the trees. It was only a sliver of moon, no bigger than a nail paring, but so brilliant that it cast an ashen light over the grass. The Officers' Club had its own light, green like verdigris, which fell from the awning and shone on the men who sat, still and contemplative, like wax figures. Most of them were growing stout but a few, still in early youth, looked lean and virile. One of these, who sat alone, was very handsome and his figure was enhanced by a uniform and riding boots of immaculate cut.

'I must say,' said Angela, 'I rather fancy him. Do you think we could get him over here.'

Harriet thought it unlikely. The officers had never been known to cross the dividing width of lawn and no one had ever thought of inviting them to do so. Though they were dressed like the cavalry officers of most European countries, they wore the fez and that set them apart. They were Orientals.

181

They were Moslems. Though they were polite to each other if they happened to meet, the English and Egyptians could not converse together for long. Angela, however, was in no way inhibited by the lack of common ground. She kept her eyes on the young officer, trying to will him to respond, but he remained impassive, looking in another direction, apparently at nothing at all.

Harriet said, 'I think they're waiting to see the last of us.'

'They may not have to wait long.'

'You think we're finished here? Is that why you're thinking of leaving?'

'No.' Angela forgot the officer and, looking at Harriet, her merriment died. 'You think I've forgotten where and when we met?'

'I was hoping you didn't remember.'

'I remember it all, and in exact detail. I remember everyone who was in that room. I remember that fellow over there. What is he called?'

'Clifford.'

'And a British officer?'

'Simon Boulderstone.'

'I brought in my boy and the room was full of people. He was a beautiful boy, wasn't he? His body was untouched – there was only that wound in his head. A piece of metal had gone into the brain and killed him. He was almost perfect, a small, perfect body, yet he was dead. We couldn't believe it, but next day, of course ... We had to bury him.'

Wishing this would end, Harriet said, 'We were upset and wondered if there was something we could do, but all we could do was go away. We knew we ought not to be there.'

'I went away, too, not long after. I couldn't stay in that house. I didn't know what to do with myself. Bertie agreed that I needed a change so I went to Cyprus. I didn't tell him, but even before I went, I'd decided never to go back. Everything ended that afternoon: child, marriage, that ridiculous life of dinner parties, gaming parties, shooting parties. It was never my life. I'd been an art student in Paris so I'd known a quite different sort of world. Do you know the English here go duck shooting on Lake Mariotis and kill the birds in thousands.

Quite literally, thousands. And when they've killed them, they don't know what to do with them. The whole set-up made me sick. I tried to escape by painting but I stopped painting after that happened. I didn't do anything. I just moped and wouldn't go out. I knew people were talking. Even Bertie thought it was better for me to go.'

'But what about him? He must have suffered terribly ...'

'Yes, but he is much older than I am. He's an old man while I'm young enough to marry again.'

'You are getting a divorce?'

'I've asked for one. Bertie will have to divorce me. It would be cruel to refuse.'

Looking into Angela's face with its delicate features and mild expression, Harriet wondered where cruelty began and ended in this painful story. And Angela could marry again. Her fine sallow skin had aged only slightly round the eyes. She might be in the mid-thirties, young enough to replace the lost child and let the new one take on the identity of the dead. For her there could be some sort of restitution but for the elderly father the loss would be with him till the end of his days.

Harriet was silent and Angela said, 'You think me ruthless, don't you? But what could I do? I blamed myself for what happened. At times I felt I'd be better dead. If I'd stayed, I might have killed myself. And Bertie was part of the trouble. He did not accuse me. In fact, he was kindness itself, but I felt his very kindness was a reproach. Do you understand?'

'I understand how you felt – but abandoning your husband, leaving him to bear it alone! Wasn't that rather hard?'

'No, because there was nothing to leave. The marriage had been over a long time. Only the boy kept us together. It is a mistake to marry an older man however charming he is. It can't last.'

While Angela was talking, Castlebar came from the club house. He glanced towards Harriet, noted her companion and crossed to them. Stopping a few feet from the table, he stood there till Angela turned to look at him.

Instantly reverting to gaiety, she laughed at the sight of him as he swayed about, a sleepy smile on his face. 'Who's this?' she asked Harriet.

'Bill Castlebar; one of my husband's time-wasting cronies. Describes himself as a poet.'

Angela gave a high yelp of laughter and Castlebar, become alert and expectant, crossed to them and asked about Guy, 'Is the old thing c-coming?'

'Yes, later.'

Castlebar, having excused himself with this question, turned to Angela and gave a little bow. Nervousness increased his stammer. 'M-may I join you?' He spoke to Angela, taking it for granted that he was free to join Harriet if he wished.

'By all means!' When he sat down, she pushed the whisky towards him.

'Oh, I s-say! Not on the house, is it? I thought not. Oh, how kind!' Castlebar's gratitude gurgled down his throat as, having filled his glass, he gulped the whisky neat. When he had drunk half the glass, he paused to set up his cigarette packet in the usual way, one cigarette half out in readiness to take the place of the one in his hand.

Harriet asked, 'Where's Jake Jackman?' because the two men were seldom apart.

'Oh, h-he's inside, phoning his stuff to Switzerland.'

'Is there any news?'

'No more than usual. He's got hold of some story.'

This was the first time Harriet had Castlebar's company without Guy or Jackman being present, and she took the opportunity to ask about Jackman's career in Spain. 'Tell me, Bill, you've known Jake for some time. Did he really fight in the International Brigade?'

'F-f-f-fight?' Castlebar, taken off guard, was too surprised by the question to do more than tell the truth. 'Jake's never fought anywhere. He's never held a gun in his life.'

'But he was in Spain, wasn't he?'

'Yes, but not to fight. Some left-wing paper sent him out, rather late in the day. Too late, as it turned out. The government front collapsed soon after and Jake jumped a car and made it over the frontier. A timely get-away. He didn't even wait to pick up his clothes. His wife wasn't so lucky.'

'So he has a wife?'

'He had a wife. No one knows what became of her. She was

running a camp for war orphans and Jake says he couldn't persuade her to leave them.'

'I see. He didn't wait to pick up his clothes but he did wait to try and persuade his wife to go with him.'

Castlebar dropped his head, snuffling at Harriet's disbelief, and said, 'Well, wives are expendable.'

Jake Jackman coming out of the club house, looked about and seeing Castlebar with Angela Hooper, his keen eyes became keener. Moving rapidly to the table, he was about to sit down when it occurred to him that Angela's presence called for unwonted courtesy. Muttering, 'OK?' he threw himself down before receiving a reply and pulled a glass towards him. 'Mind if I help myself?'

Angela pushed the bottle over. It was half-empty. She had drunk one glass, Castlebar had taken the rest.

Harriet had no love for Jackman and she feared that Angela, used to Sporting Club circles, would find both men unacceptable, but Angela was observing them with the intent amusement of one who could afford to indulge the world. Harriet thought of a story that Guy was fond of telling. Fitzgerald was supposed to have said to Hemingway, 'The rich, they're different from us,' to which Hemingway replied, 'Yes, they've got more money.' Guy saw this as a debunking of Fitzgerald but Harriet felt that Fitzgerald showed more perception than Hemingway. A person who grew up in the security of wealth was different. It seemed to her she saw this difference in the tolerant, even admiring, amusement with which Angela watched the men lowering her whisky.

Castlebar said to Jackman, 'Get your stuff away all right?'

'Yep.' Jackman, pulling at his nose, sitting on the edge of his chair, looked directly at Angela. 'Quite a story. The Vatican's come out in the open at last. The Pope's given Hitler his blessing. Said the victims of Nazism asked for all they got. I knew this would happen as soon as Russia came into the war.'

Harriet said, 'It's over a year since Russia came into the war.'

'These things take time to leak through.

'I can't believe it.'

'You can't believe it? That's how the crooks get away with

it. People are too simple-minded to credit what's going on. I can tell you this: the whole bloody dogfight is financed by the Vatican.'

Angela laughed. 'Both sides?'

'Yep, both sides?'

Harriet asked, 'Where did you hear this?'

'I've got m'sources. If you knew the financial shenanigans that went on before the war between Krupps, Chamberlain, the Vatican and a certain British bank, nothing would surprise you.'

'Which British bank?' Angela spoke as one with a knowledge of international finance and Jackman, sniffing and looking uneasily about, brought out the name of a bank which was new to Harriet. Angela made no comment and Jackman, having silenced the women, went on to describe the pre-war relationship between Allied and Axis arms manufacturers and banks, describing a corruption so complex that Harriet and Angela were lost in its machinations.

Castlebar, who had heard all this many times before, sat with eyelids down, his chin sinking into his gullet as though about to fall asleep.

Growing bored with Jackman's rigmarole, Harriet looked towards the gate, feeling it was time for Guy to arrive and divert them. Jackman came to a stop at last and Castlebar's loose, violet-coloured lips gradually trembled into speech. 'B-b-bad news from all quarters these days. My wife's pulling strings, thinks she can get back here.'

Castlebar's wife had gone on holiday to England and been trapped there by the outbreak of war. Harriet, surprised that any ordinary civilian might get passage to Egypt, asked, 'How could you wangle that?'

'Me wangle it? You don't think I want her back?'

'Then, how could *she* wangle it?'

'If you knew my wife, you wouldn't ask. The shortest known distance in the world is the distance between my wife and what she wants.'

Angela's amused gaze focussed on Castlebar as he spoke. He looked at her and their eyes held each other in serious regard for a long moment, then Angela laughed and said in a teasing

186

tone, 'So you don't want your wife here! I wonder, is there some special reason? Another lady, perhaps?'

Castlebar tittered and taking up the poised cigarette, lit it from the butt of its predecessor and propped up the one that would succeed it. He started to speak but was hindered by a fit of coughing and Harriet said, 'He has a whole library of other ladies.'

Angela raised her brows, uncertain what was meant, then suddenly screamed with laughter. 'I know, you buy those dreadful little books they sell in Clot Bey and the Esbekiya!'

Grinning, Castlebar put his hand into the breast pocket of his limp, grimy linen jacket and pulled out the corner of a limp and grimy booklet. Before he could put it back again, Angela snatched it and began to look through it. He made a half-hearted attempt to retrieve it but left it with her, looking rather proud of his sensational possession.

Angela, pushing her chair back, keeping the book out of reach, read the title: *'The Golden Member* – what have we here? The life story of some wealthy member of parliament? Hm, hm, hm ...' She turned the grey, coarse-textured pages, piecing the story together. 'Dear me! The author claims that his was so be-u-u-u-tiful that his female admirers had a model of it made in pure gold and organized a ceremony in which several virgins deflowered themselves on this object. How interesting!' Angela surveyed Castlebar, pretending wide-eyed innocence. 'Do you think it is all true?'

Jackman clicked his tongue, as bored by Castlebar's sexual fantasies as Castlebar was by Jackman's politics. Between them they had finished off the whisky and the wine and Jackman, interrupting Castlebar's play with Angela, shouted to a safragi, 'Encore garaffo.'

The safragi, taking up the challenge, replied, 'Mafeesh garaffo.'

Jackman argued and the safragi, wandering happily over to him, made a gesture of finality. 'Garaffo all finish. Not any more.'

Jackman, not reflecting the good humour of this refusal, shouted, 'You heard me, you gyppo bastard. Encore garaffo.'

'What for you say "gyppo bastard"?' the safragi asked

with dignity. 'Gyppo very good man. You go away. Party finish.'

'And a bloody awful party it was!'

Angela was talking behind her hand to Castlebar while he, enfeebled by laughter, tried to push *The Golden Member* back into his pocket. A taxi came through the gate and Harriet looked longingly towards it, but it was an empty taxi, come to take people way. She noticed how few remained. The party was indeed over. The safragi returned with the bill for the whisky. Jackman seemed too preoccupied to notice it but Castlebar made a vague move towards it. Angela, as was expected, lifted it up, saying, 'My treat.'

That settled, Jackman became more cheerful. 'Let's go on somewhere,' he said then, as a finale to the Union party, he slapped his knee and began to sing to the tune of the Egyptian national anthem:

> King Farouk, King Farouk,
> Hang your bollocks on a hook . . .

His voice was pitched high and he was directing it, with venomous intent, towards the Egyptian officers who still sat in reposeful silence under the green light.

> Oh, Farida's feeling gay
> When Farouk has got his pay,
> But she's not so fucking happy
> When she's in the family way . . .

As the verses went on, the officers seemed to awaken. One rose and went towards a table where three sat together and the four heads were bent in consultation.

Castlebar said, apprehensively, 'We'd better get out of here,' but Jackman, drunk and defiant, sang louder, then his voice trailed weakly away. The officer who had risen, a large man, was crossing the lawn towards the English group. A sick expression came over Jackman's face but the officer was friendly. When he reached the table he bowed, smiled at them all and began to speak in Arabic. Angela, the only one who understood him, was disconcerted by what she heard. 'He says the officers wish to thank us for the homage paid to their king.'

'Is he being ironical?' Harriet asked.

188

'I don't think so. He says he regrets that none of them can speak English.'

The officer had more to say and Angela translated. 'He says they have felt for some time that the Union should have a piano. They have decided to present you with one.'

The officer, thanking Angela for her help, kissed her hand, then kissed Harriet's hand and bowing to Jackman and Castlebar, departed across the grass.

Castlebar, feeling the incident called for a speedy departure, said, 'Oh, come on,' but Harriet begged them to wait saying, 'Guy always turns up at the last minute.' But the club house was dark and the safragis were waiting to lock the gates. They had to go. Angela suggested they all go and see the belly-dancing at the Extase but Harriet, with no heart now for the Extase or anywhere else, asked to be dropped off in Garden City.

'Oh, no, you don't,' Angela said forcefully. 'You're not leaving me alone with these two. Anyway, it's my first evening back in Cairo, so let's enjoy ourselves. And you men, be sports – let me be host.'

This appeal to male chivalry stirred Castlebar who mumbled, 'Can't let you ...' but as Angela insisted he agreed without further protest. Angela would be permitted to act as host.

Harriet said, 'Guy must be home by now. I really ought to go back.'

'Wouldn't bank on it,' said Jackman. 'He's probably out on the loose. You stick around with us, I bet we find him somewhere.'

The Extase, one of the largest open-air night clubs, was in a garden beside the Nile. It was always crowded. Angela's party had to wait in a queue composed chiefly of officers and their girls. As the safragi set up make-shift tables in any vacant corner they could find, the queue dwindled steadily. Moving towards the club centre, Harriet, made unreasonably expectant by Jackman's bet that they would find Guy, looked over the tables. This was the last place in Cairo she would be likely to find Guy yet, not finding him, the whole crowded, noisy, busy garden was pervaded for her by a desolating emptiness.

On the stage a man in flannels and striped blazer was imitating the sound of a car changing gear uphill. His imitation was exact and the audience, that would have objected to the sound of a real car, gave him enthusiastic applause.

The Extase served only champagne and some of the officers were hilariously drunk. The arc lights that lit the stage added to the summer heat. The audience seemed a compacted, sweating, shouting, restless, amorous mass of men and girls who, like Edwina, only wanted a good time. Harriet wondered how long she would have to stay.

A safragi led Angela's party to the furthest corner of the auditorium and there Harriet saw Guy. He was with Edwina. Harriet stood, cold with shock, and stared at them while Angela said, 'Come on, Harriet, sit down.' Harriet remained where she was, transfixed, and Angela caught hold of her arm.

'My dear, is anything the matter? You look as though you'd seen a ghost.'

Harriet sat down but had to look round again to be sure that Guy was Guy and not an apparition of the mind. She could not bear what she saw but it remained with her. Guy was leaning towards Edwina and her hand, which rested on the table, was covered by his hand. 'I had too much faith in him,' Harriet thought. She was determined not to look at them again but then it came to her: Perhaps it's not Edwina! In spite of herself, she turned her head and saw Edwina's hair falling as it always fell, over Edwina's right eye. And that was that.

Angela said, 'Don't you feel well?'

'No, not very. I get these stomach upsets.'

'We'll go as soon as Calabri's done her dance.'

The dancer, Fawzi Calabri, was in no hurry to appear. As star of the cabaret, her act came last and she delayed it until the audience was in a frenzy of anticipation. She was announced and Harriet had to move her chair in order to see the stage. Doing so, she saw the table at which Guy and Edwina had been sitting. They were no longer there. The chairs were empty. The sight of them agitated her. She wanted to run off in search of Guy but could only stay and watch.

Calabri, a plump, moon-faced beauty with flesh powdered to an inhuman whiteness, had come on to the stage. She advanced to the centre and stood there, arms lifted, hands above her head, clad in diamonds and a few gauzy, sparkling whirl-abouts, until the uproar died down. Then the diamonds began to throw off sparks of light, the gauze lifted and her abdomen moved. The movement began gently, a slight roll and swell that worked itself gradually into a strong muscular rotation so it seemed the structure of the stomach was going round in circles. The music increased with the pace while Calabri stared at her own belly as though it were an unattached object which she swirled like a lasso. Music and movement reached a convulsive pitch then began to slow until there was silence and the dancer was still.

Amid the commotion that followed, Harriet whispered to Angela that she would leave by herself.

'No, we're all going.'

A taxi was waiting outside the club. Harriet was driven to Garden City but Angela made no move to get out with her.

'I feel I must see my poet safely home,' Angela laughed at Castlebar who smiled complacently and put his arm round her.

Jackman, pulling his nose and sniffing in gloomy disgust, said, 'You can drop me at Munira while you're about it.'

Harriet could scarcely give thought to the fact, astonishing at some less anxious time, that Angela could be attracted by Castlebar. She only wanted an explanation from Guy and was relieved to find he was in the flat. Sitting up in bed, a book in his hand, he mildly inquired, 'Where have you been? It's after midnight.'

'Where have *you* been? I waited for you till the Union closed.'

'I'm sorry, darling, but Edwina begged me to take her to the Extase.'

'You went to the Extase, of all places? – when you'd promised to join me at the Union!'

'Don't be cross. You'll understand when I tell you what happened. I was going to the Union but I came back to have a shower and change, and I found Edwina in a terrible state. She had been waiting for Peter Lisdoonvarna for over an hour. When she realized he did not mean to turn up, she collapsed. I found her lying on the sofa, crying her eyes out. So what

191

could I do? I had to help her. She thought he had gone to the Extase ... And, I may say, it was all your fault.'

'How could it be my fault?'

'You advised her to put up a show of indifference and go out with someone else. She did this and went with the new boy-friend to the Extase. The first thing she saw there was Peter enjoying himself hugely with another girl – some "Levantine floosie", according to Edwina. She was convinced that Peter was at the Extase again with the same floosie and she was beside herself with jealousy. The only thing that would satisfy her was to go to the Extase and see for herself. I was really afraid she would do something desperate. I felt I had to go with her.'

'Supposing Peter had been there, what would she have done?'

'Well, I'm thankful to say he wasn't. But you can see I had to comfort her a bit ...'

'You were comforting her more than a bit. I saw you. You were holding her hand.'

Guy was jolted, but not for long. 'I felt sorry for the poor kid.'

'She's not a kid. She's the same age as I am. I went alone to the Union. She could have gone to the Extase by herself.'

'Be reasonable, darling. The Extase and the Union are very different places. And you're a married woman, you have status. She's just a frightened kid.'

'Frightened of what?'

'Losing out, I suppose. She's set her heart on this fellow, Lisdoonvarna, God knows why. Come on, darling, don't look so black. Little monkey's paws, come to bed ...' He tried to take her hand but Harriet, remembering Guy's hold on Edwina's hand, moved away. He tried to coax her to return to him but she remained on the other side of the room, and looked at the window where there was no tree to befriend her.

The sense of chill and distance between them so bewildered Guy that he started to get out of bed. She said angrily, 'Leave me alone,' and he remained where he was, watching her as though by watching he could divine what was wrong with her. He found it difficult to accept that his own behaviour could be at fault. And if it were, he did not see how it could be changed. It was, as it always had been, rational, so, if she were troubled, then some agency beyond them – sickness, the summer heat, the distance from England – must be affecting her. For his part, he was reasonable, charitable, honest, hard-working, as generous as his means allowed, and he had been tolerant when she picked up with some young officer in Greece. What more could be expected of him? Yet, seeing her afresh, he realized how fragile she had become. She was thin by nature but now her loss of weight made her look ill. Worse than that, he felt about her the malaise of a deep-seated discontent. That she was unhappy concerned him, yet what could he do about it? He had more than enough to do as it was, and he tried to appeal to her good sense. 'Darling, don't be so grumpy!'

She turned on him. 'I *am* grumpy, and with reason. I'm sick of your solicitude for others – it's just showing off. You don't show off to me. I'm part of you, as you say, so I can put up with anything. You don't come to the Union, as you promised, and where do I find you? I couldn't believe my eyes. It was ... it was incredible.'

'The girl needed help.'

'Everyone needs help. Except me, of course. I can go round alone. I can look after myself. Here I'm usually more ill than well, but that doesn't worry you, does it?'

'It does worry me. This place doesn't agree with you. You're too thin, you look peaky. I've noticed it. I've been thinking about it,' Guy said, thinking about it for the first time. 'You know, darling, there's a plan to send some of the women and children home. Why don't you apply for a passage.'

'Me? Go back without you?' She was dumbfounded and, sinking down on to a chair, she stared at him in disbelief. 'You want me to leave you?'

Made uneasy by her expression, he looked away from her. 'Of course I don't, but you said yourself that you're usually more ill than well. And you're nervous.'

'I'm no more nervous than anyone else. It's a nervous time.'

'That's true. No one knows what will happen when the Germans get their reinforcements. That could be any day. You said yourself, they could arrive almost without warning. If we ended up in a prison camp, I really don't think you'd survive.'

'At least we'd be together.'

'We wouldn't be together. We'd be in different camps. We might even be in different countries. If you were in England, at least I'd know where you were. And you would have war work – that would take your mind off things. You'd be happier, and your health would pick up there. All those bugs just die in a northern climate. Now, darling, be sensible. Think about it.'

'I don't intend to think about it.' She went to the chest of drawers that served as dressing-table and put cleansing cream on her face. 'We came here together. When we leave, we'll leave together.'

She was dilatory in preparing for bed, feeling pained and suspicious. He had never before suggested that she return to England to face life alone; why suggest it now? It came to her, with dismay, that he wished to clear the way for a possible pursuit of Edwina. Was it possible? Everything was possible. If the affair with Peter broke up as it very well might, Guy would be at hand, again the comforter and perhaps, in the end, more than comforter. She had seen many marriages fail in this place, and men whose wives were sent out of harm's way were quick to find consolation.

When she got into bed, Guy put his arms round her, imagining he could conciliate her with physical love, but her response was cool. The fact he could think of their separation, even for her own good, was not so easily forgotten.

In spite of her resolution, the thought of England had come into her mind and she recalled the vision of England that had overwhelmed her once in a Cairo street. It returned in her memory, a scene of ploughed fields and elm trees with a wind smelling of the earth; she thought if she were there, she would be well again. Here she was not only unwell, but at risk from all the diseases known to mankind. She remembered how she had danced at the Turf Club with an officer who was feverish and complained of a headache, and who went away to be sick. Next day they heard he had gone down with smallpox and everyone who had been at the party, had to be revaccinated and kept under surveillance for a fortnight.

She whispered to herself, 'That was a narrow escape.'

Guy, half-asleep asked, 'What was? What are you thinking about?'

'I'm thinking about England,' she said.

Ten

Trench was replaced by a man called Fielding. Fielding, a little older than Simon, had a plain, pleasant face and hair bleached like Trench's hair. He and Simon, being concomitants, should have been friends but Simon was becoming wary of friendship. His instinct was to avoid any relationship that could again inflict on him the desolation of loss. The only person whose company he sought was Ridley. Ridley had known Arnold and Trench and he let Simon talk about them so, for short periods, memory could overcome their nonexistence.

Not much was happening at that time. The Column went on sorties carrying out small shelling raids, but there was no more close action. Even the main positions were quiet so it seemed the fight itself had sunk beneath the load of August heat.

Ridley still brought gossip and news, but there was not much of it. In the middle of the month, when Auchinleck lost his command, the officers asked each other why this had happened. Ridley, who had once seen the deposed general standing, very tall up through a hole in a station-wagon, spoke of him regretfully as though, like Arnold and Trench, he had gone down among the dead. 'He was a big chap, big in every way, they say. He slept on the ground, just like the rest of us. No side about him, they say. A real soldier.'

'What about the new chap?'

'Don't know. Could be a good bloke but we all felt the Auk was one of us.'

Later in the month, the Column, on patrol in a lonely region near the Depression, came upon three skeletons, two together and a third lying some distance from them. The sand here was a very dark red and the skeletons, white and clean, were conspicuous on the red ground. The nomad Arabs had stripped them of everything: not only clothing but identity discs, papers, even letters and photographs, for these things could be sold to German agents to authenticate the disguises of undercover men.

The staff car stopped and Hardy and Martin got out to look them over. Simon, following from curiosity, was startled when Martin said that the skeletons were of men recently dead. Had they lain there long the sand would have blown over them. They might have been the crew of a Boston that had come down in an unfrequented part of the desert and managed, in spite of injuries, to crawl this far before giving up. He touched the bones with his toe and said: 'The kites have picked them clean.'

Simon, shocked that flesh could be so quickly dispersed, remembered his friends, dead and buried, and stood in thought until Hardy called to him, 'Get a move on, Boulderstone.'

Simon turned to him with an expression of suffering that prompted Hardy to put a hand on the young man's shoulder and say with humorous sympathy, 'You won't bring them to life by staring at them.'

That evening there was no mention of the Middle East in the radio news. 'A dead calm, eh?' Martin said. 'Wonder how long it'll last?' When he went to fetch his whisky bottle, Hardy spoke to Simon. 'I remember you mentioning your brother, Boulderstone. I couldn't let you take leave at that time but I understood how you felt. Have you any idea where he is?'

'Yes, sir. Ridley says there's a Boulderstone with the New Zealanders, near the Ridge.'

'Right. I'll give you a few days and you can take the staff car and look him up.'

When Simon began to express his gratitude. Hardy enlarged his concession. 'I don't see why you shouldn't take a week as there's nothing doing. But check up on his position. You could waste a lot of time scouting round the different camps.'

As soon as he could get away, Simon went to tell Ridley

of his good fortune but Ridley merely grumbled, 'What's he think he's doing, giving blokes leave at this time?'

'Why? Is anything about to happen?'

'Chaps down the line think so. Then there's old Rommel. He's not moving forward but he's not exactly dropping back, neither. If his reinforcements arrive, he'd be through us like a dose of salts.'

'That's not likely to happen in one week.'

'How do you know? I got a feeling it could happen any day. If it hots up, it'll hot up sudden like.'

Simon begged Ridley to keep his premonitions to himself, saying, 'This may be my only chance to see my brother,' and Ridley relented enough to admit that his 'feeling' could be 'just a twitch'. It occurred to Simon that Ridley's annoyance might come from envy of Simon's luck, or perhaps simply an unwillingness to have Simon out of his sight. Whatever it was, he began to take an interest in the vacation, saying, 'If you got a week, you could nip back to Alex. Or Cairo, even. Which'd you rather – Cairo or Alex?'

Simon did not know. He was enticed by the thought of the seaside town, but he knew people in Cairo. Had he been granted leave during his first days in the desert, he would have wanted only one thing; to return to Garden City. Now, though he sometimes thought of Edwina, she had lost substance in his mind and her beauty was like the beauty of a statue. It related to a desire he had ceased to feel.

Here in the desert, either from lack of stimulus or some quality in the air, the men were not much troubled by sex. The need to survive was their chief preoccupation – and they did survive. In spite of the heat of the day, the cold of night, the flies, the mosquitoes, the sand-flies, the stench of death that came on the wind, the sand blowing into the body's interstices and gritting in everything one ate, the human animal not only survived but flourished. Simon felt well and vigorous and he thought of women, if he thought of them at all, with a benign indifftrence. He belonged now to a world of men; a contained, self-sufficient world where life was organized from dawn till sunset. It had so complete a hold on him, he could see only one flaw in it: his friends died young.

The staff car, assigned to him for twenty-four hours, would take him first to the Ridge where he hoped to track down Hugo, then to the coast road where he could stop a military vehicle and get a lift into the Delta. His new driver and batman, a young red-haired, freckled squaddie called Hugman, had little contact with Simon. He did not expect Simon to speak to him and Simon did not wish to speak. He was wary of Hugman, as he was of Fielding, and sat in the back seat of the car, holding himself aloof. Hugman very likely thought him one of the 'spit and polish' officers that he despised, but Hugman could think what he liked. Simon was risking no more emotional attachments, no more emotional upsets. To excuse his silence, he sprawled in the corner of the car, propping his head against the side and keeping his eyes shut. They had started out early. Simon, anxious to be off before Hardy could change his mind, almost ran from Ridley who came towards him with a look of doom. 'There, what did I say, sir? The gen is that the jerries are preparing a push on Alam Halfa.'

'Christ!' Simon threw himself into the car and ordered Hugman to move with all speed. They were out of sight of the Column before he remembered he had not reported his departure to Hardy.

As the sun rose, he did not need to simulate sleep but sank into a half-doze which brought him images of the civilized world he was soon to re-enter. He no longer could, nor did he need to, exclude women from his dreams. Now that he was due for a week of normal life, he could afford to indulge his senses a little. He remembered not only Edwina but the dark-haired girl who raced him up the pyramid, and even poor forgotten Anne returned to him become, with his change of circumstances, more real than Arnold. His attention reverted to Edwina. She was the supreme beauty although he had been too dazzled to know whether she was beautiful or not. Another face edged into his mind, a woman older than the others, with a dismayed expression that puzzled him. He could not immediately recall the dead boy in the Fayoum house, but when he did he dismissed both woman and boy as intruders on his reverie. Wasn't it enough that he had lost his friends?

When he opened his eyes, the Ridge was in sight. They were driving through a rear maintenance and supply area where petrol dumps, food dumps, canteen trucks, concentrations of jeeps and ambulances, a medical unit and a repair depot were all planted in sand and filmed with sand that covered the green and fawn camouflage patches. It was a skeleton town with netted wire instead of house-walls and sand tracks instead of streets. The noon sun glared overhead and men, given an hour's respite, lay with faces hidden, bivouacked in any shade they could find. Unwilling to disturb them, Simon told Hugman to drive until he found the Camp Commandant's truck. Both men were drenched with sweat and when Simon left the car, the wind plastered the wet stuff of his shirt and shorts to his limbs. It was a hot wind yet he shivered in the heat.

The Commandant, fetched from his mid-day meal in the officers' mess, had no welcome for Simon. 'How the hell did you get leave at a time like this?'

Simon, more wily than he used to be, said, 'Only a few days, sir.'

'A few days!' The Commandant blew out his cheeks in comment on Hardy's folly, but the folly was no business of his. He advised Simon to find the New Zealand division HQ. 'About a mile down the road. Can't miss it. You'll see the white fern leaf on a board.'

The car, driven out of the maintenance area into open desert, rocked in the rutted track, throwing up sand clouds that forced the two men to close the windows and stifle in enclosed heat.

The board appeared, the fern leaf scarcely visible beneath its coating of sand, and beyond, on either side of the track, guns and trucks, dug into pits, were protected by sand-bags and camouflage nets. Simon realized they were very near the front line.

At the Operations truck, a New Zealand major, a tall, thin, grave-faced man, listened with lowered head as Simon explained that he was looking for a Captain Boulderstone. The major, jerking his head up, smiled on him. 'You think he's your brother, do you? Well, son, I think maybe he is. You're as like as two peas. But I don't know where he's got to –

someone will have to look around for him. If you have a snack in the mess, we'll let you know as soon as we find him. OK?'

'OK, and thank you, sir.'

The mess was a fifteen hundred-weight truck from which an awning stretched to cover a few fold-up tables and chairs. Simon seated himself in shade that had the colour and smell of stewed tea. The truck itself served as a cook-house and Simon said to the man inside, 'Lot of flies about here.'

'Yes, they been a right plague this month. Our CO said something got to be done about them, but he didn't say what. I sprays flit around and the damn things laugh at it.'

The flies were lethargic with the heat. Simon, having eaten his bully-beef sandwich and drunk his tea, had nothing better to do than watch them sinking down on to the plastic table-tops. He remembered what Harriet Pringle had said about the plagues coming to Egypt and staying there. The flies had been the third plague, 'a grievous swarm', and here they still were, crawling before him so slowly they seemed to be pulling themselves through treacle. The first excitement of arrival had left him and he could not understand why Hugo was so long in coming. Boredom and irritation came over him and seeing a fly swat on the truck counter, he borrowed it in order to attack the flies.

A dozen or so crawled on his table and no matter how many he killed, the numbers never grew less. When the swat hit the table, the surviving flies would lift themselves slowly and drift a little before sinking down again. He pushed the dead flies off the table and they dropped to the tarpaulin which covered the ground. When he looked down to count his bag of flies, he found they had all disappeared. He killed one more and watched to see what became of it. It had scarcely touched the floor when a procession of ants veered purpose-fully to it, surrounded it and, manoeuvring the large body between them, bore it away.

Simon laughed out loud. The ants did not pause to ask where the manna came from, they simply took it. The sky rained food and Simon, godlike, could send down an endless supply of it. He looked forward to telling Hugo about the flies and ants. He killed till teatime and the flies were as numerous as ever, then, all in a moment, the killing disgusted him. He had tea and, still waiting, he thought of the German youth he had killed on the hill. Away from the heat of battle, that killing, too, disgusted him, and he would have sworn, had the situation permitted, never to kill again.

The mess filled with officers but none of them was Hugo. About five o'clock a corporal came to tell him that Captain Boulderstone had gone out with a patrol to bring in wounded.

'Has there been a scrap, then?'

The corporal did not look directly at Simon as he said, 'There was a bit of a scrap at the Mierir Depression two days ago. Last night we heard shelling. Could be, sir, the patrol's holed up there.'

'You mean, he's been gone some time?'

The man gave Simon a quick, uneasy glance before letting him know that the patrol had left camp the previous morning. Hugo had, in fact, been away so long, his batman had gone out in the evening to look for him.

A sense of disaster came down on Simon and he got to his feet. 'They should be coming back soon. I'll go and meet them.'

'With respect, sir, you'd do better to stay. The wind's rising and there could be a storm brewing.'

Simon refused to wait. He wanted to move, as though by moving he could hasten Hugo's return to the camp. He had sent Hugman to the canteen and decided to let him stay there. The corporal told him that there was a gap in the mine fields where the track ran through the forward positions into no-man's-land and continued on to the enemy positions at El Mierir and Mitediriya. As Simon went to the car, the corporal followed him.

'You're not going alone, sir?'

'Yes.'

The car, its steering wheel almost too hot to handle, stood beside the Operations truck. The corporal said, 'Like me to come with you, sir? Only take a tick to get permission.'

'Thank you, no. I'll be all right.'

Even a tick was too long to wait while he had hope of meeting Hugo. The sand was lifting along the banks between the gun pits. Small sand devils were whirling across the track, breaking up, dropping and regathering with every change in the wind. The sky was growing dark and before he could reach the forward position, his view was blotted out. He had driven into the storm and there was nothing to do but pull to the side, stop and stare into the sand fog, watching for the batman's truck to come through it. Nothing came. He got out of the car and tried to walk down the track but the wind was furious, driving the searing particles of sand into his eyes and skin, forcing him back to shut himself in the car. He was trapped and would remain trapped until the storm blew itself out.

At sunset the sand-clogged air turned crimson. When the colour died, there was an immediate darkness and in darkness he would have to remain. He could see nothing. He could hear nothing but the roar of the wind. He opened the car door an inch expecting a light to switch on but the sand blew in and there was no light. He switched on the headlamps that showed him a wall of sand. Realizing that no one was likely to see them, he switched them off to save the battery. Then, aware there was nothing more to be done, he subsided into blackness that was like nonexistence. The luminous hands of his watch showed that it was nearly nine o'clock. He climbed over to the back seat and put his head down and slept.

He awoke to silence and the pellucid silver of first light. He was nearer the perimeter than he realized. Before him was a flat expanse of desert where the light was rolling out like a wave across the sand. Two tanks stood in the middle distance and imagining they had stopped for a morning brew-up, he decided to cross to them and ask if they had seen anything of the patrol or the batman's truck. It was too far to walk so he went by car, following the track till he was level with the tanks, then walking across the mardam. A man was standing in one of the turrets, motionless, as though unaware of Simon's approach. Simon stopped at a few yards' distance to observe the figure, then saw it was not a man. It was a man-shaped cinder that faced him with white and perfect teeth set in a charred black skull. He could make out the eye-sockets and the triangle that had once supported a nose then, returning at a run, he swung the car round and drove back between the batteries, so stunned that for a little while his own private anxiety was forgotten.

The major was waiting for him at the Operations truck, his long grave face more grave as though to warn Simon that Hugo had been found. He had been alive, but not for long. All the major could do was try and soften the news by speaking highly of Hugo, telling Simon that Hugo had been a favourite with everyone, officers and men. His batman, Peters, was so attached to him, he was willing to risk his own life to find him. And he was alive when Peters came on him, but both legs had been shot away. The sand around him was soaked with blood. He didn't stand a chance.

'And the rest of the patrol? Couldn't they have done something?'

'All dead. Young Boulderstone just had to lie there with his life-blood running out till someone found him.'

The major sent for Peters so Simon could be told all that remained to be told. Peters was a thin youth who choked on his words. 'When I found him, he said, quite cheerfully, "Hello, Peters old chap, I knew you'd come." ' Tears filled Peters's eyes and Simon felt surprise that this stranger could weep while he himself felt nothing.

Peters, regaining himself, explained that the patrol had been returning to the camp at sunset when it was attacked by German mortars. The ambulance moving against the red of the sky must have been an irresistible target. 'They knew what it was, the bastards. And they went on firing till they'd got the lot.'

Peters, having found Hugo, could not move him because movement would increase the haemorrhage. He intended to return to the camp for help but the storm blew up, so he had to spend the night with the wounded man.

'He told you what happened?'

'He did, sir. His speech was quite clear, right to the end. About two a.m., he said, "I think I'm going, Peters. Just as well. A chap's not much use with two wooden pins." I said, "You hold on, sir. They can do wonders these days with pins," and he laughed. He didn't speak again.'

'Thank you, Peters.'

Peters had brought in the body. The burial party had already set out. There was nothing for Simon to see and he felt Thank God for that. Knowing that his presence was an embarrassment in the camp, he held out his hand to the major and said he would be on his way. Hugman, who had been waiting for him, eyed him with furtive sympathy and muttered, 'Sorry to hear what happened, sir.'

Simon nodded, 'Rotten luck', then there was silence between them until they reached the coast road and he said, 'Don't wait, Hugman. The car's due back. You might tell Ridley what happened. He'll understand.'

A truck appeared on the road before Hugman was out of sight. The squaddie beside the driver offered Simon his seat but Simon refused and said he would ride in the rear. The back flap was let down for him. He threw his kit aboard, jumped after it, and the truck went on again.

Simon, sitting with his back to the cabin, looked out over the desert that had become as familiar to him as his childhood streets. He was reconciled to its neutral colour, its gritty wind, the endless stretches of arid stone and sand, but now a darkness hung over it all. He felt death as though he and Hugo had been one flesh and he was possessed by the certainty that if he returned here, he, too, would be killed.

'Both of us. They would lose both of us.'

He thought of his mother going into the greenhouse to read the wire, imagining perhaps that one of her sons was coming home on leave. He found a pad in his rucksack and began to write.

'Dear Mum and Dad, By the time you get this you will have heard about Hugo. I was there in the NZ camp when he didn't come in. His batman found him, legs blown off ...' Simon stopped, not knowing if he should tell them that, and started on another page.

'Dear Mum and Dad, By the time you get this, you'll know that Hugo is ...' but he could not write the word 'dead', and what else could he say?

Hugo was dead. The reality of Hugo's death came down on him and his unfeeling calm collapsed. He gulped and put his hands over his face. Tears ran through his fingers. There was no one to see him and the men in front would not hear his sobs above the engine noise. He gave himself up to grief. He wept for Hugo – but Hugo was safely out of it. He wept for his parents who must live with their sorrow, perhaps for years.

In the end, having stupefied himself with weeping, he lay on the floor of the truck and slept. He was wakened by passing traffic and, sitting up, he read what he had written and knew that neither letter would do.

There was nothing to be said. He tore the pages into fragments and threw them to the desert wind.

The Battle Lost and Won

To Parvin and Michael Laurence

One

Simon Boulderstone, coming into Cairo on leave, passed the pyramids at Giza when they were hazed over by mid-day heat. The first time he had seen them, he had been struck with wonder, but now there was no wonder left in the world. His brother, Hugo, had been killed. That very morning, in the dark, early hours, Hugo had bled to death in no-man's-land.

Simon had stopped a lorry on the coast road east of Alamein and, alone in the back, had cried himself to sleep. Now that he would have to face the two men in front, he tried to wipe away the marks of tears but did not do it very well. The lorry stopped outside Mena House. The driver, coming round to speak to Simon, stared at him, then said, 'You've caught the sun, sir,' as though they had not, all of them, been broiled by sun during the long summer months.

'You want anywhere in particular, sir?'

'A cheap hotel, if you know of one.'

The driver suggested the International and Simon said, 'Glad if you'd drop me there.' They drove on through the suburbs into the centre of Cairo where the lorry stopped again. They were at a modern Midan, a meeting place of three small streets where the old houses were being pulled down and replaced by concrete blocks. One of the blocks was the International and it had the unadorned air of cheapness.

Throwing down his kit, Simon thanked the two men then jumped down himself. Standing on the pavement, in the dazzling light, he seemed to be in a trance, and the driver asked him: 'You all right, sir?'

Simon nodded and the lorry went on. Left alone in the middle of the Midan, he stared at a palm tree that rose from a bed of ashy sand. As he observed it, he began to feel an extraordinary poignancy about it so for a few minutes he could not move but, forgetting Hugo, he centred his misery on this solitary palm. From its height and the length of its fronds, he could guess it was an old tree that had grown in other, more spacious days. Now, seeing it hemmed in by buildings like a bird in too small a cage, he ached with pity for it though the tree itself conveyed no sense of deprivation. A human being in similar case would have been bemoaning his misfortune but the tree, swaying in the hot wind, spread itself as though rejoicing in such air and light as came to it.

Feeling near to weeping again, he said aloud, 'Am I going crazy or something?' and picked up his kit.

The hotel, its windows shuttered against the sun, looked empty but there was a clerk in the hall, staring in boredom at the glass entrance doors. The sight of Simon brought him to life: 'Yes, please? You wan' room? You wan' bather?'

Simon, sun-parched, sweat-soaked, unshaven, sand in hair and eyes, needed a bath though he was too deep in grief to feel the want of anything. He was taken upstairs to a small room with a bathroom so narrow, the bath fitted into it like a foot into a shoe. Filling the bath, he lay comatose in luke-warm water until he heard the hotel waking up.

He could see through his bedroom window that the dusty saffron colour of the afternoon had deepened into the ochre of early evening. Time had extended itself in his desolation, yet it was still the day on which Hugo had died. At this pace, how was he to endure the rest of his life? How, as a mere beginning, was he to get through the week ahead?

He looked at himself in his shaving mirror, expecting to see himself ravaged by his emotion but the face that looked back at him was still a very young face, burnt by the sun, a little dried by the desert wind, but untouched by the sorrow of that day.

He was twenty years of age. Hugo had been his senior by a year and they were as alike as twins. Imagining Hugo's body disintegrating in the sand, he felt a spasm of raging indignation against this early death, and then he thought of those who must suffer with him: his parents, his relatives and the girl Edwina whom he thought of as Hugo's girl. He had seen Edwina when he first came to Cairo and he realized, with a slight lift of spirit, that he now had good reason to see her again.

Having somewhere to go, something to do, he shaved and dressed carefully and went out to streets that were stale with the hot and dusty end of summer.

The office workers were returning to work after the siesta. They crowded the tram-cars, hanging in bunches at every entrance, while the superior officials had taken all the taxis. Simon managed to find an empty gharry but this made so little progress among the traffic that he could have walked more quickly.

Heat hung like a fog in the air, a coppery fog coloured by the light of the sinking sun. As they came down to the embankment, the river, slowly turning and lifting the feluccas towards the sea, was a fiery gold. On the western side, the pyramids had come into view, triangles of black no bigger than a thumb-nail.

In among the ramshackle houses of Garden City, Simon breathed the evening smell of jasmin and, in spite of himself, felt the excitement of being there. Before he left England, he had received a letter from Hugo telling him to buy scent for Edwina at a West End shop. The scent was to travel in the diplomatic bag and Simon, overawed, had taken it to the Foreign Office where the young man who accepted it said, 'Another votive offering for Miss Little?' The scent was called *Gardenia* but gardenias and jasmin were all one to Simon and the whole of Garden City was for him permeated by the delicious sweetness of Edwina Little.

When the gharry reached his destination, he looked up at the balcony of the upper flat, half-expecting to find Edwina still standing there as she had stood that day, his second day in Egypt. He thought, 'Poor Edwina, poor girl!' and there was a sort of morose comfort in the fact she too would suffer their loss.

Several people lived in the flat. One of them, a young woman called Harriet Pringle, was in the living-room when he entered it. She started up, saying, 'Hugo?' but knowing it could not be Hugo.

'No, it's Simon . . .' Simon's voice broke and Harriet, giving him time to control himself, said: 'Yes, of course it's Simon. Do you remember me? We climbed the Great Pyramid together.'

He still could not speak and Harriet, sensing the reason for his grief, took his arm and led him to a chair. He sat down, blinking to keep back his tears that came in a slow, painful trickle, nothing like the fierce bout of weeping that had overwhelmed him in the back of the lorry. He scrubbed his handkerchief over his cheeks and apologized for his weakness.

'I've come to see Edwina and tell her ... Hugo has been killed.'

Hassan, the safragi, looking for drama, was peering round the door. Harriet, who had taken over the housekeeping, told him to bring in the drinks trolley. Wheeling it in, he observed Simon with furtive curiosity and Harriet ordered him away.

She gave Simon a half-glass of whisky and as he sipped it, he spoke more easily: 'He was out with a patrol, picking up the wounded. They were all killed. Hugo's legs were blown off and he bled to death. His batman found him and sat beside him till he died. There was a sandstorm, so it wasn't possible to get him back. Too late, anyway. He just lay there and bled to death.'

'I'm sorry.' Harriet was deeply sorry but not shocked. When she said goodbye to Hugo, on his last leave, a voice in her head had said, 'He won't come back. He is going to die.'

'I have to tell Edwina. It's terrible for her.'

'And for everyone who knew him.'

'But she was special. I mean: she was Hugo's girl.'

Harriet made no reply but remained silent for a while then, standing up, said, 'I'll go and find her.' As she went through the baize door that led to the bedroom corridor, Edwina was coming out of the bathroom with a white bath-robe round her shoulders. She worked at the British Embassy but that day she had stayed at home with a hang-over that she called a migraine.

'Are you better?'

'Oh, much better.' Edwina smiled at Harriet, an amused, conniving smile because, however bad her headache, she was always well enough to go out in the evening. As she hurried into her room, she said, 'Come and talk to me while I dress. Peter will be here any minute.'

She stood naked, tall and shapely, her skin glistening from the bath, and slapped herself dry with a swansdown puff. Harriet, watching her as she prepared for her night with Peter Lisdoonvarna, said, 'Edwina' with a warning emphasis that brought Edwina to a stop. She stared at Harriet, puzzled.

'What is it, Harriet?'

'Simon Boulderstone is here.'

'You mean Hugo, don't you?'

'No, it's the younger one: Simon. Edwina, he's brought bad news. Hugo has been killed.'

'Oh, no. Not Hugo? What a pity! I *am* sorry.' Edwina stood, reflectively still a moment, then, shaking her head regretfully, went to her chest of drawers and putting her hand in among her satin, crêpe-de-Chine and lace underclothes, said again, 'I am sorry,' but her mind was on other things. She had been fond of Hugo but she could not mourn him just then.

'Edwina, listen! Simon's under the impression that you were Hugo's girl. He expects you to be terribly upset.'

'But of course I'm upset. Hugo was one of the nicest boys I knew – gentle, sweet, generous. We got on well and we had a wonderful time when he came on leave. I was really fond of him.'

'Simon thinks you were in love. Don't disillusion him. Don't . . .' Harriet was going to say 'Don't hurt him' but said instead: 'Don't disappoint him.'

Edwina sighed and put a slip over her head then, crossing to Harriet, she took Harriet's hands into her own and said in a small, persuasive voice: 'Darling, I can't see him now with Peter coming any minute. Be a dear. Tell him I'm at the office. Ask him to come back tomorrow.'

'He knows you're here.'

Edwina sighed again: 'What *can* I do?' She dropped Harriet's hands and went to the wardrobe and took out a draped, white evening gown. Hanging it on the door in readiness, she looked in the glass: 'M'face – how awful!'

She touched in her eyes and lips, stepped into the dress, then returning to the chest of drawers, chose one of a long row of large, ornamental scent bottles and said, 'I think he gave me this.' She caught her breath and held her head back, trying to contain her tears. Dabbing the scent on her skin, enhancing the gardenia scent of the room, she murmured, 'These poor boys! You meet them . . . you . . .' She paused, catching her breath.

'You give them your heart?'

'Yes. And then they go back and get killed.' Edwina, putting her forefingers under her lashes to lift the wetness away, said, 'Oh, dear!' and, sniffing, gave Harriet a rueful smile that was a comment both on the futility of grief and her own incorrigible frivolity: 'What's to be done about it? Cry oneself sick? What good would that do?'

She might have given herself up to weeping were she not expecting Peter. Instead, she said anxiously, 'Can't let him see me like this,' and began to mend her make-up.

Harriet, feeling her anxiety, thought how precarious must be her hold on Peter Lisdoonvarna if she dared not betray pity for a young man's death. And it was not that Peter was prone to jealousy. She knew that any hint of affection for another man would be used by him as excuse for his own philanderings.

'How do I look?'

A current of air, bringing into the scented room the fresh smell of the tamarisks, stirred the white dress that hung like a peplos from Edwina's wide, brown shoulders.

'You look like the statue of Athena.'

'Oh, Harriet!' Edwina, a beauty but not a classical beauty, laughed at this praise. Then, hearing Peter's footsteps in the corridor, turned in expectation, putting her hands together. He was a broad, heavy man and the dry wooden floor cracked under his weight. Throwing open the door without knocking, he asked loudly: 'What's going on out there? Chap blubbing in the living-room!'

Harriet said, 'His brother's just been killed.'

'Oh, I say!' Peter, contrite, lowered his voice: 'Tough luck!' His big face with its saddle nose and black moustache, expressed as much concern as any soldier could feel after three years of desert warfare: 'Poor blighter's taking it hard, eh? Should have said a few words of sympathy.'

Peter's tone made evident his belief that his sympathy would give more than usual comfort to an inferior for he was, as everyone knew or pretended not to know, an Irish peer. Titles were out for the duration, to the annoyance of Levantine hostesses who greatly loved them, and Peter called himself Colonel Lisdoonvarna.

Now, having given a thought to Simon's condition, he looked up cheerfully: 'You ready, old girl? I've booked at the Continental roof garden. You like that?'

'You know I do.'

Peter led the two women back to the living-room where Simon disconsolately sat alone. At the sight of Edwina, he jumped up, looking at her with admiration that, for the moment, transcended grief.

Crossing to him, Edwina said quietly: 'Oh, Simon, I'm so sorry,' and Simon, longing to touch her, raised his hands. He seemed about to hold her in an embrace of commiseration but Peter, stepping forward and putting her on one side, took over the situation, dominating it as a right.

He spoke briskly to Simon: 'Sorry to hear what happened, old chap. I know how you feel. Knocks you sideways for a time, but we all have to face up to these things. Fortunes of war, y'know. You in for a spot of leave?'

'I've got seven days.'

'Good for you. Splendid. I've a table booked for supper so we have to be on our way, but see you again, I hope.'

Swinging round, Peter put a possessive hand on Edwina's shoulder and said, 'Come along, old girl.'

Simon, realizing Peter's ascendancy over her, turned on Edwina with a dazed and questioning expression that disturbed her. She said, 'I've forgotten my handkerchief,' and ran back to her room.

Peter returned his attention to Simon: 'Envy you, y'know. Long to be back at the front m'self. Can't stand the "Armchair" set-up.'

Simon stared at him for a moment then did his best to respond: 'You wouldn't want to be where I am, sir.' He explained that his unit was a 'Jock' column that patrolled the southern sector of the line: 'The fighting's always somewhere else.'

'Still, you're not in a damned silly office. You're leading a man's life.'

Simon agreed. He said the life suited him. If the patrols were uneventful he was compensated by the comradeship of the men.

Harriet, watching them as they talked, saw Peter avoiding a direct glance at Simon whose eyes were still red, while Simon was regaining his vitality. The worst, the most immediate, pain of loss was over and, soon enough, Hugo, for all of them, would be no more than a sad memory at the back of the mind.

Simon was saying there was one thing he enjoyed in the desert. He enjoyed finding his way around. 'I've got a sense of the place, somehow. I feel I belong there.' That morning, in despair, he would have been glad never to see the desert again. Now, envied and infected by Peter's approval of desert life, he said, 'To tell you the truth, I'll be glad to get back there. I'd like to have a real go at the bastards. They killed my brother when he was with an ambulance, bringing in the wounded. They shot them up. They knew what they were doing. I feel I owe them one.'

'That's the spirit.' Peter took a diary from an inner pocket: 'If you'd like a transfer, I might work it. A chap who's good at finding his way round has his uses in the desert. You could become a liaison officer. Would that appeal to you?'

Simon, feeling guilty that this day of misfortune might also be the day of opportunity, blushed and said, 'It would indeed, sir.'

Edwina, returning to the room as Peter was noting down Simon's name and position at the front, was relieved to find the men on easy terms. She gave Simon a conciliatory smile then, watching Peter as he wrote, stood, waiting, with a sort of avid patience until he was ready for her.

Putting the diary back in his pocket, he said, 'Right, I'll start things moving,' then he called to Edwina: 'Come along,' and she followed him obediently from the flat.

Simon, looking after them, at once forgot the proposed transfer, and felt only amazement that Edwina, who had been Hugo's girl, should now be subject to this heavy-featured colonel. It had seemed to him that while Edwina shared his love for Hugo, Hugo was not completely dead. Remembering Hugo's looks, his gentleness, his absolute niceness, he felt these qualities slighted – and yet, what good would they be to her now?

Harriet, pitying his downcast face, said: 'You'll stay to supper, won't you?'

'No. No thank you.' Simon felt he only wanted to get away from this room which held Edwina's lingering fragrance, but did not know where he would go. This flat, because it was

Edwina's flat, had had for him a glowing, beckoning quality, and he knew nowhere else in Cairo. He did not know the name of any street except the one in the army song: the Berka. That was where the men went to find bints.

'Well, have another drink before you go.'

Realizing he had no heart for bints that evening, Simon let Harriet refill his glass and asked: 'Who is this Colonel Lisdoonvarna? It's an unusual name.'

'It's an Irish name. He's Lord Lisdoonvarna but, as you know, we don't use titles these days.'

'I see.' Simon did indeed see. The fact that Peter was a peer solved a mystery but the solution was more painful than his earlier perplexity. He sat silent, glass in hand, not drinking, hearing the safragi laying the supper table. If he were going, he should go now, but instead he sat on, too dispirited to move.

The front door opened and another occupant of the flat entered the room. This was a woman older than Edwina or Harriet, delicately built with dark eyes and a fine, regular face.

Coming in quickly, saying 'Hello' to Harriet, she gave an impression of genial gaiety, an impression that surprised Simon who had recognized her at once. She was Lady Hooper. He had been one of a picnic party that had gone uninvited to the Hoopers' house in the Fayoum and had blundered in on tragedy.

Harriet said, 'Angela, do you remember Simon Boulderstone?'

'Yes, I remember.' Whether the memory was painful or not, she smiled happily on Simon and taking his hand, held it as she said: 'You were the young officer who was in the room when I brought in my little boy. We didn't know he was dead, you know: or perhaps we couldn't bear to know. It must have been upsetting for you. I'm sorry.' Angela gazed at Simon still smiling and waited as though there was point in apologizing so long after the event.

Harriet said, 'I'm afraid Simon has another reason to be upset. His brother has been killed.'

'Oh, poor boy!' She placed her other hand on top of his and held on to him: 'So we are both bereaved! You will stay with us, won't you?' She turned to Harriet to ask: 'Who's in tonight? What about Guy?' Guy was Harriet's husband. Harriet shook her head. 'Not Guy, that goes without saying. And Edwina's out with Peter. It's Dobson's night on duty at the Embassy, so that leaves only us and Percy Gibbon.'

'Percy Gibbon! Oh lord, that's good reason to go out. Let's take this beautiful young man into the world. Let's flaunt him.' She laughed at Simon and squeezed his hand: 'Where would you like to go?'

'I don't know. I've never been anywhere in Cairo. I haven't even been to the Berka.'

'Oh, oh, oh!' Angela's amusement was such that she dropped back on to the sofa taking Simon with her: 'You dreadful creature, wanting to visit the Berka!'

Simon reddened in his confusion: 'I didn't mean I wanted ... It's just that the men talk about it. It's the only street name I know.'

This renewed Angela's laughter and Simon, watching her as she wiped her eyes and said 'Oh dear, oh dear!' was disturbed by this gaiety and wondered how she could so quickly put death out of mind. Yet he smiled and Harriet, also disturbed by Angela's light-hearted behaviour, was relieved to see his smile.

'Let's send Hassan out for a taxi.' Angela turned to Harriet: 'If we're going on the tiles, we'll need more male protection. Where shall we find it? How about the Union? Who's likely to be there?'

'Castlebar, I imagine.'

Angela, who had left her husband after her son's death, had come to live in Dobson's flat hoping, as she said, to find congenial company. She had found Harriet and through her had met Castlebar. The mention of Castlebar was a joke between them and Harriet explained to Simon.

'Castlebar haunts the place. When he's not sitting on the lawn, it's as though a familiar tree had been cut down.'

Listening to this, Angela became restless and broke in to say: 'Come on. Let's get going.'

Hassan, told to find them a taxi, goggled in indignation: 'No need taxi. All food on table now.' Forced out on what he saw as a superfluous task, he came back with a gharry and said, 'No taxis, not anywhere.'

Angela, taking it for granted that Simon would accompany

them, led him down to the gharry and sat beside him. As the gharry ambled through Garden City to the main road, she held him tightly by the hand and talked boisterously so, whether he wanted to come or not, he was given no chance to refuse.

Bemused by all that was happening, he thought of her carrying the dead child into the Fayoum house, and felt she was beyond his understanding. He tried to ease his hand away but she would not let him go and so, still clasped like lovers, they crossed the dark water towards the riverside lights of Gezira.

There was no moon. The lawns of the Anglo-Egyptian Union were lit by the windows of the club house and the bright, greenish light of the Officers' Club that faced it. At the edge of the lawn, old trees, that had grown to a great height, crowded their heads darkly above the tables set out for the club members.

Having conducted Simon into the club, Angela let him go and walked on ahead, apparently looking for someone who was not there. When they sat down at a table, she was subdued as though disappointed.

Unlike the other members who were drinking coffee or Stella beer, Angela ordered a bottle of whisky and told the safragi to bring half a dozen glasses. Her advent at the Union a few weeks before had caused a sensation, but she was a sensation no longer. The Union membership comprised university lecturers, teachers of English and others of the poorer English sort while Angela was known to be a rich woman who mixed with the Cairo gambling, polo-playing set. Her nightly order of a bottle of whisky had startled the safragis at first but now it was brought without question.

Harriet, who did not like whisky, was given wine but Simon accepted the glass poured for him though he did not drink it. When they were all served, the bottle was placed like a beacon in the middle of the table and almost at once it drew Castlebar from the snooker table.

Harriet, from where she sat, could see his figure wavering through the shadows, drooping and edging round the tables, coming with cautious purpose towards the bottle, like an animal that keeps to windward of its prey. He paused a couple of yards from the table and Angela, knowing he was there, smiled to herself.

Though their friendship seemed to have sprung up fully grown, he edged forward with sly diffidence, still unable to believe in his good fortune. And, Harriet thought, he might well be diffident for it was beyond her to understand what Angela saw in him.

Harriet was not the only one critical of this middle-aged teacher-poet who had the broken-down air of a man to whom money spent on anything but drink and cigarettes was money wasted. As they observed his circuitous approach, people murmured together, their faces keen with curiosity and dis-approval. When he made the last few feet towards her, Angela jerked her head round and laughed as though he had pulled off a clever trick.

'H-h-hello, there!' he stammered, trying to sound hearty.

'Welcome. Sit beside me. Have a drink.'

Doing as he was bid, Castlebar made a deprecating noise, mumbling: 'Must let me put something in the kitty.'

'No. My treat.'

Castlebar did not argue. Taking whisky into his mouth, he held it there, moving it round his gums in ruminative apprecia-tion, then let it slide slowly down his throat. After this, he went through his usual ritual of placing a cigarette packet squarely in front of him, one cigarette propped ready to hand so there need be no interval between smokes. As he concentrated on getting the cigarette upright, Angela smiled indulgently. All set, he raised his thick, pale eyelids and they exchanged a long, meaningful look.

Angela whispered, 'Any news?'

'I had a cable. She says she'll get back by hook or by crook.'

They were talking of Castlebar's wife who had gone on holiday to England and been marooned there by the outbreak of war. The threat of her return hung over Angela who said, 'But surely she won't make it?'

Castlebar giggled: 'S-s-she's a p-p-pretty ruthless bitch. If anyone can do it, she will.' He appeared to take pride in having such a wife and Angela, raising her brows, turned from him until he made amends.

'Don't worry. She'll tread on anyone's face to get what she wants, but it won't work this time. Why should they send her out?' Castlebar slid his hand across the table towards her and she bent and gave it a rapid kiss.

Their enclosed intimacy embarrassed Simon, who looked away, while Harriet, feeling excluded, was envious and depressed. Guy could be affectionate but he never lost consciousness of the outside world. It was always there for him and its claim on him had caused dissension between them.

Leaving Angela and Castlebar to their communion, she asked Simon about his army life. When they had climbed the pyramid together, they had sat at the top and talked of the war in the desert. He had said, 'I don't know what it's like out there,' but now he knew and she asked him how he spent his days.

'Not doing much. We're so far from the main positions, there seems no point in being there.'

'But of course there is a point?'

'Oh yes. I asked our sergeant once. I said, "What's the use, our being here, bored stiff and doing nothing?" and he said, "What'd happen if we weren't here?" You can see what he meant.'

A taxi came in the gate and a man, jumping down and hurriedly settling with the driver, came to the whisky as though it had sent a call out to him. This new arrival was Castlebar's friend, Jake Jackman, who described himself as a freelance journalist, but what he really did, not even Castlebar could say. His aquiline face, though not unhandsome, was spoilt by an aggrieved expression that became more aggrieved when he saw Angela and Castlebar holding hands. Still, Angela was the owner of the bottle and he had to accept things as they were. Forced to show her some courtesy, he stretched his lips in a momentary smile and saying, 'Mind if I join you?' sat down before she could reply. She laughed and pushed the bottle towards him. Having taken a drink, he bent forward and pulling at his long beak of a nose, looked angrily at Simon: 'I suppose *you're* wondering why I'm not in uniform?'

Simon began to disclaim any such interest but Jackman was not listening. Having distracted Angela and Castlebar from each other, he told them: 'You know that old bag Rutter? Got too much money for her own good. Saw her at Groppi's this afternoon and what do you think she said? She said, "Young man, why aren't you in uniform?" Impertinent old cow!'

Castlebar giggled: 'What did you say?'

'I said, "Madam, if you think I'll sacrifice my life to preserve you and your bank balance, you've got another think coming." That ruffled the old hen's feathers. She said, "You're a very rude young man!" "You're dead right, missus," I said.' Having recounted his story, Jackman sat up, willing to think of other things: 'You people going somewhere to eat?'

Angela looked tenderly at Castlebar: 'What do you want to do, Bill?'

Castlebar, lowering his eyelids, smiled, conveying his future plans, but for the moment he was content to eat: 'We might get a bite somewhere.'

'The Extase, then,' Angela said and Jackman jumped up, ready to depart.

They could have walked to the Extase, which was on the river bank at Bulaq, but Angela waved to a taxi at the gate and it took them across the bridge. The fare was only a few piastres and Angela allowed Castlebar to settle it while she went into the Extase to pay the entrance fees. Simon, unused to her largesse, hurried after her, offering his share, but she closed his hand over the notes he was holding and led him inside, a captive guest.

Harriet had her own ways of repaying Angela's hospitality and so, no doubt, had Castlebar, but Jackman accepted it without question, having once said to Harriet, 'If Angela insists on taking us to places we can't afford, then it's up to her. She knows I haven't the lolly for these parties.' This might be true but, Harriet noted, he was, more often than not, self-invited.

Inside the open-air night club, there was the usual crowd of officers and such girls as they could find. The officers, most of them on leave, were drunk or nearly drunk, and there was an atmosphere of uproar.

As they queued for a table, Harriet said to Angela: 'Aren't you suffocated by all this noise?'

Angela's laughter rose above it: 'Can't get enough of it.'

The Extase, being so close to the river, was held to be cooler than other places but the arc lights poured heat down on the guests and the guests, amorous and sweating, generated more heat. It was not a place Harriet much liked. On a previous visit she had seen Guy with Edwina, and the shock of this sight still remained with her although Guy had protested he was merely comforting Edwina, who was distressed because Peter had failed to keep a date. Looking towards the table where they had been seated, she felt an impulse to run from the place – but she had nowhere to go and no one to go with.

When their turn came to be led to a table, Angela gave an excited scream and pointed to the people at the next table. One of them was a friend and Angela demanded that the tables be placed together so the two parties could become one. She introduced the friend as 'Mortimer'. Mortimer, a plain girl with a pleasant expression and a sun reddened skin, was in uniform of a sort and had with her two young captains in the regiment that was nicknamed 'the Cherrypickers'.

Looking round the double table, Angela said, 'Isn't this fun?' and Mortimer, mellow with drink, agreed, 'Great fun', but there was no response from the others.

Though the tables were united, there was division between the factions. The two hussars, called Terry and Tony, had been drinking champagne and were in an elated condition. They took no notice of Simon but the other men, Castlebar and Jackman, roused in them a hostile merriment. They stared unbelievingly at them then, turning to each other, fell together with gusts of laughter that brought tears to their eyes.

Mortimer chided them, 'Come on, now, boys!' but they were beyond her control.

To make matters worse, another non-combatant, one who had experienced Angela's liberality in the past, approached the party and stood there like a mendicant, begging to be allowed in. He was Major Cookson, who, having lost all his Greek property and knowing no life but a life of pleasure, hung around places like the Extase and provided lonely officers with telephone numbers. Harriet, meeting his humble, pleading gaze, felt discomfited but it was not for her to invite him to the table. Angela was too absorbed with her talk to notice him and so he stood, a very thin, epicene figure, much aged by his changed circumstances, the nubbled surface of his silk suit brushed with grime and his buckskin shoes, more grey than white, breaking at the sides.

223

Harriet thought 'The war has done for us all' though, in fact, she and Guy were more fortunate than many. Because they had known Dobson in Bucharest, they had been lifted out of the clutter of refugees and given a room in his Embassy flat. She looked down at her own sandals, whitened each morning by the servants, and felt pleased with them. Yet, how curious it was that they could raise her self-esteem!

Cookson's behaviour during the evacuation from Greece had given her no cause to respect him but now, seeing him there old, dry, brittle, seedy, like a piece of seaweed that circumstances had cast above the tide line, she was sorry for him. She touched Angela's arm and whispered to her. Angela, turning at once, called to him: 'Major Cookson, have you come to join us?'

A chair was found and Cookson was fitted in between Harriet and Castlebar. As he stretched a gaunt hand towards Castlebar's cigarette pack, Castlebar with a snarling glance, like a hungry dog espying another, moved it out of reach.

The Cherrypickers now found a new object for their scornful regard. As they stared at him, Cookson, probably attracted by their virile, youthful good looks, grew red and cast down his eyes. Terry, leaning towards him, enquired: 'Did Lady Hooper say *Major* Cookson?'

Cookson gave a brief, unhappy nod. His rank, acquired during the First War, was said by his enemies to have been acting and unpaid. Terry now asked with elaborate courtesy: 'Brigade of Guards, weren't you?' This time Cookson gave a brief, unhappy shake of the head.

Terry looked at Tony: 'There was a Cookson in the Guards, wasn't there? You must have known him?'

Tony heartily agreed: 'Jove, yes. Dear old Cookson. We used to call him Queenie. Had a queer way of sitting, Cookson had. Chaps used to ask "Why is Queenie like an engine?"'

Terry, knowing the answer to that one, put his hands over his eyes and howled with laughter.

Simon, too, knew the answer to that one and it increased his nervous disgust with the people about him. Because of his youth and silence, he was ignored by most of them but that did not worry him. What did worry him was their strangeness and hilarity. There were only eight of them but for all the sense he could make of the party, there might have been a couple of dozen. Even the Cherrypickers, on leave as he was, seemed to him unreal in their ribald insolence. He had never known men behave so badly in company. He was shocked. And, he remembered, it was still the day on which Hugo had died.

There was a pause while a small boy put glasses on the table, and a Nubian safragi, dripping sweat on to the customers, brought champagne in a bucket. Breaking the wire with his hand, he let the cork fly away. The ice had melted and the champagne, a gritty, sweetish German brand, was warm. Food came with the same lack of ceremony. There was a plate of steak for everyone.

'We didn't order steak,' Angela said.

'Only this meat,' said the safragi: 'All persons same. Very busy this place, this time.'

Simon knew that coming to Cairo had been a mistake. The men spoke of it as though life here was a perpetual carousal but to him it seemed a mad-house. Even the waiters were mad. When he learnt that Hugo was dead, he should have foregone his leave and returned to his unit. There, if he had nothing else, he had the comfort of familiar routine. The men would have understood how he felt but here no one understood or cared. But, of course, only two of them – Harriet Pringle and that odd, excitable woman called Lady Hooper – knew of Hugo's death. He looked at Harriet who, feeling his dejection, smiled at him and he smiled back, grateful that she had once had supper with Hugo and knew a little about him.

The table served, the Cherrypickers started up again. Discussing Queenie's favourite flower, they decided that it was a pansy. But was it a yellow or a white pansy?

Harriet was bored by the Cherrypickers yet scarcely knew with whom to ally herself. They were fighting men and, unlike Jackman, they were ready to risk their lives for others. Their trousers were purple-red in colour because – so the story went – in some early engagement, they had fought till the blood from their wounds flowed down to their feet. They could claim to have earned their amusement, but Cookson was poor game.

Moved to his defence, she said, 'Your jokes are so feeble. Can't we talk of something else?'

They gaped at her, silenced by their own astonishment, and Mortimer, looking at Harriet, nodded her approval. Feeling they were in sympathetic agreement, the two women began to talk to each other. Mortimer, Harriet discovered, was drowsy not from alcohol but from lack of sleep. She and a co-driver had driven to Iraq and back, taking it in turns to cat-nap so they could keep going through the night. This, she explained, was against regulations but gave them twenty-four hours of freedom when they got back. The co-driver had taken herself to bed but Mortimer had gone to the Semiramis bar for a drink.

'Where I met these two blighters,' she said, yawning, damp-eyed with tiredness yet keeping awake from sheer cordiality.

'I envy you,' Harriet said: 'I was about to join the Wrens but got married instead.'

They talked about the days immediately before the war when there was no longer caution or pretence that a show-down could be avoided. Realizing that war was inevitable, the English were united in a terrible excitement.

'We were all doomed, or thought we were,' said Harriet.

Mortimer asked, 'How did you get out here?' and Harriet explained that her husband, on leave, was ordered back to his lectureship in Bucharest. He and Harriet, having married in haste, travelled eastwards through countries mobilizing troops and reaching Bucharest on the day England entered the war.

Mortimer, at the same time, was embarking on a troopship for the Middle East. 'And I might have been with her,' Harriet thought, before she went on to explain how she and Guy had been evacuated to Greece and then to Egypt.

She asked, 'What is your first name?'

Mortimer, laughing and yawning at the same time, said, 'These days I have only one name, I'm Mortimer.'

The rich, red-brown of Mortimer's round face was set off by the periwinkle blue of her scarf, the privileged wear of a service that had once been voluntary and still had a scapegrace distinction.

'I suppose I wouldn't be allowed to join out here?' Harriet asked.

'No, there are no training facilities here.'

Angela said: 'You wouldn't qualify, darling. To get into

226

Mortimer's outfit you have to be a lizzie or a drunk or an Irish-woman.'

Looking at Mortimer with her cropped hair, crumpled shirt and dirty cotton slacks, Harriet asked: 'Which are you?'

'Me? I drink.'

A small man had come on to the stage wearing white tie and tails. Clasping his hands before him like an opera singer, he opened his mouth but before he could make a sound, a man in the audience bawled: 'Russian.' This was immediately taken up and from all over the audience came a clamour of: 'Russian, Russian, Russian. We want Russian.' The performer threw out his hands, in a despairing gesture, and Tony asked, 'What's all this about?'

Angela told him that the performer sang a gibberish which he could make sound like any language the audience chose, but he could not do Russian. The Cherrypickers, with expressions of concern, looked at each other and Terry said, 'Can't do Russian? M'deah, how queah!'

Jackman who had been silent, having no interest in any conversation but his own, now lost patience and said to Castlebar: 'A tedious lot, our wooden-headed soldiery!'

Apparently not relating this remark to himself, Terry asked him: 'And what are you doing out here?'

'War correspondent.'

The Cherrypickers looked him over, noted his expression of baleful belligerency, and realizing that picking on him would be much like picking on a hedgehog, they shifted their attention on to Castlebar who appeared less formidable.

'What do you do?'

'I-I-I'm a poet.'

The Cherrypickers collapsed together, clutching each other in an agony of mirth, while Castlebar, his threatening eye-tooth showing on his lower lip, watched them from behind lowered lids. He was gathering himself to speak but Jackman got in first.

'I'm surprised two priceless specimens like you haven't come under the protection of BPHA.' He ran the letters together with an explosive spit that stopped the Cherrypickers in mid-laugh.

'Come again?' Terry said.

'B-P-H-A: Bureau for the Preservation of Hereditary Aristocracy. All the dukes, lords and what-have-yous are being brought back to base for their own safety. Too many of them wiped out in the First War. Can't let it happen again, can we?'

Terry looked perplexed: 'Is this true?'

'Of course it's true,' Jackman looked at Harriet: 'Your friend Lisdoonvarna's one of them.'

'Peter? He's moving heaven and earth to get back to the front.'

'Well, he won't get back. He'll be preserved whether he likes it or not.'

Having impressed everyone at the table, Jackman, slapping his hand down on his knee, sang at the top of his voice:

> 'Queen Farida, Queen Farida,
> How the boys would like to ride her . . .'

The song had only three traditional verses but Jackman and Castlebar had added to them and as they increased in obscenity, people at neighbouring tables moved their chairs to stare at the singer and his companions. Then the Levantine manager, making a swift journey across the club floor, put a bill down in front of Jackman who came to an indignant stop.

The manager said, 'You pay. You go.'

'Go? Go where?'

'You go away. *Iggri.*'

'Like hell I will.'

Angela, picking up the bill, said, 'Yes, I think we will go.' As she took out her note-case, Jackman raged at her: 'Don't give them a cent. We'll miss the belly dance. If they turn us out, they can't make us pay . . .'

Angela, speaking with unusual quiet, said, 'Shut up. This isn't the first time we've been thrown out because of you. I'm getting tired of your behaviour.'

Jackman was thunderstruck by her severity and said nothing while she counted notes in a heap on to the bill. She let the Cherrypickers pay their share but when Simon tried to contribute, she put a hand over his and gently pushed the money away.

'Where now?' asked Castlebar.

Angela whispered in his ear. He grinned. 'Mystery tour,' she said. 'Come along,' and they all followed her out to the road. A row of taxis waited at the club entrance and Angela signalled to

228

the first two. When they were seated, the others saw that Cookson had been left standing on the pavement. Angela beckoned to him but he shook his head and sadly wandered away.

She said: 'He's guessed where we're going. Not his cuppa.'

'Where *are* we going?' Mortimer asked.

'Wait and see.'

Harriet, too, guessed where they were going and had Simon showed any inclination to leave the party, she would have asked him to see her home; but he seemed bemused by everything about him and she did not wish to leave him alone among a crowd of indifferent strangers.

They seated themselves in the first taxi. Jackman, pushing in beside Mortimer, eyed her with lewd amusement: 'So you run around in a little lorry? And how do you spend your spare time?'

'We scrub out the ambulances that bring in the dead and wounded.'

'Nice work, eh?'

'Not very nice. The other day one of the girls, who had a cut in her hand, got gas gangrene.'

Scenting a story, Jackman sat up: 'What happened to her?'

'She died.'

Jackman sniffed and pulled at his nose while Harriet thought enviously: 'They belong to a world at war. They have a part in it: they even die,' but Harriet had no part in anything. She asked Mortimer which route they took to Iraq.

They tried to vary it, Mortimer said, but however they went, they had to cross the Syrian desert. Sometimes they headed straight for Damascus then turned east. Once they went to Homs so they could visit Palmyra but it had been a rough trip and they had broken a spring. Another time they went by the Allenby Bridge over the Jordan so they could see Krak de Chevalier.

'The Levant sounds wonderful. I'd love to go to Damascus.'

'We'd give you a lift. We're not supposed to, of course, but we often pick up people on the roads. The matron says it's dangerous but women alone are safer here than they are in England. We can thank Lady Hester Stanhope for that. She impressed the Arab world so every Englishwoman has a special status in those parts.'

'I wish I could go with you.'

Mortimer smiled at her enthusiasm: 'Any time.'

The taxis had taken them past the Esbekiyah into Clot Bey where women stood in the shadows beneath the Italianate arches. From there they passed into streets so narrow that the pedestrians moved to the walls to enable the taxis to pass. No one, it seemed, needed sleep in this part of the city. Women looked out from every doorway. It was here that the squaddies came in search of entertainment and every café was alight to entice them in. Loudspeakers, hung over entrances, gave out the endless sagas relayed by Egyptian radio, while from indoors came the blare of nikolodeons or player pianos thumping out popular songs.

As the taxis slowed down in the crowded lanes, beggars thrust their hands into the windows and small boys, leaping up and clinging to the framework, shouted: 'You wan' my sister? My sister very good, very cheap.'

Jake, putting his face close to them and mimicking their infant voices, shouted back: 'My sister all pink inside like white lady,' and the boys screamed with laughter.

The taxis reached a wider street where the women put their heads out of upper windows to importune the new arrivals. Some of them, leaning out too far, betrayed the fact that, richly dressed and bejewelled from the waist up, they were naked below. Jake began to sing: 'Greek bints and gyppo bints, all around I see, Singing "Young artillery man abide with me".' He gave Simon a sharp slap on the knee: 'You a young artillery man?'

Simon, bewildered, shook his head.

Angela asked him: 'Do you know where you are?'

Simon, who had been startled by the blow, looked out and asked, 'Is it the Berka?'

She laughed. 'The very place!' The taxis came to a stop in front of a house that looked like a small old-fashioned cinema. 'If there's anything to be seen, we'll see it here.'

The house front was bright with red and yellow neon and there was the usual uproar of Oriental and western music from inside and out; it suggested pleasure, but the pleasure-seekers, queuing outside, were an abject and seedy lot. A doorman controlled the queue and Castlebar was summoned from the second taxi by Angela to negotiate with him.

The English visitors watched as Castlebar and the doorman

230

went down the line, the doorman speaking to each man in turn. Whatever he was trying to arrange did not meet with much response. At last a young man in trousers and crumpled cotton jacket, offered himself and was led away, downcast and down-at-heel, as though to his execution. Castlebar, returning, opened the door of Angela's taxi: 'All fixed up,' he said with satisfaction.

'What are they going to do with him?' Mortimer asked.

'He's the performer. In return, he'll get it for nothing.'

Holding to Simon as though fearing he would run away, Angela pushed him towards the door: 'Now, Sugar, out you get. What lots you'll have to tell the boys back in the desert.' She led the way into the house and the rest of the party, too befuddled to ask what was about to happen, followed. Harriet, knowing she would be safer inside than alone in the street with pimps, prostitutes and beggars, went with them. They were shown by a safragi into a downstair room where they stood close together, not speaking, transfixed by nervous curiosity. The room was hot and a smell of carbolic overlaid the resident smells of garlic and ancient sweat.

A half-negro woman, in a dirty pink wrapper, came in through a side door. Fat, elderly, bored and indifferent to the audience, she threw off the wrapper and lay on a bunk, legs apart.

One of the Cherrypickers whispered hoarsely: 'God, let's get out of here,' but he did not move.

The young man from the queue entered, wearing his shirt. He held his trousers in his hand and, giving the audience a sheepish glance, stood as though he did not know what to do next. The woman, having no time to waste, muttered, 'Tala hinna,' and held up her arms in a caricature of amorous invitation. The young man looked at her, then fell upon her. The union was brief. As he sank down, spent, she pushed him aside and, throwing the wrapper round her shoulders, made off on flat, grimy feet.

'Is that all?' Angela asked. She sounded defrauded but Simon felt they had more reason to feel ashamed.

The young man, left alone, was concerned to get back into his trousers. This done, he crossed to Castlebar, smiling his relief that the show was over. He said: 'Professor, sir, you do not know me, but I know you. At times I am attending your lectures.'

Castlebar began to stammer his consternation but unable to get a word out, offered the young man a cigarette.

Everyone, from a sense of chivalry, waited while cigarettes were smoked, then Angela, having given undue praise for the young man's performance, offered him a thousand piastre note.

'Oh, no, no,' he took a step back: 'I do not want. If it pleased you, that is enough.'

Castlebar, at last able to speak, asked him. 'Do you often give these performances?'

'No.' The young man looked dismayed by the question then, fearing he might seem impolite, excused himself: 'You see, we Egyptians are not like you Europeans. We are liking to do such things in private.'

'I think it's time to go,' Angela said. As they filed out, they each took the young man by the hand and murmured congratulations in an attempt to compensate him for the humiliation they had put upon him.

Two

The taxis, taking them back, stopped first outside Shepherd's where the Cherrypickers alighted, and Simon said: 'This will do for me, too.' As he thanked Angela and said his goodnights, Harriet asked if he would come to supper before his leave was up. He agreed to telephone her but it was a long time before she heard from him again.

The Cherrypickers were standing in front of the hotel. Imagining they would have no use for him he was turning to cross the road when Terry said, 'Come and have a last one.'

Surprised, taking it more as an order than an invitation, he went with them towards the hotel steps. Even at that hour, the life of the Esbekiyah went on. Dragomen, in important dark robes, carrying heavy sticks, pursued the three officers, offering them: 'Special for you, many delights.'

'Thanks, we've just had them,' Terry said, raising a laugh among the people still sitting out at the terrace tables.

Inside, Simon saw by the hotel clock that it was past midnight and he felt himself delivered from the day that had passed. No other day, ever, at any time, could be as black as that day had been. He even felt reconciled to the Cherrypickers, realizing they were not, as he had supposed, insufferably arrogant. Despite their splendid regiment and the advantage it gave them, they had, in fact, been challenged by the civilians and now, alone with him, they became simple and friendly.

He said to Terry, 'What did you think of the show, sir?'

'You mean that poor devil with the tart? I thought it pretty poor.'

Tony and Simon joined in agreeing with him and the three were united in their dislike for the exhibition. Simon was also reassured by the hotel interior which reminded him of the Putney Odeon. It was, no doubt, beyond his pocket but was not, as he had feared, beyond his dreams. The atmosphere, however, was disturbed, as though some catastrophe had taken place. Senior officers stood in the hall amid heaps of military baggage, drinking, but with an air of waiting expectancy.

Terry whispered to Tony, 'D'you think the balloon's going up? I'll mingle – see what's cooking.'

Simon watched respectfully as Terry moved among the officers looking for one of his own rank. He, himself, would not have dared to speak to any of them.

Returning, Terry said quietly, his face expressionless: 'Something's happening, all right, but they don't know what it is. Reconnaissance planes've seen preparations in the southern sector. Feeling is, jerry's all set for the big breakthrough.'

Tony permitted himself a little excitement: 'Then we'll be in at the kill?'

Simon, stuck in Cairo for a week, wondered if he would ever be in on anything. He had reached Suez during an emergency and been sent straight to the front amid the turmoil of an army that had been routed, or nearly routed. An army of remnants, someone called it.

He said, 'I suppose they had to break through sooner or later. I could see how thin our line was. I asked my CO why they didn't come on and he thought they just needed a rest.'

'Needed a rest? Like hell they needed a rest,' Terry said. 'I don't know how much action you've seen, old chap, but in our area we fought back and stopped the blighters in their tracks. That's why they didn't come on. We wouldn't give them another inch.'

'I see.' Simon spoke meekly, aware he had seen too little action to be any sort of judge of events. His sector, the great open tract south of the Ruweisat Ridge, was patrolled by mobile columns ordered to 'sting the jerries wherever and whenever they got the chance'. Simon, a junior officer in the dullest part of the line, had only once had a chance to sting anyone.

He said, 'When I was given leave, things seemed, to be at a standstill.' He had imagined the whole line becalmed for ever in the treacle heat of summer and now, it seemed, he had only to leave the desert for the war to come to life. Despondently, he said, 'My sector's south. Wish I was going with you.'

But why should he not go with them? His stay in Cairo, short though it was, had been a disaster. He wanted no more of it. At the thought of returning to the front, he rose for the first time since Hugo's death out of total desolation. To be in at the kill! To kill the killers! Everything else - Edwina's perfidy, the wretched party at the night club, the exhibition in the brothel - went from his mind and he eagerly asked: 'Can I come with you? I suppose you've got transport?'

'Yep, we managed to scrounge a pick-up. We could squeeze you in, but supposing it's only a twitch? You'd lose your leave for nothing.' Terry looked to Tony and laughed: 'If I had another week, I'd take it.'

Tony laughed, too: 'Leave doesn't come all that often!'

Simon did not explain his urgent desire to return to the desert but said, 'I'd be grateful for a lift.'

'OK. We're making an early start, so let's get that drink and call it a day.'

The Cherrypickers called for Simon at 06.30 hours next morning. Conditioned to rising at dawn, he was ready, waiting on the hotel steps. The pick-up, an eight-hundred-weight truck, was roomy enough. The three could travel in comfort.

The Cherrypickers had nothing to say that morning. Terry was at the wheel with Tony beside him. Neither had a word for Simon as he settled into the back with the baggage. He, for his part, knew he should speak only when spoken to, so they drove in silence through the empty streets in the pale morning sunlight.

The road out of Cairo was already a commonplace to Simon: the mud brick villas, the roadside trees holding out discs of flame-coloured florets, the scented bean fields, then the pyramids and the staring, blunted face of the sphinx. None of it stirred him now. He sank into a doze but outside Mena, where they ran into open desert, he was jerked awake as Terry braked to a stop. A man had been killed on the road. The body lay on the verge, wrapped in white cloth, and other men, workmen in galabiahs, seeing the truck approach, had run in front of it and held up their hands.

Terry shouted down to them, 'How'd it happen?'

The men, crowding round the truck, did not look very dangerous. Unable to understand the question, they glanced at each other then one said, 'Poor man dead', and from a habit of courtesy, grinned and put a hand over his mouth.

Saying, 'Oh, lord!' Terry put his fingers into his shirt pocket and pulled out some folded notes. Giving the man a pound, he said, 'For the wife and kids.' The spokesman, accepting it and touching his brow and breast in gratitude, waved to the others to let the truck through.

Driving on, Terry asked, 'What did you make of that?'

Tony laughed. 'Willing to wound and yet afraid to strike. They're easily bought off.'

'Fellow killed by an army lorry, I'd guess.'

Simon returned to sleep. Outside Alexandria, on the shore road near the soda lakes, Tony shook him awake, saying, 'How about brekker?'

The Cherrypickers had a picnic basket with them, packed by their hotel. The three men sat on the seaside rocks in the warm sea breeze. The food – portions of cold roast duck, fresh rolls, butter, coffee in a thermos flask – was far above the army fare to which Simon was used, but he was too self-conscious to express any opinion.

Terry asked, rather irritably, 'This all right for you?'

'I'll say. It's super.'

'Good. Thought perhaps you were tired of roast duck.'

'Never tasted it before.'

Simon was left to eat his fill while Terry and Tony discussed duck-shooting, a sport that was, they decided, carried to excess in diplomatic circles.

'Soon won't be a damned duck left,' Terry grumbled as he cleaned off a drumstick and started on a wing.

Tony gave him a sly, sidelong smile: 'Jolly nice, though, to have a bird in the fridge to pick at when you come in late.'

The meal finished, the Cherrypickers lay, eyes closed, in the sun while Simon, awaiting the order to move, threw stones into the slowly moving sea. At the eastern end of the shore road the traffic was light and the three men rested in a quiet that was almost peace. But the heat was growing and Terry, rousing himself, said, 'Better get underway.' For twenty miles or so he was able to keep a steady sixty miles an hour but reaching the forward area, they were slowed not only by trucks and cars but by infantry moving west.

Tony said, 'Certainly seems things are moving.'

When the sound of gunfire could be heard, Simon felt a familiar fear, yet, seeing about him the equipment of war, he had a sense of returning to the known world.

The petrol cans, set at intervals beside the road, indicated the direction of the different corps and divisions. None of this had relevance for the three men whose units were a good way south. Observing tanks in the distance, Terry raised his brows: 'Wonder what they're up to? Looks like training exercises.' A mile further on, he drew up by a supply dump and gave Simon a casual order: 'Care to go in and ask if they'll fill us up? Might get some gen while you're there.'

Dropping down off the back of the truck, Simon crossed to the wire enclosure. It was mid-day, the time of burning heat, and the smell of the dump hit him while he was several yards from it. The Column's signalman, Ridley, purveyor of scandals and rumours, had told him that food intended for the British civilians in Palestine was usually seized by the ordnance officers at Kantara: 'They take their whack and the rest goes into the blue to rot. Dead waste, I call it.' Ridley had no love for British officials but he had an acute dislike for ordnance officers who, he said, 'grow fat on what we don't get – which is proper grub.'

Admitted into the compound, Simon was directed to the command truck where he found the officer in charge at a desk beneath a lean-to. The stench trapped under the canvas was sickening but the officer, flushed and flustered, had other things to worry about. Hearing Simon approach, he said over his shoulder, 'What the hell do you want?'

'Petrol, sir.'

'Ah!' Simon's inoffensive request caused the officer to relax for the moment. Pushing back from the desk and wiping his face, he took out a cigarette: 'First today. Bloody circus here since that new chap took over.'

'We could see tanks in training. We wondered what was up.'

'It's the new chap, Monty they call him. He wants everyone fighting fit. Says he'll put 8th Army on its toes, so it seems things are hotting up.'

'There was a belief in Cairo that the show had started.'

'Not up here, it hasn't.'

'In the southern sector perhaps?'

'Could be. Nobody tells me anything.' The officer, not telling anything himself, took one more puff at his cigarette then squashed it into a tin where half-smoked cigarettes were twisted together like a nest of caterpillars. He stared about him, fearing some other demand would be made on him, but seeing only Simon, he lit another cigarette.

'Right. I'll give you a chitty then bring her in and fill her up. There'll be a Naafi truck round shortly if you feel like a snack.'

In mid-afternoon Ruweisat Ridge appeared like a shadow through the fog of heat with immense clouds of dust rising and turning into the sky behind it. Tony said, 'Someone's getting it over there.'

Formations of Wellingtons were going south and Terry said with delight, 'We'll drive straight into it,' but a mile further on, when they had begun to feel the vibrations of heavy artillery, a military police car blocked the route and a policeman directed them to take a barrel track that ran eastwards, away from the battle.

Terry put up an angry protest: 'That's no good to us. We're not going that way. The 11th Hussars are down in Himeimat and we've got to join them.'

'No, sir, you must get on the track and stay on it. Himeimat's under heavy fire. Doubt if any of your chaps are left there now. You follow the track and you'll get to Samaket – if Samaket's still there.'

'If there's a barney on, we ought to be in it. If the Hussars are not at Himeimat, where are they?'

'Your guess is as good as mine, sir.'

Forced to turn eastwards, the three men grumbled at each other, disappointed yet excited. Terry said, 'We were almost in it – and now where are we going? It's like being chucked out of the theatre half-way through the show.'

238

In late afternoon the track, which had dropped south, brought them into a flat stretch of sand marked out with barrels to form enclosures for tank repair units, supply dumps, vehicle workshops, dressing stations and mortuary huts. Simon had seen something similar in his early desert days and knew it was a depot for the battle in progress. They stopped at the command vehicle where a captain hurried towards them with the excited air of a man who brings good news. The enemy, he said, had attempted a breakthrough just north of Himeimat.

Terry struck the wheel in a rage: 'We've missed it. We've ruddy well missed it.'

The captain laughed. 'You haven't missed a thing.'

'Where are the jerries now, then?'

'Stuck in the mine fields.'

Terry swung round to face Tony: 'We must get in on this,' then asked the captain: 'You think they'll get any further?'

'There's no knowing. They've put in a fair bit of armour. Our reconnaissance reported a hundred or more Mark IIIs in the gap, but there's a storm blowing up. Dust so thick you can't tell sand from shit.'

In the general good fellowship, Simon found courage to enquire about his Column which he had left to the east of Ragil.

'What! Hardy's lot?' the captain gave a laugh that was almost a gibe: 'Last seen on the Cairo barrel track.'

'Not in action, I suppose?'

'Rather not. Seems like they were looking for rabbits.'

Simon jumped down from the pick-up. He could not get in on the fight and he had no excuse for staying with the Cherrypickers. He must wait for a vehicle that would take him to wherever the Column was now.

As the hussars set off again, the captain shouted after them: 'Mind you don't drive straight into the bag.' He gave Simon a look and said, 'I've known that happen before now,' then, having nothing more to say to an inexperienced second lieutenant, he walked back to the command vehicle.

Simon carried his kit into the shade of a hut and sat down beside it. He could see the pick-up disappearing down the track in a cloud of dust. He envied the Cherrypickers but felt no regrets at parting with them. He had learnt independence during his months in the desert. In early days, he had attached himself to anyone who could, in some way, replace the lost relationships of home, but the need for those relationships had died as his friends died. He had become wary of affections that seemed always to end in tragedy. This last death, Hugo's death, had, he felt, brought his emotional life to a close. He no longer wanted intimates or cronies. He told himself he could manage very well on his own.

Three

Dissatisfaction – chiefly Harriet's – was eroding the Pringles' marriage. Harriet had not enough to do, Guy too much. Feeling a need to justify his civilian status, he worked outside of normal hours at the Institute, organizing lectures, entertainments for troops and any other activity that could give him a sense of purpose. Harriet saw in his tireless bustle an attempt to escape a situation that did not exist. Even had he been free to join the army, his short sight would have failed him. He thought himself into guilt in order to justify his exertions, and his exertions saved him from facing obnoxious realities.

Or so she thought. So thinking, she felt not so much resentment as a profound disappointment. Perhaps she had expected too much from marriage, but were her expectations unreasonable? Did all married couples spend their evenings apart? She felt that their relationship had reached an impasse but Guy was content enough. Things were much as he wanted them to be and if he noticed her discontent, it was only to wonder at it. He felt concern, seeing her too thin for health, but saw no reason to blame himself. He blamed the Egyptian climate and suggested she take passage on a boat due, some time soon, to sail round the Cape to England.

She had been dumbfounded by the suggestion. She would not consider it for a moment but said: 'We came together and when we leave, we'll leave together.' And that, she thought, decided that.

Guy seldom came in for meals and when he returned to the flat one lunch-time, she asked with pleasurable surprise: 'Are you home for the rest of the day?'

He laughed at the idea. Of course he was not home for the rest of the day. He had come to change his clothes. He was to attend a ceremony at the Moslem cemetery and had to hurry.

Harriet, following him to their room, said, 'But you will stay for lunch?'

'No. Before I go to the cemetery, I have to interview a couple of men who want to teach at the Institute.'

'So you're going to the City of the Dead?' Harriet was amazed. During their early days in Cairo, when he had had time to see the sights, he had rejected the City of the Dead as a 'morbid show', so what was taking him there now? He was going from a sense of duty. One of his pupils had been killed in a car accident and he was to attend, not the funeral, but the *arba'in*, the visit to the dead that ended the forty days of official mourning.

'Can I come with you?'

Guy, harassed by the need to dress himself all over again that day, said, 'No. It's probably only for men. But why not? It won't hurt them to be reminded that women exist. Yes, come if you like.'

He was a large, bespectacled, untidy man, now much improved by his well-cut dark blue suit, but he could not leave it like that. Stuffing his pockets with books and papers, he managed to revert to his usual negligent appearance, and becoming more cheerful, said, 'Meet me at Groppi's at three.'

'But will you *be* there at three?'

'Of course. Now, don't be late. I've a busy evening ahead, so we'll go early and leave early.'

As he left the room, she saw his wallet half out of his rear pocket and shouted, 'Put your wallet in before it gets nicked.'

'Thanks. Must hurry. Got a taxi waiting. Remember, don't be late. If you're late, I'll have to start without you.'

During September, the heat of summer had settled, layer upon layer, in the streets until they were compacted under a dead weight of heat which veiled the city like a yellow fog. Groppi's garden, a gravelled, open space surrounded by house walls and scented by coffee and cakes, was like a vast cube of Turkish delight.

Wandering into it at the sticky, blazing hour of three in the afternoon, Harriet saw that Guy was not there. She asked herself why had she ever thought he would be? He was always late yet his assurances were so convincing, she still believed he would come when he said he would.

Army men saw Groppi's as a good place for picking up girls and Harriet disliked being alone there. She had chosen a table close to the wall and felt herself to be an object of too much interest. She would, if she could, have hidden herself altogether.

The sun, immediately overhead, poured down through the cloth of the umbrellas like molten brass. Creepers, kept alive by water seeping from a perforated hose, rustled their mat of papery leaves. With nothing but creepers for company, she sat with downcast eyes and told herself she could murder Guy.

Someone said, 'Hello,' and, looking up, she saw Dobson had come to sit with her. They met at almost every meal time in the flat yet she welcomed him as a dear friend unseen for months and her spirits rose.

Dobson, as usual, had an amusing story to tell: 'They say things are so bad in Russia, they've started opening the churches. What I heard was: Stalin was driving out of the Kremlin one night and the headlights of his car lit a poster that said "Religion – the opium of the masses!" "My God," said Stalin, "That's just what we want these days: opium" and he ordered the churches to be reopened.'

'Did he really say "My God"?'

Dobson's soft sloping shoulders shook as he laughed: 'Oh, Harriet, how sharp you are!' He brushed a hand over his puffs of hair and asked, 'What would he say? He'd say "Oh, Russian winter!"'

'Really, Dobbie, you're ridiculous!'

By the time Guy arrived full of excuses and apologies, Harriet had forgotten her annoyance. When he asked if she had been waiting long, she replied blandly: 'Since three o'clock.'

He took this lightly: 'Oh, well, you had Dobbie.'

Although he had earlier emphasized the need to 'go early and leave early', he sat down and ordered tea, saying, 'I've just had the greatest piece of luck. Two chaps rang the Institute last week and said they wanted work, teaching English. I saw them today and – it's almost too good to be true – they're exactly what I've been looking for. They speak excellent English. They're well read, personable, willing to take on any number of classes. In fact, they're a gift. I think they could get much better paid jobs, but they want to teach.'

'Extraordinary!' said Dobson: 'What are they? Egyptians?'

'No, European Jews.'

'Called?'

'Hertz and Allain.'

Dobson, who expected to have knowledge of the European refugees under British protection, said, 'Never heard of them. What was their last place of residence?'

Guy had not thought to ask. 'Does it matter? They may have come from Palestine.'

'Did you ask what they are doing here?'

'No, but I suppose they can come here if they want to?'

'Why should they want to? Jews who have the luck to get into Palestine are only too glad to stay there.'

Not liking these questions, Guy became restless and looked at his watch. Gathering up his books, he said, 'It's gone four o'clock,' and added; 'I cannot see why you should be suspicious of two civilized, intelligent and harmless young men who want to teach. I can now delegate the English language classes and give my time to the literature.'

Never perturbed for long, Dobson smiled and said, 'Oh, well! But keep an eye on them in case . . .'

'In case of what?'

'I don't know. I just feel they're too good to be true.'

Guy, glancing at Harriet, said, 'Darling, do hurry,' as though she was responsible for the hour. He had left a gharry waiting outside the café. When they were seated, he said to the driver, 'Qarafa,' and that was the first time Harriet heard the true name of the City of the Dead. He had learnt more Arabic than she had and was able to explain to the driver the dire need for haste. The man was so galvanized that he gave his horse a lick and the creature trotted for nearly a hundred yards before settling back into its usual lethargy.

They made their way through the old quarters of Cairo, among crowded streets from which minarets, yellow with sand, seemed to be crumbling against the cerulean of the sky. The kites, that found little of interest in the main roads, here floated, slow but keen-eyed, above the flat rooftops where the poor stacked their rubbish. As the lanes narrowed, the crowds became thicker and the enclosed air was filled with the smell of the spice shops. Guy, worried by their late arrival, had nothing to say.

Harriet, feeling the ride was spoilt by his mute disinterest in things, asked, 'Why didn't you come at three o'clock as arranged?'

'Because I had more important things to do. You don't stop to think how much I have on hand.'

His tone of controlled exasperation, exasperated her. 'Most of it unnecessary. I suppose you got so involved with the two teachers, you forgot the time.'

Truths of this sort annoyed him and he did not reply but stared ahead, his face creased as with suffering. 'This,' she thought, 'is marriage: knowing too much about each other.'

They came up to the Citadel wall and turned towards the desert region beneath the Mokattam Hills. At one time the dead had been buried in front of their homes, but Napoleon put a stop to that. Now they were carried up to their own city where there were streets and mausoleums built like houses. The relatives who escorted them took food and bedding and settled in until the spirit had become accustomed to the strangeness of the after-life.

Harriet had thought this a pleasing idea until she learnt that the dead were not buried but merely placed under the floorboards on which the family had to sit. Having gone up with friends on moonlit excursions, when the place had a macabre attraction, she had once or twice caught a whiff of mortality that brought the imagination to a standstill.

Now, in the oppressive, fly-ridden heat of late afternoon, the city looked as discouraging as death itself. The air, reflected off the naked, cinderous Mokattam cliffs, was suffocating and Harriet said, 'I suppose we won't stay long?'

'No, it's just a courtesy visit.'

The gharry wheels sank into soft ground and the only noise in the dead streets was a snort from the horse. The driver asked where they wanted to go. Guy said the tomb belonged to a family called Sarwar; the dead boy was called Gamal. None of this meant anything to the man who went aimlessly between the rows of sham houses, some of which had sunk down into heaps of mud brick. The city seemed to be deserted but, turning into a main avenue, they came on a young boy standing alone. At the sight of the gharry, he took on joyful life and ran towards it.

'Ah, professor, sir, we knew you would come.' He was Gamal's brother, posted to intercept Guy, and had been waiting an hour or more. He jumped on to the gharry step and, talking excitedly, he explained that the *arba'in* went on all day so Guy must not think he was late. It was, of course, a family occasion but the Pringles must regard themselves as part of the family. And how welcome they were! Gamal, who was, as it were, holding a reception to celebrate his inception into the next world, would be delighted.

Guy, though he did not believe in a next world, seemed equally delighted that his ex-pupil was now an established spirit.

A few streets further on, they came on the Sarwars gathered before the family tomb. It appeared to be, like most occasions in Egypt, an all-male function and Harriet said she would remain in the gharry. Gamal's brother would not hear of it. Mrs Pringle must join the party.

The Sarwar men, in European dress but each wearing his fez, stood in a close group, occasionally shaking hands or touching breasts with gestures of grief and regret. All this must have been done much earlier but now, to reassure the visitors, it was being re-enacted as though the Sarwars, like the Pringles, had just arrived.

Harriet was warmly received by the men who might keep their own wives in the background but were quick to show progressive appreciation of an educated Englishwoman.

'Where is Madame Sarwar?' Harriet asked one of the men.

'Madame Sarwar?' he seemed for a moment to doubt whether there was such a person, then he smiled and nodded. 'Madame Sarwar Bey? She is, naturally, with the other ladies.'

'And where are the other ladies?'

'They are together with Gamal in the house.'

Glancing inside the tomb, she saw dark forms in the darkness and, imagining the hot, crowded room with the corpse beneath the floorboards, she was thankful that no one suggested she should join them.

246

But something was required of Guy. After they had exchanged condolences and compliments, Sarwar Bey, a stout man in youthful middle-age, took Guy by the arm and led him close to the tomb, beckoning Harriet to follow. The other men came behind them and they all stood at a respectful distance gazing into the door from which the black-clad women retreated.

Taking Guy a step forward, Sarwar Bey called to his son: 'Gamal, Gamal! Emerge at once and witness who is among us.' He paused, then satisfied that Gamal had obeyed his command, he shouted vigorously: 'My boy, who do you see? It is your teacher, Professor Pringle, come to visit you on your *arba'in*. This is a very great honour and on your behalf I will tell him you are very much pleased.' This admonitory oration went on for some time, then Sarwar Bey turned to address Guy.

'And you, Professor Pringle, you will remember our Gamal for a long time, even when you have gone back to England. Isn't that so, Professor Pringle?'

Sarwar Bey spoke impressively and Guy was impressed. Tears stood in his eyes and at the final words, he gulped and put his face into his hands. The Egyptians, emotional people who warmed to any display of emotion, crowded round him to console him by pressing his arm or patting his back or murmuring appreciation. Sarwar Bey, holding him by the shoulder, led him away from the house and wept in sympathy.

A woman servant came from within carrying cups of Turkish coffee on a large brass tray. This strong restorative was pressed on Guy who, making a swift recovery, became the vivacious centre of the group of men.

Harriet, remaining apart, watched the men making much of Guy who beamed about him, enjoying the attention and recalling things said and done by Gamal. Gamal, he said, had written in an essay: 'My professor, Professor Pringle, is an Oriental. But if he is not, he should be because he is one of us!'

Gamal may have said that, or written it. Certainly some one had said it: and in Rumania and Greece there were people who had said the same thing. They had all laid claim to him and he had responded. He was, Harriet felt, disseminated among so many, there was little left for her.

The evening was coming down. The heat fog was turning to

umber and through it the lowering sun hung, a circle of red-gold, above the western riverbank that had been the burial place of the ancient dead.

The gharry horse stamped its feet and Harriet shared its bored weariness. She was depressed by the arid inactivity of the cemetery and wished them away. Then, as the light changed, the scene changed and she was entranced by it. The white Mohammed Ali mosque, that squatted like a prick-eared cat on the Citadel, took on the roseate gold of the sky and everything about it – the Mokattam cliffs, the high Citadel walls, the small tomb houses – glowed with evening. As the heat mist cleared, she could see in the distance the elaborate tombs of the Caliphs and Mamelukes, and thought that as they had driven so far, they might drive a little further and see the Khalifa close to.

The colours faded and twilight came down. Inside the Sarwar house, the women had lit petrol lamps and the flames flickered in the unglazed windows. The Khalifa tombs ceased to be visible but as the moon rose, they reappeared, touched in by a line of silver light.

Guy, eager enough to stay among his admirers, had to realize that time was passing. It was almost dark. The last day of mourning was coming to an end. The Sarwars themselves would soon return home and Gamal would be left alone. One after the other, the men took Guy by the hand and held to him a little longer than necessary as though, for a while, he could deliver them from the bewildering inexpedience of life.

Then they had to let him go. As he followed Harriet to the gharry, she pointed to the Khalifa monuments edged with moon light: 'Let's go and look at them.'

'Good lord, no. Who would want to see things like that?'

'They're magnificent. And they're no distance away.'

'Sorry, but I'm late as it is. I have to get to the Institute. You can go any time to see them. Ask Angela to go with you.'

'But I want to go with you.'

'Darling, don't be unreasonable. You know how I hate things like that. Useless bric-a-brac, death objects, *memento mori*! What point in making oneself miserable?' He climbed into the gharry.

Harriet stood where she was, watching the moon that heaved and rippled like liquid silver through the moisture on the horizon. Then, rising clear, it shed a light of diamond whiteness that picked out the traceries of the great tombs and lit the small houses of the common dead so that the cemeteries, arid and dreary during the day, became mysterious and beautiful.

Guy, losing patience, called to her and they drove down into the old streets where the mosques lifted themselves out of shadows into the pure indigo of the upper air. The evening star was alone in the sky but before they reached the main roads, the sky was ablaze with stars, all brilliant so the evening star was lost among them. This time of the evening, Harriet felt, compensated for the heat and glare, the flies and stomach upsets of the Egyptian summer. Her energy was renewed and feeling reconciled to Guy, she put her hand on his and said, 'Darling, don't be cross.'

He said, 'Have you thought any more about taking the boat to England?'

She withdrew her hand: 'No, I haven't thought any more because I'm not going. I don't want to hear any more about it.'

She had told him the question was settled and his bringing it up again when she was affectionate and, he supposed, compliant, gave evidence of his obstinacy and his cunning. These qualities, known only to her, were seldom manifested but when manifested, irritated her beyond bearing.

Neither spoke again until they came into the wide, busy roads with large pseudo-French buildings, shabby and dusty during the day but coming alive at night when windows lit up, and there were glimpses of rooms where anything might be happening. Pointing to some figures moving behind lace curtains, Harriet said, 'What do you think is going on in there?'

Guy shook his head. He did not know and did not care. He seemed distant and vexed, and she felt this was because she had refused to go on the boat to England. The thought came into her head: 'He wants me to go because he wants me out of the way.' But why should he want her out of the way?

When they came to the Institute, he left her to take the gharry on to the Garden City. 'I won't be late,' he said and Harriet said, 'It doesn't matter. I'll probably be in bed before you return.'

She thought, 'If I go, it will be because I want to go. And if I don't want to go, I won't go. And if he has any reason for wanting me to go, I don't care, I don't care, I don't care.'

She looked defiantly at the crowded, brilliant street where everyone seemed intent on enjoyment, and she wondered, miserably, what reason she had for staying with a husband she seldom saw in a place where she had no real home and little enough to do.

Four

Reaching the Column five days sooner than he was expected, Simon was aware of ridicule rather than approbation. When he reported his return to Major Hardy, the major said fretfully: 'What brings you back at this time, Boulderstone?'

'I thought you'd want me here, sir. In Cairo, they're all saying the balloon's going up.'

Hardy, his dark, lined face contracting as though he were in intense pain, seemed at a loss. He had been headmaster of a small school, and no doubt had been happy in his power, but the war had disrupted his life and he had manoeuvred himself, from vanity, into a position beyond his capacity. Simon, who had gathered this partly from Ridley and partly from his own observation of the man, saw now that his unnecessary return had upset Hardy by exceeding the natural order of things.

'I'm sorry, sir.'

'All right, Boulderstone.' Reassured by the apology, Hardy spoke more kindly: 'It's as well you're here. No knowing what will happen. Something could be underway, though I've heard nothing.'

Ridley, finding Simon back in camp, could hardly hide his derision. 'You handed in five days, sir? Back to the old grind for sweet damn all? Well, I hope the night you was there, you didn't waste no time.'

Simon was able to say with truth: 'I went to the Berka.'

'You didn't!' Ridley's face, burnt to the colour of an Arbroath smokie, was cut through by his lascivious smile: 'Well, good for you, sir!' He whistled his appreciation and said nothing more about the wasted five days. That evening, when they were supervising a brew-up, he asked Simon: 'Find the captain all right, sir?'

'The captain?'

'That captain you went to look up? The one you thought might be your brother?'

As Simon shook his head and walked away, Ridley called after him: 'Not the right bloke, then, sir?' but Simon pretended not to hear.

The battle at Himeimat was in its third day before the Column came within sound of it. Ridley, in touch with the news and rumours of the line, brought what he heard to Simon.

He said, 'The jerries've been taking a pasting. They were stuck all day in the mine fields with our bombers belting hell out of them and our tanks waiting to blast them when they got out.'

'And did they get out?'

'Don't know. Better ask his nibs.' Ridley jerked his head towards the HQ truck where Hardy, standing on a seat with his head through a hole in the roof, was observing the westward scene through his over-large binoculars.

Simon went to him: 'See anything, sir?'

He was risking a snub because Hardy, inclined to self-importance, preferred to keep his information to himself. This time, surprisingly, he replied with unusual friendliness: 'Not much. Plenty of smoke from burning vehicles but no sign of the hun.' Putting down the binoculars, he turned to smile on Simon who flushed, feeling a fondness for the man.

The Sunday after his return to the unit had been declared a national day of prayer: Monty's idea. Ridley said: 'They say he's a holy Joe. Thinks he's got a direct line to God.'

The padre arrived in a staff car and a squaddy set up a small portable altar in the sand. Going into the HQ truck, the padre was affable and smiling. Coming out, wearing his cassock, he was grave-faced and he made an authoritative gesture to the congregation of men seated cross-legged, awaiting him. They stood up for the hymn, 'Now praise we all our God.' The singing began but the battle did not stop. During the night the flashes and flares on the horizon, and the near gunfire, had kept the camp in a state of semi-wakefulness. Now, as the loud but tuneless praise went forth, it was drowned by flights of Wellingtons overhead.

Ridley whispered behind Simon: 'Still giving the buggers hell.'

A new distraction arrived during prayers. A messenger on a

252

motor-cycle drew up beside the group of officers and waited until Hardy, head bent, put out a hand for the signal. Opening it, still muttering his devotions, he appeared to be thunder-struck by what he read. His prayers ceased and, looking up, he stared at Simon in furious astonishment. Simon, his conscience clear, glanced uneasily round at Ridley who shrugged his ignorance of the contretemps. As soon as the padre had driven off to another camp, Hardy's batman called Simon to the HQ truck.

'Any idea what's wrong?'

'Haven't a clue, sir.'

As Simon approached the truck, Hardy, seated at an outdoor table, observed him with black indignant eyes, saying as soon as he was within earshot: 'So Boulderstone, you have friends in high places?'

'Me, sir! I don't know anyone.'

'Well, someone appears to know you. Or know *about* you. Your fame has spread beyond the Column – can't think why. I, myself, failed to recognize your superior qualities, but the fault no doubt was mine.'

Hardy went on at length until Simon, baffled and miserable, broke in: 'I'm sorry, sir, but I don't understand any of this.'

'No? Well, you're to leave us, Boulderstone. The Column is to be deprived of your intelligence and initiative. We must somehow manage without you. Its activities are obviously too limited for a man of your resource and vision.'

Simon, by remaining silent, at last brought Hardy to the point. 'You've landed, God knows how, one of the most sought-after jobs in the British army. For some reason hidden from me, someone has seen fit to appoint you a liaison officer.'

As Hardy spoke the memory of Peter Lisdoonvarna came to Simon and he murmured, 'Good heavens!' never having imagined that the social chat in the Garden City flat had meant anything at all.

Simon began, 'I did meet a chap in Cairo . . .' then came to an embarrassed stop. It must seem that he had, ungratefully, sought a transfer behind the back of his commanding officer and he tried to explain.

Hardy refused to listen: 'I don't know how you managed it,

and I don't want to know. You've got the job. Whether you're fit for it or not is another matter. It's none of my concern. It'll be up to you, Boulderstone, to prove yourself.'

'Sir! Where am I to go, sir?'

'You'll hear soon enough. They're sending a pick-up for you and you'll be taken to Corps HQ. The driver will bring your instructions. And I'd advise you to clean yourself up. Get your shirt and shorts properly washed. At Corps HQ, you'll be among the nobs.'

The other officers of the Column showed that they shared Hardy's disapproval of Simon's advancement and it was also shared by Ridley. Ridley who in early days had been Simon's guide and support, now avoided him and was vague when Simon sought him out to question him. What, Simon wanted to know, were the duties of a liaison officer?

'Don't worry, sir. You'll find out for yourself. You'll soon cotton on.'

'You don't think I'm up to it, do you?'

'It's not for me to say, sir. With respect, I'd rather not discuss it. I've got to be getting along.'

Simon, unnerved at leaving the safety of the Column, felt an impulse to stay where he was but knew that the appointment came when he most needed it. He was sick of the tedium of eventless patrols. Opportunity to escape was offered and he would not be restricted by the disapprobation of other men.

Still, he was troubled. Hardy's annoyance came of Hardy's vanity, but Ridley was another matter. Ridley was hurt by his going and this hurt resulted from affection, even love. In the desert where there were no women or animals, Ridley had to love something and he had chosen Simon. Simon was touched, but not as deeply as he would once have been. His own attachments – Trench on the troopship which brought them to Egypt, Arnold his batman and driver, and Hugo – were dead and their deaths had absolved him from overmuch feeling. He was sorry to leave Ridley, but no more than that.

The transport, which arrived two days later, was not a pick-up but a jeep. The jeep had been assigned to Simon, it was his own vehicle, and this fact, when Hardy and the others heard of it, confirmed them in their belief that Simon had been appointed above his station. They were short with their goodbyes but the men, crowding about him as he prepared his departure, showed genuine regret at his going. They liked him. Only Ridley did not join in their good wishes but stood at a distance. When Simon shouted to him, 'Goodbye, Ridley, thanks for everything,' he dropped his head briefly, then walked away. When, starting out, Simon looked back to wave, the men waved him away but there was no sign of Ridley.

For a mile or so Simon was sunk in sadness, then the Column and everyone in it dwindled behind him and he felt the exhilaration of a new beginning. He looked at the driver and asked his name.

'Crosbie, sir.'

'You attached to me permanently?'

'Yes, sir.'

Crosbie, lumpish, snub-faced, with a habit of smiling to himself, showed no inclination to talk but drove with the stolid efficiency of a man who did one, and only one, thing well. He could drive.

They passed the Ridge, almost lost in the dusty haze, and turned on to a barrel track. The track took them eastwards beyond the sound of the guns into the spacious, empty desert where the only danger was from the air. Relaxing from his usual attentive fear, Simon faced the challenge of the work awaiting him. He would have liked to question Crosbie about the corps, but his instinct was to keep himself to himself.

He had started his desert life under Hardy and had relied on Arnold and Ridley. These two NCOs, taking pity on his ignorance, had pampered him as though he were a youngster, but he had tried Hardy's patience and Hardy saw him as a fool. Well, that episode was over. Simon now had experience of the desert, and no one would treat him either as fool or youngster.

The horizon lightened as they approached the coast. There were aircraft about and Simon, seeing one of them rise, leaving in the distance a long trail of ginger-brown dust, asked from an old habit of enquiry: 'Where's that taking off from?'

Crosbie, not bothering to look at it, mumbled, 'Don't know,

sir!' Neither knowing nor caring, he was not one to answer questions and Simon decided that he would no longer be the one to ask them.

They reached the perimeter of Corps HQ in the early afternoon. Passing concentrations of trucks and equipment, and all the appurtenances of operational and administrative staff, Simon was awed by the extent of the camp. But this was where he now belonged. Its size denoted his status in the world. When the jeep jerked to a stop, they had reached the dead end of a lane and Crosbie said, 'This doesn't look right, sir.'

Simon brusquely replied: 'Get your finger out, Crosbie. You're supposed to know where you're going. The command vehicle is posted. Use your eyes.'

Crosbie might well have pointed out that Simon had eyes and could use them but, instead, he acknowledged authority with a brisk 'Sir', and backing the jeep out of the lane, brought them at last to the busy centre of the camp.

Simon was not the only new arrival. The command vehicle, a three-ton truck converted for use as an office, had a canvas lean-to, camouflaged with netting that extended on both sides. A number of officers, all senior to Simon, stood in groups under the lean-to awaiting the attention of the officer in charge. They talked with the flippant ease he had admired in the Cherry-pickers and he saw them as old campaigners to whom the desert was a second home.

Simon, who had been oppressed by Hardy's doubts and uncertainties, now felt his spirits rise as he listened to these men who had no doubts at all that, whatever happened, the allies would be the victors in the end.

The officer in charge was a major, verging on middle-age, with a thin, serious face, who tolerated the chaffing of the other men but did not respond to it. Simon, when his turn came, expected no more than an acknowledgement of his arrival, but the major, who said, 'I'm Fitzwilliams. You'll take your orders from me,' looked at him with interest and afforded him several minutes of his time.

'I'm afraid, Boulderstone, you've reached us just when the chaps are moving up from their training grounds. A deal of armour will be coming in and you'll find it a bit confusing at first, but you'll soon know your way around. Don't be frightened to ask. You're in B mess so you can go along now and get yourself a snack. Report back here at 23.00 hours. I'll probably have a job for you.'

Simon, sitting under the canvas lean-to that was B mess, wondered if he had heard right. To the men of the Column, 23.00 hours was in the middle of the night. Was he expected to start work at a time when other men were fast asleep? All he could do was report at the hour given and hope he was not making a fool of himself.

Twenty-three hours, it turned out, was the expected arrival time of an armoured division and Simon was sent to conduct the tank commander to the correct assembly point. Where that point was, Simon had to find for himself and, returning to the jeep, he said casually to Crosbie: 'I suppose you know the assembly point for tanks?'

Crosbie, who obviously did not, mumbled 'Sir' and setting out, stopped to enquire at every hut and bivouac that showed a light. The commander had found the assembly point long before the jeep reached it but Simon did not betray himself.

'Just been sent, sir, to see you've settled in.'

'Yep, all in. All tickety-boo.'

Thankful to have skirted this assignment safely, Simon relented towards Crosbie and said, 'That wasn't too bad. Now let's hope we can get some kip,' but their night's work was not yet over. Reporting back to the command vehicle, Simon found a different officer in charge. He said, 'You're the new liaison officer, are you? Well, I've got a job for you. D'you know the compound with the dummy lorries? No? I expect you'll find it easily enough. Look out the ordnance officer and give him a signal: he's to fit the dummies over the newly arrived tanks.'

'When, sir? Tomorrow?'

'No, not tomorrow. Everything here happens at night. The job's to be done before first light. Now, get a move on.'

An hour later, having tracked down the ordnance officer, Simon apologetically handed him the signal: 'I'm sorry, sir, but it's supposed to be done before daybreak.'

Amused by his tone, the officer looked at Simon, smiled and nodded; 'Received and understood,' he said.

Free now to sleep, Simon ordered Crosbie to park near the command vehicle in order to be on call. Then, Simon in his sleeping-bag, Crosbie on his ground-sheet, they dossed down on either side of the jeep.

The assembly of the camp was growing and from its proportions, Simon realized that the purpose behind it was not merely defensive. And, as he had been told, everything happened at night. The convoys and units journeyed in darkness, and in darkness took up their positions in the camp. This, he knew, would not happen on a routine training march.

Dummy equipment was collected in dumps and mysteriously moved about. He found, when delivering signals, that the dummy guns and vehicles of yesterday had been replaced by real guns and vehicles, or the real had been replaced by dummies. The purpose was to deceive, and the deceived could only be the enemy. Simon would have been glad to have Ridley with him to make sense of all this shifting and replacement. Several times he almost asked Crosbie, 'What's going on?' but kept quiet, seeing no reason for wasting words.

As Fitzwilliams had promised, he soon knew his way around but he suffered from lack of companions. Two other liaison officers were due and, sitting alone in B mess, he longed for their arrival.

The heat had dragged on into mid-September, and seemed, to tired senses, more exhausting than summer. Under the tarpaulin the air was turgid with food smells and singed by the cooks' fires. Simon was dulled by inactivity and the atmosphere, when another liaison officer came to join him. This was Blair, a captain, and Simon, standing up, said, 'Glad you've come, sir.'

Blair laughed with the uncertainty of a man who has lost his place in the world: 'Just call me Blair.'

He was soft-bodied, stoutish, puffy about the cheeks and eyes, and his hair was growing thin. Simon thought him a very old fellow to be living among the hardships of the desert. He was not the companion Simon had hoped for, but any companion was better than none.

Blair sat with Simon at meal times but had little to say for himself. When he was not eating, he would sit with his head down, his hands hanging loosely between his knees. He had been in tanks and wore the black beret, but not with pride. Whenever he could, he would take it off and fold it into his pocket.

The third liaison officer, when he turned up, had no more to offer than Blair. His name was Donaldson and although the same age as Simon, he had finished his year as a second lieutenant. With two pips up, he was able to treat Simon as an inferior. He tried at first to come to terms with Blair, but finding him sad company, he ignored both his fellow liaison officers and sat by himself.

Blair, after a few days, began to talk. Hesitant and nervous, he said he had served in the desert since the first year of the war. In those days, with only the Italians to contend with, it had been 'a gentleman's war'. His CO had said that here in the desert, they had a 'soft option', but then the Afrika Korps had arrived to spoil things. By hints, pauses and a shaking of the head, he made it clear that some unnatural catastrophe had struck him down near a place he called Bir Gubo. 'East of Retma', he said as though that meant anything to Simon. Blair mentioned other names: Acroma, Knightsbridge, Adem, Sidi Rezegh, which all, for Simon, belonged to the era of pre-history when the British still operated on the other side of the wire that marked the Egyptian frontier.

'With all that armour round you, you must have felt pretty safe?'

Blair's eyes fixed themselves on Simon: 'Safe? You ever seen inside one of those Ronsons after it's burnt out?'

'Not inside, no.'

'Imagine being packed inside a tin can with other chaps and then the whole lot fried to a frizzle. What do you think you'd look like?' Blair gave a bleak laugh and Simon said no more about tanks.

Instead, he wiped the sweat off his face and asked Blair. 'Does it ever let up?'

'I've known worse summers, but not one that lasted into October.'

October came. As though the change of month meant an automatic change of weather, the hard, hot wind stopped abruptly and a softer wind came cool out of the east and dispersed the canteen's flies. The nights became colder and jerseys were regulation wear. Those officers who owned sheepskin coats, now wore them swinging open so the long, inner fleece hung out like a fringe.

Hardy, ordering Simon to clean himself up, had said, 'You'll be among the nobs,' but 'the nobs' were much less conventional in dress than Hardy and his staff. Hardy himself always wore a carefully knotted tie but the officers at Corps HQ wore silk scarves, rich in colour, and their winter trousers of corduroy velvet – khaki and serge, apparently, were for other ranks – could be any colour from near-white to honey brown. They had for Simon a swaggering elegance and he greatly envied them. He told Blair that when he was next in Cairo he would buy some corduroy trousers and a sheepskin coat.

'Be careful about the coat,' Blair said. 'Those skins can stink to high heaven if they're not properly cured. Often, with all the smells in the Muski, you don't notice it till you get it home. If you try to return it, the chap who sold it can't be found. I had a fine Iranian coat once, best skins, embroidered all over. Was sorry to lose it.'

'You mean someone liberated it?'

'No, lost it at Bir Gubo. Lost a lot of things.'

'What *did* happen at Bir Gubo?'

Blair, biting into a bully-beef sandwich, tried to smile with his mouth full. He chewed and coughed and managed to say, 'You mean, to the coat? Got burnt.'

'Not just the coat. You and the rest of the crew? – what happened?'

Blair cleared his mouth with a gulp of tea. 'They bought it – all except me. I'd gone for a walk . . . You know, with a spade. Heard a plane go over. Didn't see it. Didn't even know whose it was. When I got back the Ronson was ablaze. Couldn't get near it. We'd been fart-arsing around, not a soul in sight. Must've taken a direct hit. I don't know. Simply don't know. I just stood there and watched till it burnt out . . . And when I went to look, you couldn't tell one chap from another.'

'And what happened to you?'

'Don't know. Wandered about . . . shock, I suppose. The Scruff found me and thought I was dead. Just going to bury me when someone saw my eyelids move. Just a twitch, as the chaps say. Saved my life.' Blair laughed so his tea cup shook in his hand, and Simon felt he knew all he need know about Blair's descent from a tank's officer to a messenger who carried signals for other men.

Simon asked him, 'Any idea what's happening here? There's a mass of stuff coming in. Do you think it's the attack?'

'Could be. Certainly looks like it.'

'When will it be, do you think?'

'Have to be soon. There's the moon, you see. And you can't keep a show like this sitting on its arse. The jerries might see it and strike first. There'll be a showdown all right.'

'You looking forward to it?'

'Don't know. Perhaps. Better than hanging about.'

The moon was growing towards the full and expectations grew with it. In the middle of the month, when anything might happen, Simon was sent south towards the point at which he had parted from the Cherrypickers. Of the big supply base, not a barrel remained but a small force of camouflaged tanks were hull down, in the wadi where the command lorry had stood. The officer in charge was lying on high ground, looking westwards through field glasses. When Simon came to him, bringing a movement order, he said in a low voice, 'Get down.' Simon crouched beside him and he pointed to a bluff of rock distorted by the mid-day heat: 'See over there; that's the salient. They've been there since Alam Halfa. If you listen, you can hear them singing.'

Lying down, Simon bent his head to extend his hearing and there came to him, faint and clear, like a voice across lake water, a song he had heard somewhere before: 'But that's an English song!'

'No, it's one of theirs: "Lili Marlene". We picked it up from the German radio.'

The two men, lying side by side, remained silent while the song lasted. Simon, moved by its nostalgic sadness, thought of the first time he had seen Edwina. She had leant over the balcony towards him, her face half-hidden by a fall of sun-bleached hair, her brown arm lying on the balcony rail, her white robe falling open so he could see the rounding of her breasts. She came back to him so vividly, he thought he could smell her gardenia scent. He was impatient of the vision and relieved when the song ended and the officer, laughing and jumping up, said, 'So we're to take the tanks up north? Gathering us all in, eh? Looks like things are hotting up?'

'We hope so, sir. The signal says: "Move only after dark".'

'Will do. Received and understood.'

As Simon drove back, Edwina was still on his mind. He tried to order her away but she stayed where she was, smiling down on him from the balcony. The desert air was a sort of anaphrodisiac, and he and the other men were detached from sex, yet he could not reject the romantic enhancement of love. He took out his wallet to distract himself, and, opening it, looked for the photograph of his wife. He could not find it. He could not even remember when he had last seen it. At some time during the past weeks, perhaps during the last months, it had fallen out, and now it was lost. He tried to recreate her in his mind but all he could see was a thin, small figure standing, weeping, on the station platform. She had no face. He struggled with his memory but no face came to him and he wondered, were he to meet her unexpectedly, would he know who she was?

Five

In October, when the evenings grew cool, Dobson ordered the servants to take blankets out of store. A smell of moth-balls filled the flat as he distributed them, saying again and again: 'So delicious to have a bit of weight on one at night.'

The Garden City foliage scarcely marked the change of season. A few deciduous trees, hidden among the evergreens and palms, dropped their leaves. These went unnoticed but one tree – the students called it the Examination Tree – made a dramatic appearance out of nowhere, feathering its bare branches with mauve blossom, mistaking the autumn for spring.

The morning air became gentle as silk and a delicate mist hung over the old banyans on the riverside walk. The heat, that had dulled the senses like a physical pressure, now lifted and minds and bodies felt renewed. Lovers, no longer suffering the wet and sticky sheets that were cover enough during the summer, became invigorated: and the one most invigorated, it seemed, was Castlebar.

The inmates of the flat were astonished when Angela first led him through the living-room to her bedroom where they remained closeted all afternoon. Castlebar, on his way out, passed Harriet and Edwina with a very smug smile. Angela, appearing later for her evening drink, was not discomposed and made no comment on Castlebar's visit. The next day he was back again.

Edwina, who had not seen Castlebar before, said to Harriet, 'Where did Angela pick up that scruffy old has-been?'

Harriet could not believe the infatuation would last, but it was lasting and becoming more fervent. Castlebar was with Angela every afternoon. She confided to Harriet that the keeper of the cheap pension where Castlebar lived had objected to her presence in Castlebar's room. The woman had demanded double payment for what she called 'the accommodation of two persons'. Angela would have paid the required sum but Castlebar argued that he had a right to bring in a friend. He said he would not be cheated by 'a greedy Levantine hag' and they settled the matter by changing ground.

Harriet and Angela were neighbours in the bedroom corridor and Harriet overheard more than she wanted of the chambering next door. She had no hope of a siesta and went to the living-room to read in peace. Dobson, whose room was in the main part of the flat, once or twice wandered out, a towel tied like a sarong round his waist, and realizing why Harriet had retreated, shook his head over Angela's fall from grace.

'The goings-on!' he grumbled after they had been going on for a week: 'To think she would take up with a shocker like Castlebar! And I'm told he's got a wife somewhere. What does she see in him?'

Harriet tried to imagine what Angela saw in him. In the picture that came to her mind, Castlebar, worn down by self-indulgence, middle-age and the Egyptian climate, had a folded yellow skin and a mouth that looked unappetizingly soft, like decayed fruit.

She shook her head: 'I don't know. But what does anyone see in anyone? Perhaps that's what Yeats meant by "love's bitter mystery"!'

Dobson, though he had never objected to Peter Lisdoon-varna's presence in Edwina's room, said he meant to be firm with Angela. 'It's going too far. You might drop her a word. Tell her I don't like it.'

When Harriet attempted to drop the word, Angela broke in to ask, 'What has it got to do with him? Perhaps he wants me to pay double expenses?'

'Angela, you're being disingenuous. He feels that Castlebar's not worthy of you – he debases you socially.'

The two women laughed and Harriet felt it best to avoid Dobson and his complaints. A few afternoons later, keeping to her room, she was startled by a ringing crash followed by Castlebar's half-stifled snuffling titter. After he had gone, Harriet, passing Angela's door, found her on her knees, mopping water from the floor.

'Sorry if we disturbed you.'

'I didn't hear a thing.'

'Bill knocked down a dish of water. He keeps it by the bed because he's inclined to come too soon so, when he's over excited, he dips his wrist in the water and it cools him down.'

This explanation, unblushing and matter-of-fact, took for granted Harriet's acceptance of the situation and she could only say, 'I see.'

'And you can tell bloody Dobson that Bill won't be here much longer. He's found himself a flat.'

'He's been very clever. When we wanted one, we couldn't find a thing.'

'The situation's easier now as some of the officers are going. And the university has a few flats for its men. Bill put his name down for one as soon as he heard his wife was determined to get back. He had to. He said if he didn't stir himself on her behalf, she'd raise hell.'

'You mean, he's frightened of her?'

'Terrified. Poor Bill!'

Angela smiled in amused contempt, and yet the enchantment remained. Their afternoons together were not enough for her, she had to see him again in the evening. If, by chance, they had not made an arrangement to meet later, she would go to the Union in search of him, always taking Harriet with her. She was generous with her friends who, in return, were required to support her in her caprices.

Now that the nights were growing cold, the Union members were retiring from the lawn into the club house and there Angela chose a corner table and held it as her own. The chief safragi, heavily tipped, would place an 'Engaged' notice on the table and she would sit for as long as need be, awaiting Castlebar.

Her friends were not the only ones to marvel at her intimacy with him. When he appeared, as he did sooner or later, those sitting around would glance askance at the two of them and then at each other.

None of this worried Angela and Castlebar, who openly held hands, Castlebar cleverly manipulating his cigarette and drink with his right hand while his left kept its hold upon Angela. They would put their heads together and whisper. They giggled over jokes known only to themselves.

Harriet, feeling an intruder, gave her attention to Jackman, tolerating him for want of better company. Jackman, himself, resenting Castlebar's preoccupation with Angela, came for the drink and pretended he had an audience of three. At that time his talk was all about movements in the desert. There were rumours of vast quantities of equipment arriving at Suez and being sent to the front. Always after dark, he said. A man with a famous name, one of a family of prestidigitators, had been flown out to Cairo and was met at parties. He was quiet and pleasant, but gave nothing away. If no one else knew why he was there, Jackman knew.

'If you hear the hun's belting back to Libya as fast as his wheels'll take him, it's because this chap has fixed up a magic show.'

'What sort of magic show?'

'Ah, that would be telling. But he creates illusions. This time, it'll be millions of them.'

'And when is this going to happen?'

'All in good time, my child.'

Meanwhile the Germans were fifty miles from Alexandria, which was exactly where they had been for the last four months. There, like the luckless engineers of some too long drawn out siege, they seemed likely to remain until boredom or starvation sent them home again.

Cookson, searching for drink and company, tracked Angela down to her table at the Union and was admitted to the company. He came intermittently at first then, thinking he had confirmed his position, began to appear nightly to the annoyance of Castlebar who whispered to Angela. Angela murmured, 'Poor old thing, I can't tell him he's not wanted.'

'Let me do it, darling.'

'Well, if you must – but be tactful.'

'Naturally, I will.'

The next night Cookson thought he could go further: he brought a friend. He knew several people in Cairo whom no one else wanted to know and one of these was a youth who had no name but Tootsie. Before the war Tootsie had come on holiday to Egypt with his widowed mother. The mother had died, her pension had died with her and Tootsie, cut off by war from the rest of the world, wandered around, looking for someone to keep him. The sight of Tootsie lurking behind Cookson caused Castlebar to lower his eye-tooth. He made a noise in his throat like the warning growl of a guard-dog about to bark.

Cookson, aware of danger, paused nervously, then made a darting sally towards the table, saying on a high, exalted note: 'Hello, Lady H! Hello, Bill! I knew you wouldn't mind poor Tootsie...'

Castlebar spoke: 'Go away, Cookson. Nothing for you here.'

'Go away?' Cookson appeared flabbergasted: 'Oh, Bill, how could you be such a meanie? Tootsie and I have had such a tiring day around the bars.'

'Go away, Cookson.'

'Please, Bill, don't be horrid!' Cookson, near tears, took out his handkerchief and rolled it between his hands while Tootsie, unaware of the contention, made himself agreeable to Harriet. He had a favourite, and, indeed, an only interest in life: the state of his bowels.

He bent over Harriet to tell her: 'It's been such a week! Senna pods every night and nothing in the morning. But *nothing*! Then, only an hour ago, what a surprise! The whole bowel emptied out, and not before time, I can tell you...'

Harriet, who had heard about Tootsie's bowels before, held up a hand to check him while she watched Cookson, now pressing the handkerchief to his cheek, shifting from one foot to the other in shame. Tootsie, taking no notice of Harriet's appeal, continued in a small, breathy voice, asking her whether she thought the recent evacuation would be a daily event.

She shook her head and Cookson, driven beyond bearing, called to Angela: 'Dear Lady Hooper, please...'

Angela, who had sat with eyes lowered, was forced to look up. She said 'I'm sorry, Major Cookson. You heard what Bill said.'

'But do *you* want me to go, Lady Hooper?'

'I want what Bill wants.'

Cookson, crestfallen, plucked at Tootsie, saying, 'I understand. Come along, Tootsie. We have to go.'

As they went in confusion, Angela said with mock severity to

Castlebar, 'You weren't very tactful, were you? You dreadful, lovely brute!' and she gave him an admiring kiss on the side of his mouth.

This incident had been observed by some thirty Union members, among them an oil agent called Clifford who had been one of the intruders present when Angela brought home her dead child. As Clifford keenly watched and heard Cookson's dismissal, Harriet remembered how he had recounted the story of the boy's death to the first people he met.

She was not surprised when Dobson complained to her a day or two later: 'Angela's outrageous. The whole of Cairo's talking about her wretched liaison. It's getting the flat a bad name. And where, oh where, will it all end?'

Six

In the third week of October, the junior officers, NCOs and men were briefed for battle. Calling his three liaison officers together, Major Fitzwilliams addressed them in his flat, pleasant voice: 'We've all known the party was due to begin. It was just a question of how soon; and with the moon already waning, it had to be damned soon. Well, no need to tell you, it's any day now. Not tomorrow. I'd say the day after. You may feel this is short notice, but that's how Monty wants it. So, keep your traps shut, even among yourselves. There'll be plenty for you to do at the off. Meanwhile, chaps, carry on.'

Blair remained sunk into silence during the next two days and Donaldson bustled about as though preparing for action. Simon, when he sat with Blair, did not attempt to break into his abstraction. In their different ways, they suffered the tension of waiting. Simon had once led a platoon into action and experienced again the accumulating apprehension of the event ahead. But this time he did not expect to face danger, and could allow himself a self-indulgent excitement.

On the second day, they saw the reconnaissance parties going out at twilight and Blair whispered to Simon: 'This is it. Their job is to mark the starting point with tape. Then there'll be the barrage. Then the infantry go in – poor fuckers!'

'Don't the sappers go first?'

'No. The sappers clear the lanes for the tanks but the infantry have to take their chance.'

The camp emptied as the different units moved forward. There was nothing for the liaison officers at that time and they stood by the command truck like stage hands waiting for the show to commence. Donaldson, having no opportunity to flaunt his superiority, walked backwards and forwards, occasionally pausing to kick at the sand with one heel. Fitzwilliams had given each of them a copy of Montgomery's message to his troops. Simon, reading by the light of a torch, was moved by the commander's invocation to 'the Lord mighty in battle' and said fervently: 'Wish I was out there with them.'

Donaldson gave a guffaw of contempt: 'Don't you know the infantry went forward at daybreak? Been stuck in the slitties all day. Had to keep their heads down, too; couldn't even come up for a piss. How'd you like that? Bet you'd soon be pretty sick. What do you think, Blair?' Blair made no reply to Donaldson's perky show of knowledge but stared before him with a distracted expression as though stupefied by the onset of action.

At 19.00 hours there had been a special treat for officers and men; a hot meal of beef and carrots. Blair had not touched it and when Simon urged him to eat up, he shook his head, 'Don't fancy it, somehow.'

The moon, the great white Egyptian moon, rising above the horizon, was sharpening every object into sections of silver or black. According to rumour the attack would start at 21.00 hours but 21.00 hours came and went and there was nothing but an expectant silence. The men that remained in the camp had gathered about the command truck, all facing westwards like sightseers awaiting a firework display.

As the brilliance increased, Simon began to feel a fearful impatience, certain that the moon would reveal to the enemy the great concourse of guns and tanks moving towards the tapes. But the night, a windless and quiet night, remained still and, imagining the Germans asleep, he pitied their unsuspecting repose.

Donaldson, making approaches to his seniors, kept looking at his watch and saying knowingly: 'It'll be 22.00 hours, you see if it isn't,' but he was wrong. The barrage started twenty minutes before the predicted time.

It opened with so deafening a roar that some of the men round the truck, a mile or more from the guns, stepped back in trepidation. The timing had been perfect. Every gun had fired on the instant.

Donaldson giggled: 'Enough to make you wet your pants. What've they _got_ out there, for God's sake?'

No one else spoke. The noise, a supreme awfulness of noise,

went on. There was no increase of volume because there could be no increase: the pitch was at its height from the start. It shocked the nerves and its effect was made more awesome by the gun-flashes that stabbed on the horizon, orange and red, an unceasing frenzy of lights.

Simon turned to Blair and found he was no longer beside him. He was leaning against the side of the truck, hands over ears, shoulders raised as though he were being beaten about the head. Simon went to him: 'You all right, Blair?'

Blair did not reply. Simon, putting a hand on his shoulder, felt the man's body shaking and left him, unwilling to be a witness to such terror.

For fifteen minutes the uproar continued without a pause, then ended as abruptly as it had begun. The sudden silence was as unnerving as the noise, then came a sense of release. The men began excitedly to discuss what might happen next but in a moment the guns started up again.

Simon looked at Blair and saw that under this ·renewed onslaught, he had sunk down and was now kneeling, head against a truck wheel, about to collapse altogether. One of Fitzwilliams's messengers was bending over him and, realizing his condition, returned to the office. The man reappeared a minute or two later and called Simon in.

Fitzwilliams said: 'I've a job for you, Boulderstone. I would have sent Blair but seems he's under the weather. Tanks are due to move in at 02.00 hours when the sappers have cleared the lanes. I want you to take a signal to CO, Engineers. You'll have to negotiate the mine field but they'll have gone over the near section by now. No great danger.' He looked at Simon and as though struck by his youth and inexperience, added: 'Sorry it had to be you. Don't take unnecessary risks. Want you back here in one piece, old chap.'

The 'old chap' produced in Simon a choking sense of grati-tude. The chance to go forward was enough. He needed no apology. He said, 'Don't worry about me, sir,' and turning, he made for the jeep at a run.

Crosbie, at the wheel, was awake simply because no living creature could sleep through the din. Yawning, he asked, 'Where are we going, sir?'

Simon scarcely knew himself but said, 'We're to take "boat" track and hope for the best.'

The tracks, each leading to a different sector of the line, were marked by symbols cut into petrol cans and lit from inside. That night there were six tracks: boat, bottle, boot and sun, moon, star. When they came on the first rough portrayal of a boat, Simon shouted, 'Get a move on, Crosbie. It'll be a piece of cake.'

Crosbie, not impressed, grunted and pressed down on the accelerator. The noise of the barrage, together with incessant flights of aircraft going in to the attack, created a sort of blanket round the jeep so that Simon, his senses muffled, imagined they were protected by a cover no enemy shell could penetrate.

For the first half mile the going was easy; then they were caught in a dust cloud that choked them and blotted out the 'Boat' signs. Not knowing whether they were on the track or off it, Crosbie dropped his pace to a crawl, peering ahead through dust and smoke until he glimpsed the rear of a stationary vehicle. He braked, jerking them against the glass, and Simon stood up to shout: 'Hi! Where are we? We're supposed to be on "Boat" track.'

A voice bawled back: 'You try and find it, chum.'

Telling Crosbie to stay where he was, Simon jumped down and felt his way ahead, holding a lighted torch. The light fell on the sand-blurred outlines of two lorries that had skidded off the track and tangled together. Other vehicles, trying to drive round them, were bogged down in soft sand. As he made his way forward, Simon began to smell the acrid smoke of bursting shells. The shells threw up immense fountains of sand that showered down on men and trucks. Realizing he was not, after all, immune from danger, Simon went back for his tin hat. Starting out again, he saw ahead of him a point of light that grew into a blaze. He was almost upon it before he could see that a truck had caught fire. Enemy mortars were bursting over it while the crew was trying to douse the flames with water from a supply tank. As he stopped, struck by the infernal confusion of the scene, an officer shouted to him: 'Get out of the way, you jackass. She's loaded with ammunition.'

'I must get through. I've a signal for CO, Engineers on "Boat" track.'

'Then get past, quick as your feet will carry you. Keep your head down. If you see a trip wire, give it a wide berth or you'll get your bollocks blown off.'

Taking this as a joke, Simon asked, 'How far do the mine fields stretch?'

'How the hell do I know. Probably twenty miles.'

Eyes streaming, throat raw with smoke, Simon sped round the ammunition truck, making for the noise of the guns. As their shapes appeared through the fog, he began to stumble on what seemed a stony beach. Lowering his torch, he saw the mardam was thickly covered with shrapnel fragments, jagged, blue-grey and crystalline from the super-heat of explosion. This shrapnel carpet stretched between the guns and many yards beyond them. There was no question of running over it and he picked his way as best he could until he was out in the open area of no-man's-land. The fog still hung in the air and even the moon was lost to sight. The mine fields were here. He expected to find the sappers somewhere ahead, but instead of the sappers, he came upon a pride of tanks, just visible, monstrous through the smoky dust. Grinding and rumbling, they were edging forward so slowly, he could pass them at a walk. The heat of the armour came out to him and he could smell, above the fumes of the explosive, the stench of exhausts.

Stumbling in the dark, he all but fell in the path of one of them and someone shouted from above, 'What d'you think you're doing down there?'

The tank commander was not much older than Simon and, bending down, his harassed young face lightened as Simon looked up. Seeing another like himself riding into battle, Simon could have cried in envy but all he said was, 'Sorry. I'm liaison. Had to leave my jeep behind and go it on foot. I'm trying to find CO, Sappers.'

'He'll be up front, where you might expect. And if you want to make it, keep clear of our treads. At the rate we're going, it'd be a slow and sticky finish.'

The rows of widely spaced tanks seemed endless but at last, dodging among them, almost blinded by the sand they threw up, Simon was suddenly out in clear air with the moon, tranquil and uninvolved, high above him. In the distance two searchlights, shifting in the sky, crossed and remained crossed, at a point a few miles forward. Someone had told him that their intersection would mark the objective of the advance and he stopped for a moment to marvel at the sight. Then he started to run with long strides, enjoying his freedom from vehicles and smoke, supposing the sappers were at hand. For a brief period he could see the western horizon agitated by flashes from the anti-tank guns then the dust clouded the air again and he realized there were men ahead of him, shadows, noiseless because their noise was lost in the greater noise of exploding shells, a field of ghosts. He had gone too far. He had reached the rear of the advancing infantry.

Walking two or three yards apart, their rifles held at the high port, bayonets fixed, the men went at a sort of drawling trudge under the shower of shells and mortars. They were on the mine fields, watching for trip wires. Each man had a pack between his shoulder blades and each pack was painted with a white cross, a marker for the man behind.

As Simon paused, uncertain what to do next, a man fell nearby and he went to him with some thought of giving help. The man, a thin, undersized youth, lay on his back and as the eyes gazed blankly at him, Simon was reminded of the death of Arnold and he wanted to take the body out of danger. Then he realized he was behaving like a fool. His job was to deliver a signal, not to get himself killed.

Having crossed the near section of the mine fields without a sight of the sappers, he was at a loss: where should he go, left or right? He ran to one of the slow, forward-pacing men and seized hold of his arm. The man, encapsulated in his own anxiety, gave a cry then stared at Simon in astonishment. Bending close to him, Simon shouted 'I've a signal for CO, Engineers. Where can I find them?'

The man twisted away as though from a lunatic and Simon let him go, then, running across the tide of the advance, came out into moonlight that whitened vast stretches of empty sand. The barrage had stopped again and despite the distant thud of guns, the effect was of silence through which he heard from somewhere far away the high whine of bagpipes. The music, as fragmentary as the singing of 'Lili Marlene', gradually faded out and he remembered there was no Scottish regiment in his corps. He knew he was lost. Having gone so eagerly into the fight, he now only wanted to get back to base.

He waited till the barrage renewed itself then, guided by the gun flashes, he ran towards the gun emplacements and came upon a group of men working intently together, lit by the star bursts of enemy shells. There were three men, one of them holding a long tube to which was fitted a plate, like a bed-warmer, which he slid over the sand surface. His companions watched with the tense attention of men to whom death was an immediate possibility. Simon stopped and stared at the mine-detector plate, fearful of interrupting the search. The man paused. He had found something. The second man marked the spot with tape and the third pinned the tape to the ground; then the three knelt and felt out the shape in the sand with questing fingers, as delicate as surgeons palpating an abdomen. Simon remained where he was till the mine was lifted, immobilized and put on one side, then he said, 'Sir!' They looked up, aware of his presence for the first time.

'I'm liaison. I've a signal for CO, Engineers.'

Without speaking, one of the three pointed to another group of men that stood darkly in the distance, then returned to the search.

The CO, receiving the signal, said, 'Have any difficulty finding us?'

'No, sir.'

'Clever lad. Report back "Detectors working OK".'

Triumphant, Simon put his head down and ran towards the barrage. Stumbling through the shrapnel fragments, he passed between the gun emplacements and found a supply truck starting back to the depot. Shouting to it to stop, he was taken back to his jeep that stood where he had left it, with Crosbie asleep over the wheel.

Crosbie, wakened, started at the sight of Simon's smoke blackened face and said, 'Where you been, sir?'

'Where d'you think? Delivering the signal, of course.'

'What's it like out there?'

'Not too good. Come on, Crosbie, let's get back.'

Expecting to be congratulated, Simon was disappointed when his safe return had so little effect on Fitzwilliams who said, 'All right, Boulderstone, get some sleep if you can. I've had to send Blair to the MO, so you and Donaldson will have to do a bit more.'

'Sorry about Blair, sir. Hope it's nothing serious?'

'I don't know. Could be that infectious jaundice. Lot of it around.' Having spoken, Fitzwilliams stuck out his lower lip so it was evident he knew exactly what was wrong with Blair.

Getting into his sleeping-bag, too tired to notice the noise of the barrage, Simon looked at his watch and saw it was four a.m., the latest he had ever been up in his life. He thought of the ghostly men, each with a white cross on his back, and imagined them still moving through the night. He almost envied them but greater than envy was his desire for sleep.

He was roused two hours later by Crosbie who handed him a mug of tea. Crosbie, wakened by the camp guard, said, 'We've got to go out again, sir. You're wanted at the command truck.'

Pulling on his jersey and gulping his tea, Simon went to the truck where a young captain called Dawson had taken over from Fitzwilliams. Simon, newly awake, was slightly unsteady and Dawson eyed him severely: 'Anything the matter?'

'No, sir. Didn't get much sleep, sir, that's all.'

'Most of our chaps'll get no sleep at all tonight. Now, we've had a signal from Corps CO. One of our armoured divisions has failed to reach its objective and the radio's haywire. No joy on the inter-com, either. So, there's nothing for it. You'll have to go and find what's holding them up.'

'Sir. Any idea where they are, sir?'

'Um!' Dawson said musingly: 'Thought you might ask that.' He straightened out a hand-drawn map of the positions, or supposed positions, of the different units and examined it with his head in his hands: 'Um, um, um! They're supposed to be in the northern corridor on their way to the final objective. That doesn't tell you much, does it?'

'What *is* the final objective, sir?'

'Up here it's Kidney Ridge, down there it's the Miteiriya. Ever heard of the Miteiriya?'

'Yes, sir.' It was fire from the Miteiriya Ridge that had killed Hugo and all the members of his patrol. But Hugo's death now seemed far in the past. Having seen what he had seen, Simon knew that if his brother had not died that time, he would, as likely as not, have died in the present battle.

Looking at Dawson's map, Simon saw the two broad arrows aimed, the one at Kidney Ridge, the other at the Miteiriya, and thought how simple and ordered the advance appeared on paper and what blinding confusion it was in fact.

'Which route shall I take, sir?'

'Find one that aims at the northern corridor. The corridor was supposed to be clear by daylight and the division on its way through. Ideally, they'd be out in the open by now, but they're not. Either they're off route and fart-arsing around, or they've been shot up by fire from Tel el Eisa. Either way, they're stuck. Your job is to contact Corps Commander and ask him what the hell? Or, in official language: "Is his division properly set up for the attack?" Got it? Any questions?'

'No, sir, no questions.'

The sun was now above the horizon. The barrage had ended at daybreak and with the main guns silent, the lesser guns – tank, machine, anti-aircraft – merged into a screen of noise so continuous the ear ceased to notice it. Seeing the dust of battle blotting out the western horizon, Simon no longer felt an eagerness for the fight. He knew what lay ahead and was reluctant to return to it. Yet he was luckier than most: he had had two hours sleep while other men, as Dawson had reminded him, had spent the night in danger and wakefulness.

They met the dust cloud where it had been the night before. Ambulances, appearing from it, were taking the severely wounded to the field hospital behind the camp. A mile further on, the jeep passed the dressing-station where men, awaiting transport, lay on stretchers on the ground itself, or sat, some alert, some with head down on knees, maimed, bloody and exhausted.

All the flies of the desert seemed to have been drawn here by the smell of festering flesh. Simon urged Crosbie to 'step on it' but there was worse to come. Less than a hundred yards further on, a mass grave had been dug to receive the dead. It was not yet full. A sickly effluvium came from it and flies hung over it like a shroud of black. Crosbie swerved, attempting to avoid its malodour, and ran off the track. The jeep ploughed into soft

277

sand. It stopped and they were at once set upon by swarms of flies, some no bigger than gnats, attacking the eyes and lips of the two men who, unable to escape, set to digging and putting mats under the wheels.

Eventually, jerking the jeep back on the track, they ran onto an empty track where Simon feared they might have driven beyond the battle area. Then two vehicles appeared on the road ahead. Distorted by the first wavering of mirage, they were difficult to identify but, seeing they were stationary, Simon told Crosbie to draw up. Walking towards them, he was disconcerted to see they were staff cars and four angry senior officers were arguing in front of them. As he approached, one of them was shouting, 'I still say it's not the way to use tanks,' and Simon hoped the tanks in question were the ones he was seeking. The four officers had an appearance of unnerving importance but one of them had noticed Simon and he felt it would be cowardly to retreat. He said, 'Excuse me, sir,' and as he spoke, all the men swung round on him in exasperated enquiry. He explained his mission and the one who had first noticed him, waved him on: 'They're about a mile up the track.'

'Are they out of the mine field, sir?'

'No, they're not out of the mine field – and if you want to know why, I suggest you toddle along and ask them.'

As Simon climbed back into the jeep, Crosbie muttered, 'Ratty bastard,' and Simon saw no reason to reprimand him.

From the churned up sand, the overturned markers, the smell of burnt oil and the thickening dust, it was soon evident that they were in the wake of an armoured division. They were also within range of enemy fire. Breathing in sand particles and the astringent smoke from mortars and shells, they bumped forward, swaying in ruts and tilting over sandhills, and passing vehicles that had been disabled and abandoned. A dispatch rider came out of the dust; Simon shouted, 'How far ahead are they?'

The rider stopped and leaning back over his dispatch box, pointed to a black cloud on the horizon: 'That's them. You'll catch them up in no time: they're down to a crawl.'

But nearly an hour passed before Simon came in sight of the rear tanks, a line spaced over so wide a field the flanking vehicles were almost out of sight. The blanket of smoke about them was

278

like the blanket of night. The tanks appeared to be motionless but coming close behind them, Simon saw they were making a very slight headway into a fog that was peppered with the star flash of bursting shells.

Crosbie braked, and turned uncertainly to Simon. He did not try to speak but his expression asked: 'Must we go into this?'

Standing up, Simon could see that one of the nearer tanks had come to a stop and the bailed-out crew was starting to dig in. He motioned Crosbie to drive towards it but as the jeep turned, shells fell about them and Crosbie stopped again. Trying to keep up his own courage, Simon bawled at him, 'Get a move on, Crosbie!' and they continued with flak hitting their tin hats and striking the sides of the jeep. At the sight of them, the tank commander waved them furiously away: 'What the hell are you doing here? Go back. You're drawing enemy fire.'

Awaiting no further encouragement, Crosbie swung the jeep round and tried to fly the field but Simon, catching hold of the wheel, forced him to stop.

Simon knew he must again make his way forward on foot. Ordering Crosbie to drive back to the track and wait, he ran to the tank crew and asked where he could find the CO. The tank commander answered with disgruntled brevity: 'Up front. 'Bout a mile,' then as Simon started forward, shouted after him: 'And don't take that bloody jeep. Everything that moves, draws fire.'

Bent almost double, finding what cover he could from each tank as he reached it, Simon went at a good pace but slackened every few minutes to ask direction from the tank commanders. The commanders, bored and irritated by the delays, sweating in the heat generated by the slow grind forward, were as perfunctory as the first man. No one knew for sure where the CO was to be found. All they could do was gesture him towards the forward sector where the leading tanks had come to a stop. The way ahead was lit by blazing tanks, and tank crews were tramping back to dig themselves in when they found a likely space. Bren carriers, looking for wounded, came out of the dust, swaying about until they made sufficient speed to steady themselves.

At the front of the advance, which was less an advance than a standstill, enemy shelling was intense. Crouching behind tanks, darting on whenever there was an instant's respite, Simon's progress was slow. As he sheltered behind one tank, a shell burst over it, not penetrating the fabric but showering it with burning oil that spattered his shoulders. Small flames sprang up over his jersey and as he gathered up sand to quench them, the whole tank was enveloped in fire and he threw himself down, rolling on the ground until he was away from the conflagration.

He found the commanding officer sitting on the lee side of his tank in an attitude of despondent impatience. Having read the signal, the commander said in a strained voice: 'The Scorpions broke down. Fault was the flails raised too much dust, damned things over-heated and the sappers had to scrap them. Half the detectors brought up were faulty and now the chaps are down to bayonet prodding. Slow business. That's why we're stuck here. Lot of sitting ducks.'

'You know your radio's packed up, sir?'

'Yep. We were shot up and shrapnel knocked it out. We've given it a shake but the damned thing's kaput . . .' He stopped then as though galvanized, shouted at the top of his voice: 'We're breaking through.' The tanks began to roll forward and at once, as though the movement had been a sign to heaven, the sinking sun cut the fog with a shaft of orange light and enemy fire became furious. The CO ordered Simon away: 'Ruddy counter-attack just as we've got the light in our eyes. Better dig in till the show's over. Goodbye. Good luck.'

Making his way back between the advancing tanks, Simon came on a trench and threw himself into it. The men in possession gave him space and they all sat together, speechless beneath the uproar of battle. Too tired now to care what was going on, Simon sank into drowsiness, imaging himself back in Garden City with Edwina, in her long, white dress, smiling her con-ciliatory smile. Now he did not feel resentment but a confused pity for her and for all womankind. In a world where men died young, what was a girl to do? Facing life alone, she had to fend for herself. He murmured, 'Poor little thing! Poor little thing!' then sleep came down on him.

He woke at daybreak to find he was alone in the trench. The noises of the night had come to a stop and, climbing out, he found the tanks had advanced out of sight. He had the field to himself – but not quite to himself. Burnt out tanks stood about him like disabled crows and the smell of burning was heavy on the air. There were dead men and men not yet dead, and the Brens were returning to pick them up.

As the sun topped the horizon, the first, subtle light of day swept like a wave over the desert and about him, and passed on, lighting desert and more desert, miles of desert that had once been no-man's-land. He was not sure now whether the division's objective had been Kidney Ridge or the Miteiriya but it was in no-man's-land that Hugo had died. He had bled to death like the dead left behind by the battle and perhaps he had lain here, on this barren ground that was now the field of victory.

Walking back among tanks as useless as the sand they stood on, stepping over the bodies of lost young men, Simon asked, 'Is this what Hugo died for? And am I to die for this?' There was no one to answer him and as he realized how hungry he was, he forgot his own questions and started to run.

Seven

Castlebar who, once a week, went to tutor a Greek boy in Alexandria, came back with the news that there was heavy combat in the desert. It vibrated through roads and pavements and at times, when the air was very still, people could hear the boom of guns. No news had been released. No one knew what was happening but Castlebar was sure that this was a major battle.

Jackman, not too pleased that Castlebar should be the bringer of such tidings, said, 'Of course it is. Didn't I tell you something was on? What do you think the preparations have been for? This is it.'

Still, there was no certainty. Alex, like Cairo, was a city of rumours. The gunfire might mean a German offensive or merely a minor skirmish, or the Afrika Korps sending a parthian shot before packing and leaving their long-held position. Ten days passed, then the civilians were allowed to know that there had been a second battle of Alamein, the greatest battle of the desert war. The allied forces were pushing Rommel back to the frontier and perhaps even further than that.

Meanwhile, an extraordinary thing happened. The sun, the great god of Egypt, disappeared and the noonday sky, so constant in its brilliance, was hidden behind cloud. A biblical darkness overhung the city and people, hastening in the streets, feared a cataclysm – the day of judgement or, at the least, an earthquake – and sought what cover they could find.

Angela and Harriet were out at the time. Harriet, finding that Angela hardly knew where the Muski was, insisted they must go there. She said, 'You should learn how the other half live,' and she led her through the narrow, dusty lanes to her favourite shop: a twilit place, like a vast tent, where old glass and china ornaments were heaped together on shelves and floor. In the centre of this disordered treasure store, there was a glass case lit by acetylene lamps and full of gleaming jewels. Harriet called Angela to it: 'Come and see the rose-diamonds.'

The rose-diamonds, set in pinkish gold, were formed into brooches, earrings, bracelets and necklaces, and Harriet, who could not afford to buy them, was attracted by their elaborate opulence. Angela, lifting the pieces and examining them, asked, 'What are rose-diamonds? They look like sugar crystals.'

Harriet repeated the question to a man in a dirty galabiah who stood guard over the case. He replied in an aloof manner, having superior knowledge: 'Rosy di'mints? - they is di'mints.'

Angela laughed, 'So now we know. Shall I buy one for Bill?' She picked among the designs, rejecting the flowers, and came upon a brooch in the shape of a heart: 'What about this? I'll give it to him for a giggle.' She did not haggle over the price but, paying what the shop-keeper asked, she laughed excitedly at the thought of giving the large, diamond-studded heart to Castlebar.

Coming out of the shop, they found the outdoors nearly as dark as the indoors. Made nervous by the unusual gloom, they hurried through the lanes, instinctively making for the European quarter as though there they might escape the ominous sky. But in the Esbekiyah the sky grew more ominous. The office workers were coming out for the siesta and the businessmen who could afford taxis were squabbling over them. As the first rain fell, one man covered his fez with his pocket-handkerchief and before the pavements were wet, every fez was protected by a covering of some sort. Drops, heavy and immense, splashed down and merged into each other, and the Egyptians began to panic at the sight. The two women, having reached the western end of the Esbekiyah, ran to Shepherd's Hotel and there, standing under the canopy, they watched the gutters flow and overflow, then cover the streets. Cairo had no main drainage and the water, speeding like a river past the hotel, could only flow down the Kasr el Nil until it lost itself in the Nile.

The shop owners, opposite the hotel, were wading up to their knees, putting up shutters as though against a riot. Cars, forced to a stop, stood in the stream with passengers waving and begging for rescue, though there was no one to rescue them.

One of the men gathered under the canopy said, 'They will be drown-ed' and this possibility was discussed around Harriet and Angela with sombre satisfaction. Angela said, 'It's too heavy to last,' but it did last and, becoming bored with it, she suggested they go inside and have a drink.

Staff officers, who regarded the place as their own, filled every chair in the main rooms and possessed every table. When they showed no sign of moving, Angela said loudly, with a gleeful contempt, 'When I was a little girl, during the First War, I heard the term "temporary gentleman". I couldn't think what it meant then, but now I know.' At this, two of the officers rose and Angela, saying, 'Oh, too kind!', smiled upon them and sat down.

Delighted by her success, she laughed and winked at Harriet, but this mood did not last. The latest communiqué from the front stated 'Axis forces in full retreat'. This news, that had rejoiced the British in Cairo, had merely perturbed Angela.

She said to Harriet: 'I don't like it. If the army leaves here, that bitch will stand a much better chance of getting back.'

'What do you think would happen if she got back?'

'Bill says he intends telling her he's finished with her.'

Pondering on the fact that both her friends were enamoured of men whom they might never have for their own, Harriet could see that uncertainty was a strong potion and said: 'Angela, would you want Castlebar so much if he didn't belong to someone else?'

Angela put the question aside with a gesture: 'Don't let's think any more about it.' Looking into her bag, she brought out the rose-diamond brooch to distract them: '"Rosy di'mints? They is di'mints." Wasn't that wonderful? Come on, let's go to the restaurant and eat.'

The noise of the rain stopped while they were at luncheon but when they returned to the terrace, they found they were trapped by the stream that still filled the street and held captive the occupants of the cars. Another hour passed before the last of it, a long, low ripple of water, slid down Kasr el Nil and away. The sun broke through the clouds, the roads began to steam, dry circular patches appeared on the paving stones, drivers struggled to restart their engines, and Harriet and Angela were released.

But that was not all. The rain had watered not only the city but the surrounding desert with remarkable consequences. The papers reported a marvel: seed that had lain for years dormant in the sand, sprang up and blossomed but the great age of the seeds prevented normal growth. The flowers were miniatures of their kind. Dobson, reading this at breakfast, said he had heard that the Saccara sands were covered with flowers.

'A garden,' he said, 'a veritable garden!' and Harriet, turning eagerly to Guy, put her hand on his arm: 'It's your free day. Do let us go and see it.'

'How would we get there?' The tram-line ended at Mena House.

'But why can't we take a taxi?'

Guy laughed at the idea of taking a taxi into the desert: 'I've better things to do,' he said and Harriet knew he had meant to refuse from the start.

'But it's your free day.'

'That's when I really work. I'm preparing my troops' entertainment. I've a hundred and one things to do.'

Guy had begun to plan the entertainment some time before and Harriet had hoped that by now it was forgotten. But it was not forgotten. 'Haven't the troops enough entertainments?'

'This will be no ordinary show.' To prevent further argument, he jumped up, his breakfast unfinished, as Hassan was putting down a bowl of fruit steeped in permanganate. He took a couple of guavas, splashing the cloth with purple fluid, and called out as he went: 'Sorry about that.'

Dobson looked after him: 'What energy! What a man! He never stops, does he?'

'No, never. How would you like to be married to him?'

'Oh, come now, Harriet. You wouldn't have him any different?'

'Wouldn't I? These entertainments worry me to death. Suppose this one fails?'

'Not likely. He's got ENSA backing.'

Harriet said, 'How do you know?': then, too late, realized she

285

was admitting her own ignorance and put in a second question to erase the first: 'Why should ENSA back Guy's show?'

'You know what he's like! He could charm the monkeys down from the trees.'

'Yes.' Harriet sat silent for a few minutes then said, 'I wish I were a man fighting in the desert.'

'You'd find it a very great bore.'

'It couldn't be worse than our life here.'

'*Here*? Most Englishwomen think they're damned lucky to be here.'

'Well, I'm not most Englishwomen.'

Edwina was supposed to be on duty at the Embassy but, coming slowly to the table, her hand on her brow, her hair dishevelled, she said in a small voice: 'Oh, Dobbie, I've got such a head. I don't think I can go in this morning.'

Dobson, in a tone of bantering commiseration, said, 'Poor thing! Then I suppose we'll have to manage without you. What about the evening stint?'

'I'll try, Dobbie dear.'

Dobson left for the Embassy and Edwina drooped over the table, sighing, until the telephone rang. Coming to instant life, she reached it before Hassan had found his way into the hall. Harriet, hearing one side of an animated conversation, gathered that Peter Lisdoonvarna had the morning off and was taking Edwina out. She came back to say, 'Oh, Harriet, to think I might have been at the office. What luck I was here!' She danced away crying, 'What luck! What luck! What luck!'

Harriet, hearing her singing as she splashed under the shower, envied her excitement. That, Harriet thought, was what women most wanted, and what risks they took to attain it. She, herself, had married and travelled to the other side of Europe with someone she barely knew. She might have been abandoned there. She might have been murdered. In fact, she had suffered no more than disappointment, finding that her husband's devotion to all comers left little room for her.

She was still sitting over her coffee when Peter Lisdoonvarna arrived, giving off vigour like a magnetic force. The shutters had been closed but the semi-darkness seemed to disperse itself as he gave Harriet a hearty kiss on the lips. All good-looking girls were Peter's girls and he approached them with such boisterous confidence, few could resist him. Edwina shouted to him from her room but he was quite happy to stay with Harriet, telling her he had just bought King Farouk's second-best Bentley.

'Magnificent job! Been angling for it for weeks. Park Ward body. Eight-litre chassis. Bonnet as long as the gun on a Panzer Mark III. I know some chaps don't think it's worth owning a car out here, but I'm the car-owning type. Like to know it's there. Get in and push off, no hanging around for taxis. You've got to have some relaxation after the stultifying, bloody chores at HQ. Care for a spin? Like to try her out?'

Harriet felt there was nothing she would like better, but what of Edwina? Hesitating, she asked, 'Where are you going?'

'Don't know. Haven't thought about it. Anywhere you like.'

'Would you go to Saccara?'

'Why not? Saccara it is!' As Edwina came into the room, he shouted: 'Come on, then, girls.'

Edwina hesitated only a moment before she smiled and said, 'Is Harriet coming with us? How lovely!'

The car, standing outside the house, was indeed magnificent. Harriet was put into the spacious back seat and, when they were under way, was soon forgotten. Edwina, having spent her enthusiasm about the car, put an arm round Peter's shoulder and her head against his head, but Peter still gave his attention to the Bentley's splendour. 'All leather upholstery,' he said.

'Leather, really?' Edwina spoke as though leather were an unheard of luxury.

Peter demonstrated the automatic opening and closing of the windows, and the button that sent the canvas roof folding back behind the seats. Harriet attempted to murmur her appreciation but anything she said was lost behind Edwina's gasps and squeals of wonder.

Unable to compete, Harriet looked out of her side window to see what could be seen. And she saw a peasant, head bound up in a scarf, mooning along the pavement. The scarf indicated that he had toothache or a cold, but she knew he was not thinking of his ailments. Instead he was telling himself one of the fantasies that compensated the poor for their poverty. A shop-keeper had once told her that a rich American lady had fallen in love with a guide at the pyramids and gone to live with him in his one-roomed village hut. Harriet had laughed at the story but the shop-keeper believed it because belief made life tolerable. She knew the peasant in the scarf, grinning, head wagging, was imagining just such a romance for himself.

Out on the Saccara road, Peter said, 'Like to travel at m'own speed,' and pressing on the accelerator, the car sped through villages, scattering children and chickens and causing the villagers to shout after him in rage. Someone must have telephoned the sugar factory at El-Hawandiyen for the factory workers had gathered outside the building with stones in their hands. The hood was down and seeing women in the car, most of them let the stones fall harmlessly but two let fly and hit the side of the car. Edwina screamed, hiding her face in Peter's shoulder, and he replaced the hood and latched it. He did this without losing speed while he grumbled: 'Damned fool country, this is! Can't take a gallop without chaps chucking stones. Wish I was back in the blue. Do what you like there.'

Edwina, folded against Peter, murmured: 'Oh, Peter, you know you don't want to leave me!'

'Perhaps not, but I'm a soldier, not a ruddy pen-pusher.'

They reached the hummocked site that had once been the great city of Memphis. Colossal statues lay among the palm groves but these held no interest for Peter who drove on rapidly, seeing no cause to stop until the track ended at Mariette's house.

It was mid-day when, even in winter, the temperature was high. Rubbing the sweat from his broad nose, Peter said, 'Let's get under cover,' and pulling Edwina with him, he made for the Serapeum, the enclosure of the sacred bulls.

Harriet, walking round, looked for the miniature flowers but they had scarcely had time to open before the sun sucked up their moisture and now nothing remained but dry stalks, like matchsticks stuck in the sand. But there were other tokens of the rain. Fragments of fallen temples had been washed to the surface and she came on a stone lotus, half of which had been buried until now. The exposed half was pitted by time but the other, newly revealed, was as smooth as flesh. The wet wind had set the sand into long, sculpted folds, washed to a salty whiteness, and Harriet felt well rewarded for her journey in the back seat.

When she first went into the Serapeum, she could see no sign of Peter and Edwina, but then she came on them, obscure in the shadows, their bodies pressed together as though each sought to merge into the other. Hearing her, they parted for an instant then at once rejoined and she moved away, feeling the solitude of those who are outside the circle of ecstasy. She wandered to the other end of the gallery and waited till the others tired of their dalliance. Edwina, giving a scream, broke away from Peter and he pursued her round the huge sarcophagi then, seizing her, he pushed her down onto a slab of black granite and threw himself on top of her. She cried out, almost smothered by his weight: 'Peter, oh Peter, you're killing me.' He let her go and she sprang up, laughing provocatively, and the pursuit began again.

Harriet, turning her back on them as they embraced, reflected that this burial place of bulls that had become lords of the western world, might well inspire Peter who was a bull himself and a lord, though of a different kind. She did not know whether the frenzy had a climax but she heard Peter say, finality in his voice: 'All right, let's go. We'll trundle back to Mena for lunch.'

They had not seen much but it did not occur to Peter that there was anything to see. As for luncheon, he took it for granted that Mena would please the women and he was right. Edwina smiled on Harriet as though she were bestowing a gift on her and Harriet smiled back, acknowledging the benefaction.

But at the hotel, the porter told them that bar and restaurant were full and they would have to wait. Harriet suggested they go and look at the matrix of the Ship of the Sun, the ship that daily crossed the heavens and at night sank down into the underworld.

Peter laughed, 'I've had enough of the bloody sun. I'm going to powder m'nose,' and left the women to go alone and look down into the concave cradle which had once held the sacred ship.

When they entered the hotel vestibule, Peter was standing with three other officers, his brows drawn blackly together. Edwina whispered, 'What do you think they're telling him?' but both women knew that the talk could only be about the desert conflict.

He was still frowning when he joined them and Edwina, trying to catch hold of his hand, asked, 'What's the matter, darling?'

Avoiding her grasp, he said, 'I'm missing the whole damned shooting match. That's all. Let's go and eat.'

Luncheon, which was to have been a pleasure, was no pleasure at all. Peter, silent in discontent, ignored Edwina who stared helplessly at him then turned to Harriet with an expression that said, 'See what I have to put up with!' Harriet, no longer excluded by their love-making, now felt an intruder upon a situation which she could do nothing to help.

Driving back between the bean fields into the Cairo suburbs, Edwina whispered, 'Honestly, Teddy-bear, do you really want to go back to the desert?'

'Yep.'

'But what would poor Edwina do without her Teddy-bear?'

'Find another Teddy-bear.'

'I only want you.'

The sweet scent of the bean fields filled the air but it meant nothing to Edwina who, in anguish, moved from one desperate manoeuvre to another. In a wheedling whisper she said: 'If we were married, or even engaged, it would not be so bad.'

'Why? What difference would that make?'

'All the difference in the world. We'd belong. I'd have a right to know if anything happened to you.'

'The old next-of-kin, eh?' Peter gave an ironical chuckle.

'Darling, I'm serious.'

'Don't be serious, old girl. I'm not worth it. Not good enough for you . . .'

Could there, Harriet wondered, be a more discouraging rejection than that? But Edwina refused to be discouraged. She protested that Peter was all she wanted. Half weeping, she pleaded her love for him while he stared at the road as though hearing nothing. At last, as her voice dissolved in tears, he said: 'Look here, old thing. The truth is, I'm all tied up.'

'You . . . you mean you're engaged?'

'Something like that.' He gave a laugh and Edwina thought he might be teasing.

'Who bothers about engagements these days? The war could

go on for years. I bet, by the time you get back, she'll have married someone else.' When Peter laughed again, Edwina persisted: 'Perhaps she *has* married someone else already.'

'Not very likely.'

'You're pulling my leg, aren't you?'

'Who could resist it?' he patted her knee: 'Such a nice, long leg!'

They were crossing the river and among the noise of the Bulaq traffic Edwina let the matter drop for the moment, but she could not resist a last triumphant shot; 'Still, you can't get back to the desert, can you?'

Peter glumly agreed: 'Doesn't look like it.'

Smiling to herself, Edwina took out her compact and looked at her pretty face. The war was on her side. It kept Peter in Egypt and the authorities kept him in Cairo. He was with her and while he was with her, she had reason to hope. The conversation, that had disturbed Harriet, seemed to have had little effect on Edwina. She powdered her face and moved close to Peter again. They were reconciled and when the women left the car in Garden City, he said, 'What are you doing tonight, old girl?'

'Nothing in particular.'

'Call for you around eight, then?'

'Oh, lovely, darling. See you soon.'

And Edwina went joyfully up the steps to the flat confident, it seemed, she would win him in the end.

Eight

On the fourth day of battle, relays of exhausted men came into the camp to be replaced by reserve troops. These men, most of them from tanks, had been lucky to get three hours sleep in a night and Simon, when he heard this, felt ashamed of his own nervous fatigue. Unable to excuse himself, he told himself that he would have done better to remain under fire and become conditioned to it. The rest periods between his sorties into action, and the fact he was liable to be wakened at any hour of the night, had demoralized him.

He had little or no idea what had been gained by the fighting and Fitzwilliams, though he questioned the returning men, could not tell him much. The general belief was that in the northern sector British armour had driven a wedge into the German defences but no sooner had this news gone round, than the commander in the sector radioed to say that his whole brigade was ringed by enemy anti-tank guns.

Fitzwilliams, like the officers Simon had approached on the road, was critical of the strategy of the battle: 'Bad show, I call it. Suppose the brass hats know what they're doing, but I've never heard of tanks being sent into a breach. Could lose the whole damn lot.'

For a while it seemed that, if not lost, the battle was petering out. There were a couple of empty days for Simon who had become used to action and felt the need for excitement. He hung around the command vehicle in a state of restless boredom; then a fresh offensive began. Given a signal to deliver, he ran gleefully to the jeep shouting, 'Come on, Crosbie, wake up. This is the life.' Crosbie, baffled as usual by Simon's moods, grunted and muttered, 'Sir.'

At the end of October, the division to which Simon belonged was withdrawn from the line. The tank crews, decimated by continuous fighting, were ordered back to reserve positions and Simon was assigned a new sector. He had to report to a coastal area where a fresh division was being prepared for an attack.

When he set out, November was beginning with dramatic splendour. The sky, that had dazzled the sight with its brazen emptiness, was filling with immense cumulous clouds. They were rising out of the sea and stretching, as though each was trying to over-top the other, until by mid-day they had reached the zenith. They were of different colours: one was a dark purple, its neighbour, swelling up behind, was azure, while on either side of them billowing curves of wool white, catching the sun on outer rims, gleamed like mother-of-pearl.

Simon, amazed by this display, said to Crosbie, 'What do you make of it?'

Raising his eyes without lifting his head, Crosbie muttered, 'Looks like trouble to me.'

The dark cloud grew until it dominated the sky. The wind strengthened in the unusual gloom and the sand lifted, but the storm did not break until the men were in sight of the camp. The rain came at them like a slanting curtain, as hard and rough as emery paper, and clattered against the jeep. The road was blotted out. Crosbie braked and flung himself round to find ground-sheets in the back of the jeep. They wrapped themselves up and waited for the deluge to slacken. The rain stopped within minutes but the camp, when they reached it, was under water.

Dawson, in the command vehicle, told Simon they were preparing to move forward. The new arrivals would be lucky if they could find themselves tea and bully.

The men, splashing through puddles, were shifting equipment. Though the water sank rapidly, the ground was left muddy and a wetness hung in the air. Dawson had been right about food. Crosbie, sent to forage, came back with mugs of tea and a couple of bully-beef sandwiches. They would have to spend the night in the jeep. Crosbie took up his favourite position, sprawled over the wheel and Simon climbed into the back seat. He wakened, cramped and chilly, at midnight when the petrol replenishing lorries went out. Then the barrage started up again, and turning on his back, staring up at the starless sky, he felt the war would never end. This, he told himself, could be his whole life and it might be a short life. He was as liable as any man in the field to be killed by the enemy. He turned towards the jeep back and tried to lose his old, abiding fear in sleep but just as he was drifting off, a messenger shook him and ordered him to report to his CO.

Dawson had gone off duty and a stranger was in charge of the command truck. He sounded as disconsolate as Simon felt. ''Fraid I've got to send you up front. The Kiwis are supposed to be advancing on Fuka but they've hit a snag. They say there's an unmapped mine field in their path. Well, here . . .' he spread out a hand-drawn sketch of the field; '. . . it's marked as a dummy, put down by our chaps last June. The commander won't take my word for it. Says it's too risky. Says he'll dig in till he gets further orders. You'll have to take this along to show him. Let him see for himself. Right?'

'Sir. Which route, sir?'

'God knows. All the routes are in a mess. Sheer, bloody shambles between here and Tel el Eisa. Try "Star", it's no worse than the others. If you can't find it, you'll have to ask as you go.'

Setting out, Simon had no more zest for the journey than Crosbie had. The battle had gone on too long and all he could feel now was a racking weariness.

The track, churned up by vehicles, had dried and hardened to the consistency of concrete and the jeep rocked on ridges and skidded through slime left by puddles. The sky had cleared and the waning moon gave a bleak, dispirited light.

The track was soon lost and they made their way guided by staccato flashes on the western horizon. They had covered little more than a mile when Simon realized the division had driven straight through an enemy position. The tanks standing idle about them were German tanks; the bodies propped in slit trenches wore German headgear and the black-clad figures that trudged past the jeep, avoiding it with blundering steps, were unarmed Germans who had given themselves up. The tank commanders, with no room or time for prisoners, had sent them back and now they were making their own way into captivity. Thankfully, Simon imagined. Once they reached the camp, they would throw themselves down to sleep and Simon wished he could do the same.

Crosbie had other thoughts. Looking askance at the burnt-out tanks, he at last reached the point of speech, 'You seen inside these ruddy Marks? God, what a sight!'

'Don't look, then. Keep your eyes on the road.'

Beyond the German positions, the first reserves of tanks waited, hidden among sand bunkers. Ahead of them was the confusion that Simon now knew and expected. The forward tanks had thrown up a screen of dust, blinding the drivers of vehicles in the rear. Lorries had bogged down in the soft sand and commanders were trying to guide their tanks round each obstruction as they came to it. They were lit by blazing vehicles that glowed through the dust like a stage effect. None of it was new to Simon. Seeing petrol leaking from a burning truck, he shouted to Crosbie: 'Make a dash for it before the whole show goes up and takes us with it.'

When they drove out of the dust belt, they found the moon had set and the overhanging face of the Fuka escarpment was just visible, darker than the prevailing darkness. Beneath it there was a gathering of torches where the tank commanders conferred. Simon, going forward on foot, reached the command tank as the sky grew pallid with first light.

The CO greeted him with little patience, saying as Simon handed him the map: 'What've you got there? Let's hope it makes sense because nothing else does. They call us a *corps de chasse* but how the hell can we chase anything with supply trucks littering the ground and now a ruddy mine field in the way.'

'It's a dummy, sir.'

'So they think, but I want to know more about it. We've lost seventeen tanks already, mostly on mines.'

'You can see it here, sir. Our chaps laid it in June when the retreat was on.'

'Damn fool thing to do.' The commander, in a fury, turned his back on Simon and Simon, in no better humour, went to the jeep, saying to himself, 'They might have let me sleep.'

He had only been gone ten minutes but Crosbie was unconscious over the wheel and Simon, with scarcely the heart to wake him, thought, 'Don't blame him, either,' then shouted 'Come on, Crosbie, lazy bastard. For God's sake, let's get back to camp.'

Nine

Winter enlivened not only the human occupants of Garden City but the cockroaches that scuttled, as big as rats, round the skirting. A green praying mantis, four inches high, was found clinging to a curtain. Bats, delighting in their new vitality, began to visit the flat. One night three of them flew together through the open balcony door and out through the window at the other end of the room. Before anyone had recovered from his surprise, they were back through the window and out at the door, giving a playful skip in mid-flight as though they were playing a game.

Dobson thought they must be attracted by the light but Angela and Harriet said bats avoided light. No one expected to see them again but next evening, while the sky still held the glow of sunset, the bats returned. This time five came in a close line and at one point each did a little caracole that seemed a salute to the humans in the room.

For the next two nights there were no bats then three – perhaps the original three – darted in and out again. Bats came at intervals for nearly a fortnight. Harriet, who used to fear them, began to see them as guardian spirits and feel affection for them. Then, just when it seemed they had adopted the place, the visits ceased. Harriet could not believe they had gone for good and waited in to see them. When they did not come, she said to Angela, 'We are bereft.'

'We can go bat watching at the Union.'

That meant they would have to go in early evening when the bats were most active and people could sit out for a little in the moist, mild air under the towering trees. In the officers' club opposite, the Egyptian officers also sat out at sunset, wearing their winter uniforms, but as soon as the evening star showed in the copper green after-glow, they gathered themselves together and went indoors. As the cold came down, Angela said, 'We should go in, too.'

Harriet, who had been watching the short, darting flight of the bats among the trees, sadly agreed: 'We might as well. They're not our bats. They don't know us.'

Angela laughed at her and stood up, eager to go in search of Castlebar.

Although the two women were not expected at that hour, Castlebar and Jackman reached the table almost as soon as the whisky bottle. Angela, laughing, pushed it towards them, pretending that that alone was the attraction.

Having set up his cigarette pack and lit a cigarette, Castlebar put his hand in his pocket and brought out the heart of rose-diamonds. He smiled at Angela, saying, 'Pin it on for me.'

Angela gave a little scream of shocked delight: 'You wouldn't dare!'

'Oh, wouldn't I?' Castlebar, his eye-tooth out to meet the challenge, glanced round to see who was watching him, and pinned the heart to his lapel then slid his hand under the table in search of Angela's hand, and so they sat with the heart between them.

Several people were watching them but Jackman looked the other way. Harriet thought he was showing disapproval but, following the direction of his gaze, she saw a short, heavy, square-built woman looking for someone among the tables. Her light clothing marked her as a newcomer, whose blood had not been conditioned by the Egyptian summer. Jackman made no sign but his expression, a slightly malicious expression, suggested to Harriet that he knew who she was.

Catching sight of Castlebar, she came straight to him, watching him with a purposeful and sardonic smile. She called out, 'Hello, Wolfie!'

At the sound of her strong, carrying voice, Castlebar's eyes opened. Seeing who had spoken, his startled stare changed to alarm. He grew pale. Dropping Angela's hand as though he could not imagine what he was doing with it, he half lifted himself from the chair and tried to speak. His stammer increasing so he was barely intelligible, he began, 'M-m-m-Mona ... L-L-L-Lambkin!' then too shocked to support himself, he fell back and tried again: 'H-h-h-how...'

'How did I get here?' Mona Castlebar's eyebrows rose in triumph. She placed a chair firmly at the table and sat upon it: 'By air, of course. Didn't you get my cable?'

'N-n-n-no.'

The company was silent, looking at this weighty woman who had once been Castlebar's Lambkin: then they saw the horror her arrival had roused in him. Of course there had been no cable. She had come without warning, intending to catch him in some misdeed, and she had caught him. With her sardonic smile fixed, she looked first at Harriet then at Angela, not sure which had been the lure. Returning to Castlebar, she said: 'What a splendid decoration! Is it meant for me?'

As she put out her hand to take the brooch, Angela, roused from her first dismay, spoke with spirit: 'No, it's not meant for you. It was a present for my friend Harriet here. Bill put it on for a joke.'

'Y-y-yes ... just a l-l-l-little joke.' Castlebar's fingers shook as he undid the brooch and handed it to Angela. Angela passed it to Harriet who put it into her handbag, then they all looked again at Mona Castlebar.

'Well, well!' she said and the rest were silent. She observed each in turn as though summing them up. She did not like them and she knew they did not like her. She met their antagonism with a bellicose smile.

Harriet wondered how any woman, newly arrived after a long journey, could seem so confidently in control of a situation. Did her appearance, perhaps, mask her diffidence? Harriet thought not. But, of course, she was not in a strange place. She had lived in Cairo before the war and had known exactly where to come to find her husband.

Her dress was cut to display her only attraction: fine shoulders and bosom. She was older than the others at the table, even older than Castlebar. Her square face with its short nose, small eyes and heavy chin, was already falling into lines. Newly arrived from a temperate climate, her pallor seemed ghastly to the others and it was accentuated by the unreal red of her hair.

Castlebar put out a hand for another cigarette and could scarcely lift it from the box. He poured himself the last of the whisky and his wife said, 'You've had about enough,' then added as one demanding her due: 'If anyone's buying another round, mine's a strong ale.'

'Now, Lambkin, you won't get strong ale here – you know that. Have this,' Castlebar pushed his glass across to her: 'Come on. Tell us how you got here.' His wheedling tone suggested a hope that somehow an explanation would send her back where she came from.

'You do want to know, don't you, Wolfie?'

He nodded and Harriet realized that 'Wolfie' was a reference to the tooth that overhung his lip when he was angry or when, as now, he was hopelessly at a loss.

Provokingly, she went on, 'Hmmm,' as though about to tell but taking her time and then, apparently revealing something too precious to be lightly given away, she said: 'ENSA. They sent me out with a party.'

Neither Angela nor Castlebar had ever thought of ENSA. Angela glanced at him but he was careful not to glance at her.

Harriet asked, 'You sing, do you?'

'Of course. I'm a pro. Hasn't Bill told you about me?'

Evading the question, Harriet turned to Angela: 'Mrs Castlebar ought to meet Edwina as they're both singers. Perhaps we could arrange an evening?'

Angela did not reply. Castlebar nervously asked: 'Where are you staying, Lambkin?'

'With you, I hope.'

'Yes. Oh, yes. I just thought ENSA might be putting you up in style.'

'They probably would if I wanted it, but I don't intend having much truck with them.'

'Surely, if they brought you out . . .'

'Don't be soft, Wolfie. Now I'm here, they can't do anything. They can't send me back. I've got the laugh on them. Anyway, you know I've a sensitive larynx. Anything can upset it, so if I can't sing, I can't.' Mona emptied the glass as though to say, 'That's final,' then, fixing her yellow-brown eyes upon him, gave an order: 'Better get a move on, Wolfie. I left my bags at the

299

ENSA office. We must pick them up, and I want to buy a few things. So come along.'

Castlebar rose, promptly but shakily, holding to the edge of the table. Instinctively, Angela rose with him and made to steady him, then drew her hand away, realizing she had been displaced. Observing this movement, Mona stared at Angela with narrowed eyes. Angela had betrayed herself.

As the Castlebars went ahead, the others followed, having nothing else to do. Jackman, who had not spoken since Mona's appearance, stared at her back view and gave a snigger of contempt. Her short dress was made shorter by being stretched over her massive backside.

'Look at that woman's legs,' he said. 'They're solid wood. Not even a slit between them.'

Angela tried to smile but her misery was apparent. She walked with head hanging and Harriet took hold of her hand. They left the Union and went across the bridge to the taxi rank outside the Extase. Mona was already seated inside a taxi when they arrived and Castlebar, peremptory in his agitation and guilt, said to Angela, 'Got to call it a day. Have to collect the luggage . . . s-s-s-see her to the flat. She looks all in.'

'Does she?' Angela's tone was sullen but in spite of herself, she put a hand on Castlebar's arm and looked appealingly at him.

From inside the taxi came a warning call: 'Wolfie!'

'M-m-m-must go.' Castlebar sped from the company, fearing to be detained, and struggled into the taxi. Angela watched after it as it drove away.

Jackman, tittering, said to her: 'Think of it! There's only one bed at his place. He'll have to sleep with her.' When Angela did not reply, he asked: 'Where are we going now?'

She turned abruptly from him and put out her hand to Harriet: 'Nowhere. I'm tired. I want an early night.'

Abandoning Jackman, the two women walked slowly under the riverside trees towards Garden City.

'He won't stay with her long,' Harriet said.

'Perhaps not, but they've been married for twenty years. If he can't bear her (as he says) why didn't he leave her long ago?'

'He had no incentive. It's different now.' Harriet took the rose-diamond heart from her bag: 'Here's the brooch. At least, she didn't get that.'

'I gave it to you.'

'But you didn't mean me to keep it.'

'Yes. Why not? You like those stones. What good is it to me?'

'Thank you.' Harriet paused and holding the brooch cupped in her hand looked at the diamonds catching the embankment lights: 'Thank you, Angela. I love it.'

A week passed without news of Castlebar. He may have gone to the Union but Angela would not go in search of him. She said to Harriet, 'He knows where I am. If he wants to see me, he can ring me,' but he did not ring.

Harriet, aware of Angela's disquiet, suggested they invite the Castlebars in: 'We said she should meet Edwina. So let's fix an evening!'

Angela, sprawled on the sofa, shrugged, as though indifferent, but, looking up, her expression brightened and she at once gave Harriet Castlebar's telephone number. 'If you want to ask them, it's all right with me.'

Harriet rang Castlebar's flat but there was no reply. She decided to settle the matter by going to the Union.

'Why not come with me? You've no reason to stay away.'

'No. I couldn't bear seeing him there with her.'

Harriet disliked appearing alone in public places, but, feeling that any action was better than the dejection that kept Angela inactive, she sent Hassan out for a gharry. It was early in the evening and she expected to find Castlebar at the snooker table with Jackman, but there was no sign of Jackman. Castlebar was seated at a table with Mona beside him.

So there they were: Wolfie and Lambkin: the lamb and the wolf! Harriet went straight to them.

At the sight of her, Castlebar grinned and his grin was both feeble and defiant. He knew she condemned him for his neglect of Angela, but what could he do? His wife had whistled him back and now held him helpless in their old relationship. He looked trapped and ashamed of himself but prepared to bluster it out. Mona, in possession, was smugly conscious of the legality of her own position.

301

They seemed to expect Harriet to accuse them but Harriet was not there to make accusations. Uninvolved and apparently friendly, she offered them the invitation.

Mona, not expecting it, bridled slightly as though unsure how to deal with it, then answered in a lofty tone: 'I'm not sure. What are we doing that night, Wolfie? I think we're engaged.'

'Oh, Lambkin, of course we're not. Why shouldn't we go?'

'Very well, if you're so keen.'

Harriet said, 'Then you accept?'

Mona nodded a graceless, 'All right.'

Harriet, having come only for Angela's sake, refused the offer of a drink and left at once. Although she knew Angela would be on edge until she heard the result of her approach to the Castlebars, she walked back to Garden City. Having seen him in the grasp of his wife, she felt she had been unwise to foster Angela's infatuation with anyone so futile.

Angela was still lying on the sofa, her head buried in her arms. She jerked herself up as Harriet entered and demanded, 'Well?'

'It's all right. They've accepted.'

'So they were there? What are they doing?'

'Nothing much. Just sitting, drinking beer.'

'How did he look?'

'Not happy. I would say he was trapped.'

'Trapped? Ah!' Angela gave a long sigh of agonized relief then, throwing her arms into the air, she shrieked with a laughter that was very near hysteria.

Guy, when he heard that Mona Castlebar was a singer, became interested in the supper party and said, 'I'd like to ask Hertz and Allain.'

'Oh, darling, they wouldn't fit in.'

'Of course they'll fit in. They're well-mannered and agreeable and help out whenever needed. Everyone likes them. You couldn't find a nicer couple of guests.'

Dobson said, 'Wouldn't it be better to ask them on their own?'

'No, they'll get on with Castlebar. They'll have a lot in common.'

'Oh, well, if they're as charming as you say, I look forward to meeting them.'

Edwina agreed to be in to meet Mona but when the evening came, she said she was sorry, 'terribly, terribly sorry,' but Peter was taking her to supper at the Kit-Kat. As a result of this defection, Harriet felt more inclined to welcome Hertz and Allain.

They and Guy, having evening classes, were expected to arrive late. The Castlebars, with nothing to detain them, would probably be first. Angela, awaiting them, moved restlessly between the living-room and her bedroom, looking as though she might, at the sound of the doorbell, disappear altogether. Harriet said, 'Do sit down, Angela. Keep calm. When they come, don't let them see you're worried.'

Guy brought home the two men, both young and good-looking, with a muscular grace, like athletes in training, and Harriet hoped they would distract Angela, but Angela seemed scarcely aware of them. As time passed and no one else arrived, her vacant stare became more vacant. She had nothing to say.

The young men, refusing alcohol, drank iced lime-juice. Dobson, entertaining them with diplomatic ease, congratulated Guy on finding two such employees at such a time.

'You must be very fond of teaching,' he said to them.

Hertz and Allain appeared gratified by Dobson's attention. Carefully enunciating each word, Allain told him: 'Yes, we are very fond of teaching.'

'You see it as a vocation, no doubt?'

'A vocation, certainly. We see it as a vocation,' Allain looked to Hertz for confirmation and Hertz, as though eager to please, smiled and vigorously nodded his head.

Guy, delighted with both of them, would have been content to sit drinking and talking for the rest of the evening, but it was nearly nine o'clock. The food was ready and Hassan was lurking, aggrieved, in the doorway.

Harriet said, 'I think we'll have to eat.'

As they moved to the table, the front-door bell rang and Angela paused, paralysed by anticipation. Hassan, answering the door, came back with a telegram addressed to Harriet.

She read: 'Please excuse. Mona not too well, Bill' and handed it to Angela who gave it a glance, dropped it on the floor and made for the baize door to the bedroom. Harriet called after her: 'Won't you have supper?'

'No, I'm not hungry.'

Guy, talking at the table, expressed his enthusiasm for a Jewish National Home in Palestine. He was particularly impressed by the idea of kibbutzim, based he believed on the Russian soviets, and the possibility of turning the Negev into arable land. The teachers, although Jews themselves, smiled politely but had, it seemed, no great interest in these ambitious schemes.

Dobson, who knew more than Guy did, discussed them from a practical viewpoint: 'It all sounds fine,' he said. 'But these things can't be carried out without money, a great deal of money. Well, the Jews have money – much of it comes from the States – and they can buy tractors and fertilizers and combined harvesters, while the wretched Arabs are still scraping the ground with the same ploughs they used in biblical times. They'd go on doing this, quite happily, if they weren't made envious by the equipment the Jews have got. As it is, they are resentful and likely to make trouble, so, to keep them sweet, HMG has to fork out to give them tractors and pedigree bulls and other rich gifts . . .'

'But this is magnificent,' Guy broke in. 'Thanks to the Jews, the Arabs are being provided for.'

'My dear fellow, it has to be paid for. And who pays? The poor, old British tax-payer. As per usual.'

'Oh, come, Dobbie! You surely don't object to a rich country like Britain helping the poor Palestinians?'

Dobson laughed: 'I don't object, but your Jewish friends do.'

Reminded of his guests, Guy was quick to defend the Jews: 'I don't believe it. I'm sure they don't object. It's up to all of us to share the sum of human knowledge and advance the underdeveloped peoples of the world.' His eyes glowing with faith in all-pervading human goodness, he looked to Hertz and Allain for support, and they both solemnly nodded their agreement with his sentiments. It looked like dispassionate agreement but Harriet, who had watched them while they were listening to Guy, had seen on their faces an intent expression that did not accord with their apparent detachment from the subject in hand.

Guy pursued it, fervently postulating ethics that Dobson good-humouredly amended, while Harriet, not much interested in polemics, waited for a chance to go to Angela. When she went to the room, she found her lying in darkness, made more dark by a large mango tree that blotted out most of the sky.

Harriet said, 'Shall I put on the light?'

'No.'

Harriet sat on the edge of the bed: 'This is Mona's doing, of course.'

'Yes, but he let her do it,' Angela raised herself on her elbow. 'He's frightened of her and she despises him. She despises him, yet she'll keep her hold on him simply to prevent anyone else getting him. Her "Wolfie"! – God help us! Harriet, what's the cure for love?'

'Another love.'

'Not so easy. You want one person, not another. I must get away for a while. I don't want to go to the Union – which I will, sooner or later, if I stay here. So I must go where he isn't. I want to be out of sight. I want to get away from him. The truth is: he's a dead loss.'

'Where can you go?'

'I've been thinking. When I was with Desmond, we used to spend every winter in Luxor. I could go back there. Would you come with me?'

'I don't know, I'll have to see what we have in the bank.'

'Don't be silly, it's my treat.'

'No. It can't always be your treat.'

'Well, it is this time. And what the hell does it matter? I can afford it. If you come to please me, why shouldn't it be my treat?'

They argued it out and agreed that Angela should pay for the train journey but Harriet would settle her own hotel bill. By now it was taken for granted that they would go to Luxor and Angela, seeing herself escaping from an obsession, became excited and putting her arms about Harriet, she promised her, 'We'll have a riotous time. We'll see everything there is to see down there. We'll go to a hotel with the best food in Egypt. We'll live it up, and to hell with bloody Bill Castlebar and his even bloodier wife.'

Angela's euphoria remained with her on the train to Luxor. When they were in the dining-car, she ordered a bottle of whisky although she would be the only one to drink it. In flight from Castlebar, she could talk of nothing but Castlebar – and Castlebar's wife. She had heard at Groppi's, where she sometimes took tea with friends from her married days, that Mona Castlebar was already a subject for gossip. She had been invited to a musical evening arranged by the American University in aid of the Red Cross. Edwina was also invited and both women were expected to sing for the cause. Edwina complied willingly, singing song after song, until she became aware of Mona's critical stare, at which she broke off and turning to Mona, said, 'But I'm being selfish. I must stop. It's your turn now.'

'And what do you think?' Angela squealed with delight: 'Mona refused to sing. She seemed to think she was being tricked into performing and she said "I only do it for money".'

'Did she really say that?'

'Well, no.' In the face of Harriet's disbelief, Angela moderated her story: 'What she actually said was "I don't give my services free". *Her services*! Heaven help us!'

As Angela paused in her laughter to wipe her eyes, Harriet asked: 'Was Bill there?'

'Yes. And they say he was horribly embarrassed and begged her to sing "just one little *Lieder*" – *Lieder*'s her thing – but she wouldn't, and there she sat on her big bottom, in a long green dress, with that mantelpiece of a bosom sticking out of it, her face grim, as obstinate as a pig. No one could get a squeak out of her.'

'How did Bill come to marry such a woman in the first place?'

'Oh, he's a simple soul. She paraded the bosom and kept the legs out of sight. He told me he thought she was "the Great Earth Mother", now he says she's a lout. Yet she's only got to turn up and he's at her heels. It makes me sick.'

'He'll rebel sooner or later.'

'Too late for me. I've finished with him.' Angela emptied her glass and put the cap back on the bottle. 'This'll do for tomorrow.' Her merriment had started to flag – and a desperate merriment it was, Harriet thought. She looked haggard and weary and said, 'Let's go to bed.'

They had first-class sleepers and slept well, but next morning the excursion took on a different aspect. At breakfast in the dining-car, Angela would take nothing but coffee and had little to say. They looked out of the window at the disturbing sight of graves beside the track, dozens of them, each one a mound of sand with a palm leaf stuck at the head. The train was running through a cemetery and at stations, where a lively crowd usually gathered to gape at the tourists, the platforms were deserted except for a few forlorn villagers who stood about listlessly with dejected eyes.

Angela, to whom Upper Egypt was well known, could make nothing of this desolation. And the graves continued: new graves, not simply dozens of them but hundreds. She called a waiter and spoke to him in Arabic then translated his reply: 'He says there's been an epidemic and many people have died.'

'But of what?'

'He doesn't know. He just says "a bad sickness".'

'Why weren't we told about this? There was nothing in the papers. Ask him why it was kept secret.'

The waiter, a small, light-coloured man with a gentle face, was unable to answer this question. He knew nothing of newspapers and the deceits of governments, but his expression as he looked from the window was uneasy and Harriet, seeing the other waiters gathered at the end of the car, said, 'They're all frightened.' The visitors came here in ignorance but the waiters came because they could not afford to refuse.

The few officers and nurses at the other tables seemed unaffected by the conditions outside the train. Seeing that one of the men wore the insignia of a medical officer, Angela called to him, 'Doctor, what's the matter here? The whole place is a graveyard.'

The doctor, looking out, appeared to see the graves for the first time. 'Rum go,' he said and shouted for the head waiter. Why, he wanted to know, had the epidemic not been reported to the army?

'Hotels want people to come,' the head waiter earnestly explained.

'They do, do they? And what have they got here? Plague, smallpox, spotted fever? – some little thing like that?'

The head waiter grinned. Taking the doctor's angry humour for facetiousness, he tried to make light of the trouble: 'It is nothing. It is a thing they have here.'

The doctor's tone changed: 'Come on, what is it?'

Challenged by this important-sounding officer, the head waiter went back to his subordinates and they conferred together. He returned to say: 'Malaria, effendi. Not too bad. You take quinine, you all very well.'

The doctor rejected malaria and made his own decision. He told his fellow diners: 'It's probably cholera. Nothing to worry about if you're careful. Eat only cooked food, and eat it hot. Avoid tap water, salads, fresh fruit. Drink bottled spring water. French, if you can get it.'

Reassured, Harriet and Angela began to discuss the dangers of life in the Middle East. Harriet told how she had danced at the Turf Club with an officer who was sickening for smallpox. Angela, becoming more animated, said she had been to a dinner-party where a certain Major Beamish was expected but did not arrive: 'Then another guest, an MO, said, "I did a PM on a chap called Beamish this morning" and the host said "It couldn't be our Beamish. He was alive and well when we saw him last night." But it was their Beamish. While we waited for him, he was in his grave, dead in the night of poliomyelitis.'

Harriet had never heard of poliomyelitis. Angela said, 'If you get it here, it hits you hard. You're gone in no time.' Though she essayed this information herself, it had a dire effect upon her. She sat silent, staring out at the graves and the palm fronds that were drying and turning yellow. Soon they would be blown away and the graves with them. They would be sifted by the wind, one into the other, until the ground was flat again and the dead forgotten. She whispered, 'People can die so suddenly,' and she was distraught by her own fancies.

They drew into Luxor. Outside the station, a funeral was passing: a flimsy, open coffin, held aloft by four men, was followed by the family and professional mourners who enacted grief by howling and throwing dust over their heads.

Angela, about to call a gharry, stopped and said, 'Harriet, I can't stay. I must go back.'

'Oh, Angela, surely you're not afraid?'

'Not for myself – of course not. I just can't bear being so far from Bill. Anything might happen to him. Suppose he died in the night as Beamish did?'

'It's not very likely. And even if you went back: what could you do? What difference would it make?'

'Only that I was there. I would be near him, not four hundred miles away.'

Harriet tried to reason with her: 'Be sensible, Angela. Beamish was only one person. Think of all the English people who haven't died here, so why should Bill be in peculiar danger?'

'In this place, we're all in peculiar danger. Any one of us might die any minute.' Angela's face, with its delicate, dry skin, was taut with fear, and Harriet saw that reasoning was useless. Even if she could be persuaded to stay, she would be miserable. Persuading her against her will would be a cruelty.

Harriet, reconciling herself to their return, said, 'Very well. If we must go back, we must. Let's find when the train goes.'

'No, not you. You must stay. I'll go alone. It doesn't matter about me, I've seen all the sights, I know the place inside and out. But it's all new to you. You must stay and enjoy it.'

Harriet, who had no wish to enjoy it alone, tried to argue but Angela insisted that Harriet remain in Luxor while she went back to Cairo. Finding that the train would not return until late in the evening, she decided to go to the hotel with Harriet. She must wait for time to pass.

Angela had booked them into the old Winter Palace, a pleasant building beside the Nile, its portico heavily embowered with verdure, its terrace overhung by palms.

The day was still early, the light pale and the soft, cool air scented by some flowering tree. Harriet said, 'What a delightful place,' and driving in the gharry, silent on the sandy roads, she longed for Angela to remain with her. But the funerals, passing one after the other, aggravated Angela's nervous condition. She explained to Harriet that only the bodies were buried, the coffins were kept to be used again. Some of them, padded, draped and fringed, denoted victims from affluent families but others had been too poor even to hire a coffin. The bodies, closely wrapped in cloth, were carried on a board with a symbol to denote the sex: a fez for the male and a flow of hair for the female. But each, whether rich or poor, male or female, had its dusty crew of women mourners, the wails of one procession scarcely fading before those of another could be heard.

The piercing ululations followed Harriet and Angela even into the haven of the hotel. As they sat under the palms, watching the traffic on the narrow waterway between the quay and the island opposite, Angela was too distracted even to order a drink. Seeing her with her face set in a mask of suffering, Harriet knew she was thinking of her son, a beautiful boy for whose death she had, in a way, been responsible. In those days she had painted pictures and while she was too intent on her work to notice, he had picked up a live grenade which had exploded in his hand.

As she remembered this, Harriet could understand Angela's state of mind. After such a tragedy, how could she trust anyone to remain alive? - least of all Castlebar whom she loved and longed for.

They went in to luncheon where, for a while, she discussed the question of what they should or should not eat, but this did not last long. Throwing the menu aside, she said, 'What does it matter? If I could die, it would be the easiest way out.'

Somehow they got through the day. After supper, the gharry called as arranged and Harriet, glad of something to do, went with Angela to the station. At the station, she made a last appeal: 'Don't you think you could stay for a couple of days?'

'No. I'm sorry, Harriet. I know it's mean to leave you alone here. But I must go back.'

There was no one else in the first-class compartment. Angela was given a berth in a long row of empty berths and, standing in the doorway, she said, 'Don't wait, Harriet. Goodbye,' then shut herself in to suffer through the night.

As she returned in the gharry to the hotel, an intense loneliness came down on Harriet. At that time of night, the streets were empty, the river empty of shipping. The gharry driver, and the horse plodding silently through silence, seemed to be the only other creatures in a deserted world.

Above the low houses the sky appeared vast and its great staring but indifferent expanse enhanced the solitude. Her bedroom, when she reached it, looked as void as the town. It was very large and her bed, shrouded in a sand-fly net, was islanded in the middle of the floor. Getting into it and covering herself with a sheet and a single blanket, she closed the net against the dangers of the night. Angela's flight had reduced her to a sense of friendlessness but as she lay down to sleep, she, too, said, 'What does it matter?' though she did not intend to die. Instead, she said, 'I've survived other things. I'll survive this,' and so went to sleep.

The desk clerk offered her a number of sight-seeing trips and she accepted them all. The first started immediately after breakfast. The tourists gathered beneath the riverside palms in air so cool, it seemed to blow off the sea. Harriet thought, 'Paradise must be like this,' then the funerals started again. Those who had died during the night must be buried before the heat of mid-day.

A string of gharries stood outside the hotel. Harriet, seated alone in the first of them, found funerals passing beside her. She could look into the open coffins and see the dark, peaked faces of people who appeared to have died of starvation. This went on until the dragoman, appearing to take charge of the tourists, ordered the mourners to the other side of the road. They shifted ground without protest and without a pause in their lamentations.

The dragoman, complacent in his authority, was a large Nubian, his size enhanced by a full, dark blue kaftan, lavishly trimmed with gold. His stick was taller and heavier than those usually carried and it was topped by an ivory head as big as a skull. He chose to ride in Harriet's gharry and though he sat beside the driver, it was evident he saw himself as superior to the members of the party.

The gharries went from hotel to hotel, picking up nurses and army officers. At the last hotel there was only one person waiting, an officer, and as he, too, was alone, he was directed by the dragoman to the leading gharry. He paused, his foot on the step, and staring at Harriet, asked, 'Are you real? – or have I conjured you out of a dream?'

It was a rhetorical question, expressively spoken, and Harriet laughed at it: 'Get in, Aidan. If I'd never seen you before, I would have known you were an actor.'

'*Was* an actor,' the officer corrected her as he sat down beside her. On the London stage he had taken the name of Aidan Sheridan but in the army had reverted to his real name which was Pratt. He was a captain in the Pay Corps, based in Syria but as often as he could, came to Egypt on duty or pleasure. In the past, Harriet had heard him speak bitterly of his broken career but that morning his tone was one of humorous resignation to his present position.

As soon as he could without appearing precipitant, he asked, 'I suppose Guy isn't with you?'

It was the question Harriet expected. When he came to Cairo, it was in hope of seeing Guy, and though she pitied him, she could only say, 'I'm afraid not.'

'So you're here alone?'

'I didn't come alone, but I'm alone now. I was abandoned.'

He gave her a startled glance, suspecting some interrupted liaison, and she laughed again: 'A woman friend came with me, but at the sight of the funerals, she went straight back to Cairo.'

'I can't say I blame her. I, too, felt scared when I realized what was going on here.'

'Oh, Angela wasn't scared, at least not for herself. She began thinking of death – someone else's death – and she couldn't bear to stay.'

Aidan, aware that the only death he had thought of was his own, grew red and, taking her words for a reprimand, turned away. She had forgotten how easy it was to upset him and regretted what she had said. He was morbidly sensitive but, more than that, he had been marked by some experience that he promised one day to reveal to her. He was a young man, still in his mid-twenties, but his large, dark eyes were set in hollows of dark skin and their expression suggested a rooted unhappiness. They had seldom met yet they had become friends. She had taken him to the Muski where he had bought a small votive cat made of iron and mounted on a block of cornelian. It was a gift for his mother but he had asked Harriet to keep it for him, saying he lost things because he no longer had the sense that anything was worth keeping. Speaking of the experience that had so terribly impaired him, he had said, 'There are some memories that are beyond bearing, except that we have to bear them.'

Now, meeting him again in this delectable place, she saw he was still burdened by a memory beyond bearing.

A long, riverside road was leading them to the site of Karnac.

The gharries stopped outside the walls and the dragoman, walking impressively, led his party into a compound and, making a circular movement with his stick, required its members to stand about him at a respectful distance. He pointed to the temple of Ammon.

'This am very great place. Biggest building in the world. This avenue is sphinxes, only not sphinxes. They is sheep.'

'Rams, surely?' Aidan murmured.

Ignoring him, the dragoman swept round like a whirling dervish and strode towards the main complex of buildings: 'You alls follow me.'

In the Hypostyle Hall, while the others were held by a rigmarole about Ramses xii, Harriet slid behind the group and made her way among the crowded pillars that stood, calm but watchful, like trees in a forest. She felt that their number and closeness were designed to puzzle, for apart from puzzlement she could see little point in congestion simply for congestion's sake. As for the puzzle: she had the curious illusion that she had, at one time, solved it but had forgotten the solution. Gazing up at the capitals, she saw that only some of them were bud capitals, the others were decorated with the papyrus calyx, and she imagined that in the irregular placing of these two designs there was a clue to the mystery. But the heat was growing and as she wandered about, all she could feel was wonderment without hope of understanding.

Aidan, coming to look for her, said, 'Our dragoman's a mine of misinformation. I'm not surprised you made off. Come with me. The sun's almost overhead – there's something I want to show you.'

She followed him out to the courtyard and across to a small building that was lit by a hagioscope in the front wall. Putting his eye to the hole, Aidan smiled his satisfaction then gestured to her to come and look for herself. She, too, put her eye to the hole and saw inside, lit by a shaft of sunlight from the roof, the head of a cat. It was the same cat whose image Aidan had bought in the Muski but this was more than life-size, a black basalt head on top of a column, gazing with remote, mild gaze into its own eternal seclusion.

'The god in the sanctuary.'

'Yes,' Aidan looked pleased: 'I thought you would recognize it.'

The afternoon excursion was to the tombs on the other side of the river. Crossing in a boat, Harriet felt on her bare head a pressure that was almost painful, and she realized how soon the respite of winter would be over and this paradisal little town would become an inferno for those not born to it.

On the opposite bank, in a field that had once been inundated by the Nile, two ruined figures sat enthroned among the sugar beet. Their dark colour, their immense height, their worn and featureless faces looking towards Karnac, imparted such an impression of regal dignity, Harriet would have chosen to contemplate them in silence. The dragoman was not permitting that.

'Them, all two, is Memnon, not singing any more. Memnon very brave Greek man killed in battle. Him buried here.'

Aidan said, 'Nonsense.'

A nurse with a guide book, agreed. 'It says here they're statues of Amenophis III.'

The dragoman stood in front of nurse and book as though to obliterate them and pushed his face towards Aidan. His eyes, brown, in balls of glossy white, started in anger from their sockets. He shouted, 'You is guide, then, Mister Officer? O K. You go guide your own self. I finish. I go.'

He swept off and went at a furious pace back to the river's edge but there had to stop. The ferry had returned to Luxor.

The nurse, dismayed by his departure, said to the others, 'Oh dear! I didn't mean to hurt his feelings. Should I go and tell him I'm sorry? I might persuade him to come back.'

Before anyone else could speak, Aidan, assuming an ironical air of authority, said, 'Certainly not. He doesn't know his arse from his elbow. We're better off without him,' and the others, impressed by the act, let themselves be conducted to where some donkeys and old taxis stood ready to take them into the Valley of the Kings. The drivers, seeing the dragoman dismissed, were jubilant while the dragoman himself, realizing what was happening, came running back, bawling at the top of his voice, 'You no go without guide. Law says no one go without guide,' but the tourists were already in the taxis and the drivers, gleefully starting up, were away before he reached them. While he raged behind them, they went bumping and swaying up the rocky track to the valley where the kings and queens of Upper and Lower Egypt had left their earthly remains.

On the quay, when they returned there, Aidan asked Harriet if she would have dinner with him that evening. It was arranged that she should go to his hotel by gharry but the evening was so pleasant, she decided to walk. The sun was setting in a lustre of crimson and gold and the Nile, small compared with the great river of Cairo, ran in loops of coloured light under the brilliant sky. She paused to look down into the walled hollow that held the Temple of Luxor. There was a mosque among the jumble of remains and a man, probably the attendant, looked up, grinning, and said, 'Ghost, ghost.' He seemed to expect her to run and was disconcerted when she leant over the wall and asked, 'Is there *really* a ghost?' but he could only repeat, 'Ghost, ghost,' and she laughed and went down to the quayside to walk under the palms.

The terrace of Aidan's hotel was built out over the water and served as a dining-room. It was roofed with greenery but closely netted against flying creatures and insects. One end was open to reveal the evening colours of the river but the inner area was shadowed and candles, their flames motionless inside tulip shades of engraved glass, were on the tables. There were less than a dozen diners, senior officers and their women, but the menu that Aidan held in front of his face was of a size that might have catered for a hundred. Hearing Harriet arrive beside him, he looked suspiciously round it, then reassured by the sight of her, he put it down. He had placed a lily beside her plate, a white blaze bigger than the evening star, its central petals tied into a cone with thread. She knew he was trying to be gallant, but it was not easy for him. Yet they were oddly in sympathy, both wanting the same person and wishing he were here.

Aidan said, 'How about lobster? The waiter tells me it was flown in this morning from Aqaba.'

The lobster, when it came, was cold under a mayonnaise sauce and Harriet thought it delicious until she realized the danger of eating it. She put her fork down, her appetite gone, and Aidan asked with concern, 'Are you all right? I thought you

315

looked strained, and you've lost weight, haven't you? How do you feel?'

'Not well. In fact, I gave up feeling well when I came to this country. Guy eats anything and everything, and he's never ill. I am careful with food and yet my inside's always upset.'

'Egypt is unpredictable. You never know what it will do to you. I hated it at first, then it grew on me. It's like a mother you detest, yet are tied to in spite of yourself. I think it's the place where we all began. It's here where we were born first and lived out the infancy of the soul.'

Harriet was surprised, not by what he had said but the fact he had said it, then she laughed: 'So you believe in reincarnation? Which pharaoh were you?'

Aidan did not laugh. He seemed affronted for a moment, then, remembering she was Guy's wife, he did his best to smile. Because she was Guy's wife, he had been happy to find her in Luxor, he had invited her to dinner and now he permitted her to laugh at him.

She responded by asking seriously: 'Is that why you are drawn to Egypt? Would you stay on here after the war?'

'Oh, no, it's too far from the centre of things. If you're an actor, you have to live in the world.'

'And this isn't the world?'

'Not my world, though I am, as you say, drawn to it. I intend to see what I can of it while I'm out here. Tomorrow I'm going to Assuan to visit the gardens of Elephantine. They're so ancient, they were there when Alexander came to Egypt three hundred years before Christ.'

'What is Elephantine? An oasis?'

'No, an island in the river. It's called Elephantine because some king or other sacrificed an elephant there.'

'Sacrificed an elephant? How abominable!'

'It would be dead by now, anyway. It was a long time ago.' He laughed to show her he was being humorous and when she smiled, he said, 'Why don't you come to Assuan tomorrow?'

'I can't,' Harriet's money did not allow for a visit to Assuan. Angela, with her usual belief that the dearest thing was the cheapest in the end, had chosen one of the most expensive hotels in Luxor. Harriet said, 'I can't stay long.'

Aidan sighed enviously: 'I suppose Guy wants you back.'

Not sure what to say to that, Harriet smiled and Aidan, sympathizing with her uncertainty, said he would walk with her to her hotel. They stopped by a row of small riverside shops that sold Egyptian antiquities and African curios. Although it was nearly midnight and there were few customers these days, the windows were lit and the owners still inside. Aidan bent down, intently examining objects made of ebony or of ivory trimmed with gold. Harriet wondered if he were thinking of a gift for his mother and reminded him: 'You know, I still have that little cat you bought in the Muski!'

'A cat? Yes, I did buy a cat, but what did I do with it?'

'You gave it to me to keep till you asked for it.'

'So I did. Yes, so I did.'

They left the shops and came to the Temple of Luxor. Harriet said, 'A man told me there is a ghost here.' They leant against the wall and peered down into darkness but no ghost moved through it. She said, 'You said you had lost the sense that anything was worth keeping. You said that one day you would tell me what caused it. Suppose you tell me here and now, while it's dark and I can't see your face!'

'I don't know . . . I don't think I can tell you.' He hung his head over the temple site that was like a pit of darkness where nothing could be discerned except a faint star-glimmer on one of the colossi of Ramses II. When it seemed he had nothing more to say, she urged him:

'Whatever it was: if you keep it to yourself, you'll never get over it.'

'I don't expect to get over it. But what happened has no bearing on life as we know it. The dead are dead. There's nothing to be done about it now.'

'You mean, you don't want to tell me?'

'There's no reason why I shouldn't tell you. It's not a secret. It's only that I feel . . . I feel it's unjust to burden another person with the story.'

'Enough has happened to me. I don't need to be protected. And you promised.'

'Yes, that's true. I did promise,' he considered this fact for some minutes before saying, 'It's not what happened to me: that wasn't important. It's what happened to other people, most of them children.'

'That made it more terrible, of course.'

'More terrible, yes. And yet I don't know. As we have to die sooner or later, does it matter when we die?'

Leaving that question to answer itself, Harriet waited and eventually he went on: 'It was early in the war and I had declared myself a conscientious objector. I thought, being an actor, they might let me go on with my own work but, instead, I was directed on to a ship going to Canada. I had to act as a steward and waiter. I suppose the idea was to humiliate me. The other stewards were lascars, but we got on all right. In fact, I was rather enjoying the trip. There was a crowd of kids on board, being evacuated to Canada . . .'

'I think I can guess which ship that was. You were torpedoed?'

'Yes, just when we thought we were out of range of the u-boats. Our escorts had turned back. We took that to mean we were safe but the truth was, they turned back because they had used their quota of fuel. As soon as we were hit, the convoy scattered. That was according to orders. Whatever happened, the other ships had to save themselves and we were left to sink or swim. We were holed in the side and there was no hope for the ship itself. We had to get the kids into the boats and quick about it. We were going down fast. We tried to be cheerful – told the kids it was an adventure and we'd be picked up in no time. But there was no one to pick us up. It was a miserable night, cold, blowing a gale, pouring with rain. When daylight came, the convoy had vanished and there was no sign of the other boats. We were alone on the Atlantic. Nothing to be seen but the grey, empty sea. Absolutely alone.' Aidan paused to swallow in his throat, then he asked, 'Do you want to hear any more?'

'Of course.'

'The children were in their night clothes. We'd got them into life-jackets but when we realized how bad things were, there was no time to go down for blankets. The storm went on, the sea slapping up on us so there was a foot of bilge water in the boat. The kids were seasick but everyone was packed together so they couldn't get to the side. No one could move. There were nineteen children in our boat and two women helpers, volunteers.

318

Then there were the lascars, fourteen of them ... And there was an elderly man who was joining his wife in Canada. We had one of the officers with us, a retired navy man who'd been recalled to active service. Kirkbride. He was splendid. Without him, we'd all have died. He knew how to propel the boat, which no one else did. There were no oars. Instead, there were handles like beer-pulls that had to be worked backwards and forwards. We tried to put the lascars on to that job but all they would do was pray and beseech Allah to rescue them. Not that it mattered. There was nowhere to go. We had no idea where we were. Kirkbride said he could navigate by the stars, but there were no stars. Only the black sky and the sea and the wind howling round us. God, the cold! It was bitterly cold. I'll never forget it.'

'Did you have any special job?'

'I doled out the food, what there was of it. There were iron rations in the boat: some tinned stuff and water. Not enough water. By the fourth day the ration was one mouthful of water and a sardine or a bit of bully on a ship's biscuit. The women did what they could to keep the kids amused – played games: "Animal, vegetable and mineral", that sort of thing, and got them to sing "Run rabbit" and "Roll out the barrel". The old man told them stories. Then one night one of the women disappeared; no one knew what happened to her. The water ran out and the kids couldn't swallow the biscuits because their throats were dry. I'd saved some condensed milk to the last but that wouldn't go down, either: it was too thick. After we'd been in the boat a week, the lascars gave up and began to die . . .'

Aidan stopped again and startled Harriet by laughing. She said 'Yes?'

'The storm got worse. We threw the dead lascars overboard and the waves threw them back again. We pretended this was funny but the kids had lost interest. They were dying, too. We always knew when a boy or girl was about to die, the kid would start having visions. One of them described an island covered with trees and kept pointing and saying, "Look, it's just over there. Why don't we go there?" Several times one of them would think he saw a ship coming to rescue us and the others would say they saw it, too.'

'I suppose they died of thirst?'

'Thirst and exposure. Their feet would go numb, then they'd sink into a coma and that was the end. Each morning, we'd find two or three of them dead. We used the tins to collect rainwater but it wasn't enough. After about ten days – I'd lost count by then – the second woman died. She'd wrapped her coat round one of the dying girls and she died herself. Hypothermia. Next day the last two children died. There was no one left but Kirkbride, the old man, three of the lascars and me. We'd had nothing to eat for a week. The rain stopped so we hadn't even rainwater. We decided we'd had it and Kirkbride began to wonder where the boat would be cast up. He thought Iceland or the Faroes, but we knew it would probably just break up and no one would know what had happened to any of us. We'd rigged up a shelter for the smallest children and when there were no children left, we took it in turns to sleep there. The last time I crawled in, I said to myself "Thank God, I needn't wake up again!"'

Aidan's voice broke and Harriet, seeing the outline of the Ramses statue, wondered what it was doing there out in the dark Atlantic. After a long pause, she said, 'But that wasn't the end of the story?'

'Not quite, no. Kirkbride didn't go to sleep. He stayed on watch and he was awake when a Sunderland flew over us and dived to see what we were. He stood up and waved his shirt and they dropped us a tin of peaches. He woke me up . . . forced me back from another world by pouring peach juice down my throat. The Sunderland radioed all the snips anywhere near – I think the nearest was two hundred miles away – and the first one that reached us, picked us up.'

'And they were all alive: Kirkbride, the old man and the lascars?'

'Yes, I was the only one who died. And I should have stayed dead like the poor little brats we threw overboard. Some of them too light to sink. It was ghastly, seeing them floating after us. I should have died. Instead I woke up, safe and warm, in a bunk on board an American destroyer. The very smell of peach juice makes me sick . . .' Aidan pushed himself away from the wall and said in disgust: 'Now, you've heard it. That's the whole story.' He had told it in a flat voice with none of the dramatic force of his profession. The story itself was enough.

Harriet said, 'And you ceased to be a conscientious objector?'

'God, yes. One experience of that sort and I realized I'd be safer in the Pay Corps.'

His bitterness kept her silent and she told herself she would never laugh at him again.

As they walked on to Harriet's hotel, he regained his composure and saying 'goodnight', he took her hand and persuasively asked, 'Why not come to Assuan tomorrow?'

'I'm afraid it's impossible.'

'Then what about Damascus? You thought you might visit me there.'

'I would if I could persuade Guy to come with me.'

'Yes, *do* persuade him!' In his eagerness for Guy's company, he took a step towards her: 'And don't forget to remember me to him.'

'I'll give him your love,' Harriet said as she went into the hotel, and she realized she was laughing at him again.

Harriet's money ran out. There was nothing left for her to see in Luxor so she returned to Cairo a day earlier than expected. When she reached the flat, it was pervaded by an empty silence and she went to Angela's room in the hope of finding her there. Angela, too, was out but her suitcases were there, piled so high under the window they partly hid the mango tree that stared into the room.

Harriet went to her room and, lying on her bed, listened for someone to come in. She did not expect Guy, who seldom ate luncheon, but Angela, Edwina and Dobson were likely to arrive. She could imagine Angela laughing at the folly of her flight back to Cairo, or perhaps rejoicing because Castlebar had discovered he needed her. As for Harriet: all she wanted was a sense of welcome and an assurance that she was not as ill as she felt.

The bedrooms, barely tolerable in summer, were now cool but the wood that had been baked and rebaked during the hot weather, still gave out a smell like ancient bone. From the garden outside the window came the herbal smell of dried foliage and the hiss of the hoses. She had been repeatedly wakened during the night by the railway servants who were under orders to spray the berths with disinfectant. She had argued that this was no way to prevent the spread of cholera but that did not stop them rapping on her door until she opened it. Half asleep on her bed, she heard a sound of sobbing and knew it came from the room of that other suffering lover: Edwina. She sat up with the intention of going to her, then realized she was not alone. Peter Lisdoonvarna, with joking gruffness, was telling her to 'shut up'. The sobbing grew louder and gave rise to a slap and scuffle and Peter's voice, contused with sexual intent, spoke hoarsely: 'Come on, you little bitch. Turn over.'

Harriet pushed her bedside chair so it crashed against the door, but the noise did not interrupt the lovers who, with squeaks, grunts and a rhythmic clicking of the bed, were locked together until Peter gave out a final groan and there was an interval of quiet before Edwina, in honeyed appeal, said 'Teddy-bear, *darling*, you don't really mean to go back to the desert?'

'Fear so, old girl. Damned lucky to get back. Thought I was stuck in that God-damn office for the rest of the war.'

'Oh, Peter!' Edwina's wail was anguished but it was also resigned. She knew she could not prevent Peter going back to the desert but behind her appeals there was covert intention. She changed her tone as she said: 'When I passed the Cathedral yesterday, there was a military wedding and I waited to see them come out. The bridegroom was a major and the bride looked gorgeous. Her dress must have come from Cicurel's. I *did* envy her. I'd love to be married in the Cathedral.'

'In that yellow edifice beside Bulacq Bridge? You must be right off your rocker.'

'Well, where else is there?'

'I don't know. I've never thought about it.'

Peter's indifference to the subject was evident and Harriet wished she, too, could tell Edwina to 'shut up'. But time was short and Edwina was desperate. However unwise it was, she had to force the pace: 'Teddy-bear, darling, before you go . . .' she paused then rushed her proposal: '*Do* let's get married!'

There was a creaking noise as Peter got off the bed. Abrupt with embarrassment, he said, ''Fraid I can't do that. Sorry. Blame m'self. Know I should have told you sooner, but didn't want to spoil things. Been a brute. Not fair to you. Didn't realize you cared in that way.'

322

'*Peter*! You're not married already?'

''Fraid so, old girl. Married m'cousin, Pamela. Great girl. Childhood sweethearts.'

'But how could you be married? People would know. Dobson would have told me.'

'Oh, I see. You think it was a big affair: St Margaret's, fully choral, dozen bridesmaids and pictures in the *Tatler*? Well, it was nothing like that. Didn't tell a soul. Just slipped into the Bloomsbury Registry Office and then had a week-end at Brown's. Only the family knew. With a war on, who cared, anyway?'

'But, Peter, there were dozens of marriages like that and they're breaking up all the time.'

'Perhaps, but I'm not breaking up this one. Pamela and I always knew we would marry. It's the real thing. So, be sensible. No reason why we shouldn't go on being friends.'

Edwina began to sob again, no doubt thinking that with Peter at the front and the British advancing towards Libya, there would not be much scope for friendship. Touched by her tears, Peter became impatient.

'Oh, come on, old girl! We've had a lot of fun, haven't we? Don't make a fuss now it's over.'

At the words 'it's over', Edwina broke down completely. Peter, unable to bear her violent weeping, opened the bedroom door and Harriet heard him mumbling as he went: 'Got to go, old girl. Sorry and all that. See you some time. 'Bye, 'bye.' He made off, his steps heavy in the corridor, then was gone, banging the front door after him. The departure was conclusive and Edwina was left to cry herself sick.

Knowing no way to comfort her, Harriet took herself out of hearing. When Dobson came in, he found her lying on the sofa in the living-room and said, 'Hello, you safely back?'

'Not really. I feel worse than usual. Dobbie, it couldn't be cholera, could it?'

He had, of course, heard about the cholera from Angela. Harriet felt, rather than saw, his movement away from her and felt his fear that she had brought the disease into the flat. Still, he did his best to reassure her.

'When I heard there was an epidemic down there, I made enquiries and was told there was no cholera anywhere in Egypt.

The minister said there had been an outbreak of food poisoning in the south.'

'That's absurd. There were miles of graves and the funerals were passing the hotel all day.'

'You were nowhere near them, I hope?'

She was alarmed, remembering the corpse she had viewed from the gharry: 'Why, are the bodies infectious?'

'I don't think so, but I don't know much about it. You'd better have a drink.'

With matter-of-fact kindliness, he gave her a half-tumbler of brandy which she gulped down. Becoming more cheerful, she said, 'If I have to die, I might as well die drunk.'

Dobson went out to the telephone. When he came back, he told her there was a taxi waiting for her at the door. He was sending her to the American Hospital for a check-up. He expected her to go at once and she did not blame him. The flat was an embassy flat and the last thing he wanted was to be responsible for spreading the epidemic in Cairo.

It was mid-day with the crowds pushing through the streets. On the bridge to Zamalek, she saw that soldiers were on duty directing people going east to walk on one pavement and the westward stream on the other. The taxi driver told her that this had been the king's own idea and was being enforced on his orders.

She thought, 'Silly, fat king.'

Coming in sight of the long, white hospital building, she felt she would be thankful to hand herself over to anyone who would accept responsibility for her tired and constantly ailing body.

Ten

The camp was on the move again. Allied forces had broken through the enemy front and Rommel was retreating.

Dawson told Simon: 'When we catch up with the old fox, we'll finish him for good and all.'

'It's been a great battle.'

'And a killing battle. The Jocks and the Aussies have had the worst of it.'

Simon told Dawson how one night, when he was lost among the forward troops, he heard bagpipes playing as a Scottish regiment advanced under enemy fire. He felt a catch in his throat as he remembered the thin wail of music but Dawson was not impressed.

'Foolhardy lot! That piper you heard was a boy with no more idea of modern warfare than his ancestors at Culloden. He walked at the head of the advance, unarmed, playing for dear life.'

'But did he get through?'

'Get through? Of course he didn't get through. He was down in the first ten minutes with his pipes dying out under him. A kid, a mere boy! His CO should've known better. Hopeless, these heroics!'

'Still, it was a pretty good show!'

'Good enough, but who paid the price? D'you know that one division reached Kidney Ridge led by a corporal? Every officer and NCO killed and no one left to lead except a ruddy corporal! But they got there.'

'Didn't the Jocks?'

'They got there all right, but not because they had a kid blowing bagpipes at the front.'

The forward troops advanced on Matruh and the camp followed them. Now there were only allied aircraft overhead, all travelling westwards to bomb the retreating enemy and the coast road jammed with Italian vehicles. Vast dust clouds on the horizon marked daily skirmishes but there was no major battle to finish Rommel 'for good and all'.

Simon asked, 'Where do you think the jerries are?'

Dawson could not say but it was his belief that 8th Army intended to cut the road ahead of the Afrika Korps. 'And then we'll have 'em all in the bag.'

Simon admired Dawson's prediction but nothing came of it. The Germans were retreating too rapidly to be overtaken and trapped.

Torrents of rain blotted out the ruins of Mersa Matruh and the yellow Matruh sand was spongy with yellow water. To make matters worse, the advance British tanks ran out of petrol and the reconnaissance planes reported: 'No sign of Rommel in the next eighty miles.'

Simon asked Dawson, 'Where do you think he's got to?'

'Seems like the desert fox has gone away.'

The rain stopped and the tarmac coast road gleamed and steamed in the afternoon sun. The sea, that had been leaden, regained colour and brilliance, and Simon, driving beside it, felt the excitement of the chase. During all his time in Egypt, the regions beyond the frontier had been enemy territory. Now he felt the whole of North Africa was opening to him.

The wire, great barbed rolls of it, put up by the Italians to keep the Senussi tribesmen out of Libya, was blasted with holes through which the allied armour and transports followed the defeated enemy out of Egypt. Simon, pursuing the pursuers, came to Sollum and Crosbie drove them up the escarpment through Halfaya Pass amidst a jam of military vehicles. This was the famous pass that the troops called Hellfire. The story was that a grounded airman was likely to be seized and held for ransom by the Bedu who would send his testicles to GHQ in proof of his sex and colour. Now it seemed petrol fumes rather than the risk of castration justified the nickname. At the top, they came on the white crenellated fortress of Capuzzo, much shot about, its ornamental gateway declaring itself to be: 'The Gateway of the Italian Army'.

The camp leaguered behind the mud-brick remains of Upper Sollum and Simon, with nothing to do till supper-time, walked down the escarpment to the lower village. From the distance, it looked a pretty place. A collection of small villas had been built on pink rocks beside a curving bay of pink sand. It was early evening and a mist, like fine powder, overhung the translucent green of the sea.

Coming down into it, he saw that the place was deserted and in ruins. The villas were collapsing into heaps of raw clay but plant life had sprung up after the rain. Bougainvillaea mantled the broken walls and the garden areas were furred over with new grass. During the five months' lull, while the contestants faced each other at Alamein, the splintered trees had regained themselves and the bougainvillaea had flowered. In one pit, that had once held a house, poinsettias covered the ground so thickly, they formed a counterpane of scarlet lace.

The town was a small, seaside town and the fact made Simon think of Crosbie. He was beginning to like Crosbie better and had even learnt something about him. Crosbie's parents kept a shop in a small seaside town on the Lincolnshire coast. It was some time before Crosbie was brought to reveal that the shop was a fish shop and when the war started, he was just beginning to learn the trade.

'Did you like being a fishmonger?' Simon asked.

'Well, it's a job, isn't it?'

'You wouldn't rather do something else?'

'I did do something else. Sometimes, I drove the van.'

That, so far, was all Simon had learnt about Crosbie but it had roused his curiosity. Somewhere behind his blunt, blank face Crosbie had memories of another life lived before the war brought him here. In spite of his determination to avoid emotional relationships, Simon was becoming attached to Crosbie because, like Ridley, he felt the need for an attachment of some sort.

He wandered down to a small central square where a jacaranda, earliest of flowering trees, had covered itself with blue rosettes as though to hide its own desecration. He came to a café where a single chair had been left standing on a mosaic floor. The mosaic surprised him, then he realized this must have been an Italian town, an Italian seaside town.

He tried to imagine Crosbie's small town shattered as this place was shattered, and he said to himself, 'Lord, the things we do to other people's countries!'

Eleven

The American Hospital had one of the most pleasing aspects in Cairo. Harriet, put to bed in a white, air-conditioned room with a balcony, lay for a long time with her eyes shut, waiting for someone to come and investigate her condition. When no one came, she opened her eyes and staring out at the empty sky, she thought of her death in a foreign place. The poet Mangan had died of cholera and that death seemed nearer than all the deaths in Upper Egypt. Like Yakimov, who had died in Greece, she would be buried in dry, alien earth where her body would quickly turn to dust and she would never see England again. The prospect did not greatly upset her, she felt too tired. She thought of Aidan crawling into the canvas shelter to die and could not see that she, herself, had much more reason to go on living.

She was roused by the Armenian nurse who told her in an awed whisper: 'Doctor come.'

The doctor was not, as she had expected, an American, but an Egyptian who spoke with an American accent. He announced himself: 'Shafik,' and bowed slightly.

'You have thrown up, yes?'

'No.'

'But your insides are upset? For how long?'

'A long time, on and off.'

'And now worse?'

'Yes.'

Dr Shafik examined her critically, without sympathy, almost resentfully, as though annoyed that she should be there. She found his manner disconcerting and his appearance more disconcerting. Most Egyptians put on weight and looked middle-aged when they were thirty. Dr Shafik, who was thirty or more, had preserved his facial good looks as well as the slim elegance she had occasionally noted among young officers at the Officers' Club. He picked up her hand and examined it as though it were an entity all on its own.

'How much do you weigh?'

'Seven stone. That's one hundred pounds.'

'I think not. I think you weigh not even eighty pounds, but we shall see. One thing I can say: you haven't cholera.' He obviously thought her a fool for choosing such a sickness: 'There is no cholera in this part of Egypt.'

'I've just come from Upper Egypt where people are dying in hundreds.'

'Not of cholera. Malaria, more likely. Upper Egypt is malaria country.'

'Is there an epidemic form of malaria?'

Harriet's spirit broke the severe calm of Shafik's face. His long, firm mouth twitched slightly but he turned away before the twitch could become a smile. Leaving the room, he said, 'To-morrow we will make tests, then we can see if you are ill or not.'

The possibility that she was not ill heartened Harriet and, seeing no reason to stay in bed, she rose, put on her dressing-gown and went out on to the balcony. The balcony overlooked the Gezira sports grounds. A grove of blue gums lined the hospital drive and looking down on them, she could see the crowns of blue-grey leaves moving and glittering in the wind. A couple of long cane chairs were on the balcony and sitting out in the brief splendour of the evening light, she was less inclined to contemplate death in Egypt. Instead she reflected on the recent news: the fact that Tobruk had been recaptured and Mont-gomery's claim that he had smashed the German and Italian armies, and she began to think of the war ending and a normal life beginning again. They could go back to England. With all that before her, why should she think of dying?

The crickets, brought out by the cooling air, were noisy in the grass below. As the sun sank, the different playing-fields – the polo ground, the golf course, the cricket field, the race course – merged into a greensward so spacious, it was like an English parkland. The club servants came out with lengths of hose and began to spray the grass with Nile water. As the light failed and mist rose from the ground, the white robes of the men glimmered through the twilight. The haze deepened over the acres of green but even when it had turned to dark, the servants were still visible, drifting about in their dilatory way, an assembly of shadows.

The nurse, who called herself Sister Metrebian, came looking for Harriet. Speaking in a small, gentle voice, she said, 'You should not be out here in the cold, Mrs Pringle,' but she left it for Harriet to decide whether she would go in or not. She was a yellow-skinned, plain, very thin, little woman with a solemn expression that, whatever her emotions might be, never altered. She simply stood and watched Harriet until Harriet rose from the chair and returned to bed. She was sitting up, her supper finished, when Guy entered amid his usual clutter of books and papers, and with his usual air of having made a temporary landing during a flight round the earth.

He kissed her, sat on the bed and said he could not stay long. Pushing his glasses up into his hair, he gazed quizzically at her and asked, 'What are you doing here? What's the matter?'

'I don't know, but it isn't cholera.'

'No one thought it was, did they?'

'Yes. Dobson couldn't get me out of the flat quickly enough.'

He shook his head, smiling with a frown between his brows. Worried by her loss of weight, he had wanted her to apply for a passage on the ship taking women and children to England, but that did not mean that, here and now, he could believe she was really ill.

'How long will they keep you here?'

'If there is nothing much wrong, I might be out tomorrow.'

This sensible reply cheered him and at once convinced that there was no cause for concern, he lifted her hand and said, 'Little monkey's paw! You won't be here long.'

That settled, he put aside the question of her health and talked of other things. It was not simply that he wished her to be well. Sickness of any sort was an embarrassment to him because he did not believe in it. Forced to accept that whether he believed or not, it existed, he saw it as a self-imposed condition, a mental aberration related to witchcraft, religion, belief in the supernatural and similar follies. So far as Harriet herself was concerned, he suspected a deep-seated discontent but as this could not relate to him or his behaviour, he preferred to forget about it.

'What happened in Luxor? Why did Angela come back so soon?'

Harriet told him of Angela's sudden anxiety and need to return and assure herself that Castlebar was alive and well.

'She's crazy,' Guy said. 'You do realize that, don't you? The woman's mad.'

Harriet laughed and went on to the subject of Aidan Pratt, describing their meeting and dinner at his hotel.

'He told me how he had been torpedoed in mid-Atlantic . . .'

'Yes, he told me, too. When we first met in Alexandria.'

So the confidence had not been, after all, a confidence. She could not doubt Aidan still suffered from the experience but she suspected that now he preserved his suffering and, relating it, felt himself enhanced by it.

She said, 'He tells it very well,' but Guy had lost interest in Aidan and would not discuss him or his misadventure.

'I've a lot on at the moment: not only the entertainment for the troops but Pinkrose's lecture is in the offing. He's fussing a lot. My idea had been a reasonably sized audience in the Institute hall but he thinks we should hire the ballroom at the Semiramis or the Continental-Savoy.'

Professor Lord Pinkrose had been sent out from England to give an important lecture in Bucharest but had arrived amidst political disorder so no lecture was possible. He had hoped to make up for this in Athens where there had been the same difficulty in finding a hall. In the end he had lectured at a garden luncheon given in Major Cookson's Phaleron villa. 'A glittering party', he had described it: 'A sumptuous affair'. He clearly expected the Cairo lecture to be something of the same sort.

Harriet laughed: 'Why not get the ambassador to lend the Embassy ballroom?'

'Yes, he thought of that, too, and made me speak to Dobson who said it's been shut up for the duration. Pinkrose says if I don't make it a big social occasion, he won't give the lecture. I've got to humour him because the university people are impressed by him. He's a bigger name than any of us realized.'

As Guy lifted his wrist to look at his watch, Harriet said, 'Don't go. When your evening begins, mine will end. So stay a little longer.'

Guy settled back on his chair but it was evident he would go soon. 'I've a rehearsal with Edwina this evening. I promised I'd pick her up.'

Remembering the interlude she had overheard that afternoon, Harriet said, 'I'm not sure she'll feel like going.'

'Yes, of course she will.' Guy spoke with easy certainty, having found that people usually did what he wanted them to do.

'I suppose you're right.'

She had seen that, caught in the radiance of his enthusiasm, everyone proved to be a player at heart. Everyone, that was, except Harriet. She had been cast for the main part in his first production but after a couple of rehearsals, he had put her out of it. He said she was too involved with him but the truth was, she suspected, he felt she was not impressed, as the others were, by his personal magnetism. She was inclined to be critical.

For her part, she not only resented the time spent on the productions but she dreaded their possible failure. He had managed well enough so far. In Bucharest he had drawn in the whole of the British colony: a ready-made audience. In Athens, where every serviceman was a hero, he had had almost too much help and support. But here, in this big heterogeneous and indifferent city, where the soldiers were provided for and entertained till they were tired of entertainment, who would care?

She made a last appeal to him: '*Must* you go on with this show? Haven't you enough to do?'

'I never have enough to do.' He jumped up, enlivened by the thought of the evening ahead: 'You wouldn't want my energy to go to waste, would you?'

She saw that only his constant activity enabled him to live with himself and she felt helpless against it. She began to see their differences as irreconcilable. He was never ill and did not understand illness. She wanted a union of mutual devotion while he saw marriage merely as a frame to hold an indiscriminate medley of relationships that, as often as not, were too capacious to be contained. She sighed and closed her eyes and this gave him excuse to go.

'It won't hurt you to have a rest in bed. I expect you overdid it, sight-seeing in Luxor.'

As he was leaving, Sister Metrebian came in with sleeping-tablets for Harriet. The sight of her with her plain face, her small chocolate-brown eyes, her reticence and air of enclosed sadness, brought Guy to a stop.

She offered the tablets to Harriet who said she did not need them. Sister Metrebian gently persisted: 'I am sorry, but you must take them. Dr Shafik wants you to sleep very well so to-morrow you will be fresh for the tests.'

Feeling he must make a gesture towards the nurse, Guy said cheerfully: 'I can see the patient is in good hands,' and as he smiled admiringly on her, Sister Metrebian's sallow cheeks were tinged with pink. Although she was by nature quiet, conveying her requests by movements rather than words, she said when Guy had gone: 'What a nice man!'

Growing drowsy, Harriet, lying in darkness, drifted in memory till she seemed back again in the haunted strangeness of child-hood. She had had pneumonia when she was a little girl. At first it was thought to be merely influenza and she had been put to rest on the living-room sofa, facing the fire. She remembered how the fire and the fireplace and the clock above it and the ornaments had become insubstantial, as though made of some glowing, shifting, magical stuff that enhanced the luxury of lying there, wrapped in warmth and comfort, drifting in and out of consciousness.

Her mother, becoming anxious, had put a hand on her fore-head and said to someone in the room, 'She has a fever.' That, too, was part of luxury for her mother was not given to tender-ness. She sometimes said, as though describing a curious and interesting facet of herself: 'I don't like being touched. Even when the children put their arms round me, I don't really like it.'

But Harriet was different and as sleep came down on her, she told herself, 'I want more love than I am given – but where am I to find it?'

Her first visitor next morning was Angela who arrived with an arm full of tuberoses that scented the room. She asked with intense concern, 'What is it? What is the matter with you?'

'Apparently nothing serious.'

'Oh, Harriet, what a fool I was dashing back to Cairo and leaving you on your own.'

'I was all right. I met a friend and saw the sights. But what came of your dash? – did you find Bill alive?'

'Need you ask? I went to the Union and there he was: smirking, with his bloody Mona smirking at his side. I realized then he'd never leave her. He dare not. He hasn't the guts. Harriet! I've decided, I'm going on that boat for women and children. I may go to England, or I may get off at Cape Town, but whatever I do, I'm going.'

Harriet could not take this declaration seriously: 'You can't go. You couldn't leave me without a friend.'

'I *am* going. I've already applied for a passage. I have to get away from Bill and I won't get away unless I do something drastic. So, to hell with him and his God-awful wife. Let him sit there and smirk. I have my own life to lead and I intend to have a rattling good time.'

'If you go to England, you'll be conscripted.'

'Not me. I know what to do about that. When they call you up, you just say, "I'm a tart." Tarts are exempt (God knows why). They say, "Oh, come now, Lady Hooper, you don't want us to think you're a common prostitute, do you?" and you say, "Think what you like. That's what I am: a tart," and if you stick to it, there's not a thing they can do about it.'

'But you're not a tart. You couldn't keep it up.'

'I could and, if necessary, I shall.'

'So you really mean to go?' Harriet became dejected as she saw Angela lost to her. 'You've made me feel miserable.'

'Then come with me.'

Harriet smiled. 'Perhaps I will,' she said.

No one was in a hurry at the American Hospital. Once there, Harriet was expected to stay there and when she asked Sister Metrebian if she could soon go home, the nurse shook her head vaguely: 'How can I say? First, they must examine the specimens.'

'And when will we get the verdict?'

'Tomorrow, perhaps. The day after, perhaps.'

But the result of the tests was slow in coming and when Harriet enquired about it, Sister Metrebian became distressed: 'How can I say? You must wait for Dr Shafik.'

'When will he be back?'

Sister Metrebian shrugged: 'He is a busy man.'

That was not Harriet's impression of Dr Shafik. Sometimes, from boredom, she went out in her dressing-gown and wandered about the passages of the hospital, seeing no one and hearing nothing until, passing through a gate marked 'No Entry', she came into a cul-de-sac where there was only one door. Behind the door a man was shouting in delirium, expressing a terror that seemed to her more terrible because it was in a language she did not understand. As she hurried back to her own room, she met Sister Metrebian and asked her what was wrong with the man.

Sister Metrebian shook her head in sombre disapproval: 'You should not go near. He is very ill. He is a Polish officer from Haifa where they have plague.'

'*Plague*? He has got plague?'

'How can I say? He is not my patient. I can say only: you must not go near.'

Trembling, Harriet sat on her balcony, gulping in fresh air as though it were a prophylactic, and she thought of England where there was no plague, no cholera, no smallpox, and the food was not contaminated. If she went with Angela, she would regain her health – but how could she leave Guy here alone?

She had said to Angela, 'You know what happens when wives go home? We've seen it often enough.'

Angela took this lightly: 'You know you can trust Guy. He's not the sort to go off the rails.'

Perhaps not, but it was Guy who had first suggested she ask for a passage on the boat and she was suspicious of the fact he wanted her to go. She thought, 'Everything has gone wrong since we came here.' The climate changed people: it preserved ancient remains but it disrupted the living. She had seen common-place English couples who, at home, would have tolerated each other for a lifetime, here turning into self-dramatizing figures of tragedy, bored, lax, unmoral, complaining and, in the end, abandoning the partner in hand for another who was neither better nor worse than the first. Inconstancy was so much the rule among the British residents in Cairo, the place, she thought, was like a bureau of sexual exchange.

So, how could she be sure of Guy? When she married him, she scarcely knew him and, now, did she know him any better? How rash she had been, rushing into marriage, and how absurd to imagine it, on no evidence at all, a perfect, indestructible marriage! Every marriage was imperfect and the destroying agents, the imperfections, were there, unseen, from the start. How did she know that Guy, under the easy-going, well-disposed exterior, was not secretive and sly, suggesting she return to England for his own ends, whatever they might be?

It was noon, the most brilliant hour of the day, when the Gezira playing-fields looked as dry as the desert. The sky was colourless with heat yet to her it seemed to be netted over with darkness. The world seemed sinister and she felt she could put no trust into it. Aidan Pratt had said of life: 'If it has to end, does it matter when it ends?' The same could be said of life's relationships. If Guy were a deceiver, then the sooner she found out, the better.

Later that afternoon, when she had returned to bed, Dr Shafik entered with a springing step and, standing over her, looking satisfied with himself, he said, 'Well, madame, we have discovered your trouble. You have amoebic dysentery. Not good, no, but not so bad because there is a new drug for this condition. The American Embassy has sent it to us and you will be the first to benefit by it.'

'And I will be cured?'

'Why, certainly. Did you come here to die?' Tall and handsome in his white coat, Dr Shafik smiled an ironical smile: 'Could we let a member of your great empire die here, in our poor country?'

'A great many members of the empire are dying here. You forget there is a war on.'

Harriet could see from his face that Dr Shafik had forgotten but he hid his forgetfulness under a tone of teasing scorn: 'Call that a war? Two armies going backwards and forwards in the desert, chasing each other like fools!'

'It's a war for those who fight it. And may I ask, Dr Shafik, why you have to be so unpleasant to me?'

Surprised by the question, he stared at her then his smile became mischievous: 'Are you aware, Mrs Pringle, that we have here another English lady?'

'No.' Harriet had not heard of an Englishwoman being in hospital but there were a great many English people not known to her in Cairo. Some lived half-way between the Orient and the Occident, avoiding the temporary residents brought here by war. Some had adopted the Moslem religion and its ways. Some had married Egyptians and others, though they went to England to find marriage partners, had lived here so long, they had become a race on their own.

'Is she very ill?'

'She was, but now she is recovering. Would you wish her to come and talk to you?'

Harriet knew that he meant to play some trick on her but asked from curiosity, 'What is her name?'

Shafik was not telling: 'Perhaps when you see her, you will know who she is.'

He went, promising that the lady would visit her, and an hour later a very old woman came sidling into the room, wearing a hospital bath-robe and a pair of old camel-leather slippers that flapped from her heels. She crept towards the bed and Harriet, seeing who she was, said, 'Why, Miss Copeland, what are you doing here?'

She had last seen Miss Copeland in the pension where the Pringles lived before moving to Dobson's flat. She came in once a week to lay out a little shop of haberdashery which, to help her, the inmates bought, whether they needed the goods or not. She had not changed; her skin, stretched over frail, prominent bones, still had the milky blueness of extreme age. At some time during her long sojourn in Cairo, she had become deaf and had shut herself into silence, seldom speaking.

Though she knew the old woman could not hear her, Harriet said to encourage her: 'Why are you here? You look quite well.'

Miss Copeland sat on the edge of the chair. Her pale, milky eyes observed the things about her and when they came to Harriet, she whispered: 'They found me in bed. I couldn't get up.'

'What was the matter?'

'I was riddled with it.'

Much shocked, Harriet could think of nothing to say. Seeing that her lips did not move, Miss Copeland leant towards her and enquired: 'What did you die of?'

Before Harriet need answer, Miss Copeland jumped down from the chair: 'It must be time for lunch. It's nice being dead, they give you so much to eat.' She was gone in a moment, her slippers flapping behind her.

Almost at once, Dr Shafik came in to discover how Harriet had taken the visit: 'So, you have seen the lady? You know her, I think?'

'I know who she is. Has she really got cancer?'

'No. That is her little fantasy. But is she not charming? An old, harmless lady, living here among other ladies of her own country – and yet she nearly starved to death. She lay in bed, too ill to move, and no one called to see how she was. It was a poor shop-keeper, where she bought bread, who asked himself, "Where is the old English lady? Can she need help?" – and so she was found.'

Discomforted, as Dr Shafik intended her to be, Harriet said, 'We knew nothing about her. She made some money by selling little things: tapes, cottons, needles, things like that. She was independent. She lived her own life and did not seem to want anyone to call on her . . .' Harriet's defence faded out because, in fact, no one knew how or where Miss Copeland lived, and she wondered whether anyone cared.

Shafik nodded his understanding of the situation: 'So you left her alone and it was an Egyptian peasant who showed pity! You see, here in Egypt, we live together. We look after our old people.'

'Miss Copeland didn't want to live with anyone. She wanted to be alone so, when she needed help, there was no one at hand to give it.'

Shafik gave a scoffing laugh: 'Now you know she needs help, will you, with your large house and many servants, take her in?'

'I might, if I had a large house and servants, but I haven't. My husband and I have one room in someone else's flat.'

'Is that so?'

'You did not answer my question, Dr Shafik. I asked why you are so unpleasant to me?'

He again left the question unanswered but later in the day, when Edwina came to see her, she had an answer of sorts.

Edwina, her tear-reddened eyes hidden behind dark glasses, said, 'Oh, Harriet, I couldn't come before. I couldn't . . .' She put her head down and sobbed again and it was some minutes before she could continue; 'Peter's gone back to the desert. I'll never see him again . . . I'll never . . .'

'Don't worry, you will see him again. The next thing will be a counter-offensive and they'll all be belting back to Sollum and coming to Cairo on leave.'

'That's not what he thought. He said, "This time we've got them on the run."'

'They say that every time.'

Harriet brought out a bottle of whisky, given her by Angela, and said, 'Let's have a drink. It'll do us both good.' As Edwina sniffed and drank her whisky, Harriet said, 'Even if he doesn't come back, there are other men in the world.'

'That's true. Guy's been terribly kind to me.'

'He's kind to everyone,' said Harriet who had no intention of offering Guy as one of the 'other men'.

But Edwina was not to be discouraged: 'You know, I think Guy arranged this whole entertainment just to take my mind off Peter.'

'He arranged it long before Peter became troublesome.'

A number of people, Aidan Pratt among them, had imagined they were the sole recipients of Guy's regard. And yet . . . And yet . . . It was Edwina's singing voice that had induced him to plan a troops' entertainment.

Warned by Harriet's silence, Edwina said no more about Guy but diverted her by giggling: 'I see you've got that gorgeous Dr Shafik! How romantic, lying here pale and interesting, with Dr Shafik taking your pulse!'

'Amoebic dysentery is not a romantic condition.'

'*Condition du pays.* I bet he's had it himself.'

'And he's not gorgeous to me. He's downright disagreeable.'

'Oh, he's disagreeable to all of us. He's violently anti-British.

He belongs to the Nationalist Party and that's worse than the Wafd. They'd cut our throats tomorrow if they had the chance.'

'Good heavens, Dr Shafik has every chance in the world here. I hope Sister Metrebian will protect me from him.'

Edwina, having finished her whisky, became wildly amused by this but her laughter changed in a moment and she choked with sobs: 'Oh, Peter, Peter, Peter! I long to have him back!' She was desolate but not to the point of admitting that Peter was married to someone else.

Harriet, knowing what she did know, said, hoping to pull her together, 'I'm sorry, Edwina dear, but I think you're well out of it. He'd make a terrible husband. All that fooling about! What a bore!'

'You're probably right. Yes, I know you're right. There were times when I could have murdered him. Although he's got a title, he's a brute, really.'

Edwina dabbed her eyes, then murmured, 'Still . . .'

A brute, but, still, no ordinary brute! He was a catch – alas, already caught! Edwina sighed. Her golden beauty drawn with disappointment, she saw herself setting out again to find another 'catch'. There were a great many lonely men in Cairo but few who matched up to Edwina's aspirations.

Her regimen of emetine capsules and a bland diet seemed so simple, Harriet thought she could treat herself at home but Sister Metrebian would not hear of it: 'We have to carefully watch you. Emetine is very dangerous. A toxic drug. You take too much and you kill yourself. Do you understand?'

And, Harriet thought, how easily Dr Shafik could kill her! When she had been in hospital a week, he entered the room in a businesslike way and said he needed a sample of her blood. Sister Metrebian was at his heels, carrying a knife in a kidney dish. He lifted the knife and Harriet was startled to see it was sharp-pointed like a kitchen knife.

'What is this?' he asked: 'We have here an edge like a consumptive's temperature chart!' He threw the knife back with elaborate disgust and she realized it had been another joke. He did not mean to use it, yet, in her distrust of everyone and everything, she felt a particular distrust of Shafik. She thought, 'The smiler with the knife', and asked: 'Why do you want a sample of blood?'

'For a little test, that is all. You are afraid?'

'No, of course not.'

She expected him to draw off the blood with a syringe but he had found another instrument which he wished to try. She felt he was experimenting on her. He pressed the point of a metal scoop into the artery of her inner arm. As the blood flowed down the scoop to a test-tube, she felt she could bear no more. Tears ran down her cheeks and Dr Shafik spoke with surprising kindliness: 'There, there, Mrs Pringle, don't cry. You are a very brave girl.'

Knowing she was not a brave girl, Harriet laughed but he did not laugh with her. The blood taken and the small wound covered, he pressed his long, strong fingers into the region round her liver and asked, 'Does that hurt?'

'Yes, but it would, anyway, you're pressing so hard. Why? What else is wrong with me?'

'That is a thing I must find out.'

When doctor and sister had gone, Harriet asked herself how it was she had sunk so low, she wept at the sight of her own blood? She despised herself and yet she wept again. Hunting round for a handkerchief, she found among the detritus at the bottom of her handbag, the heart made of rose-diamonds. She had forgotten it and now, holding it above her head, she was entranced by the radiance of the diamonds and was amazed that they were not merely in her keeping, like Aidan's votive cat, but were her property. The heart had been given to her: an object from a richer, grander, altogether more opulent world than any she had inhabited. She put it on the bedside table where it lit the air, a talisman and a preserver of life.

When Guy came in that evening, Dr Shafik was in the room, making a routine visit. He was about to rush away when it apparently occurred to him who Guy was. He came to a stop, held out his hand and said with awe: 'But, of course, you are the Professor Pringle that people speak of. You are a lover of Egypt, are you not? You are one who would urge us towards freedom and social responsibility?'

The revelation of his breadth of vision surprised even Guy but, pink with pleasure, he seized on Shafik's hand and admitted that he was indeed that Professor Pringle, saying, 'Yes, Egypt must have freedom. But social responsibility? That, I imagine, can come only through a Marxist revolution.'

Whether the doctor agreed or not, he moved closer to Guy and said in a quiet voice: 'You know, there are many of us?'

'Of course. I've talked to students . . .'

'Oh, students! They act and so are useful, but they do not think, and so are dangerous. But enough for now. We will talk another time, eh? Meanwhile, I have this case of your wife. She is not well.'

Guy, forced to revert to the discouraging subject of Harriet's health, asked: 'Aren't you satisfied with her progress?'

'Not so much. These amoebae are insidious animalcule. They move from organ to organ.'

Guy stared and kept quiet while the doctor, supposing the matter to be of intense interest to him, described the dangers of amoebic infection: dangers comprehensible by a male brain but not, of course, by a female.

'You must know that the amoebae can be carried in the portal stream to the liver and cause hepatitis and the liver abscess. If they reach the gall bladder that, too, can be bad. But I do not think she has the liver abscess.'

'Oh, good!' Guy, his dismay rapidly dispersed by this assurance, said, 'Then she's all right. There's nothing to worry about?'

'Sooner or later, she will be all right.'

'Splendid!' That decided, Guy was eager to return to the subject of social responsibility but Shafik seemed equally eager to evade it.

'Such talk would bore a lady, and you and your wife must have much to say to one another.' With an amused expression, lifting his hand in an adieu, the doctor made a swift departure.

Guy gazed regretfully after him: 'Why did he go off like that?'

'Sister Metrebian says he is a busy man.'

'I suppose he is.'

Now that the chance to discuss social responsibility had been snatched from him, Guy looked tired. He, too, was a busy man and he seemed to have about him the oppression of the dusty, noisy Cairo streets. He sat down and, as he looked at Harriet, she felt he reproached her for remaining in a country that was destroying her health.

'Dobson was telling me that before the war, anyone who contracted this sort of dysentery was shipped home. In England, the amoebae leave the system and you are not re-infected. Here, if you're prone to it, you're liable to get it again.'

'So Dobson wants to ship me home? He's absurdly self-important at times. He thinks he's only to say the word and I'll get straight on to the boat. Well, I won't. It would simply mean you were alone here and I would be alone in England. A miserable arrangement!'

'He's only thinking of your good. He says when people are depleted by acute dysentery, they pick up other diseases and . . .'

'And die? Well, let's wait till I show more signs of dying.'

He was about to say more when he noticed the rose-diamond brooch on the table beside her and he became animated: 'Where did you get this?'

'Angela gave it to me. She bought it in the Muski.'

He picked it up and laughed as he examined it: 'It's vulgar but it has a sort of panache. Let me have it. I'll give it to Edwina to cheer her up.'

'But it's mine. It was given to me.'

'Surely you don't want it. You couldn't be seen wearing a thing like that. It's a theatrical prop: just right for Edwina when she sings, "We'll meet again" or "Smoke gets in your eyes".'

'She doesn't sing those sort of songs.'

'She does in the show. It's for troops and the troops will love this thing.'

'It's a valuable piece of jewellery. They're real diamonds and cost a lot of money.'

'Even so, it's tawdry. It looks cheap.'

Smiling his contempt, he held the brooch away from him and she saw it degraded from a treasure and a talisman into a worthless gewgaw. She could not defend it, yet she did not want to lose it.

She said, 'Give it back,' unable to believe he would take it from her, but he slipped it into his pocket.

344

'Darling, don't be silly. You know you don't want it. Let Edwina have it. Well, I must go.'

She watched, silent in disbelief, as he left with the brooch, delighted that he had something to give away.

'But what he gives, he takes from me!' She went to sit on the balcony, feeling, as the first shock of the incident wore off, a sense of outrage that the brooch was gone. Gazing over the greensward where she sometimes saw men on polo ponies and other men swinging golf clubs, she asked herself, 'What is there to keep me here?'

When Angela came to see her again, she said, 'I've been thinking about England. I could get a job there. I'd be of some use in the world.'

'Do you mean you might come with me?'

'Yes, I do mean that. I've been watching those men out there playing ridiculous games while other men are being killed, and I thought how futile our life is here. I felt I wanted to get away.'

'If you're serious, you'll have to apply at once. There's a rumour that the ship's over-full already. Shall I speak to Dobson? Get him to use his influence?'

'Yes, speak to Dobson.' But though she agreed, Harriet was still half-hoping that the ship was too full to take her and she would have to stay.

Still, she had put the matter into Angela's hands and before they could say anything more about it, she was visited by Major Cookson. He had not come alone. His companion, whose function had probably been to pay for the long taxi drive to the hospital, did not follow him to the bed but stood just inside the room as though bewildered at finding himself there.

Cookson sat on the bed edge and whispered to Harriet and Angela: 'I've brought an old friend, very distinguished. I knew you'd be pleased to meet him.' He turned and summoned the friend in a commanding tone: 'Humphrey, come over here.' Then returning to the women, he whispered again: 'It's Humphrey Taupin, the archaeologist. You were in Greece, Harriet. You must have heard of him.'

They all looked at Humphrey Taupin as he managed to make his way to the bedside where he stood, swaying, as though about to crumple to the floor.

Cookson brought a chair for him, saying, 'Sit down, Humphrey, do!' but Taupin remained on his feet, looking at Harriet, a smile reaching his face as though from a great distance.

Harriet had heard of him. He had been a famous name around the cafés in Athens. When he was very young, on his first dig, he had come upon a stone sarcophagus that contained a death-mask of beaten gold. The mask, thought to be of a king of Corinth, was in the museum and Harriet had seen it there. This find, that for some would have been the beginning, was for him the end. She could imagine that such an achievement at twenty might leave one wondering what to do for the next fifty years. Anyway, confounded by his own success, he had retired to the most remote of the Sporades; and no one had thought of him when the Germans came.

But he had escaped somehow and here he was, in Cairo, standing beside her bed. When she smiled back at him, he moved a little closer to her and a smell of the grave came from his clothes. His light alpaca suit hung on him as on a skeleton. He was in early middle-age but his hair was already white and his face was crumpled and coloured like the crust on old custard.

She asked him how he had escaped from Greece. When it occurred to him that she was speaking to him, he did not reply but bent towards her and offered her his hand. She took it but not willingly. She had heard that he had been cured of syphilis, but perhaps he was not cured. Feeling his hand in hers, dry and fragile, like the skeleton of a small bird, she remembered the courteous crusader who took the hand of a leper and became a leper himself. When Taupin's hand slipped away, she felt she, too, was at risk.

Cookson plucked at his jacket, telling him again to sit down but his senses seemed too distant to be contacted He smiled then, turning, wandered back across the floor and out of the room.

Cookson tutted and said, 'He really is a most unaccountable fellow. I'm sorry. I thought he would amuse you.'

Harriet, still feeling on her palm the rasp of Humphrey Taupin's hand, asked, 'How did he get here?'

'He's just arrived from Turkey. His Greek boys managed to

get him to Lesbos in a caique in the middle of the night. He went on to Istanbul and he hung around there till the Turks threw him out.'

'Why did they do that?'

'Hashish, y'know. They're sticky about that.'

Angela asked: 'Is that why he's so vague?'

'Oh, my dear, yes. I went to that island of his once. Quite an ordeal, getting there and even more of an ordeal staying there. He kept you sitting up, talking, all night and if you got any sleep, it was during the day. Only one meal was served and not very good either. He called it breakfast. It arrived about ten in the evening and then the talk began.'

'I suppose he was more *compos mentis* in those days?' Harriet asked.

'Much more. He was quite the tyrant before he got on to hashish. He had three subjects: sex, literature and religion. You discussed one a night and then you were told the boys would row you back to Skiros. There was no knowing how long you would have to wait for the boat back to Athens.'

'And that was the routine?'

'Yes. Invariable. Everyone who went, talked about it.'

'But they did go?'

'Yes. Out of curiosity, as much as anything. We formed quite a little élite, those of us who'd braved the island. We felt we'd done something remarkable.'

'Yet when the Germans were coming, you all forgot about him?'

'Oh!' Major Cookson's mouth fell open, then he tried to excuse himself: 'It was so sudden, the German breakthrough. They came so quickly.'

'Still you had time to prepare your get-away.'

Major Cookson hung his head, knowing that the manner of his departure from Greece might be forgiven, but it would never be forgotten.

Having discovered that Harriet was the wife of a professor who was a lover of Egypt, Dr Shafik changed towards Harriet. Whenever he had nothing else to do, he would stroll into her room and entertain her with flippant and flirtatious talk. He did not suppose her capable of discussing an abstruse problem but he would gaze at her thoughtfully, even tenderly, and accord her his especial care. Harriet knew that Arabs, when not laughing at the female sex as a ridiculous aberration in nature, were romantic and generous, but she became bored by his levity. She broke into it to ask, 'Is your plague patient still alive?'

'Yes, he is alive. How did you know I have such a patient?'

'I heard him crying out in delirium. It was frightening. And he's still alive! Is there a new drug with which to treat bubonic plague?'

'Yes.' He was rather sulky at being forced into this conversation and she had to question him before he would tell her: 'There is a serum which is effective, sometimes. But his heart will be weak.'

'You are not afraid for yourself?'

'Naturally I have been inoculated. We wear special clothing and so on. The danger is not great.'

'The man is a Polish officer, isn't he? Why was he brought to a civilian hospital?'

'He had to be isolated, and the military have no suitable place. You know, on this spot, a long time ago, there was the old quarantine station and hospital. The island was only half formed then, and it was desert.'

Harriet's interest, arising out of her horror of contagion, led Shafik to talk in spite of himself. He told her it was there that patients were brought during the plague epidemic of 1836. 'There was a Dr Brulard. He wanted so much to know how plague was transmitted, he took the shirt from a dead man and wore it himself. Was he not brave?'

'My goodness, yes. And did he catch plague?'

'No, nor did he solve the mystery of how it was transmitted. And there was typhus – now, how did they catch typhus?'

Harriet laughed nervously and Shafik refused to tell her any more about plague and typhus, but, leaning towards her, said, 'You are getting better. Are you glad you did not die and go to heaven?'

'I thought there was no heaven for women in your religion.'

'Wrong, madame, wrong. The ladies have a nice heaven of

their own. They are without men but there is a consolation: they are beautiful for ever.'

'If there are no men, would it matter whether they were beautiful or not?'

'Ha!' Dr Shafik threw back his head and shouted with laughter: 'Mrs Pringle, I am much relieved. You are, after all, a true woman.'

'Why "after all"?'

'I wondered. I thought you were too clever for your sex.'

'And you're not as clever as you think you are.'

'Oh, oh, oh!' Shafik shook his hand as though it had been burnt: 'How ungrateful, after I have so cleverly cured you!'

'Perhaps you didn't cure me. Perhaps I cured myself. You see, I have given in. I'm going back to England.'

'You are going to England?' he stared with concern and dismay: 'Just when we have become friends! And Professor Pringle? – he, too, is going to England?'

'No. He has to stay here till the war ends.'

'But does he want you to go?'

'He thinks I will never be well while I remain here.'

'I'm sorry you are going.'

'I'm sorry, too.'

Before she left the hospital, Harriet asked if she might see Miss Copeland again, but Miss Copeland was no longer there. When he suggested that the Pringles should give her a home, Dr Shafik had been making fun of Harriet. A home already had been provided by the Convent of the Holy Family and there Miss Copeland could stay for the rest of her life.

Shafik, saying goodbye to Harriet, held her hand between his two strong, slender hands and said, 'One day you will come back to Egypt and then you will come to see me. Yes?'

Harriet promised that she would. Looking into his large, dark, emotional eyes, she almost wished she had an Oriental husband, especially one who looked like Dr Shafik.

Twelve

For a fortnight before the lecture, Pinkrose telephoned Guy several times a day, demanding to know what progress had been made in finding a hall that would reflect his importance. He rejected the assembly rooms of the American University, the cathedral, Cairo University and the Agricultural Museum. None of these was grand enough for the occasion he had in mind. He wanted a large and ornate hall, one suited for the entertainment of royalty and the Egyptian aristocracy.

Cairo offered nothing to suit him. The Egyptians themselves when gathering for a wedding or the funeral of a notable, employed a tent-maker to erect a tent in a Midan or some other open area. These tents, large, square and appliquéd all over with coloured designs, had appealed to Harriet and she suggested that one be hired for the lecture.

Pinkrose was appalled by the idea: 'Lecture in a tent, Pringle! Lecture in a tent! Certainly not. What do you think I am! – Barnum's Circus?' He insisted that the Embassy be again approached and asked to open up the ballroom.

To please him, Guy had another word with Dobson who only laughed: 'The place is under dust sheets. It would take an army of servants to get it ready.'

In the end, Guy approached the management of the Opera House and found it was available if the sum offered were large enough. But even the Opera House did not please Pinkrose. Forced to accept it, he frowned at the bare stage and said, 'I expect you to pretty it up, Pringle.'

'We'll surround the podium with flowers and ferns.'

'Fair enough, Pringle; see to that. Now, about the reception. You know I've invited the king and court? Well, we can't ask them to sit on kitchen chairs, can we?'

The reception was to be in the Green Room which looked well enough to Guy but did not satisfy Pinkrose who went off on his own and found a shop that hired out theatrical furniture. He chose crimson plush curtains with gilt tassels and a large gilt and plush-seated chair that looked like a throne. These, together with two dozen gilt reception chairs, were delivered to the Opera House. When the curtains were hung and the chairs crowded into the room, Pinkrose called Guy in to admire the effect: 'What do you think of it, eh, Pringle? What do you think of it?'

'I think it's tawdry and ridiculous.'

'No, Pringle, it's regal. His majesty will think he's in a corner of Abdin Palace.'

'You know we've had no acceptances from the palace?'

'Oh, they'll come. They'll come.'

Guy had promised to call for Harriet when she left hospital but was too busy. He telephoned her at the flat to excuse his defection: 'By the time this lecture's over, I'll be as loony as Pinkrose.'

Losing patience, Harriet said, 'Why do you pander to the old egoist? Who cares whether he lectures or not?'

'You'd be surprised. The whole university staff is coming. And you'll come, too, won't you?'

Still toxic from the drugs that had killed the amoebae, Harriet had been thinking of going to bed. Persuaded to dress and attend the reception, she asked Angela to go with her.

'Oh, no, darling, I can't bear lectures. I forget to listen and I start talking and people around get shirty . . .'

'Do come, Angela, we'll sit at the back and laugh.'

'No, darling, no.'

Angela was firm in her refusal and suspecting she had some other engagement, Harriet went to the Opera House alone.

The Green Room was filled with gilt chairs but the guests, edged in among them, were neither numerous nor very distinguished. Pinkrose, ignoring the university staff and the government officials, waited, in a state of peevish anxiety, for someone worthy of his attention. He was wearing an old, greenish dinner suit with a grey knitted shawl over his shoulders.

351

Usually he kept the shawl up to his mouth but now he had pulled it down in readiness for a royal welcome and his lips opened and shut in agitation.

Guy came to say the lecture should begin. Pinkrose, refusing to listen, shook his head: 'You must telephone the king's chamberlain, Pringle. I insist. I *insist*. Make it clear that this is no ordinary lecture. I'm not just a don, I'm a peer of the realm. The palace owes me the courtesy of royal patronage.'

Guy, mild in manner but determined, refused to telephone the palace while the guests listened, transfixed by Pinkrose's behaviour.

'If you don't ring the palace, I won't go on. I won't. I won't. I won't.'

'Very well, I'll give the lecture myself.'

Pinkrose did not reply but stared at his script which shook in his shaking hands. When Guy asked the guests to follow him into the theatre, Pinkrose made a rush and pushed ahead of him. Trotting at a furious pace, he went down the aisle and up some side steps to the stage. Guy was to take the chair but before he could reach it, Pinkrose had positioned himself at the forefront of the stage. An oval figure, narrow at the shoulders and broad at the hips, he stared at the audience, his eyes stony with contempt. A stage light, shining down on his dog-brown hair, lit the ring on which his hat usually fitted.

He took a step forward. He was about to begin but before he could say anything, there was a report and he stood, looking astonished, saying nothing. The noise had not been very great and some people, thinking he was waiting for silence, shushed at each other. Then they saw that he had a hand pressed to his side and his body was slowly folding towards the floor. As he collapsed, Guy hurried to him and pulling the shawl away, revealed Pinkrose's dress shirt soaked in blood. There was hubbub in the auditorium.

Harriet, going towards the stage, saw Guy's face creased with amazed concern. An army doctor ran up the steps to join him. Guy shook his head and the doctor, putting an ear to Pinkrose's chest, said, 'He's dead.'

This statement reached the people in the front row and was quickly passed back. A crowd of students leapt up and began bawling in triumph. One of them shouted: 'So die all enemies of Egypt's freedom.' The others, excited by the possibility of a political demonstration, repeated this cry while more sober members of the audience began pushing their way out before trouble should begin.

Harriet, standing below the stage, felt someone touch her arm and, looking round, saw a young woman who said, 'Remember me?'

'Yes, you're Mortimer.'

'Tell me, why are they saying Lord Pinkrose was an enemy of Egyptian freedom?'

Harriet could only shake her head but the student nearest to her answered: 'Not Lord Pinkrose. Lord Pinkerton. Minister of State. Very bad man.'

Another corrected him: 'Not Minister of State. Minister of War.'

Harriet said, 'Pinkrose isn't any sort of minister. You've killed the wrong man.'

Taking this as an accusation, the students began a clamour of protest: 'We did not kill any man.' 'Who is wrong man?' 'What's it matter, all British lords bad men. All enemies of Egypt,' and having found an excuse for a riot, they began tugging at the theatre seats in an effort to get them away from the floor.

The stage was empty now. Guy and the doctor had carried Pinkrose into the wings. Mortimer, holding to Harriet's arm, said: 'You don't look well.'

'It's the shock, and I've just come out of hospital.'

'Better get away from this rampage. No knowing what they'll do next.' Capable and strong, Mortimer put her arms about Harriet and led her out to the street. They stood in the cool, night air, listening to the uproar inside the theatre and waiting for Guy to emerge. He did not come but the students, defeated by the clamped-down seats, came running out, bawling every and any political slogan that came into their heads. Two of the young men, recognizing Harriet, stopped, becoming suddenly cautious and polite. She asked them if they knew who fired the shot.

Speaking together, showing now vehement disapproval of what had happened, they told her that Egyptians were good people: 'Believe me, Mrs Pringle, we do not kill. We talk but killing is not in our nature.'

'Then who do you think did it?'

They looked at each other, hesitant yet unable to keep their knowledge to themselves. One said, 'They are saying a gun was seen. They are saying that Mr Hertz and Mr Allain were beside the door. When the shot came, they at once went out.'

'But who fired the shot?'

'Ah, who can say?'

An ambulance pulled up at the kerb. The watchers became silent, waiting to see what would happen next. Men went inside with a stretcher and when they came out, Guy was walking in front of them. The body, even more protected in death than in life, was muffled up like a mummy with Pinkrose's old, brown, sweat-stained trilby lying, like a tribute, on the chest. The body was put into the ambulance and Guy got in with it. Harriet moved to speak to him but he was driven away.

'So that's that,' Mortimer said: 'I could do with a drink. How about you? Shepherd's is too crowded. Let's get a taxi and go to Groppi's.'

Harriet, exhausted, was happy to let Mortimer find a taxi and help her into it. They found Groppi's garden nearly empty. The Egyptians were nervous of the winter air at night and the staff officers were thinning out as the desert war moved westwards. Cairo was no longer a base town though the townspeople, especially those who lived off the army, daily expected the British back again.

The two women sat in a secluded corner and Mortimer, attentive and concerned for Harriet, recommended Cyprus brandy as a restorative for them both. They talked about Pinkrose and the manner of his death.

'He was advertised as Professor Lord Pinkrose,' Mortimer said: 'What was he doing here? Was he sent out to do some sort of undercover work?'

'I don't think so.' Harriet described Pinkrose's arrival to lecture in Bucharest, his move to Athens and then on to Egypt: 'I don't think he dabbled in anything. I imagine, like Polonius, he was mistaken for his better. The students mentioned a Lord

Pinkerton. That may have been the one the assassins were after. But how was it you were at the lecture?'

'Oh, I'm addicted to lectures. I was a student myself when war broke out. I was at Lady Margaret Hall. Seeing that a Cambridge professor was to talk on Eng. Lit., I thought, "This will be quite like old times." I went in with some idea of taking notes. Keeping in training, as it were. I'll go back to study when the war's over. Strange to think of it, though.'

'Did you know that Angela and I are leaving Egypt? We've got berths on the ship going round the Cape to England.'

'Really, you're going? Both of you. Soon there'll be no one left here. You sound sad. Do you mind leaving?'

'I do, strangely enough. When I first came here, I hated the place. Now I feel miserable about leaving it. And, of course, I'm leaving Guy. I won't see him again till the war's over – that is, if it ever is over.'

'If you feel like that, why are you going?'

'I don't know. Out of pique, as much as anything.' Harriet told Mortimer how Guy had taken the rose-diamond brooch and Mortimer shook with laughter.

'You couldn't go because of that. It's too silly.'

'Not as silly as you think. He took the brooch to give to a girl who's had an unhappy love affair. He thought it would comfort her.'

'But it's not serious? – with the girl, I mean?'

'Perhaps not – but that detonated my feelings. I wanted to change my life and did not know how to do it. This will be a change. We know nothing about war-time England. I want to go back and see for myself. I want to be in the midst of it.'

Mortimer ordered more brandy and they drank sombrely, Mortimer despondent at the departure of Angela, and Harriet despondent at having to depart. Buttoning her cardigan against the wind that rustled the creepers and shook the coloured lights, Harriet pictured England as a cold and sunless place, no longer familiar to her and so far away, it had become an alien country.

Mortimer said, 'I'm off to Damascus tomorrow. We leave at first light.'

'And when do you get back?'

'We never know for sure. We thought, this time, we'd go as far north as Aleppo.'

'Aleppo!' Harriet's fancy expanded through the Levant and hovered over a vision of Aleppo. She had come so far and seen so little: and, in spite of Dr Shafik's entreaty, she was not likely to return. But it was too late for regrets. She finished her brandy and said she had better go home to bed.

Walking with her down to the river, Mortimer said, 'I suppose you haven't been told the sailing date?'

'No. That'll be kept dark, for security reasons. We'll just have to wait till we receive a summons.'

'You'll go from Suez, of course. When you hear, give me a ring. Angela has my number. Leave a message if I'm not there; I'll ring you back. We often take the lorry to Suez to pick up supplies so, if we can, we'll come and wave you both goodbye.'

Thirteen

The German rearguards fought a delaying action outside Gazala and Dawson said, 'I think we've got him now.' The British infantry broke through but Rommel had already gone.

Simon, sent forward to check fuel supplies, drove into the refuse of war, seeing among the seaside rocks upturned rusting vehicles. On the other side of the road, where the desert ran towards Knightsbridge and Sidi Rezegh, the abandoned hardware dotted the sand like herds of grazing cattle. Except for an old Lysander that chugged, slow and harmless, like a big daddy-longlegs, in the sky, the whole field of past battles was silent.

Simon was content as he drove with Crosbie who, sitting beside him, had for him the wordless but companionable presence of a cat or dog. The familiar ordinariness of Crosbie was a comfort as the camp moved again and again, following the action as it went westwards into country Simon did not know.

On this quiet coast, with the sea lapping at their elbow, it seemed the war was as good as over. He said, 'We might be home for Christmas. D'you want to go back to fishmongering?'

'Don't know that I do,' Crosbie said.

Thinking of his return to a wife he had almost forgotten, Simon wondered how he would fit into a world without war. He would have to begin again, decide on an occupation, accept responsibility for his own actions. What on earth would he do for a living? He had been trained for nothing but war.

Outside Gazala, near the remains of a walled house, a tall palm marked the site of a water-tank. The palm attracted him, though he did not know why. Then he remembered the single palm he had seen and pitied in Cairo. This similar palm, swaying in the wind, was like something known and loved.

'A good place to eat our grub,' he said.

'Stop here, sir?'

'Yes. Get into the shade.'

As Crosbie ran the jeep under the palm, the ground rose about them and he rose with it. Simon, watching Crosbie's grotesque ascent, scarcely heard the explosion. He shouted, 'Bloody booby trap!' expecting Crosbie to shout back, then he was struck himself. Part of the mine's metal casing cut across his side and he was flung from the jeep.

This, he thought, was death, but it was not his death. Dragging himself round the jeep, seeing Crosbie sprawled a dozen yards away, he called to him: 'Crosbie. Hey, Crosbie!' but the man's loose straggle of limbs remained inert.

Simon tried to lift himself, with some idea of dragging Crosbie into the shade, but the lower part of his body would not move. And there was no shade. The palm, cracked through the stem, had broken in half and its fine head of plumes hung like a dead chicken. The jeep, too, was smashed and Simon's first thought was, 'How are we going to get back?' Oddly detached from his condition, he put his hand to his side and felt the wet warmth of blood. He said to himself, as though to another person: 'You were afraid to die like Hugo, and now this is it!' For some minutes death seemed like a fantasy then he realized it could be a reality. The action had moved so far forward, he was very likely to bleed to death before help came.

Putting his head in his hands, waiting for unconsciousness, he heard the sound of a vehicle and looked up. A Bren was lumbering and swaying out of the rubble, having collected the Gazala wounded, and he watched with little more than curiosity as it stopped beside Crosbie. Closing his eyes again, he heard a voice coming as from the other side of sleep: 'Let's take a shufti at that one over there.'

As they were lifting him into the Bren, Simon whispered, 'Never thought you'd come in time.'

The driver laughed good humouredly: 'Oh, we like to be in time, sir. That's our job.'

Inside the Bren with the wounded, Simon called out: 'What about my driver?'

'That chap over there? Mungaree for the kites, that one.'

'Can't we take him?'

'No, sir, can't take him. Got to get you and the others back to the dressing station.'

The Bren started up. Propped on his elbow, Simon stared out through the open flap at Crosbie's body till it became no more than a spot on the sand and then was lost to sight.

Fourteen

Only the English language papers reported the murder of Pinkrose. The *Egyptian Mail*, reputedly pro-British, published a leader entitled 'A Mystery'. Who, the editor asked, would wish to kill this great and good lord who was giving his lecture 'free and for no payment but love of his *confrères*?'

'Who, indeed?' asked Dobson when he read the article at the breakfast table, and he turned on Guy with an expression of ironical enquiry.

Everyone knew that Hertz and Allain had left the Opera House immediately after the shooting and had not been seen since.

Guy, seldom confused, was confused now. He could not believe that Hertz and Allain were guilty; he could not believe that anyone was guilty, yet he could not deny that someone had killed Pinkrose. He could only say that Hertz and Allain were the two best teachers he had ever employed.

'And, anyway, it was a mistake,' Harriet said: 'The students were talking about a British minister with a similar name.'

Dobson sniffed, trying to contain his laughter: 'Is there a minister with a similar name? I don't think so. But a fellow did pass through Cairo a few days ago, on his way to Palestine. He was called Pinkerton.'

'Yes, the students mentioned Pinkerton. Who was he?'

'I can't say. Something very hush-hush, apparently. He said he was an official in the Ministry of Food. The only thing the British have to eat in Palestine are sausages, made by an English grocery shop called Spinney's. Very good they are. But this chap has been sent out to teach Mr Spinney how to make them out of bread instead of meat. To think of it! Poor old gourmandizing Pinkers bumped off in place of a sausage-maker.'

Disliking Dobson's jocosity, Guy asked: 'Why should anyone want to murder a sausage-maker?'

'Who knows? Perhaps he wasn't a sausage-maker. He may have been an MI6 man in disguise'.

'This is all nonsense. I don't believe Pinkrose was mistaken for anyone. He was on the platform, a target, and some fellow with a gun couldn't resist taking a pot at him.'

Dobson, becoming serious, nodded agreement: 'That's possible. Now the heat's off here, all the killers will be coming out of their holes.'

Guy and Major Cookson were the only people to follow Pinkrose's coffin to the English cemetery and neither could be described as a mourner. Guy went from a sense of duty and Cookson because he had known Pinkrose in better days. For Cookson even the dull ride into the desert outside Mahdi was a diversion. Coming back together into Cairo, Guy, who could not maintain enmity for long, decided that the major was not, after all, a bad fellow and stood him several drinks.

Harriet, thinking she might have died herself, asked what the English cemetery was like.

Guy said, 'A dreary place behind a heap of rubble. Poor old Pinkrose, with all his pretensions, would have demanded something better.'

In mid-December, the prospective passengers were informed that the ship – it was still known merely as 'the ship' – would sail early in January. English women and children from neighbouring countries began to congregate in Cairo, awaiting the exact date which would be announced twenty-four hours before the sailing.

A diplomat called Dixon wrote from Baghdad, asking Dobson to put his wife up during this waiting period. The flat being an Embassy flat, Dobson felt bound to comply and it so happened that a room was temporarily vacant. Its occupant, Percy Gibbon, had been sent on loan to the 'secret' radio station at Sharq al Adna, so Dobson wrote back saying he would welcome Mrs Dixon as his guest.

Without further notice, Mrs Dixon arrived as Hassan was setting the breakfast table. Six months pregnant, with a year-old son, a folding perambulator, a high chair, a tricycle, a rock-ing-horse and ten pieces of luggage, she stumbled into the living-room, exhausted by a long train journey, and sank on to the sofa. Dobson, called to attend her, went to look at Percy's room. It was only then that he realized it was locked and there was no spare key. He was ordering Hassan to go out and find a locksmith when Percy Gibbon let himself in through the front door. Percy stopped in the living-room to stare at the strange woman and her impedimenta then, sniffing his disgust, went to his room, unlocked it and shut himself inside it.

Dobson said, 'Good God, who was that?'

Guy, who had seated himself beside Mrs Dixon in an attempt to cheer and comfort her, told him: 'It was Percy Gibbon.'

Dobson stood for a moment in helpless perplexity, then beckoned Guy into the bedroom. He whispered, 'You know, this is very awkward for me. I agreed to put her up, but where can I put her? Her husband's a colleague, so I can't tell her to go, but you, my dear chap, with your charm – you could, in the nicest possible way, of course, explain things to her. Tell her she'll have to find a room in an hotel.'

Guy was aghast at this request: 'I couldn't possibly. I've been talking to her, saying how pleased we all are to have her here. It would be such a shock for her if I told her to go. You see, everyone likes me. I'm not the person to do it. Ask Harriet. She's better at things like that.'

Harriet, appealed to, came from her room, thinking she could deal with the situation. Then she saw Mrs Dixon. Limp and near tears, trying to soothe her fretful child, she was a frail, little woman, her thin arms and legs incongruously burdened with her heavy belly, her fair prettiness fading, her apprehensions heightened by the awful appearance of Percy Gibbon.

She gazed at Harriet with anxious eyes and Harriet, saying 'Don't worry. We'll manage somehow,' went to speak to Dobson. 'Someone has to be sacrificed and it must be Percy Gibbon. Your room is big enough for two. You'll have to get a camp-bed in here and share with him.'

'Oh, dear God, no! I couldn't bear it. And how could I persuade him to give up his room?'

'It's your flat. Don't persuade him, order him.'

Dobson again appealed to Guy: 'Come with me and help me deal with Percy,' but Guy was in a hurry to get away. Agitatedly rubbing his soft puffs of hair, Dobson went to speak to Percy.

Hearing uproar from the bedroom passage, Mrs Dixon sat up in alarm then turned piteously to Harriet: 'Oh, this is my fault. I must go. We're not so poor we can't afford a room at Shepherd's.' She began gathering up the child and its belongings and Harriet had to explain that it was not a question of what one could afford. In Cairo, the few main hotels were so full that even senior officers had to share rooms and sometimes share beds. As for inferior hotels, she would find them intolerable.

Mrs Dixon remained on the sofa, watching fearfully as Percy passed through, carrying his belongings to Dobson's room. He looked blackly at her, muttering his rage as he went. His room vacated, Harriet went to look at it. It was the only one on the right of the corridor and it faced the blank wall of a neighbouring house. She now understood why Dobson had allowed Percy to remain in it. Who else would want it?

She said to Mrs Dixon, 'I'm afraid it's not much of a room.'

Lifting a hand, Mrs Dixon said, 'What does it matter? Anything will do.'

After Harriet had helped her unpack her immediate necessities, she dropped on to the bed and cried, 'Oh, to be safely on board ship.'

'Well, we will be soon, Mrs Dixon. But, meanwhile, you'll find the flat isn't so bad.'

Mrs Dixon smiled weakly: 'My name's Marion,' she said.

Marion Dixon, though grateful for Harriet's support, was chiefly admiring of Angela. Of the three women, united by the prospect of their long sea voyage, Angela was the most expectant of pleasure. Her hopes animated Marion and persuaded her that they were in for what Angela called 'a rattling good time'.

Angela, herself, having heard that many things in England were in short supply, spent much of the day shopping, coming back with parcels that she opened to amuse Marion. Marion had few interests, apart from the boy Richard, but she loved clothes and fingering Angela's silks and new dresses, she said, 'I long to get my figure back so I can wear things like that.'

While Edwina and the men were leaving for work, the three women lingered on at the breakfast table, suspended in the nullity of the present but promised a future of stimulating newness.

Angela often said, '*Bokra fil mish-mish.*'

First hearing it, Marion, who spoke a different Arabic, asked: 'What does that mean?'

'Apricots tomorrow: good times to come.'

Marion smiled her wan smile: 'I was so frightened but I'm not any more,' and she told her new friends that if, by some mischance, her baby was born at sea, their presence would console her.

Dobson laughed at them: 'You three, really! You're like a cluster of schoolgirls discovering sex.'

Edwina, feeling left-out, said, 'I wish I could go with you. But, of course, I can't. There's the show and I couldn't let Guy down.'

Harriet, putting her on trust, said, 'You'll look after Guy for me, won't you?'

'Oh, darling, you know I will. I'll see he doesn't get into mischief. You can rely on me.'

When the others had gone, the three sat in the darkened living-room where, even in winter, the shutters were put up against the sun that splintered in through the cracks. Some previous resident had had a fireplace built into a corner, a very inadequate fireplace. The only fuel to be found was cow-cake, which gave off more smoke than heat. The curious, bland smell of the smoke filled the flat and seemed to Harriet a part of the futility of her life in Cairo. She told herself she was thankful to be leaving it and yet, at times, she was furious because she had agreed to go. It had all been decided too quickly. She should have dwelt upon it. She should have taken time to think. And now it was too late and she thought, 'At least, I'm getting away from this bloody show. I needn't care whether it fails or not.'

In her bleakest moods, she wondered what would happen to her in London. Angela talked as though their friendship would survive the displacement but Harriet realized, if Angela did not, that their social spheres were very different. Angela, who was wealthy, had wealthy friends. She jokingly spoke of them as the 'Q and G', the Quality and Gentry, and said they were brilliantly entertaining. 'You'll love them,' she told Harriet, but Harriet would have to work, not only as a reason for living. She would need the money. Guy could make her only a small allowance.

When she mentioned this to Angela, Angela said, 'I intend to work, too. I shall start painting again. You know, when he was killed, I was painting. That's why I didn't see what he had picked up. I thought I would never paint again, but it will be different in England. A new life, a fresh start. We'll find a flat with a studio. I'm told everyone's left London so you can get flats and studios for the asking.'

Harriet, sharing Marion's faith in Angela, said, 'Then we'll both work. Something to do: that's the most important thing in life.'

Flaunting her emotional independence, Angela said one evening, 'Let's go to the Union.'

'But Bill and Mona will probably be there.'

'What if they are? All that's in the past now. I'm indifferent to Bill. Let's go and say goodbye to the Union and thanks for the fun we had there.'

Marion refused an invitation to accompany them. Guy and Edwina were at a rehearsal. Dobson was out and having heard stories of children being raped by frustrated servants, she would not leave Richard alone with the safragis.

At the Union, Angela gave her usual order for a bottle of whisky and several glasses. Smiling mischievously, she said to Harriet, 'Let's see who we can pick up.'

They were soon joined by Jackman who seated himself as a right: 'Haven't seen you for ages. Not surprised. That rhinoceros, Bill's wife, would drive anyone away.'

'I don't see her here tonight.'

'No, Guy's talked her into that show of his. She's rehearsing, I believe.'

'And Bill? What's he up to?'

'Oh, he's around. I'm inclined to keep clear when he has Mrs C in tow.'

Hearing that Castlebar was alone in the club, Angela became silent and did not move till some instinct told her he was nearby. He came with his usual tentative, wavering walk and paused a few yards away. She slid her eyes to one side, observed him, then gave her whole attention to Jackman. He had been telling the women that in his opinion the 'Alamein business' had been a 'put up job': 'The order was "stretch them to breaking point" and they stretched them.'

Angela laughed flirtatiously at him: 'Come off it, Jake. You're a terrible liar. I never believe a word you say.'

Jackman, who had not noticed Castlebar, went on protesting his 'inside information' while Castlebar stood twitching and shivering like a hungry pariah dog that longs for sustenance but dares not approach too near. Angela, pretending to be absorbed by Jackman, again gave him an oblique glance and aware she was aware, he edged nearer and put his long, yellow hands together as though in prayer. Angela spoke sternly to him: 'Bill, come here at once.'

He advanced eagerly, his hands still held up, and muttered: '*Mea culpa. Mea maxima culpa.*'

'I agree. Sit down beside me. I require, as a penance, that you drink a very large whisky.'

Grinning delightedly, Castlebar sat where he was told while Jackman, realizing he had been fooled, frowned and indignantly asked: 'Where did you come from?'

While Castlebar was setting up his cigarettes, Harriet said, 'So Mona is singing in the show? How did Guy manage that?'

Castlebar snuffled and giggled and said, 'You know what your old man's like. He buttered her up till he had her eating out of his hand.'

When, Harriet wondered, did all this happen? – and where? She had the despairing sense of being completely outside Guy's life and she thought, 'At least I'm going in good time. I'm young enough to start another life.'

Angela, having permitted Castlebar to return to the circle, kept her head turned from him while he watched her, willing her to face him. At last, forced to look round, she met his eyes and for a long minute they gazed at each other in meaningful intimacy, then Angela stood up. She said to Harriet, 'I think we should go.'

Flustered and disappointed, Castlebar wailed, 'You going already? The bottle's only half empty.'

'I'll leave it for you and Jake. We girls need our beauty sleep. I suppose you know we're going on the boat to England. We'll be away in a few days.'

Castlebar's mouth opened with shock and his cigarette fell between his knees. While he was scrabbling for it, Angela gripped Harriet by the arm and hurried her out to the gate where a taxi had just put down a fare. The two women got into it and, all in an instant, they were away.

'I thought you and Bill were about to be reconciled.'

Angela laughed: 'Never in this world. He won't have the chance to ditch me again. I said I was going and, I'm going. Tomorrow to fresh woods and pastures new.'

'You're very wise,' Harriet said, thinking that Angela was a great deal wiser than she expected her to be.

Dobson told the waiting women that, as another security measure, the ship might leave earlier than intended. He guessed the sailing date as 28 December.

With time so short, Harriet suggested to Angela that they visit the places they had always meant to visit. They should see the great mosques, the Khalifa and the zoo.

'Oh, what fun, yes,' Angela agreed, having the ability to find fun in everything. But next morning, when they were setting out for the zoo, the telephone rang. The call was for Angela who stood so long in the hall, talking in a low voice to the caller, she lost all interest in the zoo.

Coming back to Harriet, she said, 'I'm sorry darling, but I don't think I can "zoo" it today. I've still so much shopping to do.'

'Shall I come with you?'

Angela ignored the question. Wherever she was going, she meant to go alone. A taxi was waiting for them and she said in agitated apology: 'You don't mind if I take it? Hassan can get you another one.'

Not waiting for an answer, Angela hurried from the flat and Harriet, at a loss, telephoned Mortimer to tell her their probable departure date.

'So you're really going? It sounds a bit mad to me,' Mortimer said.

'It is mad, but it's a solution, I can't go on living in limbo.'

'Well, if it's at all possible, we'll be there to see you off.'

It seemed then that everything was settled and, forgetting the zoo, Harriet went out to do some shopping on her own. Returning for luncheon, she found Marion in the sitting-room, gazing dully at Richard who was whimpering and throwing his toys about.

'Angela not back yet?'

Marion shook her head and Harriet asked, 'What have you been doing all morning?'

'Nothing. Richard's got nettle-rash. It makes him so cross, poor little fellow. Oh, Harriet, to be in England!'

England, it seemed, was a solution for every difficulty met here.

When Angela had not returned by tea-time, Harriet went to her room and was relieved to see her splendid cases still piled against the wall. Without reason, she had feared Angela had gone for good. Reassured, she told Hassan to bring in the tea-tray.

When he put down the tray, he said, 'Man here' and he handed Harriet a grimy slip of paper. It authorized the bearer to collect Lady Hooper's luggage. Going back to the room, Harriet opened the wardrobe and found it empty. At some recent time, Angela had packed her clothes in expectation – of what? – perhaps only of a sudden summons to the boat.

The man stood humbly in the doorway and Harriet asked him: 'Where is Lady Hooper?'

He was one of the itinerant porters who sat about in the bazaars ready to transport furniture and heavy objects to any part of the city. He said, 'Lady say she send letter.'

'But where are you taking her luggage?'

'Lady say no say.'

Harriet motioned him to the cases. He was naked to the waist, short, square and strong-smelling. He belonged to the strict

Moslem sect that believes the Messiah will be born of a male and he wore baggy pantaloons in order to catch the babe should it present itself without warning. He was dark-skinned but not negroid. The rope of his trade, his greatest and perhaps his only possession apart from the pantaloons, encircled his neck and massive shoulders. His air was savage but his manners were gentle and looking over the cases to compute their number, he touched them with an amiable, almost loving, respect. He regretfully shook his head. He could not carry them all at one time but would have to make two journeys. He asked would the lady be willing to pay so much? Harriet said she was sure she would.

He sorted the luggage into two heaps then, grunting and muttering instructions to himself, he roped cases on to his chest, back and sides, and hoisted others up to his shoulders.

Laden like a pack mule, he grunted his way out of the flat, leaving behind him a stench of stale sweat. Harriet threw open the verandah doors and went out into the fresh air. Looking down at him as he went among the poinsettias to the front gate, she saw that from bearing so much weight, his feet had become almost circular and appeared to have toes all round. She watched until he reached the road where he set off at a fast trot and turned the corner out of sight.

An hour passed, then he came back with the promised letter: 'Harriet, darling, you can guess what has happened. Bill has escaped but he's terrified she'll track him down. So we're going into hiding until she gets used to the separation. If she comes howling to you, tell her nothing. Sorry to miss the good times on board ship, but you and Marion have fun for me. See you again one day. Love, Angela.'

'What good times, what fun?' Harriet asked aloud, angry that she had not foreseen what had happened. Angela had said she would not give Castlebar a second chance but Harriet, abandoned once, had not had the sense to see that the same thing could happen again.

No other word came from Angela. Rumours went round Cairo that she and Castlebar had been sighted in Jerusalem, in Haifa, in Tel Aviv and in Upper Egypt but their disappearance remained as much a mystery as the killing of Pinkrose.

369

Mona Castlebar did call at the flat, not 'howling' but in such fury, she could scarcely get a word out of her clenched face. When she found her voice, she accused Harriet: 'You know where they are, don't you?'

'No. Nobody knows.'

'My God, I'll do for them, you wait and see if I don't. He'll lose his job. He'll have nothing to live on. I hope they starve.'

'No danger of that. Angela has more than enough for both of them.'

'So that's it? She bought him with her money? I thought there must be something. He wouldn't have gone otherwise. She *bought* him.' Bitterly satisfied by this explanation of her husband's perfidy, she sat brooding on it as though she had nowhere else to go.

It was Christmas Day and everyone except Percy Gibbon had given presents to Richard. They littered the floor, to the annoyance of Percy who would, if he dared, have kicked them out of the way.

Mona watched Richard pushing the wheeled toys about then overturning them pettishly and whimpering his discontent. She looked as though she liked the scene no better than Percy did and at last, rising, she said, 'Well, there are some things to be thankful for,' and she took herself off.

Everyone was home for Christmas luncheon which was no different from any other luncheon. Richard, put into his high chair, struggled and cried and spewed out the soft-boiled egg which his mother tried to spoon into him.

Percy had seen this exhibition often enough but now, irritated by the toys on the floor, he stared at it with incredulous distaste so Marion became more nervous than usual. Her hand shook and the egg yolk went over Richard's chin and bib.

'Disgusting!' Percy said with feeling and Dobson remonstrated with him:

'Really, Percy, the child has to be fed.'

Brought to the point of open complaint, Percy hit the table: 'He needn't be fed in public. She could take him into her room – *my* room, I should say.'

Guy tried to reason with him: 'Oh, come now, Percy, the child has to be with adults in order to learn table-manners.'

Percy leapt up: 'Well, he won't learn them from me.'

'That's only too evident,' Harriet said.

At this, Percy strode into the room he shared with Dobson, slamming the door so violently, Richard began to scream and Marion to weep, asking: 'What am I going to do? What am I going to do?'

Harriet said: 'Put him in his pram and we'll take him to the zoo,' but Marion could not face the excursion. Weary of the petulant child, Harriet went to the zoo alone.

She walked across the river among crowds to whom Christmas Day, under the brilliant sky, was no better and no worse than any other day.

Just inside the zoo gates were the parrot stands, a long row of gaudy colours, each bird different from its neighbours. They gave occasional squawks but were too busy with preening and fussing and fluttering over their feathers to make much noise.

Harriet wandered round, desolate that, leaving Egypt, Angela was not going with her. There was no reason now for going at all. She had said to Dobson a few days before: 'I know you were kind, getting me a berth on the ship, but would it make any difference if I changed my mind?'

Dobson observed her reflectively: 'It would make a difference to you. You look as though a puff of wind would carry you away. You might catch anything in this condition. I recently heard of a chap who got tertian malaria and was gone in a matter of hours.'

And Harriet had taken on the responsibility of Marion who had been dismayed by Angela's flight and, in near panic, all her incipient apprehensions aroused, had said to Harriet, 'But *you* are coming, aren't you? You won't leave me. I don't know what I'd do if I lost you both.'

'Yes, of course I'm coming,' Harriet said and sighed.

She wondered now how long Marion would require her support. Angela had planned a life for herself and Harriet but neither thought to ask what Marion would do in England. Harriet, who often heard Marion sobbing behind the closed door of her room, had decided to find out.

She asked her, 'When you get to England, where will you go?' and was dismayed when Marion, her voice breaking, replied, 'I

371

don't know.' She told Harriet that her parents were in India and her husband was expecting her to stay with his mother: 'But I know she doesn't want me. She's only got a small flat and there'll be nowhere for Richard to play. I keep asking myself, "Where will I go?" and I don't know. I don't know.'

'Why are you going at all?'

'It was Jim's idea. Richard's always unwell in Iraq and he gets on Jim's nerves. The truth is, Jim *wanted* me to go.'

This confession had a fatal ring for Harriet who, remembering it as she walked round the paths among the captive animals, thought, 'They want to get rid of us.' The friend who had made all possible, had deserted her. Left with an ailing woman, a complete stranger, who clung to her simply because there was no one else, she wondered, 'What on earth will I do with Marion all the way round the Cape and perhaps in England as well?'

She paused before one cage and another. The animals, comatose in the afternoon heat, seemed content enough. Then she came to a polar bear and stopped, appalled at finding an arctic animal in this climate. The bear was in a circular cage, not very big, an island of concrete surrounded by bars that rose up to a central dome from which water trickled constantly. The bear, sitting motionless under the stream, hung its head, torpid in its heavy white coat. Harriet felt it was in despair and leaning towards it, she whispered, 'Bear,' but it did not move. She was about to move on but, unwilling to leave the creature unaided, she went closer to the cage and stood for a long time, trying to contact the animal's senses through the medium of her intense pity for it. It did not move. She knew she could not stand there for ever but before she went, she said aloud, 'If I could do anything for you, I would do it with my whole heart. But the world is against us. All I can do, is go away.'

As Dobson had predicted, word came that the ship would sail on 28 December. The passengers were to board the boat train for Suez at ten a.m. on the sailing date.

'I'm sure you're thankful,' Guy said: 'You must be tired of all this hanging about.'

'I'm tired of the whole situation, but it's too late to argue about it. I suppose you'll come with me to Suez?'

'Come to Suez?' Guy was abashed by the very suggestion: 'How could I possibly come to Suez? You know the show is on New Year's Eve, and I'll be rehearsing day and night till it goes on.'

Harriet, expecting no other reply, was not even disappointed by it but said, 'The train is at ten a.m. tomorrow. I suppose you *will* come to the station to see me off?'

'Of course.' Guy, stung by the ironical inexpectancy of Harriet's tone, became apologetic: 'I'm sorry I can't come to Suez, darling. It never entered my head you would want me to, but I will be at the station. I'll dash into the office first thing then, when I've looked through my letters, I'll go straight to the station. I'll get there before you arrive.'

Next morning, left alone in the flat, Harriet and Marion sat in the living-room, waiting to depart. The flat was silent; even Richard, tensed by the unusual atmosphere, had ceased to cry. Hassan had been sent out to find two taxis, the extra one to take the excess luggage.

The others had said their goodbyes after breakfast. Edwina, flinging her arms round Harriet, burst into tears: 'What shall I do without you?' and Harriet, remembering Peter's answer to the same question, breathed in Edwina's gardenia scent and wondered what would become of her.

Its sweet redolence still hung in the air. The curtains and shutters were closed for the day and the two women, seeing each other, shadowy across the room, were on edge, facing the change from a known world to one where everything would be different.

Hassan returned. The taxis had been brought to the door and now the travellers could start on their journey. It was the congested hour of the morning and as the taxis were held up in traffic, Harriet became perturbed, imagining Guy losing patience at the station and perhaps going away. But they arrived in good time and he was nowhere to be seen. She put Marion into a carriage then ran from one end of the platform to the other, searching among groups of people, unable to find him. The guard, coming towards her, shutting the carriage doors and unfurling his green flag, called to the passengers to get on board.

The train was full of young mothers and children and Harriet, finding her carriage, was greeted with unusual buoyancy by Marion, happy at being in the company of others like herself.

Hanging from the window, feeling the train about to start, Harriet saw Guy making his way along the platform, searching short-sightedly for her face among the faces at the windows. She shouted to him and he came running, his glasses sliding down his nose, already beginning a lengthy excuse for failing to be there sooner. Someone had come into the office just as he was about to leave.

'Had to have a word with him ... Didn't realize ... So sorry...'

The little time left to them was taken up by these excuses, yet what else was there to be said? Harriet stretched her hand down to him and he was able to hold it for a second or two before the train moved and drew it from his grasp. He followed the carriage at a jog-trot, still trying to tell her something but, whatever it was, it was lost in noise as the train gathered speed.

Leaning out further, waving to him, she could see him pushing his glasses up to his brow and straining to see her, but almost at once she was too far away to see or be seen.

Marion had kept a seat for her and she sank into it, unaware of the people about her, still holding to a vision of Guy standing, peering after the train, looking perplexed because he had lost sight of her. She did not suppose he would be perplexed for long. She could imagine, as he turned back to his own employments, his buttocks and shoulders moving with the energetic excitement of having so much to do.

And what could come of all that activity? He ate himself up. He dissipated himself in ephemeral entertainments like this show that would be a one-day's wonder and just about pay its way. To someone moving so rapidly through life, reality and unreality merged and were one and the same thing. There were times when she felt he drained her life as well as his own, but he had physical strength. He could renew himself and she could not.

He had said the climate was killing her but now, seeing the relationship from a distance, she felt the killing element was not the heat of Cairo but Guy himself.

*　　*　　*

Marion was sitting next to a woman Harriet did not know, but knew about. She was the Mrs Rutter who had once reproached Jake Jackman for being a civilian. A rich widow, she had about her the confident certainty of one who knew that her world was the only world that mattered. The war had not changed it much. She lived in one of the great houses on Gezira and kept a retinue of servants. Harriet wondered why she was leaving this land of plenty for their beleaguered homeland where she would be no more privileged than any other woman.

She was asking Marion probing little questions, keeping herself at a distance until she discovered that Marion's husband was a diplomat in Baghdad. At this, Mrs Rutter became affable and looked approvingly at Marion and made advances to Richard who was persuaded to give her a smile. She had on her knee a large shagreen jewel-case and Marion, returning favours, said, 'What a beautiful case!'

'Yes, it is beautiful,' Mrs Rutter warmly agreed: 'I *treasure* it. Whenever I travel, I carry it myself, heavy though it is.'

As they talked about the jewel-case, Marion, holding Richard on her knee, put her cheek down on the top of his head, knowing she had the greater treasure.

They were now out in the desert and Mrs Rutter, saying the light was too keen for her, pulled down the dusty, dark blue oil-cloth blind over the carriage window. The window was open and the blind flapped in the wind. Richard closed his eyes, thinking night had fallen, and lay like a little ghost in Marion's arms.

The other passengers fell silent in the steamy penumbra and Mrs Rutter, not wishing to be overheard, whispered to Marion, apparently conveying facts too sacred to be widely circulated. In England, she said, she had a married daughter the same age as Marion. '*And* three little grandchildren. I've never seen them, so I'm going home to enjoy them while they're still babies.'

Enthralled by this information, Marion talked about her coming confinement: 'I'm sure Richard will be easier to deal with when he's not the only one. I always think one should have two or three.'

Mrs Rutter fervently agreed: 'What is a home without children?' she asked.

Harriet, not included in the conversation, thought '... or without a husband?' She could see between Marion and Mrs Rutter a swift growing up of friendship that was likely to intensify until, on board the ship, Marion would be a surrogate daughter to the old lady, Mrs Rutter a surrogate mother to the pregnant woman. As she felt the burden of Marion slip away from her, Harriet could see even less reason now for being on a train where the younger children were peevish, the older obstreperous and the grown-ups suffocating in semi-darkness.

Hours had passed, or so it seemed, when, pulling aside the blind, she saw the canal: a flat ribbon of turquoise water lying between dazzling flats of sand. They were coming into Suez. Between the grimy house-backs, hung with washing, she could see the bazaars and wished she could visit them. But the passengers were not here on a sight-seeing tour. The train ran straight on to the quay and they had their first sight of the ship. It had a name at last. It was called the *Queen of Sparta*.

For some reason, the classical allusion jolted Harriet with fear: an elusive fear. She could make nothing of it as they climbed down to the quay and stood in the sea wind with the sea, itself, lapping the quayside. Then another departure came to her mind, the departure from Greece. The refugees had embarked at the Piraeus among the burnt-out buildings, the water black with wrecks and wreckage. Only two ships rode upright: the *Erebus* and *Nox*.

They had been used to transport Italian prisoners-of-war to Egypt. They were vermin-ridden, filthy, red with rust, the life-boats useless because the davits had rusted. They were nearly derelict but the refugees had no choice. The situation compelled and they were thankful to have ships of any kind. They had to trust themselves to the *Erebus* and *Nox*; and the two old tankers had carried them gallantly across the sea to Alexandria.

The *Queen of Sparta*, painted umber, was the same colour as the tankers, but she looked trim enough. She was altogether a more seaworthy craft than the *Erebus* and *Nox*, yet Harriet, who had trusted the tankers, was afraid of her. While the other women busied themselves collecting children together, ordering their baggage and getting into line to embark, Harriet stood apart from them, feeling that no power on earth could get her on to the

Queen of Sparta. But this, she knew, was ridiculous. She had had forebodings before without any resultant disasters and she must swallow back this foreboding and go with the others.

The queue stretched down the quay to the ship's gangway. Seeing Marion and Mrs Rutter about mid-way, she went reluctantly to join them, thinking, 'I want an excuse to escape. I want a last-minute reprieve.' And what hope of that?

Harriet's companions, still fused in the comfortable stimulation of their new relationship, scarcely saw that Harriet was with them. A truck was collecting the baggage. It had almost reached Harriet when she heard her name called.

Mortimer and her co-driver were walking towards her. Breaking from the queue, Harriet ran towards them, her arms outstretched, shouting, 'Mortimer! Mortimer! God has sent you to save me.'

Mortimer laughed: 'Save you from what?'

'I don't know. All I want is to get away from here. Take me with you.'

Harriet, seeing her luggage about to be thrown on to the truck, ran to retrieve it. She told Marion: 'I'm not going with you. You'll be all right, won't you? Mrs Rutter will look after you. I hope you and Richard have a pleasant journey.'

Baffled by Harriet's decision, Marion asked: 'You mean, you're going back to Cairo?'

'No, I'm going to Damascus.'

'Damascus!' Marion, parting her lips in disapproval, looked like a good little girl confronted by some piece of peccant naughtiness. She breathed out a shocked, 'Oh dear!' then, seeing the queue had moved forward, she hurried on as though fearing Mrs Rutter, too, might forsake her.

Mortimer came over to Harriet: 'We're driving through the night. I expect you can get some sleep among the ammunition in the back. Hope you won't mind a bumpy ride across Sinai? The road's in a bad way.'

Harriet laughed and said she did not mind how she crossed Sinai for all the wonders of the Levant were on the other side.

Coda

A week after the ship sailed, rumours reached Cairo that the *Queen of Sparta* had been torpedoed off Tanganyika with the loss of all on board. Then another, more detailed, report reached the *Egyptian Mail* from a correspondent in Dar-es-Salaam. One life-boat, crowded with women and children, had got away from the sinking ship. The steering was faulty. The boat was drifting when the German U-boat surfaced and the commander took on board a heavily pregnant woman and her small son. They were put to rest on the commander's own bunk but, a British cruiser appearing on the horizon, the U-boat had to submerge and the woman and child were returned to the life-boat. The cruiser did not sight the boat that drifted for ten days until found by fishermen who towed it into Delagoa Bay. By that time most of the children and many of the adults had died of thirst and exposure. No names were given.

That was the last that Cairo heard of the *Queen of Sparta* and, the times being what they were, only the bereaved gave further thought to the lost ship.

VOLUME THREE

The Sum of Things

To the memory of Jim Farrell
taken by the sea August 1979

One

In December, when the others, the lucky ones, were advancing on Tripoli, Simon Boulderstone was sent to the hospital at Helwan. Before that he had been held in a field dressing-station then moved to a makeshift first-aid station at Burg el Arab. The desert fighting had so crowded the regular hospitals that no bed could be found for him until the walking wounded were moved on to convalescent homes. While he waited, he was attended by orderlies who gave him what treatment they could. He did not expect much. His condition, he felt, was in abeyance until he reached a proper hospital where, of course, he would be put right in no time.

The Helwan hospital, a collection of huts on the sand, was intended for New Zealanders but after the carnage of Alamein anyone might be sent anywhere. Simon was carried from the ambulance into a long ward formed by placing two huts end to end. Because he was an officer, even though a very junior one, he was given a curtained-off area to himself. This long hut was known as 'The Plegics' because few of the men there could hope to walk again.

Simon did not know that but if he had known, he would have seen in it no reference to his own state. At that time, he exulted in the fact he was alive, when he might so easily have been dead.

He and his driver, Crosbie, had run into a booby trap and, like an incident from a dissolving dream, he could still see Crosbie sailing into the air to land and lie, a loose straggle of limbs, motionless on the ground. In his mind Crosbie would lie there for ever while he, Simon, had been picked up by a Bren and taken back to the living world. And here he was, none the worse for the curious illusion that his body ended half-way down his spine.

The wonder of his escape kept him, during those first days, in a state of euphoria. He wanted to talk to people, not to be shut away at the end of the ward. He asked for the curtains to be opened and when he looked down the long hutment, its walls bare in the harsh Egyptian sunlight, he was surprised to see men in wheel-chairs propelling themselves up and down the aisle. He pitied them, but for himself – he'd simply suffered a blow in the back. It was a stunning blow that had anaesthetized him, so, for a while, he thought more about Crosbie than about himself. It was not until he reached Burg el Arab that he realized part of his body was missing. It seemed he had been cut in half and wondered if his lower limbs were still there. Sliding his hand down from his waist, he could feel his thighs but could not raise himself to reach farther. Speaking quite calmly, he told the man on the next stretcher that he had lost his legs below the knees. He was not surprised. The same thing had happened to his brother Hugo and accidents of this sort ran in families. He had dreaded it but now it had happened, he found he did not mind much. Instead, for some odd reason, he was rather elated. He talked for a long time to the man on the next stretcher before he saw that the man was dead.

The male nurse who dressed his wound asked him if he needed a shot of morphine. Cheerfully, he replied, 'No thanks, I'm all right. I'm fine.'

'No pain?'

'None at all.'

The nurse frowned as though Simon had given the wrong answer.

Brens were arriving every few minutes with wounded from the front lines. Simon was at the first-aid station a couple of days before a doctor was free to examine him. When the blanket was pulled down and he saw his legs were there intact, he felt an amazed pride in them.

'Nothing wrong with me, doc, is there?'

The doctor was not committing himself. He said he suspected a crushed vertebra but only an X-ray could confirm that.

'It'll mend, won't it, doc?'

'It's a question of time,' the doctor said and Simon, taking that to mean his paralysis was temporary, burst out laughing. When the doctor raised his brows, Simon said, 'I was thinking of my driver, Crosbie. He looked so funny going up into the air.'

At Helwan, he was still laughing. Everything about his condition made him laugh. After the early days of no sensation at all, he became subject to the most ridiculous delusions. At times it seemed that his knees were rising of their own accord. He would look down, expecting to see the blanket move. Or he would imagine that someone was pulling at his feet. Once or twice this impression was so strong, he uncovered his legs to make sure he was not slipping off the end of the bed.

And then there was his treatment. His buttocks were always being lifted and rubbed with methylated spirits: 'To prevent bedsores,' the nurse told him. Every two hours he was tilted first on one side and then on the other, a bolster being pushed into his waist to keep him there. The first time this happened, he asked, 'What's this in aid of?'

The nurse giggled and said, 'You'd better ask the physio.'

The physio, a young New Zealander called Ross, did not giggle but soberly told him that the repeated movements helped to keep his bowels active. Not that they were active. The first time a young woman had given him an enema, he had been filled with shame.

She had said, 'We don't want to get all bogged up, do we?' Soon enough the enemas were stopped and suppositories were pushed into him. He became used to being handled and ceased to feel ashamed. He had to accept that his motions were not his to control but after a while, he recognized the symptoms that told him his bladder was full. His heart would thump, or he would feel a pain in his chest, and he must ask to be relieved by catheter.

Ross came in three times a day to move his knees and hip joints, performing the exercises carefully, with grave gentleness.

Everything they did to him enhanced for him the absurdity of his dependence. 'You treat me like a baby,' he said to Ross who merely nodded and tapped his knee.

The tap produced an exaggerated jerk of the leg and Simon, interested and entertained, asked, 'Why does it do that?'

'Just lack of control, sir. Your system's confused – in a manner of speaking, that is.'

Once when his left leg gave a sudden move, he called for Ross, saying, 'I must be getting better.'

Ross shook his head: 'That happens, sometimes, sir. It means nothing.'

Even then, Simon's laughter went on, becoming, at times, so near hysteria that the doctor said, 'If we don't calm you down, young man, your return to life will be the death of you.'

He was given sedatives and entered an enchanted half-world, losing all inhibitions. Seeing everything as possible, he asked the staff nurse to telephone Miss Edwina Little at the British Embassy and tell her to visit him.

'Your girlfriend, is she?'

'I'd like to think so. She was my brother's girlfriend. I don't know whose girlfriend she is now but she's the most gorgeous popsie in Cairo. You wait till you see her. D'you think I'll be out of here soon? I'd like to take her for a spin, go out to dinner, go to a night club...'

'Better leave all that till you're on your feet again.'

'Which won't be long now, will it, nurse?'

'I can't say. We'll have to wait and see.'

'You mean it's just a matter of time?'

The nurse, making no promises, said vaguely: 'I suppose you could say that,' and Simon was satisfied. So long as he felt certain he would eventually recover, he could wait for time to pass.

Two

Now that 8th Army had left Egypt, a slumberous calm had come down on the capital: Cairo was no longer a base town. The soldiers that had crowded the pavements, wandering aimlessly, disgruntled and idle for lack of arms, had all been given guns and sent into the fight.

The British advance after Alamein had been impressive but no one thought it would last. Everyone expected a counter-attack that would bring the Afrika Korps back over the frontier. But this time the counter-attack failed and by January, the Germans had retreated so far away, they seemed to be lost in the desert sand.

The few British officers who still took tea in Groppi's garden had an apologetic air, feeling they had been cast aside by the runaway military machine.

It was a pleasant time of the year. Winter in Egypt was no more than a temperate interval between one summer and the next. It did not last long and there was no spring though a few deciduous trees that dropped their leaves from habit were now breaking into bud again. They went unnoticed in Garden City, lost as they were among the evergreens and palms and the dense, glossy foliage of the mango trees. The evenings were limpid and in the mornings a little mist hung like a delicate veil over the riverside walks.

The mid-days were warm enough to carry the threat of heat to come. In the flat that Edwina Little shared with Dobson and Guy Pringle, the rooms that looked on to the next-door garden were already scented by the drying grass.

Dobson, who held an embassy lease, had a room in the cool centre of the flat. The others, in the corridor under the roof, were let to friends. Now only two friends remained. Guy Pringle's wife, Harriet, had left Cairo to board an evacuation ship at Suez.

This ship, the *Queen of Sparta*, was bound for England by way of the Cape. It had sailed a few days after Christmas and now, in January, there was a rumour that she had been sunk in the Indian Ocean with the loss of all on board. Guy, when he heard it, refused to credit it. Rumours were the life of Cairo and usually proved to be wrong. Dobson and Edwina, also suspicious of rumours, agreed behind Guy's back that, until the sinking was confirmed, they would not speak of it or commiserate with him.

He was glad of their silence that seemed to prove the whole thing was a canard. He began to feel it was directed at him because his wife had not wanted to be evacuated. He half suspected his friend Jake Jackman, a noted source of rumours, who had been fond of Harriet and may have resented her going.

Sitting with Jake at the Anglo-Egyptian Union, he said as though to justify himself: 'You know, this climate was killing Harriet. I doubt whether she would have survived another summer here.'

'Yep, she looked like a puff of wind,' Jake agreed then, unable to resist his own malice, he sniggered and pulled at his thin, aquiline nose: 'You know what they say: if you want to know a man's true nature, look at the health of his wife.'

Guy was indignant: 'Who said that? I never heard a more ridiculous statement.'

Jake, having delivered his shaft, was ready to be conciliatory: 'You don't believe these rumours, do you? Leave them be and they'll die of their own accord.'

But they did not die. People who had friends or relatives on board the ship approached Guy and asked if he had any information. Dobson received a letter from a diplomat in Iraq whose wife, Marion Dixon, had sailed on the ship. He appealed to Dobson for news and at last the matter was brought up at the breakfast table, the one place at which the three inmates of the flat met and conversed.

Guy was the first to speak of it. He, too, appealed to Dobson: 'You must have heard this about the *Queen of Sparta* being lost! If it's true, surely you would have had official confirmation by now?'

'Yes, in normal times, but the times aren't normal. The ship had passed out of our sphere of influence so we might not hear for months.'

Edwina, eager to reassure Guy, said: 'Oh, Dobbie, you would have heard by now. Of course you would!'

'Well, we *should* have heard by now, I agree.'

Dobson's tone suggested they might still hear and Guy, disturbed, left the table and went to the Institute where, by keeping himself employed, he could put his anxiety behind him.

After he had gone, Edwina said: 'You know, Dobbie, Guy's not a bit like himself. You can see he's terribly worried but trying to hide it. If Harriet is dead – of course I'm sure she isn't – I know she'd want me to console him. I feel I should, don't you?'

Dobson, regarding her with an ironical smile, asked: 'And how do you propose to do it?'

'Oh, there are ways. I could ask him to take me out. He once took me to the Extase when he found me crying because Peter hadn't turned up. He was really sweet.'

'And what did Harriet say about that?'

'I don't think she said anything. You know we were great friends. I was thinking we might go to a dinner-dance at the Continental-Savoy. I suppose Guy does dance?'

'I don't know. I've never heard of his dancing.'

'I'm sure he can. He's very clever, you know. I sang in his troops' concert and he was wonderful. He said I sang like an angel.'

'I hope, in the midst of this mutual admiration, you won't forget he's married to Harriet.'

'Dobbie, how could you say that? I'll never forget Harriet. But when you're doing a show together, a special relationship grows up. That's what Guy and I have: a special relationship.'

Dobson laughed indulgently and Edwina remembered another special relationship. 'You remember that nice boy Boulderstone who was killed, the one I liked so much? What was he called?'

'I can't remember.'

'Well, now his brother's been wounded. He's in hospital at Helwan and I've promised to go and see him. It's quite a journey, so if I'm late this evening at the office, you'll understand, won't you, Dobbie dear?'

Dobson laughed again and said: 'Don't worry. We'll forgive you, as we always do, my dear.'

Edwina's appearance in Plegics caused a wondering silence to come down on the men. Anyone who could move his neck, followed her as she walked the length of the long ward to find Simon at the farther end. She was wearing a suit of fine white wool and the heels of her white kid shoes tapped on the wooden floor. The whiteness of her clothing enhanced the gold of her hair and skin. Becoming aware of the intent gaze of the men, she shook her hair back from her right eye and smiled, kindly but vaguely, from side to side.

Simon, as she approached, shared the wonder of the ward. When she reached him and sat beside him, saying: 'How are you, Simon dear?', he sank back against his pillows, benumbed, without power to reply.

She put some white carnations on the table then leant towards him so he was enveloped both by the scent of the flowers and the heavy scent she was wearing. He remembered that Hugo had ordered him to buy perfume for her at an expensive little West-End shop: *Gardenia* perfume. For some moments its aroma was more real than her presence. Though he had been expecting her, he could only marvel that a creature so beautiful, so elegant, so far removed from the desert suburb of Nissen huts and sand, should come to visit him.

Misunderstanding his silence, she asked in a tone of concern: 'You haven't forgotten me, have you?'

'Forgotten you?' He gave a laugh that was nearly a sob: 'How could I forget you? I've thought of no one else since I first saw you.'

'Oh, Simon, really!' His vehemence disconcerted her. That he was infatuated with her, did not surprise her, but she was not quite the girl she had been at their last meeting. She, too, had been infatuated, not with this poor boy but with a man, an Irish peer, who, having pursued their affair in a carefree, generous manner, had ended it by telling her he was already married. He had returned to the desert and she had lost not only him, but some inner confidence. And all the time she had been yearning for Peter Lisdoonvarna, this young lieutenant had been yearning for her! At the thought, she smiled sadly and he asked anxiously:

'What's the matter, Edwina? You aren't cross with me for saying that?'

'Cross? No, not a bit cross, but do you remember that colonel, Lord Lisdoonvarna? He was in the flat when you came to tell us about your brother's death.'

'You bet I do. Because of him, I got a liaison job. He put my name up for it. Jolly decent of him, wasn't it?'

'I didn't know about that.'

Now, knowing, this act of kindness made her loss seem the greater. Tears blurred her eyes and she said in a breaking voice: 'Oh, Simon, you've no idea how he treated me. It was dreadful. I haven't got over it.' She paused, shaking her head to control herself: 'He deserted me. Yes, deserted. For months we went everywhere together. He simply appropriated me, so I never had a chance to see anyone else. Then, would you believe it, he felt he'd had enough and he wangled his return to his unit.'

'That's monstrous!' Simon stretched out his hand and she put her hand into it. He had been outraged when he believed she had rejected Hugo, and he was outraged now because Lisdoonvarna had rejected her. He could only say, 'I am sorry,' but it was such heartfelt sorrow that Edwina squeezed his hand.

'Dear Simon, what a comfort you are!' She looked into his face that was so like his brother's face and, seeing in it the same youth and sensitivity and absolute niceness, she was moved to something like love for him. She said: 'Let's forget Peter. There are other men in the world, aren't there? You're so sweet, you restore my faith in myself. I'd begun to think no one would ever find me attractive again.'

'Good lord! Why, my brother Hugo said . . .'

'Yes, Hugo,' Edwina seized on the name that had been evading her: 'Hugo was wonderful. You know, he was the one for me. I was just dazzled by Peter, that was all. He was a lord and a colonel and . . . well, I was silly, wasn't I?'

Simon felt there was some confusion in this protest but said: 'So you were Hugo's girl, after all?'

'Oh, yes, I was. Of course I was. And you know, Simon, you're so like him. Your face, the way you speak, everything about you. Just like Hugo.' She smiled encouragingly at him.

Though good-looking officers did not offer much of a future, they were a lot of fun while they lasted.

Smiling back at her, Simon said: 'We used to be mistaken for twins. My mother said that sometimes she couldn't tell us apart.'

'But how are you, Simon. You seem quite well. There can't be much wrong with you. You weren't badly wounded, were you?'

'No, it's nothing much. I was hit by a piece of flak. I'll soon be out and about, and I wonder! If I got hold of a car, would you let me take you for a drive?'

'I'd love it.'

The word 'love' spoken by Edwina quite overthrew him. He flushed as a thought came into his head, probably the most daring thought of his whole life. If he seemed to her so like Hugo, might she not feel for him as she had felt for his brother? After all, he was the survivor and the survivor was, by right, the inheritor. As his blush deepened, he had to explain that he was still running a temperature. Because it was winter, it did not worry him much but in summer it would be tiresome.

Edwina, not taken in, responded to his hopeful, aspiring gaze as she had responded to many other young men. She smiled a smile that was enticing and slightly mischievous, and seemed to Simon full of promise. He remembered that like Peter Lisdoonvarna, he was already married, but what did that matter? He had been married for only a week before he was sent to join the draft. Now that week had sunk so far out of sight, it might never have existed.

They were still holding hands but Edwina felt she could now loosen her fingers. As she did so, Simon gripped them tighter and said, 'Don't leave me yet.'

'I'm afraid I must.' Laughing, she slid from his grasp and picked up her gloves and handbag: 'I'm a working girl, you know. I have to go back to the Embassy.'

'But you'll come again?'

'Of course I will.' She touched his cheek with her finger-tips: 'Again and again and again. So, just for now: goodbye.'

Choked with gratitude for this promise, he could scarcely say, 'Goodbye.'

Watching her as she walked away down the ward, his mood changed. His exaltation had reached its apogee during her visit and as she departed, his excitement went with her. He saw the men in wheel-chairs shift to let her pass and for the first time, he identified himself with them. He realized what sort of ward it was and why he was in it. Terror formed like a knot in his chest and he moved restlessly against his pillows, in acute need of reassurance.

For some time the only person who came near was the orderly with his tea. Simon caught at his arm and tried to question him, but the orderly only said: 'Don't ask me, sir. Afore I come to this kip, all I'd ever done was shovel coal.'

'Where's the doctor? Why hasn't he come round? I must see him.'

The orderly, a big, red-haired fellow, looked pityingly at him and said: 'Don't you get upset, sir. It'll be all right. The physio'll be here in a minute.'

Simon let the man go then lay, impatient for Ross to arrive. He realized that all his laughter, all his high spirits, had been a screen to divide him from the poor devils in the wheel-chairs.

He heard them singing an old troops' song that they had adopted as their theme song. He had taken it to be, 'Beautiful Dreamer, Queen of my song/I've been out in Shiba too fucking long . . .'

Now, hearing it again, he realized it was something different:

> Beautiful Dreamer, Queen of my Song,
> I've been here in Plegics too fucking long . . .

and this ward was Plegics – paraplegics, quadraplegics! They sang mournfully, going on to the next lines:

> Send out the *Rodney*, send the *Renown*,
> You can't send the *Hood* for the bleeder's gone down.

How long, he wondered, had some of them been in Plegics? How long was he likely to be there?

When Ross came to his bedside, Simon could appreciate his solemnity.

Ross, seeing his distraught face, made a noise in his throat as though acknowledging the change in him, but said nothing. With his usual gentle efficiency, he uncovered Simon's legs and began to manipulate them.

Looking down at them, Simon could now see how strange they were. Not his legs at all. Having lost their sunburn, they looked to him unnaturally white; marble legs, too heavy to move; lifeless, the legs of a corpse.

The exercises finished, Ross pulled a pencil along Simon's right sole, from heel to toe: 'Feel that?'

'No.'

As the blanket was pulled back over them, Simon imagined his legs disappearing into the darkness of death. He said: 'Wait a moment, Ross. I want you to tell me the truth.' He nodded towards the chairbound men who seemed in the sunset light to be moving in a limbo of infinite patience: 'Am I going to be like them?'

Ross regarded him gravely: 'How long since you copped it, sir?'

Simon had lost count of time since he had been picked up at Gazala but he said: 'About a month.'

'You begin worrying when it's five weeks.'

Ross went to his other patients and Simon, with nothing to do but worry, realized it must be all of four weeks since he and Crosbie ran into the booby trap. The Gazala dogfight had been in the middle of December and he had followed the advance not much later. Now it was January. Early January, but still January. Facing up to the passage of time, his desolation became despair.

The sister, paying her evening visit, came in cheerfully: 'And how are we today?' Meeting with silence, she asked: 'What's the matter? Girlfriend not turn up?'

He did not reply till her ministrations were ended, then he said: 'Sister, if that young lady comes again, I don't want to see her.'

'You'd better tell her that yourself.'

'Please close the curtains.'

The sister, who understood the change in him, pulled the curtains round three sides of his bed and left without saying anything more. On his fourth side there was a window without shutters. He had to tolerate the light but if he could, he would have blotted it out and closed himself into wretchedness as in a tomb.

Three

The *Egyptian Mail* confirmed the sinking of the *Queen of Sparta* but in its report there was reason for hope. A correspondent in Dar-es-Salaam had informed the paper that one life-boat, crowded with women and children, had got away. Its steering was faulty and it drifted for ten days before being sighted by fishermen who towed it into Delagoa Bay. By that time the children and some of the adults had died of thirst and exposure.

But not all. Not all. There had been survivors.

Edwina said earnestly to Guy: 'I'm sure, I'm *absolutely* sure, that Harriet is alive.'

Guy became as sure as she was and his natural good-humour returned. His nagging fears and anxiety were displaced by the certainty that any day now Harriet would cable him from Dar-es-Salaam.

He said: 'She's a born survivor. After all she's been through since war began, ten days in an open boat would mean nothing to her.'

Dobson agreed: 'She looked frail but these frail girls are as tough as they come.'

Guy said, 'Yes,' before being caught in an accusing memory of why she had been persuaded on to the boat in the first place. But all that was past. When she returned to Cairo, neither he nor anyone else would talk her into going if she did not want to go.

Seeing Guy himself again, Edwina said: 'Oh, Guy darling, do let's have an evening out together!'

'Perhaps, when I have some free time.'

'Let's go to the dinner-dance at the Continental-Savoy.'

'Heavens, no.' Guy was aghast at the suggestion. He said he would celebrate Harriet's return, preferably when Harriet was safely back, but nothing would get him to the Continental-Savoy.

'Oh!' Edwina sighed sadly: 'Didn't you ever go dancing with Harriet?'

'No, never.'

'Poor Harriet!'

Not liking that, Guy left her and she set out for Helwan where she expected more cordial entertainment.

Certain of her welcome, she did not enquire for Simon at the office but went straight down the ward to where he lay, hidden behind curtains. Parting the curtains, she said, 'Hello,' but there was no reply. Simon gave her one glance, filled with a suffering that disturbed her, then turning away, pulled the cover over his face. She was perplexed by the change in him. He was no longer her ardent admirer but a shrunken figure that seemed to be sinking into a hole in the bed.

'What is it, Simon?' She bent over him, trying to rouse him: 'Don't you want to see me?'

His silence was answer enough. It occurred to him that his legs were not the only part of him that might never function again. He not only hid under his blanket but turned his face into the pillow. Standing beside him, she said several times: 'Simon dear, do talk to me. Tell me what's the matter.'

He at last mumbled, 'Go away,' and unable to bear the misery that hung over the gloomy little cubicle, she left him. At the other end of the ward, she went to the sister's office and asked what had caused this dramatic change in Mr Boulderstone.

The sister said, 'He'll get over it. It happens to all of them. First, they're up in the air, thankful to be alive, then they realize what being alive probably means. It's not easy to accept that one may never walk again. Still, if he's worth his salt, he'll meet the challenge. Next time you come, I expect he'll be trying to cheer *you* up.'

'Cheer me up? But he told me he'd be out of here in no time.'

'Even if he recovers – and I don't say there isn't still a chance – it'll be a long haul before we get him on his feet again.'

The sister, a homely, vigorous, outspoken woman, gave Edwina a critical stare, weighing her ability to face up to this information, and Edwina could only say, 'Poor Simon, I didn't know. I thought . . .' but she did not say what she thought. She was dismayed to learn of Simon's condition and dismayed, too, that the sister had summed her up correctly. They both knew she would not come to Helwan again.

Returning to Cairo, she told herself the visit had been too painful and what could she do for a man so lost in misery, he would only say, 'Go away'? Yet she was hurt by the sister's judgement and wondered how to discount it. By the time the train reached the station, she had found a way out of her discomposure. She could not go to Helwan again but someone could go in her place. She decided that Guy, so warm, so magnanimous, was the one to take Simon in hand.

When this was put to him next morning, Guy agreed at once. He was always ready to visit people in hospital. Of course he would see the poor boy.

'I'll go on my day off.'

Guy's day off was often a day of work but the following Saturday would be given up to Simon Boulderstone. He was leaving the flat to catch the Helwan train when Dobson came in the front door. Dobson had gone to the office and, for some reason, had come back again.

He said, 'Guy!' The unusual solemnity of his tone stopped Guy with a premonition of evil tidings. Dobson put an arm round his shoulder.

'Guy, I didn't telephone – I had to come and tell you myself. We've had official confirmation that the evacuation ship was sunk by enemy action. Only three people survived in the life-boat. We had their names this morning. Harriet was not among them.'

Guy stared at him: 'I see, Harriet was not among them,' then shifting his shoulder from under Dobson's arm, he hurried from the flat.

Four

On the day before Edwina's second visit, Simon had come of age. He had once thought of his twenty-first birthday as the summit of maturity, a day that would change him from a youth to a man. Having climbed up to it through the muddle of adolescence, he would find himself on a proper footing with the world. His parents would give him a party and someone important, like his Uncle Harry who was a town councillor, would make a speech and hand him a golden key, saying it was not only the key of the door but the key to life.

As it was, the day passed like any other day. He did not mention it even to Ross. Here in Plegics it had no meaning, but that night he had a dream. He dreamt he was running through the English countryside, running and leaping over miles of green grass. When he came to a hedge, he took a very high leap, a preternatural leap. It lifted him so high into the air, he felt he was flying and when he came down he said as he woke: 'That was to celebrate.' The elation of the dream remained with him for several seconds then faded, and he knew there was nothing to celebrate.

After Edwina's second visit, he began to think of suicide. Death would solve everything, but how to achieve it? Nothing lethal – no sleeping pills, no poisonous substances, not even the meths bottle – was ever left within his reach. They saw to that. He was like a child in their hands and he had begun to feel like a child, dependent, obedient, resentful.

He was wondering if he could smother himself, or refuse to eat till he died of starvation, when someone came fumbling through the curtains. He expected a nurse but the newcomer was not a nurse. He was a padre.

'Thought you'd like to see one of us,' the padre said. 'I'd've come sooner but we're in demand these days. Was talking to your quack and he said you were in high old heart. Glad to be alive and all that. Expect you'd like to give thanks, eh?' Getting no reply, the padre explained himself: 'Give thanks to the One Above I meant, of course. Eh?'

Still no reply. The padre's red-skinned face, like a badly shaped potato, remained amiable but he was puzzled by Simon's silence. 'C of E aren't you?'

Simon nodded. He knew he had made a mistake in putting down 'C of E'. He had been warned often enough by his old sergeant in the desert: 'Don't never admit to nothing, sir. Whatever they ask you, you say, "Don't know," then they can't get at you, see!' But 'don't know' had not seemed the right answer when one was asked to state one's religion. Anyway, it was too late to retract now. The padre, satisfied by the nod, took out his pipe and gained time by stuffing the bowl.

'Can't get round much, can you?'

Simon shook his head.

'That's all right. We've got a special arrangement for chaps like you. We bring the Eucharist right here to your bedside. Chaps find it a great comfort. Now, how about after Sunday service?'

Simon shook his head again.

'You mean you're not a regular communicant?'

'I mean, I want to be left alone.'

The padre, undefeated, put his pipe in his mouth and began to deal with the situation: 'Depressed, are you? What's the quack been saying?'

'Nothing. He didn't need to. My legs are useless.'

'But it's not permanent.'

'It probably is. They've been like it a bit too long.'

'Oh, cheer up, old chap. Keep your pecker up. Even if it comes to the worst, you're only one chap among a lot of chaps who've been unlucky. You must remember Him. Think of His sacrifice. Think of the sparrow's fall. Think of His love.'

Simon began to feel sorry for the padre. It could not be easy preaching the love of God to young men whose future had been ended before it began.

The padre went on: 'You're down now, but it won't last. You'll jump out of it, see if you don't. And if the old legs don't shape up, well, it's not the end of the world. You can be thankful you're a para and not a tetra. There's still plenty you can do. You can earn a living, you can swim, you can play games . . .'

'*Games!*'

'Yes, you'd be surprised. They'll teach you all sorts of larks. And everywhere there'll be people to help you.'

What people? Simon asked himself when the padre had gone. Who would have time for a legless man? – a legless, impotent man? He had an appalled picture of Edwina, driven by pity, pushing him round in a chair like a baby in a perambulator. Everyone using the soothing, patronising, simplified speech reserved for infants and invalids.

'Not for me,' he told himself, but what was to become of him? His brother had bled to death in No-man's-land when his legs were blown off. Had he lived, he could have been fitted with two artificial legs but what happened to a man whose legs were in place but no use to him? He was simply the prisoner of their existence. No doubt people would help him. Some girl might even offer to marry him but no, one life wasted was enough.

He wondered why the ward looked so bare. When he had been with men on the troopship and in the desert, each had kept, like a private reredos, his pictures of women. But there were no pictures in the ward. It occurred to him that this fact was a symptom of the loss of manhood. When the sister next came round, he said to her: 'No pin-ups.'

'No what?'

'Bare walls. No pin-ups.'

'I should think not, indeed! We don't want our nice, clean walls cluttered with that sort of rubbish.'

So that was it! Perhaps, after all, some spark would remain to torment him.

That day another visitor came fumbling through the curtains. He was afraid the padre had returned, or perhaps it was one of those welfare workers who imposed themselves on the other ranks. But the newcomer was not the padre and did not look like a welfare worker. Peering short-sightedly into the shadowed cubicle, he did not seem sufficiently purposeful or righteous of manner, and there was a largeness about him, not only of the flesh but of the spirit, that did not suggest to Simon any sort of organized mission. The pockets of his creased linen jacket were stuffed with books and papers, and he held under his arm some bags of fruit and a bunch of flowers, all badly crushed.

His appearance startled Simon into sitting up and saying: 'Hello.'

'Hello. I'm Edwina's deputy. I live in the same flat. My name's Guy Pringle. She asked me to come because she could not come herself.' Guy dropped the flowers and bags of fruit on to the table and sat down: 'I've brought you these things. If there's anything else you need, let me know.' He began to pull books from his pockets: 'I thought these might interest you. I can get more from the Institute library.'

'Thanks, but I'm not much of a reader.' Then, feeling he must acknowledge Guy's gifts, he picked up a book: 'Still, I'd like to look at them.'

While Guy talked about the books, Simon's dejection lifted a little. Here, he supposed, was one of those who would help him but more important than that, one from whom he was not unwilling to accept help. He wondered how this large man fitted into the Garden City flat. When he went there, just after Hugo's death, the inmates had all been women. There was Edwina, of course, and a strange woman called Angela Hooper, and there was the dark girl Harriet.

He said: 'You're called Pringle? Then you must be the husband of Harriet Pringle?'

Guy's head jerked up. He caught his breath before he said: 'You knew her?'

'Yes, we went together on a trip into the desert. And we climbed the Great Pyramid and sat at the top talking about Hugo. He was alive then. She said you met in Alex and had supper with him. He was killed a month later.'

'Yes, I heard. I was very sorry. Harriet is dead, too.'

'Harriet! Your wife?'

'Yes, she was lost at sea. She went on an evacuation ship that was torpedoed and only three people were saved. But not Harriet. Not poor Harriet.' Then, to Simon's consternation, Guy choked and put his face into his hands, giving way to such an anguish of grief that Simon stared at him, forgetting his own misery. He had seen men weep before. He himself had wept bitterly over Hugo's death, but the sight of this man so violently overthrown by sorrow shocked him deeply.

Guy gasped: 'Forgive me. I've only just heard . . .'

'But if three were saved, there might be more somewhere . . .'

'No.' Guy tried to dry his face with a handkerchief but his tears welled out afresh: 'No, only one boat got away. The steering was broken and it drifted until it was taken into Dar-es-Salaam. By then there were only three people left alive.'

'There could have been other boats that went to different places.'

'I would have heard by now. Wherever she was, she would have cabled me. She wouldn't leave me in suspense.'

Simon, not knowing what other comfort he could offer, shook his head despondently: 'People are dying all the time now. Young people. I mean not people you might expect to die. People with their lives before them.'

'Yes, this accursed war.'

They were silent, contemplating the calamity of their time, while Guy scrubbed his handkerchief over his face and looked, red-eyed, at Simon. Simon looked back in sympathy but as he did so, he felt – not quite a sensation, rather a presentiment of sensation to come, then there was a stirring in his left upper leg as though an insect were crawling under his skin. He put his hand down and touched the spot but the skin was smooth. No insect there. He tried to disregard it, knowing Ross would say, 'It means nothing.'

'I suppose it will end one day,' Guy was saying, 'but that won't bring them back . . .'

Simon was about to say that grief did fade in time; that it became no more than a sadness at the back of the mind, but he was distracted as the insect movement repeated itself in his thigh. Then a trickle, slow and steady, rather sticky, like blood, ran down to his knee and he again touched the spot. He looked at his fingers. There was no blood. He was afraid to hope that the trickle was a trickle of life. Guy was speaking but he could not listen. His whole consciousness was gathered on the area of the sensation. A pause, then the insect moved in his other leg and the same sticky trickle went down to his knee. Cautiously, he tried to

400

press his thighs together and for the first time since his injury, he felt his legs touch each other. He held his breath before letting it out in his excitement, and he knew this was the sign he had longed for, the sign that one day he would walk again.

In his relief, he wanted to shout to Guy, expecting him to rejoice with him, but he was checked by the sight of the other man wiping tears from his face.

Simon repressed, or tried to repress his joy, but his joy transcended his sense of decorum and he could not hide his laughter.

Guy was too absorbed by his own emotion to notice Simon's and Simon bit his lip to control himself. Guy said it was time for him to go. He dried his eyes and gathering up the books Simon did not want, put out his hand. Taking it, Simon said, 'You'll come again, won't you?'

The invitation was vivaciously given but Guy felt no surprise. Most people, having met him once, were eager to see him again.

Five

Unaware that she was mourned for dead, Harriet was alive in the Levant. She had not boarded the evacuation ship. Instead, she had begged a lift on an army lorry that would take her to Damascus. The two women with whom she absconded, members of a para-military service, made regular trips to Iraq, taking ammunition and other supplies.

They would admit only to surnames. For the duration they were Mortimer and Phillips, or rather Mort and Phil, two strongly-built young females, their faces burnt by the sun and wind and worn down to a ruddy-brown similarity. Sitting together in the cabin of the lorry, they took it in turns to drive or sleep so they could keep going all day and all night.

Harriet, in the back among cases of ammunition, hardly slept at all. The road over the desert was little more than a track and full of pot-holes. Each time she drifted into sleep, she was jolted awake as the lorry bumped or skidded or swayed into the sandy verge. In the end, she sat up and stared into darkness, seeing waterfalls tumbling black through the black air, huge birds sweeping to and fro across the night, enormous animals that paused to stare back at her before lumbering away out of sight. When the dawn came, she saw none of these things, only the empty road stretching from her, away into the desert hills.

Soon after daybreak, they stopped at a frontier barrier, then the lorry moved on to tarmac and Harriet, exhausted by the uneasy night, fell into a heavy slumber. When she woke again, the lorry was standing on a rocky shoulder that overlooked the sea. There was no sign of Mort and Phil.

She had left Egypt and was in another country. In Egypt the sun shone every day in a cloudless sky. Here the sky was blotted over with patches of cloud and the wind had an unfamiliar smell, the smell of rain. Because of the rain, grass was coming up, a thin shadow of green over the pinkish hills. In Egypt there had been rain only once during her time there: a freak storm that hit Cairo like a portent and turned the roads to rivers. Winter in Egypt was like a fine English summer but here it was really winter, wet and cold. Revived by the freshness of the air, she stood up, stretched her stiff muscles, then jumped down to the road. She had been ill but now she felt well, and free in a new world.

The rocks hid the foreshore but she could see, rising above them, the bastion of a castle that breasted the water of a bay. The water, glassy smooth, reflected every stone and crevice in the wall so there seemed to be two castles, one inverted below the other.

Climbing up the rocks, she saw Mort and Phil barefoot by the edge of the sea. She was about to call out to them but was checked by the sense of intimacy between them. She realized how little she knew about them. Of Phil she knew nothing at all. Mortimer she had met only twice but each time there had come from her such a sense of warmth, that, seeing her on the quay at Suez, she had run to her, calling out: 'Mortimer! Mortimer! God has sent you to save me.'

She walked away from them towards the other side of the bay. The sand was firm and brown, like baked clay, and her feet sank into it, leaving behind her a string of footprints. She took off her shoes and waded into the torpid water and walked until she came on a half-buried piece of fluted pilaster. Sitting down, she could observe Mort and Phil from a safe distance. They were standing close together, looking into each other's faces and she began to suspect that they would have preferred to be alone. When she asked Mortimer to save her from the evacuation ship, she had not considered Phil as an obstacle. She had not considered Phil at all. That was a mistake. Turning away from them, she wondered what she would do if they decided to drive off without her. Some time passed, then she glanced back at them. As the sun came and went among clouds, the figures merged and wavered against the dazzle of the sea. They remained locked together for several minutes then began to walk back towards the lorry.

As she watched them go, she realized how precarious her position was. She had fifty pounds that was to have been her spending money on board the ship. Now she would have to live on it while she found herself a job of some sort. She had one friend in

403

Syria, Aidan Pratt, who was a captain in the Pay Corps and might find her work. He was, in a way, responsible for her escapade because he had suggested she visit him in Damascus. He had hoped Guy would come with her. Now she would have to explain why she was alone and why she had to earn her own living.

She kept her face turned to the sea, giving Mort and Phil the chance to go without her, and was startled by Mortimer's lively, baritone voice speaking behind her: 'How d'you feel after that bumpy ride?'

Harriet rose, again caught up in Mortimer's friendly warmth: 'It wasn't too bad.'

'Come on, then.' Contrite perhaps at having left her alone so long, Mortimer linked her arm and walked her back to the lorry: 'I expect you're hungry? We brought food with us. We'll have a picnic.'

There were packets of sandwiches in the cabin and two flasks of canteen tea. They sat on the rocks to eat their meal. The sandwiches, slabs of corned beef between slabs of bread, were dry and roughly cut but Mort and Phil devoured them with the appetite of old campaigners. Harriet, who was recovering from amoebic dysentery, envied their vigour and wondered if she would ever feel well again.

After eating, they sat for a while, made sleepy by the food and sea air, until Phil started up: 'Holy Mary, what's that?'

A grunting and rustling was coming from behind the slopes on the other side of the road, then a large, dark, dirty pig swaggered towards them, followed pell-mell by a dozen other pigs and a swine-herd equally dirty and dark. Midges clouded about them and a strong smell of the sty filled the air.

The man's eyes shone out from behind a fringe of black curls. Bold and curious, he stared at the three women. He was naked to the waist, his broad shoulders and chest burnt to a purple-red, his bare feet grey with dust.

Mort shouted: 'Hello there. How are you and all the pigs?'

Hearing a strange language, the man grunted and hurried his herd down to the sea.

'I say!' Mort's eyes opened in admiration: 'What a splendid figure! He might be Ulysses on the island of the Phaeacians.'

Phil asked in her wondering Irish voice: 'Did Ulysses keep pigs?'

'Not exactly, but his followers were turned into pigs somewhere along the line. This is an heroic shore, isn't it? I bet that castle was built by the Crusaders.'

Harriet said: 'Have you ever been inside?'

'Yes, but there's not much to see. The Bedu have taken it over. They've burrowed into it like rabbits and live in holes in the wall, but there's a café. Phil and I had coffee there once. We might go in again.'

They entered through a gateway. Large hinges showed where the gates had hung but the gates had gone and as Mortimer said, there was not much to see. A lane followed the outer wall, pitted with dark cells that served as dwelling places. At the sight of the strangers, children ran out to clamour for baksheesh and followed the women wherever they went. They came to a cavern that was no more than a hole in the original fabric. This was the café. Inside men in grimy galabiahs sat at grimy tables. The place depended for light on a break in the wall through which gleamed the motionless silver of the sea.

Mortimer led Harriet and Phil inside and ordered coffee. The men stared in silence, obviously confounded by this female presumption and Harriet felt proud of Mort and Phil and their confidence in the world.

On their way back to the lorry, a sharp burst of rain sent them running and Mortimer, climbing up among the cases of ammunition, pulled out a tarpaulin to shelter Harriet who was wearing only the blouse, skirt and cardigan that had been her winter wear in Egypt. Sitting with the tarpaulin over her hair, she looked out on wild and empty hill country patched light and dark by the sun and cloud. On one side the sea, disturbed by the wind, rolled in on a deserted shore. On the other were hills, rocky and bare except for the fur of grass. Black clouds and white clouds wound and unwound, sometimes revealing a stretch of clear blue sky. The rain slanted this way and that, cutting through broad rays of light, one moment pouring down, the next coming abruptly to a stop.

It was evening when they reached the Haifa headland and

skirting the town by the coast road, drove up on to the downs before the Lebanon frontier. The officials, who saw Mort and Phil once a week, waved them on.

As the wet sunset faded into twilight, the lorry was stopped on the verge of the road and driver and co-driver, without a word to Harriet, jumped down and walked away among the shadowed hills. Some twenty minutes later they returned and, looking up at Harriet, Mortimer said: 'How about some supper?'

Descending, Harriet took the tarpaulin with her, intending to spread it out for the three of them but Mort and Phil, whose slacks were already soaked by the wet ground, laughed at her precaution.

There was a tinkle of bells in the distance and Phil said: 'More pigs?' But this time the visitants were camels laden with bundles and decked out with fringes and tassels and camel bells. One after the other, tall and stately, they came swaying out of the twilight to cross the road. As their feet touched the tarmac, they grumbled and grunted then, catching sight of the women, they shied away and the drovers, shouting, pulled at the lofty heads. The men made a show of ignoring the women but came to a stop nearby. The camels, forced to kneel, gave indignant snorts as though even rest was a form of servitude.

While they ate corned-beef sandwiches and drank the second flask of tea, the three women watched the camp's braziers being lit and skewers of meat being laid across the charcoal.

Phil said: 'How about Arab hospitality? D'you think we'll get an invite to supper?'

'Heaven forbid,' said Mortimer, 'I've heard pretty hair-raising stories about these chaps. Some British officials stopped their car to watch a Bedu wedding party and were invited to join in. They said they were in a hurry and after they'd driven off, the Bedu got together and decided the refusal was an insult. They galloped after them, and slaughtered the lot.'

'Women as well?' Harriet asked.

'There weren't any women but if there had been they would have escaped.'

'Why, I wonder?'

'Apparently Lady Hester Stanhope so impressed the Arab world, English women have been treated as special ever since.'

Harriet laughed: 'That's a comfort. I'll feel safer now.'

But alone in the back of the lorry, she did not feel very safe. The countryside was silent, the sky heavily clouded and there was no light but their own head-lights. There were few houses and those were in darkness. The villages seemed to be deserted yet twice, passing through a village street, there were conflagrations, produced by lighted petrol poured into the gutters of some main building. If these displays marked an occasion, there were no witnesses, no one to rejoice. Each time, after the raw brilliance of the flames, they returned to dense and silent darkness. Harriet became nervous at the thought of leaving Mort and Phil, and wished she could keep the comfort of their company.

Perhaps they, too, were unnerved by the black, endless road to Damascus for they began to sing together, loudly and aggressively:

> Sing high, sing low,
> Wherever we go,
> We're Artillery ladies,
> We never say 'No'.

There was another verse that ended:

> At night on the boat deck
> We always say 'Yes'.

They sang the two verses over and over again, their blended voices conveying to Harriet a union she could never hope to share.

Damascus appeared at last, a map of lights spread high on the darkness. As the road rose up among gardens and orchards, a scent of foliage came to her and her fears faded. Here she was in the oldest of the world's inhabited cities. The oasis on which it was built was said to be the Garden of Eden. Adam and Eve were created here and here Cain killed Abel. Damascus had been a city before Abraham was born and had been one of the wonders of the Ancient world. Who knew what pleasures awaited her in such a magical place?

A sound of rifle fire came to them. As they drove into the main square, they saw through the yellowish haze of the street lights that men were rushing about, screaming and firing pistols into the air. The large buildings on either side looked ominous and unwelcoming.

The lorry stopped at the kerb. Harriet could go no farther and perhaps Mort and Phil would not want her to go farther. Whether she liked it or not, she had arrived.

They were outside a shabby, flat-fronted building that had the word 'Hotel' above the door. Mortimer jumped down and lifted Harriet's suitcase to the pavement. She said: 'I know it doesn't look very encouraging, but it's the only hotel I know. I expect it will do till you find something better.'

Harriet nervously asked: 'Is there revolution here?'

'Oh no, this usually goes on at night. It's a demonstration against the Free French but it's harmless.'

Harriet was not so sure. She remembered Aidan Pratt telling her that his friend had been killed by a stray bullet during one of these demonstrations. She appealed to Mortimer: 'Couldn't you stay here just for one night?'

Mort and Phil shook their heads. Standing together, smiling their farewells, they said they must press on to Aleppo where they planned to stay at the Armenian hospital. For a moment she thought of asking them to take her with them, but wherever she went she had to leave them sometime. Here at least she had Aidan Pratt.

Seeing her trying to lift her heavy case, Mortimer took it from her and carried it easily into the hotel hallway. There was a small night-light on the desk but no one behind the desk.

Mortimer said: 'The clerk will come when you ring. You'll be all right here, won't you?'

Eager to be back on the road, she took a quick step forward and kissed Harriet's cheek: 'You're not staying here long, are you? We'll meet again back in Cairo. Take care of yourself.'

Harriet watched through the glass of the door till the lorry was out of sight, then she struck the bell on the desk. There was a long interval before the clerk appeared, looking aggrieved as though the bell were not there for use. He seemed disconcerted by the sight of a solitary young woman with a suitcase and he shook his head: 'You wan' hotel? This not hotel.' He pointed to a notice in French that said the building had been requisitioned by the occupying force. It was now a hostel for French officers.

Dismayed, Harriet asked: 'But where can I go? It's late. Where else is there?'

The clerk looked sympathetic but unhelpful: 'Things very bad. Army take everything.'

Having nothing to offer, he waited for her to go and she, having nowhere to go, went out and stood on the pavement. There must be someone, somewhere, who could direct her to an hotel. Eventually a British soldier sauntered by with the appearance of abstracted boredom she had seen often enough in Cairo. She stopped him and asked if he knew where she could stay. He gave a laugh, as though he could scarcely believe his luck, and lifting her bag, said, 'You a service woman?'

'More or less.'

'That's all right then. There's a hostel over here.'

He led her across the square and into a side street. There was more rifle fire and she asked what the trouble was.

'Just the wogs. They're always ticking.'

'What's it like here in Damascus?'

'Same as everywhere else. Lot of bloody foreigners.'

They came to another shabby, flat-fronted building, this one distinguished by a Union Jack hanging over the main door.

When Harriet thanked him, the soldier said: 'Don't thank me. It's a treat seeing an English bint.'

Harriet thought she had found a refuge until she was stopped in the hall by an Englishwoman with scrappy red hair and foxy red eyes. She looked Harriet up and down before she said accusingly: 'This hostel's for ORs.'

'Does it matter? I've come a long way and I'm very tired.'

'I don't know. Suppose it doesn't matter if you aren't staying long. I've got to keep my beds for them as they're meant for.'

Harriet followed the woman through a canteen, a stark place shut for the night, to a large dormitory with some thirty narrow, iron bedsteads.

'Which can I have?'

'Any one you like. There's a shower in there if you care to use it.'

The beds had no sheets but a thin army blanket was folded on each. The shower was cold, but at least she had the place to herself; or so it seemed until the early hours of the morning when she was wakened by a party of ATS, all drunk, who kept up a ribald criticism of the men who had taken them out. They finally subsided into sleep but at six a.m. a loudspeaker was switched on in the canteen.

Raucous music bellowed through the dormitory. Harriet, giving up hope of sleep, rose and went to the shower. As she passed the ATS, one of them lifted a bleared, blood-shot eye over the edge of the blanket, and observed her reproachfully.

The person in the canteen was a half-Negro sweeper who seemed as baleful as the red-haired woman. When Harriet asked about breakfast, he mumbled, 'Blekfest eight o'clock,' and went on sweeping.

With an hour and a half in which to do nothing, Harriet set out to look at Damascus. Independence had not begun well for her and she was inclined to blame herself. If she had taken the woman into her confidence, charmed her, flattered her, she might have been set up as the hostel's favourite inmate. But she had no gift for ingratiating herself with strangers. And she was sure that if she tried it, it would not work.

The square, ill-lit and sinister the previous night, was at peace now in the early sunlight. The ominous buildings were no longer ominous. There were towers and domes and minarets, sights to be seen, a new city to be explored. She could imagine Aidan escorting her round and helping her to find employment and lodgings. She would warn him to keep her presence a secret. She could not have Guy coming here out of pity to rescue her and take her back to Cairo. Later, perhaps, she would contact him but while the evacuation ship was at sea – the voyage around the Cape would take at least two months – no one would expect to hear from her.

She sat for a while in a garden beside a mosque, watching the traffic increase and the day's work beginning. The city was set among hills as in the hollow of a crown. The highest range, to the west, was covered in snow and a cold wind blew towards her. She was not dressed for this climate. Shivering, she rose and found a café where she could drink coffee at a counter among businessmen to whom she was an object of curiosity. Cairo had become conditioned to the self-sufficiency of western women but she was now in Syria, a country dominated by Moslem prejudice. In spite of the bold gaze of the men, she remained on her café stool until the military offices were likely to start work.

Seeing nothing that resembled the Cairo HQ, she took a taxi and was driven to the British Pay Office. This was a requisitioned hotel where the walls had become scuffed and the furniture replaced by trestle tables. Here, among her own countrymen, she felt at ease. The worst was over. She had only to find Aidan Pratt and he would take care of her.

When she asked for him, a corporal said: 'Sorry, miss. He's been transferred.'

'Can you tell me where he's gone?'

'Sorry, miss, can't help you. Not allowed to reveal movements of army personnel.'

'But I'm a friend. Surely, under the circumstances . . . At least, tell me, is he in Syria?'

The corporal conceded that he was not in Syria but beyond that would disclose nothing. He said apologetically: 'Security, you know, miss.'

She said: 'Do you know anywhere I can stay? A hotel or guest-house?'

The corporal shook his head: 'Haven't heard of one. Sorry.'

Harriet returned to sunlight that was beginning to fade. Clouds were drifting over the snow-covered mountains and fog dimmed the towers and minarets. She said aloud: 'So you really are on your own!' and as the first drops of rain hit her face, she started back to the hostel, hoping for breakfast in the canteen.

Six

Guy was going through a period of stress unlike anything he had known in his life before. There had been only one death in his family and that was in his childhood. When told his grannie had gone to a much nicer place, he had said, 'She'll come back, won't she?' She did not come back and he had forgotten her. But after his outburst in Simon's ward, he could not forget Harriet. He was haunted by her loss and the haunting bewildered him. He was like a man who, taking for granted his right to perfect health, is struck down by disease. But the loss was only one aspect of his perplexity. He had to consider the fact that going, she had gone unwillingly. He refused to blame himself for that. He had suggested she go for her own good. He told himself it had been a sensible suggestion to which she had sensibly agreed. In fact, in the end, she had *chosen* to go.

But however much he argued against it, he knew he had instigated her departure. He could not cope with her physical malaise and air of discontent. There were too many other demands upon him. He simply hadn't the time to deal with her. So he had persuaded her to return to her native air where, sooner or later, she would regain her health. No one could blame him either for her illness or her deep-seated discontent. She needed employment and in England she would find it. He had expected, when he eventually joined her at home, that once again she would be the quick-witted, capable, lively young woman he had married.

Her going, too, was to have been a prelude to their post-war life. She was to be the advance guard of their return. With her particular gift for doing such things, she was to find them a house or flat and settle all those problems of everyday life which he found baffling and tedious.

Now it was not simply that Harriet would not be there when he returned, she would never be there.

Faced with the finality of death, he could not accept it. In the past, he had had many an easy laugh at those gravestone wishes: 'She shall not come to me but I shall go to her,' 'Not lost but gone before . . .' and so on. As a materialist, he still had to see the absurdity of belief in an after-life. He could not tell himself that Harriet had gone to a 'much nicer place' but, in his confusion of grief and guilt, he almost convinced himself she had not gone at all. Perhaps, at the last, she had decided against the journey to England and had come back to Cairo. She had hidden herself from him but when he turned the next corner, he would find her coming towards him. Then, not finding her there, he went on expectantly to the next corner, and the next.

If he had no extra classes, he would spend his afternoon walking about the streets of Cairo in search of someone who was not there. When people stopped to condole with him, he listened impatiently, imagining they had been misinformed, and that she was somewhere, in some distant street, if only he could find her.

One day, coming into the lecture hall, he was shocked to see an immense wreath of flowers and laurel propped up against the lectern. Refusing to acknowledge it, he took his place as though it were not there. But, of course, his students could not let him escape like that. They all rose and their elected spokesman stepped to the front of the class.

'Professor Pringle, sir, it is our wish that I express our sorrow. Our sorrow and our deep regret that Mrs Pringle is no more.'

He said briefly, 'Thank you,' angry that they had blundered in to confirm a fear he had rejected. The student spokesman, respecting his reticence, retired and nothing more was said, but in the library he found the librarian, Miss Pedler, waiting for him.

'I'm so sorry, Mr Pringle. I've only just heard.'

Guy nodded and turned away but she followed him to an alcove where the poetry was stacked: 'I wanted to say, Mr Pringle, I know how you feel. I lost my fiancé soon after the war started. He contracted TB. If he could've got home, he would have been cured, but there was no transport. It was the war killed him just as it killed your wife. I know it's terrible but in the end you get over it. The first three years are the worst.'

Aghast, he murmured, 'Three years!' and hurried away from

her. Back in the lecture hall, he found the wreath still propped against the lectern. What was he supposed to do with it? He thought of Gamal Sarwar, one of his students, who had been killed in a car accident and buried in the City of the Dead. He could take the wreath up for Gamal, but he knew he would never find the Sarwar mausoleum among all the other mausoleums. And the cemetery, though at night it took on a certain macabre beauty, was in daytime a desolate, cinderous place he could not visit alone. The thought of it reminded him of the afternoon when he and Harriet had attended Gamal's *arba'in* and the Sarwar men had made much of him. Harriet had waited for him, and then, as the moon rose, she had asked him to go with her to see the Khalifa tombs. It had meant only a short drive in a gharry but he had refused. When he said she could go with someone else, she had pleaded: 'But I want to go with you.'

Angry again, he said to himself: 'I hate death and everything to do with death,' and picking up the wreath, he threw it into the stationery cupboard and shut the door on it.

Guy felt betrayed by life. His good nature, his readiness to respond to others and his appreciation of them had gained him friends and made life easy for him. Now, suddenly and cruelly, he had become the victim of reality. He had not deserved it but there it was: his wife, who might have lived another fifty or sixty years, had gone down with the evacuation ship and he would not see her again.

Edwina, thinking that Guy was becoming resigned to Harriet's death, said to Dobson: 'He can't go moping around for ever. I think I should try and take his mind off it.'

'If I were you, I'd leave it a bit longer.'

'Really, Dobbie, anyone would think I had designs on him. I only want to help him.'

That was true but Edwina, too, felt betrayed by life. She had had a lingering hope that she would see Peter Lisdoonvarna when he came on leave but the British army was now so far away, the men no longer took their leave in Cairo. Guy was a prize that had come to hand just when she had begun to fear her first youth was passing. Before she became obsessed with Peter, she had taken life lightly, receiving the rewards of beauty. But what good had

414

they done her? She had been offered only futureless young men like Hugo and Simon Boulderstone, or men like Peter who would not leave their wives. Now, just when she needed him most, here was Guy bereft and available and much too young to remain unmarried.

'You know, Dobbie dear, I was very fond of Harriet, but she's dead and the rest of us have to go on living.'

'I still think you'd be wise to leave it for a bit.'

'And have some Levantine floosie snap him up?'

Dobson laughed: 'I agree, that could happen. They're great at getting their hooks into a man, especially when he's feeling low.'

'There you are, then! I'm not risking it.'

On Saturday, Guy's free day, Edwina said in a small, seductive voice: 'Don't forget, Guy dear, you promised to take me out.'

'Did I promise?'

'Oh, darling, you know you did! I'm not doing anything tonight so wouldn't it be nice if we had a little supper?'

Guy, who would have refused Harriet without a thought, felt it would be discourteous to refuse Edwina. Edwina, unlike Harriet, was the outside world that called for consideration.

He said: 'All right. I'll be back for you about seven.'

Edwina's voice rose in joyful anticipation: 'Oh, darling, darling! Where shall we go?'

'I'll think of somewhere. See you later, then.'

Returning at a time nearer eight o'clock than seven, Guy found Edwina waiting for him in the living-room. She was wearing one of her white evening dresses and a fur jacket against the winter chill. Both seemed to him unsuitable for a simple dinner but worse was the jewel on her breast: a large, heart-shaped brooch set with diamonds. He frowned at it.

'You can't wear that thing. It's ridiculous.'

'You gave it to me.'

He was puzzled then, looking more closely at it, he remembered he had indeed given it to her to wear at his troops' entertainment. He had no idea where it came from.

He said: 'It's vulgar. It's just a theatrical prop.'

'It's not a theatrical prop. They're real diamonds. It's a valuable piece of jewellery.'

This protest recalled for him another protest and he realized the brooch had belonged to Harriet. She had said: 'It's mine. It was given to me,' but that had meant nothing to him. He had taken the brooch from her because it was exactly right for the show. He recalled, too, her expression of disbelief when he pocketed the absurd object. And soon after that she told him she would go on the evacuation ship.

He said to Edwina: 'Please take it off.'

'Oh, very well!' She unpinned it with an expression of wry resignation and offered it to him: 'I suppose you want it back?'

'It belonged to Harriet.'

Deciding that nothing must spoil their evening, she smiled a forgiving smile: 'Then, of course, you must have it back.'

He did not want the thing yet did not want Edwina to have it. He wished it would disappear off the face of the earth. Edwina, still smiling, slipped it into his pocket and not knowing what else to do with it, he let it remain there.

A taxi took them to Bulacq Bridge and Edwina supposed they were going to the Extase night club. Instead, they stopped at one of the broken-down houses on the other side of the road.

'What is this?'

'The fish restaurant,' Guy said as though she ought to know.

They went down into a damp, dimly-lit basement where there were long deal tables and benches in place of chairs. The other diners, minor clerks and students, stared at Edwina's white dress and white fur jacket, and she asked nervously: 'Do Europeans come here?'

'My friends do. The food is good.'

'Is it? It's very interesting of course. Quite a change for me.' Edwina, trying to suffer it all with a good grace, looked about her: 'I didn't even know there was a fish restaurant.'

Before she could say more, Guy's friends began to appear. The first was Jake Jackman. When he came to the table, Edwina thought he only wanted a word with Guy but he sat down, intending to eat with them. She had not expected anything like this. Her evening with Guy was to be an intimate exchange of sympathy that would lead to   well, there was no knowing!

Still, Jackman being there and meaning to stay, she would have to put up with him. She had never liked him. She supposed he was, in his thin-faced fashion, attractive, but her instinct was against him. She knew that in a sexual relationship, the only sort that interested her, he would be unscrupulous. But there he was: a challenge! She acknowledged his presence with a sidelong, provocative smile that had no effect upon him. He was intent on Guy to whom he at once confided his discovery of a 'bloody scandal'. The western Allies were uniting themselves against Russia and he had inside information to prove it.

'What sort of information?'

Sniffing and pulling at his nose, Jake leant towards Guy, lifting his shoulder to exclude Edwina: 'This "Aid to Russia" frolic – it's all my eye. The stuff they're sending is obsolete and most of it's useless. They don't want the Russkies to advance on that front. They want them wiped out. They want the Panzers to paralyse the whole damn Soviet fighting force.'

'I can't believe that. It would mean German troops pouring down through the Ukraine and taking our oil.'

'Don't be daft. We'd have made peace long before that. Or the Hun would've exhausted himself. It's the old policy of killing two birds with one stone. It was the policy before Hitler invaded Russia and it's still the policy . . .' Jake dropped his voice so Edwina could not hear what he said and she felt not only excluded but despised.

Guy had forgotten they were there to eat and the waiter, leaning against the kitchen door, was quite content to let the men talk. Hungry and neglected on her comfortless wooden seat, Edwina sighed so loudly that Guy was reminded of her presence. He turned but at that moment there was another arrival at the table. This was Major Cookson, a thin little man without income, growing more shabby every day, who followed after anyone who might buy him a drink.

He said to Jackman: 'I've been looking for you everywhere.'

Since his friend Castlebar had disappeared from Cairo, Jackman had admitted Cookson as a minor member of his entourage. He looked at him now without enthusiasm and said: 'Sit down. Sit down.'

Hearing him called 'major', Edwina gave him a second glance, but he did not relate to the free-spending young officers she had known in the past. As he sat beside her, he enveloped her in a stench of ancient sweat and she felt more affronted by him than by Jackman.

Giving up his revelations of Allied intrigues, Jake said: 'I suppose we're going to eat some time?' imposing on Guy the position of host.

'Good heavens, yes.' Guy, becoming alert, called the waiter and gave Edwina the menu.

It was a dirty, handwritten menu that listed three kinds of river fish. Guy recommended them all but advised Edwina to choose the *mahseer* which, he said, was a speciality of the house. Edwina did not like fish but concurred from a habit of concurring with the male sex.

Jackman had now become the joker. Giving Edwina a smile full of malice, he said: 'Something funny happened today. Was passing Abdin Palace and saw a squaddie, drunk as arseholes, his cock sticking out of his flies. He'd got hold of an old pair of steel-rimmed specs and having perched them on the said cock, was saying, "Look around, cocky boy, and if you see anything you like, I'll buy it for you."'

Knowing he meant to offend her, Edwina ignored Jackman's laughter and gave her attention to the plate in front of her. The fish, if it tasted of anything, tasted of mud.

'Which,' Jackman went on, 'reminds me of lover-boy Castlebar. But he's not bought anything, has he? He's been bought.'

Guy shrugged: 'If they're happy, why worry?'

'Happy? You think Bill's happy acting the gigolo? I bet he's sick to his stomach.' Jackman turned to Cookson for agreement and Cookson, giggling weakly, said:

'Live and let live.'

'What a bloody amoral lot you are!' Jackman sulked for a while then began another story but was interrupted by yet another arrival at the table.

The newcomer was a dark, gloomy-eyed man who incongruously wore the uniform of an army captain. Guy introduced him as, 'Aidan Sheridan, the actor. He's now in the Pay Corps and calls himself Pratt.'

Edwina caught her breath: 'Oh, Aidan Sheridan!' she said, and widened her eyes at him.

Aidan viewed her with distaste then turned accusingly on Guy: 'Where's Harriet?'

There was dismay at the table. Edwina and Jackman glanced at Guy who did not speak.

'What's the matter? You haven't split up, have you?'

Guy shook his head and said: 'I would have written but I didn't know where you were.'

'I've been transferred to Jerusalem. But where is she?'

'I should have told everyone who knew her. I didn't think...'

'Whatever it is, tell me now. Where is she?'

'She's dead. She was on an evacuation ship that was sunk... She's dead. Drowned.' Unable to say more, Guy shook his head again.

Aidan sank down to the bench and after a moment said: 'You're sure? There are so many false reports going round.'

Guy could only shake his head and Edwina, speaking for him, said: 'I'm afraid it was confirmed. I'm at the Embassy and I saw the report. The ship was torpedoed off the coast of Africa. Poor Harriet, it was terrible, wasn't it? Three people were saved but she...'

Guy broke in, frowning: 'What's the good of going over it again! She's lost. Nothing will bring her back, so let's talk of something else.' He looked at Aidan who stared down at the table as though not hearing what was being said: 'You'll have something to eat?'

The others were trying to talk of something else but for Aidan the news was too sudden to be put aside: 'No, I can't eat. I'll go... I'll walk to the station.'

'You're going back tonight?'

'Yes, I've a berth booked...'

'Then I'll walk with you.' As he rose, Guy remembered he was Edwina's escort and he said: 'Sorry, I must go. I want to talk to Aidan. Jake will see you home.'

'Look here,' Jake put in quickly: 'I've come out without cash. I'll need something for a taxi.'

Guy paid the bill and handed Jackman a pound note then went off with Aidan.

'A disastrous evening,' Jake said.

For Edwina, too, it had been a disastrous evening. Hiding her resentment, she said: 'Yes, poor Harriet!' but her mind was on the treatment she had received. She added: 'And poor Guy! I suppose that actor not knowing brought it all back.' At the same time she was telling herself that Guy and the company he kept would not do for her.

Seven

Guy was surprised by Aidan's reaction to Harriet's death and at the same time felt grateful to him. That others grieved for her in some way lightened his own burden and the debt he owed her. Out in the street, he said: 'I didn't realize you felt any special affection for her.'

'We had become friends.'

That also surprised Guy. Though he rewarded him by going with him to the station, Guy was bored by Aidan and could not imagine he would have had much attraction for Harriet.

'She used to tease me,' Aidan said: 'I deserved it, of course. I know I'm a bit of a stick. You remember, I came on her in Luxor and we saw some of the sights together.'

Guy said, 'Yes,' though he had forgotten Harriet's trip to Luxor. Thinking about it and about her association with Aidan, he began to imagine her with a whole world of interests about which he knew nothing. He did not begrudge them but had a disquieting sense of things having happened behind his back. Not that anything much could have happened. He had taken her away from her friends in England and, abroad, she had had few opportunities to make more. For the first time, it occurred to him that while he had kept himself occupied morning, noon and night, she had been often alone.

He said: 'She was on that boat the *Queen of Sparta*. I thought she ought to go – this climate was killing her.'

'When we were in Luxor, she didn't look well, but she didn't look happy, either. I would say the unhappiness was more destructive than the climate.'

'Unhappiness? Did she say she was unhappy?'

'No. There was no mention of such a thing, but she seemed lonely down there. I wondered why you didn't go with her.'

'Go with her?' Guy disliked this hint of criticism: 'She did not suggest it. The whole thing was fixed up by that woman Angela Hooper. She took Harriet to Luxor then went off and left her there. It was typical of the woman. She's unbalanced. I couldn't have gone, anyway. I had much too much to do.'

'You do too much, you know.' Aidan spoke gently but his tone expressed more censure than sympathy and Guy felt annoyed. He was not used to criticism and he said:

'I suppose you are blaming me because she's gone. Well, there's no point in it. Anyway, the past is past. We have to manage the present, even if it is unmanageable. We can't stay becalmed in memories.'

'No, I suppose not.'

Aidan's agreement was not wholehearted and Guy walked in silence until they reached the station then, saying a curt, 'Goodbye,' he swung round and walked back to Garden City. Aidan, he told himself, was not only a stick but a prig. He put him out of his mind but for all that, he felt the need to make some amends to Harriet. He began to look about him for an image to adopt in her place. The only one that presented itself at that time was the young lieutenant, Simon Boulderstone. Harriet was beyond his help but the injured youth had to remake his whole life.

Now that he showed signs of recovery, Simon ceased to be the helpless object of everyone's devotion. He was expected to contribute towards his own progress but the progress seemed to him depressingly slow.

As soon as he could flex the muscles of his hips and lift his knees a few inches off the mattress, parallel bars were brought to his bedside and Ross said: 'Come on now, sir, we've got to get you out of bed.'

Ross and the orderly lifted him into place between the bars and told him to grip them with his hands. He was expected to hold himself upright and swing his body between them. This was agony. His arm muscles were so wasted, he could scarcely support his torso but, encouraged by Ross, he found he could move himself by swinging his pelvis from side to side.

Ross said: 'You're doing fine, sir. Keep it up. A bit more effort and you'll get to the end of the bars.'

Simon laughed and struggled on, but in all these exercises

there was a sense of fantasy. Without ability to walk, he seemed to be acting the part of a man who could walk. It was a hopeless attempt. He was troubled by the illusion that he had only half a body and was holding it suspended in air. Yet he had legs. He could see them hanging there, and he lost patience with them, and shouted: 'When on earth will they start moving themselves?'

'Don't you worry, sir. They'll come all right in time.'

His feet, from lack of use, had become absurdly white and delicate. 'Look at them,' he said to Ross: 'They're like a girl's feet. I don't believe I'll ever stand on them again.'

Ross laughed and running his pencil along Simon's left sole, asked: 'Feel that?'

'Nope.' He was disgusted with himself; with his legs, his knees, his feet, every insensate part of himself.

Guy, who visited him two or three times a week, decided that he needed mental stimulation and told him that to recover, he had only to decide to recover. Guy believed in the mind's power over the body. He said he had been ill only once in his life and that was the result of Harriet's interference. His father, an admirer of George Bernard Shaw, had refused to have his children vaccinated in infancy. Coming to the Middle East where smallpox was endemic, Harriet had insisted that Guy must be vaccinated. He had reacted violently to the serum. He had spent two days in bed with a high temperature and a swollen, aching arm, whimpering that he, who had never known a day's illness before, had had illness forced upon him. He had been injected with a foreign substance and would lose his arm. He was amazed when he woke up next morning with his temperature down and his arm intact.

'You see, I was a fool. I allowed Harriet to influence me against my better judgement and, as a result, became ill.'

Simon protested: 'But I'm not ill. I was injured when we ran into a booby trap – that was something different.'

'Not so very different. There are no such things as accidents. We are responsible for everything that happens to us.'

Simon was puzzled yet, reflecting on all Guy said, he remembered how he had been attracted to the palm tree where the trap was laid. The tree had seemed to him a familiar and loved object and he had said to Crosbie: 'A good place to eat our grub.' Guy could be right; perhaps, somehow or other, one did bring catastrophe upon oneself.

'What should I do?'

'Make up your mind that having got yourself into this fix, you're going to get yourself out of it.'

Whether because of this conversation or not, he became aware of his feet in a curious, almost supernatural, way. They had entered his consciousness. He could almost feel them. When he spoke of this to the sister, she said: 'Oh? What do they feel like?'

'Not exactly pleasant. Funny, rather!'

She threw back the blanket and put her hand on them: 'Cold, eh?'

'No, I don't think it's cold.'

'Yes, it is. You've forgotten what cold feels like.'

Simon waited for Ross, intending to say nothing of this development until Ross said: 'Feel that, sir?' then he would say: 'Yes, my feet feel cold.'

But it did not happen like that. That day, when Ross ran the pencil along his sole, an electrical thrill flashed up the inside of his leg into his sexual organs and he felt his penis become erect. He turned his buttocks to hide himself and pressing his cheek into the pillow, did not know whether he was relieved or ashamed.

Ross, seeing him flush, threw the blanket over him, saying: 'You're going to be all right, sir.' He laughed and Simon laughed back at him, and from that time a new intimacy grew up between them. Ross, losing his restraint, ceased to look upon Simon as a dependant and began to treat him as a young man like himself. He took to lingering at the end of each session and talking about small events in the hospital. This gossip led him on to a subject near to his heart: his disapproval of the 'Aussies'. He felt the need to impress Simon with the respectability of New Zealanders that contrasted with the wild goings-on of the Australians.

'A rough lot, sir,' he said. 'Some of 'em never seen a town till they were taken through Sydney to the troopship. And take that Crete job? The Aussies blamed us and the Brits for lack of air-cover. Well, you can't have air-cover if you haven't got aircraft, now can you, sir? They just couldn't see it. They weren't reasonable. When they got back, they took to throwing things out of windows. In Clot Bey they threw a piano out. And they threw out a British airman and told him: "Now fly, you bastard!" From a top floor window, that was. Not nice behaviour, sir.'

'No, indeed. What happened to the airman?'

'I never heard.' Ross shook his head in disgust at his own story.

Simon sympathized with Ross but, secretly, he envied the Aussies their uninhibited 'goings-on'. They had frequently to be confined to barracks for the sake of public safety. And at Tobruk, ordered to advance in total silence, they had wrecked a surprise attack by bursting out of the slitties bawling, 'We're going to see the wizard, the wonderful wizard of Oz'. He had to put in a word for such lawless men.

'After all, Ross, they needn't have fought at all. We started the war and they could have told us to get on with it.'

'Oh, no. With respect, you're wrong there, sir. It's our war as much as yours.'

To the sister, Simon said: 'You know that young lady who came here, the one I said I didn't want to see? Did she come back?'

The sister answered coldly: 'How do I know? I'm not on duty every day and all day, am I?'

'Sister, if she does come, you won't stop her, will you? I want to see her.'

'*If* she does come, I'll bring her along myself.'

A few days later, having had no visitor but Guy, Simon appealed to him: 'Could you ask Edwina to come and see me?'

'Of course,' Guy cheerfully agreed: 'I'll speak to her. I expect she'll come tomorrow or the day after.'

But Edwina, when he spoke to her, blinked her one visible eye at him and seemed on the point of tears: 'Oh, Guy, I really can't go to Helwan again. It's so embarrassing. Simon's got it into his head that I was his brother's girlfriend and I find it such a strain, playing up to him.'

'Why play up? Just tell him the truth.'

'Oh, that would be unkind. Besides, the place upsets me. When I went last time, I had a migraine next day. I do so hate hospitals.' Edwina gave a little sob and Guy, afraid of upsetting her further, said no more but he decided there would be a meeting somewhere other than the hospital.

He arranged to hire a car and asked the sister for permission to take Simon for a drive. They would go to the Gezira gardens. He asked Edwina to meet him there, telling her that he would see there was no distressing talk about Simon's brother. Edwina said: 'Of course, I'll come, Guy dear. How sweet you are to everyone.'

Much satisfied, Guy put his plan to Simon who was upset by it. Closeted in his cubicle, he had become like a forest-bred creature that is afraid to venture out on to the plain. Even Edwina's promise to join them in the gardens had its element of disappointment.

'So she won't come here?'

'She says hospitals have an unfortunate effect on her.'

'I'd rather not go to the gardens, Guy. I don't think she wants to see me.'

'Oh, yes, she agreed at once,' Guy persuaded Simon as he had persuaded Edwina and a day was fixed. By the time the car was outside the Plegics, Simon had worked himself into a state of restless anticipation. He several times asked Guy: 'Do you really think she'll be there?'

'She's probably there already. So, come along!'

Simon's chair, brake-locked, stood beside his bed and Guy and Ross watched while he manoeuvred himself into it. He shifted to the edge of the bed and pushed his legs over the side then, gripping the chair's farther arm, he swung himself into the seat. Comfortably settled, he looked at his audience and grinned: 'How's that?'

Both watchers said together: 'Splendid.'

Ross came to the car where Simon, depending on the strength of his arms, lifted himself into the back seat. His movements were ungainly and Guy and Ross were pained by the effort involved but they smiled their satisfaction. Simon was progressing well.

Heat was returning to the Cairo noonday. The drive over the desert was pleasant and Simon, looking out of one window or the other, said: 'Funny to be out again. Makes me feel I'm getting better.'

The gardens, that curved round the north-eastern end of the island, were narrow, a fringe of sandy ground planted with trees.

Constantly hosed down with river water, the trees had grown immensely tall but their branches were sparse and their leaves few. They were hung with creepers that here and there let down a thread-fine stem that held a single pale flower, upright like an alabaster vase. Nothing much grew in the sandy soil but it was sprayed to keep down the dust and the air was filled with a heavy, earthy smell.

Simon moved his chair noiselessly along the path with Guy beside him. They were both watching for a sight of Edwina but they reached the end of the gardens without meeting anyone.

Simon said in a strained voice: 'She hasn't come.'

'She will. She will.' Guy was confident she would. They turned back and mid-way between the garden gates found a seat where Guy could sit. He said it was four o'clock so she would probably come in on her way to the office. She would have to make a detour and cross by the bridge, all of which would take some time. An hour passed. The afternoon was changing to evening and Simon's expectations began to fail. He could not respond to Guy's talk and soon enough Guy, too, fell silent. They faced the opposite bank of the river where Kasr el Nil barracks stood, its red colour changing as the light changed until it was as dark as dried blood. The long, low building, so bug-ridden that only fire could disinfest it, was hazed by river mist and looked remote, a Victorian relic, a symbol of past glory.

Gazing across at it, Simon remembered his first days in Egypt, when Tobruk had fallen. Ordered to join his convoy at dawn, he had taken a taxi to the barracks, fearing that the other men would laugh at him for his extravagance. He soon realized that no one knew or cared how he got there. Hugo had been alive then. Now, with Hugo dead and Edwina uncaring, he looked back on those early days as a time of youth and innocence he would never know again.

He sighed and glanced at Guy who also seemed lost in some vision of the past. He said, perhaps unwisely: 'You loved her very much, didn't you?'

Surprised and startled by the question, Guy said: 'You mean Harriet? I suppose I did. Not that I've ever thought much about love. I've always had so many friends.' He stood up to end this sort of talk: 'You ought to be back at the hospital by now.'

When they reached the main gate, two people were descending from a taxi: Edwina and an army officer.

Looking round, seeing Simon in his chair, Edwina ran in through the gates, holding out her hands: 'Oh, Simon! Simon darling, I was so afraid we'd be too late.' She seized his hands and gazing warmly into his face, asked: 'How are you? Dear Simon, you're looking so much better!'

Simon, glancing over her shoulder, could see her companion was a major, an old fellow, thirty-five or more; much too old for Edwina. But the major had two good legs and he came strolling after her with a possessive smile, conveying to the world the fact that he and Edwina had spent the afternoon in intimate enjoyment.

He was introduced as Tony Brody, recently appointed to GHQ, Cairo – a tall, narrow-shouldered man with a regular face that was too fine to seem effectual. Edwina, her eyes brilliant, her voice halted by a slight gasp, seemed elated by her new conquest.

She kept saying: 'Oh dear, I'm sorry I'm late,' and even Simon could guess why she was late. He wanted to get away from her. Guy, meeting his appealing glance, said they had no time to talk. Simon was due back at Helwan. Cutting short Edwina's excited chatter, he helped Simon back into the waiting car and took him away from her.

Eight

Harriet had settled into a pension recommended by the waiter behind the café bar. It was called the Anemonie, a large, draughty building, dark inside and, in wet weather, very dark. It had a garden where a mulberry tree spread its crinoline of branches over a long table and half-a-dozen rickety chairs. The rain lay in pools on the table-top but Harriet could imagine the tourists sitting out to dine in the long, indolent twilights of peace-time summers.

The war had ended all that. The pension proprietors, Monsieur and Madame Vigo, were surprised when Harriet arrived at the door but they admitted her. They lived in an out-building and kept themselves to themselves, so Harriet had the whole pension to herself. Madame Vigo, who served her meals, spoke French and Arabic but she could make nothing of Harriet's anglicized French or her Egyptian Arabic.

Harriet knew the Vigos were curious about her and wondered what she was doing there, alone in Syria. Now that her escapade had lost impetus, she wondered herself.

The dining-room, where she ate alone, could have accommodated fifty or sixty guests. At night a single bulb was lit behind her seat and the large room stretched from her into total darkness. She would have been glad to have her meals with the Vigos but they maintained their privacy and were not relenting for Harriet's sake. The food, that was cooked by Monsieur Vigo, was served in a businesslike way by Madame Vigo who put the plates on the table and immediately made off.

After supper, Harriet would sit on at the table, afraid to go up to the bedroom floor where thirty or more empty rooms led off from a maze of corridors. Wherever she went, there was silence except for the creak of the boards beneath her feet.

She wondered how long she could bear to stay there? How

long, indeed, could she afford to stay there? And when she went, where would she go?

During the day, she walked about the streets or sheltered in doorways from the rain. The shopping area was much like that of any English town except for the Arabic signs. The real life of the place was in the covered souks. When the sun shone, she could see the Anti-Lebanon with its sheen of snow, but this was not often. It was winter, the rainy season, and most days a foggy greyness overhung the town. Harriet's suitcase was filled with light clothing intended to see her across the equator. Her winter clothing had been forwarded to the ship and she could imagine it going to England and lying unclaimed at Liverpool docks. She could not waste what money she had to buy more and so, conditioned to the heat of Egypt, she shivered like an indoor cat turned out in bad weather.

Wandering aimlessly beneath the sodden sky, she felt persecuted by the Abana, a river in flood, that would scatter out of sight into a drain only to reappear round the next corner, its rushing, splashing water enhancing the air's cold. She began to forget that she had been ill most of her time in Egypt and she longed for the sumptuous sunsets, the dazzling night sky, the moonlight that lay over the buildings like liquid silver. She remembered how the glare of Cairo produced mirages in the mind, so vivid they replaced reality, and she forgot the petrol fumes and the smell of the Cairo waste lots.

There were no mirages in Damascus. Instead, there was rain and she could escape that only by returning to the pension or by pushing her way through the crowds in the big main souk, the Souk el Tawill, the Street called Straight where Paul had lodged in his blindness. Here there were tribesmen, hillmen, businessmen in dark, western suits, peasants, donkey drovers and noise. She was astonished by the energy of the crowds and after a while, she realized her own energy was returning. The Syrian climate was restoring her to health. She felt she could walk for miles but wherever she went, she was on the outside of things, a female in a city where women were expected to stay indoors.

One morning she found the souk in a state of uproar. Something was about to happen. The roadway had been cleared and the crowd pressed back against the shops. The shopkeepers had pulled down their shutters and become spectators, straining their necks and bawling with the rest of them. Harriet, at the back of the crowd, stood on a piece of stone, remnant of a Roman arcade, and looked over the heads in front of her, eager to see what was to be seen. While she waited, she became aware that one man in the crowd was not looking expectantly down the souk but looking up at her. He wore a dark suit, like the businessmen, and was holding a flat, black case under one arm. He was a thin man with a thin, sallow face and a way of holding himself that denoted a self-conscious dignity. Catching her eye, he bowed slightly and she, tired of her own company, smiled and asked him: 'What are they all waiting for?'

'Ah!' He pushed his way towards her, speaking in a serious tone to make clear the honesty of his intentions: 'They are waiting for a political leader who is to drive this way.' He paused, bowed again and said: 'May I offer you my protection?'

'Good heavens, no,' she was amused: 'I don't need protection. I'm an Englishwoman.' Then, the noise becoming a hubbub, she looked for the political leader and saw him being driven slowly between the two rows of excited onlookers. He was standing up in the back of an old, open Ford, and, as the enthusiasm became frantic, he waved to right and left, grinning all over his fat, jolly face, seeming to love everyone and being loved in return. His followers screamed and applauded and, drawing revolvers from waistbands, fired up at the tin roof of the souk. There was a frenzy of gunfire and pinging metal and Harriet felt she had been unwise in refusing any protection she could get. She looked to where the sallow man had stood, holding his black case, but he was no longer there and she feared her answer had driven him away.

As the Ford passed, the crowd pressed after it and Harriet could safely get down from the stone and walk back to her solitary meal in the pension. If she had replied to the man in a more encouraging fashion, she might have made a friend. But did she want a friend who looked like that? She liked large, comfortable men. She wanted a large, comfortable man as friend and companion, like Guy but without his intolerable gregariousness. If Guy were with her, he would not be a companion. Nothing would get him into the Ummayad Mosque or the El Azem Palace. She had spent too much time bored by left-wing casuists; she thought marriage with Guy had been hopeless from the start. They had never enjoyed the same things.

But without Guy, she was not enjoying herself very much. And her money would not last long. Having paid for her first week at the pension, she realized she would soon be in need of help. And where could she find it? The only person to whom she could turn was the British consul and he would advise her to go back to her husband. She thought: 'What a fool I've been! If I'd gone on the evacuation ship, my whole life would have changed. In England, I would have been among my own people. I would have found work. I would have had all the friends I wanted.'

A few evenings later, coming down to supper, she heard voices in the dining-room. Several more lights had been switched on and three people – a man and two women – were sitting at the table next to hers. The man was talking as she took her seat and went on talking, though he gave her a covert stare, then broke in on himself to say: 'You were wrong. We aren't alone here. There's this young lady: black hair, oval face, clear, pale skin – Persian, I'd guess!'

Harriet did not blink. His words having no effect on her, he returned his attention to his two companions and talked on in an accent that at times was Irish and at other times American. He was large but Harriet would not have called him comfortable. The women seemed insignificant beside him. His milky colouring and heavy features produced the impression of a Roman bust placed on top of a modern suit. It was a talking bust. Served with pilaff, he forked the food into his mouth and gulped it as though it were an impediment to be got out of the way. The pilaff finished, he threw aside his fork and gestured, shooting his big, white hands out of his sleeves and waving them about as he discoursed on the origins and cultures of the people of the eastern Mediterranean. The two women gave him so little attention they might have been deaf but Harriet, having been cut off from conversation for a week, listened intently.

'Now, take the Turks and Tartars of the Dobrudja,' he said. 'And the Gagaoules – Mohammedans coverted to Christianity and then converted back to Mohammedanism! They speak a language unknown anywhere else in the world.'

At this statement, Harriet could not help catching her breath and the man instantly swung round. Pointing his fork at her, he said: 'Our Persian lady is asking herself what on earth we're talking about.'

Harriet laughed: 'No, I'm not. I know what you're talking about. I used to live in Rumania.'

'Hey, d'ya hear that?' he gawped at the women: 'The Persian lady speaks English.'

'I am English.'

'Well, what d'ya know!' He stared at Harriet then told the two women: 'She's not Persian after all.' Quite unaffected by this revelation, the women went on with their meal.

Harriet said: 'May I ask what you are? Irish or American?'

'I'm neither. I'm both. I'm an Italian who's lived both in Dublin and in the States. I acquired an Eire passport because I thought it was the answer to life in these troubled times, but it's been a goddam bother to us. No one in the occupied countries will believe that Eire isn't part of England and as much at war as you are. To tell you the truth, we've stopped trying to stay in Europe. It's too much trouble. So we've shaken the dust and here we are monkeying around the Levant gathering material for my book. You've probably heard of me: Beltado, Dr Beltado, authority on ancient cultures. And this here's m'wife, Dr Maryann Jolly, another authority, and this is our assistant, Miss Dora O'Day.'

Dr Beltado looked at Dr Jolly and Miss Dora as though expecting them to carry on from there, but neither showed any interest in Harriet.

Dr Beltado spoke to cover their silence: 'You are called . . .?'

Harriet said: 'Harriet.' Dr Beltado again referred to his wife but she remained unmoved. She was a small, withered woman and, Harriet now saw, not to be disregarded, and Miss Dora, physically like her, was her handmaiden. Together they owned the large, flamboyant Dr Beltado. They might ignore him, they might even despise him, but no one else was going to get him. Harriet need not try to enter the group.

Having no wish to compete for Dr Beltado's attention, Harriet looked away from him and pretended not to hear when he directed remarks towards her. Their meal finished, Dr Beltado

433

asked Madame Vigo for Turkish coffee and he and Dr Jolly lit Turkish cigarettes. The warm, biscuity smell of the smoke drifted towards Harriet like an enticement and Dr Beltado said: 'How about coffee for the Persian lady?' Harriet did not reply. She would remain apart but in her mind was the thought: 'In one minute, Guy would have had them eating out of his hand.'

The dining-room door opened a crack and someone looked in. Beltado said under his breath: 'Here's that guy Halal.' There was no welcome in his tone but lifting his voice, he shouted: 'Hi, there, Halal, nice to see ya. Come right in.'

Glancing up through her eyelashes, Harriet saw that Halal was the man who had offered his protection in the souk. He gave her a swift look and she suspected she was the reason for his visit, but he went directly to Beltado's table and, bowing, said: 'Good evening, Dr Jolly and Miss Dora. Good evening, Dr Beltado. Jamil has asked me to deliver an invitation. This evening he has a party and would ask you to his house.'

'Is that so?' Dr Beltado beamed and was about to accept when Dr Jolly's thin, dry voice stopped him: 'No, Beltado, we are all too tired.' She lifted her eyes to Halal: 'No. We have spent the day driving from Alexandretta.'

Dr Beltado began: 'Perhaps if we just looked in to say "hello" . . .' but Dr Jolly interrupted more firmly: 'No, Beltado.'

Beltado shrugged his acquiescence then, as though not wishing to waste the occasion, pointed to Harriet: 'Why not take Mrs Harriet! Believe it or not, she's English.'

'I am aware of that.' Halal looked towards Harriet and bowed. A slight smile came on his face as he remembered her avowal in the souk: 'If she would care to come, she would be made most welcome.'

'Thank you, but I'm just going to bed.'

'Bed! At nine o'clock, a young thing like you!' Beltado waved her away: 'Go and enjoy yourself. See one of the big Arab houses. It will be an experience.'

Yes, an experience! Knowing it would be faint-hearted to refuse, Harriet smiled on Halal and said: 'Thank you, I will come.'

'That's right,' said Beltado approvingly and as she passed him, he patted her just above the buttocks as though encouraging her towards an assignation.

A large car stood outside the pension gate. 'I suppose this is Dr Beltado's?'

'Certainly, yes. Few own such cars in Syria.'

'Do you know him well?'

'No, I cannot say well. He has been here twice before, working on his book.'

'The book about comparative cultures? He seems to have been working on it a long time.'

'Yes, a long time.' Halal spoke respectfully and there was an interval of silence before he next said: 'Mrs Harriet, you were displeased, were you not, when I offered my protection. I meant no discourtesy. I am myself a Christian and I know that among Moslems one must be circumspect.'

'Was I not circumspect? You mean my standing up on the stone? I'm sorry if I sounded ungrateful.'

'No, not much ungrateful. It is only, I would not wish to be misunderstood. Now, let me tell you where we are going. We are going to a khan. Do you know what a khan is? No? It is a private souk owned all by one man. This one is owned by Jamil's father who rents out the shops and is very rich. Jamil is my friend. He is very handsome because his grandmother was a Circassian. He tells me his wife, too, is very handsome but, of course, I have not seen her. They are Moslems. Yes, Jamil, a Moslem, was my great friend at Beirut. We went together to the American University so, you see, you will be with an advanced circle.'

'Is it so remarkable for a Moslem and a Christian to be friends?'

'Here, yes, it is remarkable. In the past the Christians suffered much persecution and hid their houses behind high walls. But Jamil and I are advanced. We mix together as our parents would not dream of doing.'

'I look forward to meeting him.'

'Yes, you will like him. He is a superior person. I am fortunate in knowing him.'

Halal spoke modestly but Harriet understood that, as proved by his association with Jamil, Halal, too, was a superior person.

Glancing aside at him, seeing he still carried his black leather case, Harriet asked him: 'What did you study at the university?'

'I studied law.'

'So you are a lawyer? You work in an office?'

'I am a lawyer but I do not work in an office. My father owns a silk factory and I conduct his legal affairs. That gives me more time than working in an office.'

They had reached the Souk el Tawill, deserted now and half-lit, at the end of which was the khan, walled and protected by decorated iron gates. Halal pulled a bell-rope, a shutter was opened and an ancient eye observed them before the gates were opened. Inside, a spacious quadrangle, under a domed roof, was lit by glass oil-lamps.

'See, is it not fine?' Halal pointed to the tessellated floor and the Moorish balcony that ran above the locked shops: 'If it were summer, Jamil would entertain out here, but now too cold.'

Halal was so eager for Harriet to appreciate the splendours of the khan that he kept her for several minutes in the cold before taking her to a door in the farther wall. Passing through a court-yard, they entered the family house. In the reception room, a plump young man came bounding towards them with outstretch-ed arms: 'Ha, ha, so you found the lady, eh?'

Halal said reprovingly: 'I went as you requested to invite Dr Beltado . . .'

'Who could not come but sent this lady instead? That is good. See,' Jamil shouted joyfully to the other men in the room, 'we have a young lady.'

Jamil was a much more ebullient character than Halal. He had the rounded, rose-pink cheeks and light colouring of the Circassians and an air of genial self-indulgence. He took Harriet like a prize round the room. The guests, all men, were Moslems, Christians and Jews.

'A mixed lot, are we not?' Jamil asked, taking a particular pride in the presence of the Jews whom he introduced simply as Ephraim and Solomon. Before Harriet could speak to them, she was hurried over to a large central table where there was food enough to feed a multitude.

Jamil tried to persuade her to take some pressed meats or cakes or sweets but she had already had supper.

'Then you must drink,' he said.

There were jugs of lime juice and bottles of Cyprus brandy, Palestine vodka, wines and liqueurs.

Harriet took lime juice and Halal, under pressure, accepted a small brandy but protested: 'Why, Jamil, are you drinking nothing? You are not so abstemious when you come to visit me.'

'Shush, shush!' Jamil, giggling wildly, covered his face with his plump hands. 'Do not speak of such things. I know I can be a little devilish at times, but in my own house I consider the servants. If they saw me drink brandy, I could never lift my head among my people.'

The men crowded around Harriet, treating her with ostentatious courtesy so all might see how enlightened was their attitude towards the female sex.

Conducted to a place of honour on the main divan, she unwisely asked: 'Is your wife not coming to the party?'

Jamil, disconcerted, said: 'I think not. She is a little shy, you understand! But if you will come to meet her, she would be very much honoured.'

Harriet would have preferred to stay with her group of admiring men but Jamil, taking for granted that a woman would prefer to be with women, helped her to her feet and led her through a passage to another large room where she was left to sit while Jamil found his wife. The room was empty except for a number of small gilt chairs closely ranged round the walls.

Jamil returned. 'This is Farah,' he said and hurried back to his friends.

Farah was not, as Halal said, very handsome but she looked amiable and was very richly dressed. As she spoke little English and could not understand Harriet's Arabic, she could say nothing at first. The two women sat side by side on the gilt chairs and smiled at each other. After some minutes, Farah touched Harriet's skirt and gave a long, lilting, 'Oo-oo-oo-oo,' of admiration. Harriet, with more reason, returned admiration for Farah's kaftan of turquoise silk encrusted with gold. Even if too shy to attend the party, she seemed to be dressed for it.

A servant brought in Turkish coffee and dishes of silver-coated sugared almonds. They drank coffee, still marooned in smiling silence. Several more minutes passed, then Farah, gesturing gracefully in the direction of the Anti-Lebanon, said: 'Snow.'

Harriet nodded: 'Yes, snow.'

'In England snow every day?'

'Not every day, no.'

Farah regretfully shook her head and sighed.

When an hour, or what seemed like an hour, had passed, Harriet rose to say 'Goodbye'. Farah gave a moan of disappointment, then smiled bravely and went with Harriet to the door of the room. There she held out her hand and said slowly: 'Please come again.'

The party was over when Harriet returned to the reception room. Halal, waiting for her, stood with Jamil beside the table where the food and drink had hardly been touched.

Jamil, escorting his last guests across the khan to the gate, insisted that Harriet must return 'many times'. 'It is a great treat for my wife to talk with an English lady.'

'I'm afraid we could not talk much. We have no common guage.'

'What does that matter? Ladies do not need language. They look at each other and they understand.'

Walking back through the souk, Halal eagerly asked: 'Was she beautiful, Halal's wife?'

Harriet replied: 'She was very nice' and Halal was satisfied.

Reaching the lane that led to the pension, Halal stopped and said: 'I wish to show you something' and led her to a cul-de-sac at the side of the souk: 'Come. Look in here.'

Harriet peered into an area of darkness that might have been the interior of a great cathedral. There was light only in one corner where three Arabs sat with their camels round a charcoal brazier.

'What is it?' she asked.

'The greatest caravanserai in the world. Once, at this time of night, it would have been filled with camel trains settled in round their fires, all eating, all talking, then lying down to sleep. Here every route converged and it was called the Hub of the World. But now, you see: only the one small caravan, and soon no more. Perhaps that is the last to come here. It is sad, is it not?'

'Yes.' Harriet gazed into the vast darkness with its one corner of light and felt the sadness of things passing.

438

Halal said: 'Mohammed must have slept on this ground many times. His caravan went from Mecca to Aqaba and back to Mecca. When he conquered Damascus, he called it Bab Allah, the Gate of God, because from here the road runs straight to Mecca.'

'No doubt you have seen many things in Damascus?' Halal asked as they went towards the pension. When Harriet had to admit that as a woman and alone, she had been nervous of entering the Moslem sites, he said: 'If you would permit, I could be your escort. There is, I assure you, much to see.'

Harriet, not wanting to encourage Halal, said: 'Thank you,' and was glad that a distant burst of rifle fire interrupted him when he started to speak again.

'What are these demonstrations about?'

'Oh, it is just doleur. Food is scarce, prices keep rising and they blame the military, the Free French or the British. They do not harm. It is nothing to worry you. But, Mrs Harriet, you have not said "Yes" or "No". So tell me, may I call tomorrow and take you to see the Azem palace?'

'Well, not tomorrow. Perhaps another day.' Harriet knew she should be thankful for his company but leaving him, she hoped he would understand that that 'another day' was meant as a refusal.

Nine

Ross was the first to tell Simon that he would be transferred to the 15th Scottish hospital.

'But why?'

'Can't say, sir. Not exactly. I believe they've got a rehabilitation unit there where you'll get proper treatment.'

Simon, heartsick over Edwina's defection, felt this move was another blow. He was so despondent that Ross tried to coax him into a better humour: 'You wouldn't want to stay here for ever, now, would you, sir?'

'No, but I don't want to go anywhere else. I want to stay with the people I know. I thought they'd keep me here till I was back on my feet.'

Of the people he knew – the doctor, the sister, the nurses – Ross was the one who meant most to him. Ross had become a friend, more than a friend. He was like a faithful lover whom he might hope to keep about him for the foreseeable future. Now, for no reasonable reason, he would be taken from him, not by enemy action, against which there were no arguments, but on the orders of some administrator who had never seen Simon or Ross, and cared nothing for either of them.

But it was not only the separation from Ross that vexed him. Here, in his small area of Plegics, he was an important patient. The doctor, nurses and Ross were all concerned for his recovery and so closely related to his needs, emotions, fears and uncertainties, they were like members of his own family. To break with them would cause him anguish.

Simon took his appeal to the doctor: 'Surely, sir, I could stay till I'm better? It shouldn't take long.'

The doctor agreed that Simon was 'on the mend'. He could now get around on crutches. 'But when you can walk without them, I just cannot say. You need exercises and there's a proper unit at the 15th Scottish. There you'll get better faster, you wait and see.'

Simon's next appeal was to the sister who was brisker and blunter than Ross or the doctor: 'You've got to go, young man. We need your bed. This is a New Zealand hospital and we must put our own lads first. We've had a signal warning us to prepare for casualties. Our lads have taken a beating on the Mareth Line and they'll be coming in soon from the dressing-stations. So, there's nothing for it. We have to accommodate them.'

'The Mareth Line? Where is it? I've never heard of it.'

'Somewhere in Tunisia. That's where the Kiwis are now.'

Simon had to realize that while he had been lying there disabled, the fighting had moved a long way west. He felt resentful that he had been left behind and he was eager to be back in the desert. He asked Ross: 'How long before I'm fit again for active service?'

'That depends, sir. It's what the doc said. The thing you need now is exercise. If you keep at it, you'll be fit sooner than you think.'

Simon still hoped that the move, if it must come, would be delayed so he was shocked when Ross told him the ambulance was waiting for him. Sitting on the edge of the bed, he put on his clothes and fitted his few possessions into the box that held his dress uniform. Then he swung himself on to his crutches and made his way out of Plegics. The other men, though his officer status had kept him separate from them, said goodbye to him. One even said: 'Sorry to see you go, sir.'

Simon could only nod, too affected to speak.

The ambulance men helped him up the steps and sat him on a bunk. There, looking out at Ross, he said: 'You'll come and see me, won't you, Ross?'

'You bet, sir.' Ross smiled and saluted, then turned away. He did not look back as the ambulance was started up. Instinctively, Simon knew that Ross had finished with him. The physio had other work to do. New patients were due and there would be another special case in Simon's cubicle. So far as Ross was concerned, Simon had ceased to exist.

The 15th Scottish was bigger and better equipped than the New Zealand hutments but Simon disliked it from the start. The place seemed to him impersonal. The new team attendant on him had no great interest in him. They had had no part in his recovery. To them he was merely another wounded man half-way to health.

As the hospital was only a tram-ride from the Institute, Guy could visit Simon more often now. He found him peevish and resentful of his changed life. He was passing through a difficult stage of convalescence when he was expected to do more for himself and make an effort to adjust to the normal world. He longed for Ross to take responsibility for him and knowing he would never see Ross again, he turned to Guy, looking to him as to a much older man on whom he could lean. Guy could not have this. Simon had to face his own independence and his own future. He had too much time in which to feel sorry for himself and Guy urged him to spend it in study of some sort.

'What was your job before you were called up?'

'I didn't have a job. I'd just left school when the war started. My dad was keen for me to become a teacher. I was entered for a teachers' training college but I never got there.'

Guy said: 'Splendid!' He would have encouraged Simon to prepare for any profession but none seemed to him as worthy as teaching. He said with enthusiasm: 'I'll apply for the preliminary examination papers and you can begin work here and now. What were your best subjects at school?'

Simon shook his head vaguely: 'I was all right at some things, I think.' Looking back at his last days in the sixth form, he could remember only the excitement of waiting for the war to break out. He had excelled in the officers' training course and he had come to see warfare as his natural occupation.

He said: 'I was never keen on mugging up school books. I liked games. I liked the OTC.'

'Well, now's your chance to train your mind. There's a well-stocked library at the Institute and I've a collection of books on teaching methods. I'll give you all the help I can.'

'What's the point?' Simon was dismayed by Guy's plans for his further education: 'It may be years before I'm demobbed. I'd forget everything I'd learnt. It would just be a waste of time.'

'Learning is never a waste of time. Even if the war does drag

442

on, you should keep your mind active so when you return to civilian life . . .'

'But I don't want to return to civilian life. The army's my life. All I want now is to get back into the fight. Out there no one thinks of the future because, well, there may not be any future.'

Guy argued but all Simon would say was: 'Let's leave it, Guy. Just now I've got to concentrate on getting better.'

And he was getting better, but not as fast as his new physio wished. Though he now had every sort of exercising device, his feet would not support him on the floor. The physio, Greening, had him fitted with callipers and ordered him to take his hands off the parallel bars. The result was he toppled forward and struck his chest on a bar. Greening, barely suppressing his anger, knelt down and savagely pulled Simon's feet forward, one after the other, requiring him to place them firmly on the ground.

Simon was out of sympathy with Greening who had been a sergeant drill-instructor in the regular army. Middle-aged, more experienced than Ross, he had a habit of command rather than persuasion. He was irascible, even brutal, and had little patience.

'It's up to you,' he told Simon: 'You've got to work at it.'

As Simon strained to keep himself upright, his hands would return to the bars and Greening would bawl: 'Take your hand off.' His face distorted with the effort, Simon managed at last to shift his right foot forward but the left refused to follow.

Greening, relenting, said more amicably: 'All you have to do is forget you can't do it. You can feel your feet, can't you?'

'Yes, I know they're there but they're sort of ghostly.'

'Well, you think of them as solid flesh and blood, and tell them to get on with it.'

That night he again had the dream of running across fields unbroken except for some giant trees that rose out of the ground and quivered in front of him. As he ran, he could see the flash of his feet but not the feet themselves. Suddenly fearful, he slowed down to look and seeing them there, solid flesh and blood, he sped on in sheer delight of being whole again. He shouted out and waking himself, realizing his condition, he gave a cry that brought the night nurse running to him.

Now that he was regaining energy, he was bored by the claustrophobic routine of hospital life. Details of his time in the desert came back to him and he felt an intense nostalgia for events that had once meant nothing to him: brewing-up, making a fire of scrubwood between stones, boiling the brew can and throwing tea in by the handful; the whiplash crack of bursting shells, even the sandstorms and the pre-dawn awakening.

When Guy again tried to interest him in a teaching course, he said: 'I know teaching's fine. My dad thought the same, but it's not for me. I want to be with the chaps. I'd like to join a regiment stationed somewhere like India or Cyprus. I want to see the world.'

'But you'll want to settle down later. You'll want to marry and have a home of your own.'

'Later, perhaps.' Simon had not told Guy that he was already married because that marriage did not count, but another thought came into his head and he said as lightly as he could: 'How's Edwina? Is she still seeing Major Brody?'

'I expect so but she'll soon get tired of him.'

'Really? You think so?'

'Oh, yes. Edwina aspires towards a title. She's looking for another Lord Lisdoonvarna.'

Simon laughed. He did not consider that Edwina's aspirations lessened his own chances but was happy to think that Major Brody would soon be out of the way.

Guy sometimes asked Greening about Simon's progress and discussed what could be done to hasten his recovery. Greening said he intended trying electrotherapy and thought it a pity there was no swimming-pool at the hospital. Hydrotherapy often proved useful in these cases.

Giving this some thought, Guy decided to take Simon to the Gezira pool, a place he would not visit on his own. Having grown up far from the coast, he could not swim and saw water as an unreliable element. He had first thought of taking Simon to Alexandria but realized the dangers of the open sea. He applied to the Gezira Club for temporary membership and when this was granted, he thought all difficulties were at an end.

Intending to surprise Simon, Guy did not say where they were going. The winter was petering out and the afternoons were very warm. When they reached the club garden, a sound of laughter and splashing came from the pool and Simon looked alarmed.

'We're not going in there, are we?'

'Yes. We'll probably see Edwina. She's always in the pool.'

Simon left the car unwillingly and self-conscious on his crutches, let himself be led inside the enclosure. As he feared, the pool was full of girls and able-bodied men and he would, if he could, have fled, but Guy wanted him to be there and saying nothing, he sank into the deck-chair that Guy placed for him.

Guy had imagined that the sight of Simon would arouse sympathy and there would be willing helpers to induce him into the water, but those who noticed the disabled man seemed discomforted and embarrassed by his presence. And Guy realized he had not thought the plan through. Before he could swim, Simon had to undress. Bathing trunks and towels would have to be found for him and he would need a clear stretch of water in which to try and propel himself. As it was, there were not two square feet of it free of bodies.

Sitting beside Simon, Guy said: 'Later, when they've gone into tea, there'll be more room for you . . .'

Realizing what was intended, Simon said fiercely: 'Good heavens, I'm not going in there.'

'But some of them will help you.'

'I don't want their help. I'd only be a nuisance among that crowd.'

That, Guy feared, was true. Simon, gazing with sombre fixity at the merriment in the water, twitched as though in pain. Guy, following his gaze, saw that Edwina had appeared on the diving-board. In a white bathing-dress, her hair caught up in a white cap formed of rubber petals, she stood, a tall, golden girl, poised to dive. Tony Brody was clearing a space in the water, officiously asserting his claim on her. She dived, came up, saw Guy and swam across to him: 'Hello. I haven't seen you here before.'

'I've never been before. I brought Simon for an airing.'

'*What* a good idea!' Edwina, startled to see Simon with his crutches, said: 'Oh Simon, how well you look!'

Simon knew that was not true. Thin and pallid from his days in bed, he was also exhausted by his efforts under Greening. He blushed, hung his head and did not reply.

Edwina cajoled him: 'It's great fun here, isn't it?'

Guy began to say: 'Can't you persuade him to join in?' But Edwina, whether she heard or not, pushed off from the side and went to join Brody who was waiting for her, a medicine ball held above his head. She jumped up to seize it and they scuffled together, churning the water and shrieking in their excitement.

Simon watched so intently he did not hear when Guy spoke to him.

'Shall we go?'

Simon, becoming aware of the question, shook his head. Miserable though he was, he could not leave while Edwina was there, and so they sat until the sun began its descent towards the west. Near them lay one of the young women known to officers as 'Gezira lovelies'. Plump, round-faced, not pretty but with a bloomy look, she stretched and roused herself as a safragi came to serve her with iced coffee.

To Guy, the whole idle, sensual, self-indulgent ambience of the pool was unbearably boring. Had it not been for Simon, nothing would have kept him there, and as the afternoon advanced, he felt he could tolerate no more of it.

'I'll have to take you back. I'm due at a staff meeting at five.'

In the car, fearing he had cut short Simon's pleasure, Guy said: 'We'll come again another day.'

'No, thank you. I don't want to go there again.'

'I expect you felt as I did: messing about there is just a waste of time?'

Simon was surprised: 'No, I didn't think that. I felt envious. I longed to be like them.'

Guy was surprised but said to encourage him: 'You will be, soon enough. It's only a question of time.'

'That's what they all say,' Simon said bitterly, thinking of the time he had lost, the time that had been taken from him.

Ten

A few days after the party at the khan, Halal turned up at the pension with a taxi. The inmates of the pension were still at breakfast and Beltado, seeing Halal making his shadowy, uncertain way into the room, began: 'Hi, there, Halal!' then realized the visitor was not for him. Watching Halal, his case under his arm, moving warily towards Harriet, Beltado smiled a salacious smile.

'Mrs Harriet, may I sit down?'

'Yes, but my name is not Mrs Harriet. I am a married woman. My husband is called Guy Pringle.'

'Ah, I understand – so you are Mrs Pringle. I have come to ask if you would care to make a visit to some place of interest? The big mosque, or the castle, perhaps? I can tell you about them. I would be your guide.'

Unable to think of a reason for refusing, Harriet said: 'I would like to see the mosque.' As she left the pension in Halal's company, she heard Beltado chuckling with satisfaction.

In the taxi, Halal said: 'I have made bold to hire this driver for a week in the hope we may make many excursions together.' After a pause, he added: 'So your husband is in this part of the world? Where, may I ask?'

'He is in Cairo.'

'So! I presume you are here for a short holiday only? Tell me, Mrs Pringle how long are you planning to stay in our city?'

'I suppose till my money runs out.'

Taking this for a joke, Halal made a slight, choking noise intended for a laugh: 'Then I may hope you will be here a long time.'

Harriet laughed, too, but she knew he felt there was something odd about her presence in Syria though he had not the courage to ask what it was.

447

The taxi stopped at the mosque and Halal announced: 'We are now outside the great mosque of the Ummayad.'

An attendant, lolling half asleep on a bench, leapt into life as he saw Harriet and, reaching into a closet, brought out a black robe which he held out to her.

Halal said: 'I fear you must wear this. He says to put the hood over your head so it hides your face.'

Disliking the robe, which was dusty and not over-clean, Harriet asked: 'Why must I wear it?'

'I'm sorry but they fear a lady will distract the men from their devotions. The men have, you understand, strong desires.'

'You mean they are frustrated. Tell him that you can't make men chaste by keeping women out of sight.'

Halal stared at her, disconcerted, then smiled, not knowing what else to do: 'You are an unusual lady, Mrs Pringle. Very unusual. You think for yourself.'

'Where I come from that's not unusual.' Harriet shook the robe and laughed: 'This is ridiculous but if I must, I must.' She adjusted it about her, trying to give it some dignity, then started to walk away. The keeper croaked a protest and pointed to her shoes. Halal said:

'Ah, I forgot. We must enter barefoot.'

'In Cairo they give you felt slippers to put over your shoes.'

'Here they are more strict.'

At last they were admitted to the spacious, sunlit courtyard where the marble flooring was cold beneath their feet. They paused under the porticos to admire the mosaics.

'See, they are very old, very beautiful,' Halal said, as though Harriet might not be aware of these facts: 'You must understand, the cities they portray are not real. The buildings, the forests, all are fanciful. You will observe that there is no human figure, no animal, no creature that could be mistaken as an object of worship.'

'Because of the ancient Egyptians, I suppose?'

'I suppose, yes. You can hit the nail very nicely, Mrs Pringle.' Halal smiled again, more warmly, beginning to approve Harriet's habit of independent thought. 'Now we enter the mosque proper.'

The vast interior hall, lit only by the glow from stained-glass windows, was in semi-darkness so Harriet had no clear view of the men whose devotions were to be protected against a female form. A few were at prayer but most of them seemed to treat the mosque as a social centre. They sat on the floor in groups, talking and slipping their amber chaplets through their fingers.

'Do the women ever come here?'

'Oh, yes,' Halal pointed to a heavy curtain stretched across a corner: 'They may sit behind there.'

Harriet was glad to have an escort. No one gave her curious looks or nudged against her or stared into her face with bold, provocative eyes. She was hidden, the concern only of her protector who was probably mistaken for her husband. Halal, for his part, held himself with an air of importance. As guide, he was almost too knowledgeable. Harriet became weary, standing about while he talked. He required her to 'give attention' to the lamps of which there had once been six hundred, each hanging from a golden chain. He started to count them but on reaching a hundred, gave up, saying apologetically, 'Many have been plundered, I fear. At times there has been much destruction, massacres and such things, and the mosque is very old. It was first a Greek temple – the temple of Rimmon spoken of in the Bible – then a Christian church, and now a mosque. They have beneath this floor a precious relic: the head of John the Baptist.'

'I'd like to see that.'

'I, too, but it is put away, I think because of the war. Still, there is another relic. Very interesting. Follow me.'

They came to an ancient doorway, the main doorway of the early Christian church. Halal stretched out his right arm: 'Behold what is written above! Can you read it?'

'No. I never learnt ancient Greek.'

'Then, I will translate for you.' Holding himself stiffly, his black case under his arm, he proclaimed with reverence: 'Thy kingdom, O Christ, is an everlasting Kingdom and thy dominion endureth through all generations.' He relaxed and smiled on her: 'That was true in the fourth century and still true, is it not?'

'Why do you think Christ let the Moslems take over?'

Halal thought it best to evade this question: 'We must not question the will of God. Now we will visit the old castle.'

Taken for a walk round the castle walls, Harriet was surprised by her own energy. She was recovering what she had lost in

Egypt: the will to exert herself. When Halal proposed 'a little drive into the Ghuta' next day, she said: 'That sounds pleasant.'

'It is pleasant,' Halal earnestly told her: 'The Ghuta is the Garden – the Garden of Damascus. You will come, then, Mrs Pringle? Good! I will call for you.'

That evening Dr Beltado leant towards her to say with a conniving smile: 'I see you have made a conquest.' Knowing he suspected a liaison had started, she was discomforted, chiefly because Halal had no attraction for her. She decided that the outing to the Ghuta must be their last.

The next day Harriet wished she had rejected it. The sky was overcast and the suburban greenery, heavy with the night's rain, seemed to her oppressive. She had become conditioned to desert, the nakedness of the earth, and the orchards and market gardens worried her. Anything might be hidden among their massed, lush leaves.

'We owe all this,' Halal complacently said, 'to our great rivers that in the Bible are called Abana and Pharphar.'

'The ones that couldn't cure Naaman?'

'Ah, I could take you to the house of Naaman. It is now a leper colony.'

'No thank you.'

Halal smiled but, discouraged by her manner, kept silent until they were beyond the town and driving into the grassy slopes of the Anti-Lebanon. The sun broke through, the mists cleared and the green about them became translucent. Harriet, now more appreciative of Halal's hospitality, said: 'It is beautiful here.'

'Yes, yes,' Halal became eagerly talkative again: 'And now we come to a very nice café from where we can see Damascus encircled by gardens as the moon by its halo.'

Harriet laughed: 'You're quite a poet, Halal.'

'Alas, it was not me but another that wrote that deathless tribute to our city.'

The café, a white clap-board bungalow, was hung on the hillside, its terrace built out over the slope below. Three young men, one with a guitar, were seated on the terrace and called to Halal as he passed them: 'You're out early Halal,' and they looked, not at Halal, but at Harriet.

Halal gave them a cold 'Good morning' and led Harriet to the rail so she might see rising above the 'halo' of foliage, the battlements of the castle and the gold-tipped domes and minarets of the Ummayad mosque.

'Mohammed was right, was he not? This is paradise. Some say it was indeed the Garden of Eden.'

When Harriet did not speak, he asked, 'Could you live your life in this place?'

'Yes, if I had to. I feel well here.'

'That is good. And now observe,' Halal pointed towards the minarets: 'See the very tall one? There Christ will alight on the Day of Judgement.'

'Christ? Not Mohammed?'

'No, not Mohammed. Mohammed will return to the rock in Jerusalem from which he leapt up to Heaven. It is in the Mosque of Omar and still bears the mark of his horse's hoof.'

Behind them, the young man with the guitar had started to strum a popular Arabic song. He sang quietly: 'Who is Romeo? Who is Julietta?' Harriet noticed two tortoises crawling near her feet and as she bent towards them, she caught the eye of the guitarist who gave her a sly, sidelong glance and smirked. So the song was directed at her.

Halal, seeing her attention diverted, frowned and spoke to regain it: 'The spring is already here! The anemones are coming out.'

Looking down at the grass, Harriet saw that a few buds were breaking and one, more sheltered than the rest, was opening, a gleam of scarlet.

'In summer, when the evenings are long, we walk by the river and many young men bring musical instruments. Such things are common here.'

Before Halal could instruct her further, a waiter called to him and he led her to a table set with cakes and coffee: 'I took the precaution of ordering by telephone so there would be no delay.'

The young men put their heads together in wonder at this precaution. Halal, becoming more confident, asked boldly: 'May I ask you, Mrs Pringle, why you came here alone to Damascus?'

Ready now for this question, Harriet said: 'Because I was ill in

Cairo. The climate did not agree with me. I developed amoebic dysentery and was advised to come here to regain my health.'

'Ah, I understand. And your husband could not come with you?'

'No, his work kept him in Egypt.'

'So you will stay till you are restored, is that it?'

'I will if I can but, to tell you the truth, I need to earn some money.'

'You need to earn money? E-e-e-e-e!' Halal made a noise that expressed his astonishment. 'But that is very difficult for an English lady. And yet it might be possible. I may have an idea.'

'Really?'

'We will say no more. I would not raise false hopes.'

Driving back into the city, Halal stopped the taxi and said to Harriet: 'Let us take a little stroll. There is something that may please you.'

The stroll, up a lane between the backs of houses, ended at the gate of a graveyard. The graves were so old, the stones had sunk almost out of sight but in the centre there was a prominent tomb, an oblong protected by iron railings. A rambler rose, just coming into leaf, sprawled over the rails and covered the tomb's upper surface. Halal crossed to it and put his hand affectionately on the stone.

'This is a Christian graveyard and this is the burial place of Al-Akhtal, a poet and a wild fellow. Because he was a Christian, he was free to drink wine and he loved to go with singing slave girls. These things inspired him and he wrote about them.' Halal tittered: 'It was very shocking, of course, but perhaps enjoyable. What do you think?'

'It sounds very innocent to me.'

'Indeed?' Halal looked pleasurably surprised: 'That, I agree, is how we should see it but most people here are not very advanced.' He smiled and lifted his eyes to the sky: 'There is the new moon. Do you know what the Moslems call it? The prophet's eyebrow.'

The moon was brilliant, a sliver of crystal in the green of the evening sky. Halal, lowering his gaze to her, said solemnly: 'You know, Mrs Pringle, you are like the new moon.'

'Meaning I'm thin and pale?'

'Meaning you are very delicate. When I saw you in the souk, I thought, "She is so delicate, these ruffians will sweep her away." Yet, though you are delicate, you shimmer like the moon. You are, if you will permit me to say it, the wife I wish I had.'

'Oh dear! Surely there are a great many ladies in Damascus who would do as well?'

'Yes, there are ladies here, very nice but very simple. For myself, I like them less nice and more intelligent. Tell me, will you come tomorrow and see the ravine through which the Abana flows?'

Harriet replied firmly: 'No. You have been very kind to me, Halal, but I cannot go out with you again. People will misunderstand.'

Halal's face lengthened with an expression of tragic melancholy and he slowly shook his head: 'It is true, they observe and do not understand. And I know, you are afraid of your husband. Gossip will reach him and he will be angry.'

Harriet laughed at the idea of Guy's anger. 'Nothing like that,' she assured Halal but he knew better.

'Believe me,' he said: 'I respect your prudence.'

Harriet laughed again but left it like that. Before they parted, she asked him: 'Please tell me, Halal, what do you keep in your black case?'

He gravely answered: 'My diplomas.'

As the days passed without Halal, Harriet wished she had not given him such a definite dismissal. Almost any company was better than none. In her solitude, it seemed to her that Dr Belta-do was ignoring her, perhaps in disapproval of her separation from Halal. The women, once she had an escort of her own, had relented somewhat and had even given her a glance or two. Now all three seemed determined to stress her loneliness. But perhaps she imagined this for one evening Dr Beltado, his coffee cup in his hand, came over and sat in the chair beside her.

'Our friend Halal tells me you might like to help me out with my book?'

'Why, yes, I would.'

'Say, that's fine. You know we have the big room on the top floor? Every morning we work there together. Well, little lady, any time you feel like it, come up and join us.'

Overwhelmed by this proposal, Harriet wished Halal were there so she might show her gratitude.

The room that Beltado spoke of was very big; a long, low attic with two dormer windows. It was as sparsely furnished as Harriet's bedroom but the Beltados had brought in their own folding chairs and tables and the floor was heaped with their books.

Dr Jolly who had her work space at one end of the room, sat bent down in concentrated study and apparently deaf to her husband's voice. Dr Beltado and Miss Dora held the centre of the room where there was most light. Beltado dressed for breakfast and then apparently, undressed in order to do battle with his enormous task of correlating all cultures. The bed had been pulled forward to accommodate him and, resting on one elbow, he lay, wearing a Chinese robe that exposed more of him than it covered. He was dictating to Miss Dora when Harriet tapped on the door. He called to her to come in, obviously irritated by the interruption. He stared at her, bemused for some moments before he remembered why she was there.

Rather exasperated, he said: 'What are we going to do with you?' He ordered Miss Dora to show Harriet her shorthand notes: 'Think you can make a rough typescript of that?'

The shorthand was unlike any Harriet had seen before: 'I'm sorry, I can't.'

'You can't, eh? Sit down then and we'll find you something else.'

Harriet sat and listened and learnt about different cultures but she never learnt what she was employed to do. Or, indeed, if she were employed at all for, from first to last, there was no mention of a salary.

Forgetting Harriet, Dr Beltado dictated, waving his arms about and letting his robe slip so all might view his white legs, his belly and his large pudenda. Miss Dora, obviously used to this display, ignored it and meekly scribbled on. Advocating the co-ordination of all cultural disciplines, Dr Beltado said that the experts should work together like an orchestra gathered under the baton of one supreme conductor.

'And who,' Beltado asked, 'should that conductor be? I think I may, without undue conceit, suggest myself, a man widely travelled and experienced, and not one to flinch from responsibility. If invited to fill the role . . .' Gazing round, he caught Harriet's eye and came to a stop.

'What are you doing here?'

'I'm waiting for a job.'

Miss Dora was told to find Harriet a job. She produced a box of photographs that had to be sorted according to their countries of origin. There were some five hundred photographs and sorting them gave Harriet three days' work. That finished, she was set to making a fair copy of Miss Dora's rough typescript. At the end of the first week, she hoped Dr Beltado would mention money, but nothing was said. She spent the next week typing each day from nine in the morning until six in the evening and once, when Dr Beltado had gone to relieve himself, she spoke quietly to Miss Dora: 'Does Dr Beltado pay one weekly or monthly?'

'Pay?' Miss Dora seemed never to have heard of pay. Her homely face with its small eyes and thin, red nose quivered in embarrassment, but she asked: 'What did you arrange with him?'

'I didn't arrange anything but I need to earn some money.'

'If I get a chance, I'll mention it to Dr Jolly.' Miss Dora turned away as though the subject were distasteful and nothing more was said for the next three days. Then Harriet managed to trap her in the passage.

'Miss Dora, please! Have you asked Dr Jolly about my salary?'

'You're to send in your account.' Miss Dora dodged round Harriet and was gone. Harriet, used to a system of wages paid weekly for work done, had no idea what to charge or for how long. She bought some ruled paper and spent Friday evening in her room, concocting an account so modest no one could question it but when, on Saturday morning, she went up to the Beltado work-room, she found no one there.

Dr Beltado, Dr Jolly and Miss Dora, folding chairs and tables, books and papers – all had gone. The bed was back against the wall. The whole place had the abject nullity of a body from which life had departed. And Harriet, on the floor below, had not heard a sound.

She hurried down to ask Madame Vigo where Dr Beltado had

gone? He and his ladies had departed the pension soon after day-break, leaving no forwarding address.

'And when are they coming back?'

'One year, two year. I not know.'

'They did not pay me for my work.'

'They forgot?'

Perhaps they did forget; and Harriet felt the more disconsolate to think herself forgotten.

Eleven

The news reached Cairo that British and American forces had made contact in North Africa. At the same time Guy received official confirmation of Harriet's death. The letter stated that the name of Harriet Pringle was on a list of 530 persons granted passage on the evacuation ship, the *Queen of Sparta*, that sailed from Suez on 28 December 1942. The *Queen of Sparta* had been sunk by enemy action while in the Indian Ocean. Harriet Pringle, together with 528 other passengers, had been declared missing, believed drowned. One passenger and two members of the crew had survived. The passenger's name was given as Caroline Rutter.

Guy took the letter to Dobson who was still in his bedroom. 'It's been a long time coming.'

Dobson, quick to defend authority, said: 'There could be no absolute certainty about the ship's fate till it failed to turn up at Cape Town.'

'What about the survivors? Wouldn't they be conclusive proof?'

'No. We've had a longer report. The crewmen were lascars who scarcely knew what ship it was. The woman was too ill for weeks to tell anyone anything. Until there was proof, the rumours had to be treated as – well, rumours.'

'I see.' Guy put the letter into his pocket.

That morning, at breakfast, Edwina said she was thinking of marrying Tony Brody.

'Good heavens,' said Dobson; 'not Tony Brody!'

'Why not? He's a major and a nice man.'

'I should have thought you could do better than Brody.'

Edwina, sniffing behind her curtain of hair, said dismally: 'There's not much choice these days. The most exciting men have all gone to Tunisia and I don't think they're coming back.'

'Even so. Be sensible and wait. Someone will come along.'

'I have waited, perhaps too long. I'm not getting younger.'

Dobson observed her with a critical smile: 'True. The bees aren't buzzing around as they used to.'

'Oh, Dobbie, really! How beastly you are!' Edwina gave a sob and Dobson patted her hand.

'There, there, pet, your Uncle Dobbie was joking. You're still as beautiful as a dream and you don't want to marry Brody.'

'Oh, I might as well. If you can't marry the man you want, does it matter who you marry?'

'Why not stay peacefully unmarried, like me?'

'Because I don't want to spend the rest of my life working in a dreary office.'

While this conversation skirted his consciousness, Guy was thinking of Harriet missing, believed drowned. At an age when other girls were thinking of marriage, she was lying at the bottom of the Indian Ocean.

The letter, though it told him nothing he did not already know, hung over him during his morning classes. It was as though a final shutter had come down on his memories of his wife and he realized that all this time some irrational, tenuous hope had lingered in his mind.

He thought of another ill-fated ship, the ship on which Aidan Pratt had served as a steward when he was a conscientious objector. On its way to Canada, with evacuees, it was torpedoed and Aidan had shared a life-boat packed with children in their night clothes. They had died off one by one from cold and thirst and when thrown overboard, the little bodies had floated after the boat because they were too light to sink. Harriet had weighed scarcely more than a teenage girl and Guy could imagine her body floating and following the boat as though afraid of being left alone on that immense sea.

Still disconsolate when he reached the hospital, he found Simon in a mood very different from his own. That morning, Simon had managed to walk a few yards without a crutch. He had walked awkwardly but he had done it – he had walked on his own.

'You see what that means?'

Guy laughed, trying to lift his own spirits up to Simon's level: 'No wonder you're so cheerful.'

Simon, lying in a deck-chair on the veranda of his small ward, was cheerful to the point of light-headedness. Delighted with himself, he said: 'I was like this once before, when I first went into Plegics – but more so. In fact, I was pretty nearly bonkers and for no reason. But now I have a reason, haven't I? I *know* I'm going to walk like a normal man. I told you about those dreams I get, when I'm running for miles over green fields? Well, one day, after the war, I'm going to do that! I'll go into the country and run for miles, like a maniac.'

'Just to show you're as good as the rest of them? You could run in the desert just as well.'

'No, it has to be over fields. I want that green grass, that green English grass.'

'So it's England now, not India or Cyprus?'

Simon laughed wildly. He was in a state where everything amused him but he was particularly pleased by a joke he had heard the previous evening. There had been a lecture in the main hall of the hospital, intended for patients who were near recovery. They were told they would leave the hospital in perfect health and the army had expected them to stay in perfect health. They were to avoid brothels and street women and to keep themselves clean and fit.

'Just like a school pi-jaw,' Simon said, 'Except that the chap was funny. Oh, he was funny! What do you think he said at the end? He said: "Remember – flies spread disease. *Keep yours shut!*"'

Simon threw his head back in riotous enjoyment of this statement and Guy, smiling and frowning at the same time, thought: 'What a boy he is! Little more than a schoolboy in spite of all he's seen.' Guy himself was not yet twenty-five but, suffering the after-effects of bereavement, he felt a whole generation or more older than Simon. It occurred to him, too, that Simon returning to normal vitality, was a different person from the disabled youth whom he had adopted as a charge. Simon, helpless and dependent, had had the appeal of a child or a young animal but now, growing into independence, he had qualities that set him apart from his protector. Guy remembered his own boredom at the

Gezira pool while Simon felt only envy of an activity in which he could not join. Even now Simon, with his carefree ambition to run over green fields, was growing away from him and Guy, with the letter in his pocket, wondered what consolation he would find when Simon was gone altogether.

For some weeks now he had been avoiding public gatherings and the condolences of friends but that evening, feeling a need to talk to someone who had known Harriet, he went to the Anglo-Egyptian Union where he found Jake Jackman practising shots at the billiard table. They played a game of snooker then went into the club-room for drinks. Sitting with Jake at a table, Guy took out the letter and said casually: 'This came this morning.'

Jackman, as he read, grunted his sympathy until coming to the name of Caroline Rutter, he burst out: 'So that old crow Rutter's still alive!'

'Who is this Caroline Rutter?'

'Why, the impertinent old bloody bitch who had the cheek to ask me why I wasn't in uniform. To think of it! A nice-looking girl like Harriet dead and that old trout survives! She probably lived off her fat. The rich are like camels. They grow two stomachs and spend their time filling them so they've always got one to fall back on in case of emergencies.'

Jackman, drinking steadily, spent the evening dwelling on this fantasy and enlarging it until Castlebar's wife came to the table. He was now in a rage against the perversity of chance and he looked at Mona Castlebar with hatred. Not disconcerted, she sat down beside Guy. She had sung in his troop's entertainment and felt she had as good a right as anyone to his company. Having no quarrel with her, he bought her a drink.

She said: 'I suppose you've heard nothing from Bill?'

'I'm afraid, not a word.'

'Neither have I, and I haven't had a penny from him since he went. He neither knows nor cares how I'm managing.'

Jackman asked with gleeful malice: 'How *are* you managing?'

'That's my business.'

Both men knew that the university was allowing Mona to draw Castlebar's salary so Guy did not speak but Jackman, who had been eyeing her breasts and legs as though unable to credit their bulk, said: 'You're not starving, that's obvious.'

Mona, her glass empty, was tilting it about in her hand as though inviting a refill. Jackman said: 'I'll buy you a drink if you buy me one.'

'I'm not buying you anything. You've had more than enough as it is.'

'Oh!' Jackman straightened himself, his eyes glinting for a fight: 'No wonder Bill went off with the first woman who asked him. He always said you were a mean-natured lout.'

'He said you were a scrounging layabout.'

'That's good, coming from Lady Hooper's fancy man.'

Guy said: 'Shut up, both of you,' and Jackman, grumbling to himself, looked around as though seeking better company. Seeing Major Cookson at another table, he said: 'If that cow's staying, I'm going.'

Guy felt he, too, had had enough of Mona. As a taxi came in at the Union gates, he said he had to go home and correct students' essays.

Taking the chance, Mona rose with him: 'As you're going to Garden City, you can drop me off on the way.'

So it happened Guy missed an event that was long to be a subject of gossip in Cairo. Or, rather, he did not miss it, for had he remained it would never have occurred.

What Jake Jackman did after joining Major Cookson was recounted by Cookson whenever he found himself an audience.

Cookson had not been alone at his table. He had with him his two cronies: Tootsie and the ex-archaeologist Humphrey Taupin. Shouting so all could hear, Jackson told this group that he would not spend another minute with that 'grabby monstrosity' Mona Castlebar and continued to vilify her till she and Guy were gone. Then, curving forward in his chair, his right hand pulling at his nose, his left hanging between his knees, he subsided into morose silence. Cookson, who was spending Taupin's money, asked what Jake would drink.

'Whisky.'

Cookson called on Taupin to replenish funds but Taupin said he had nothing left. Jackman losing patience, called a safragi and ordered a double whisky: 'Put it down to Professor Pringle's account.'

'Not here Ploffesor Plingle.'

'He's coming back. And bring another for him. Put them both down to his account.'

Still pervaded by grievances, Jackman drank both whiskies rapidly and they brought him to the point of action. Leaning confidingly towards Cookson, he said: 'You know that Mrs Rutter who lives down the road?'

'I don't think I do.'

'She owns a swell place. Big house and garden, crowds of wogs to wait on her. Generous old girl, keeps open house. Told me to drop in for a drink any time. "Bring your friends," she said, "I'm always ready for a booze up."'

'Really!' Major Cookson's grey, peaked face lit with interest. 'She sounds a charming woman.'

'Charming? She's charming, all right. Like to come?'

'What, now? Oh, I don't think I can leave my friends.'

'All come, why not?' Jackman slapped the table to emphasize his magnanimity and jumped to his feet: 'It's no distance. We can walk there in half a minute.'

Cookson and Tootsie, unusually animated, got to their feet but Taupin was unable to move. He lay entranced, sliding out of his chair, eyes shut, a smile on his crumpled, curd-white face.

'Leave him,' Jackman said and walked off. After a moment's uncertainty, Tootsie and Cookson followed.

The house was, as Jake had said, no distance away. It was one of the privileged mansions of Gezira that shared the great central lawn with the Union, the Officers' Club and the Sporting Club. It stood dark amid the clouding darkness of tall trees and Cookson, seeing no light in any windows, said doubtfully: 'I don't think the lady's at home.'

'She's there all right. She's always home. Probably in the back parlour. Come on.' Jake led them through the cool, jasmine-scented garden to the front door where he gripped a large lion-headed knocker and hammered violently on its plate. If the noise roused no one else, it troubled Cookson who said: 'Oh dear, do you really think we should?'

They all peered through the coloured glass of the front door and saw the outline of a staircase curving up from a spacious hall. Jake hammered again and at last a light was switched on at the top of the stair. A white-clad figure began to make an uncertain descent.

'I'm afraid we've got her out of bed,' Cookson whispered.

'Nonsense. She's up till all hours.'

The figure, reaching the hall, paused half-way to the door and a nervous female voice called out: 'Who is it? What do you want?'

'We're friends. Open up.'

'If you want Mrs Rutter, she's not here. You can leave a message at the servants' quarters – they're at the bottom of the garden.'

Losing patience, Jackman bawled: 'I don't want the bloody servants. Open the door.'

'No. I'm just looking after things while she's away.' The girl began to back towards the stairs and Jackman became more persuasive:

'Look, it's important. I've something to deliver to Mrs Rutter. I'll leave it with you.'

The girl returned and opening the door a couple of inches, asked: 'What is it?'

The two inches allowed Jackman to force his foot in, then, using his shoulder, he flung the door open, sending the girl staggering back. Jackman was inside.

The destruction, Cookson said, began there and then. A six-foot-high Chinese ornament stood in the hall. Jackman overturned it with the decisive competence of a cinema stuntman and it crashed and splintered on the stone floor. He then marched into the drawing-room ('A treasure house' according to Cookson) and here he went to work as though carrying out a plan that had been burning in him for months.

Cookson and Tootsie had followed him, making weak protests, while the girl sobbed and asked: 'Why are you doing this? Why are you doing this?' Getting no reply, she tried to reach the telephone but Jake flung her away and then pulled the wire from the wall.

'Then,' said Cookson, 'he just went on smashing the place up.'

When everything breakable had been broken, he took a pair of cutting-out scissors the girl had been using and tried to cut up the velvet curtains. The scissors were not strong enough and, said

Cookson: 'Raging around, he found a diplomat's sword, a valuable piece, the hilt and sheath covered with brilliants, and pulling it out, he slashed the curtains, the upholstery and the furniture. Fine Venetian furniture, too. I kept saying: "For God's sake, stop it, Jake," but it was like trying to stop a tornado. For some reason the girl was more frightened by the sword than the general destruction. She started to scream for help and ran out of the house, but you know what Gezira's like at that time of night! There should have been a boab on duty but he'd cleared off somewhere. And even if she'd found a policeman, he'd simply have taken to his heels at the idea of tackling a lunatic.'

The girl reached the Anglo-Egyptian Union. The gates were shut but the safragis were still inside. She persuaded the head safragi to telephone the British Embassy and so, eventually, a posse of embassy servants arrived in a car and took charge of Jackman who by that time had fallen asleep, exhausted by his own activity.

Guy asked Dobson: 'Is it true Jackman's a prisoner at the Embassy?'

'Not any longer.'

'Then where is he?'

'At the moment in a military aircraft. If you must know, but keep it under your hat, he's been sent to Bizerta HQ for questioning.'

'To Bizerta HQ on a military aircraft! Why should the military concern themselves with Jackman? You don't mean he really was doing undercover work?'

'My dear fellow,' said Dobson, 'Who knows? Anybody could be doing anything in times like these.'

Twelve

During the three weeks that Harriet had spent working for Dr Beltado, Halal had come to the pension five times. These were social visits. He would arrive just as supper was ending and bowing to the doctor and the two women, would say: 'I hope I see you well!'

Dr Beltado always responded with a weary effort at good-fellowship, saying: 'Hi, there, Halal, how's tricks?' or, 'How's the world treating you?' and push forward a chair: 'Take the weight off your feet, Halal.'

Protesting that he had no wish to intrude, no wish to impose himself, Halal would sit down and Miss Dora would be sent to order coffee for him. While Beltado went on talking, Halal would give Harriet furtive glances, transmitting the fact that there he still was, patiently waiting, in case she had need of him.

Now, if she did not need Halal himself, she needed help of some sort. She was nearly penniless and, walking up and down the souk, she longed for circumstance to befriend her. She loitered at each stall, with the crowd pushing about her, and when she came to the Roman arcade, she turned and walked all the way back again. No one took much notice of her now. She had become a familiar figure, an English eccentric with endless time and no money to spend.

Three days after Beltado's departure, when she was nearing desperation, Halal came to the pension. She had finished breakfast and was wondering what to do with herself, when he edged round the dining-room door and without approaching further, began at once to explain and excuse his presence. Jamil had heard of Beltado's departure and had seen her walking in the souk, apparently with nothing to do.

'I asked myself "Could Mrs Pringle be bored? Would she care to look over the silk factory?"'

'That would be nice.' Harriet's manner was so subdued that Halal crossed to her, saying with concern: 'I hope, Mrs Pringle, you are not ill.'

'Sit down, Halal. No, I'm not ill, but I'm very worried. Have you any idea where Dr Beltado has gone?'

'I know nothing, but I see all is not well with you. Please, if I can help, what can I do?'

'I'd be glad of anyone's help but I don't know what you can do. Dr Beltado went without paying me for the work I did.'

'No?' Aghast, Halal declared in fierce tones: 'Such a thing is not heard of in our world.'

'You mean the Arab world? But Beltado isn't an Arab. Madame Vigo thinks he just forgot.'

'To forget one who has worked for three weeks! It is not possible.' Frowning, he considered the matter for some moments then said: 'This should be told to Jamil. He will be in his café at this time, discussing business. May I take you to see him?'

'Would it do any good?'

'Perhaps. He has known Dr Beltado longer than I have. He may know where to find him.'

Jamil's café was not, as Harriet supposed, one of the bazaar cafés where men sat all day over a cup of coffee. It was in the new city, a large modern establishment with marble table-tops and tubular chrome chairs. Jamil, as proprietor, sat among an admiring crowd of young men, one of them the guitarist who had sung 'Who is Romeo?' They all shouted Halal's name and Jamil, springing to his feet, placed a chair for Harriet, making it clear to the others that he was already acquainted with her. She realized that if they had not actually seen her with Halal, they had heard of her. Their welcoming laughter was not for Halal alone, it was for Halal accompanied by a lady. She might have a husband somewhere but if so, the fact merely enriched the drama of Halal's relationship with a foreign woman, and the courtesy bestowed on her was all the more courteous.

Halal's manner was serious but that did not affect the humour of his friends and several minutes passed before he could tell them of Beltado's perfidy. Even then, from habit, Jamil went on laughing, saying: 'That Beltado! It is like him, isn't it? You remember last time he was here he had long treatment for his stomach from Dr Amin, then one day he was gone and Amin was not paid?'

One of them prompted him: 'Tell us again what Amin said.'

'Yes, what he said!' This was so funny that Jamil could hardly speak for laughing: 'He said of Beltado: "Pale, bulky and offensive like a sprue patient's shit."'

'*Jamil*!' Halal raised his voice in anger: 'To tell such before a lady!'

Jamil collapsed in shame, red faced and abashed to the point of speechlessness. Harriet pretended that Dr Amin's remark had been beyond her comprehension and so Jamil gradually recovered and was able to discuss Beltado's departure. But the discussion did not help Harriet. Beltado with his large, powerful car might have gone anywhere. He might even have returned to Turkey and, as he had done in the past, disappeared into Axis territory. Soon the talk ceased to relate to Harriet's predicament and became an acclamation of Beltado's mysterious, almost supernatural, ability to cross frontiers closed to the subjects of the Allied powers.

'How is it done?' they asked each other. 'Is he British or American? If not, what is he?'

Harriet told them that Beltado had an Eire passport.

'But what is it, this Eire passport? How does it give him such powers?'

'It means he has Irish citizenship and as Ireland is not at war with the Axis, he can enter occupied countries, but he doesn't find it easy. The Axis officials can't believe that Ireland, being part of the British Isles, isn't an enemy country.'

This explanation merely puzzled them further and led them a long way from Harriet's problem. Halal, seeing that there was no help from Jamil, said: 'I am taking Mrs Pringle to see my father's silk factory.' They left amid regrets and good wishes.

Alone with her in the street, Halal said sadly: 'I fear now you will return to Cairo.'

'I don't know what I'll do. To tell you the truth, I can't return to Cairo. My husband thinks I'm on a ship going to England. I was supposed to go but instead of boarding the ship, I came here.'

Halal, baffled by this confession, stopped and stared at her:

'What you tell me is very strange, is it not? Do I mistake your meaning? Did you say you were to go in a ship to England but did not go? Ah, I understand! You could not bear to travel so far from Mr Pringle and yet, afraid to go back, you came here. Was that what happened?'

'That may have been the reason.'

The indecision of this reply puzzled him still further but sensing there was a rift between the Pringles, he walked on, staring down at his feet as though pondering what he had been told. He said at last: 'Do you wish to come to the silk factory?'

'Yes.'

The factory was in a series of sheds behind the souk. For a while she was distracted by the young workmen – very like Halal's friends except that the friends were idle while these men had to work – and the large spools of brilliantly coloured silks. She was shown rolls of the finished materials in ancient patterns, some enhanced with gold and silver. She forgot Beltado but Halal did not forget his concern for her. Walking with her back to the pension, he said earnestly:

'Mrs Pringle, my friends do not understand why I seek your company. They say: "Halal, you are foolish. We know such English ladies. They seem free but there will be nothing for you. All you do is waste your money." But I know better. I have in me ideals they do not know of. They talk much of romance but they are afraid. In the end they marry within the family. It is usual with them to marry a cousin.'

'And does it work out?'

'Oh yes, well enough. The girls do not expect much. There is something simple and good in these women. They have the childish outlook of nuns. And what criteria have they? What do they know of men? They know only a father or a brother. A cousin is the nearest thing; he is safe. And the female relatives are tactful. When the bridegroom is seen, they are full of admiration, or pretend to be, so the girl is content.'

'I suppose it is the criticism of the world that spoils things.'

'Well, for me, I don't fear criticism. I know what I want. I know what I am doing. I say to Jamil and the others: "If I spend money on this lady, I shall make a friend. One day I think she will reward me."'

468

He looked into Harriet's face, expecting her to applaud him and perhaps give him hope, but she had no hope to give. The rain started as they reached the pension garden and they stood for a few minutes under the mulberry tree. Halal put his hand out to her but she would not take it.

He said again: 'May I offer you my protection?'

She looked away, wondering how to escape him. When he tried to touch her arm, she said 'I'm sorry,' and hurried into the pension. Reaching her room she locked the door, not from fear that he would follow her but because she had to isolate herself. She had to face her own situation. She lay on the bed and closing her eyes, she projected her thoughts into space. With the resolution of despair, she cried to such powers as might be there: 'Tell me what to do now.' After a while she sank into a drowsy inertia, stupefied by her own failure.

In London, she had earned her own living and had told herself that any girl who could survive there, could survive anywhere in the world. Now she knew she had been wrong. Here her attempt at an independent life had reduced her to penury. She slept and woke with a name in her mind: Angela.

She knew only one Angela, her friend in Cairo who had gone off with the poet Castlebar. Remembering her with affection, she thought: 'Dear Angela, I know if you were here you would help me. But you're not here and I must help myself.' She jumped up and packed her suitcase. When she went to the dining-room, she told Madame Vigo she was leaving next day.

Unperturbed, Madame Vigo said: 'You want taxi?'

'No. I'll go to Beirut by train.'

'Not good train. Better taxi.'

Harriet could not afford a taxi to Beirut but she had to take one to the station. Driving through the main square, she saw Halal at the kerb, his case under his arm, his sallow, vulnerable face grave, waiting to cross the road. Safely past him, she said to herself: 'Goodbye, Halal. I'm afraid your friends were right.'

At the station, she spoke to the stationmaster who knew a little English. When was the next train to Beirut? He shrugged, putting out his hands: 'Mam'zell, who knows? Trains very bad. All stolen by army, better take taxi.'

'I can't. It would cost too much.'

'Then go Riyak and then go Baalbek. In Baalbek many tourists, some English. They take you Beirut.'

Here was a solution of a sort. She felt pleased, even excited, at the thought of seeing Baalbek. There was a local train to Riyak at one p.m. and she waited on the platform, fearful of missing it. There was no buffet, nowhere to sit, but she was getting away from Halal.

The train arrived at two o'clock and stood for an hour in the station before setting out again. As it climbed the foothills of the Anti-Lebanon, she could see through the dirty windows the foliage of the Ghuta and the golden crescents of the mosque, and she said again: 'Goodbye. Goodbye, Halal.' The oasis, a thick green carpet, was sliced off abruptly and then they were in the desert, grey under a grey sky. The train, like a mule unwilling to go farther, jerked and jolted and stopped every few miles.

Two old countrywomen shared Harriet's carriage, speaking a language that was strange to her. Halal had told her that in some outlying villages the people still spoke Aramaic and she listened intently, wondering if she were hearing the language of Christ.

When at last the train dragged itself into Riyak, the sky had cleared and a small tourists' shuttle marked 'Baalbek' stood at the next platform. The ease of this transfer brightened everything for her. As the shuttle ran between orchards burgeoning in the sunlight, she felt sure that succour awaited her in this brilliant and fruitful land.

Thirteen

Dobson said at breakfast: 'The navy's been bombarding Pantellaria. I think we can guess what that means.'

As Guy and Edwina had never heard of Pantellaria, he told them: 'It's an inoffensive little island shaped like a sperm whale. I suppose the Wops have it fortified.'

'So you think we're preparing to cross the Med?' Guy asked.

'My guess is as good as yours, but we're certainly preparing for something. The gen is that Axis troops have folded up in North Africa. Not a squeak out of them. So we're due for the next move which would be northwards. It could all be over quicker than anyone thinks. Home for Christmas, eh?'

'Not this Christmas, I shouldn't think.' Remembering the wet, empty streets of London at Christmas, Guy knew he had no home there. On his last Christmas in London, on his way to an evening party, he had passed men standing at street corners, waiting for the pubs to open. Lonely men, men without homes. But he would not be like that. He would always have friends. He had friends wherever he went, but the truth was: friends had lives of their own and were liable to disappear. Castlebar had gone off with the mad woman Angela Hooper and Jackman had been sent to Bizerta under arrest. And perhaps even Simon would not need him much longer. He was beginning to feel that the only permanent relationship was the relationship of marriage, if death or divorce did not end it. He sighed, thinking that his had been as good as any yet he had not known it at the time.

Fourteen

Baalbek was the end of the line. Though the little train still went hopefully to its destination, tourists were few and Harriet was the only passenger. When she descended at the empty station, it seemed that even the engine driver and the guard had disappeared. There were no porters. The platforms were empty. She was alone. She dragged her case out to the road then stopped, unable to take it farther. She hoped to find a taxi but there were no taxis.

At one side of the station entrance there was a primitive café with an outdoor table and bench. Pushing the case in front of her, she reached the bench and sat down in the late afternoon sunlight. Though the whole place looked unpopulated, she felt pleasure in being there.

A wide road ran from the station into the distance where rust-coloured hills rose from among green foliage. The road was light-coloured, dusty, and on either side stood trees, very tall and slender, drooping towards each other. There were a few old buildings here and there and neglected fields. Beyond the fields there were the remains of ancient ramparts. At one side of the road a clear and brilliant stream ran into a pool. The place, what there was of it, conveyed a sense of tranquillity and broken-down grandeur.

Tired, not knowing where to go, she let herself drift into the pleasing languor of the spirit that the Arabs called *khayf* and was startled when a man came out of the café and stood looking at her. He was short and though still young, stout. His dress, white shirt and black trousers, told her that he was a Christian. He asked in French what he could do for her. When she said she was looking for somewhere to stay, his plump, brown face became troubled.

'I bring you *mon frère* George.'

George, a large, red-haired, fair-skinned fellow, came from the café. From his appearance, he might have been an English yeoman and, as was fitting, he spoke some English. Harriet, deciding that the brothers were descended from a red-haired Crusader, was delighted with them for proving the Mendelian theory and tried to explain heredity, pointing out that while one brother was a brown-skinned Arab, the other was a copy of his English forebear. They did not know what she was talking about and she realized she was being absurd. Her situation was now so hopeless, she was almost light-headed.

She said to George: 'Where can I find an hotel?'

George stared at her for some moments before reaching the point of speech: 'Not any more hotel. Before war, two, but now all two are close-ed.'

'Is there a train to Beirut?'

'Tonight no train. Train tomorrow.'

A third brother, very like the first, appeared now and the three of them, speaking in Arabic, discussed her situation with expressions of concern. It did not occur to them to abandon her. Here was a young woman alone, in need of a bed for the night, and something must be done for her. They appeared to reach a conclusion and the red-haired brother, saying 'Come with me', beckoned her into the white-washed interior of the café. She was led upstairs to a landing that had the smell of an unaired sleeping place. He opened a door and showed her a small room with a bunk, a broken-backed chair and some hooks for clothing. There were no sheets but a grimy, padded cover thrown to one side showed that this was a bedroom. One of the brothers had given up his room to her.

The red-haired man offered this accommodation with a smile, apparently imagining it was as good as anything to be found in the world. She returned the smile, saying: 'Thank you, it is very nice.' What else could she do? Where else could she go? At least she had shelter for the night and next day there would be a train to Beirut.

The first brother carried up Harriet's suitcase and, left to herself, she went to look for a washroom. She found only a privy with a hole in the floor, high smelling and not over clean.

When she went downstairs, the brothers were waiting for her and George asked: 'You like to eat? We make kebabs.'

'Yes, but later. I must see the temples first.'

George came out to the road with her and waving at the long avenue of trees, said: 'Baalbek very old.'

She looked at the ruined remnant of fortifications and asked: 'Roman?'

He shook his head in forceful denial: 'No, no. Much more old. Cain lived here. He built a fort to hide in after he murdered Abel. Noah lived here. King Solomon sat beside this water. He built the temples for his ladies. You know he had many ladies, all many religions.'

Harriet laughed: 'Are you sure Solomon built the temples?'

'What other could do it?. Solomon had them built by his genii. Not men.'

Harriet laughed again and started down the road. As she went, she could see columns rising in the distance, dark and ponderous, looking less like classical monuments than menhirs from a more primitive age. The sun was beginning to sink, the light was deepening and she hurried to see what she could before the night came down.

Inside the temple enclosure, she came to the steps on which the columns stood. Standing below them, she gazed up at them, overawed by their height and massive girth. Against the dense cerulean of the evening sky, their hot colour looked almost black.

Although there were walnut trees coming into leaf and pigeons taking flight and lizards rustling between the stones, there was a sinister atmosphere about the site. The platform had been a place of sacrifice: human sacrifice. Terror was imprinted on the atmosphere and Harriet felt afraid as she climbed up the steps and passed between the pillars on to the stretch of massive stones that now reflected the orange-gold of the sinking sun. She contemplated her own solitude and thought of the room in which she would have to spend the night. The men, however good their intentions, were strangers and she had seen no sign of a woman about the café.

Tomorrow she could go on to Beirut, but what would she do there? Without money and without future, she would be no better off than she had been in Damascus. Unnerved by her own situation, she cried out: 'Guy, why don't you come to look for me?'

But no one was coming to look for her. No one knew where she was to be found. For all anyone knew, she might be dead.

She walked to the temple at the other end of the platform. The interior was dark and, pausing at the entrance, she thought she heard a car come to a stop. She stood, listening intently, and after a few minutes heard someone coming up the steps to the platform. She felt the solace of not being alone, then she realized that she was alone and anything could happen to her.

She watched apprehensively as a fat man limped into view. He had on a faded khaki shirt and brown corduroy trousers and only his cap, worn at a jaunty angle, showed that he was an army officer. She recognized him and laughed at her own fears. Seeing her, he lifted his stick and waving it excitedly, shouted: 'What are you doing here?' Astonished by her presence, he came towards her, moving as quickly as he could, his round, pink face beaming at this unlikely encounter. She felt too much relief and thankfulness to say anything.

'You remember me, don't you? Old Lister who used to take you out to lunch at Groppi's?'

'Of course I remember you. It's just . . . I'm a bit stunned. It seems too good to be true.'

Delighted at seeing her, Lister scarcely heard this declaration but chattered on: 'It's amazing, how things happen. Only yesterday I saw a friend of Guy's, that poet fellow I met in Alex. I didn't speak to him because he's not alone. He's got a bint with him. Nice-looking, dark-haired girl, not too young.' Lister's round pink nose and fluff of fair moustache quivered as he spoke of the girl: 'Lucky chap, eh? Lucky chap!'

'Do you know where they're staying?'

'At my hotel. That's where I saw them.'

Lister, not understanding her wonder at this news, went on: 'And where's Guy? Not on your own, are you?'

'Yes, on my own. I was trying to get from Damascus to Beirut and arrived here. There's no train till tomorrow.'

'So you're stranded? Pretty god-forsaken place, if you ask me. Where are you staying?'

'There's no hotel but I've found a room, not very nice.'

'I bet it's not very nice. If you want to get to Beirut, how about coming back with me? Have a night at my hotel, see your friend

Castlebar and take the bus tomorrow. Have a convivial evening in the bar with old Lister. What do you say?'

A few hours ago this suggestion would have seemed to her her salvation, but now she thought of the brothers and their kindness and said: 'The people who've given me a room – I don't want to hurt their feelings.'

'Oh, don't worry. I'll explain to them.'

'And then, your hotel – I don't think I could afford it.'

'If you're short, I can lend you a few quid. Guy will always pay me back. Now, let's look round. Spooky place, isn't it? But those columns are pretty impressive. What's this temple?' Lister had a guide-book and led her from temple to temple, determined to see everything: 'Good lord, look at this – just like the inside of a city church. Wonder where the oracle had its abode!' Limping and groaning from the pain in his foot, Lister kept her among the temples till the air became chilly and the sun began to set. Then in twilight that was beautiful and pleasant now she was not alone, they went out to the waiting taxi and drove towards the station.

'Where's this pension of yours?'

'It's not exactly a pension. I'm in this café.'

The brothers showed only satisfaction that Harriet had found someone to look after her. Lister went upstairs to fetch her suit-case and came down looking blank. George, putting the suitcase into the taxi, said happily: 'You go Beirut. You like very much.'

Once out of hearing, Lister said in a shocked tone: 'My dear girl, you couldn't have stayed in a place like that. What do you think would have happened to you there?'

'What would be likely to happen?'

'God knows. You're too trusting.' Lister gasped and began to titter: 'A girl alone with three randy A-rabs! No wonder they said. "Come into my parlour . . ."'

'Really, Lister! I'm sure they only wanted to help me.'

'Perhaps, perhaps,' Lister dropped the subject and said: 'I wish we could have found the oracle. It was much brighter than that affair at Delphi. Much more – well, what's the word? Snide. The Emperor Trajan tried to trick it by handing it a blank sheet of paper and in return, he got another blank sheet of paper. Then he asked about his expedition to conquer Parthia and the oracle handed him a bundle of sticks wrapped in a piece of cloth.'

'What did that mean?'

'What indeed! Probably nothing, but he died on the way and his bones were sent to Rome wrapped in a piece of cloth.'

'Did oracles ever give anyone good news?'

'I doubt it. They were always hinting at something nasty.'

The road carried them in deepening twilight over the bare rocky pass between the Anti-Lebanon and the Lebanon. The journey was not long and there was still a glint on the western horizon as they dropped down among gardens and orchards, and Lister pointed: 'There! That's the hotel, The Cedars.'

Seeing the hotel, its windows radiant, set on a hill spur above Beirut, Harriet said: 'It's much too grand for me.'

'Nonsense. Guy's not badly off. We can't have you staying in places like that café.' As the taxi stopped, Lister struggled out, saying: 'I'll see you're properly fixed up. Room and bath, eh?'

He was gone before Harriet could reply and she stood in the garden, among a scent of orange blossom, and wondered how she would manage to pay.

She entered the vestibule as Angela Hooper was coming down the stairs. Angela glanced at Harriet, glanced away then jerked her head back and gave a scream: 'Harriet Pringle! But you went on that evacuation ship.'

'No, I didn't go. I came to Syria instead.'

'Good heavens, what a shock you gave me! And you're staying here?'

'Only for one night . . .'

'No, you must stay longer than that. I want to hear what's been happening in Cairo and a lot of other things.'

'I'll have to find a cheaper place. The truth is, I'm almost out of cash.'

'Oh, cash. You're always worrying about cash . . .'

Angela stopped abruptly as Lister, coming from the desk, joined them. Stiffening slightly, she looked suspiciously at him then said to Harriet: 'I thought you were alone.'

Angela did not move but Harriet felt that in her mind she took a step away and a distance of disapproval had come between them. Harriet said: 'I was alone but I met Major Lister in Baalbek and he was kind enough to give me a lift in his taxi. And now I'm here.'

'So you are!' Angela smiled but there was still uncertainty in her manner: 'And where's Guy?'

'In Cairo.'

'Too busy to come with you, I suppose.' Angela gave Lister another look and realizing that her suspicions were absurd, laughed: 'Well, it's lovely to have you here. Let's all have a drink after supper. See you in the Winter Garden.'

When she had left them, Lister said: 'I don't think your friend liked me.'

'It was just that she thought at first I'd gone off with you.'

Lister shook with wheezy laughter: 'Would it were true! Dear me, dear me! Would it were true!'

Harriet laughed too: 'She went off with Castlebar. It's funny how often people disapprove of others doing what they have done themselves.'

Angela and Castlebar were seated at a small table in an alcove of the dining-room that Angela, with her habit of lavish tipping, had probably kept reserved for them. Glancing across at their enclosed intimacy, Harriet could not suppose that Angela would want her to be with them for very long. She had found friends but that did not solve anything. She might borrow from Angela, she might even borrow from Lister, but borrowing merely put off the day when she must face up to her situation. She glanced again towards the lovers and caught Castlebar's eye. As though he understood her dilemma, he smiled and raised his hand reassuringly. She had never understood his attraction for Angela but now, warmed by his greeting, she felt him to be an old friend in a strange, unhelpful world.

'What are we going to drink?' Lister offered her the wine list.

'Not for me.'

'Oh, come on,' Lister rallied her: 'must have a glass,' and added as though admitting to a curious virtue, 'I always have wine with my meals.' He ordered a bottle of Cyprus red and watching the cork being drawn, he flushed with impatience and pushed his glass forward.

Harriet remembered his eagerness for food and drink. Based in Jerusalem, he would come to Cairo whenever he could to treat himself to what he called 'the fleshpots'. He sometimes took Harriet out for a meal, feeling that a companion gave him licence to indulge himself.

His glass filled, he lifted it quickly and drank, holding the wine in his mouth and sluicing it round and round his teeth, then as he swallowed it, giving a long drawn 'Ah-h-h.' Before the meal was over, Lister had drunk the whole bottle.

As Angela and Castlebar left the room, Angela called across: 'See you in the Winter Garden.'

'You think they want me?' Lister asked with tremulous lips and bulging wet blue eyes.

'Of course. You saw she meant both of us.'

The Winter Garden, that stretched out from the main building, was a large, glass gazebo that gave a view of the lights of Beirut and the dark glimmer of the distant sea. Lister followed Harriet with timorous expectancy as though fearing Angela would order him away.

Angela and Castlebar were seated in a corner behind a screen of blue plumbago flowers. Again Harriet felt they had made this seclusion their own, but Castlebar rose eagerly to welcome her and went to find extra chairs. During his absence from Cairo, it seemed he had taken on the function of host while Angela, who paid the bills, kept in the background. Their nightly bottle of whisky was on the table. Angela pushed it towards Lister who, after conventional demur, filled his glass and lifting it towards her, said: 'Here's seeing you, mem.'

Angela watched him with critical attention as he put down the whisky and refilled his glass. She did not look at Harriet but Castlebar, devoting himself to an old friend, insisted that evening she must have something more festive than her usual glass of white wine: 'How about a Pimm's? They do it very nicely here.'

When the Pimm's arrived, expertly dressed with fruit and borage, he handed it to her with a conniving smile and she felt he would not be at all displeased if she remained to share Angela's liberality. She was sure they had discussed the oddity of her presence here when she was supposed to be on the *Queen of Sparta*. And why was she short of money when she could send to her husband for help? She realized that if she stayed there, she would have a lot of explaining to do.

Angela, leaning her delicate, pretty head back among the flowers, gave Harriet a quizzical smile then, perhaps remembering their past friendship, suddenly leant forward and squeezed Harriet's hand: 'Dear Harriet, I thought I would never see you again.'

Angela had not changed in appearance since she left Cairo but Castlebar was not quite the Castlebar of the Anglo-Egyptian Union. He not only had more confidence and more to say for himself but he had lost the seedy look of the alcoholic for whom any money not spent on drink was money wasted. He was wearing an expensively tailored suit and silk shirt. Rich living had enhanced his looks but he still chain-smoked, placing the pack open in front of him with a cigarette pulled out ready to succeed the one he held in his hand. He still hung over the table, his thick, pale eyelids covering his eyes, his full, mauvish under-lip hanging slightly with one yellow eye-tooth tending to slip into view. Not really very different from the Castlebar of the Anglo-Egyptian Union.

Harriet asked where they had been since leaving Cairo.

'W-w-we went to Cyprus,' Castlebar said. 'S-s-stayed in Kyrenia.'

'At the Dome?' asked Lister: 'Great hotel the Dome. Got more public rooms, and *bigger* public rooms, than anywhere else in the Eastern Med. And the teas,' Lister's eyes watered at the thought of them, 'real old English teas – scones, jam, cream, plum-cake! Oh, my goodness!'

'Yes, we stayed at the Dome. But Cyprus is a small place and we got b-b-bored. We took the boat back to Haifa and Angie bought a second-hand car and drove us up here.'

Angela said: 'We thought we'd stay here a bit.' She smiled at Harriet: 'It's quite a nice hotel, isn't it?' and Harriet wondered what she would have thought of the Baalbek café.

Offered the bottle again, Lister said: 'Can't drink all your booze,' but, pressed, took a larger glass than before and, sipping, sighed: 'Back to the grindstone tomorrow. Only had four days' leave but managed to see a few things. Ever been to the Dog River?'

Angela, beginning to relent towards him, asked: 'What is the Dog River?'

'Oh, quite fantastic. There's this great headland where all the conquerors since Nebuchadnezzar have carved inscriptions. I wanted to see the earliest, the Babylonian one, but it's all overgrown with bramble. Silly people these Lebanese, no sense of history. I'd've climbed up and cleared it but couldn't get across the river. I've been told that at the river mouth there's a dog – not a real dog, of course – that used to howl so loudly at the sight of an enemy, it could be heard in Cyprus.'

Castlebar lifted his eyelids with interest: 'W-w-what was it? Some sort of siren?'

'Don't know. Drove down and looked for it but couldn't see hide or hair.' In an absent-minded way, Lister refilled his glass again and fell silent. He was beginning to droop and had to cling to his stick to keep himself from falling. He sighed and lifted the bottle but finding it empty, he put it down and his infantile nose and fat cheeks fell together with disappointment: 'Walked a long way . . . foot very bad . . . no dog anywhere. Never been able to find anything, really. Always deprived, always ill-treated. My nurse – what d'you think she used to do? She used to pull down m'knickers and beat m'bum with a hairbrush. Bristle side. Used to pull down little knickers and beat little bum. Poor little bum! What a thing to do to a child!' He drew in a long breath and let it out painfully: 'Never got over it. Never. Never shall.'

He sniffed and as he gave a sob, Angela sat up briskly and looking from Castlebar to Harriet, said: 'Time for bed.'

Making their excuses and goodnights, the three left Lister to brood on his wrongs and went out to the hall, where Angela asked: 'How did you come to pick that one up? Or, rather, how did Guy pick him up? I take it, it was Guy.'

'Of course. And how does Guy come to pick anyone up?'

'Well, Major Lister's going tomorrow, thank goodness, but Harriet you must stay on. I can't let you go so soon. We haven't had a chance to talk yet.'

'Angela dear, I've less than five pounds in the world.'

Angela went upstairs. Putting a hand out to stop the argument, she said: 'I'll settle your bill and you pay me back in Cairo,' then passed from view.

Harriet turned to Castlebar: 'You know, Bill, I can't afford to stay here.'

Castlebar grinned: 'Leave it to Angie. You're silly to worry, she loves to do the honours.' He followed Angela upstairs.

He did not worry himself. His attitude towards Angela's money had been determined early on when his friend Jake Jackman told him: 'If Angela takes us to places we can't afford, there's nothing for it. We'll have to let her pay.'

For Harriet, too, there was nothing for it. She had to borrow or starve. She could only hope that one day she would be able to repay what she owed.

When she went down to breakfast next morning, she found that Lister had already gone. There was no sign of Angela and Castlebar so, having eaten alone, she walked round the hotel garden that was lush with semi-tropical plants and early orange trees. The end, unfenced, fell for several hundred feet sheer to the road into Beirut. She saw Beirut itself stretched beneath her, a sharply-drawn maze of streets set with pink and cream buildings, delicately coloured in the early sunlight. The streets, flashing with traffic, converged towards the water-front where ships were gathered on the glittering Mediterranean. On the southern side of the town, beside the road, there was a wood of dark trees, each a stiff arrangement of branches with wings of closely packed foliage, standing like crows in affected attitudes. These, she realized, were the Cedars for which the hotel was named. And the hotel, of course, was one of the most famous in the Middle East – and here she was, living in idleness with no means of keeping herself. How long could it go on? Angela had said 'pay me back in Cairo' and now that their relationship had established itself, she and Castlebar would, sooner or later, return to Egypt. Then what would become of Harriet? The future was too ominous to contemplate and, turning her back on it, she went out to the road and walked between the orchards.

Angela and Castlebar were down for luncheon. Angela had asked for a larger table and, leaving their alcove, they seemed content to have Harriet with them. If they had suffered headaches or hangover, they had had time to recover and Angela began to consider the afternoon.

'Supposing we go and find this Dog River! What do you think, Harriet?'

Harriet said she was ready for anything. After luncheon, Angela said:

'Let's have our coffee in the Winter Garden. You, Bill darling, you want to work on a poem, don't you?'

Castlebar said, 'Yes', and went upstairs, as no doubt prearranged, and Angela took Harriet to the secluded spot behind the plumbago plants.

'Now, Harriet, when you say you're near penury, you're playing a little game with yourself, aren't you? I'm sure if you write to your husband, he'll send you what you need?'

'I can't write to him, that's the trouble. I can't ask him for anything.'

'Well, you can rely on me. I'll do all I can to help – but I must know the truth. What are you doing here? You're obviously not on holiday. Have you left Guy?'

'I think you could ask, rather, has he left me. Things happened that made me feel I'd be better elsewhere. I decided to go to England but, instead, I came here.'

'What happened? What sort of things?'

'Small things that seemed important at the time. You remember that brooch you gave me: the rose-diamond heart? Guy took it from me and gave it to Edwina.'

'To Edwina?' Angela gave a shocked laugh but added: 'If he did, surely it didn't mean anything?'

'It meant something to me.'

'I'm sorry. Oh, Harriet, I'm truly sorry. I wish I'd never bought the wretched thing.'

'I loved it. But if it hadn't been that, it would have been something else. I was ill and depressed. Guy's devotion to the outside world was more than I could stand. I felt I was tied up to him yet I was always alone. I sometimes think I would have done better to go on the evacuation ship. In England I could have earned a living. I would have had a life of my own.'

'But how did you get here from Suez? Not by train, I'm sure.'

'I was given a lift in a lorry. I came on an impulse, without stopping to ask myself how I was going to live when I got here. I had fifty pounds with me but it didn't last long. I'm in a silly predicament which I've brought on myself and I don't know what to do next.'

'Well, I won't abandon you, now that I've found you. As for money, you needn't worry about that. We're moving around and if you'd like to come with us, then come with us.'

'I'd like nothing better but I'd feel like an intruder. You and Bill are soon going to get tired of having me trailing after you.'

'No, you wouldn't be an intruder. We see quite enough of each other, and when we surface, we're glad to have someone else to talk to.'

'Yes, but for how long?'

Angela laughed and said: 'You know, Bill likes you, and he's not averse to having two females in tow. Men are like that. Women, too, probably. I wouldn't mind having an extra man around if he were amusing. But, for goodness' sake, no more Major Listers. He was impossible. Bill and I may not be very exciting company but at least we don't cry about our little bums.'

'Angela darling, it is lovely to be back with you. My only fear is I'll never be able to repay you.'

'Oh yes, you will. I'll chalk it up, every penny. But, please, no more about money. You've no idea how boring it is. It's a bore to be without it, and a bore to have it and have to look after it. There should be a more satisfactory system of exchange.'

Angela stood up and now, with explanations over, Harriet supposed they were going to the Dog River, but no. Angela said, 'I'd better see how Bill's getting on', and going upstairs did not come down again.

Harriet, giving up hope of her, returned to the garden to look at Beirut far below. Wondering how much it would cost to take a taxi down to the sea-front, she went and asked the hotel clerk who said: 'There and back, a wait for you between? I fear, very much.'

'More than five pounds.'

'More, yes, I fear. The taxis are not here. They come up from Beirut and they must return. It is a bad mountain road so they charge more. And then this very nice hotel and drivers think, "All rich people," and charge more. So it is.'

Harriet, contemplating the penalties of affluence, said: 'I see. Thank you,' and gave up the idea of going to Beirut on her own.

The days passed in monotonous inactivity. Angela might say: 'Let's go to Baalbek,' or the Beirut bazaars, or the Dog River, but in the end, she and Castlebar would retire to their room and not reappear until suppertime. Harriet's only diversion was to walk along the country road to a small village where there was nothing to do or see.

Still, here, on the seaward side of the mountain, the spring was advancing. The fruit trees were beginning to flower and small cyclamen were opening in the grass verges. The middays were so warm that Angela and Harriet could take their coffee in the garden. Castlebar, who did not take coffee, always went upstairs 'to work' and Angela would follow him there.

It had not occurred to Harriet that Castlebar was entertaining but now, escorted by what he called his 'two birds', he would tell stories and repeat conversations he had overheard and, at Angela's request, repeat his limericks, all of them well known to Harriet. The first hour after dinner was the time for these performances. Later his stammer grew worse, his speech slurred and he began to yawn. When he was at his best, Angela kept him going, reminding him of this story and that.

'Darling one, tell Harriet about the two officers at the Mohammed Ali Club.'

Castlebar snuffled and tittered, apparently reluctant until coaxed further: 'Do tell it, darling, it's my favourite story.'

'W-w-well, it was like this. These two young officers were discussing the arrival of a Sikh regiment in Cairo: "Nuisance their being here. Means, if the city's overrun, we'll have to shoot our women."

'"Shoot our women, old chap, why'd we do that?"

'"Done thing, old chap. Obligatory, y'know."'

Delighted, Angela threw her arms round Castlebar: 'You'd enjoy shooting me, wouldn't you, you great, big, glorious brute?'

Every night, she insisted on at least one of Castlebar's own limericks and she was as indignant as he was that the Cairo poetry magazine *Personal Landscape* had rejected them as too obscene for publication.

Harriet had discovered that beneath the mists of alcohol, Castlebar's creativity had its own separate life. During their days at The Cedars, he was, he said, working on a poem.

'When do you do it? In the afternoon?'

'W-w-well, no. Angie and I tend to get drowsy in the afternoon.' He took out of his pocket a page from a small, ruled note-book: 'I have it here. Before lunch, when I'm shaving, I put it up on the shaving-mirror and look at it, and I alter a word here and there, and gradually it builds up. In a couple of weeks, it will be a poem.'

'When it's finished, what will you do with it?'

'Just keep it, and one day I'll have enough for a slim vol.'

As Harriet gazed at him in a wakening admiration, Castlebar patted her knee: 'Don't worry about money. You'll be all right with us. Angie's a great giver. She loves to feel she's got us captive.'

'And you don't mind being a captive?'

'I don't mind anything so long as I can work at my poetry.'

He smiled and put the paper back in his pocket. She could see he had his own integrity and though he might be under Angela's heel, a part of him remained aloof and intact.

She envied him his talent and decided that an occupation so intensive it made all else unimportant was very much what she needed herself. She wondered if she could write. During the empty afternoons, she read through the books in the writing-room bookcase. They had been left behind by visitors and were mostly forgotten French novels, stilted and dull, but there was a Tauchnitz edition of *Romolo*. Though she thought it laboured in style and lifeless in content, she read it for lack of anything else to do.

A week after her arrival, Harriet heard a familiar voice as she entered the dining-room. Dr Beltado, seated with Dr Jolly and Miss Dora, was declaiming on the possible fusion of all cultures. Glancing up at Harriet as she passed, he looked puzzled as though wondering if he had seen her before. Dr Jolly did not notice her but she saw that Miss Dora had seen her and had no wish to see her.

As the doctor's voice filled the room throughout dinner, Harriet questioned herself whether she dare intercept him before he got away again. Angela, seeing her abstracted, asked what was the matter and heard the whole story.

Swinging round, giving the trio a fierce stare, she asked at the top of her voice: 'You mean that lot over there? You must make them pay up. If you don't, I will.'

The other diners, alerted to an interesting situation, stared at Angela then at Beltado, and again at Angela and back to Beltado, until Beltado, his voice failing him, began to realize he was a centre of unwelcome attention.

'I'll just have a word with him,' Angela said and, crossing to his table, she made her accusations in a voice that could be heard by all. He had bolted without paying the sum owed to an employee.

Beltado gave Harriet another look and recalled what this was all about. He began to bluster: 'How was I to know what I owed her? She was told to put in her account . . .' Bluster had no effect on Angela. Extravagant though she was, she would not tolerate misdealing, and she demanded that the money be paid there and then. She came back to Harriet with more than was due to her.

'But I didn't earn all that.'

'Never mind.' Angela closed Harriet's fingers over the bundle of notes and, alight with victory, kissed her on the cheek: 'You take it. It's your money plus interest. Next time he'll decide it's cheaper to pay when the money is due.'

Fifteen

Simon was reaching the point of complete recovery. Guy, on his next visit to the hospital, found he had given up his crutch and was moving firmly on a stick. His walk was normal except, as he explained to Guy, his left foot tended to drag a little and his right toe had a trick of doubling under itself.

The trick came at unexpected moments but he had it under control. Whenever the toe seemed about to pitch him forward on to his face, he squared his shoulders and jerked them back and the toe was frustrated.

Simon laughed as though he had outwitted an enemy: 'Neat that. Greening says the toe's the last hurdle. He said: "Get your muscles into trim and your feet will serve you OK." He told me to just go on working at it, so I'm working at it. I say to myself: "See that rope over there? You've to shin right to the top."'

'And can you do it?'

'I have done it. It's a bit of a sweat but I make myself do it. I think Greening's pretty pleased with me.'

'You like him better these days?'

'Oh, Greening's all right.'

Simon was not only physically better, he had thrown off the shock to his system and had a new belief in himself.

'I'll be out of here as soon as the toe clears up. I don't intend to hang around in the convalescent centre. Lots of chaps stay there for weeks, afraid of going back to the desert, but I'm not like that. I want to go back.'

Guy still hired the car and took Simon to the Gezira gardens or the sports fields, but the heat was becoming too oppressive for these afternoon outings and Simon no longer wanted to be treated as an invalid. As for Guy himself, he had other things he should be doing.

When he next arrived with the car, Simon said: 'I want to go to the pyramids.'

Not much drawn to the pyramids, Guy said: 'We could go to Mena and have a drink in the bar.'

Driving through the suburbs where flame trees held out plates of flowers the colour of tomato soup, Simon was reminded of his first day in Cairo and his first trip into the desert. That had been a month or so later than this, but already the wind blowing into the car had the sparking heat of mid-year and the chromium was too hot to touch. The climate had seemed to him intolerable yet during his year in Egypt, he had learnt to tolerate it.

The car stopped outside Mena House. When they stepped into the brazen sunlight, Guy's one thought was to reach the air-conditioned bar but Simon, without pause or explanation, hurried away in the opposite direction. Guy followed him, calling, but he did not look round. Striding across the stone floor on which the pyramids were built, he stopped at a corner of the Great Pyramid where the stone showed white from the scraping of many feet. This was the usual place of ascent. Shielding his eyes with his hands, he looked up to the apex above which the sun was poised, blazing and scintillating in a sky white with heat.

When Guy caught him up, he said: 'I'm going to climb it.'

'Not now, surely?'

'Yes, now.' He turned to look at Guy with an exultant determination and Guy could only try and reason with him.

'Simon, you know, this is foolhardy. If you slipped, you could undo all the work they've done on you.'

'I won't slip.' He held out his stick: 'If you'd just look after that . . .'

Guy took the stick and put it on the ground: 'You don't imagine I'd let you go alone?'

Simon laughed: 'Good show. Let's see who gets there first.'

The blocks that formed the pyramid were about three feet in height. Guy, with his face towards the stonework, put his hands on the first block and pulled himself up till he could kneel on top of it. He got to his feet and tackled the second block.

Simon shouted to him: 'Look, this is how Harriet did it.' Turning his back on the pyramid, he jumped his backside up on to the block, swung his legs after him, stood up and sat himself on the second block.

To Guy, watching, it seemed to be done with one movement and he remembered Harriet going up in the same way, wearing her black velvet evening-dress that had never been the same again.

'It's easy,' Simon said and Guy agreed. It looked extraordinarily easy but he preferred to keep his eyes on Simon and laboured up in his own way, keeping immediately below his companion with some idea of acting as a safety net.

Simon, in high spirits, laughed with pleasure at the speed of his ascent and the noise brought out the 'guides' who bawled: 'Not allowed. Must have guide,' and shook their fists when they were ignored. But it was too hot for indignation and they soon retreated to whatever shelter they had found.

Half-way up, Simon's pace slackened. Both men were soaked with sweat and Simon, pausing to get his breath, took off his shirt and spread it on the stone. Guy did the same thing and while they stood for a few minutes, he hoped Simon would now give up. Instead, he went on at a less furious pace. Guy, below him, could see the scar of his wound rising above the waistband of his slacks. It was red and the skin looked thin. Guy, fearing it might break open, wondered where he could go for help if help were needed. But Simon did not need help. He was well ahead of Guy and reaching the top where the apex stones had been removed, he passed out of sight. Guy, moving more quickly, followed and found him lying spreadeagled on his back, his arms over his eyes.

Throwing himself down beside him, Guy asked: 'How do you feel?'

'Fine.' He was too breathless to say much and lay for so long without moving that Guy became uneasy again. How was Simon to be transported down if he could not transport himself? Before this unease could become anxiety, Simon lifted his arms and seeing Guy's worried expression, burst out laughing.

'I did it.'

'Yes. It was pretty impressive.'

'I feel a bit dizzy, though.'

Guy felt dizzy, too. Looking around him at the dazzle of the desert, he wondered why anyone should want to come up here. There was little to see. In the distance, wavering and floating in the liquid heat, were the odd shapes of the Saccara Pyramids. Not much else. The two men might have been on a raft in a yellow sea; or rather, on a grill beneath an intense and dangerous flame.

He shook Simon by the shoulder: 'Come on. If we don't move out of this, we'll both get sun-stroke.'

Without speaking, Simon rolled over and over till he reached the edge of the floor then he let himself down to the step below. Here an edge of shade was stretching out but not enough.

'If you can manage it,' Guy said, 'we'd better get down to the hotel and have that drink.'

'Oh, I can manage it.' Standing up, Simon staggered slightly and made a face at Guy: 'Muscles stiff. Not yet in tip-top form, but they soon will be.' He sat on the edge of the block and dropped down to the one below: 'Piece of cake, this. I wish Greening could see me.' His shirt was dry again and at the bottom, he picked up his stick: 'I don't think I'll need this much longer.'

'What about the toe?'

'The toe? Good Lord, I'd forgotten about it. That's what Greening said. I'd only to forget I couldn't do it.'

He talked on a note of triumphant assurance but for all that, he was glad enough to sink into a chair in the bar and take the glass Guy put into his hand: 'Cheers. Just the job.'

There were half a dozen or so officers in the bar and Guy noticed that as Simon entered, leaning lightly on his stick, they had reacted very differently from the men at the swimming-pool. There, pallid and strained, he had been a dismal reminder of the reality of war. Here, his young face still flushed from the climb, he was the shining hero.

He and Guy sat for a while, silent and glad of rest, drinking their chilled beer, then Simon put his hand into his shirt pocket and took out a thin piece of card: 'This came two days ago.'

It was one of the new air-mail letters, photographed and reduced, and Guy had to tilt his glasses in order to read the miniature handwriting:

Dear Simon, Sorry I can't say 'darling' any more. I know you'll be upset but it's a long time since you went away and you didn't write much, did you? I don't suppose it was much fun in the desert but it isn't much fun here, either. I've been lonely and what did you expect? Well, the long and the short of it is I've met someone else. Not getting letters from you, my thoughts turned to Another. I like him very much and he makes me happy and I want a divorce.

It wasn't much of a marriage, was it?

Ever yours,

ANNE

P.S. Your mum tells me you were wounded. I'm sorry but you didn't even let me know that.

Guy read it through twice before he said: 'You didn't tell me you were married.'

'Yes. We rushed into it before I went to join the draft. We only had a week at the Russell Hotel before I left. She's right, it wasn't much of a marriage. She came to see me off at the station. All I remember is her standing there crying and waiting for the train to take me away. I thought: "poor little thing" – that's all: a girl crying and me looking at her out of the carriage window. I wouldn't know her now if I passed her in the street.'

'Have you a photograph?'

'No. I had a snap but it fell out of my wallet somewhere in the desert. I don't even know when it went. I just found one day it wasn't there. Well, I don't need to feel sorry for her any more. I'm glad she's found someone who makes her happy. I only hope he's a decent bloke.'

'I wouldn't take it too seriously. People get carried away in wartime. Probably, when you get back, you'll find she's waiting for you.'

'Oh, no. It's better as it is. She can have a divorce and welcome. It's the best thing for both of us.' Simon, with Edwina's face glowing in his thoughts, smiled and pushed the letter back into his pocket.

'Have you decided yet what you'll do when the war's over?'

'I don't know. What is there left to do?'

'Everything. You've got a whole lifetime ahead of you. Even if you were accepted for the regular army, it would only be a short-term commission. You still have to face the future. I suppose, whatever happens, you'll return to England?'

'I suppose so, but I'm not going to stay any longer than I can help. It's my Mum and Dad. Every letter I get from them, they say they're just waiting for me to come back and tell them about Hugo. They say that's all that's keeping them alive. They say, "We know you'll tell us everything," as though there was something secret about his death. I've told them everything. Everything I know, that is. What else is there to tell? It's all in the past now. I don't want to talk about it. I don't want to be reminded of it. I feel I can't go through it all again.'

'But if it means so much to them . . .'

'They should try to forget it. Instead, they keep on as though I'd be bringing him back with me.'

'In a way you will be bringing him back, because you looked so much alike.'

'Still, I'm not Hugo. When they see me, it will make things worse for them. They'll realize they used to have two boys and now there's only one. They make me feel responsible. Can't you imagine what it will be like, going over it all again and again. I feel sorry for them but somehow, I don't know, they've become strangers.'

'It will be different once you get home. You'll feel you've never been away.'

'I don't know that I want to feel like that. I can't pretend nothing has changed. I've changed. I don't feel I belong there any more.' Simon's mouth, that during the days of his dependence, had seemed tenderly young and defenceless, now closed itself firmly. He had been a sick, despondent boy; now he was a young man conscious of his strength and his individuality in the world. Guy did not feel altogether pleased by this developing self-reliance which hinted of selfishness and he said sternly: 'Still, they are your parents. You will have to let them talk about Hugo; you owe it to them. It will be a comfort to them. And, remember, you're all they've got now.'

Simon finished his beer and put down his glass: 'Yes, I suppose you're right. Of course I'll go home and do what I can for them. I didn't mean I wouldn't, but I'm not staying in England. I feel now as though the whole world's waiting for me.'

Driving back to the hospital, he said gleefully: 'You know, I told myself if I did it, if I got to the top, I'd apply for a return to active service. They may stick me in an office at first but anything's better than hanging round being treated like an invalid.'

'I suppose you'll be sent to Tunisia.'

'Hope so. I wouldn't want to be kicking my heels like those chaps we saw in the bar.'

Guy felt a drop in spirits, thinking that Simon, too, would be lost to him. But that had to happen sooner or later. Simon had reached the last stage of recovery and must return to normal life; or rather, to the killing, destruction and turbulent hatred that these days passed for normal life. As he considered the emotions of violence that must blot out all other emotions, Guy said: 'War is an abomination yet I could almost envy you.'

Sixteen

The day after they were routed, the Beltados left the hotel and Angela and Harriet, returned to the ease of their old amity, began to talk of going elsewhere, but it was only talk. Angela was content at The Cedars and the days went on as before with the after-dinner whisky bottle and the drowsy retreat to bed. Then one day she said: 'We'll leave tomorrow. Where shall we go?' She turned to Castlebar: 'Where do you want to go, you great, domineering brute?'

Castlebar beamed on her: 'Wherever you take me, my pet.'

'We'll go back to Palestine. We'll make an early start and drive to Jerusalem. Bill, tell them to wake us at eight a.m.'

Castlebar nodded: 'Right. Troops will parade at eight a.m.' But when Harriet, having been wakened, went down to breakfast, there was no sign of Angela and Castlebar. They appeared, as usual, for luncheon and the party set out at three in the afternoon.

Angela's car was an old Alvis and as she drove, she complained continually: 'Wretched car. Steering all wrong. On the way here it nearly had us over a precipice.' Yet it brought them safely up on the downlands of the frontier and Angela stopped for a rest beside a curious pair of rocks that rose like horns from the grass.

Castlebar said: 'This was where the great battle was fought in 1187 when Saladin defeated the Crusaders and captured the true cross.'

Whether this was true or not, they stood and admired the innocent rocks because men had fought around them.

They were in Galilee. The new grass that Harriet had seen on her way through Palestine had now grown tall and the whole countryside had become a rich meadow choked with flowers. She exclaimed in wonder at a field of blue lupins and Angela, stopping the car, said they would walk for a while and see what was to be seen.

Hidden among the lupins were irises of a maroon shade so deep they looked black. Farther on there were other irises, purple and pink, and a buff colour veined with brown. The field ended in a downslope of grass starred like the Damascus Ghuta with red, white and purple anemones, and in the distance there was a lake of pure lapis blue.

'Do you realize what that is?' Angela said: 'It's the Sea of Galilee.'

Castlebar, who had been trailing after the women, stopped at the edge of the lupin field and said he needed a drink.

'Yes, my poor lamb needs a drink and I feel I've driven far enough. That little town down there looks entrancing. It might do us for the night.'

The town, when they drove down to it, was less entrancing than it had seemed from the heights. Like everywhere else in the Levant, it had been blighted by war. The hotels were boarded up. A notice said 'Thermal baths' but another notice said 'Closed'. The whole place, with its white villas and waterside buildings, had the air of a resort but it was a rundown resort and most of the inhabitants had gone away. Castlebar was sent to enquire about accommodation in a shop and came back to say there was a pension somewhere in the long, lakeside main road. The pension was owned by a very old Jewish woman who talked with Angela in Arabic, explaining that people usually came there in summertime but nowadays hardly anyone came. Still, she agreed to put up the English visitors and she opened rooms where the blinds were drawn, the bedding folded away and the air smelled of dust. She smiled at them, friendly and encouraging, and said if they cared to walk round the town, all would be ready for them on their return.

Angela appealed to Castlebar: 'What do you think, loved one?'

Castlebar did not think at all but shook his head and said: 'Won't it do, darling? We don't want to drive all night.'

The old woman asked for their passports and required Castlebar to sign a register. His fountain-pen was dry and she said, 'Wait, wait,' and brought a small ink bottle. When the bottle was opened, there was nothing inside but a little black sediment.

Resignedly spreading her hands, she said, 'Never mind,' and shut the register up.

The English visitors started down the main street but did not get very far. Coming to a stone quay where an Arab café owner had put his tables and chairs by the lake edge, Castlebar sat down and took out his cigarette pack.

The sun was low, the water placid. There was no noise except the click of the tric-trac counters from inside the café. A slight breeze blew cool across the lake and Castlebar, drinking arak and smoking his cigarettes, smiled contentedly and put his hand out to Angela. She slipped her hand into his, then he smiled at Harriet and she smiled back. She knew he did not want her to be excluded and she had begun not only to appreciate him but to feel affection for him. She could understand Angela's love for him. He might not dazzle the outside world but he was Angela's own man. He devoted himself to her and to her comfort. He was kind, and not only to Angela. He carried his kindness over to Harriet so she, an admirer of wit, intelligence and looks in a man, was beginning to realize that kindness, if you had the luck to find it, was an even more desirable quality.

They sat for some time with nothing to say then Castlebar, no doubt prompted by their being in the Holy Land, told the women a story he had not told before: 'Y-y-you know that in the Far East every Jew is called Sassoon? Well, it's the Jewish name there. Someone told me that one of the embassy chaps was coming back from safari on a Good Friday and saw the embassy flag at half-mast. He said to his bearer: "What d'you think's the matter, Chang?" And Chang told him: "Two thousand years ago, Sassoon man kill white man's joss. White man still velly solly."'

Angela gave a shriek of appreciation: 'Oh, Bill, you are wonderful!' and leaning towards him, she kissed his ear.

How pleasant it would be, Harriet thought, if Guy were here with them, not talking his head off or looking around for additional company, but happy to be with her in the way Angela and Castlebar were happy.

As the sun sank lower, a remarkable thing happened. First, Mount Hermon appeared, its silver crest hanging in mid-air, a disembodied ghost of a mountain, then the hills round the lake were emblazoned with colour, turning from an orange-pink to crimson then a crimson-purple so vivid it scarcely seemed a part of nature.

They had all seen the splendours of the Egyptian sunsets and Harriet had seen the famed violet light on the Athenian hills, but none of them had seen before this luscious, syrupy richness of light that suffused the hills, the town and the waters of the lake. Their faces were brilliant with it and Angela cried: 'If this is Galilee, we will stay here for ever!'

They sat, amazed, until the colour faded and the wind blew cold, then they went to a restaurant where a card in the window said: 'Steak sandwiches.' Steak sandwiches, Castlebar said, were just what his inside had in mind. His inside was also thinking of a privy and while he was away, Harriet said: 'I can understand why you are so fond of Bill. He's kind. Perhaps the kindest man I've ever known.'

'Wasn't your Guy supposed to be the epitome of kindness?'

'Supposed to be, yes.'

Angela laughed, saying quietly: ' "If he be not kind to me, what care I how kind he be?" To tell you the truth, I thought he was the most selfish man I've ever known. I often wondered why you didn't box his ears.'

Harriet smiled. She knew if Guy were to hear Angela's opinion of him, it would merely confirm his belief that she was mad.

'It's not exactly selfishness. It's . . . well, he doesn't stop to think.'

'You should pull him up short: *make* him think. The trouble is that with his charm, he has had things too easy.'

'That's true; but at the same time he feels deprived. He feels he should have fought in Spain. He venerates the men who did go there, especially the ones who died. I don't know why it should have been more heroic to fight in Spain than, say, the western desert, but apparently it was.'

'Is that why some of them bolted to the States when the war started?'

'Probably. They didn't want to be involved in anything so trivial as a Second World War.'

Angela, laughing, put her hands on Harriet's shoulder: 'Dear Harriet, I'm so glad you're with us. You really do add to the gaiety of nations.'

498

The restaurant was a long room with a row of tables against each wall. There was a bar at one end with a surprising variety of bottles. Small though the place was, it appeared to be the centre of life in Tiberias. Local boys were gathered there, drinking beer and mead. Angela was able to buy her bottle of whisky and Harriet was served with white Cyprus wine. The steak sandwiches were very good and Castlebar was able to buy a new pack of Camels. He and the two women imagined themselves comfortably settled in for the evening when there was a commotion in the street. Dozens of Australian soldiers were making an unsteady way down the centre of the road. The restaurant door crashed open and a bunched crowd of men elbowed each other into the narrow path between the tables. After staring about, befuddled and belligerent, they settled down at the few unoccupied tables and the arguments began.

The men wanted whisky. The young waitress, a refugee Jewess with little English, tried to tell them there was no whisky but they pointed to Angela's bottle and the other bottles behind the bar.

The girl appealed to Castlebar: 'What to do? Officers say no whisky for troops. Troops have beer but troops say: "Give whisky." What to do?'

Castlebar, feeling himself in a weak position, grinned uneasily at the angry men but had no suggestion to make. More Australians were crowding in but there was nowhere for them to sit. They lurched about, vaguely threatening, before wandering out again. One, as he left, scooped up a heap of small change from a table by the door. The rightful owner, finding it gone, began to shout that no change had been given to him. The waitress argued and wept while more arrivals pushed her this way and that.

Getting no help from her, the Australians took over the bar and began to serve themselves. They filled tumblers with spirits and started to sing. The girl brought out an older woman who demanded: 'You pay, you hear? You drink our drink and now you pay,' while the men, ignoring her, quarrelled, shouted and sang in hard, throaty voices.

In the midst of this uproar, Angela said: 'Let's go.' Castlebar hid the half-empty whisky bottle under his coat and they tried to push out between the tables but the way was blocked by a solitary Australian who had taken the empty fourth chair, which was beside Harriet. As she rose, he pushed her back into her seat and said: 'You're not going.'

Finding themselves trapped, Angela and Castlebar sat down again. The Australian, having looked Harriet over, said: 'Like to dance?'

'There's not much room for dancing.'

'Y'could be right.' He brought out a wallet and offered Harriet pictures of his parents. When she had admired them, she asked, 'What are you all doing here?'

'Three-day tour,' he said but could not tell her where they had been or where they were going. The men, it seemed, had arrived drunk the night before and having spent the day asleep, were intent on getting drunk again.

'So you haven't seen much?'

The Australian shook his head and again brought out his wallet: 'Wan' to see m'old mum and dad?'

'I've seen them. How long will you be here?'

'Don't know. Three-day tour.'

At that moment, a local boy at the next table, over-stimulated by events, gave a scream and fell to the floor. Shuddering, snorting, chattering, foaming at the mouth, he lay near Harriet's feet, a piteous and horrible sight. When she tried to move out of his way, the Australian pushed her down again.

'Take no notice of him; he's showing off. Wants to get ya to notice him. 'Ave another look at me old mum and dad.'

'For God's sake,' Angela shouted to Castlebar, 'make them let us out.'

Rising, holding the table before her like a battering ram, Angela thrust it into the aisle, pushing Harriet and the Australian in front of her. The Australian tried to force her back, but with the strength of anger, she gave him a violent blow across the mouth and he burst into tears. Castlebar, taking Harriet by the hand, pulled her after him while the Australian wailed: 'Nobody loves poor Aussies. Nobody loves poor Aussies.'

Somehow or other, the three English reached the street.

Harriet said: 'They'll be gone tomorrow.'

'So will we,' Angela spoke with furious decision and Harriet began to feel resentful of Angela's directives. The lakeside town

500

attracted her and she wanted to stay there a few days. At the pension, finding her room cleaned and the bed made, she thought of saying to Angela: 'You go. I will stay. I'm used to making my own decisions and I'm tired of being told where I shall go and when.' But supposing she did stay, how would she live? If she could not find work in Damascus, she certainly would not find it here.

During the night a storm broke and, wakened by the thunder, she went to the window and looked out on a small garden that ran down to the lake. She could see the water in tumult and a palm tree, lashed by the wind, bending from side to side, pliable as rubber, its fronds touching the ground this way and that. Serpents of lightning zig-zagged across the sky and flashed in sheets, illuming the scene with unnatural brilliance. The grass had been flattened by rain and, as she imagined the lupin field laid low by the torrent, she ceased to think of staying on in Galilee.

Next morning, the air glittered and the palm tree stood upright in the sun. No sound came from the room occupied by Angela and Castlebar. The next door was marked 'Bad' but when Harriet tried to open it, the old woman ran from her kitchen, holding up ten fingers to indicate the cost of a bath. Inside there was no bath but an old, rusted shower that creaked and gasped and gave out irregular bursts of cold, brown water.

The restaurant was shut till mid-day. Walking in the opposite direction, Harriet found beside the lake an open area planted with pepper trees. Beneath the trees were some iron tables and chairs, wet from the storm and as they dried, a mist rose into the delicate, lacy foliage of the trees. The lake water was flat and clear as glass and the surrounding trees motionless in the early morning air. A few people were sitting at the tables drinking coffee and as Harriet waited, a waitress came with a towel and mopped the rain from a chair and offered it to her.

Sitting happily alone beneath the shifting sun and shade of the trees, Harriet was diverted by a flying-boat that circled the lake and settled on the surface some fifty yards away from her. A rowing-boat went out to pick up the passengers. They were brought to the café, a collection of civilians with one army officer. The civilians, government officials or journalists, passed quickly between the tables and were gone while the officer, trudging up over the sandy floor, was left behind. He stopped in front of Harriet.

'Well, I never, I know the Middle East is a small world but surely the hand of fate is bringing us together.'

Wheezing and coughing through his big, fluffy moustache, Lister dropped on to a chair and tried to seize Harriet's hand. She slid it away from him, asking: 'What are you doing, arriving by sea-plane? Who were the other men?'

'Box-wallahs,' Lister panted, exhausted by the walk through the heavy sand: 'Secret mission. Trying to solve the food situation. Very hush-hush. Everyone knows about it, of course. Everyone knows everything here.' He coughed and spluttered before finding his voice again: 'The other day I got into a taxi and said to the driver: "Take me to the broadcasting station." "What you want, sah?" he asked. "You want PBS or you want Secret Broadcasting Station?" I said: "How d'you know there's a secret broadcasting station?" and the fellow roared with laughter: "Oh, sah, everyone know secret broadcasting station."' Lister, too, roared with laughter, his big, soft body straining against his washed-out khaki shirt and faded corduroy trousers. His eyes streamed and as he began coughing again, he took out a hip flask and drank from it: 'That's better. Have to go. There's a bus picking us up at 10.00 hours. See you in the Holy City, I expect. Oh, by the way, that actor fellow Pratt is there. Did I tell you?'

'No. If we come, where can I find him?'

'He's at the same bunkhouse as I am, the YMCA. I see a lot of him but he doesn't approve of poor old Lister. Thinks I'm fast or something. Look me up, won't you? We'll have a blow-out. Must go. Must go.' Shifting about and squirming, he managed to rise from his chair then, with a wave of his stick, he plodded on, his desert boots sinking into the sand, his trousers splitting over his big buttocks.

Jerusalem, Harriet decided, was the place for her. With the help of Aidan and Lister, she would be able to find work in a government office. Imagining all her problems were solved, she hurried back to the pension and found Angela, too, preparing to set out for Jerusalem. Castlebar had been sent to buy steak sandwiches and, soon after midday, they had left behind them the flowers and meadows of Galilee. Angela drove up on to the central ridge of hills to reach Nazareth where Castlebar thought they might stop for a drink. Angela said: 'Not here. Dim little place. We'll go on to Nablous.'

Nablous did not look much better but there was a pool, a large tank, where boys were splashing about and making a lot of noise.

'Now this is fun,' Angela said, 'we'll stop here.' When they had eaten their steak sandwiches, she wandered down and spoke to the boys in Arabic. She asked how they had come by the pool and the boys told her that a rich man had presented it to the town.

She asked when did the girls have their turn in the water?

The girls? The boys looked confounded until one, older than the others, as though talking to someone simple-minded, told her the girls did not come to the pool. The girls had to stay at home and help their mothers.

Angela came back to the car in a rage and said: 'This is a one-sex town. Let's push on to civilization.'

As they reached the end of the ridge, they glimpsed distant towers and spires but it was not till they overlooked the valley of Latrun that they saw the Holy City complete and radiant on its hills. It seemed to float on a basin of mist and within its crenellated walls, the golden dome of the Mosque of Omar radiated the evening sunlight.

There was a downdrop of hairpin bends. 'The Seven Sisters,' Castlebar told the women. 'Notorious place for accidents, designed by the silly Turks. This is where the horses would smell the stables and make a dash and take the whole caboose over the edge. I hope our old moke doesn't smell a garage.'

Angela smiled indulgently on him. 'You awful idiot,' she said and bending to kiss him, nearly took the Alvis over the edge.

They drove down into olive groves then, rising again, reached the outskirts of the city and came on to the Jaffa Road.

'Here we are,' Angela said and stopped the car outside the King David Hotel.

Seventeen

The Jerusalem weather was still unsettled. Heavy showers came and went, leaving on the air the scent of rosemary, but the rains were nearly over. The sun, when it appeared, had the pleasant heat of an English summer.

Settling down to their old routine, Harriet, Angela and Castlebar would sit before dinner in the hotel garden and watch the mist clear over the Jordan valley and the mountains of Moab appear, purple-brown and wrinkled like prunes.

On the first evening, Angela was so pleased by her surroundings that she said: 'We might spend the summer here,' and Harriet, hoping soon to find work and pay her way, said she could think of no more agreeable place.

'What about you, loved one?' Angela turned to Castlebar and Castlebar, as usual, agreed with Angela.

But at dinner, her enthusiasm waned at the sight of the strange, dark meat on her plate. She called their waiter, an Armenian, and said: 'What on earth is it?'

The waiter was not sure. He said it could be mutton or it could be camel.

'Mutton? Camel?' Angela cried out indignantly, attracting the attention of the other diners: 'No one eats mutton these days. As for camel!'

'Here, madam, we must be glad for what we can get.' The waiter explained that the different communities conserved their food for their own people. The Arabs fed the Arabs, the Jews the Jews, but the British, having no one to provide for them, were always half-starved and the hotels had to take what they could get. He, an Armenian, was not much better off than the British so he was lucky to work where food was provided. His manner, modest and considerate, disarmed Angela who smiled into his old, sad, wrinkled face and said with humorous resignation: 'There's always a something, isn't there? And I suppose you're going to tell me there's no Scotch whisky.'

'Oh, madam, there is whisky. Many kinds. You like whisky, madam?' He asked as one asking a child if it liked chocolate. Angela threw back her head and laughed, then said to all the interested diners: 'Isn't he sweet!' She told him he was her favourite waiter, her favourite of all the waiters she had ever known and he smiled at her with gentle, adoring eyes.

The Holy City was protected by a town planner. The city was built of grey, local stone, and new buildings had to conform, but opposite the hotel there was a red, stark structure that had somehow evaded regulations. It was fronted by the small, neat rosemary hedges that scented the air in wet weather. Harriet thought it was a block of municipal offices but found it was the YMCA.

When Angela and Castlebar were settled in the bar, she crossed the road to enquire for Aidan Pratt.

The porter told her: 'Captain Pratt gone away.'

'And not coming back?'

'Yes, indeed, coming back. We keep his room. He come when he come. When? Any time now, I think.'

Harriet, eager to start work, left with a sense of hope deferred. Outside on the steps, she met Lister who gave her a riotous welcome: 'Here she is, my lovely girl. Come to find her old Lister.'

'Well, not exactly. To tell you the truth, I was looking for Aidan Pratt but he's away.'

'That one is always away. He thinks the War Office sent him out on a joy-ride. Do you want him for anything special?'

'Only to see him. It's just that he's a friend of Guy.'

'Aren't we all? Everyone's a friend of Guy.'

'When do you think Aidan will be back?'

'I don't know but I could find out. Why worry about him when you've got your old Lister to show you round. How long will you be in Jerusalem?'

'I'm not sure.' There was, Harriet realized, a flaw in her plan to live and work here. Guy had friends in the city and sooner or later, one of them would tell him where she was. She had been prepared to take Aidan into her confidence but Lister was another matter. She could not trust him to keep her presence secret.

He said: 'Come over to the bar and have a drink.'

Having no reason to refuse, Harriet went with him to the hotel, discomforted by the thought that Angela did not want to see him again. But Angela seemed to be amused by the sight of him and when he pressed his damp moustache ardently against the back of her hand, she asked: 'And how's the little bum tonight?'

'Ho, ho, ho,' Lister shook all over and on the strength of their previous acquaintance, sat down and helped himself from the whisky bottle. His hand was shaky. It was obvious he had already reached the talkative stage of inebriation but he said: 'First to-day.' Then: 'Just met this girl looking for that actor fellow Pratt. She said he was a friend of Guy. "Aren't we all?" I said: "Aren't we all?" Eh, eh? Not surprising, eh?' He eulogized Guy's good fellowship, his gift of making people feel wanted, his readiness to help anyone who needed help and so on. While he talked, his eyes slid loosely in their sockets and several times looked to Harriet for confirmation of what he said, expecting her to be gratified.

And, in a way, she was. Guy deserved this praise, she could even feel proud of his deserving but the fact remained, she had not been included in this widely bestowed generosity.

Angela listened but said nothing. Castlebar smiled and gave Harriet a sly glance. Lister, catching the glance, shouted: 'Eh, you poetaster? What do you think? Do you agree or disagree?'

'I agree, of course.'

'Ever hear that story about the two men on the desert island? Neither knew the other but they both knew Guy Pringle?'

'Oh, y-y-yes, frequently.'

'There you are, then! The man's a legend. Isn't he a legend, eh?'

'Y-y-yes. Very lively legend, though.'

Mollified, Lister subsided: 'Glad you've turned up. Nice to have someone who talks one's own language. You'll be here most nights, I expect. Nowhere else to go, is there?'

Lister helped himself again from the bottle and in return for hospitality, set out on a survey of Palestine as it looked to him.

'Ideal climate this, never too hot, but awful place, everyone hating everyone else. The Polish Jews hate the German Jews, and the Russians hate the Polish and the German. They're all in small communities, each one trying to corner everything for themselves: jobs, food, flats, houses. Then there's the Orthodox Jews – they got here first and want to control the show. The sophisticated western Jews hate the Old City types with their fur hats and kaftans and bugger-grips. See them going round on the Sabbath trying the shop doors to make sure no one's opened up on the quiet. All they do is pray and bump their heads against the Wailing Wall. Their wives have to keep them. Then all the Jews combine in hating the Arabs and the Arabs and Jews combine in hating the British police, and the police hate the government officials who look down on them and won't let them join the Club. What a place! God knows who'll get it in the end but whoever it is, I don't envy them.'

Castlebar said: 'I s-s-suppose things'll settle down when the Jews feel more secure?'

'Don't know,' Lister had said his piece and had now started to droop. 'Hatred,' he muttered. 'Terrible thing: hatred! My nurse used to hate me, never knew why. She used the brush on me. Bristle side. Used to pull down m'little knickers . . .'

'Not that little bum again,' Angela interrupted sharply and Lister gave her a hurt look, then sank forward on his stick. A tear trickled down his cheek.

'No sympathy. No understanding . . .'

'Come on,' Angela ordered Castlebar who protested: 'But the bottle's still a quarter full.'

'Let him have it. You drink too much, anyway. How about you, Harriet?'

'I'm coming.' Looking back, Harriet saw Lister abstractedly refilling his glass. She expected a reprimand from Angela but Angela said only: 'I suppose we'll have him every night,' and sighed as she went into the lift.

Lister was, as she had feared, a nightly visitor to the bar but he also escorted Harriet on sight-seeing trips while Angela and Castlebar spent the afternoons in their room. Angela lent Lister the car and he drove Harriet to Bethlehem to see the Church of the Nativity and a cave made gaudy with velvets, brocades, ikons, holy pictures and bejewelled gewgaws that claimed to be the manger where Christ was born. They went westward down through the orange groves to Jaffa and eastward through the desert to Jericho and the Dead Sea. All these trips were described in the evening to Angela who was content to listen and see nothing, but there was one event that roused her interest. The Armenian waiter had told her about the great ceremony of the Greek church, the Ceremony of the Holy Fire.

Lister eagerly agreed: 'Mustn't miss it, even if you have to camp in the church all night.' He said nothing more but a few days later he arrived with an air of smiling complacency that had in it a slight hauteur. Even his limp had acquired majesty. Bowing first to Angela, then to Harriet and to Castlebar, he said: 'I have done the impossible. I have obtained tickets for the Holy Fire; and ask you to honour me by coming as my guests.'

Gratified by their grateful acceptance, he went to the bar and bought drinks for everyone. 'This year,' he explained in a somewhat lofty fashion, 'the police are going to control the show. There will be no fighting to get in, no violence or people getting killed. Admission will be by invitation only.'

'But won't that spoil things?' Angela said.

'Not a bit. The hoi-polloi will simply have to wait till the ticket holders are seated then they'll be admitted in an orderly manner. There'll be a special entrance for distinguished visitors, among whom will be . . .' he lifted Angela's hand, then Harriet's, and having kissed them both, simpered at them: '. . . will be these two lovely ladies.'

Harriet asked: 'How did you get the tickets?'

'Never mind. There are ways and means, *if* one has influence.' Lister maintained his dignity for the rest of the evening, leaving the bar while still reasonably sober and making no further mention of his little bum. He refused to disclose how he had obtained the tickets but Angela learnt from her friend, the Armenian waiter, that batches of invitations had been sent out to the different orders of Jerusalem society: the government officials, the military and the religious sects – the Greeks, the Roman Catholics, the Copts, the Armenians and even the lowly Abyssinians who were so poor, they had been pushed out of the interior of the church but had managed to keep a foothold on the roof.

'The roof of what?' Angela asked.

'Why, madam, the roof of the church. The Holy Sepulchre.'

Lister, when tackled by Angela, admitted he had applied for four of the military allotment and had been granted them. 'Quite an achievement, eh? Getting all four?' He produced the tickets and allowed his guests to examine them then, with the air of a munificent host, put them back in his wallet. He impressed on them the need to make an early start. Though the onlookers would be organized, nothing could organize the Greek patriarch.

'The show begins when the old boy chooses to turn up, and that could be any time. Want to get in at the start, don't we? It'll be a great occasion, a great occasion.'

Lister, in his state of expansive authority, remained as near sober as he ever was. The only thing troubling him was his gout.

Eighteen

Edwina had announced her engagement to Tony Brody but she still had doubts about the marriage. Creeping her hand towards Guy and gently touching his arm, she sighed and said: 'Guy darling, what do you think? *Should* I marry Tony?'

'Don't you want to marry him?'

'I wish I knew. I'm fond of him, of course, but he's so stingy about money. I told him I wanted a big wedding in the cathedral and an arch of swords but he won't hear of it. He says a simple ceremony at the Consulate will do for him. Isn't that mean? I've always wanted an arch of swords but he refuses to speak to his colonel. Just think of it! A simple ceremony at the Consulate! We might as well not be married at all. What was your wedding like, Guy?'

'Very simple. We went to a registry office.'

'Oh yes, people did that in England with the war coming. But next time you'd want something better than that.'

'There won't be a next time.'

'Oh Guy, really!' The evening in the fish restaurant had faded into the past and Edwina again considered Guy as a likely match: 'You're too young to be on your own. I keep thinking how silly it would be if I married Tony and then you changed your mind and started looking . . . well, you know what I mean!'

Guy smiled: 'I won't change my mind. I'm not the marrying kind.'

'You married Harriet.'

'Harriet was different.'

'How horrid you are!' Edwina, growing pink, shook her hair down to hide her face and said in a small voice: 'Well, Harriet's gone, now. Poor Harriet! You weren't all that nice to her when she was alive. She must have spent a good many nights alone here just as I do when Tony's on duty. I know how beastly it is.'

Guy rose without speaking and went to his room to sort his books. Dobson said to Edwina: 'That was cruel and uncalled for, Edwina.'

'I don't think it was uncalled for. Why is Guy so rude and horrid these days? He used to be sweet but now you never know what he'll say.'

'Then don't provoke him. If you've settled for Tony Brody, you must put Guy out of your mind.'

'You don't care what happens to me, do you? It's miserable being engaged. Nobody takes me out now except Tony.'

'You mean there's loyalty among men even in these lean times?'

'No, it's not that. All the best men have gone to Tunisia.'

'If you're marrying Tony simply because there's no one else, you'd be wise to wait. There are always better fish in the sea.'

'Oh, but we can't wait because we're going to Assuan. I've always wanted to stay at the Cataract and it'll soon be too hot.'

Marrying in haste, Edwina went around in taxis, shopping for her trousseau, buying evening dresses at Cicurel and having fittings for her bridal gown. She occasionally looked in at her office because she had decided to keep her job. It was, in its way, war work and, in a less enthusiastic mood, she admitted Tony had said the money would be useful. As she was still arguing and pleading for a cathedral wedding and a reception at the Semiramus, Tony had to tell her that he was a divorced man. Though there might be no ban by the cathedral authorities, he felt that a quiet civil ceremony would be more fitting for a second marriage. Edwina, stunned by this disclosure, was left with nothing but the honeymoon at the Cataract; and Upper Egypt was already uncomfortably hot.

'Poor girl,' Dobson said to Guy: 'I'll have to do something for her. We could have a little reception here. It won't be very grand but it will be better than nothing.'

Offered a party of thirty guests with Cyprus champagne and a cake from Groppi's, Edwina was moved to tears: 'Oh, Dobbie, what a darling you are! What a darling you've always been to me! Guy, too.' She dabbed at her eyes and both men felt the pathos of lost hopes. All her lavish plans had gone down in disappointment. She had hoped to marry Peter Lisdoonvarna and have a title, even if only an Irish one, and she had ended with a major past his first youth who already had one wife to keep.

Meanwhile Dobson had decided to write his memoirs. 'With the war out of the way, one has to do something,' he said and at the breakfast table, while Edwina was trying to discuss the details of her reception, he would call on Guy to approve some theory about empire or advise on some anecdote or other. He kept a collection of used envelopes on which he made notes.

Guy, giving an ear to each of them, inclined towards Dobson, having some interest in the uses of diplomacy and none in Tony Brody.

It was Dobson's belief that the British empire began to decay when the speed-up of communications gave the Colonial Office dominion over the colonial governors.

'That will be my theme,' he said.

Guy considered it: 'You mean, individuality became answerable to the machine?'

'Excellently put,' Dobson scribbled on an envelope: 'We no longer have great men like Bentinck, the Wellesleys, Henry Laurence, James Kirk: men who developed their initiative by exercising it. Now the service is dependent on a pack of nonentities. You agree?'

'I'm not sure that I do. One can develop bad judgement as well as good.'

'True, but now we have no judgement at all. We administer by statistics.'

'That's not necessarily harmful. Think of the mayhem that's been caused by putting a Hitler in control.'

'Well, yes. Strong measures don't always work. Would you say that HE did any good when he drove a tank through the gates of Abdin Palace?'

'You know more about that than I do.'

Dobson consulted another envelope: 'I've said the results weren't up to much. HE thought he'd taught Farouk a lesson but Farouk has his own ideas. He's no fool. The other day he said to HE: "When are you going to take the last of your damn troops out of my country." HE gave him a lecture on Egypt being the front line of defence of the Gulf oil-fields. Farouk listened in sulky silence and at the end said: "Oh, stay if you must, but when the war's over, for God's sake put down the white man's burden and go." '

When Guy laughed, Dobson added quickly: 'But keep that under your hat. It's my story. Those bloody journalists are a pack of thieves. If you're fool enough to tell them anything, they'll print it as their own next day. Your friend Jackman is the biggest crook.'

'Jackman's no longer here.'

'Umm, I forgot. Now listen to this: King Farouk said to me: "Egypt, you know, is part of Europe." "Indeed," I replied: "Which part?" I wasn't going to put it in but I think it's too good to leave out.'

Edwina, weary of this talk, broke in on it: 'Oh, Dobbie, you're becoming a bore. No wonder Harriet described you as a master of impersonal conversation.'

'Did she?' Dobson spoke in a high note of satisfaction and scribbled down: 'Master of impersonal conversation.'

'I don't think you've any real feeling for anyone. You know how worried I am. Here am I on the very eve of marrying Tony and I'm not sure I'll go ahead with it.'

'Then I'd better cancel the order for champagne.'

'Oh, I don't think you should do that,' Edwina said.

When Edwina had accused him of leaving Harriet too much on her own, Guy had been offended, yet the accusation was justified. Harriet must have spent many nights on her own and he had never asked her what she did with herself. Loneliness was something outside his experience. He had his work and his friends, and he had sacrificed Harriet to both. The truth was, the war had given his work too much importance. Work had condoned his civilian status. Its demands had left him no time for his wife and he had instigated her return on the doomed ship. But had the demands of his work been so intensive? Didn't he inflate them to save his civilian face?

Now, no longer challenged by the nearness of war, he could see the futility of his reserved occupation. Lecturing on English literature, teaching the English language, he had been peddling the idea of empire to a country that only wanted one thing; to be rid of the British for good and all. And, to add to the absurdity of the situation, he himself had no belief in empire.

But if he did not have his work, what would be left to him? He thought it no wonder that people were giving themselves to such absurdities as Dobson's memoirs and Edwina's perfunctory marriage. The war had abandoned them, leaving them in a vacuum that had been filled by everyday worries. But everyday worries were not enough. They had to invent excitements to make life bearable. Now it seemed to him the only excitement left in life was work.

He still had friends, of course. Almost everyone who knew him, claimed him as a friend. Simon was still on hand, glad of an outing now and then. And Aidan Pratt, though given little encouragement, came to Cairo with the sole purpose of seeing him.

Aidan, taking two weeks' leave, had spent the whole time at Shepherd's, telephoning Guy every day and begging his company when Guy had time to spare.

On his last day, he invited Guy to dinner at the Hermitage. 'Just to say "goodbye",' he said with unconvincing cheerfulness and Guy, feeling bound to him by his affection for Harriet, accepted the invitation but said he would probably arrive late.

'However late you are, I'll wait for you,' Aidan replied and Guy, tired of his company, felt the relationship was being augmented by a sort of blackmail.

Crossing the Midan to the restaurant door, Guy could see through the glass into the brightly-lit interior where Aidan was sitting on a sofa. He was, as he promised, waiting for his guest, looking for him but looking in the wrong direction, his dark, sombre eyes betraying a longing that brought Guy to a stop.

Guy, reaching the pavement, paused in the darkness of the street, reluctant to enter, knowing he was the longed-for object. He had tolerated Aidan, feeling indebted to him for grief shared, but now he had had enough. As he stood, half inclined to make his escape, Aidan turned, saw him and at once played another role. He had been sitting in the sofa corner like a caged, unhappy bird. Now, rising with an actor's grace, he lifted a hand as Guy joined him and said: 'So there you are!'

'Sorry I'm late.'

'I'm quite used to your being late,' Aidan spoke lightly, with a self-denigratory smile as though resigned to his unimportance in Guy's scheme of things. The smile still lingered on his face as they went to the table he had booked and sat down.

During dinner, he did not try to establish any sort of intimacy. He talked, as most people did, about the war. He had heard, he said, that plans were in hand for a combined British and American attack across the Mediterranean.

Guy said: 'I knew it was on the cards but if it's imminent, surely it would be top secret?'

'It is top secret. Naturally. But things get round. That fellow Lister who works at Sharq al Adna, you've only to give him a few drinks and he'll tell you anything. He got a signal about the preparations for an attack across the Med, but there's more to it than that. There's a rumour that the Vichy government has started to evacuate children from the Channel ports. That could mean a concerted attack, north and south. If there were two sudden blows, the whole centre could disintegrate quite suddenly. It might mean a complete German collapse.'

'You think so?' Guy could not believe it. He did not even want to believe it. He was in no fit state to face peace at that time: 'If by the centre, you mean the occupied countries, an area of that size doesn't collapse in a hurry. Except for Switzerland and Sweden, it's the whole of Europe.'

'What about Spain?'

'Spain's part of the Axis.'

'I wouldn't say that. The Germans haven't found Franco as docile as they'd hoped, and we should be grateful for it. If the government had won, Spain would have been occupied when war broke out. It would have been an important stronghold for the enemy. We would certainly have lost Gibraltar.'

Guy, frowning, said: 'That's merely supposition.'

Aware that he had annoyed Guy, Aidan left the question of Spain and said mildly: 'I have a feeling the war could be over this year.'

'That's ridiculous. The Germans will fight from town to town, from house to house, doorway to doorway. It could drag on for years. By the time we get back – if we ever do get back – there may be nothing left of Europe but rat-ridden, plague-stricken ruins, and, don't forget, there are other war zones. I can't imagine the Japanese ever giving in. It could be like the Hundred Years War. There may never be peace in our time.'

Aidan gave a bleak laugh: 'You're very gloomy tonight. Why shouldn't we pull out? – make a separate peace?'

'Pull out? We're allied to Russia and the United States. Do you imagine we could pull out and leave them to fight without us? Would you want such a thing?'

'I don't know. Perhaps.'

Guy could see that Aidan did want it, though he had little hope of it. The smile that had lingered on his face faded as he contemplated a lifetime of war and he said: 'I believe a good many people want it but, of course, they won't admit it. Look what the war has done to us all! You've lost Harriet. I've lost my future as an actor, everything that mattered to me. Do you remember that night in Alex when Harriet said she had seen me as Konstantin in *The Seagull*? How moved she had been! She said she was spellbound. On the first night, I said to myself, "Now it's all beginning," and less than three months later, it had ended. I declared myself a conscientious objector and I was directed on to that ship taking the children to Canada . . .' Aidan's voice failed and Guy, not unfeeling, said: 'It'll end sometime. We'll begin again.'

'But too late for me. I'll just be another out-of-work actor.'

'You think you'll be forgotten so soon?'

'I'd scarcely done enough to be remembered as more than promising. And I'll be edging into middle-age. Too late to be promising. In the theatre, if you don't start young, you might as well not start at all.'

Guy shook his head slowly, having no consolation to offer. As they walked to the station, Aidan broke their silence to ask: 'Did you mean that about the Hundred Years War?'

'Not really, no. But however long it lasts, what is lost, is lost. Things won't be returned to us. I forgot to tell you: Harriet left something for you – one of those Egyptian votive figures. A cat. She said you'd asked her to keep it for you.'

'Yes, I bought it for my mother.'

'Well, it's at the flat. I'll send it to you.'

They became silent again for some minutes then Guy said:

'I've been reading Pater's *Imaginary Portraits*. He says that the Greeks had a special word for the Fate that leads one to a violent end. It's Κήρ – the extraordinary destiny. It comes out to the cradle and follows the doomed man all the way: "over the waves, through powder and shot, through the rose gardens . . ."'

'The rose gardens!' Aidan jerked out a laugh: 'Aren't we all being followed through the rose gardens? One way or another, we're all due for a violent end. But do you think Harriet suffered an extraordinary destiny?'

'Who knows what happened on that ship?'

'Do you mean cannibalism? I assure you that in our boat, no one even thought of it.'

'No, I didn't mean cannibalism. She probably didn't even get into the life-boat. Just think of them all fighting for their lives. She was thin and weak. She'd been ill. She wouldn't've stood a chance.'

Aidan did not answer. They had reached the station and when he had found his berth in the sleeping-car, he stood in the corridor to say goodbye. Guy, looking at him from the platform, said: 'If you give me your address in Jerusalem, I'll post the cat to you.'

'Why don't you bring it yourself? You must have some leave due to you. Come and spend a week in Palestine. Jerusalem is a lovely place, just like a Cotswold town. A holiday will do you good. Take your mind off things.'

'No.' Guy spoke firmly. He had seen enough of Aidan for the time being and the remarks about Spain still irked him. He had decided to see less of him in future. There would be no scope for personal fantasies about a relationship that could never exist. Stepping back from the carriage, he said: 'I won't wait any longer. I'll be off.'

Aidan could not let him go so easily. Putting his arm out through the open window, he leant forward to touch Guy, pleading with him: 'Do come to Jerusalem . . .' Before Aidan's hand could touch him, Guy took another step back.

Looking at Aidan's eager, unhappy face, he shook his head: 'It's out of the question. I'm much too busy. What is your address?'

'I'm at the YMCA. Are you sure you won't come?'

'Quite sure.'

'Perhaps later. In the summer. It's an ideal summer climate.'

'No, I haven't time for holidays.'

'Or for me?'

Guy laughed, treating the question as a joke, and Aidan, his dark eyes pained, stared at him and gave a long sigh. Saying, 'Then goodbye, Guy,' he turned and shut himself in his berth.

Guy sensed the finality in that 'goodbye' and approved it. He would prefer not to see Aidan again. He had no wish to hurt him but what was more hurtful than the pursuit of hopeless illusions? Outside the station, he realized he had not answered Aidan and he said to himself: 'Goodbye, goodbye'.

A clean break, a tidy break, he thought as he set out on the long walk through the town to Garden City.

Nineteen

The invitation to the Holy Fire completely changed Angela's attitude towards Lister. Castlebar sometimes grumbled about him, saying: 'Do we want that fat fool drinking our whisky every night?' Angela now put a stop to these complaints. 'I won't hear a word against him. He's my favourite man.'

Lister, flattered by her, seemed to melt into self-satisfaction and was constantly lifting her hand to his wet moustache. Everything he did seemed to amuse her. She made him repeat his limericks that were less witty and more scatalogical than Castlebar's. Harriet thought them abject but to Angela they were wildly funny and she demanded more and more. Lister's pride rose to such a point, he decided to give a party.

'Small party. Nothing grand. Hope to see you in my room at 18.00 hours. Eh?'

Lister's room could not have held a larger party. He had invited a Wren officer on leave from Alexandria and the guests were somehow packed in with the bed, wardrobe, small table and single chair. The Wren, as newcomer, was given the chair and Castlebar stood, hanging over her. A strip of carpet ran from chair to table and on the table there was a bottle of gin.

Harriet and Angela were to sit beside Lister on the bed. Before sitting down, Angela examined the ornamental label on the gin bottle and read:

IN MEMORIAM GIN

Bottled by H M King George VI at Balmoral, England and Shipped by Messrs Ramatoola, New Delhi, India.

She asked: 'Where on earth did you get that?'

In a lofty tone, Lister said: 'I have my contacts.'

Angela told Castlebar: 'Gin doesn't agree with you,' but Castlebar was not listening. Standing very close to the pretty Wren, he said that as she was a sailor, she ought to know some sea shanties. Cheerful and obliging, the girl sang 'Roll out the Barrel' while Castlebar kept time with his forefinger. Though he seemed absorbed by the singing, he slipped away every few minutes and tip-toed along the carpet to top up his glass. Returning with the same tip-tippity step, he kept his finger waving to cover his excursions to the bottle.

Angela watched anxiously as the line of his steps was impressed on the carpet and whispered to Harriet: 'That stuff will kill him.'

It was also having an effect upon Lister who was beginning to hark back to ancient wrongs. He told the room that there had been a 'super tart' staying at the King David the previous Christmas. He had decided to give himself a Christmas present of a session with the lady but – here his voice started to break: 'She wanted so much money, I couldn't afford it. I said: "Season of good-will. Come on, do a chap a good turn," but she wouldn't drop her . . .' Lister ended on a sob.

'Wouldn't drop her what?' Angela asked crossly.

'Price,' Lister gulped.

Angela shouted to Castlebar: 'Time to go, Bill.'

He was led out of the YMCA in a dazed state and half-way across the road he sank down on to his knees. Pulling him to his feet, Angela demanded: 'What was that stuff you were drinking? Some sort of bootleg poison, from the look of it.'

'Very strong,' Castlebar mumbled: 'Only needed a sip to knock a fellow out.'

Angela ordered him to bed. When he was not well enough to appear for supper, she confided to Harriet: 'I don't know what I'd do if anything happened to Bill.'

The next day was the day of the ceremony. Before Harriet had finished her breakfast, Lister arrived, eager to be off. In his impatience, he left the hotel and walked up and down in the early sunlight while Harriet telephoned through to Angela, urging her to come down.

Lister was wearing his cap at a jaunty angle, the peak over one eye, but beneath it, his face was strained and he paused every now and then to look down at the desert boot which held his gouty toe.

It was nearly nine before the party set out. When they reached the Jaffa Gate, crowds were passing through it on their way to the Holy Sepulchre – or so Lister said. He had forgotten that the ceremony had been organized by the police and kept saying there would be no room for them in the church.

Just inside the gate, where meat stalls imbued the air with a smell like a rotting corpse, Angela stopped to laugh at a single piece of black meat which hung in a mist of flies. The owner, supposing her to be a customer, hurried out with his flit gun and sprayed the meat. Angela started to chaff him in Arabic and Lister, beside himself with anxiety, gripped her upper arm and urged her on, saying: 'It'll be your fault if we miss the show.'

Elbowed by all the races of Palestine, they pushed a way through the main alley that ran deeply between buildings that almost touched in the upper air. Lister, hurrying his party on, realized he did not know the way to the basilica. He began to force them wildly this way and that, first through the fruit market, then the spice market, then into the bazaar of the metal workers where the air rasped with the smell of white hot steel.

Lister, his voice thin, cried: 'This isn't right. Where are we? Where are we?'

Angela stopped at a curio shop and began to pick over antique fire-arms, their butts decorated with silver and brass and semi-precious stones. When she said: 'One of these might frighten Bill's wife,' Lister limped on in disgust.

'We're lost,' he said. 'We've taken the wrong turning,' and he looked for someone who might give them directions. A camel passed, shaking its tasselled head; donkeys were pushed through spaces too small for their loads. Female beggars, their faces covered with black and white veils, plucked at his arm and he shied away, thinking they were lepers. At last a man in a European suit came round a corner and Lister stopped in front of him. The man was a Greek. Finding that Lister understood modern Greek, the man began to rage at him then, suddenly becoming all courtesy and smiles, directed him to the basilica.

'What was that about?' Angela asked.

'Oh, he was complaining about police interference. He said no person of decent feeling would go near the basilica this year. It's his opinion that if people want to be trampled underfoot, no one has a right to stop them. Anyway, he thinks we should go through the Via Dolorosa.'

In the Via Dolorosa a procession was advancing slowly over the spacious, creamy flagstones, led by a bespectacled cardinal in magenta canonicals. Lister saluted and the cardinal bowed towards him.

'Who was that?' Harriet whispered.

Lister replied with modest satisfaction: 'Spellman. Friend of mine.'

They came into the Greek quarter which was strangely clean, empty and silent. Immense black coffin lids stood upright by the doors of undertakers and small shops were filled with silk vestments and olive wood camels. There was a scent of incense in the air and Lister said: 'At last.'

Somewhere, hidden by the buildings that crowded about it, was the basilica. They found it at the bottom of a narrow turning. Seeing the great, carved door amidst the crumbling splendour of the façade, Lister gave a shout of triumph: 'Here we are, and not a soul going in. We'll have the whole place to ourselves.'

But the door was shut. A barrier had been erected across it and two policemen sat in front of it. They observed Lister with a contemptuous blankness as he took out his tickets and advanced upon them. The door was not an entrance; it was an exit. Lister and his party must return to the Via Dolorosa and start again.

Lister stood for a moment, stunned, then tried to pull rank. He claimed friendship with the Greek Metropolitan and with Cardinal Spellman. He said he knew the Chief of Police. He said the ladies were tired and one of them had been very ill. The police could not be moved. Ticket-holders, like everyone else, must enter by the main door.

Lister, who had advanced so confidently, now limped back with a pained and foolish air. Reaching his guests, he said in a low voice: 'Damned self-important nobodys. Just as I told you. Everyone despises them so they try to get their own back. Bunch of conchies, most of them. Shipped out here because they're no good for anything else. One of them was a ballet dancer. Think of it, a policeman ballet dancer!' Lister tried to laugh and Harriet was sadly aware that he had suffered such defeats all his life.

The din around the main door was heard long before they

found the way to it. Almost at once they came up against a closely packed crowd and could go no farther. Lister, trying to push
through, demanded passage for ticket-holders. No one moved.

A Greek in the back row turned to tell him that people were
wedged together for half a mile or more. Some had been waiting
since dawn. Some had been there all night.

'But why are they waiting?' Lister asked: 'Why don't they go
into the church?'

'Because the door's locked and there's a barrier across it. A
police barrier,' said the Greek, spitting his contempt.

'How long are they going to keep us here?'

He was told they would have to remain till the Armenian
patriarch arrived. The door belonged to the Armenians, the
patriarch kept the key, and only he had the right to unlock it.

While this talk went on, more people had arrived so Lister's
party had ceased to be at the back of the crowd and now was in
the midst of it. As those at the rear tried to push forward, the
English visitors were wedged into a solid mass of bodies and Harriet, more frail than the others, could not free her arms. Her face
was pressed against sweaty clothing and she had to rise on tiptoe
to get air to breathe.

More and more people arrived and as the pressure grew, some
of the older women began to moan, fearful of what would happen
when there was a move. A batch of Greek soldiers, finding the
way blocked, tried to prise themselves into the crowd with their
elbows. Eyes were struck, arms came down like hammer blows
on heads and shoulders, and there were screams of pain and
wrath. A woman began to pray and others took up her prayer.
The screaming, the prayers of the women, the moans of those
held prisoner and gasping for breath, caused waves of panic to
pass backward and forward through the congested bodies.

Angela clung to Castlebar. Harriet, crushed and nearly sense-
less, remained upright simply because there was no room to fall.
Lister, pressing his arm in between her body and the one behind,
gripped her round the waist and catching her elbow on the other
side, whispered: 'When the rush starts, hold on to me.'

There was a cannonade of hisses and enraged insults and word
came back that the Armenian patriarch was about to unlock the
door. Lister, a head taller than those about him, laughed and

said: 'The old fool's skipped inside pretty quick. Scared out of his black socks. *Now*! Keep hold of me!' But the door was shut again and the enraged Greeks shouted: 'Break down the barrier!' As a drive like a battering ram struck the rear of the crowd, one old woman began to call on God and her cry was taken up by men as well as women. People pleaded: 'Let us out. Let us out,' and Harriet, clinging to Lister, felt the same primitive urge to call on God, the last resort of them all.

The barrier crashed down. The crowd toppled forward and as the police shouted warnings and the Greek soldiers howled as though rushing into battle, Lister gathered Harriet into his arms and shouted to her: 'Stay upright. Whatever you do, don't let them knock you down.'

People pelted past them, striking against them like rocks rushing downhill. One furious blow knocked Harriet out of Lister's arms but he caught her wrist as she fell and held on to her until she was afraid the bone would break. Then another blow sent them spinning together into a curio shop. Crashing through the candles that hung over the doorway, scattering rosaries, crucifixes, olive wood boxes, baskets of Jericho roses, they fell into a corner with a table on top of them.

Shaken but unhurt, they were helped up by the shopkeeper who said: 'The police will pay for this. They caused this trouble, so we'll make them pay.'

'And serve them bloody well right,' said Lister.

Laughing and forgetting to limp, he kept his arm round Harriet as they made their way to the churchyard where the soldiers were breaking up a paling intended to keep the visitors in an orderly queue. The police had taken themselves off, leaving the Greeks free to smash whatever could be smashed. The front of the basilica, riven by age and earthquakes, was held up by wooden struts and these, too, were attacked until a priest came out and demanded a stop.

There was no sign of Angela and Castlebar. 'How will they get in?' asked Lister anxiously as he brought out his tickets, but no one was taking tickets. Inside the porch, a black-clad Armenian monk stood guard over the Armenian door, fiercely observing everyone who passed through it. Inside the church there was chill and quiet. To add to the drama of the occasion, all the candles had been extinguished and the place was in darkness. As Harriet and Lister made their way blindly forward, they were met by a major-domo with a silver-headed stick. Finding they had tickets, he conducted them in a formal manner to the chairs reserved for distinguished visitors. So far the only distinguished visitor present was Angela. She had lost Castlebar and Lister was sent off in search of him.

Angela had seated herself in the centre of the front row and Harriet, discomposed by the fall, sank down beside her. There were about fifty chairs, placed in a square and roped in with a heavy cord. Outside the cord, a mass of people stood together, awaiting events. For the first half an hour, they waited patiently, then the soldiers and young men, growing restless, began to climb the scaffolding that shored up the interior walls. Boredom produced noise and the noise grew as time passed. Occasionally someone, seeing himself more privileged than the rest, attempted to breach the cordon and sit on the empty chairs. Some were sternly ordered back to the crowd, others, for no obvious reason, were allowed to remain. An Egyptian family, the father in a fez, was left undisturbed while an old, fat Greek, gasping, sweating and pleading, was helped to a chair by one major-domo and thrown out by another.

After a long interval, Lister returned with Castlebar, both men smelling strongly of arak. They sat on either side of the two women and at first were circumspect, quietly gazing at the monument of gold and coloured marbles that was said to mark the burial place of Christ. Lister told them that the rotunda over it, shored up by girders and struts, had been placed there by the Crusaders. They returned to silence. Fifteen or twenty minutes passed then Castlebar, beguiled by the twilight, put his arm round Angela and Lister fumbled for Harriet's hand. Harriet, grateful for the protection he had afforded her, let him hold it for a while. Lister was kind but, thinking of his fat, pink face, his ridiculous moustache, his wet eyes and baby nose, she told herself that kindness was not enough.

The church was now so full that people were taking places in the topmost galleries and some had managed to join the poor Abyssinians on the roof. Faces were pressed against the small windows in the dome. The young men on the girders climbed higher to allow others to take their places. The most adventurous went up and up until one slipped and fell screaming to the crowd below. The girders, hung with a weight of humanity, creaked and shuddered and some of the women shouted warnings and the young men shouted back. Gradually losing all restraint, the congregation talked and laughed and began to sing Greek songs.

Lister's hand was plump and small with small, fat fingers, an enlarged baby's hand, that seemed to Harriet much too soft. He was not more than thirty but was deteriorating early. Defeat, though he resented it, had got its hold on him and Harriet felt sorry for him. She, too, could be kind and when he squeezed her hand, she squeezed back. Lister whispered: 'You may get a better-looking one but a more loving one, you'll never find.' Harriet laughed and slid her hand away.

The hubbub came to an abrupt stop. A minor procession was entering the church. Representatives of leading Greek and Christian Arab families, all male of course, were making a circuit of the sepulchre, the more prosperous in dark suits and pointed, patent leather shoes, the very poor in dirty galabiahs.

'A ruffianly lot,' Lister whispered as rich and poor went round with no sense of status, linking fingers and smiling at each other.

Seeing three people led to the doorway of the sepulchre, Lister became grave: 'My goodness, look who we've got here! Prince Peter and Prince Paul. The woman is Peter's Russian wife. He's a nice chap; looks like an English gent.'

Harriet, turning her head away from Lister's arak smell, saw a group of English officials being led to the chairs, among them a woman she had seen somewhere before. But where? The woman chose to sit by herself in the front row. Harriet watched her as she took her seat. She had a large crocodile handbag which she placed on her knee, putting her hands on it as though to shield it from all comers. This gesture confirmed Harriet's certainty that the woman was known to her. Some occasion when there had been a similar shielding of an object stirred vividly at the back of her mind but would not present itself. The occasion, she knew, was associated with unhappiness. She felt the unhappiness again, but that was all. The occasion itself eluded her.

She remained puzzled until distracted by the excitement around her. The major-domos were clearing a passage for the

Greek patriarch. Using their silver-headed sticks, they pushed and prodded people out of the way. The congregation moved, if it moved at all, unwillingly, craning necks for a sight of the great figure of the day.

As he appeared in the doorway, a shout of welcome filled the church and he stopped, making the most of his entry, then moved slowly forward. In robes of white brocade, wearing a large, golden, onion dome on his head, the patriarch held himself with dignity, his white beard parted from chin to waist so all might see the display of gold and gems that covered his chest. The priests behind him were in cloth of gold, some of it ragged with age, some new and gleaming. After the priests, came the choir boys. They were singing, mouths opening and shutting, but the sound was lost in the general din. After the choir boys, it was just anyone who happened to own a religious banner. These rearguard upstarts were treated with little respect. The crowd closed in on them, swamping them, throwing down their banners which they used as weapons to keep the mob at bay.

The patriarch, with an eye open for press photographers, pulled back his beard and arranged his jewels whenever he saw a camera. The procession was to go three times round the church but in the third round, all was confusion. The patriarch himself was untouched but his retinue had degenerated into a rabble of shouts, scuffles and blows. Arriving intact at the door to the sepulchre, he shook hands with the royal visitors then, mounting the steps to the door itself, he stood benign and smiling, while acolytes removed his onion dome and outer robes, leaving him in a black cassock, a humble priest like any other priest. Then came the search for matches or any means of making fire. He lifted his arms and the acolytes patted him lightly on either side. No matches were found.

The search completed, the door to the tomb was unsealed. The patriarch, with two priests to act as witnesses, entered the sepulchre. The door was shut. There was silence as everyone awaited the miracle.

'How long will it take?' Harriet whispered.

Lister nodded portentously: 'A decent interval.'

It was scarcely that. There were two smoke-blackened holes through which the fire would appear. As it shot out, a wild paean

527

of joy bellowed from the crowd. A man had waited at each hole to seize the cylinders that held the fire and at once, as the church vibrated with the yells of the faithful, the fire was passed from hand to hand. The cordon was broken and the congregation, stumbling over chairs and falling against the distinguished visitors, rushed forward, holding out candles and tapers to receive the fire. All inhibitions were lost in the intoxication of the miracle. The patriarch had brought them the divine gift of fire.

Faintly above the uproar, the church bells could be heard pounding away, telling the world the miracle was accomplished and bringing down the plaster from the ceiling. Bunches of lighted candles were given to the men on the scaffolding and passed up and up to the topmost balconies and out to the Abyssinians on the roof so, in no time, the whole interior of the church was festooned with light.

Two enormous, painted candles, guardians of the tomb, lit only on this special occasion, spouted enormous flames. Dark outlying chapels became bright with the fire and the crypt, where Helena had discovered the true cross, threw a refulgence from the depths.

Harriet, caught up in all the excitement, jumped on to the seat of her chair and stood among a dazzling swirl of lights.

The door of the sepulchre opened and the patriarch, his hands full of lighted candles, burst forth just ahead of the witness priests who, holding him on either side, ran him from the church and out of sight.

But that was not the end of the ceremony. A sort of burlesque or harlequinade followed the miracle. Priests in tattered, grimy robes now walked round shaking poles from which hung silver plates surrounded by bells. After the priests came men with boys perched on their shoulders. The boys had whips and lashing out, struck anyone who could not dodge away from them. The men on the scaffolding leant forward to lunge at the boys and two of them lost their footing and went down among the crowd.

A new, less pleasing animation had come over the scene. The royal visitors prepared to leave and the English thought it best to follow them. As Harriet stepped down from the chair, the woman at the end of the row glanced towards her and she knew it was Mrs Rutter.

528

Mrs Rutter did not recognize Harriet. Their only meeting had been brief. With her jewel case on her knee, she had sat near Harriet in the train going to Suez. She had been in the queue moving on to the *Queen of Sparta* when Harriet saw Mortimer and Phillips. By now she should have been half-way to England.

She hurried towards her friends and Harriet went after her, catching her up in the church porch.

'Excuse me.'

Mrs Rutter, turning and seeing what she took to be a stranger, frowned to discourage her: 'Yes?'

'Surely you are Mrs Rutter?'

'I am Mrs Rutter, yes.'

'We went to Suez in the same carriage. I was with Marion Dixon and her little boy.'

Mrs Rutter let out her breath and, lifting a hand to ward Harriet away, she went at a half-run out to the churchyard where her friends awaited her. Disturbed and puzzled, Harriet pursued her and caught her by the shoulder.

'Mrs Rutter, please, you must tell me why you are here. You boarded the ship for England, didn't you? Then how did you get back? Is Marion here, too?'

'Don't speak of it.' Mrs Rutter had lost what colour she had and her voice was hoarse: 'I can't speak of it. I don't want to speak of it. Go away,' then seeing Harriet's perplexed face, she relented a little: 'Anyway, I can't speak of it here.' She moved over to the churchyard wall and leant against it as though about to faint.

The casualties of the ceremony – two men on stretchers, one shrouded in death – lay nearby but she seemed unaware of them. Her friends, standing apart, stared at Harriet, realizing there was something very odd about the encounter.

Breathless and still hoarse, Mrs Rutter said: 'You didn't know what happened? You don't know that we were torpedoed? Some of us got into a life-boat. Marion and me and poor little Richard . . .' She choked and gasped before asking: 'You didn't know any of this?'

'No.'

'But it was in the *Egyptian Mail*.'

'I didn't return to Egypt. I heard nothing.'

'The boat drifted. There was something wrong with the steering. We had two lascars on board but they didn't know what to do. We had no water, nothing to eat . . . It went on for days. We caught some rainwater in a tarpaulin and drank it, but it wasn't enough. People started dying . . . Poor little Richard was one of the first.'

'And Marion?'

Mrs Rutter shook her head, unable to speak, then whispered: 'All dead except me and the lascars. The children first, then the women . . . I don't want to talk about it. I came here to forget it.'

'I'm sorry if I've upset you but I had to know.'

Mrs Rutter, like an invalid in need of help, looked towards her friends and one of the men, giving Harriet a look of reproach, crossed to her and led her away.

Harriet remained by the wall, shock-bound by Mrs Rutter's story. Angela, seeing she was alone, came to ask: 'What's the matter?'

'Guy thinks I'm dead.'

'Is that what that woman told you?'

'No. She told me the evacuation ship was torpedoed and she was the only woman who survived. Marion and Richard were lost. Guy thinks I was on the ship.'

'But he may not have heard . . .'

'Yes, it was in the *Egyptian Mail*.' As Harriet absorbed this fact, tears came into her eyes and she broke down, sobbing: 'Poor Guy. Oh, poor Guy, he thinks I'm dead.'

Angela led her over to Castlebar and Lister. Walking back to the Jaffa Gate, all three tried to comfort her by giving different unfounded reasons for supposing Guy would know nothing of the sinking. Harriet was too tense to listen. She wanted only one thing: to contact Guy and assure him she was alive and well.

They stood together in the foyer of the King David discussing how best to deal with the situation. Lister had been invited to luncheon at the hotel but Harriet would not join the party. She said: 'I'd better ring the Institute first.'

Castlebar said: 'It's Saturday. Isn't that Guy's day off?'

Angela said to Lister: 'Is it easy to ring Egypt?'

'Not very. The lines are always engaged. The military used to have an emergency line but that closed down when the army moved west. Better put the hotel porter on to it. Tell him to ring every two minutes till he gets a line.'

Angela said to Harriet: 'It may be ages before he gets through You might as well come and eat.'

'I can't eat.'

Harriet sat through the afternoon in the foyer, awaiting a summons to the telephone. It was six in the evening before the porter was connected to the Garden City flat. Smiling at his achievement, he called Harriet and handed her the receiver. Her impatience, that had lapsed during the hours of waiting, now filled her with such perturbation, she felt sick. A strange safragi answered the telephone. In a remote, small voice, she asked for Professor Pringle.

'Not here, Blofessor Blingle.'

'Where is he?'

'How do I know, lady?'

How, indeed! How did anyone ever know where Guy was?

'Who is there?'

'Not no one. All out, lady.'

Desperately, she asked for the safragi she had known: 'Where's Hassan? Tell him to come to the 'phone.'

'No, no Hassan. Hassan gone away. Me Awad, me do all now.'

'I see. Thank you, Awad.'

Downcast with disappointment, she went to the bar to join Angela and Castlebar. She said: 'He's not at the flat. I can't find anyone.'

Angela looked at Castlebar: 'If we took the train tonight, we'd be in Cairo tomorrow morning.'

Scarcely understanding, Harriet stared at her: 'Do you mean you'd come with me?'

'Of course. We can't let you go alone.'

- 'Angela, you're the best friend I've ever had.'

'Thanks: but the truth is we want to go to Cairo. Bill can't stand the food here. If it hadn't meant leaving you to fend for yourself, we would have gone before this.'

After supper, when Lister came to the hotel, he found Harriet, Angela and Castlebar packed and ready to set out for the station. They would take the train to Jaffa and there change to the Kantara train which would reach the canal before day-break. They would not be in Cairo as soon as Angela supposed, but they would be there soon enough.

'And you're taking all this baggage? You travel like a Russian princess.' Lister smiled at Angela but his manner was unusually subdued. He offered to arrange sleepers for them. Most of the wagon-lits were permanently reserved for army officers and usually left empty. He went to the telephone and came back saying: 'I've fixed it,' then he helped carry the bags to Angela's car. At the station, Angela put the car keys into his hand.

'I'll leave it with you.'

'A loan?'

'In a way. I don't suppose I'll ever ask for it back.'

'A car's always useful.' Lister looked down at the keys for some moments before he said: 'I'm afraid I've bad news for you, Harriet. Your friend Aidan Pratt has been shot.'

'But not dead?'

'Well, yes. It was on the train coming back from Cairo. In the corridor.'

'Who would shoot him? He had no enemies.'

'No, no enemies. He shot himself.' Lister raised his wet, blue eyes and looked at Harriet: 'I'm sorry. Bad time to tell you, but thought you ought to know.'

The whistle blew and Harriet, too confused by her own problem to give Aidan the attention due to his memory, embarked with Angela and Castlebar on her return to Egypt.

Twenty

The news of Aidan Pratt's suicide reached Guy with unusual speed. The commanding officer at Kantara had telephoned the Embassy where Dobson was on night duty and Dobson, coming in to breakfast next morning, said: 'You know that actor chap, Aidan Sheridan! He seems to have gone berserk on the train to Palestine. Killed himself in the corridor of the sleeping-car. Put his gun to his head and blew his brains out. I imagine we'll hear from the Minister of Transport about the mess. Why couldn't he have waited till he got to his own quarters.' Then, observing Guy's face, he apologized: 'Didn't mean to upset you. He wasn't a particular friend, was he?'

'I saw him fairly often. He used to ring up when he came here. In fact, I had supper with him last night. He was attached to Harriet and upset by her death, but not to that extent. I'm afraid he was rather a one for dramatic gestures.'

'Unstable sort of chap, was he?'

Bemused by this second tragedy, Guy said: 'I don't know. I don't think I'd say unstable. The war had trapped him in an intolerable situation and he probably took this way out.'

'The war's trapped a good many of us but death's a pretty desperate escape route.'

Guy could feel little more than exasperation at Aidan's death. Too much was being imposed on him. He tried to put it out of his mind but for the rest of the day Aidan's dark, appealing gaze followed him as he went about his work. Aidan had wanted response, reassurance and affection, perhaps even love, and Guy had made it clear that he would give none of those things. He remembered that Harriet had accused him of taking up with inadequate people so for the first time they felt understood and appreciated. Then, their dependence becoming tedious, he would leave her to cope with them. She had, apparently, coped with Aidan. Guy, having talked him out of his defences, had become bored with him and wished him away. He had gone, and gone for good.

Edwina, told of his death, dismissed Aidan without a tear: 'You mean that actor who came to the fish restaurant? I'm not surprised he shot himself. He was an absolute misery.'

It was the eve of her wedding and she passed at once to the much more important subject of the reception.

'You're coming, aren't you, Guy darling?'

Guy, in no mood for parties, tried to excuse himself: 'I'm afraid I can't. I promised to go and see Simon.'

'Oh, but Guy, you can see Simon any time. This is a special occasion; I don't get married every day.'

'Well, the arrangements have been rather sudden, and I'm committed to Simon. He's leaving the hospital. It may be some time before I see him again.'

'Bring him with you. I'd love him to come. Now, Guy, you've no excuse. You're to come to my reception. I'll never forgive you if you don't. You're such a close friend, if you weren't there, people would think we'd had a row or something.'

Realizing it would be wise to put in an appearance, Guy telephoned Simon at the hospital and asked if he would like to come to a party in Garden City.

'Will Edwina be there?'

Simon's voice was eager and Guy said: 'Of course,' forgetting to tell him that the party was to be Edwina's wedding reception.

Simon was hoping to leave the hospital soon. He refused all offers of rest in convalescent homes and intended to take himself to Kasr el Nil barracks before being posted to an office job. What the job would be, he did not know but it was to be temporary. The party in Garden City had come at the right time. It would be for him a celebration of his complete recovery.

He had brought from England, as part of his kit, a dress uniform of fawn twill which, packed in an insect-proof tin trunk, had followed him about in the regimental baggage train. Now, for the first time, he had a use for it. The tin trunk had been sent after him to the hospital. He dragged it out from under his bed and Greening found him trying to smooth out the creases in the twill.

'Dressing ourselves up, are we, sir? Come on, I'll get that pressed for you.'

Guy, when he reached the hospital, found Simon dressed and ready, a handsome and elegant young officer, in high spirits and aglow with health. Guy had brought a taxi which took them to Garden City earlier than they were expected.

Simon, breathless at the thought of seeing Edwina again, bounded up the long flight of steps to the upper flat with Guy some way behind. Shown into the living-room, Simon was deflated at finding they were alone.

'But where is Edwina?'

'Don't worry. She'll be along soon.'

They waited with the appurtenances of the party all round them. There was a table with cold meats and a cake from Groppi's, five rented champagne buckets and three cases of champagne. There were also vases of tuberoses, white asters, lilies and ferns.

'I say, it's quite a party, isn't it?' Simon said.

It was some time before the other guests came, and they came all together. Simon, unaware of the nature of the occasion, was surprised that there should be so much laughter in the street; then came an inrush of young people, mostly from the British Embassy, all wearing white carnations. There was still no sign of Edwina but her name was repeatedly mentioned and when most of the guests hurried out to the balcony, Simon realized they were watching for her. He guessed that this was a wedding party yet it did not occur to him that it could be Edwina's wedding.

There was the sound of a car door banging below. The guests on the balcony shouted a noisy welcome. Two girls entered, dressed in pink chiffon and carrying bouquets of Parma violets. Then, at last, Edwina herself appeared. She stood posed in the doorway of the room so all might admire her in her dress of white slipper satin, a veil thrown back, a wreath of gardenias crowning her resplendent hair. She remained there for nearly a minute, the day's bright star, then the dazzled audience thought to applaud. She burst out laughing and the young men crowded about her, clamouring for a kiss.

Simon, stunned, realized there was a man looking over her

shoulder: the dim, grinning face of Major Brody, the man in possession. As Edwina was drawn into the room, the safragis started bringing round the champagne in ice buckets. Simon, given a glass, whispered to Guy: 'You didn't tell me.'

Edwina was now making her way round the room. The effusive hostess, she greeted each guest in turn, kissing the girls who were her office friends. The guests embraced her and she gave squeals of excitement, declaring her love for all of them. Coming to Simon, she was stopped, astonished by the change in him. She gasped before she said: 'But you look wonderful!'

As she bent to kiss him, a confusion of emotion strained her face and she said under her breath: 'You're so like Hugo . . . so like Hugo!' then turned quickly away and gave her attention to Guy. '*Dear* Guy, so glad you're here,' speaking his name as though there existed between them a particular intimacy. He kissed her lightly and she passed on.

The cake was a large cream sponge but Edwina, using Tony Brody's dress sword, cut it as though it were a real bridal cake. As this performance went on, Simon said pleadingly to Guy: 'Please, let's go.'

Guy was about to make their excuses to the wedded couple when he became aware that the room had grown silent. People were staring towards the door and a figure, apparently uninvited and unexpected, was sidling into the room, self-consciously smirking, as surprised at finding himself at a party as the party was at seeing him. The new arrival was Castlebar.

Guy pushed forward, saying: 'But this is wonderful! Jake's been taken from us and you've come to console us.'

'Y-y-yes,' Castlebar was fumbling for his cigarette pack: 'Y-y-you're right. I have come to console you.'

Edwina, asserting her importance, said: 'Good gracious, where have you come from? Where have you been all this time?'

'Oh, swanning around,' Castlebar managed to get a cigarette into his mouth and his speech became clearer, 'I came to see Guy. Didn't know there was something on. Angie's downstairs in a taxi and she sent me up to break it to you. She thought I should come up first and t-t-tell you, she's not alone.' Whatever Castlebar intended to say to Guy, he had obviously been warned

536

to say it without undue haste. He lit his cigarette before adding: 'It . . . it's about Harriet.'

There was an uncomfortable movement throughout the room. This was no time for recalling the dead and Guy, going close to him, said urgently: 'You don't know, of course, but Harriet was lost . . .'

'But that's just it. That's what I came to tell you. She wasn't. She kept trying to telephone you yesterday but couldn't get hold of you, so we thought we'd better come straight here and . . .'

Dobson asked sternly: 'What are you talking about, Castlebar?'

'I'm not doing very well, am I? I wanted Angela to come up first but she decided to stay with Harriet.'

'What do you mean?' Guy, agitated, took Castlebar by the shoulders and shook him: 'Are you trying to say Harriet is alive?'

'Yes. I've been telling you – she's downstairs with Angela.'

Dobson pulled Castlebar away from Guy and gave him another shake: 'If you're lying, I think I'll murder you.'

'I'm not lying. Don't be an ass. Who would lie about such a thing? She *is* alive. She didn't get on to the ship for some reason, I don't know why. She went to Syria and we found her there and brought her back. That's the truth. If you go downstairs, you'll find her with Angie in the taxi.'

Guy did not seem able to move and Edwina, elevated by all that had happened that day and was still happening, darted forward: 'I'll go. I'll bring her up. I was her best friend.'

Guy, his face creased in an expression of longing and disbelief, stared at the door until Edwina returned holding Harriet tightly, Angela following behind. Edwina cried out to the room: 'Isn't this marvellous! To think it should happen at my wedding! The whole of Cairo will be talking about it.'

Harriet took a step towards Guy then stopped in uncertainty: 'I wasn't sure you'd want me back.'

Guy put out his arms. She ran to him and he clutched her against his breast and broke into a convulsive sob. Dropping his head down to her head, he wept loudly and wildly while people watched him, amazed. He was known as a good-humoured fellow, a generous and helpful fellow but no one expected him to show any depths of emotion.

Harriet kept saying: 'I'm sorry. I didn't know the ship went down. If I'd known, I wouldn't have stayed away.' She tried to explain her action but Guy did not want an explanation. His paroxysm subsided and, finding his voice, he said: 'What does it matter? You're safe. You're alive. You're here,' and, his face still wet with tears, he started into laughter.

Simon, caught up in the drama of Harriet's return, no longer wanted to leave the party. Had Guy offered to go with him, he would have said: 'It doesn't matter,' and it did not matter. A part of his mind had been returned to him. His vision of Edwina had dropped out of it, just as Anne's photograph had dropped from his wallet, and he knew he was free of her. His sudden freedom produced in him an emptiness like an empty gift box that in time would be filled with gifts.

Looking at her now, he saw the glow had faded. Her hair was still lustrous, her skin smooth, yet it was as though a film of dust had settled on the golden image.

She had been a fantasy of his adolescence but now he had not only reached his majority, he was verging on maturity. He had been the younger son, Hugo's admirer and imitator, and Edwina's attraction had lain not only in her beauty but the fact he had believed her to be Hugo's girl. He had wanted to be Hugo and he had wanted Hugo's girl, but now he was on his own. And Edwina had been no more Hugo's girl than she could be his.

He realized he was becoming less like Hugo. He was losing the qualities that had made him Hugo's counterpart. He was becoming less simple, less gentle, less considerate of others. He had, he feared, been tainted by experience, but he did not greatly care. Hugo did not have to face the future; he could remain innocent for ever. But there was no knowing what he, Simon, might still have to endure.

Harriet came over to speak to him. Not knowing he had been wounded, she asked: 'How are you, Simon?'

'Very well, thank you.' And that was the truth. He had passed through the ordeal of slow recovery and he was very well.

There was a flurry as Edwina, having gone to change, reappeared in a suit of white corded silk; a pretty girl, a very pretty girl, but the magic was no longer there. Her departure left Simon unmoved. For him, she had already gone.

The party dwindled; the guests went off to their different offices. Dobson, before returning to the embassy, came close to Harriet and, surprisingly, squeezed her round the waist.

There remained only Guy and Harriet, Simon, Angela and Castlebar, together with the debris of the feast. They sat down with little to say, exhausted by events.

Guy began to think of the day's work. He said he would take Simon back to the hospital and then go on to his class at the Institute.

'Oh no!' Angela sat up in protest: 'You can ditch the Institute for one night. We'll all take Simon back and then we must do something special. Mark the occasion. Make a night of it.'

Guy, looking blank, said nothing. For him the excitement was over. Harriet was safely back and there was no reason why life should not resume its everyday order. But Angela, imagining he would agree with her, had other plans for the evening. She and Castlebar intended to book in at the Semiramis, so she said: 'We'll have dinner at the hotel and then go on somewhere, perhaps to the Extase.'

Guy frowned but still said nothing. Harriet, with the Semiramis in mind, said she must go and change. Awad had put her suitcase in the room she had shared with Guy. Now it was her room again.

She thought: 'Our room. Our very own room!' She had gone away in despair but could not think why she had ever despaired. The room was as it had always been; very hot, the woodwork like parched bone, the air filled with the scent of the dry herbage in the next-door garden. It was the day for the snake-charmer and the thin, wavering note of his pipe rose above the hiss of the garden hose.

She opened her case and threw the clothes out. They were the summer things she had intended to wear while voyaging down the coast of Africa. They were very creased but one dress, a light mercerised cotton, was still fit to wear. She shook it out and spread it on the bed, then opened the top drawer of the chest. It had been her underwear drawer and Guy had left it unused. There was only one object in it – the diamond heart brooch that Angela had given her. She ran with it to the living-room.

'Look what I've found.'

She held it out to Guy who gave it an uninterested glance. She asked: 'Did Edwina return it to you?'

'I don't know. I think I asked for it.'

'Why did you ask her for it?'

'I can't remember.' Guy turned to Simon, saying: 'We must go', then to Angela: 'I'm afraid dinner isn't on tonight. I've too much to do. After the Institute, I have to meet some young Egyptians and give them a talk about self-determination. I was invited by Harriet's doctor, Shafik, and I can't let him down. You can see that. We'll have dinner another night.'

This did not satisfy Angela who said: 'This is absurd. Surely on a night like this, you can ditch all this nonsense you get up to. So far as you're concerned, Harriet has returned from the dead and you want to leave her and go and talk to a lot of Egyptians.'

'They're expecting me.'

'You can put them off.'

'It wouldn't be fair to them.'

Defeated by his belief in his own reasonableness, Angela gave up the argument. Guy, bending to kiss Harriet, became aware of her despondency and relented enough to say: 'Very well. I won't stay long at the meeting. You go and have dinner at the Semiramis and I'll come and join you afterwards. We'll all have a celebratory drink. How's that?'

'Try not to be late.'

'No. I'll come as soon as I can.'

When Guy had gone cheerfully away, taking Simon with him, Harriet said: 'Nothing has changed.'

'No. I told you you ought to box his ears. It would serve him right if you went away again.'

'Where would I go? I'm not much good at being alone. My home is where Guy is and the truth is, he's more than he seems to you. You saw how he cried when he saw me. And he made Edwina return the brooch.'

'I'd like to know how that happened,' Angela said, then she turned to look at Castlebar who had fallen asleep with his mouth open: 'Poor Bill, champers doesn't agree with him.' She kissed the top of his head and he, lifting his pale, heavy eyelids, smiled at her. 'Wake up, you gorgeous brute,' she said. 'We're going to the Semiramis. And you, Harriet, if you're going to change, hurry up. We must feed Bill. He badly needs a proper meal after all those awful weeks in the Holy Land.'

At the Semiramis, Angela booked into a famous suite on the top floor that was called the Royal Suite. There, protected by the hotel servants, she hoped they would be safe from the assaults of Castlebar's wife. The main room overlooked the Nile and Angela decided that before they went down to the dining-room, they would have drinks by the window and wait for the pyramids to appear.

Castlebar, lying on a long chair, smiled in lazy content and said: 'Suppose we just stay here! Have supper sent up!'

'What a good idea!' Angela went to the house phone and asked for the menu.

The little black triangles of the pyramids came out of the mist as they had done every evening for some four thousand years. They came like the evening star, magically, just as the red-gold of the sunset was changing to green. Twilight fell and the star was there, a single brilliance that for a few minutes hung in the west then was lost among the myriad stars that crowded the firmament. While all this was happening, Castlebar kept his eyes on his plate, eating smoked salmon, veal cutlets and a mound of fresh, glistening dates. Harriet, who had not yet regained her appetite, ate frugally and watched the spectacle outside.

Angela's whisky bottle had come up with the meal and, when they had eaten, the two of them sat over it as Harriet had seen them sit so many evenings before. The lights of Gezira came on and darkness fell. It was time for Guy to arrive. Castlebar, replete, yawned once or twice and Harriet became anxious, feeling she should leave but having to stay. At last, when the bottle was nearly empty and Angela and Castlebar were nodding with sleep, Guy was shown into the room.

'Sorry I'm late.'

Angela roused herself and laughed towards Harriet: 'You're right: nothing has changed.'

Guy, surprised by the laughter, asked: 'What should change?' He was himself again, relieved not only of grief but remorse and a nagging sense of guilt, free to pursue his activities without being tripped at every turn by the memory of his loss. He said:

'Life is perfect. Harriet and I are together again. No one would want things different, would they?' He took Harriet's hand and bent to kiss her.

'And how were your Gyppos?' Angela asked.

'Fine!' Guy had had a brilliant evening and being given a vote of thanks, the leader of the group had said: '"Blofessor Blingle has blought his influence to bear on many knotty bloblems."'

Guy reproduced the Egyptian accent with such exactitude that Angela had to laugh as she said: 'Knotty problems, indeed! Do they hope to solve anything? The Gyppos play around with hazy ideals instead of learning to govern themselves.' She had given Guy the last of the whisky and when he had drunk it, she said: 'We must go to bed.'

'I've only just arrived. I want to talk with my friend Bill.'

'Not now. Bill's exhausted. It's nearly midnight. I'm afraid you'll have to talk another night.'

Guy, feeling he had been uncivilly ejected, said when they were in the street: 'You see what I mean about Angela? She asks me to dinner then turns me out as soon as I arrive.'

'You were very late.'

'Not unreasonably. She really is the most irrational of women. Crazy. Pixillated. Mad as a hatter. I don't know what you see in her.'

Twenty-one

In July, while Cairo wearied under its blanket of heat, the British and American forces left North Africa and crossed the sea to Sicily. So far as the Egyptians were concerned, the war was over. But the British, bored and restless, with no hope of going home till hostilities ceased, knew it was not over.

Guy, who now took a much more favourable view of the future, told Harriet it might be over in year or eighteen months, then what were they going to do?

That was something to be thought out. Harriet said to Angela: 'What will you and Bill do when the war ends?'

Angela smiled and said: 'Humph!' as though the end of the war were a remote and fantastic concept. Still, she was willing to consider it.

'Bill ought to start work again. They've kept his job open here but I doubt if he'll go back. He'd be willing to live like this for ever but is it good for him? I'd like him to apply for a lectureship in England. Of course he'd only get one in a minor university but what fun to settle down in a provincial town and act the professor's wife: make friends with the vicar and the local nobs, have a nice, old house and cultivate one's garden! Would you come and see us?'

'Of course. We might even come and live near you.' Harriet, too, could see herself settling down in a provincial town. 'Make it a cathedral town,' she said. 'What about Salisbury?'

'You goose, Salisbury has no university. I'm afraid we'll all end up in somewhere grimmer than that.'

Harriet was the only visitor admitted to the Royal Suite. News that the runaways had returned, bringing Harriet with them, had been spread by the wedding guests. When it was known that Angela and Castlebar were living in opulent seclusion at the top of the Semiramis, Angela's old friends called at the hotel but were turned away.

Angela said: 'One of them might prove to be Bill's wife in disguise. She'd do anything to get in here. Even dress up as a man.'

'With her figure,' said Harriet, 'she'd look extremely odd.'

'Still, I'm not risking it. I've got Bill in safe-keeping and that's where he's going to stay.'

'For how long?'

'As long as need be. If she gets in here, it'll be over my dead body.'

The suite was air-conditioned and during the fiery days of summer, while the British and American forces occupied Sicily, Angela and Castlebar scarcely moved from their retreat. The windows were fitted with jalousies in the far-eastern manner. During the day, while the city shimmered in a glare of sunlight, the rooms were shaded and the occupants as cool as sea-creatures in a rock pool.

The hotel servants, heavily tipped, would allow no intruder to reach the suite. Harriet they saw as belonging to it and she came and went as she pleased. She need no longer spend her evenings alone in Garden City. When the sun began to sink, she could take the riverside walk to the hotel and join her friends on the top floor for a drink, for supper, for as long as she cared to stay. As the heat slackened, a safragi came to pull back the jalousies and they could watch for the pyramids on the western horizon. When it became dark, the safragi returned to open the windows and admit the evening air.

It was a pleasant routine but on the night that Italy surrendered, there was a disturbing break. When Harriet arrived, Castlebar was not in the long chair with his drink and cigarettes, but sprawled on the bed with Angela pouring iced water for him and persuading him to take two aspirin.

'What is wrong with Bill?'

'He has a headache. I think we've been shut in here too long. He needs a change of scene. Why don't we all go out for a drive?' Angela, looking anxiously at him, put her hand to his brow: 'Better?'

He gave her a languid smile: 'A little better.' He had taken the aspirin and after a while said: 'The pain's lifting. We'll go out if you like.'

A gharry was sent for and they drove by the river beneath the glowing sky. As they turned on to Bulacq Bridge, boys jumped on to the gharry steps and offered them necklaces made of jasmin flowers. Begging and laughing, they swung the heavily scented necklaces into Castlebar's face and Castlebar, usually amused by this sort of play, shuddered back: 'Tell them to go away.'

Angela paid off the boys then asked: 'Where shall we go?' When Castlebar said he did not care, she turned to Harriet who remembered an excavated village she had seen during her first days in Cairo. She said: 'If we drive to the pyramids, I'll show you something you've never seen before.'

They passed through the delicate evening scent of the bean fields out to Mena where the pyramids stood and beyond them to the desert that stretched away to the horizon. Angela said: 'Surely there's nothing to see here?'

'Wait.' Harriet stopped the gharry and Angela descended with her, but Castlebar shook his head. Smiling slightly, he put his face against the grimy padding at the back of the seat and closed his eyes.

The two women crossed the flat, stony mardam and reached a depression that was invisible from the road. Below they could see a whole village of narrow streets and empty, roofless houses that had been excavated from the sand.

Angela jumped down at once and said: 'Let's explore.' Watching her, Harriet felt an odd apprehension. She and the others had been shown this village on the day Angela's child had died. Putting this from her, she followed Angela. They wandered about the lanes and looked into small rooms, amazed that lives had once been lived here in these confined quarters. They asked each other why this isolated village should exist at all, without water or any reason for being there.

'But, of course,' Angela said, 'before the dam was built, the Nile would have come very near. There could have been culti-vated land here. Or, more likely, the people who lived here built the pyramids. You know they were not slaves as scholars once thought. They were peasants, ordinary workmen, doing a job for a daily wage. And they were fed on onions and radishes – not much of a diet, if you had to lug blocks of stone about.'

The twilight had begun to fall between the houses and as the women returned to the road, a wind sprang up and sand hit their faces. They started to run as the storm roared upon them, the sand grains striking into their flesh and blinding them. Clinging together, lost in the dark enveloping sand, they heard the gharry driver shouting to them above the noise of the wind.

They found Castlebar still lying back, eyes closed, unaware of sand and wind, while the driver gestured wildly, warning them that they must get back before the road was covered. Castlebar did not move and Angela, sitting close to him, lifting his limp hand, said: 'The aspirin have made him sleepy.' At Mena, she said they must go into the cloakroom and tidy themselves before facing the guests in the Semiramis foyer. In the cloakroom, the women looked at each other, seeing their faces coated with a grey mask of sand. Angela threw back her head with a howl of laughter and it was to be a very long time before Harriet heard her laugh again.

At the Semiramis, Castlebar said he did not want supper. He would go straight to bed.

'But you'll have a whisky, won't you?'

'No, I don't fancy it. I might take a drop of vodka.'

'Oh well, so long as you have something!' Angela was relieved.

Food for Harriet and Angela was sent up to the living-room. As they ate, Angela said: 'It's probably just a touch of gyppy. What should he take, do you think?'

Harriet recalled all the remedies that were part of the mythology of the Middle East. She recommended that great comforter Dr Collis Browne's Chlorodyne, but it was not easy to find. One cure was to eat only apples and bananas and drink a mixture of port and brandy. Then there was kaolin, intended to block the gut, but a more rapid cure, in Harriet's opinion, was a spoonful of Dettol taken neat.

'Neat?'

'Yes. It's not difficult to swallow, and it's nice and warming.'

'I'd never get Bill to swallow it.' Angela sent down for apples, bananas, port and brandy and when they arrived, said: 'Let's go and look at him and see what he'll take.'

546

Castlebar, in bed, his throat visible above his pyjama jacket, looked gaunt and tired but not seriously ill. Harriet left early and Angela, walking with her to the lift, said: 'Do you think it might be jaundice? A lot of officers have had it. He might have picked it up in one of these low bars.'

'Good heavens, does he go to bars?'

'I know he sneaks out when I'm in the bath. Poor old thing, he wants a drink with the boys. I don't say anything.'

Harriet agreed with Angela that Castlebar would be all right in a day or two, but two days passed and his condition was unchanged. He was indifferent to food, and nauseated by the things that had once pleased him most. And there were other symptoms.

Castlebar did not want company so Angela now came down to sit with Harriet in the foyer or the dining-room. She said: 'His temperature goes up and down; up in the evening and down in the morning. He says his tum is sore. He doesn't like me to touch it. I want him to see a doctor but he says "No".'

'Gyppy is painful, you know.'

'His stomach is not so much painful as tender, and it's swollen – or, rather, it's puffy.'

'It could be food poisoning.'

'I thought of that. He sometimes slips into a place that sells shell-fish. I've told him not to touch it but he doesn't always do what he's told.'

At the end of a week Castlebar had developed a rash that covered his chest and belly and Angela, now agitated, rang Harriet and said he must see a doctor whether he liked it or not.

She shouted into the telephone: 'It could be smallpox.'

'No. Believe me, he'd be much more ill. He'd have high fever and be delirious; and he'd be vomiting. I know because I read it up when I was in quarantine.'

'He has been vomiting. Oh God, Harriet, what am I to do?'

'Is he well enough to walk? Could we get him into a taxi?'

'Yes, he goes to the bathroom. He even took a few bites of chicken at lunch time.' Angela's voice shook with the attempt to reassure herself: 'He says he's not ill, only not well.'

'Then let's take him to Shafik at the American Hospital. Shafik is a good doctor; he'll set your mind at rest.'

'You'll come with me?'

'Of course I'll come with you. Get him dressed and I'll be round by the time you're ready to go.'

Harriet was uneasy, less for Castlebar who might not be very ill, than for Angela who had known despair and could not face it again. Harriet had seen her in a state of anxiety that was near frenzy and knew that at such moments she was, as Guy maintained, crazy. It was important to get Castlebar's illness diagnosed before Angela again lost control of her reason.

She took a taxi to the hotel and waited in the hall. As Castlebar came from the lift, she was shocked by the sight of him. He could walk, but with the shuffle of an old man, leaning on Angela who was maintaining a precarious calm. He looked weary beyond endurance. The sweat of exhaustion beaded his face and when Harriet spoke to him, he could scarcely lift the lids from his sunken eyes. He smiled at her but it was a weak and frightened smile.

The porter took his arm and helped him to the taxi. Angela, following behind, whispered to Harriet: 'His temperature's up again. It's 102°.'

Harriet said: 'That's not bad,' but she knew it was bad enough.

The white hospital building and the avenue of gum trees glimmering in the afternoon sun gave them the sense that all would now be well. There would be no more doubts and confusion of hope and dread. Help was at hand. Castlebar's ailment, whatever it was, would be treated and cured.

The hospital porter, opening the taxi door, insisted that the patient must stay where he was till a wheel-chair was brought for him. Then, with the sympathy that the Egyptian poor show to the sick, three male nurses came out to lift him into the chair. Castlebar tried to grin, suggesting that all this attention was a joke, and inside the hospital, took out his cigarettes but did not try to light one.

Harriet sent her name up to Dr Shafik. Shafik came down at once, his handsome face beaming with astonished delight: 'How is it you are here, Mrs Pringle? Have you been so quickly to England and back again? Or did you decide you could not leave your Dr Shafik after all?' He was eager to renew their past flirtatious

548

relationship but Harriet was too worried to respond to him. She said: 'Dr Shafik, I've brought my friends to you because they need your help.'

Shafik turned to observe Harriet's friends and his manner changed at once. He crossed to Castlebar, stared at him and asked: 'How long has he been like this?'

Angela said: 'About ten days.'

'He should have been brought here sooner.'

'What is it?' Angela's voice was shrill with alarm: 'What is the matter? What can you do for him?'

'That, madam, I do not know.' Shafik had reverted to the ironical formality that was his professional manner. 'We must make tests. May I ask: are you his wife? No? I understand. Well, it is necessary that he remain here and when his malady is known, we will do what we can.'

'May I stay with him?'

'No, no. Impossible. He must be alone. He needs rest and quiet.'

Castlebar, languishing in his chair, showed no awareness of what was being said. He did not open his eyes or move as Angela clung to him for some moments before he was wheeled away. The chair was put into a lift. Angela stood so long, staring as the lift rose up out of sight, that Harriet put an arm round her shoulder: 'Angela dear, I think we should go.'

'Go? Go where?'

'We could have tea at Groppi's and then come back and ask if there's any news!'

'No, I can't leave here. I must stay until I know what is wrong with him.' She looked round for Shafik but Shafik had left them.

'Stay with me,' she said to Harriet.

At the farther end of the hall there was a waiting area where french windows opened on to the hospital grounds. The grounds joined up with the Gezira polo fields and they sat and stared out at the great vista of grassland that floated and wavered in the haze of heat. Angela, by nature a restless woman, was so still that no creak came from the basket chair in which she sat.

Harriet, remembering how long she had had to wait for the result of her own tests, said: 'You probably won't hear anything until tomorrow or even the day after.'

Angela turned her head slowly and looked at Harriet, her eyes glazed and uncomprehending. So they sat on. Sister Metrebian, who had nursed Harriet through amœbic dysentery, came down to speak with her: 'But you are looking very well!'

Harriet, rising and leading the nurse away from Angela, whispered: 'The new patient – is he as ill as he looks?'

'Yes, he is ill, but it is for Dr Shafik to say. He must first make the diagnosis.'

'What do you think yourself?'

Sister Metrebian shook her head and was soon gone, unwilling to talk. Angela and Harriet sat in silence until six o'clock when the porter told Angela she might go to Castlebar's room. While she was away, Shafik came and spoke to Harriet in a subdued voice: 'Mrs Pringle, you must look after your friend. She is, I think, of an hysterical temperament and will need support. I have allowed her to see the patient but I cannot let you go up. You have been ill too recently. You must not risk an infection.'

'What infection? What is wrong with him?'

'I cannot say yet. He has what is called the "typhoid" state. That is: he has a fever, rapid pulse, low blood pressure and other symptoms we will not speak of.'

Harriet could guess that the other symptoms were, in Shafik's opinion, either too distasteful or too profound for the female mind. Cutting through his constraint, she said: 'So he has typhoid?'

'I did not say so. He has been ill only ten days. It is the second week which is critical.'

'Poor Angela, what can I do for her? She will be beside herself.'

'I will prescribe sedatives. I have told her nothing but if she suspects, you can say that typhoid is endemic here and we know how to treat it. Tell me, do you know, has Mr Castlebar been injected against typhoid?'

'He probably was when he first came out. We're supposed to have a booster each year but I'm afraid most of us forget.'

'So I feared. Mrs Pringle, you and your friend must go today to the Out Patients' Department and be given an anti-typhoid injection. You, please, go now and I will send your friend to join you.'

★

Angela, sedated, remained as though benumbed until the end of the second week when she telephoned Harriet and begged her in a frantic whisper: 'Come, Harriet, come at once.'

It was nine in the morning and Harriet asked: 'Come where?'

'To the hospital.'

'What has happened?'

'You will see when you come.'

Harriet, her taxi delayed again and again by the early morning traffic, was taut with apprehension. Shafik had said the second week was critical but typhoid, notorious for its long fever, was not necessarily fatal. In spite of Angela's entreating tone, she could not believe that Castlebar was dead. As she entered the main hospital door, Angela rushed at her and said hoarsely: 'That woman! That terrible woman!' She pointed to the waiting area where a woman was sitting, upright and purposeful, her massive, tubular legs planted so she could rise in an instant.

Harriet recognized the red hair that accentuated the clammy pallor of the face: 'Mona Castlebar! How long has she been here?'

'She was here when I came this morning. As soon as she saw me, she bawled: "Clear out, you bitch, you're nothing better than a whore." She tried to push me out through the door but I fought back and the porter went to fetch Shafik. Shafik ordered us both out. She said she'd fetch the consul to prove that she's Bill's legal wife and Shafik said he didn't care what she was, she must go. But she wouldn't go and I wouldn't go, either. Bill needs me. He's mine. I can't be kept from him. Harriet, Shafik's your friend. He'll listen to you. Please, Harriet, *please* go and explain that Bill left that woman months ago. She has no right to claim him. He never wants to see her again.'

'But is he well enough to see anyone?'

'The sister says he's a bit better today. I know if that woman forces her way in on him, he'll have a relapse. Oh, Harriet, please go.'

Harriet found Shafik still indignant at the uproar caused by the two women. Before she could speak, he shouted at her: 'So Mr Castlebar has two wives! That is nothing to me. He can have three. If he is rich enough, he can have all the prophet allows, but he is a sick man. I will not allow these ladies to come and disturb him.'

551

'Is he very sick?'

'Yes, he is very sick. He is now entering the third week and any day there will come the crisis. There could be perforation, peritonitis, pneumonia, cardiac failure – all such things are brought on by shock. These ladies must be kept from him.'

'But his wife! Can she be kept out – legally, I mean? She has threatened to call the British Consul to establish her rights.'

Dr Shafik, angry that the consul or anyone else might try to broach his authority, brought his hand down on his desk: 'In a case of life or death, the doctor's decision is final.'

'Dr Shafik, I'd be grateful if you'd let Lady Hooper just look in on him. She will be quiet, I promise you. They love one another. The sight of her will help him.'

Shafik, placated as Arabs usually were by a suggestion of romance, reflected for a moment then said: 'Very well. If you take her to the back entrance, I will send the porter to show her to his room. She will have five minutes, no more.'

Returning to the hall, Harriet said: 'Come, Angela, there is no point in staying here.' Angela, realizing that this summons meant more than was said, followed Harriet out to the porch and gazed hopefully at her.

'Back entrance. He's letting you see Bill for five minutes.'

Angela held on to Harriet's hand as they went up the staff staircase and were led to the door of Castlebar's room. As the door opened, Harriet had a glimpse of the patient propped up with pillows, ice bags on his head and brow, his eyes shut, his skin yellow, his face drawn. A low muttering was coming from his lips that hung open, swollen, cracked and dark with fever.

The door was shut behind Angela and Sister Metrebian stood guard before it.

Harriet said: 'Lady Hooper told me he is a little better today.'

'Not much better. His temperature will not come down. That is bad.'

'Is he in pain?'

Sister Metrebian put her thin little hand on to her abdomen: 'He is . . . pouf!' She moved her hand out to show how Castlebar's middle was distended: 'Here is discomfort.'

'Poor Bill!' Harriet said, thinking of his gentle compliance with

Angela's demands, his kindness and his sympathy: 'Will he recover?'

'I cannot say.'

Angela came out, too perturbed to weep, and Harriet led her down to the taxi. Put to bed in the Royal Suite, she lay so long silent that Harriet thought she was asleep and began to leave. Alert at once, she said: 'Don't go, Harriet, don't go.' She rang down for smoked salmon and a bottle of white wine. When it was brought up, she refused to eat.

'No, Harriet, it is for you.'

She lay as before until late in the afternoon when the telephone rang. The hospital porter had promised to keep in touch with her. After a few words, she replaced the receiver with a sigh.

'How is he, Angela?'

'No change.' After another period of silence, she raised herself on her elbow and said in a firm, clear voice: 'He will get better. I have faith. They say if you have faith, you can move mountains. I have profound faith.'

Angela was not allowed in to see Castlebar again. The porter, who rang two or three times a day, told her that Mrs Castlebar was always at the hospital but excluded from the sick room. Three days after Angela's profession of faith, it seemed that faith had prevailed. The porter told Angela that the patient's temperature had fallen at last. It was under 100°.

Angela, in a state of euphoria, telephoned Harriet, who was at breakfast, and told her to come at once to the hotel. She was to bring a taxi and together they would enter the hospital by the back door and, unknown to Shafik and unseen by Mona, make their way to Castlebar's room.

As soon as she saw Harriet, Angela began to talk at manic speed, and went on talking all the way to the hospital, planning Castlebar's convalescence. They would go back to Cyprus and stay at Kyrenia in the Dome, or perhaps he would prefer to remain in Famagusta where the sands were perfect and white lilies grew on the dunes. Or they might go to Paphos where Venus rose from the sea.

When they reached the corridor that led to Castlebar's room,

Angela came to a stop. Mona Castlebar was stationed outside the door. Angela, pulling Harriet round a corner, out of sight, said: 'Get her away somehow. Tell her Shafik wants her in his office.'

'Wouldn't she wonder what I was doing here?'

'You can tell her you were a patient here once. You've come in for a check-up. Go on, *do*!'

'She wouldn't believe me.'

'She would. Oh, Harriet, get rid of her. Flatter her, charm her, fool her for my sake.'

'For your sake, then . . .'

Harriet approached Mona with a smiling attempt at friendliness: 'I hear Bill is improving. I'm so glad.'

'I don't know who told you that.' There was cold aggression in Mona's tone but before anything more could be said, Sister Metrebian came from the room.

Harriet asked her: 'How is Mr Castlebar?'

Sister Metrebian answered gravely: 'He is in the operating theatre. The bowel perforated. He was in much pain. I heard him cry out and went at once to Dr Shafik. Now they perform the laparotomy.'

'So he has a chance?'

'A chance, yes. There was no delay.'

Mona, asserting her position as Castlebar's wife, said: 'I was allowed in for a minute but he did not recognize me.'

Which was as well, Harriet thought. Aloud she said for the sake of saying something: 'Do you think he'll get better?'

'Your guess is as good as mine.' Mona's manner was suitably serious but she could not suppress a hint of triumph, a twitch of satisfaction that Angela should lose out in this way.

Harriet returned to Angela who was avid for news of her lover: 'He's not in his room.'

'Why? Where is he? He's not dead, is he?'

'No. We can't talk here. Mona is full of suspicion. I'll tell you outside.'

Standing under the gum trees that shivered and glistened in the early sunlight, Harriet said: 'They're having to operate. There was no delay – Sister Metrebian says he stands a chance . . .' As Angela's lips trembled, Harriet added: 'A *good* chance.'

'What shall I do? What *can* I do?'

'Angela dear, you can't do anything. Only wait.'

'Stay with me, Harriet.'

'Of course I will stay,' Harriet said.

Castlebar died just after three a.m. the following morning.

The porter, when he telephoned Angela the previous evening, said: 'Mis' Castlebar not so well,' and Angela, going at once to the hospital, was told that Mona had been admitted to the sick room. Angela herself was refused entry. Prepared for any contingency, Mona had obtained from the consul written confirmation that she was Castlebar's legal wife. She must be permitted to visit him and in the event of his death, she alone had the right to dispose of his remains. Angela, having no rights at all, walked back to her hotel.

Dobson, as usual the first to hear whatever news there was, received from the consul an entertaining account of 'the whole damn fool imbroglio – two women squabbling over a dying man. And one of them no less a person than Lady Hooper. Now that he's gone, he's eluded both of them but Mrs C will be awarded the cadaver.'

Harriet felt it unlikely that the porter, with the Arab dislike of conveying bad news, had told Angela that Castlebar was dead. Harriet went at once to the Royal Suite and found Angela lying, fully dressed and awake, on the bed.

'What have you come to tell me, Harriet?'

'I'm afraid you've guessed right.'

'He's dead?'

Harriet nodded. Angela stared at her with an expression of distraught vacancy bereft, it seemed, of anything that made life possible. Knowing there could be no comfort in anything she might say, Harriet sat on the edge of the bed and held out her arms. Angela collapsed against her.

Harriet remained with her till late in the evening. For most of the time Angela lay as though in a stupor but twice she started to talk, rapidly, almost vivaciously, going over the details of Castlebar's illness and its possible cause.

'The shellfish! If I had been with him, he would be alive now. But, who knows, it may not have been the shellfish. Yet I'm sure it was the shellfish . . .'

When she lapsed into silence the second time, Harriet persuaded her to undress and take her sedative táblets. Leaving her sleeping, Harriet walked to Garden City by the river and was astonished to find Mona Castlebar with Dobson in the livingroom. She had a drink in her hand and from her manner, seemed to see it as a gala occasion. Having no one else on whom to impose herself, she had come to the flat, ostensibly seeking advice about the funeral.

Had Castlebar died anywhere but in the American Hospital, he would have been already buried. The hospital, with all its modern equipment, had a refrigerated mortuary cabinet and there the dead man could stay till Mona claimed him.

This, she said, was very satisfactory. She would have time to arrange a funeral befitting a well-known poet and university lecturer.

'The service will be in the cathedral, of course. Fully choral. I'm having invitations printed but these will only go out to a select few. If other people want to attend, they can sit at the back. Now, as to timing, I suggest we have the coffin carried in about mid-day then allow an interval of, say, fifteen minutes, after which I'll walk slowly up the aisle. There should be someone for me to lean on,' Mona glanced at Harriet, 'Guy would do.'

Harriet did not speak. Dobson, who had maintained a decorous face until then, could scarcely keep from laughing: 'My dear lady, this is a funeral, not a wedding. If you must make an entrance, you should come in immediately after the coffin.'

Mona's face fell. She tried to argue but had in the end to agree that Dobson, an authority on protocol, probably knew best.

Angela, to Harriet's surprise, wanted to attend the funeral service. 'I must go. Of course I must. What would Bill think if he didn't see me there? You'll come and call for me, won't you? We'll go together.'

Harriet, calling for Angela, found her in a short dress that looked too fashionably chic for a funeral.

She said: 'It's my only black. I know it's not suitable, but what does it matter? I suppose I'll have to wear a hat!' She pulled a milliner's box from the wardrobe and brought out a wide-brimmed hat of black lace trimmed with pink roses: 'This will do, won't it?' She sat it on her head without looking in her glass. 'Is it all right?' she turned to Harriet, her face red, swollen and dejected beneath the pretty hat.

'It will do,' Harriet said.

In the cathedral, the three front rows of pews were filled by Mona's selected guests: a few members of the embassy staff and some senior lecturers from the university.

Guy, though he had received an invitation, had chosen to sit at the back and Harriet and Angela sat beside him. Almost at once the congregation rose. There was a shuffle of feet in the porch, then the coffin began its journey down the aisle. Mona's invitations had said 'No flowers by request' but did not state whose request. Her own wreath, a large cross of red carnations, was conspicuous on the coffin lid. As Dobson had directed, she followed the coffin in, walking slowly, her head bowed, her legs hidden by a black velvet evening skirt that crawled like a snake on the ground behind her. Her corsage revealed to advantage her broad, heavily powdered shoulders and full bosom.

Guy, his face taut with distaste, whispered: 'If she were a better actress, she'd manage to squeeze out a tear.'

Angela remained calm until the cortège reached her then, looking askance, seeing the coffin a few inches from her, she broke into agonized sobs that could be heard beneath the thumping and grinding of the organ. There was some furtive glancing back by the distinguished guests in the front row. Aware of nothing but her own grief, Angela sank down to her seat and buried her face in her hands, abandoning herself to heart-broken weeping that went on throughout the service.

The service over, Mona left the cathedral in front of the coffin, her head now raised to denote a ceremony completed. As the seats emptied, Guy and Harriet remained with Angela, making no move until it seemed likely that the hearse would have set out for the English cemetery. But Mona was in no hurry to curtail her advantage as hostess. When Guy supported Angela out to the porch, the hearse still stood by the kerb while Mona moved about among her select guests. She had found no one to escort her behind the coffin but there were several prepared to companion her for an evening's drinking. She gave a quick, elated glance at Angela's bedraggled hat and defeated figure, then she seized Guy by the arm: 'You're coming to Mahdi, aren't you?'

Guy excused himself, saying he had an appointment at the Institute.

She still held to him: 'You know there's to be an evening reception, don't you? I've arranged for a tent to be put up behind Suleiman Pasha. I thought we'd get our first at the Britannia Bar then move on to Groppi's and the George V, and reach the reception about six o'clock. You can pick us up somewhere, can't you?'

Though Harriet and Angela were standing on either side of him, Mona made it clear that the invitation was for Guy alone. He muttered discouragingly: 'I'll come if I can.'

The hearse was an old Rolls-Royce decorated with black ostrich plumes and black cherubs holding aloft black candles. Angela kept her eyes on the coffin with its great carnation wreath and as the equipage moved off, stared after it as though by staring she could bring Castlebar back alive.

Watching the string of cars that took Mona and her guests away, Harriet said: 'She's spending a lot of money, isn't she?'

Guy told her: 'It's all on the university. She's not only getting her widow's pension but a large grant from funds. She's had to put up some sort of show, and she thinks Bill would have wanted it.'

Guy conducted the women to the Semiramis and left them there. Harriet sat in the shuttered gloom of the Royal Suite, keeping watch over Angela, imagining she had no consciousness of time, but at exactly six o'clock, she sat up: 'Let's go and look at the reception tent.'

Still in her black dress but without a hat, Angela held to Harriet's hand as they went in a gharry through the crowded streets. The fog of heat still hung in the air. The faded pink of the evening sky was streaked with violet. It was the time when windows, unnoticed during the day, were lighted up, revealing a world of mysterious life behind the dusty, gimcrack façades of buildings. For Angela none of this existed. There were no crowds, no sky, no windows, no life of any kind. She sat limp, waiting to see the tent, the last vestige of the lover she had lost.

The tent was not easy to find. There were a number of small midans behind Suleiman Pasha and the gharry wandered around, up one lane and down another, until at last they came on it: a very large, square, canvas tent appliquéd all over with geometrical designs and flowers cut from coloured cloth. The flap was tied back to catch what air there was and the two women could see something of the interior. Carpets overlapped each other on the ground and there were a great many small gilt chairs. The scene was lit by the greenish glow of butane gas. The guests were near the open flap. There were not many of them and those that Harriet recognized were the hardened remnants of Mona's drinking acquaintances. She could see Cookson with his hangers-on Tootsie and Taupin. Then, to her surprise, an unlikely figure moved into sight.

'Look who's there – Jake Jackman!'

Angela did not care who was there. She stared at the tent and beyond the tent into emptiness, her face a mask of hopeless longing.

When Mona came near the entrance, her black hem still snaking after her, Harriet felt they had better go. They drove back to the hotel where Angela refused to eat but, worn out by despair, went willingly to bed.

Harriet, walking home, met Major Cookson and Tootsie. Cookson was in a nervous state and very eager to talk: 'My dear, the funeral! It began so well but ended, I fear, on an unpleasant note.' He told her that Mona, finding she was entertaining not the select few but Jake Jackman and others like him, became bored and resentful. She allowed them a couple of drinks each then told them if they wanted any more, they would have to pay for them.

'Dear me!' said Cookson. 'What a scene! Just imagine how Jake reacted to such an announcement! I am afraid there was a bit of a fracas. Tootsie and I felt it better to leave.'

'What was Jake Jackman doing there? Is he back for good?'

'Well, no. To tell you the truth, he's being sent to England under open arrest. He's to go on the next troopship.'

'What do you think will happen to him there?'

'I don't know. Probably nothing very much.'

Returning to the Royal Suite next morning, Harriet found

Angela surrounded by all her sumptuous luggage and clothing. She was attempting to pack and said: 'I can't stand this room a moment longer. It's so . . . so vacant. I haven't slept all night. The place depresses me. I really hate it. Look at that beastly view. I'm sick of the sight of it.'

'Where will you go?'

'God knows. Nobody needs me now.'

'Angela, I need you.'

Angela shook her head, not believing her, and Harriet said: 'Come back to Garden City with me. Your room is just as you left it. There's only Guy and Dobson now and if you don't come, I'll be alone most evenings. So, you see, I need you. Will you come?'

'Would Dobson have me back?'

'You know he would. Will you come?'

Angela dropped the clothes she was holding and sighed. Like a lost and trusting child, she put out her hand, 'Yes, if you want me. You know, this is the end of my life. No one will ever love me again.'

'I love you.' Feeling that enough had been said, Harriet stuffed the clothes into the gilt-bound crocodile and pigskin cases then rang down to the porter and ordered two gharries. When Angela first arrived in Garden City she had brought two gharries, one to take her excess luggage, and she would return with two gharries.

Awad spent the morning piling the cases under the window in Angela's old room that looked out on the great, round head of a mango tree. The air was very hot and filled with the scent of drying grass.

'Home again,' Harriet said.

Angela smiled and, putting her head down on the pillow she had so often shared with Castlebar, she said: 'I think I can sleep now,' and closed her eyes and slept.

Twenty-two

It was some days before Guy, wrapped up in his many interests, realized that Angela had become a permanent inmate of the flat. He had seen her at mealtimes and had imagined she was seeking the consolation of company: then he met her coming out of the bathroom wrapped up in a towel and it occurred to him to ask Harriet: 'Is that crazy woman back here for good?'

'If you mean Angela – yes, she is.'

'How did she manage that? I'm sure you didn't encourage her?'

'I did encourage her. In fact, I persuaded her to come.'

'Then you must be as mad as she is. She took poor Bill Castlebar away and finished him off. Heaven knows what she will do to you.'

Guy was angry but Harriet was not affected by his anger. She said firmly: 'Angela helped me when I needed help; now, if I can, I'll help her. So don't try and influence me against her. You have your friends; let me have mine.'

Guy was startled by her tone and she remembered how Angela had advised her to box his ears. And that, in a sense, was what she had done. After his first surprise, he was clearly uncertain how to deal with the situation. Harriet was moving out from under his influence. She had gone away once and had, apparently, managed very well on her own. He was unnerved by the possibility she might go away again. Even more unnerving was the possibility that Angela, who had taken Castlebar from him, should now attempt to steal Harriet.

He said: 'Apart from anything else, Angela is rich. She's used to a completely different way of life. It would be a mistake to put too much trust in a woman like that. Sooner or later, she'll go off as she did last time.'

Guy waited for Harriet to relinquish her independent attitude

561

and agree with him, but she did not agree. She said nothing and Guy, taking hold of her hands, felt it best to be generous: 'I know you are lonely sometimes and if you're fond of Angela and feel she's a friend, well and good. But don't forget our life will change when the war ends. It will all be different then. I'll have much more free time and we'll do everything together.'

'Will we?' Harriet doubtfully asked.

'Of course we will.' Lifting her hands to his lips, he murmured: 'Little monkey's paws!' Then remembering some pressing business elsewhere, he put them down, saying: 'I have to go but don't worry; I won't be late.'

Twenty-three

It was mid-September before Simon was declared fit for active service. Impatient and eager for action, he went straight from the MO's office to his ward and started to put his belongings together. He wanted to leave the hospital at once but would have to stay until he was posted somewhere.

Greening, who had been waiting for him, said: 'We'll be sorry to see you go, sir,' but Simon was too excited to regret his separation from Greening or anyone else.

Laughing, he said: 'This time next week, I'll be in the thick of it.'

'I wouldn't bank on that, sir. The MO recommends you take it easy for a bit. They'll find you a nice, cushy office job, I expect.'

'Not for me. "Active service" means "active service" and that's what I want. I've been pampered long enough.'

'Don't forget we had to remake you – that takes time.'

'I'll tell them I've been remade good as new. I need a fresh start. Fresh country. I've had enough of Egypt.'

The country Simon had in mind was Italy. Recently Allied forces had landed near Reggio, taking the precaution to come ashore in the middle of the night. It proved unnecessary for the Italians were only waiting to surrender. As a result the Germans occupied Rome, sank their battleship, the *Roma*, and sent the whole Italian fleet full speed for Malta.

Italy was where things were happening. It was the place for Simon. Ordered to Movement Control, he said gleefully to Greening: 'I know a chap there who'll wangle anything for me.'

The chap was Perry, a fat, jovial major, smelling of whisky, to whom Simon had had to report the day after Tobruk fell. Impressed by his youth and eager desire to reach the front, Perry had promised to send him into the desert 'at the double'.

563

The promise had been kept. Perry would see to it that Simon was properly fixed up.

But times had changed. Army personnel had been cut to a minimum and many offices had closed. Movement Control, once at Helwan, was now in Abbasia Barracks again and Simon found that Major Perry had been posted to Bari. The middle-aged captain who interviewed him was far from jovial. He stared a long time at the medical report and said: 'I see you're down for an office job, Mr Boulderstone.'

'Well, sir, I'd much rather see some action. I'm no good at office work and I'm perfectly fit. I want to be back in the fight.'

The captain, not unsympathetic, gave him a glance: 'You look all right to me, but we've got to fall in with the MO's advice. We've arranged for you to go to Ordnance. Stationery Office. You won't find it too bad.'

'How long will I have to stay there, sir?'

'Not long. It's just a token job. Anyway, we'll all be out of here soon.'

Appeased, Simon asked for accommodation in the barracks and was given a room identical with that he had occupied on his first night in Egypt: bare, with three camp beds and reeking of fumigating smoke. The sense of life repeating itself made him the more determined to get away.

Simon was now drawn to the Garden City flat, no longer in hope of seeing Edwina, but because it was the only place he could call a home.

Guy and Harriet had taken over Edwina's room at the end of the corridor, which for months remained redolent of Edwina's gardenia scent, and Harriet suggested that Simon move into their old room. He said: 'It's not worth the bother. I'll be off any day now.'

She knew what he meant for they all felt themselves transient, living on expectations though not knowing what to expect. The events that occurred about them no longer related to them. Like the captain at Abbasia Barracks, they all believed they would be 'out of here soon'.

Edwina came only once to the flat after her marriage. Finding Dobson and Harriet in the living-room, she confided to them that

Tony was a bore with no sense of fun and, giggling ruefully, she said she was already pregnant. After she left, Dobson shook his head sadly: 'I suppose that accounts for the hasty marriage! Poor girl! To think that men once waved guns about and threatened to kill for her sake, and here she is stuck with a dull dog like Tony Brody!'

'I don't imagine she'll be stuck for very long,' Harriet said. 'I bet, once the baby's born, she'll find another major; one with a more highly developed sense of fun. But *did* men threaten to kill for her sake?'

'I believe someone waved a gun about once, but it was a long time ago, when she was eighteen and quite exquisite.'

Dobson stared unseeing, distracted by the memory, and Harriet marvelled that beneath his ironical sufferance of Edwina's foibles, he had kept hidden this knowledge of her dramatic past.

Simon's job, that he described as 'stamp licking', did not last long. Early in October he was ordered to Alexandria to take charge of two hundred men bound for an unnamed destination. So far as Simon was concerned there could be only one possible destination. He would be off to Italy at last.

Guy, who went to the station with him, said: 'I envy you going to Alex at this time of the year,' but Simon, all prepared to fight his way up to Rome, had no interest in Alex. He was now a full lieutenant, rising into authority, but to Guy he was still a charge and one he did not want to lose.

'How long are you likely to be in Alex?'

'I don't know. Probably a week.'

'We might come up and see you.'

'Yes, do come.'

As the whistle blew, Guy put his hand on Simon's arm and Simon, covering it with his own hand, said: 'Thanks for everything.' It was a detached valediction – he felt as remote from Guy as he had from Greening – but to Guy it was gratitude enough. The visit to Alexandria, posed as a vague possibility, now became an imperative and as soon as he saw Harriet, he asked her to come with him. He was surprised that she did not immediately agree.

'You want to go, don't you?'

'I've wanted to go to a good many places since we married, but you've never had time to go with me.'

'Oh, darling, this is different. Don't be unreasonable. We may never see Simon again.'

They set out on the following Saturday, starting early when the light, now fading into the cool topaz of winter, gave a particular delicacy to the delta. Looking out at the belt of green cut into sections by glistening water channels, Harriet thought of their arrival in Egypt and said: 'Do you remember our first camel?'

Guy, intent on the *Egyptian Mail*, murmured 'Yes' and Harriet watched for a camel. One appeared, led by a boy on a very long rope. It moved slowly, planting leisurely feet into the dust beside the railway track, and slowed down when the rope was jerked, holding its head back, refusing to be hurried.

'Guy, look!'

Guy, coming out from behind the paper, adjusted his glasses and tried to see what she was showing him: 'You said something about our first camel – what did you mean?'

'Don't you remember? After we left the ship at Alex, when we were on the train, we saw a camel. Our first camel. It could have been the very same camel.' After a pause, she said: 'Egypt is beautiful,' and she felt sorry that they must one day part from it.

Guy laughed and went back to his paper and Harriet realized he could not see what was beyond the window. Beneath his confident belief in himself, beneath his certainty that he was loved and wanted wherever he went, he was deprived. She saw the world as a reality and he did not. She put her hand on his knee and he patted it and let it lie there, keeping his gaze on the lines of newsprint. Deprived or not, he was content; but was she content?

She was free to think her own thoughts. She could develop her own mind. Could she, after all, have borne with some possessive, interfering, jealous fellow who would have wanted her to account for every breath she breathed?

Not for long.

In an imperfect world, marriage was a matter of making do with what one had chosen. As this thought came into her head, she pressed Guy's knee and he patted her hand again.

Alexandria, when they arrived, was nothing like the city Harriet had visited during the 'flap'. Then, with the Afrika Korps one day's drive away, people were on edge, speaking German yet buying up food against a probable occupation, or else piling goods on cars, ready for a getaway. It had been a grey city under a grey sky, the shore deserted beside the grey, plashy sea. Now in the breezy, sparkling October air, people looked carefree, the most carefree being the young naval men still in their summer uniforms of white duck.

'I'm glad we came.'

Guy answered with serene certainty: 'I knew you would be.'

They were to meet Simon in the bar of the Cecil and they found him already there, a lone khaki figure among the naval crowd. He did his best to greet them cheerfully but they saw his spirits were low. Something, no doubt to do with his transfer, had disappointed him, but he was not free to speak of it and they were not free to question him. Though they might never see him again, there was nothing to talk about but the war and the Italian surrender.

To relieve the atmosphere of dejection, Harriet said: 'I think things will go our way in future.'

Simon asked: 'What makes you think that?'

'The Italians wouldn't have changed sides if they weren't pretty certain we'd win. Won't it be wonderful when the war ends? We'll be able to go wherever we like. Think of seeing Greece again!'

Struck by the mention of Greece, Simon said: 'You lived there, didn't you? What was it like?'

'We loved it.' Harriet turned to Guy: 'Do you remember how we climbed Pendeli on the day the Italians declared war?'

'Will I ever forget it?'

'Or those two old tramp steamers, the *Erebus* and *Nox*, that took us from the Piraeus? You sat on the deck singing: "If your engine cuts out over Hellfire Pass, you can stick your twin Browning guns right up your arse." Did you really think we'd make it?'

'Yes. I knew we'd make it somehow or other. We always do.'

Guy and Harriet smiled at each other, aware that they were joined by these shared memories and the memories would never be lost. Then Harriet looked at Simon for he, too, was part of their memories and they of his. She said: 'When we climbed the pyramid, the war was at its worst. Now it's turned round.'

'Yes, you're right. Things *are* going our way.' He laughed and for a moment he looked like the very young man of a year ago who, newly off a troopship, said of the desert: 'I don't know what it's like out there' and next day was sent to find out.

Then, giving his watch a glance, he sobered and stood up. 'I've got to rush. Sorry to leave you so soon, but we'll meet when it's all over.'

'Yes, when it's all over,' Guy and Harriet both agreed.

They watched him go. A shadow of anxiety had come down on his face and as he passed between the tables, he seemed older than the white-clad naval officers who might never have had a care in the world.

He went out through the door and the Pringles were left looking at the room's faded cream and gold, and its war-weary fawn carpet.

Guy dropped his gaze and sighed. There was another friend gone. As he called for the bill, he said: 'We might as well take the next train back to Cairo.'

Outside, where the light was deepening, they walked along the Corniche, watching the silver kidney shapes of the barrage balloons rising into position above the docks.

Putting his arm through Harriet's, Guy said: 'You'll never leave me again, will you?'

'Don't know. Can't promise.' Harriet laughed and squeezed his arm: 'Probably not.'

That morning, Simon had been briefed about his impending move. He was not, after all, conducting his men to Italy. They were bound for an island in the Aegean called Leros where they might never hear a shot fired.

Noting his downcast expression, the commanding officer said: 'This is an important assignment, Boulderstone. You'll be accompanied by a military mission with orders to put heart into the chaps on Leros.'

'I'd been hoping for a bit of a barney, sir.'

'You may well get it. The island is to be defended at all costs.'

Simon assented: 'Sir,' but he was not impressed. He was to be

568

marooned in the Aegean and likely to be left there till the war ended.

After his luncheon with the Pringles, he spent the rest of the day organizing his men and their equipment on to the destroyer. Told where they were going, the men grinned and one of them said: 'Piece of cake, sir.'

Remembering how Harriet had said of Greece, 'We loved it,' he began to think that Leros might not be so bad after all. The convoy that was taking provisions to the Leros garrison sailed at midnight. Standing at the rail of the destroyer, Simon watched the glimmer of the blacked-out shore, the last of Egypt. He felt he had left his youth behind and was taking with him nothing but his memory of Hugo; and even that was sinking back in his mind like a face disappearing under water.

'Not a lucky place,' he said aloud, then, tired from the day's activity, he took himself to his bunk.

Coda

Two more years were to pass before the war ended. Then, at last, peace, precarious peace, came down upon the world and the survivors could go home. Like the stray figures left on the stage at the end of a great tragedy, they had now to tidy up the ruins of war and in their hearts bury the noble dead.

FIND OUT MORE ABOUT PENGUIN BOOKS

We publish the largest range of titles of any English language paperback publisher. As well as novels, crime and science fiction, humour, biography and large-format illustrated books, Penguin series include *Pelican Books* (on the arts, sciences and current affairs), *Penguin Reference Books, Penguin Classics, Penguin Modern Classics, Penguin English Library, Penguin Handbooks* (on subjects from cookery and gardening to sport), and *Puffin Books* for children. Other series cover a wide variety of interests from poetry to crosswords, and there are also several newly formed series – *King Penguin, Penguin American Library, Lives and Letters* and *Penguin Travel Library*.

We are an international publishing house, but for copyright reasons not every Penguin title is available in every country. To find out more about the Penguins available in your country please write to our U.K. office – Dept EP, Penguin Books Ltd, Harmondsworth, Middlesex UB7 ODA – unless you live in one of the following areas:

In the U.S.A.: Dept DG, Penguin Books, 299 Murray Hill Parkway, East Rutherford, New Jersey 07073.

In Canada: Penguin Books Canada Ltd, 2801 John Street, Markham, Ontario L3R 1B4.

In Australia: Marketing Department, Penguin Books Australia Ltd, P.O. Box 257, Ringwood, Victoria 3134.

In New Zealand: Marketing Department, Penguin Books (N.Z.) Ltd, P.O. Box 4019, Auckland 10.

In India: Penguin Overseas Ltd, 706 Eros Apartments, 56 Nehru Place, New Delhi 110019.

OLIVIA MANNING

Olivia Manning's *Balkan Trilogy* and *Levant Trilogy* form a single narrative entitled *Fortunes of War*, which Anthony Burgess described in the *Sunday Times* as 'the finest fictional record of the war produced by a British writer. Her gallery of personages is huge, her scene painting superb, her pathos controlled, her humour quiet and civilized. Guy Pringle is certainly one of the major characters in modern fiction.'

Penguins also publish the three volumes in *The Balkan Trilogy*:

THE GREAT FORTUNE
THE SPOILT CITY
FRIENDS AND HEROES

and

SCHOOL FOR LOVE

In wartime children have to grow up quickly. One small boy, waiting to return to England, finds himself in Jerusalem in the care of Miss Bohun, whose house offers a refuge to others washed up by the freak tides of destruction.

There he can watch the unaccountable wayward progress of the feeling called love – and there his real education in life can begin.

'Through the clear light of Miss Manning's sympathy ... we feel for this horror [Miss Bohun] some of that emotion, part amusement, part revulsion, part admiration for a triumphant assertion of life, that we feel for other comic horrors in literature, Tartuffe, Squeers, Mrs Proudie' – C. P. Snow in the *Sunday Times*

THE FATE OF MARY ROSE

Caroline Blackwood

Raped and horribly murdered, the body of ten-year-old Maureen Sutton is eventually discovered in woods near a sleepy commuter village in Kent. With nerve, inspiration and deadpan brilliance Caroline Blackwood draws us into the village to witness the macabre and devastating effects of this story on a local family: the historian Rowan Anderson, his wife Cressida and their sickly daughter, Mary Rose.

'A winner . . . guaranteed to disturb' – Victoria Glendinning in the *Sunday Times*

THE LITTLE GIRLS

Elizabeth Bowen

'Resonant, beautiful and often very funny . . . Eva is triumphantly real, a creation of great imaginative tenderness . . . Elizabeth Bowen is a splendid artist, intelligent, generous and acutely aware, who has been telling her readers for many years that love is a necessity, and that its loss or absence is the greatest tragedy man knows' – Julian Webb in the *Financial Times*

'Rarely have I come across a novel in which sexual frustration (and sexuality) have been so richly and powerfully conveyed' – Roger Barker in *Books and Bookmen*

MOTHER'S HELPER

Maureen Freely

The Pyle-Carpenter household comes complete with three children who can do what they like as long as they have Thought It Through, an intercom that never turns off, with Weekly Family Councils and with the television padlocked into a bag. Like Kay Carpenter herself, it was a totally liberated, principled, caring, warm, nurturing nucleus . . . And at first, Laura was completely fooled.

'A novel to weep over or laugh with. Whichever will stop you going mad' – *Literary Review*